WINE IN AMERICA

ASPEN ELECTIVE SERIES

WINE IN AMERICA: LAW AND POLICY

Richard Mendelson
Director, Program on Wine Law and Policy
University of California at Berkeley

Published by Wolters Kluwer Law & Business in New York.

Wolters Kluwer Law & Business serves customers worldwide with CCH, Aspen Publishers, and Kluwer Law International products. (www.wolterskluwerlb.com)

To contact Customer Service, e-mail customer.service@wolterskluwer.com, call 1-800-234-1660, fax 1-800-901-9075, or mail correspondence to:

Wolters Kluwer Law & Business
Attn: Order Department
PO Box 990
Frederick, MD 21705

Printed in the United States of America.

1 2 3 4 5 6 7 8 9 0

ISBN 978-0-7355-9974-1

Library of Congress Cataloging-in-Publication Data

Mendelson, Richard, 1953-
Wine in America : law and policy / Richard Mendelson.
p. cm.
ISBN 978-0-7355-9974-1 (perfectbound : alk. paper)
1. Wine and wine making—Law and legislation—United States. I. Title.

KF3924.W5M468 2011
343.73′07864122—dc22

2011013753

Front cover image: *La Vigne*, a steel sculpture by Richard Mendelson, 2000; photography by Kurt-Inge Eklund, 2010.

About Wolters Kluwer Law & Business

Wolters Kluwer Law & Business is a leading global provider of intelligent information and digital solutions for legal and business professionals in key specialty areas, and respected educational resources for professors and law students. Wolters Kluwer Law & Business connects legal and business professionals as well as those in the education market with timely, specialized authoritative content and information-enabled solutions to support success through productivity, accuracy and mobility.

Serving customers worldwide, Wolters Kluwer Law & Business products include those under the Aspen Publishers, CCH, Kluwer Law International, Loislaw, Best Case, ftwilliam.com and MediRegs family of products.

CCH products have been a trusted resource since 1913, and are highly regarded resources for legal, securities, antitrust and trade regulation, government contracting, banking, pension, payroll, employment and labor, and healthcare reimbursement and compliance professionals.

Aspen Publishers products provide essential information to attorneys, business professionals and law students. Written by preeminent authorities, the product line offers analytical and practical information in a range of specialty practice areas from securities law and intellectual property to mergers and acquisitions and pension/benefits. Aspen's trusted legal education resources provide professors and students with high-quality, up-to-date and effective resources for successful instruction and study in all areas of the law.

Kluwer Law International products provide the global business community with reliable international legal information in English. Legal practitioners, corporate counsel and business executives around the world rely on Kluwer Law journals, looseleafs, books, and electronic products for comprehensive information in many areas of international legal practice.

Loislaw is a comprehensive online legal research product providing legal content to law firm practitioners of various specializations. Loislaw provides attorneys with the ability to quickly and efficiently find the necessary legal information they need, when and where they need it, by facilitating access to primary law as well as state-specific law, records, forms and treatises.

Best Case Solutions is the leading bankruptcy software product to the bankruptcy industry. It provides software and workflow tools to flawlessly streamline petition preparation and the electronic filing process, while timely incorporating ever-changing court requirements.

ftwilliam.com offers employee benefits professionals the highest quality plan documents (retirement, welfare and non-qualified) and government forms (5500/PBGC, 1099 and IRS) software at highly competitive prices.

MediRegs products provide integrated health care compliance content and software solutions for professionals in healthcare, higher education and life sciences, including professionals in accounting, law and consulting.

Wolters Kluwer Law & Business, a division of Wolters Kluwer, is headquartered in New York. Wolters Kluwer is a market-leading global information services company focused on professionals.

SUMMARY OF CONTENTS

Contents ix

Authors xxi

Foreword
Mike Thompson xxv

Introduction and Acknowledgments
Richard Mendelson xxix

1. ***U.S. WINE LAW: AN OVERVIEW***
Richard Mendelson **1**

2. ***TRADE PRACTICES***
James M. Seff and Carrie L. Bonnington **43**

3. ***LABELING AND ADVERTISING***
Wendell Lee **73**

4. ***BUSINESS MODELS FOR MAKING WINE AND GROWING GRAPES***
James W. Terry and Erik W. Lawrence **149**

5. ***THE COMMERCE CLAUSE AND THE TWENTY-FIRST AMENDMENT: AN EVOLVING CONSTITUTIONAL PUZZLE***
Margot Mendelson **183**

6. ***WINE BRANDS AND APPELLATIONS OF ORIGIN***
Richard Mendelson and Scott Gerien **217**

7. ***LAND USE: RURAL WINERIES AND URBAN BARS***
Richard Mendelson and Lynne Carmichael **281**

8. ***LITIGATING A CASE OF COUNTERFEIT WINE***
William J. Casey and Andrew G. Wanger **329**

9. ***PUBLIC HEALTH AND SOCIAL RESPONSIBILITY***
Richard Mendelson **349**

10. ***INTERNATIONAL INSTITUTIONS AND ACCORDS***
Jacques Audier **395**

For Further Exploration
Richard Mendelson *441*

Index *445*

CONTENTS

Authors — *xxi*

Foreword
Mike Thompson — *xxv*

Introduction and Acknowledgments
Richard Mendelson — *xxix*

1. U.S. WINE LAW: AN OVERVIEW

Richard Mendelson — 1

A. HISTORICAL OVERVIEW — 1

B. REGULATORY STRUCTURE AND APPROACHES — 13

1. Local Option — 14
2. The States — 15
   (a) License States — 15
   (b) Control States — 17
3. The Federal Government — 19

C. REGULATING THE WINE INDUSTRY, FROM GRAPES TO WINE TO THE CONSUMER — 22

1. Viticultural Practices — 22
2. Wine Production — 23
3. Distribution and Marketing — 29

D. CONCLUSION — 33

2. TRADE PRACTICES

James M. Seff and Carrie L. Bonnington 43

A. HISTORICAL BACKGROUND 43

B. FEDERAL TIED-HOUSE REGULATION 45

1. Federal Alcohol Administration Act 46
2. Code of Federal Regulations 47
3. Preemption 49

C. CALIFORNIA TIED-HOUSE REGULATION 50

1. Restricted Ownership Laws and Exceptions 50
2. Restricted Benefits Laws and Exceptions 53
3. Tied-House Case Law 54
4. California Free Goods Law 57
   a. Statute and Regulations 57
   b. Free Goods Case Law 58

D. WASHINGTON STATE TRADE PRACTICE LAW 59

E. NEW YORK STATE TRADE PRACTICE LAW 65

F. CONCLUSION 70

3. LABELING AND ADVERTISING

Wendell Lee 73

A. INTRODUCTION 73

B. JURISDICTION: WHO GOVERNS WINE LABELS? 74

C. FEDERAL LABELING REGULATIONS ARE DESIGNED TO PREVENT CONSUMER DECEPTION 75

D. WINE LABELS: PRIOR APPROVAL REQUIRED 77

1. Exemption from Label Approval 78

E. BARE BONES WINE LABEL CONSTRUCTION 79

1. Initial Glossary of Terms 82

a. Appellations of Origin 83
Viticultural Area Appellations of Origin 84
The "Estate Bottled" Designation 86
Foreign Appellations 87
b. Vintage Date 88
c. Varietal Term 88
2. Mandatory Label Information 88
a. Brand Names 88
Geographic Brand Names 89
Brand Names of Viticultural Significance 90
Brand Name can be Overtaken by A Viticultural Area 95
State Appellation Controls 95
b. Standards of Identity 98
Grape Varietals in Lieu of Class and Type 101
Validating Foreign Varietal and Geographic Label Claims 107
c. Alcohol Content 108
d. Net Contents 110
e. Contains Sulfites 114
f. Government Warning 115
g. Name and Address 117
h. Vintage Date 117
F. PROHIBITED PRACTICES 121
a. Therapeutic Claims 122
G. WHAT'S TO COME? 127
1. Serving Facts 127
2. Allergen Labeling 135
H. ADVERTISING 138
1. New Media 143
2. "Do Not E-Mail" Laws 145
3. Green Claims 146
I. CONCLUSION 147

4. BUSINESS MODELS FOR MAKING WINE AND GROWING GRAPES

James W. Terry and Erik W. Lawrence 149

A. THE TRADITIONAL MODEL: BRICKS-AND-MORTAR WINERIES 150

1. Developing a New Winery Facility 150

a. The Acquisition Process 150

Negotiating the Sale 150

Term Sheet or Letter of Intent 150

Purchase and Sale Agreement 150

Investigating the Property: Due Diligence and Title Review 151

b. The Development Process 152

2. Acquiring an Existing Winery Facility 153

Structuring the Acquisition 153

Asset Purchase 153

Equity Purchase 154

Merger 154

The Acquisition Process 154

3. Leasing an Existing Winery Facility 156

4. Licenses and Permits for Traditional Bricks-and-Mortar Wineries 156

a. State Regulation 156

California Department of Alcoholic Beverage Control 157

California Department of Food and Agriculture 158

California State Board of Equalization 159

b. Federal Regulation 159

Alcohol and Tobacco Tax and Trade Bureau 159

Food and Drug Administration 161

B. "NON-TRADITIONAL" WINERIES 161

1. Custom Crush 161

a. Federal and State Regulation of Custom Crush Arrangements 163

b. Custom Crush Agreements 163

c. The Négociant Model 164

2. Alternating Proprietorship 165
a. Federal and State Regulation of Alternating Proprietorships 166
TTB Scrutiny 166
Scope of the Bonded Premises 167
b. The Alternating Proprietorship Agreement 167
3. The Unintentional Vintner: Grower Custom Crush 168
a. Sale of Wine? 168
b. Sale of Grapes? 168
C. GRAPE SOURCING 169
1. Purchasing Raw Land or an Existing Vineyard 169
a. Raw Land 169
b. Existing Vineyard 169
c. Acquisition Process 170
d. Legal Due Diligence Concerns 170
Zoning 170
Material Contracts and Water Rights 170
Neighbors 171
Title Issues 171
Williamson Act Contracts 171
Conservation Easements 171
e. Non-Legal Due Diligence Concerns 172
2. Leasing Raw Land or an Existing Vineyard 172
a. Vintner's Motivation to Lease 173
b. Landowner's Motivation to Lease 173
c. A Side Note on Sale-Leaseback Transactions 173
d. Process 174
e. Unique Vineyard Development Lease Elements 174
f. Subdivision Map Act Concerns (California Only) 174
g. Lease Term Issues 174
h. Rent Issues 175
i. Vineyard Improvements 175

3. Purchasing Grapes 175
a. Grape Purchase Agreement 176
Preamble and Recitals 176
Term and Termination 176
Quantity 177
Quality 177
Pricing and Payment 178
Price per Ton 178
Per-Acre Pricing 178
Bottle Pricing 179
Other Price Adjustments 179
Timing of Payment 179
Vineyard Designation 180
Farming Practice and Viticultural Control 180
Harvest, Delivery, and Risk of Loss 181
A Brief Note on Grower's Liens 181
D. CONCLUSION 182

5. ***THE COMMERCE CLAUSE AND THE TWENTY-FIRST AMENDMENT: AN EVOLVING CONSTITUTIONAL PUZZLE***
Margot Mendelson 183
A. INTRODUCTION 183
B. THE DORMANT COMMERCE CLAUSE: HISTORY AND DOCTRINE BEFORE THE EIGHTEENTH AMENDMENT 186
C. ALCOHOLIC BEVERAGES AND THE COMMERCE CLAUSE IN YOUNG AMERICA 189
D. PROHIBITION, REPEAL, AND THE JUDICIAL AFTERMATH: THE COMMERCE CLAUSE AND THE TWENTY-FIRST AMENDMENT 195
1. Dormant Commerce Clause Jurisprudence 198
2. The Dormant Commerce Clause and Twenty-First Amendment Jurisprudence 202
E. GRANHOLM v. HEALD AND BEYOND 206
F. IS THE THREE-TIER DISTRIBUTION SYSTEM CRUMBLING? 214

6. *WINE BRANDS AND APPELLATIONS OF ORIGIN*

Richard Mendelson and Scott Gerien 217

A. TRADEMARK LAW 218
1. Classification of Marks 225
2. Protectability and the Spectrum of Marks 227
3. Adoption and Registration of Marks 232
a. Use in Commerce Requirement for Federal Registration 233
b. Trademark Screening 234
c. The Application Process for a Federal Trademark Registration 236
d. State Trademark Registration 240
e. Legal Systems That Provide No Statutory Trademark Protection 241
4. Enforcement of Marks 241
5. Licensing of Marks 244

B. COPYRIGHT 246

C. APPELLATIONS OF ORIGIN 248
1. Defining Wine Appellations 249
a. American Viticultural Areas 251
i. AVA Naming 256
ii. AVA Boundaries 257
iii. Viticultural Distinctiveness 257
iv. Amending AVA Names or Boundaries 258
2. Protecting Wine Appellations 259
3. Other Geographical Designations on Wine Labels 260
a. Brand Names of Geographical Significance 260
b. Generic, Semi-generic and Non-generic Names of Geographical Significance 267
c. Varietal Names with Geographical Significance 268
4. The Future of Wine Appellations in the United States 268

a. Revisiting the Regulations 269
b. Privatization 274
D. CONCLUSION 280

7. ***LAND USE: RURAL WINERIES AND URBAN BARS***
Richard Mendelson and Lynne Carmichael 281
A. RURAL WINERIES 282
1. Land Use Basics 283
2. California 285
a. Napa County, California 286
3. Virginia 292
a. Source of Authority for Virginia Localities 293
b. Statutory Benefits of Licensed Farm Wineries in Virginia 294
c. Right to Farm 295
d. Statutory Protection for On-Site Marketing and Sales 296
e. Building Code Exemption and Ancillary Uses 297
f. Virginia Agritourism Liability Act 299
g. Case Study: Paradise Springs Winery in Fairfax County 299
4. Oregon 300
B. URBAN RETAILERS 304
1. New Locations 305
a. Washington 306
b. Texas 308
c. New York 310
d. California 312
New Establishments 312
Limits on the Number of Licenses Issued 312
Zoning 314
Use Permits and Conditions 315
Public Convenience or Necessity 316
ABC Notifications: Mailing, Posting, and Publication 317
Neighborhood Groups 318

Protests and Protest Hearings 318
ABC- and Police-Imposed Conditions 319
Entertainment Commission 320
Entertainment Zones 321
Summary: California's Controls on New Establishments 321
2. Controls on Existing Businesses in California 322
a. Non-Conforming Uses 322
b. Disorderly House Action 323
c. Deemed Approved Ordinances 324
d. Alcohol Impact Fees 325
C. CONCLUSION 327

8. *LITIGATING A CASE OF COUNTERFEIT WINE*
William J. Casey and Andrew G. Wanger 329
A. INTRODUCTION 329
B. RECENT HISTORY 332
C. LAWSUITS 334
1. Koch v. Rodenstock 334
2. Koch v. Greenberg 334
3. Koch v. Chicago Wine Company 335
4. Koch v. Acker Merrall & Condit Company 336
5. Koch v. Rudy Kurniawan 336
6. Koch v. Christie's International PLC 337
D. INDUSTRY TECHNIQUES TO RESPOND AND PROTECT AGAINST COUNTERFEIT WINE 338
E. LEGAL ISSUES AND LITIGATION OF A COUNTERFEIT WINE CASE 339
1. Who is an Expert in Counterfeit Wine? 340
2. Legal Claims Associated With Counterfeit Wine 341
a. Breach of Contract 341
b. Breach of Warranty 341
c. Negligence 341
d. Fraud 342
e. Negligent Misrepresentation 342
f. Unfair Business Practices 342

3. Discovery 342
4. Case Law Impacting the Counterfeit Wine Claim 343
5. Damages 344
    a. Negligence and Negligent Misrepresentation 344
    b. Breach of Contract 345
    c. Fraud 345
    d. Punitive or Exemplary Damages 345
    e. Interest 346
6. Trial 346
    a. Jury selection 346

F. CONCLUSION 347

9. *PUBLIC HEALTH AND SOCIAL RESPONSIBILITY*

Richard Mendelson **349**

A. HEALTH EFFECTS 350

B. PUBLIC SAFETY 359

C. REGULATIONS AND INTERVENTIONS 360
1. Access and Availability 360
2. Taxation and Pricing 364
3. The Drinking Context 368
4. Drunk Driving 372
5. Advertising and Marketing 374
6. Prevention 381

D. A MODEL OF SOCIAL RESPONSIBILITY 383

10. *INTERNATIONAL INSTITUTIONS AND ACCORDS*

Jacques Audier **395**

A. INSTITUTIONS 395
1. The OIV 395
    a. Historical Overview 395
    b. Participation 399

i. Members 399
ii. Observers 402
iii. Guests 403
c. Constituent Bodies 404
i. The General Assembly 404
ii. Executive Committee 406
iii. Scientific and Technical Committee 406
d. Governance 407
e. Scientific Work and Heritage 408
f. OIV Standardization 412
i. Viticultural Standards 413
ii. Oenological Standards 413
iii. Economic Standards 414
g. Relations with Other International Organizations 416
i. Codex Alimentarius Commission 417
ii. World Intellectual Property Organization 418
iii. World Trade Organization 418
B. MULTILATERAL AND BILATERAL AGREEMENTS 419
1. Multilateral Agreements 420
a. The WTO 420
i. The SPS Agreement 420
ii. The TBT Agreement 422
iii. The TRIPS Agreement 423
iv. Dispute Settlement Body 424
b. The WIPO 427
i. The Lisbon Agreement 427
ii. Standing Committee on the Law of Trademarks, Industrial Designs and Geographical Indications 428
c. World Wine Trade Group 429
2. Bilateral Agreements 429
a. The U.S.-EC Wine Accords 430
3. Others Bilateral Wine Accords 438
C. CONCLUSION 438

For Further Exploration
Richard Mendelson *441*
Index *445*

AUTHORS

Jacques Audier is Professor Emeritus at the University of Paul Cezanne/ Aix-Marseille III. He specializes in rural law and in vineyard and wine law and was the former director of the Master's degree program in vineyard and wine law. He presently is the legal advisor to the Director General of the International Organization of Vine and Wine (OIV) and is a member, and President since 2002, of the Scientific Committee on Designations of Origin, Geographical Indications and Traditional Specialties at the European Commission. He also serves as a consultant to the European Commission and the World Intellectual Property Organization. He is the author of several books on rural law and over 60 articles, of which 21 have been published in the *OIV Bulletin*. Université Paul Cezanne-Aix en Provence-Marseille, Diplôme d'Etudes 1964; Maîtrise en Droit Privé 1965; Diplôme d'Etudes Supérieures de Droit Prive 1966, de Sciences Criminelles 1967 et d'Histoire du Droit et des Faits Sociaux 1967; Docteur en Droit 1975.

Carrie Bonnington is a Senior Associate at Pillsbury Winthrop Shaw Pittman LLP, where she has been practicing since 2003. After concentrating in general civil litigation early in her practice, she began specializing in alcoholic beverage control law, focusing on litigation and advice relating to trade practices, responsible beverage service, and special events. She has presented at seminars and conferences throughout the nation. She is an adjunct professor at the University of the Pacific, McGeorge School of Law, where she coaches a mock trial team and lectures in trial advocacy. University of California Davis, BA, 2000; University of the Pacific, McGeorge School of Law, J.D., 2003.

Lynne Carmichael, a partner for 20 years at Hinman & Carmichael LLP in San Francisco, was previously a partner in the Corporate and Financial Services Group at Brobeck, Phleger & Harrison. Her current practice focuses on alcoholic beverage licensing for all business ventures, licensed business acquisitions, and trade practice counseling. She is a past president of Women for WineSense and a member of the International Wine Law Association.

She wrote the CEB treatise on transferring retail liquor licenses in California (2000) and was included in *Northern California Super Lawyers 2006*. Occidental College, B.A., 1965; University of California Berkeley Law, J.D., 1978.

William Casey is the managing partner of the San Francisco office of Clyde & Co US LLP. Bill's practice is in the area of business litigation, insurance coverage and counseling, and the defense of lawyers in legal malpractice actions. Bill is a civil litigation trial lawyer, who has tried cases to verdict, and regularly is involved in mediation practice. Bill also regularly counsels clients on the topic of risk management and loss prevention. He has also lectured at University of California Berkeley Law regarding authenticity issues surrounding rare and fine wines. Bill is a 1984 graduate of Santa Clara University School of Law, J.D., where he was editor-in-chief of the Santa Clara Law Review, and a graduate of Stanford University, A.B., 1980.

Scott Gerien is a Director of Dickenson, Peatman & Fogarty in Napa, California, where he heads the firm's Intellectual Property Department. Since his first case in 1996, *Kendall Jackson v. Gallo*, Scott has represented hundreds of wineries in intellectual property matters. Scott is very active with the International Trademark Association (INTA) and helped author the INTA Proposal for a Multilateral Register for Geographical Indications for Wines and Spirits. He is also a board member of the International Wine Law Association. In 2006, 2007, and 2009, Scott was identified by *Trademark Insider* as one of the top 50 trademark attorneys in the United States, and in 2009 *Wine Industry Business Journal* named him one of the top wine lawyers in Northern California and described him as "one of the most knowledgeable wine trademark-protection attorneys in the nation and the world." Trinity College, B.A., 1990; University of California Berkeley Law, J.D., 1996.

Erik Lawrence is an Associate at Dickenson, Peatman & Fogarty, where he has practiced since 2008. His practice focuses on business and real estate transactional law, specializing in servicing clients in all areas of the beverage alcohol industry. Prior to his legal career, he was an Associate Vice President in Wells Fargo's Commercial Banking Group. He received a Bachelor of Science degree in Managerial Economics from the University of California Davis in 1997 and a Juris Doctor degree from the University of California Davis School of Law in 2007, where he was Managing Editor of the *UC Davis Law Review* and a member of the Order of the Coif.

Wendell Lee is General Counsel to Wine Institute, the public policy advocacy group consisting of more than 1,000 California wineries and affiliated businesses. Wine Institute represents 85 percent of U.S. wine production and 90 percent of U.S. wine exports. He has been with Wine Institute since 1980 and deals with all legal matters for the organization. Additionally, he oversees the Wine Institute website, computer database, and technical support. For four years prior to joining Wine Institute, Wendell was a criminal trial attorney serving in the Office of the District Attorney for the City and County of San Francisco. He is a graduate of Hastings College of the Law and the University of Hawaii and has been a member of the California Bar since 1977.

Margot Mendelson is a law clerk for the Honorable Diana Gribbon Motz on the U.S. Court of Appeals for the Fourth Circuit. She worked previously at the University of Arizona Rogers College of Law and the Migration Policy Institute. She has published works in the *Yale Law Journal*, the *Berkeley Women's Law Review*, and the *Harvard Review of Latin America*. She is a graduate of Harvard College (B.A., 2003), Yale Law School (J.D., 2009), a member of the California Bar, and an Arthur Liman Public Interest Law Fellow (2009-2010).

Richard Mendelson directs the Program on Wine Law and Policy at the University of California, Berkeley, School of Law, where he teaches classes on wine law and geographical indications. He is counsel to the law firm of Dickenson, Peatman & Fogarty in Napa, California, where he has practiced wine law since 1986. He is past president and current director of the International Wine Law Association, headquartered in Paris. He is the author of *From Demon to Darling: A Legal History of Wine in America* (University of California Press 2009), which was awarded the Law Prize in 2009 from the International Organization of Vine and Wine, and *Spirit in Metal* (Val de Grâce 2011), on his work as a metal sculptor. He owns Mendelson Wines and sells a Pinot Noir and two dessert wines under that label. Harvard College, B.A, 1975; Oxford University, Magdalen College, M.A., 1977; Stanford Law, J.D., 1982.

James Seff heads the Wine, Beer & Spirits Law practice at Pillsbury Winthrop Shaw Pittman in San Francisco and previously was Wine Institute's chief counsel. He is a professional member of the American Society for Enology and Viticulture, a former chair of the American Bar Association Alcoholic Beverage Practice Committee, and a founding member of the International Wine Law Association. His practice deals with all wine industry legal issues, including regulatory matters, trade practices, mergers and acquisitions, litigation, and internal investigations. *Chambers USA* rates him Tier 1 in Food and Beverages: Alcohol. His publications include chapters in the *UC/Sotheby Book of California Wine; Successful Wine Marketing*; and *Inside the Mind: Food, Beverage & Drug Law*. He was president of the San Francisco Bar Association, was a governor of the California State Bar, and is a retired U.S. Navy Captain. University of Michigan, A.B. with Honors in English, 1963; University of California Berkeley Law, J.D., 1966.

James Terry is a Director of Dickenson, Peatman & Fogarty, where he has practiced since 1995. Jim has represented buyers in numerous vineyard and winery acquisitions throughout California. His wine industry–related practice includes alcoholic beverage law, business entity selection and formation, business planning, sales and acquisitions, grape purchase agreements, and vineyard leasing. He has lectured extensively on wine law subjects in California. His publications include "Grapes to Wine: Business Models and the Regulation of Wine Production," published in the Organisation Internationale de La Vigne et Du Vin's *Le Bulletin de L'OIV* in 2006. Jim is past president of the Napa County Bar Association and a member of the Real Property and Business Law sections of the California Bar Association. He is the current Managing Director of Dickenson, Peatman & Fogarty. University of California Berkeley,

A.B., 1972; Santa Clara University School of Law, J.D., 1976; New York University School of Law, LL.M, 1978, where he was awarded the Donald L. Brown Fellowship in Trade Regulation.

Andrew Wanger is a partner with Clyde & Co US LLP. He is a trial lawyer practicing in the area of civil litigation. His practice regularly includes the representation of businesses in contract disputes and of other legal professionals in malpractice actions, and the defense of insurers in complex insurance coverage disputes. Andrew has extensive civil and criminal trial experience, having tried numerous cases to verdict. He previously served as a Deputy District Attorney for Fresno County from 1995 to 1996. Andrew is a 1993 graduate of Santa Clara University School of Law, J.D., and a graduate of Santa Clara University, B.S., 1990.

FOREWORD

Mike Thompson

As the congressman from Northern California's premier wine growing region, I've been introduced to some of the world's top wine aficionados. They've talked extensively about how wine is more than just a beverage; it's a gateway to a better food experience, to a place's culture, to a vineyard's soil and climate, and to a winery's technique.

When they talk, I nod and smile. I'm truly appreciative of the passion they bring to wine. But when you were born and raised in the Napa Valley, when you are the third generation in the wine community, and when you have done every job in the industry from fixing tractors to washing out barrels to growing grapes, you *know* that wine is so much more.

In my congressional district, which includes the Napa Valley and Sonoma, Lake, Mendocino, and Yolo Counties, wine is life. It's an economic backbone, spreading jobs beyond wineries and vineyards to restaurants, retail, and tourism. It's the taxes that pay for our schools and roads. It's the business name on the back of the little league uniforms and the patron of the new hospital wing. It's the farmer who religiously monitors the rain and temperature. It's the winery owner who grew an internationally recognized brand out of a few barrels in her cellar.

For us, great wines are more than just tasting notes. They are a testament to the hard-working people and incredible natural resources that make up our home. But they are also a product of the policies, laws, and regulations that govern how wine is made and sold.

When Richard Mendelson asked me to write the foreword to his comprehensive book on the policy and law behind wine, I saw it as an amazing opportunity to help tell the story of what I taste when I drink a wine from my congressional district—the people, the agriculture, as well as the tax policy, trade laws, and labeling regulations. A book like this goes beyond the wine in the bottle and back through the story of the economic, political, and legal factors that brought the wine into existence. And I believe that once you learn how these factors can be as complex and engaging as a 98 point Napa Valley cabernet, the wine on your palate will taste even better.

That is exactly what drove me to form the Congressional Wine Caucus when I first came to Congress in 1998. Most Members of Congress had no idea of the impact their policy decisions have on wine, but I soon found out they were eager to learn—and taste—more. The Wine Caucus, which today is one of the largest bipartisan and bicameral groups on Capitol Hill, meets regularly to discuss policies pertaining to wine, such as efforts to control agricultural pests, barriers to increasing American wine's presence in the global market, and wine's impact on public health. But with those discussions, I also like to introduce my fellow representatives to the people behind the wine, whether it's the independent winemaker, the fifth-generation grape grower, or even the sommelier at a hip new restaurant. These are the people who bring the policies to life.

Over the years, I've seen congressional interest in wine grow as vineyards have taken root across our country. Now that wine is made in all 50 states, every representative and senator has reason to be invested in the success of American wine. And, like me, they are quickly learning that wine is more than a beverage or even an experience; it's an economic driver and community builder.

As a result, these Members of Congress have joined the people from my district, who know wine is not just a matter of what tastes good and what doesn't. They've seen how laws, policies, and court decisions such as the ones discussed in this book make a big difference in whether the wines from their congressional districts succeed or not. A recent issue they grappled with was a proposal in Congress to increase the federal excise tax on wine by a massive amount. Most people know intrinsically that an increase in the excise tax means higher prices on the wine shelves. But what members of the Congressional Wine Caucus discussed were the thousands of winery and vineyard jobs that would be lost as a result of the increase. We also talked about the vineyards that would be eaten up by development when the price of the excise tax eclipsed the value of the grapes. Fortunately, we were able to point out the consequences of the legislation for jobs and our agricultural lands, and the proposal was defeated.

But this example is exactly why the stories behind wine—the jobs, the land, and the communities—are so important to understand. Since Prohibition, an arcane and idiosyncratic maze of policies and laws has been erected around wine, to the point that most people who consider themselves oenophiles know very little about, and have been given few opportunities to understand, such critical elements of the wines they love to drink. The complex subject matters involved, such as constitutional law, intellectual property, taxation, and international trade, are often addressed by people far removed from the wineries and vineyards. Yet to someone like me or my neighbors at home, these subject matters are at the very center of American wine. And we know that the disconnect between people's understanding of wine and the policies and laws that govern it is a real threat to our way of life.

That is what makes this book—the first of its kind in America—such a critical read. Written by experienced wine law attorneys Richard Mendelson and colleagues, it provides valuable information and insights into the laws and policies that make American wine what it is. This book should be studied by any American student, scholar, government regulator, or policymaker who wants to truly understand wine.

Examples of why this book is so important abound. As this book goes to press, the wine community is embroiled in another important policy battle. Legislation was introduced in Congress again this year that would strip the federal government of its power over interstate commerce in alcoholic beverages and put it entirely in the hands of states, in essence allowing the Twenty-first Amendment to trump the Commerce Clause. Although this is a subject traditionally more familiar to Congress watchers than wine drinkers, it is central to the ability of wine lovers everywhere to buy and receive wines directly from wineries in interstate commerce. Since its introduction, the legislation has been amended to limit its scope, but its future direction is unpredictable. Wineries, legislators, and consumers must remain vigilant and oppose attempts to limit consumer wine choices or to unreasonably restrict the rights of wineries to access these consumers.

A topic this complex, yet incredibly important to the future of American wine, requires a deep understanding of wine policy and law, one that few have. Yet this policy proposal is just one example of many that are being brought before policymakers and regulators on the federal, state, and local levels. Richard Mendelson's book is exactly the place to begin for those who want to quickly gain this understanding without having to immerse themselves in tens of thousands of pages of legal text.

For most wine drinkers, taste is all that matters. And for those of us who are involved in making wine, that's fine by us. But anyone who wants to know the story behind the wine needs to look at the people, the land, the history, and the laws and policies that brought the wine to your table. This book is where to start.

Mike Thompson
Member of Congress and
Co-chair, Congressional Wine Caucus
March 2011

INTRODUCTION AND ACKNOWLEDGMENTS

What is wine law? Technically, it is a branch of administrative law concerning the regulation of wine, as a subset of alcoholic beverages. But this definition is altogether too narrow. In my wine law practice, spanning more than 25 years, I have handled a wide variety of legal matters of vital interest to the wine industry in areas such as land use, intellectual property, international trade, torts, specialized contracts (distributor agreements, grape purchase and sale agreements, vineyard leases), environmental law, tax law, constitutional law, and administrative law.

This being what I learned, this also is what I have taught. My Wine Law class at the University of California, Berkeley, School of Law ("Berkeley Law") is essentially a survey class covering diverse legal fields, all focused on wine. We also address important wine policy issues such as promoting public health, preserving agriculture, preventing wine counterfeiting, and eliminating international trade barriers. For embracing such a wide vision of wine law and allowing me to teach at their universities, I thank Berkeley Law and Pam Samuelson in particular, the University of Aix-Marseille Law Faculty (Jacques Audier), the University of Bordeaux Law Faculty (Dominique Denis, Antoine Vialard, and Jean-Marc Bahans), the University of Reims Law Faculty (Theodore Georgopoulos), and the University of California, Davis, School of Management (Bob Smiley).

Wine law is arcane and often counter-intuitive. Without an understanding of the history of temperance and Prohibition in our country, one cannot begin to comprehend the spirit or the letter of wine law. This is why I wrote my first book, *From Demon to Darling: A Legal History of Wine in America* (University of California Press 2009). As that book shows, our laws are deeply rooted in our history, and a firm grasp of that history is essential. For example, were it not for the saloons of the pre-Prohibition and Prohibition eras—those dens of iniquity that infuriated women temperance crusaders—we might not have special laws that prohibit trade practices such as tied-houses, free goods, and consignment sales, practices that are commonplace in other industries. And if we had not begun in the 1830s to devolve control over alcoholic beverages to local communities, we might not have local option elections on the sale and service of alcoholic beverages across the United States today.

Despite these deep historical roots, wine law is evolving rapidly as the wine industry expands at home and abroad. Nowhere is this more evident than in the area of Twenty-first Amendment jurisprudence, particularly in relation to direct-to-consumer interstate shipments of wine, and intellectual property, where wine brands and appellations of origin are important focal points in the ongoing discussion at the World Trade Organization about geographical indications.

Wine law is idiosyncratic, as anyone who has dealt with the subject quickly realizes. It is a world unto itself, with its own constitutional provisions (intoxicating liquors are the subject of not just one, but two, constitutional amendments—the Eighteenth and the Twenty-first), its own language (tied-house, primary source, semi-generics, to name a few), and its own regulators at the state, federal, and sometimes local levels.

Finally, wine law is fun, in large part because wine itself is fun. My Berkeley Law students always look forward to our class wine tasting, which focuses on appellations of origin. Are appellations meaningful to consumers? Can consumers tell the difference between wines made from grapes grown in distinct appellations? The only way to know is to taste the product.

This book follows the general outline of my Wine Law class at Berkeley Law. We begin with an overview of the subject, followed by individual chapters on wine industry trade practices (Jim Seff and Carrie Bonnington), wine labeling and advertising (Wendell Lee), business models for grape growing and winemaking (Jim Terry and Erik Lawrence), Twenty-first Amendment jurisprudence (Margot Mendelson), intellectual property involving wine brands and wine appellations (Scott Gerien and me), land use in the context of rural wineries and urban bars (Lynne Carmichael and me), wine counterfeiting (Bill Casey and Andrew Wanger), public health and social responsibility (myself), and international institutions and accords that deal with wine (Jacques Audier). My co-authors are my colleagues and friends and, in the area of constitutional law, my daughter. I have the utmost confidence in their abilities and their experience. Most of them have lectured to my students, so their presentations have been classroom tested. I thank them all for their valuable contributions.

Finally, I thank my students, past and present, for their questions, opinions, and feedback; Alexis Burgess, Negin Iraninejadian, and Kim Lehmkuhl for their research and editorial assistance; my secretary, Jaymie Kilgore, who coordinated the manuscript preparation; the very capable staff of Berkeley Law Library; and my wife, Marilyn, for her patience and support, for reviewing every chapter, and for sharing with me a love of wine and culture.

Richard Mendelson
Napa, California
March 2011

CHAPTER 1

U.S. WINE LAW: AN OVERVIEW

Richard Mendelson

The system of laws controlling the production, marketing, distribution, and sale of wine in the 50 states that comprise the United States is of recent origin compared to its foreign counterparts. This body of law has evolved rapidly from a set of liquor licensing and anti-drunkenness laws in colonial America to the present complex and interrelated set of local, state, and federal regulations that govern all aspects of the wine business.

Section A of this overview presents a brief history of American wine law. Section B discusses the modern-day federal and state wine laws and the regulatory authorities that enforce them. Section C focuses on the various operations and activities that are central to the wine business, beginning with viticulture, then wine production, and finally marketing, distribution, and sales. Many of these topics are addressed in greater detail in other chapters of the book, and those particular chapters are referenced where appropriate.

A. HISTORICAL OVERVIEW

While the first tax on wine in the United States did not appear until 1862,[1] evidence of grape growing and wine production can be traced back to the first

1. In 1862 Congress imposed an internal revenue duty on domestic producers of wine made from grapes that was produced, sold, or removed for consumption in the U.S. Revenue Act of 1862, ch. 119, §75, 12 Stat. 432, 462, 465. No duty was imposed on artificial or imitation wines under that Act. In 1864 Congress expanded the coverage of the duties on internal and imported wine. Regarding imports, the statute imposed a duty on wines of all kinds based on the value of the product; the statute imposed special duty rates on champagne and sparkling wines. Act of June 30, 1864, ch. 171, §2, para. 1, 13 Stat. 202, 203 (increasing duties on imports). By a separate act on the same day, Congress expanded the coverage of the domestic duty on wine products. While the Act continued to impose the same domestic duty on wine made from grapes, it also provided for a duty "[o]n all other wines or liquors known or denominated as wine, not made from currants,

European settlers who established the American colonies. As civilization brought wine and winemaking to Europe, it did the same for America. Early settlers, however, were unsuccessful in producing quality wine from native grapes. Their efforts to cultivate European vines also failed because of the harsh climate on the east coast, with its excessively cold winters and its high humidity during the growing season.[2]

In the late 1700s some progress was made in the utilization of native vines. However, it was not until the 1820s, after the introduction of American hybrids,[3] that decent domestic wines began to be produced that did not require fortification (the addition of spirits) or adulteration (the addition of extraneous substances). By the middle of the nineteenth century, winemaking had become an important but relatively small industry in the United States, with Ohio, Missouri, New York, and California leading the way. The consumption of wine was minuscule compared to that of beer and spirits; wine represented only 4 percent of the total volume of alcoholic beverages consumed in the United States in 1869.[4]

Wine could not escape the growing temperance movement in America,[5] despite the fact that temperance advocates targeted, at least initially, "ardent spirits."[6] Spirits, with their higher alcohol levels, were thought to be unhealthy by Dr. Benjamin Rush, a leading physician of the era. By contrast, Dr. Rush regarded wine as a temperate beverage, reinforcing Minister Increase Mather's

---

rhubarb or berries produced by being rectified or mixed with other spirits, or into which any matter whatever may be infused to be sold as wine, or by any other name, and not otherwise provided for in this act. . . ." Revenue Act of 1864, ch. 173, §94, 13 Stat. 223, 264, 269.

2. Maynard A. Amerine, American Wine Industry to 1960, in Wine Production Technology in the United States 1, 1 (Maynard A. Amerine ed., 1981), describes the causes of these failures:

> Some plantings of the European grapes succeeded for a time but sooner or later most died. It was not for lack of care. Or interest. The problems were primarily climatic: excessively cold winters for cold-sensitive *V. vinifera* varieties and high humidity during the growing period. The periodic cold winters partially, and sometimes completely, killed the vines. The humid growing seasons fanned the growth of endemic cryptogamic diseases: downy and powdery mildew, anthracnose, black rot, etc. The death of the vine in the South Atlantic states may have been attributable to Pierce's disease, a bacterial disease that we will later find in California. Fungicides to control mildew, etc. were still far in the future. Finally, in many areas the native root louse, phylloxera, probably destroyed the susceptible *V. vinifera* varieties.

3. Hybrids are the offspring of two different grape species, occurring naturally by cross-pollination or induced by man "to combine in the progeny some of the desirable characteristics of the parents." Oxford Companion to Wine 499-500 (Jancis Robinson ed., Oxford University Press 1994). Many of today's commercial rootstocks are hybrids.

4. S. W. Shear & Gerald G. Pearce, Supply and Price Trends in the California Wine-Grape Industry, table 2 and figure 2 (Giannini Foundation of Agricultural Economics, Mimeographed Report No. 34, 1934). Today wine accounts for 9.2 percent of the total domestic consumption of alcoholic beverages. National Institute on Alcohol Abuse and Alcoholism, Volume Beverage and Ethanol Consumption for States, Census Regions, and the United States, 1970-2007, Oct. 2009, http://www.niaaa.nih.gov/Resources/DatabaseResources/QuickFacts/AlcoholSales/consum02.htm (accessed December 18, 2010).

5. The genesis of the temperance movement in the United States is beyond the scope of this chapter. For further details, *see* Richard Mendelson, From Demon to Darling: A Legal History of Wine in America 6-49 (University of California Press 2009).

6. Ardent spirits, now an obsolete term, refers to the fiery taste of spirituous liquors. Liquor is used throughout this section to refer to any alcoholic beverage.

statement that "the wine is from God."[7] Gradually the temperance movement, like its members' pledges, became more severe, moving from opposition to spirits to a demand for teetotalism (complete abstinence from all alcoholic beverages).

The reasons for abstinence were numerous: religious dogma, moral concerns, cultural norms, social order, public health and safety, and worker efficiency, to name a few. Not surprisingly, there was and still is no consensus in the United States on what constitutes responsible use of alcohol — which beverages and in what quantities and contexts — and its opposite, harmful and hazardous use. The appropriate legal and policy prescriptions therefore have varied widely over time. Thomas Jefferson, for example, envisioned an agrarian society in which domestic wine was cheap and plentiful, and spirits were heavily taxed to dampen demand for them. One hundred years later Wayne Wheeler, as "boss" of the Anti-Saloon League, cleverly combined the forces of business and the church to pressure Congress to enact, and the states to ratify, National Prohibition. Wheeler's goal was to annihilate all the "booze brothers" — beer, wine, and spirits.

During the colonial period, long before the nation's experiment with prohibition, Americans had made drunkenness a crime. The city of Baltimore, for example, defined drunkenness in 1638 as "drinking with excess to the noticable [sic] perturbation of any organ or sense or motion."[8] No arrest was more common than that for drunkenness. It also was a crime in many American colonies and later in early states to pay for labor with alcohol;[9] to sell alcoholic beverages on Sundays or during the hours of "divine service"; or to sell alcohol to a minor, an idler, a felon, a habitual drunkard, an actual drunkard, or a Native American, or to sell it within a given distance from a university or a church.

To regulate the lawful trade in alcoholic beverages, Americans relied on liquor licensing. The model was the English licensing system that applied, beginning in the sixteenth century, to public houses ("pubs"), alehouses (where beer was sold), dram shops (bars at which spirits could be sold in measured quantities (drams) of less than one gallon),[10] and other places where alcoholic beverages were sold. Sidney and Beatrice Webb, in *The History of Liquor Licensing in England Principally from 1700 to 1830*, summarized the purposes of liquor licensing in England:

> The device of licensing — that is, the requirement that any person desiring to pursue a particular occupation shall first obtain specific permission from a governing authority — may be used to attain many different ends. The licence [sic] may be merely an occasion for extracting a fee or levying a tax. It may be an

---

7. Increase Mather, Wo to Drunkards, Two Sermons Testifying against the Sin of Drunkenness: Wherein the Woefulness of that Evil, and the Misery of all that are addicted to it, is discovered from the Word of God 4 (Boston: Marmaduke Johnson, 1673).

8. Gallus Thomann, Colonial Liquor Laws, Part II: Liquor Laws of the United States; Their Spirit and Effect 71 (New York: U.S. Brewers' Ass'n 1887).

9. *Id.* at 11.

10. Ronald S. Beitman, Practitioner's Guide to Liquor Liability Litigation 3 n.2 (Philadelphia: American Law Institute 1987).

> instrument for registering all those who are following a particular occupation, in order, for some reason or another, to ensure their being brought under public notice. It may be a device for limiting the numbers of those so engaged, or for selecting them according to their possession of certain qualifications. Finally, the act of licensing may be the means of imposing special rules upon the occupation, or of more easily enforcing the fulfillment either of these special rules or of the general law of the land.[11]

Liquor licenses in the young United States were granted by local officials at their sole discretion, sometimes with the requirement of letters of support from the immediate neighborhood or the local community. Unlicensed purveyors were subject to criminal prosecution. Licenses were conditioned on compliance with a host of measures. Pricing measures figured prominently. Price controls were used for various purposes, depending on the community's goals: to reduce consumption by raising prices, to eliminate price competition though fixed prices, or to encourage customers to drink wine and beer rather than spirits.[12] The licensing laws frequently specified which trade practices were allowed or banned. For example, there were restrictions on tippling (habitual drinking, sometimes referred to as soaking), free rounds, profanity, gambling, and other disreputable practices.

Licensing had one other important benefit. From the government's perspective, licensing generated significant revenues from various fees, taxes, and other instruments, including license stamps, surety bonds, duties, and excise taxes.[13] Because the taxes and other sumptuary laws[14] were designed, in part, to curb excessive drinking, they became known as "sin" taxes.

Over time, the problem of drunkenness grew more severe, leading historian W. J. Rorabaugh to describe the United States of the early 1800s as "a nation of drunkards."[15] The apex of American drinking was between 1805 and 1830, when per capita consumption of absolute alcohol hovered around seven gallons.[16] In response, states and local communities adopted more stringent regulations. The number and locations of licensed premises were carefully controlled. Both civil and criminal nuisance actions against purveyors of liquor were authorized. Communities began to pass dram shop laws to circumvent the common law theory of tort liability, which held that the owner of a

---

11. Sidney Webb & Beatrice Webb, The History of Liquor Licensing in England Principally from 1700 to 1830, at 4 (London: Longmans, Green and Co. 1903).

12. Phinizy Spalding, Oglethorpe in America 49 (Athens: University of Georgia Press 1984). In the colony of Georgia, General James Oglethorpe, the colony's founder, proposed and the colony's trustees passed a law in 1735 that prohibited the importation and sale of rum, brandy, and other distilled spirits. Wine and beer were excluded.

13. An excise is a tax on manufacture or sale or for a business license or charter. In the case of alcoholic beverages, the amount of the redundantly named "excise tax" depends on the alcoholic content of the particular beverage.

14. Sumptuary laws are defined in Black's Law Dictionary as "limit[ing] the expenditures that people can make for personal gratification or ostentatious display" or, "[m]ore broadly, any law whose purpose is to regulate conduct thought to be immoral, such as prostitution, gambling, or drug abuse." Black's Law Dictionary 1574 (9th ed. 2009).

15. W. J. Rorabaugh, The Alcoholic Republic 3-22 (New York: Oxford University Press 1979).

16. *Id.* at 233, table A1.2. By contrast, average per capita alcohol consumption today is less than 10 liters. One gallon equals 3.785 liters.

liquor establishment could not be held liable for any damages caused by a drunkard because the proximate cause of the damage was the intoxicated person, not the seller. Under the common law, even if the liquor store were to supply drinks to a minor or an obviously intoxicated person, the owner would not be liable.[17] The dram shop laws imposed statutory as opposed to common law liability on the owner for selling or serving alcohol to a minor, a habitual drunkard, or an intoxicated person who was subsequently involved in an accident. Some states required liquor purveyors to post a bond to pay for the actual damages sustained in such an accident, the support of injured parties and their families, and punitive damages.[18] Sometimes the recovery under the dram shop law was limited to the amount of the bond.

In the 1830s local jurisdictions began to hold "local option" elections at which the voters would decide whether beer, wine, or spirits could be sold within the jurisdiction's borders and, if so, at which types of establishments (for consumption on the premises with or without food or for takeout), on which days, and at what hours. In this way, the community would set its own drinking standards. Not surprisingly, the rise of the local option coincided with the growing politicization of the liquor issue in the United States.

In 1851 Neal Dow, the mayor of Portland, Maine, and an ardent prohibitionist, spearheaded the adoption of a state law that prohibited the manufacture and sale of intoxicating liquor in Maine, with only minor exceptions.[19] The Maine Law became the model for the first wave of prohibitory liquor laws in America. Now not only local jurisdictions but entire states were "dry." These laws, however, raised important constitutional questions regarding individual liberties,[20] private property rights, and substantive and procedural due process. Prior to the

---

17. The modern rule of common law liability on commercial servers of alcoholic beverages began with the decision of the New Jersey Supreme Court in *Rappaport v. Nichols*, 31 N.J. 188, 156 A.2d 1 (1959). In its holding, the court stated,

> We are fully mindful that policy considerations and the balancing of the conflicting interests are the truly vital factors in the molding and application of the common law principles of negligence and proximate causation. But we are convinced that recognition of the plaintiff's claim will afford a fairer measure of justice to innocent third parties whose injuries are brought about by the unlawful and negligent sale of alcoholic beverages to minors and intoxicated persons, will strengthen and give greater force to the enlightened statutory and regulatory precautions against such sales and their frightening consequences, and will not place any unjustifiable burdens upon defendants who can always discharge their civil responsibilities by the exercise of due care.

Id. at 205.

18. Beitman, *supra* note 10, at 4.

19. The exceptions were for liquor used for mechanical and medicinal purposes, sold by an agent of the city or state government, and liquor "of foreign production . . . imported under the laws of the United States . . . contained in the original packages." 1851 Me. Acts 211 (repealed 1856).

20. John Stuart Mill believed that prohibition was an illegitimate interference with the rightful liberty of the individual. In *On Liberty* (1869), he acknowledged that prohibition was based on the doctrine of social rights and described the argument in its favor as follows:

> I claim, as a citizen, a right to legislate whenever my social rights are invaded by the social act of another. . . . If anything invades my social rights, certainly the traffic in strong drink does. It destroys my primary right of security, by constantly creating and stimulating social disorder. It invades my right of equality, by deriving a profit from the creation of a misery I am taxed to support. It impedes my right to free moral and intellectual

adoption in 1868 of the Fourteenth Amendment to the U.S. Constitution, state courts decided these cases based on the provisions of the particular state's constitution. After 1868 the Supreme Court established the law of the land with respect to whether prohibition violates the privileges or immunities of U.S. citizens; deprives any person of life, liberty, or property without due process of law; or denies any person the equal protection of the laws. In the key case of *Mugler v. Kansas*, 123 U.S. 623 (1887), the Supreme Court upheld Kansas's prohibitory law as a valid exercise of the state's police power under the Tenth Amendment[21] and found that it did not infringe on the Fourteenth Amendment.

Liquor commerce was another subject altogether. Article 1, §8 of the Constitution, known as the Commerce Clause, gives Congress the authority to regulate interstate and foreign commerce.[22] When the state of Maryland in 1827 imposed a license requirement and a licensing fee for the privilege of importing wine, among other goods, into that state from abroad, the Supreme Court by a vote of 6 to 1 invalidated the state law in light of Congress's express authorization of these imports.[23] According to Chief Justice John Marshall, who wrote the decision in *Brown v. Maryland*, only when the imported goods were "mixed up with the mass of property" in the state could Maryland exercise its police power. "While remaining the property of the importer in his warehouse in the original form or package in which it was imported," the imported good was not subject to state interference.[24] This became known as the "original package" doctrine.

But Congress never explicitly authorized interstate commerce in liquor. Where Congress is silent, can the states legislate under their police power in matters affecting interstate commerce? In *The License Cases* of 1847, the Supreme Court in six separate opinions upheld a New Hampshire law requiring a license for the sale in that state of spirits in their original package imported from Massachusetts.[25] Because of the diversity of opinions, it was difficult to interpret the Court's Commerce Clause jurisprudence. Subsequently, the Court clarified its position and reversed its decision in *The License Cases*, holding that a state could neither prohibit the transportation of liquor from one

---

> development, by surrounding my path with dangers, and by weakening and demoralizing society, from which I have a right to claim mutual aid and intercourse.

But he quickly dismissed these arguments as well as prohibition, writing,

> So monstrous a principle is far more dangerous than any single interference with liberty; there is no violation of liberty which it would not justify; it acknowledges no right to any freedom whatever, except perhaps to that of holding opinions in secret, without ever disclosing them. . . . The doctrine ascribes to all mankind a vested interest in each other's moral, intellectual, and even physical perfection, to be defined by each claimant according to his own standard.

John Stuart Mill, On Liberty 160-161 (London: Longman, Roberts & Green 1869).

21. The Tenth Amendment provides that "[t]he powers not delegated to the United States by the Constitution, nor prohibited by it to the States, are reserved to the States respectively, or to the people." U.S. Const. amend. X.

22. Article I, §8, clause 3 states, "The Congress shall have a Power . . . to regulate Commerce with foreign Nations, and among the several States, and with the Indian Tribes."

23. *Brown v. Maryland*, 25 U.S. 419 (1827).

24. *Id.* at 441-442.

25. *The License Cases*, 46 U.S. 504 (1847).

state to another nor require a license for an importer of liquor from another state if the liquor remained in its original package.[26]

The original package doctrine opened a major hole in the states' prohibitory laws. Only Congress, through the exercise of its Commerce Clause authority, could change the situation. As prohibitionists grew more powerful, they exerted pressure on Congress to act. Ultimately, Congress did so, not by setting specific standards for interstate and international trade in liquor but by deferring to state authority over the distribution and sale of alcohol within the state's borders. First, Congress passed the Wilson Act in 1890, which provided

> [t]hat all fermented, distilled, or other intoxicating liquors or liquids transported into any State or Territory or remaining therein for use, consumption, sale, or storage therein, shall upon arrival in such State or Territory be subject to the operation and effect of the laws of such State or Territory enacted in the exercise of its police powers, to the same extent and in the same manner as though such liquids or liquors had been produced in such State or Territory, and shall not be exempt therefrom by reason of being introduced therein in original packages or otherwise.[27]

When the Wilson Act failed to halt interstate liquor shipments into dry states for personal use rather than for resale,[28] Congress passed the Webb-Kenyon Act of 1913, which remains in effect today.[29] The Webb-Kenyon Act is subtitled "An Act divesting intoxicating liquors of their interstate character in certain cases." It provides:

> [t]hat the shipment or transportation, in any manner or by any means whatsoever, of any spirituous, vinous, malted, fermented, or other intoxicating liquor of any kind, from one State, Territory, or District of the United States, . . . into any other State, Territory, or District of the United States, . . . or from any foreign country into any State, Territory, or District of the United States, . . . which said spirituous, vinous, malted, fermented, or other intoxicating liquor is *intended*, by any person interested therein, *to be received, possessed, sold, or in any manner used, either in the original package or otherwise*, in violation of any law of such State, Territory, or District of the United States . . . is hereby prohibited.

(Emphasis added.)

Despite its extensive reach, the Webb-Kenyon Act did not halt the transportation of liquor through a state for delivery elsewhere.[30]

---

26. *Bowman v. Chicago Nw. Ry. Co.*, 125 U.S. 465 (1888) (states do not have the right to prevent the importation of liquor from another state); *Leisy v. Hardin*, 135 U.S. 100 (1890) (invalidating Iowa's ban on the sale of liquor imported from another state in its original package). The Court in *Leisy* stated clearly that liquor importers have the right to import beer from another state and to sell it, "by which act alone it would become mingled in the common mass of property within the state. Up to that point of time, we hold that, in the absence of congressional permission to do so, the state had no power to interfere by seizure, or any other action, in prohibition of importation and sale. . . ." 135 U.S. at 124.

27. Wilson Act, ch. 728, 26 Stat. 313 (1890) (codified at 27 U.S.C. §121 (2006)).

28. *See Rhodes v. Iowa*, 170 U.S. 412 (1898).

29. Webb-Kenyon Act, ch. 90, 37 Stat. 699 (1913) (codified at 27 U.S.C. §122 (2006)).

30. *See, e.g., Alcohol Div. of Dep't of Fin. & Taxation of Tenn. v. State ex rel. Strawbridge*, 63 So. 2d 358, 360 (Ala. 1953). The court reasoned as follows:

> Transportation of intoxicating liquors from one state through another state is within the protection of the commerce clause of the federal constitution and not subject to state interference. And this is true regardless of whether the state to which the liquor is being

Historian Anne-Marie Szymanski has described the history of prohibition in America as a process of "local gradualism," essentially a step function from local to state to federal regulation of alcohol, growing stricter with each step.[31] But not all cities and states moved in the same direction at the same time. Jack Blocker concluded in *American Temperance Movements: Cycles of Reform* that there were three distinct cycles of prohibition: 1805-1840, 1851–1865, and 1907-1913.[32] Whether by step or cycle, prohibitionist sentiment in America advanced. With the Anti-Saloon League (ASL) at the helm, wary about future changes of people and policies in Congress and at the Supreme Court, prohibitionists pushed for a constitutional amendment to prohibit trade in liquor across America and make the country forever dry.

The perpetual symbol of the social evils surrounding alcohol and the rallying cry for the ASL was the saloon. The infamous Carrie Nation called attention to the sordid saloons through her hatchet attacks on them across the United States. Frances Willard was just as tireless a temperance reformer who spoke of "a war between the rum shops and religion."[33] However, she eschewed violence, telling the members of her Woman's Christian Temperance Union to be "wise as serpents and harmless as doves"[34] when they filed into saloons, Bibles in hand. All the while, the ASL, a single-issue, politically astute, well-funded organization, applied political pressure to advance the prohibitionist cause.

When the United States entered World War I, the country's enthusiasm for prohibition accelerated. The spirit of sacrifice and hostility to all things German were constant themes. Sacrifice meant the conservation of grain used to produce alcoholic beverages; beer and brewers were demonized because of their association with the Kaiser. In the midst of the national emergency, Congress adopted wartime prohibition and then, on December 18, 1917, passed a joint resolution proposing the Eighteenth Amendment to the Constitution, known as National Prohibition or simply Prohibition (with a capital *P*). That resolution was sent to the states for ratification. On January 16, 1920, the amendment went into effect. The Eighteenth Amendment reads in pertinent part as follows:

> §1. After one year from the ratification of this article the manufacture, sale, or transportation of intoxicating liquors within, the importation thereof into, or

---

shipped prohibits the sale and traffic in such liquors. The Twenty-first Amendment to the Federal Constitution, together with the Webb-Kenyon Act, 27 U.S.C.A. §122, which prohibits the transportation or importation of intoxicating liquors into any state for delivery or use therein in violation of its laws, does not render such liquor contraband while passing through Alabama into another state for disposition in violation of the laws of the latter state, nor authorize seizure and condemnation of such liquors and the transporting vehicles under Alabama statutes.

31. Anne-Marie E. Szymanski, Pathways to Prohibition (Durham, NC: Duke University Press 2003).

32. Jack S. Blocker, Jr., American Temperance Movements: Cyles of Reform (Boston: Twayne Publishers 1989).

33. Let Something Good Be Said: Speeches and Writings of Frances E. Willard 4 (Carolyn DeSwarte Gifford & Amy R. Slagell eds., University of Illinois Press 2007).

34. Mary C. Johnson, Our Method of Saloon-Visiting, in Hints and Helps in our Temperance Work 26 (Frances E. Willard ed., New York National Temperance Society and Publication House 1875).

> the exportation thereof from the United States and all territory subject to the jurisdiction thereof for beverage purposes is hereby prohibited.
>
> §2. The Congress and the several States shall have concurrent power to enforce this article by appropriate legislation.[35]

Intoxicating liquors were defined in the implementing legislation — titled the National Prohibition Act and popularly known as the Volstead Act after its author, Andrew Volstead, Chairman of the House Judiciary Committee — as those containing one-half of 1 percent or more alcohol by volume that were fit for use for beverage purposes.[36]

With Prohibition came the cessation of virtually all commercial winemaking in the country. For the next 14 years only limited winemaking was authorized, for the production of medicinal wine, wine for other non-beverage purposes, sacramental wine, and home winemaking for personal use.[37] Interestingly, the possession and consumption of alcoholic beverages were not unlawful during Prohibition. In colloquial terms, Prohibition America was not "bone dry." The Eighteenth Amendment killed the lawful liquor trade, but not drinking.

The "iron law of prohibition" explains a great deal about alcohol consumption during Prohibition.[38] The theory states that, when a drug or alcohol is banned, particularly when it is part of a social or cultural custom (what Graham Sumner calls a "folkway"[39]), consumers turn to the stronger and more concealable form of it. Thus, spirits in flasks and hidden in boots, from which imagery is derived the term "bootlegger,"[40] gained popularity. Spirits consumption rose by 10 percent during Prohibition, while beer consumption fell by 70 percent. Surprisingly, wine consumption rose by 65 percent, largely because of the specific exemptions for home winemaking and sacramental wine.[41]

Despite the obvious failure of the prohibitionists to change the thinking and drinking habits of Americans, Prohibition continued because it was thought to be good for the country. Amending the federal Constitution was considered a dim prospect, which is why the ASL had pressed for its passage, even after the adoption of the Webb-Kenyon Act.

---

35. U.S. Const. amend. XVIII, §§1-2 (repealed 1933).

36. National Prohibition (Volstead) Act, ch. 85, tit. 2, §1, 41 Stat. 305, 308 (1919) (repealed 1933).

37. *Id.* at tit. 2, §29, 41 Stat. 305, 316. After prescribing penalties for certain violations of the Act, including illegal manufacture and sale, the Volstead Act declares that "the penalties provided in this Act against the manufacture of liquor without a permit shall not apply to a person for manufacturing nonintoxicating cider and fruit juices exclusively for use in his home, but such cider and fruit juices shall not be sold or delivered except to persons having permits to manufacture vinegar."

38. Richard C. Cowan, How the Narcs Created Crack, Nat'l Rev., Dec. 5, 1986, at 30-31.

39. William Graham Sumner, Folkways: A Study of the Sociological Importance of Usages, Manners, Customs, Mores, and Morals 2-3 (Boston: Ginn and Co. 1906).

40. Although the term "bootlegger" explicitly refers to one who carries liquor in his bootleg, it has come to refer more generally to an illicit trader in liquor, and "bootlegging" to the illicit trade itself.

41. Mendelson, *supra* note 5, at 50-51.

Prohibition, known widely today as "the noble experiment that failed," was costly for the country. The expense of enforcement at the federal and state levels was small to begin with and then skyrocketed; even then the prohibitory laws could not be effectively enforced. Bootlegging flourished, and criminal syndicates developed a large illegal liquor industry to service the demand of the public for alcohol. Public corruption was widespread, and many Americans ignored the Prohibition laws and, as a consequence, developed contempt for the law itself. Certain states passed anti-Prohibition referenda.

Repeal happened relatively swiftly. Just as World War I had accelerated National Prohibition, the Great Depression of 1929 led the government to search for new means of federal revenue and new sources of employment. The drys were unwilling to exempt beer and wine in order to save Prohibition. The election of 1932 was widely perceived as a Prohibition referendum. Franklin Roosevelt, who supported repeal, defeated Herbert Hoover, the incumbent, in a landslide. True to his word, President Roosevelt urged Congress to pass the repeal amendment and, even before that, requested modification of the Volstead Act to permit the sale of beer and wine with less than 3.2 percent alcohol by weight. Congress obliged on both counts.

National Prohibition ended on December 5, 1933, when three-quarters of the states ratified the Twenty-first Amendment to the U.S. Constitution, repealing Prohibition. The Amendment reads in pertinent part as follows:

> §1. The eighteenth article of amendment to the Constitution of the United States is hereby repealed.
>
> §2. The transportation or importation into any State, Territory, or possession of the United States for delivery or use therein of intoxicating liquors, in violation of the laws thereof, is hereby prohibited.[42]

The Twenty-first Amendment vests the states with broad power to regulate the importation and use of intoxicating liquor within their borders. This approach was not dictated by law or policy. The federal government, if it wished, could have controlled liquor production and commerce through the exercise of its Commerce Clause authority. But history has shown time and again that liquor is a politically divisive issue in the United States, and no politician wants to face the voter's scorn by setting national drinking standards. This explains the popularity of the local option — then and now. Let the voters decide! In addition, at the time of Repeal many states wanted to remain dry, and without the ability to close off their borders to alcohol through the exercise of their constitutionally delegated Commerce Clause authority, this would have been impossible.

Pursuant to the Twenty-first Amendment, each state adopted its own liquor laws and regulations and its own administrative machinery after Repeal, leading to the adage that the U.S. is not a single wine market but 50 separate markets. Some states remained dry entirely or partially. Other states reverted to liquor licensing or instituted government-run liquor monopolies.

---

42. U.S. Const., amend. XXI, §§1-2.

Despite the diversity of approaches, which are described in detail in a later section, the states shared many goals. Foremost among them was the desire to promote temperance, defined as the moderate use of alcohol or, in the negative, the avoidance of excess. Equally significant, state governments looked to liquor as an important revenue source through excise and sales taxes and licensing fees. To accomplish both goals and ensure an orderly market for alcoholic beverages, the states established controls over alcoholic beverage trade and consumption.

The states realized that the social evils surrounding alcohol in the pre-Prohibition and Prohibition eras had numerous causes — economic, cultural, genetic, and otherwise. But a primary culprit in terms of market structure was the power wielded by the vertically and horizontally integrated liquor "trusts." Trusts were common in the spirits and beer sectors but less so in the wine business. Best known was the Whiskey Trust (the actual name of which was the Distillers' and Cattle Feeders' Trust), which in the late 1800s acquired numerous small-scale distilleries in an effort to control the price and quantity of whiskey on the market. Once a small distillery became part of the Trust, its production was carefully controlled, or the acquired plant was closed down entirely. The Trust also controlled its own distribution and sales outlets and insisted on "exclusive dealing" arrangements whereby the distributor or retailer could sell only the Trust's brands of liquor. The same held true for the large brewers who owned their own saloons. The goal was to maximize corporate profits, which meant more drinking.

Rather than relying solely on "antitrust" laws to break up these monopolies (Congress had passed the Sherman Antitrust Act in 1890), the states took steps after Repeal to ensure that private liquor monopolies could not arise or, if they did, that they could not use their market power to ply consumers with alcohol in the quest for maximum profit. "Tied house" laws prohibited suppliers — including liquor producers, importers, and wholesalers — from owning or controlling the retail shops at which their own beverage brands would be sold. And "free goods" laws prohibited aggressive sales techniques, including commercial bribery, gifts of money, and other "things of value" that could lead to over-consumption of alcohol. The classic free good is the "free lunch" strategically packed with salt to stimulate thirst. Tied-house and free goods laws are discussed in more detail by Jim Seff and Carrie Bonnington in Chapter 2.

The states also sought to restore citizens' faith in the law and to banish criminals from the lawful liquor trade. The common theme was that there was no place for criminal syndicates and bootleggers in post-Prohibition America.

Finally, states took steps to stimulate their agricultural sector as a way to promote economic development. Wine, unlike beer and spirits, is tied directly to agriculture. Wine is made from grapes with little else, if anything, added. The finished wine is thought to reflect the *terroir* (site) where the grapes are grown; that distinctive taste is known as *goût de terroir* (taste of the site). Wine also contributes directly to agro-tourism. Beginning in the 1970s, many states adopted "farm winery" laws granting special privileges to local wineries that made wine from grapes grown in the state, including the privilege of direct sales to in-state consumers.

These and other measures favoring in-state liquor businesses over out-of-state businesses were upheld by state and federal courts in the first several decades following Repeal, despite the discriminatory effects of these laws on interstate trade. Judges relied on the Twenty-first Amendment, which gives states broad authority to regulate alcoholic beverages notwithstanding the constraints of the Commerce Clause.

Margot Mendelson explains in Chapter 5 how the Supreme Court's Twenty-first Amendment jurisprudence has changed over time. Beginning in the 1980s, the Court explored the core purposes of the Twenty-first Amendment, such as temperance, establishment of an orderly market, and the avoidance of social evils. The Court then balanced the benefits of the state's preferential laws in serving those purposes against the harm to interstate commerce.

Around the same time, wine became a significant industry in the United States, with consumption growing steadily from 0.26 gallon (around one liter) per person in 1934 to 2.11 gallons (eight liters) per person in 1980.[43] Rising out of the ashes of Prohibition, this growth in wine consumption (see Table 1-1) along with the increasing sophistication of the American palate and the ever-improving quality of domestic wines were astounding. Author Leon Adams, in his seminal book *The Wines of America*, first published in 1973, aptly called it the Wine Revolution.[44]

Table 1-1 U.S. Per Capita Wine Consumption Since 1934

Year	U.S. Population, in Millions	Wine Consumption, in Millions of Gallons	All-Ages Per Capita Consumption, in Gallons
1934	126	33	0.26
1940	132	90	0.68
1950	152	140	0.93
1960	181	163	0.91
1970	205	267	1.31
1980	227	480	2.11
1990	249	509	2.05
2000	282	568	2.01
2009	307	767	2.50

With the development of the Internet in the 1990s, coupled with the expanding number of wineries (1,800 in 1995 and over 5,000 in 2008) and the consolidation of wholesalers (3,000 wholesalers in 1995 and only 700 in 2008), wineries — particularly smaller ones that could find no wholesaler to carry their wines — began to ship more wine directly to consumers in interstate

43. The consumption statistics here and in Table 1-1 are from Wine Institute, www.wineinstitute.org/resources/statistics/article86 (accessed December 18, 2010), and the U.S. Department of Commerce, Bureau of the Census, Current Population Reports, Series P-25, Nos. 311, 917, 1095.

44. Leon D. Adams, The Wines of America 38 (4th ed., McGraw-Hill 1990).

commerce, bypassing wholesalers and retailers.[45] Certain states allowed direct-to-consumer sales and shipments, some only if the producer's state granted reciprocal shipping rights to wineries located in the destination state.

New York and Michigan, along with many other states, adopted a different approach. They allowed in-state wineries to sell and ship their wines directly to in-state consumers but prohibited out-of-state wineries from doing so. The out-of-state wineries had two options: in New York, they could establish a physical presence as a licensed New York branch winery and sell their out-of-state wines to consumers from that location; or, in either state, they could sell their wines to an in-state wholesaler who, in turn, would sell the wines to an in-state retailer who would sell them to in-state consumers. With a mark-up at each step of the so-called three-tier distribution system, the out-of-state producer received less money for its wines, and the consumer paid directly or indirectly for the higher cost of fulfillment. Finally, a few states prohibited direct-to-consumer shipping from in-state or out-of-state wineries; all wine shipments in those states had to pass through the three-tier distribution system.

Ultimately, these distribution schemes were challenged on Commerce Clause grounds. Different circuits reached different conclusions, making the issue ripe for resolution by the U.S. Supreme Court. In the seminal 2005 case of *Granholm v. Heald*,[46] the Court decided in a 5-4 decision that the Twenty-first Amendment does not authorize a state to allow in-state wineries to sell and ship directly to in-state consumers while withholding that same privilege from an out-of-state winery. Such facial discrimination, said the Court, cannot be sanctioned under the Commerce Clause.

Granholm did not require any state to provide wineries with the right of direct-to-consumer sale and shipment; indeed, the Court fashioned no remedy in the case. The Court's mandate was to end discrimination and level the playing field between in-state and out-of-state wineries with respect to direct shipments. Following *Granholm*, some states "leveled down" by prohibiting any winery, in-state or out-of-state, from shipping wine directly to in-state consumers; most states "leveled up," allowing all wineries to ship their wines to in-state consumers. The significance of *Granholm* cannot be underestimated, both for its holding and for the simple fact that, unlike the earlier liquor law cases decided by the Supreme Court, this case concerned wine, not beer or spirits. Wine had come of age.

B. REGULATORY STRUCTURE AND APPROACHES

Because the Twenty-first Amendment explicitly authorizes the states to control the delivery and use of alcoholic beverages within their borders (that is, intrastate commerce), each state had to develop its own alcoholic beverage regulatory scheme after Repeal. Some states, in turn, ceded this control to

---

45. Jack Heeger, Industry Trends Discussed at Wine & Grape Symposium, Napa Valley Reg., February 8, 2008, available at http://napavalleyregister.com/lifestyles/food-and-cooking/wine/article-5e8eb15a-3185-5a37-bf4f-94677eedc366.html.

46. 544 U.S. 460 (2005).

local jurisdictions through the local option. The federal government retained jurisdiction over interstate commerce in alcoholic beverages and developed a separate and independent regulatory regime. Only in the sphere of intrastate retail sales did the states have exclusive jurisdiction. As a result, three levels of government — local, state, and federal — are intimately involved in regulating the wine business in the United States. This concurrent authority is a hallmark of U.S. wine law.

1. LOCAL OPTION

After Prohibition, many states reestablished the local option, a practice that had begun in the early 1800s. Under the local option, local jurisdictions (counties, cities, even voting precincts) vote on whether, when, and where beer, wine, or spirits can be sold within their respective boundaries. Typical local option ballots include one or more of the following questions:

(a) Shall the sale of [beer, wine, or spirits] be prohibited within this [local voting unit]?
(b) Shall the sale of [beer, wine, or spirits] be prohibited within this [local voting unit] on any Sunday?
(c) Shall the sale of [beer, wine, or spirits] be prohibited within this [local voting unit] for consumption on the premises where sold?
(d) Shall the sale of [beer, wine, or spirits] be prohibited within this [local voting unit] between the hours hereafter specified?

Sometimes the local option questions are more specific. For example, Kentucky in 2000 authorized local option elections for the service of alcoholic beverages at golf courses. The Kentucky local option law provides:

> (1) To promote economic development and tourism in a county containing a city that has, in whole or in part, voted to discontinue prohibition, with the exception of a territory that has discontinued prohibition in accordance with KRS 242.1292, a local option election for the limited sale of alcoholic beverages may be held in any precinct containing a nine (9) or an eighteen (18) hole golf course that meets United States Golf Association criteria as a regulation golf course, notwithstanding any other provisions of the Kentucky Revised Statutes.
>
> (2) A local option election for the limited sale of alcoholic beverages held under subsection (1) of this section shall be conducted in the same manner specified in KRS 242.020 to 242.120, except that the form of the proposition to be voted upon shall be "Are you in favor of the sale of alcoholic beverages by the drink at (name of golf course) in the (name of precinct)?"
>
> (3) Upon approval of the proposition, the Department of Alcoholic Beverage Control may issue a license to the golf course for the sale of alcoholic beverages by the drink as provided in KRS 243.030 and KRS 243.040.
>
> (4) No alcoholic beverage license shall be issued to any applicant within the precinct except the nine (9) or the eighteen (18) hole regulation golf course named in the proposition.[47]

47. Kentucky Revised Statutes §242.123 (2009).

Jurisdictions that have wet establishments inside dry territory often are referred to as "damp" or "moist."[48] There is no common term to describe dry cities within wet counties. Suffice it to say that the local option is still prevalent across the United States, in both control and license states. Appendix 1-1 lists the various local option jurisdictions in the United States today.

2. THE STATES

The states employed two basic methods to regulate the wine industry and protect the public health, safety, and welfare: licensing private individuals to distribute and sell alcoholic beverages in the 32 "open" or license states and the District of Columbia, and establishing state monopolies in the wholesale and/or retail distribution of alcoholic beverages in the 18 "control" states. The control states, in alphabetical order, are Alabama, Idaho, Iowa, Maine, Michigan, Mississippi, Montana, New Hampshire, North Carolina, Ohio, Oregon, Pennsylvania, Utah, Vermont, Virginia, Washington, West Virginia, and Wyoming.

(a) License States

In an open or license state, the chief function of the state alcoholic beverage control agency, often referred to as ABC,[49] is the issuance of licenses to all individuals and business entities in the distribution channel — manufacturers, importers, wholesalers, and retailers. This authority is granted by the state constitution[50] and/or the state legislature.

Generally speaking, each owner of an alcoholic beverage business and each place of business in the state must be qualified by the state before the business commences and must post a bond to assure the state that all taxes, fines, and penalties will be paid. The applicants for a liquor license must be of good moral character and without a criminal record.[51] And the prospective licensee cannot hold a prohibited tied-house ownership interest in another tier of the distribution channel. Tied-house laws vary considerably from state to state in terms of their proscriptions and their exceptions.

Sometimes the tied-house rules and exceptions seem to defy logic. For example, in California a wine wholesaler or importer cannot own an interest

---

48. In Connecticut "damp" towns, although not defined by state statute, are municipalities that allow some liquor to be sold within an otherwise dry city. The Town of Wilton is an example of a damp town. In 1992 residents repealed the town's prohibition law to allow restaurants to obtain permits to serve alcohol in the town but did not extend that right to grocery stores or package stores. *See* Meghan Reilly, Connecticut General Assembly Office of Legislative Research, "Damp" Towns (Feb. 5, 2009), http://www.cga.ct.gov/2009/rpt/2009-R-0101.htm (accessed October 31, 2010).

49. Thus, the California Department of Alcoholic Beverage Control is the California ABC. Other abbreviations are used in other states (e.g., the SLA for the State Liquor Authority of New York).

50. *See, e.g.*, Cal. Const. art. XX, §22.

51. Criminal convictions for misdemeanors and even certain felonies may not be disqualifying. Even with a disqualifying conviction, a person may be awarded a liquor license upon proof of rehabilitation or expungement of the conviction, depending on the laws of the particular state.

in an on-sale retail license of any type. An on-sale license allows the sale of beer, wine, and/or spirits (depending on the license type) with or without food (again, depending on the license type) to members of the public for consumption on the licensed premise. By contrast, a winery, known as a winegrower in California licensing lexicon,[52] can hold one or more on-sale retail licenses for a bona fide eating place (restaurant) so long as the winery's brands are not sold at more than two restaurants owned by the winery, and even then, the winery's brands cannot constitute more than 15 percent of all wine brands offered for sale at those restaurants.[53]

Many states limit the maximum number of retail establishments in a given area (based on population or reported crimes) or restrict the number of licenses issued to a particular person. In California, retail licenses cannot be issued in areas of "undue concentration of licenses" unless the applicant can show that public convenience or necessity requires issuance of the license.[54] "Undue concentration" includes areas of high crime and census areas where the density of licenses is greater than the county average. This concept is discussed in more detail in Chapter 7.

Typically, the proposed alcoholic beverage premise must be posted with a notice prior to commencing business so that there is an opportunity for interested persons to object to the issuance of the license. Special consideration often is given to residences, churches, and schools that are near a proposed licensed premise to ensure that the business operations do not interfere with those existing uses.

Licenses generally are not freely alienable. They are not subject to attachment or execution, and they do not follow the laws of descent or distribution upon the death of the licensee. In fact, the state, subject to the legitimate exercise of its police power and the constitutional mandates of due process, may grant or withhold alcoholic beverage licenses at will. Often the state seeks the input of the local jurisdiction in which the licensed premise will be located before it will issue an alcoholic beverage license. Sometimes the state delegates its licensing authority to the local jurisdiction. If a license is refused, the applicant generally has the right to a public hearing on the merits of the particular case. Such administrative hearings generally do not follow common law or statutory rules of evidence. Most states, however, do provide for a review of administrative proceedings by an administrative appeals board or by a court of competent jurisdiction.[55] A similar process is followed for license revocation. Common grounds for revocation are violation of the alcoholic beverage laws, misrepresentation of material facts in the licensing applications, the conviction of any offense involving moral turpitude, and bankruptcy.

---

52. Jefferson E. Peyser, longtime counsel of Wine Institute, the trade association of California wineries, coined the term "winegrower" to underscore the agricultural roots of the wine industry.

53. Cal. Bus. & Prof. Code §25503.15(b) (2009).

54. *Id.* §§23958, 23958.4 (2009).

55. In California, a three-person ABC Appeals Board, the members of which are appointed by the governor and confirmed by the state senate, hears administrative appeals "from a decision of the department ordering any penalty assessment, issuing, denying, transferring, suspending or revoking any license for the manufacture, importation or sale of alcoholic beverages." Cal. Const. art. XX, §22(d).

To conduct an interstate business in the open states, the out-of-state manufacturer or the manufacturer's national distributor generally must obtain a permit as an out-of-state shipper or nonresident seller that allows it to sell alcoholic beverages directly to wholesalers in the particular state. The manufacturer or distributor may be required to register its brands in that state, obtain a bond to secure payment of the state's excise tax, designate its wholesalers there, post its wholesale prices, and submit to the state liquor control authorities monthly reports of wines shipped into the state. This information allows the state to track the whereabouts of all alcoholic beverages in the state and to prevent unlawful production (moonshining) and unlawful sales (bootlegging). This is part and parcel of ensuring an orderly market for alcoholic beverages. The information also is used by the state to enforce state franchise laws (discussed below) and, in those states with "primary source" laws (also discussed below), to ensure that state wholesalers are importing only those brands for which the manufacturer has designated them as authorized agents.

The state ABC, or in some states a separate Department of Revenue or Board of Equalization, is responsible for collecting excise taxes and enforcing the state's laws, regulations, and rules concerning industry business practices (also known as trade practices). This agency also is often involved with maintaining public health and safety surrounding alcohol, a subject discussed in Chapter 9. One area that receives considerable attention is responsible beverage service at licensed establishments, including the prevention of liquor sales to minors. ABC officials typically work closely with local law enforcement officials.

(b) Control States

In the 18 control or monopoly states, the state government (or, in certain counties of Maryland, the county government[56]) participates directly as a wholesaler and/or retailer of alcoholic beverages. This system, based on research funded by John D. Rockefeller Jr. and modeled after the state liquor monopolies of Finland, Norway, and Sweden (among other nations), eliminates the role of private enterprise in the liquor market in whole or in part.[57] Only in this way, monopoly states contend, can the states protect the public health, safety, and welfare with respect to the sale and consumption of alcoholic beverages.

The extent of the government monopoly varies from jurisdiction to jurisdiction. Today, in fact, most control states are hybrids — part monopoly, part open — rather than pure monopolies. For example, some state monopolies extend only to beverages with higher levels of alcohol such as spirits, fortified wines, and malt liquor (sometimes referred to as "heavy beer" or "strong beer"), leaving other wines and beers to be sold by private individuals, who

---

56. Montgomery County, Maryland, is an example of such a local control jurisdiction.

57. No state engages directly in the manufacture of alcoholic beverages, although the regulations of some states would allow it.

obtain licenses from the state's liquor authority. As Harold Holder and Kathleen Janes write:

> One of the legacies from the end of Prohibition in the U.S. has been to target distilled spirits for monopoly control. The beverage next most controlled is wine. Beer is rarely a part of the monopoly control or involvement of the state.
>
> This beverage distinction in the U.S. reflects which beverages are viewed as the most subject to abuse in the eyes of elected officials, i.e., which beverages are considered the "most dangerous." These distinctions reflect the amount of ethanol per liquid ounce rather than the amount of ethanol typically consumed per drinking occasion by type of beverage.[58]

Other states operate a retail monopoly but leave the wholesale tier open to private enterprise. The control states also differentiate between on-premises sales (for consumption on the seller's premises, such as a restaurant or bar) and off-premises sales (for take away, such as a liquor store), with the state monopoly often covering the latter but not the former. In that situation, privately licensed hoteliers, restaurateurs, and bar owners sell alcoholic beverages to their customers.

Appendix 1-2 lists the control states that participate in the marketplace as wholesalers or as retailers. As mentioned previously, the role of the state may vary depending on the particular beverage, but the states, not surprisingly, do not maintain uniform definitions of the beverage types. An example is the different definitions of wine and fortified wine. In Maine, wine includes any fortified wine whose alcoholic content does not exceed 24 percent by volume. In Montana, a wine can contain no more than 16 percent alcohol by volume, and fortified wine can contain more than 16 percent up to 24 percent alcohol. Washington uses a cutoff of 14 percent to distinguish a wine from a fortified wine, but in this era of high-alcohol wines, the state exempts wines over 14 percent that have a cork closure and have been aged for at least two years or that are produced solely as the result of natural fermentation without any added spirits, brandy, or alcohol.

Over the past several decades, there has been a marked trend to privatize wine sales in the control states, allowing wines to be sold at retail in a variety of licensed premises such as bottle shops, grocery stores, convenience stores, drive-through establishments, and sometimes even shops attached to gas stations. A similar expansion of available retail sales outlets has occurred in the license states. Some control states decided to privatize at the wholesale level but to maintain "state stores," sometimes referred to as state-operated "package stores," where wine and other liquors are sold at retail for off-premises consumption. Some control states established "agency stores" operated by third parties under contract to the state that follow the state's rules regarding beverages sold, pricing, hours of operation, etc. And sometimes state stores and private retailers sell the same alcoholic beverages. The variations are seemingly endless.

---

58. Harold D. Holder & Kathleen Janes, Control of Alcoholic Beverage Availability: State Alcoholic Beverage Control Systems Having Monopoly Functions in the United States, in State Monopolies and Alcoholic Prevention 355, 361 (Timo Kortteinen ed., Report from the Soc. Research Inst. of Alcohol Studies No. 181, 1989).

To conduct interstate commerce with a control state, the out-of-state manufacturer or the out-of-state wholesaler must obtain a wine shipper's or seller's permit to sell their wines to the state monopoly (often through an agent) or, in some states, to a licensed wholesaler, and the products must be listed with the state control boards prior to their importation.

Control states have the legally prescribed mission to protect and benefit the public. Their primary means of accomplishing this goal is to control the availability and price of alcoholic beverages. Because many, if not most, retail outlets are state owned, the state is able to control directly their number and location. Generally, there are fewer retail outlets in a control state, although some control states establish state stores or agency stores in rural areas where alcohol otherwise would be unavailable. In terms of pricing, the control states impose fixed prices, mandatory price markups, and/or taxes that generally result in higher retail prices than one finds for the same products in the license states.[59] This is why the popular Charles Shaw wine, known commonly as "Two Buck Chuck," may be "Four Buck Chuck" in a control state. As with every other maxim in the field of wine law, there are exceptions. New Hampshire, for example, keeps its markups and taxes low and its range of offerings high to encourage wine sales, leading consumers from nearby states to travel there for the sole purpose of purchasing wine.

The credo of most control states is that less availability and higher prices for alcoholic beverages translate into a lower average alcohol consumption rate among the states' consumers. This, in turn, is said to be associated with fewer injuries, less risk of certain diseases such as cirrhosis and fetal alcohol syndrome, less crime, and increased worker productivity. Chapter 9 reviews the evidence in support of this argument, as well as various alternative means of liquor control.

3. THE FEDERAL GOVERNMENT

When the Twenty-first Amendment took effect and the states adopted their own laws and regulations governing the delivery and use of alcoholic beverages within their jurisdictions, many observers thought that there would be no place for federal liquor law. But the Twenty-first Amendment did not grant the states complete and exclusive control over commerce in intoxicating liquors.[60] Congress believed that federal involvement was necessary to eradicate criminal operations like bootlegging and racketeering that crossed state lines. Just as important, the federal government had grown accustomed to its

---

59. The control states' pricing measures vary but generally include fixed wholesale or retail prices (with price changes allowed up to four times a year on advance notice ranging from 45 to 75 days, unless the state control board rejects the change) and minimum or percentage markups. State excise taxes on table wine in the control states range from $0.30 per gallon in Ohio to $1.70 per gallon in Iowa. *See* Federation of Tax Administrators, State Tax Rates on Wine (Jan. 1, 2010), http://ww.taxadmin.org/fta/rate/wine.pdf (accessed October 31, 2010), for a list of all the states' excise tax rates on wine).

60. *William Jameson & Co. v. Morgenthau*, 307 U.S. 171, 172-173 (1939).

liquor tax revenue and did not want to relinquish its excise taxes on wine,[61] beer, and spirits. In fact, the federal government had begun taxing spirits in 1794 to help pay the debts of the Revolutionary War and for a related social purpose — to restrain consumption of spirits.[62]

The U.S. Treasury Department, through the monitoring and oversight activities related to the exercise of its tax authority, has a long and intimate involvement with the alcoholic beverage industry in America. This explains why the Treasury rather than the Department of Agriculture or the Food and Drug Administration has the primary responsibility for regulating the alcoholic beverage industry. Today that responsibility resides in the Department's Alcohol and Tobacco Tax and Trade Bureau (TTB).[63]

The TTB administers two principal laws related to alcoholic beverages — the Internal Revenue Code (IRC)[64] and the Federal Alcohol Administration (FAA) Act.[65] The IRC governs the taxation and production of wine. The internal revenue laws are designed primarily to protect and secure the government's tax revenue. The IRC regulations are designed to ensure that no alcoholic beverage subject to tax escapes taxation.

In addition to the extensive system of control over the production and treatment of wine that exists under the IRC, the FAA Act established a system of controls designed to protect the wine consumer from fraud and deception and to foster fair marketing practices. The focal points of the FAA Act are the permit requirements for producers, wholesalers, and importers (but not retailers) of alcoholic beverages; the trade practice provisions that regulate unlawful economic practices in restraint of trade; and labeling, advertising, and marketing practices.[66]

---

61. An excise tax applicable to all still and sparkling wines was levied by the U.S. Congress in 1914. Wine Tax Law of 1914, ch. 331, §2, 38 Stat. 745, 746. The 1914 Act taxed still wines at the rate of 1 cent per pint, 2 cents per quart, and 8 cents per gallon. Sparkling wines were taxed at 10 cents per pint and 20 cents per quart. In 1916 the present system of classifying still wines for tax purposes by alcoholic content was adopted. Revenue Act of 1916, ch. 463, 39 Stat. 7546, 783-787. Since that time, the tax rates for various wines have been changed; the last rate change for wines occurred in 1991, when the excise tax on wine was increased by $0.90 per gallon with the exception of sparkling wine. Revenue Reconciliation Act of 1990, 104 Stat. 1388-415, §11201 (1990). That law also provided for a tax credit of up to $0.90 per gallon for small domestic producers of wine, other than sparkling. 26 U.S.C. §5041(c) (2006). In fiscal year 2007, federal excise tax collections from alcohol totaled $7.23 billion. By contrast, excise tax collection on tobacco in that same year was $7.19 billion. Joint Committee on Taxation, House Committee on Ways and Means, The Jurisdiction and Responsibilities of the Alcohol and Tobacco Tax and Trade Bureau, Hearing Before the Subcomm. on Oversight of the H. Comm. on Ways and Means, 110th Cong., 6, tbl.1 (2008) (report prepared by the staff of the J. Comm. on Taxation).

62. The distilled spirits tax did not sit well with the farmers of southwestern Pennsylvania, who opposed it by spearheading the Whiskey Rebellion. President Washington responded by sending in federal troops to quell the uprising.

63. The TTB was created by the Homeland Security Act of 2002, Pub. L. No. 107-296, §111(d), 116 Stat. 2135 (2002) (codified at 6 U.S.C. §531(d) (2006)). Its predecessor agency, the Bureau of Alcohol, Tobacco, and Firearms, commonly known as ATF, had broader authority than the TTB. Essentially, ATF's functions dealing with firearms, explosives, and arson, as well as the smuggling of tobacco and alcohol, were kept in ATF, which was transferred to the Justice Department and renamed the Bureau of Alcohol, Tobacco, Firearms, and Explosives. The TTB assumed regulatory and tax oversight of the wine industry.

64. 26 U.S.C. §§5001-5691 (2006).

65. 27 U.S.C. §§201-219(A) (2006).

66. The federal regulatory requirements to establish a winery are discussed in more detail below and in Chapter 4.

The IRC and the FAA Act are the principal pillars of federal supervision and oversight of the wine industry.[67] Under each act, the TTB is vested with the authority to promulgate additional rules in the form of regulations. The issuance of these regulations is controlled by the Administrative Procedures Act,[68] which requires that rules be issued through a procedure called informal rulemaking, commonly referred to as Notice and Comment Rulemaking. The TTB first publishes rules as proposals and then solicits public participation through public hearings or the submission of written comments. Only after this process is completed will the TTB issue new regulations. This openness in the rulemaking process enables the TTB to acquire the widest possible range of views, which is critical to informed decision-making and protects the public against closed-door decision-making.

In terms of its operations and internal structure, the TTB is headed by an Administrator and divided into several divisions. The Trade Investigations Division, Tax Audit Division, and Trade Analysis and Enforcement Division, collectively known as Field Operations, ensure that the members of the regulated industry comply with federal laws and regulations. These divisions conduct audits, investigations, and product analyses in an effort to eliminate tax diversion, fraud, and evasion and to prevent unfair competition in the industry. The Regulations and Rulings Division develops regulations, rulings, and internal regulatory interpretations. The Advertising, Labeling and Formulation Division reviews the labels of all alcoholic beverages offered for sale in the United States, both foreign and domestic; issues certificates of label approval (COLAs) for those beverages; and monitors alcoholic beverage advertising for deceptive practices. Wendell Lee discusses wine labeling and advertising in Chapter 3.

The TTB also has an International Trade Division that facilitates worldwide trade in wine by educating foreign governments about U.S. alcoholic beverage laws and regulations and by offering technical assistance to domestic producers wishing to export their products to other countries. This division also works with the Office of the United States Trade Representative and represents the interests of domestic alcoholic beverage producers in international negotiations, such as the Wine Accords between the United States and the European Union, discussed by Jacques Audier in Chapter 10.

The TTB's statutory mandate often overlaps with that of other federal agencies. Customs and Border Protection aids the TTB by ensuring that importers of alcoholic beverages have a valid basic permit, that excise taxes are paid, and that alcoholic beverage products carry labels that the TTB has approved prior to release of the products into interstate commerce. The TTB also consults with the Food and Drug Administration (FDA) for expert advice on health and safety issues related to alcoholic beverages. As an example, the TTB incorporates in its regulations on winemaking processes and materials the FDA's

67. The TTB also enforces the previously mentioned Webb-Kenyon Act, 27 U.S.C. §122 (2006), and the Alcoholic Beverage Labeling Act, 27 U.S.C. §§213-219(a) (2006), which prescribes a "Government Warning" on all alcoholic beverage labels (27 U.S.C. §215(a)).

68. 5 U.S.C. §§551-559 (2006).

"Generally Recognized as Safe" (GRAS) standards,[69] and the TTB has worked closely in recent years with the FDA on rulemaking for allergen labeling on alcoholic beverages. The TTB and the FDA occasionally have sparred (for example, over ingredient labeling for alcoholic beverages), and the two agencies have entered into several agreements outlining their respective areas of authority over alcoholic beverages.[70] The TTB and the U.S. Department of Agriculture exercise concurrent jurisdiction over alcoholic beverage labels that bear an organic claim. The jurisdictions of the TTB and the U.S. Patent and Trademark Office intersect in matters of brand names (trademarks) and appellations (certification marks), as explained further in Chapter 6. Finally, the TTB and the Federal Trade Commission each enforce their own regulations concerning alcoholic beverage advertising.

C. REGULATING THE WINE INDUSTRY, FROM GRAPES TO WINE TO THE CONSUMER

The combination of federal and state wine laws makes for a complicated regulatory environment. To better understand the interaction of these laws, in this section I focus on the state and federal legal provisions governing each aspect of the wine business, from grape growing to winemaking to wine distribution and sales. First, I examine the laws governing viticultural practices, that is, the cultivation of vines and the growing of grapes. Second, I discuss the laws and regulations pertaining to wine production. Third, I address the laws relating to the distribution and marketing of wines. With respect to state law, I focus in this section on California, where 90 percent of all domestic wines are produced.

1. VITICULTURAL PRACTICES

The federal and state governments exercise limited control over viticultural practices. Unlike many other countries, the United States does not regulate the acreage used for grape growing or the harvesting practices adhered to by grape growers. However, information on wine labels regarding the designation of a geographic area where grapes are grown (appellations of origin) and representations of varietal content and vintage dates are regulated by the federal government. At least two states, California and Oregon, supplement the federal labeling laws with their own stricter standards on grape origin; Oregon also has a stricter rule on varietal content.[71]

---

69. 27 C.F.R. §24.246 (2010).

70. *See, e.g.*, Alcohol and Tobacco Tax and Trade Bureau, U.S. Department of the Treasury, Alcohol Beverages Containing Added Caffeine, Industry Circular 2010-8 (Nov. 23, 2010); Major Food Allergen Labeling for Wines, Distilled Spirits and Malt Beverages, 71 Fed. Reg. 42329, 42331 (proposed July 26, 2006); Memorandum of Understanding, 52 Fed. Reg. 45502, 45503-04 (Nov. 30, 1987); Food and Drug Administration, Trade Correspondence No. 224 (1940); *see also* Mendelson, *supra* note 5, at 132, 167-172.

71. *See, e.g.*, Cal. Code Regs., tit. 17, §§17010(a)(3), 17015 (2010); Or. Admin. R. 845-010-0915 (varietal content) and 0920 (origin) (2010).

In California, the Department of Food and Agriculture (CDFA) seeks to ensure the orderly marketing and distribution of farm products, including grapes, by licensing all processors of those products (wineries) as well as produce dealers (resellers of grapes or must). The California Food and Agriculture Code spells out the payment obligations of processors and dealers and provides the grower a lien on grapes and the resulting wine until the grower receives payment for its fruit.[72] The CDFA, assisted by its Wine Grape Inspection Advisory Committee, also establishes "objective criteria and inspection procedures for all quality conditions that have an effect on the acceptance of, or on the amount of the purchase price of, fresh grapes for wine and byproduct purposes."[73]

California permits growers to have wines made from their own grapes by qualified wineries. The growers, after obtaining the proper licenses, can sell those wines in intrastate or interstate commerce. These are referred to as "custom crush" operations, which are discussed in more detail in Chapter 4.

At the state and local levels, there also are extensive environmental, resource conservation, and land use laws governing vineyard development and operations. For example, local zoning laws may prohibit grape growing in industrial or commercial zones or, conversely, may limit commercial and industrial operations in exclusively agricultural zones. Land use laws are discussed in more detail in Chapter 8. States may promote grape growing through various tax benefits. Grading permits, erosion control plans, and other local, state, and federal approvals also may be required in order to plant a vineyard. In California local permits, if discretionary, require compliance with the California Environmental Quality Act, which considers the environmental impacts of the particular development proposal.[74]

2. WINE PRODUCTION

The two major federal laws administered by the TTB, the IRC and the FAA Act, control the production and labeling of wine. The IRC governs the taxation and production of wine. The FAA Act regulates the distribution, labeling, and advertising of wine.

The internal revenue statute is the oldest and most extensive law in the United States regulating the wine industry. Although the present law was enacted in 1954, with significant amendments in 1958, this statute actually dates from 1862, when Congress first imposed an internal revenue tax on domestic producers of "wine, made of grapes."

Over the years, Congress has expanded the coverage of other products taxed as wine, and today the wine tax is imposed on "all wines (including imitation, substandard, or artificial wine, and compounds sold as wine)."[75] However, when a wine product is in excess of 24 percent alcohol by volume, it is classified as a distilled spirit and taxed accordingly.[76] By using such terms

72. Cal. Food & Agric. Code §§55631-55653 (2009).
73. *Id.* §41207.5(b).
74. Cal. Pub. Res. Code §§21000-21177 (2009).
75. 26 U.S.C. §5041(a) (2006).
76. *Id.*

as "imitation," "substandard," "artificial," and "compounds sold as wine," Congress intended, for tax purposes, that the term "wine" would apply to a broad category of products.[77]

The rate of taxation, which is the same whether the wine is imported or domestically produced, is determined by the alcoholic content of the product and the quantity and source of its effervescence, if any. But the tax rates do not vary in direct proportion to alcoholic content. This is true not only within the wine category but across all alcoholic beverages. Distilled spirits are taxed at the highest rate and beer at the lowest (see Table 1-2). For wine, the excise tax rates range from a low of $0.17 per gallon on still wine having not more than 14 percent alcohol by volume (taking into account the "small producer's tax credit") to a high of $3.40 per gallon for sparkling wines that are naturally effervescent (that is, wine containing more than 0.392 gram of carbon dioxide per hundred milliliters of wine).[78]

Table 1-2 Federal Excise Tax Rates for Alcoholic Beverages

Item	Current Tax Rate
Distilled spirits	$13.50 per proof gallon[79]
Wine[80] –	
Still wines	
No more than 14 percent alcohol	$1.07 per wine gallon[81]
More than 14 percent but not more than 21 percent alcohol	$1.57 per wine gallon
More than 21 percent but not more than 24 percent alcohol	$3.15 per wine gallon
More than 24 percent alcohol	Taxed at the distilled spirits rate
Hard apple cider	$0.226 per wine gallon
Sparkling wines	
Champagne and other naturally sparkling wines	$3.40 per wine gallon
Artificially carbonated wines	$3.30 per wine gallon
Beer	$18.00 per barrel[82]

77. Some of these classifications, such as "substandard," are rarely seen or used.

78. 26 U.S.C. §5041(a)-(c) (2006).

79. A "proof gallon" is a U.S. liquid gallon consisting of 50 percent alcohol. 26 U.S.C. §5002(a)(10)-(11) (2006). Credits are allowed for wine content and flavors content of distilled spirits. *Id.* §5010(a)(1)-(2).

80. Small domestic wine producers (i.e., those producing not more than 250,000 wine gallons in a calendar year) are allowed a credit of $0.90 per wine gallon ($0.056 per wine gallon in the case of hard cider) on the first 100,000 wine gallons (other than champagne and other sparkling wines) removed from the bonded premises. The credit is reduced by 1 percent for each 1,000 wine gallons produced in excess of 150,000 wine gallons per calendar year. 26 U.S.C. §5041(c)(1)-(2) (2006).

81. A "wine gallon" means a U.S. gallon of liquid measure equivalent to a volume of 231 cubic inches. *Id.* §5041(d).

82. A "barrel" is equal to 31 gallons, with each gallon equivalent to a volume of 231 cubic inches. A domestic brewer who produces not more than 2 million barrels in a calendar year is subject to a per-barrel rate of $7.00 on the first 60,000 barrels produced in that year. 26 U.S.C. §5051(a)(1)-(2) (2006).

In order to protect the government's source of revenue, the internal revenue law authorizes the federal government to impose various requirements on producers of wine. Since the tax on wine is paid by the producer on the final wine product at the time of its removal from the winery, most controls are focused there.[83]

Every person desiring to establish premises for the production, blending, cellar treatment, storage, bottling, packaging, or repackaging of non-tax-paid wine must qualify at the federal level as a bonded winery or bonded wine cellar.[84] The applicant must file the permit application with the TTB prior to commencing operations. In that application, he or she provides the location of the wine premises and describes the land, buildings, and equipment. If the premises consist of one or more entire buildings, the applicant must describe the size of each building, the material of which it is constructed, and the purpose for which it will be used.[85] The details can seem picayune, such as the need to describe all windows, doors, and other means of ingress and egress, as well as the means of securing them. This is necessary to allow the TTB to "secure the revenue," that is, to ensure that its excess tax revenue is protected by preventing theft of the underlying wine. Generally, the applicant attaches a drawing illustrating the layout of the bonded premises and all equipment there.

The federal government also protects its tax revenue through a "bond" requirement.[86] A bond is a guarantee, usually given by an insurance company, that covers the potential tax liability on the wines stored on the bonded premises, should the winery fail to pay its taxes. Taxes are paid by filing a tax return with an accompanying tax payment after the wine has been removed from the bonded premises. Returns are filed and payments are made twice each month, unless the tax is prepaid or no tax is due.[87]

Many of these same qualification requirements reappear under state and local law. A prospective winery must contact various local (city or county) and state agencies as well as the TTB and abide by their respective regulations. Only after the applicant has qualified with the TTB and obtained any required state and local licenses and permits may operations commence.

The IRC also imposes an extensive system of controls over production practices, cellar treatment, and classification of wine. These controls date back well into the nineteenth century. Federal law defines proper cellar treatment as those practices and procedures in the United States, whether historical or newly developed, that employ various methods and materials to correct or stabilize wine in order to produce a finished product acceptable in good

83. Historically, occupational taxes were imposed on sellers of wine, including wine producers, wholesalers, and retailers. 26 U.S.C. §§5081 (producers), 5111 (wholesale dealers), 5121 (retail dealers). Although these taxes were recently repealed, occupational tax registration still is required.

84. 26 U.S.C. §5351 (2006). Any premises engaged in the production operation may be designated as a bonded winery as opposed to a bonded wine cellar. The latter may be involved only in non-production operations such as blending and bottling.

85. 27 C.F.R. §24.166 (2010).

86. *See, e.g.*, 27 C.F.R. §24.146(a) (2010).

87. *Id.* §24.271.

commercial practice.[88] This law specifically identifies particular winemaking methods and materials used in customary commercial practice as lawful cellar treatment in the absence of regulations finding them to be improper.[89] These provisions are designed to ensure that all wines sold in the United States are safe to consume and, by extension, that the federal government will receive its tax revenue when the wine is "removed from bond." Were it never removed from bond, no taxes would be due.

The TTB imposes extensive recordkeeping requirements on wineries and has authority to enter the business premises of a winery during all business hours. The producer must be able to account for all wine on the bonded premise and to prove the veracity of every label claim by reference to detailed production, processing, and storage records. Inspections are conducted on a regular basis, at which time TTB inspectors ensure that the proper taxes have been paid and that proper cellar treatment and production practices are being followed. Generally speaking, TTB audits are of three types: a product integrity audit, a tax audit, or a trade practices audit.

Present federal law contains specific provisions governing the cellar treatment, amelioration, and sweetening of wines. These requirements are very technical in nature. The standards on amelioration and sweetening are based on the classification of the wine involved. Classifications of wine include "natural wine"[90] made from grapes or fruit; "specially sweetened natural wine,"[91] which is wine produced by adding sugar; "special natural wine,"[92] which is wine flavored by herbs, spices, or other natural essences; "agricultural wine,"[93] which is wine made from agricultural products other than grapes; and "effervescent wines," which include natural sparkling wines and artificially carbonated wines.

California and certain other states supplement the TTB's list of authorized winemaking practices. For example, California prohibits the addition of sugar to wine, although the addition of concentrated grape must is allowed.[94]

Together, these state and federal laws are designed to prevent fraudulent winemaking which, along with label fraud, is the primary means of counterfeiting wine. Bill Casey and Andrew Wanger address this topic in Chapter 8.

In addition to the extensive system of control over the production and treatment of wine that exists under the IRC, the FAA Act introduces into the marketplace a system of controls designed to protect the wine consumer from fraud and deception and to eliminate unfair competition. The focal point of the statute is its permit requirements for producers, wholesalers, and importers of wines and spirits, but not beer, and its trade practice provisions.

---

88. 26 U.S.C. §5382(a) (2006); 27 C.F.R. §§24.175-218 (2010).

89. In the case of imported wines, 26 U.S.C. §5382(a) (2006) requires certification by the government of the producer's country that the wine has been produced in accordance with practices and procedures approved in the United States or that it is covered by an international agreement. The content, validity and use of such certifications are described in Treasury Decision Labeling and Advertising of Wine, 27 C.F.R. §§4.1-4.101 (2010); Wine, *Id.* §§27.1-27.221.

90. 26 U.S.C. §5381 (2006).

91. *Id.* §5385.

92. *Id.* §5386.

93. *Id.* §5387.

94. Cal. Code Regs. Tit. 17, §17010(a) (2010).

The FAA Act, enacted in 1935, is the other primary pillar of federal wine authority.[95] This statute requires the approval of the United States Treasury Department before anyone can engage in the business of importing, producing, or blending wine, or purchasing wine at wholesale for resale to a trade buyer. This approva1, in the form of a basic permit issued by the TTB,[96] is given only if an extensive background investigation by the TTB indicates that the applicant is likely to maintain business operations in conformity with federal and state laws. Once the permit is issued, it remains in force unless and until it is revoked, voluntarily surrendered, or automatically terminated.[97] Since the permit cannot be sold or transferred, it automatically terminates if there is a change in control of the entity holding it.[98] However, in the case of a winery sale, operations are allowed to continue under the seller's basic permit until a new permit is issued to the buyer.[99]

In California, a license to engage in the wine business is required in addition to a federal basic permit.[100] However, unlike the federal permit system, the responsible state agency — here the California ABC — issues licenses to wine retailers as well as wine producers, importers, and wholesalers. California ABC licenses are particular to a person, premise, and type of beverage.[101] For example, a winegrower (winery) licensee cannot brew beer under that license, although a separate beer manufacturer's license can be obtained; a beer and wine wholesaler cannot sell distilled spirits; and an off-sale beer and wine retailer cannot allow wine to be consumed on the premise without a separate on-sale beer and wine license. That being said, California affords winegrowers perhaps the broadest privileges of any licensee. Along with the right to produce and blend wine, winegrowers can offer wine tastings, sell their wine for on-premises consumption, and even operate a restaurant at the winery where any producer's wine, beer, or brandy may be served.[102] A winegrower's license application, like the application for any other ABC license, must include detailed personal and financial information, which is thoroughly examined by ABC prior to license issuance.

The trade practice provisions of the FAA Act and the California ABC Act prohibit all producers, importers, and wholesalers of alcoholic beverages from engaging in specified practices that tend to produce monopolistic control over retailers. Federal and state tied-house and free goods laws are discussed in more detail in Chapter 2.

---

95. Before the passage of the FAA Act, President Franklin Roosevelt established by executive order the Federal Alcohol Control Administration (FACA) to guide the post-Prohibition wines and spirits industries through the development of voluntary industry codes. The National Industrial Recovery Act, ch. 90, 48 Stat 195 (1933), *amended by* Act of June 14, 1935, ch. 246, 49 Stat. 375, under which authority Roosevelt established the FACA, was ruled unconstitutional in *A.L.A. Schechter Poultry Corp. v. United States*, 295 U.S. 495 (1935). Subsequently, Congress adopted the FAA Act, ch. 814, 49 Stat. 977 (1935) (codified as amended at 27 U.S.C. §§201-219(a) (2006).

96. 27 U.S.C. §203 (2006).

97. 27 U.S.C. §204(g) (2006).

98. *Id.*

99. 27 C.F.R.§1.44 (2010).

100. Cal. Bus. & Prof. Code §23300 (2009).

101. *See, e.g., id.* §23320.

102. *Id.* §§23356.1, 23358.

The FAA Act is also a consumer protection law, as is evident from a reading of §5(e) of the Act, controlling the labeling of wines.[103] This section makes it unlawful to sell, ship, receive in interstate or foreign commerce, or remove from customs custody any wine,

> unless such products are bottled, packaged, and labeled in conformity with such regulations, to be prescribed by the Secretary of the Treasury, with respect to packaging, marking, branding, and labeling and size and fill of container (1) as will prohibit deception of the consumer with respect to such products or the quantity thereof and as will prohibit, irrespective of falsity, such statements relating to age, manufacturing processes, analyses, guarantees, and scientific or irrelevant matters as the Secretary of the Treasury finds to be likely to mislead the consumer; (2) as will provide the consumer with adequate information as to the identity and quality of the products, the alcoholic content thereof . . . ; (4) as will prohibit statements on the label that are disparaging of a competitor's products or are false, misleading, obscene, or indecent; and (5) as will prevent deception of the consumer by use of a trade or brand name that is the name of any living individual of public prominence, or existing private or public organization, or is a name that is in simulation or is an abbreviation thereof, and as will prevent the use of a graphic, pictorial, or emblematic representation of any such individual or organization, if the use of such name or representation is likely falsely to lead the consumer to believe that the product has been endorsed, made, or used by, or produced for, or under the supervision of, or in accordance with the specifications of, such individual or organization.

At the hearings before the House Ways and Means Committee on the bill proposing the FAA Act, Mr. Choate, Administrator of the Federal Alcohol Control Administration, made the following statement concerning the objectives of §5(e):

> The purpose was to provide such regulations, not laid down in statute, so as to be inflexible, but laid down under the guidance of Congress, under general principles, by a body which could change them as changes were found necessary.
>
> Those regulations were intended to insure that the purchaser should get what he thought he was getting, that representations both in labels and in advertising should be honest and straight-forward and truthful. They should not be confined, as the pure food regulations have been confined, to prohibitions of falsity, but they should also provide for the information of the consumer, that he should be told what was in the bottle, and all the important factors which were of interest to him about what was in the bottle.[104]

The TTB enforces §5(e) through a label approval process that must be completed prior to the product's sale by the winery or, in the case of imported wine, prior to its removal from customs custody.[105] The label approval is known as a

---

103. 27 U.S.C. §205(e) (2006).

104. Federal Alcohol Control Act: Hearing on H.R. 8539 Before the H. Comm. on Ways and Means, 74th Cong. 10 (1935) (statement of Joseph H. Choate Jr., Chairman and Director, Federal Alcohol Control Administration).

105. 27 C.F.R. §4.50(a) (2010).

COLA (its full title is Application for and Certification/Exemption of Label/ Bottle Approval). States can and do supplement the federal labeling regulations with rules of their own. Oregon, for example, has perhaps the most rigorous labeling standards in the country for appellation grape source content[106] and varietal content.[107]

Although the TTB has regulations similar to those for labeling that apply to the advertising of wines,[108] the FAA Act does not mandate prior approval of wine advertisements. However, the law does prohibit any advertisement that is inconsistent with any statement on the wine label.[109] The labeling and advertising regulations for wine are covered in Chapter 3.

3. DISTRIBUTION AND MARKETING

I previously described the three-tier distribution system, involving separate and distinct manufacturers, wholesalers, and retailers, with alcoholic beverages passing from one level to the next and ultimately to the consumer. This system is enforced by state licensing laws that grant specific sales privileges to specific licensees and by so-called at-rest laws. The latter laws, which exist in around 30 states, require that wine shipped from out of state physically arrive and remain at the premises of an in-state wholesaler before it is transferred to a retailer. The retailer in turn must take physical possession of the wine before shipping it to a consumer.

The three-tier system is not mandated by the TTB, and it is not the only way to sell wine in the United States. Depending on the laws of the particular state, manufacturers might be authorized to sell their wines directly to retailers, with or without the assistance of a broker,[110] or to consumers. This is the case in California. Winery sales to retailers are known as self-distribution; winery sales to consumers are called direct-to-consumer sales.

As mentioned above, tied-house laws at the federal and state levels prohibit the vertical integration commonly found in the pre-Prohibition era. Whereas many state tied-house laws present "bright-line" standards — such as the California provisions that prohibit an alcoholic beverage manufacturer, importer, or wholesaler from having "any interest, direct or indirect,"[111] in a retailer and vice versa (subject to enumerated exceptions that have expanded greatly in recent years) — the FAA Act prohibits any supplier from *inducing* a retailer to purchase his products to the *exclusion* of other products in interstate

106. Or. Admin. R. 845-010-0920 (2010).
107. *Id.* 845-010-0915.
108. 27 U.S.C. §205(f) (2006).
109. 27 C.F.R. §4.64(b) (2010).
110. *See, e.g.*, Cal. Bus. & Prof. Code §23377 (2009) (licensed wine brokers). The main distinction between a broker and a wholesaler is that the former does not take title to the goods but typically solicits an order and forwards it to the winery. By contrast, a wholesaler buys wine from a winery for purposes of resale, typically to other wholesalers and retailers.
111. *See, e.g.*, *id.* §25500. Such interests include corporate control over, or financial interests in, the alcoholic beverage business, business property, or alcoholic beverage license. Depending on the state's attribution rules, the tied-house prohibition may extend to spouses, affiliates, agents, subsidiaries, or others.

commerce.[112] The federal Act specifically prohibits suppliers from obtaining preferred treatment from retailers by acquiring an interest in the retailers' license or property; by giving those retailers money, equipment, or services;[113] by guaranteeing the retailers' financial obligations; by extending excessive credit to them; or by giving the retailers any "other thing of value."[114] Federal law also prohibits a variety of other unfair trade or marketing practices by suppliers that can restrict interstate commerce, deceive consumers, or jeopardize government revenue. These practices include consignment sales, exclusive outlets,[115] and commercial bribery.[116] In each instance (other than consignment sales), federal law is violated only if the practice occurs in interstate commerce and there is evidence of exclusion of competitors' wines in the marketplace. As a practical matter, the exclusion requirement makes federal enforcement of trade practices laws substantially more difficult than similar state laws that do not require exclusion.

States have their own trade practice provisions relating to alcoholic beverage sales that may or may not mirror those of federal law. Most states, for example, have regulatory controls over sales promotion devices that might stimulate alcohol consumption. California, for example, prohibits any licensee from giving "directly or indirectly, any premium, gift, or free goods in connection with the sale or distribution of any alcoholic beverage," except as specifically authorized by the California ABC. Authorized exceptions include retailer advertising specialties (such as coasters, menu cards, calendars, and napkins) and consumer advertising specialties (such as ashtrays, corkscrews, posters, and bottle stoppers).[117] These specialty items are limited in unit cost and in the total dollar amount of the giveaway to any single retailer. While most exceptions like these are established administratively by the alcoholic beverage regulatory agency itself, through rulemaking or interpretations of existing laws, sometimes a special law is required. As an example, the California legislature passed a law to permit manufacturers to give to on-premise retailers "paper beverage coasters less than 25 square inches in size and having a value of less than five cents ($0.05) per coaster."[118]

Some states ban credit sales altogether. And most states control advertising in some fashion, effectively limiting standardized national advertising content. Other states control the methods of contacting purchasers (solicitations, phone and mail orders, auctions, etc.).

---

112. 27 U.S.C. §205(b) (2006).

113. An important exception to the general prohibition of payments to retailers is for consumer-related activities such as wine tastings and coupons. For other exceptions, *see* 27 C.F.R. §§6.81-6.102 (2010).

114. 27 U.S.C. §205(b) (2006).

115. An exclusive outlet is created when a retailer agrees to purchase and sell only the products of one supplier. *Id.* §205(a).

116. Commercial bribery occurs when a supplier induces the employees of a retailer through various means, including gifts and payments, to purchase the supplier's products to the exclusion of products sold by other suppliers. *Id.* §205(c).

117. Cal. Bus. & Prof. Code §25600(a)(1) (2009); Cal. Code Regs., tit. 4, §106(e)(1)-(2) (2010).

118. Cal. Bus. & Prof. Code §25501(a).

Separate and apart from specific state and federal alcoholic beverage laws, relations among manufacturers and wholesalers often are regulated by specific state alcoholic beverage franchise laws.[119] The original purpose of these franchise laws was to protect the in-state wholesaler from what were perceived to be unfair requirements imposed by the typically larger out-of-state producer.[120] Recently, the wholesale tier has contracted and consolidated; many wholesalers are now far larger than the producers whose products they carry.

California has no alcoholic beverage franchise law, but among the states that do, wine is not always a covered product. Some franchise laws cover beer and/or distilled spirits but not wine; other, broader franchise laws cover both alcoholic and non-alcoholic products. Presently, 21 states have some type of franchise law provision concerning wine. Most franchise laws regulate the territories in which wholesalers and manufacturers may conduct business. Some states require exclusive territories, that is, the appointment of one wholesaler per manufacturer in a given area. Other states permit multiple, non-exclusive territorial appointments, referred to as dualing. Oklahoma requires manufacturers to sell wines to all licensed wholesalers in that state.

State franchise laws also regulate the business relationship between a manufacturer and wholesaler. Many state laws require a showing of "good cause," as defined under local law, to make any change in a distribution relationship, including the termination, replacement, or addition of wholesalers. Good cause may include a wholesaler's bankruptcy, the sale of substantial assets of the wholesaler's business, repeated violations of state or federal law, or the wholesaler's failure to meet reasonable performance standards following notice of non-performance and an opportunity to cure. The practical effect of these laws is to make it difficult, if not impossible, for a winery to terminate an out-of-state wholesaler. In states where there are no specific statutory termination provisions, as in California, general legal principles apply, including the covenant of good faith and fair dealing, which is implied in all California contracts and related unfair competition and antitrust laws.

Many states have adopted another mechanism to eliminate tax evasion and ensure product integrity. These are known as "primary source" laws that require an out-of-state winery or wholesaler that wishes to sell its wine in that state to establish that it lawfully produced the wine (in the case of a winery) or purchased the wine (in the case of the importer or wholesaler) and by written contract has the sole right to distribute the wine in the United States. This applies to both domestic and foreign wines. Florida's primary source law is typical; wine shipments into the state must come from "a licensed primary

---

119. As background reading on alcoholic beverage franchise laws, *see* Douglas Glen Whitman, Strange Brew: Alcohol and Government Monopoly (Oakland: Independent Institute 2003) and Susan C. Cagann, Contents Under Pressure: Regulating the Sales and Marketing of Alcoholic Beverages, in Social and Economic Control of Alcohol 57, 67-69 (Carole L. Jurkiewicz & Murphy J. Painter eds., Public Administration and Public Policy No. 135 (2008)).

120. The concerns are essentially about adhesion contracts imposed by the out-of-state franchisor with greater economic might and a superior bargaining position. Today, however, many wineries are dwarfed in size and muscle by the out-of-state wholesalers. Assuming a small winery can even find a wholesaler to represent its brand in a particular state, it rarely can dictate the terms of the producer-wholesaler relationship.

American source of supply," which must be the manufacturer or the primary importer.[121] Primary source laws effectively close off the "secondary market," also known as the gray market, to wines and other alcoholic beverages that otherwise could enter the market lawfully — for example, from a wholesaler in another state or from abroad.

Antitrust laws, which date from the period of massive industrialization following the Civil War, apply to the alcoholic beverage industry as they do to other sectors of the economy. The Sherman Act of 1890[122] prohibits all contracts, combinations, and conspiracies that unreasonably restrain trade. This Act has been the basis of lawsuits involving price fixing, allocation of customers and territories, and refusals to deal. The Clayton Act[123] and particularly the Robinson-Patman Act[124] prohibit, *inter alia*, price discrimination, exclusive dealing, and tie-ins. Violations of both federal laws are punishable as felonies, with the violator also subject to civil actions for treble damages and attorney's fees. Several states have enacted ancillary or parallel laws.

Under federal and state antitrust laws, a few actions automatically are presumed to be anticompetitive and hence are per se illegal. Other business conduct is judged case by case, based on the "rule of reason." The choice between these methods of analysis depends largely on the nature of the restraint and whether the agreement or conduct in question is "horizontal" or "vertical." Horizontal agreements are made between parties on the same level of distribution. For example, an agreement between two wineries to fix the prices they charge wholesalers would be classified as a horizontal price restraint, which is per se unlawful under the Sherman Act. Vertical agreements, by contrast, involve parties on different levels of the distribution system. For example, an agreement between a winery and a wholesaler to allocate customers, products, or territories in a given market is a vertical non-price restriction, subject to the rule of reason.[125] Resale price management, in which a manufacturer requires a reseller (e.g., a wholesaler or a retailer) to sell the manufacturer's product at a specific price, used to be classified as per se illegal but, following the Supreme Court's decision in *Leegin Creative Leather Products, Inc. v. PSKS, Inc.*, 127 S. Ct. 2705 (2007), is now judged by the rule of reason.

Under the Robinson-Patman Act, a manufacturer may not sell the same product to two different customers in the same tier of distribution at different prices unless there is a commercially justifiable reason. Valid reasons include a cost justification (such as volume discounts or variable sales costs) and the need to meet the competition. Additionally, tying arrangements, whereby a customer must purchase an undesired product to obtain a desired product, and full-line forcing, whereby a customer must handle all product lines even if he

121. Fla. Stat. §564.045(1), (4) (2010).

122. Sherman Anti-Trust Act, ch. 647, 26 Stat. 209 (1890) (codified at 15 U.S.C. §§1-7 (2006)).

123. Clayton Anti-Trust Act, Pub. L. No. 63-212, 38 Stat. 730 (1914) (codified at 15 U.S.C. §§12–27; 29 U.S.C. §§52-53 (2006)).

124. Robinson-Patman Price Discrimination Act, Pub. L. No. 74-692, 49 Stat. 1526 (1936) (codified at 15 U.S.C. §§13-13b, 21a (2006)).

125. Today almost all vertical non-price restraints are judged by the rule of reason.

or she desires only one product, are subject to close antitrust scrutiny concerning their commercial impact and the manufacturer's economic power.

Antitrust laws and principles often conflict with state franchise laws. For example, many franchise laws mandate contract terms in an alcoholic beverage distribution relationship that entrench incumbent wholesalers appointed on an exclusive basis in given market areas and that restrict market entry by new and possibly more efficient wholesalers. As such, these laws have a potentially anticompetitive effect, which permits the survival of inefficient distributional arrangements. State franchise laws and many state pricing schemes for alcoholic beverages have been protected from antitrust attack because, under common law, state action for specific state purposes is immune from antitrust attack.[126] This is known as the *Parker* immunity doctrine, established by the Supreme Court in *Parker v. Brown.*[127]

D. CONCLUSION

Wine law in the United States is not a single body of law administered by a single governmental agency. It exists at the local, state, and federal levels in the form of specific alcoholic beverage laws and regulations, as well as in countless related fields of law. This complexity is the result of our nation's complicated history of regulating alcoholic beverages and our state and federal governments' efforts to protect their revenues and the public at large. Like our country's wines, wine law is organic, diverse and sophisticated, and always exciting.

126. *Parker v. Brown,* 317 U.S. 341, 352 (1943).
127. Id.

APPENDIX 1-1

LOCAL OPTION JURISDICTIONS IN THE UNITED STATES[128]

State	Number of Jurisdictions: Counties: Wet	Counties: Dry	Cities and Municipalities: Wet	Cities and Municipalities: Dry	Comments
Alabama	41	26			
Alaska	14	2 Damp	55	107 Dry 18 Damp	Alaska's dry communities ban alcohol importation and possession. Communities that ban sale but allow importation and possession are referred to as "damp." Regional local government in Alaska here includes boroughs or unified municipalities, not counties.
Arkansas	33	42			Once an entire county has been voted dry, no particular portion of that county can vote

128. National Alcohol Beverage Control Association, NABCA Survey Book 2009, at 253-255 (2010).

State	Number of Jurisdictions				Comments
	Counties		Cities and Municipalities		
	Wet	Dry	Wet	Dry	
					to make itself wet. However, a county that has been voted wet can have within its borders, by local option election, smaller dry subdivisions.
Colorado	All		All		Local option available but not exercised.
Connecticut			168	1	Local option is available in cities and towns only.
Delaware	3		All		
Florida	62	5			
Georgia					Sale of liquor is allowed by local referendum; sale of beer and wine by local ordinance. Only two counties are completely dry: Union and Echols.
Honolulu Co., Hawaii	4		1		
Idaho		1		1	All Idaho counties now permit private table wine sales.
Iowa	99		1,000+		
Kansas	73	32			59 with 30% food requirement; 11 with no food requirement.
Kentucky	30	52			Moist: 17 wet cities are located in dry counties.
Louisiana	41	1		68	Louisiana has parishes, not counties. Dry municipalities refer to election districts or wards. 22 parishes

	Number of Jurisdictions				
	Counties		Cities and Municipalities		
State	Wet	Dry	Wet	Dry	Comments
					contain both wet and dry areas; 41 parishes are totally wet; 1 parish is totally dry.
Maine	16				
Maryland	21	2	2	2	Two counties have geographically defined dry areas.
Massachusetts			342	9	
Michigan	All		1,513	261	There are 261 municipalities where spirits and mixed spirit drinks are prohibited. Beer and wine for consumption on the premises may be sold in these municipalities.
Minnesota	87				To the best of [NABCA's] knowledge, there are no dry cities in Minnesota.
Mississippi	48	34			Alcohol sales are allowed on Indian reservation — MS Band of Choctaws.
Missouri					Local option is available for liquor by the drink in cities with less than 19,500 population. Cities may not prohibit the sale of malt liquor by the drink or package, but they may limit the number of licenses by ordinance.
Montana	All		All		Two dry Indian reservations.

	Number of Jurisdictions				
	Counties		Cities and Municipalities		
State	Wet	Dry	Wet	Dry	Comments
Nebraska					Unknown. Local option exists, but there is no reporting requirement to state.
New Hampshire			All cities and all but 5 munici-palities		Four local option questions for voter input: shall state stores be operated by permission of the State Liquor Commission in this town/city; shall malt beverages be sold by permission of the State Liquor Commission; shall wines containing not less than 6% or more than 15.5% alcoholic content by volume (table wine) be sold by permission of the State Liquor Commission; shall liquor be sold for consumption on the premises where sold by permission of the State Liquor Commission.
New Jersey			530	37	Local option available in cities and towns only.
New Mexico	31	2			
New York					13 totally dry towns; 37 partially dry towns.
North Carolina	63	37			15 counties allow beer/ wine only, no spirits. There are 135 wet cities in the dry counties.
North Dakota	52	1			

State	Number of Jurisdictions: Counties		Cities and Municipalities		Comments
	Wet	Dry	Wet	Dry	
Ohio					Local option as to the sale of beer and intoxicating liquor is controlled by ward/precinct within a municipality or township. There are approximately 3,195 wards and 8,460 precincts in Ohio. Because there are annexed areas in many wards and precincts, a precinct may be partially wet or dry. A particular premise may be wet in an otherwise dry area.
Oklahoma	41	36	N/A	N/A	Off-premise stores and bottle clubs exist in dry counties.
Oregon	36		242		
Pennsylvania			1,888 are wet in some fashion (beer, spirits or both)	690 are totally dry but for voter single exception	
South Carolina					Must have referendum for Sunday sales.
South Dakota	65	1			
Tennessee	2	93	56	287	
Texas	203	51			Texas authorizes local option elections by county, city, or justice precinct. The County Clerk of each county certifies the wet/dry status of a particular location.

	Number of Jurisdictions				
	Counties		Cities and Municipalities		
State	Wet	Dry	Wet	Dry	Comments
Vermont		246	5		
Virginia	All		All		No jurisdictions dry, but local option votes are allowed on whether a store may be located in a county, whether mixed beverages may be sold in restaurants, or for limiting Sunday beer and wine sales.
West Virginia	47	8		6	There are 6 wet districts within the 8 dry counties.
Wyoming	23	0	190	2	A national park is licensed in addition to the wet cities, counties, and municipalities.

APPENDIX 1-2

CONTROL STATES: WHOLESALE AND RETAIL PRODUCT DISTRIBUTION[129]

129. Id. at 284.

This table shows who wholesales and retails wine, fortified wine, beer, and spirits in each control state.

S = Spirits, W = Wine, FW = Fortified Wine, B = Beer, N/A = Not Applicable

State	State Wholesale	Private Wholesale	State Retail	Agency Retail	Private Retail
Alabama	S + FW	W + B	S + FW	N/A	S + W + FW + B
Idaho	S + W + FW + Beer: Malt liquor only	W + B	S + W + FW	S + W + B	W + B
Iowa	S	W + FW + B	N/A	N/A	S + W + FW + B
Maine	S + FW	FW + W + B	S + FW	S + B + FW + W	W + FW + B
Montgomery County, MD	S + W + FW + B	N/A	S + W + FW + B	S + W + FW + B	B + W + FW
Michigan	S	W + FW + B	N/A	N/A	S + W + FW + B
Mississippi	S + W + FW	B	N/A	N/A	S + W + FW + B
Montana	S + FW	W + B	N/A	S + W + FW	S + W + B + FW
New Hampshire	S + W + FW	B	S + W + FW	S + W + FW + B	W + FW + B
North Carolina	S	W + FW + B	N/A	S through county and municipal boards	W + FW + B and mixed beverages
Ohio	S	W + FW + B	N/A	S through contract sales agents	W + FW + B
Oregon	S	W + FW + B	N/A	S	W + FW + B
Pennsylvania	S + W + FW	B	S + W + FW	N/A	B
Utah	S + W + FW	B	S + W + FW	S + W + FW	B
Vermont	S + FW	W + B	N/A	S + FW	W + B

State	State Wholesale	Private Wholesale	State Retail	Agency Retail	Private Retail
Virginia	S	W + FW + B	S + W + only native Virginia wines	N/A	W + FW + B
Washington	S	W + FW + B	S + W + FW + B	S + W + FW + B	W + FW + B
West Virginia	S	W + FW + B	N/A	N/A	S + W + FW + B
Wyoming	S + W + FW	B	N/A	N/A	S + W + FW + B

CHAPTER 2

TRADE PRACTICES

James M. Seff and Carrie L. Bonnington

Trade practices laws in the wine, beer, and spirits industries regulate relationships among industry members and with consumers. Nearly every state and the federal government have enacted trade practices laws. The laws are designed to prevent domination of retailers by suppliers (generally, producers, importers, and wholesalers[1]) ("tied-house laws") and to prohibit commercial bribery and other unlawful inducements designed to promote the aggressive sale of licensed beverages[2] ("free goods laws"). The laws are arcane, complicated, sometimes contradictory, often frustrating, and, in many jurisdictions but especially in California, riddled with exceptions. They are subject to varying regulatory interpretations and have, not surprisingly, engendered their own jurisprudence. Because these laws regulate practices involving the sale and distribution of licensed beverages, wine lawyers must understand them in order to steer their clients through what are often treacherous waters.

In this chapter, we address the federal and state tied-house and free goods laws. In the state section, we focus on three of the principal markets where wine is produced and sold in the United States: the states of California, New York, and Washington. Our primary focus is California, which accounts for 90 percent of domestic wine production.

A. HISTORICAL BACKGROUND

The Twenty-first Amendment to the Constitution allows the states greater latitude to regulate the sale and distribution of wine and other licensed

1. In the licensed beverage industry the terms "wholesaler" and "distributor" are synonymous.

2. The term "alcoholic beverages" is frowned on by the industry because it could suggest misuse of its products by alcoholics. For this reason the industry has generally adopted as an alternative the term "alcohol beverages." This chapter uses the term "licensed beverages" instead.

beverages than for any other consumer product.[3] Each of the states has gone its own way in enacting laws governing the sale and distribution of licensed beverages.[4] However, in 1935, when the states turned their attention to such regulation after Repeal, there was widespread agreement that they should adopt laws to curtail the excesses that led to Prohibition in the first place.

The "drys" blamed aggressive marketing of licensed beverages for many of these excesses. Breweries controlled bars in their local markets and worked hard to encourage consumption of their products.[5] As a first step in curbing such alleged abuses, most states adopted a three-tier system of distribution, with the intent of separating the three tiers from each other: "Manufacturing interests were to be separated from wholesale interests; wholesale interests were to be segregated from retail interests."[6] However, in most states the separation is between "suppliers" (producers, importers, and distributors) on the one hand and retailers on the other. The three-tier system exists in all areas but the 18 states and two counties[7] known as "control" or (less flatteringly) "monopoly" states, which themselves participate in some aspect of the sale or distribution of licensed beverages.[8]

Having separated the three tiers, the states sought to strengthen and protect each tier from the others. Tied-house laws are the most notable example of this protection.[9]

One of the most notorious practices that led to the enactment of Prohibition was the so-called tied-house evil. Bars and restaurants, tied by ownership to their parent breweries, often offered free meals as long as the patron ordered a drink.[10] The temperance movement attributed numerous social evils to tied-houses, including "political corruption, proliferation of saloons, increase in alcohol consumption, and irresponsible ownership of retail outlets."[11] The tied-house laws were "aimed to prevent two particular dangers: the ability and potentiality of large firms to dominate local markets through vertical

---

3. Indeed, licensed beverages are the only presently traded commodities the Constitution specifically addresses; and not only once, but twice. The Eighteenth Amendment enacted Prohibition and the Twenty-first Amendment repealed it.

4. Such diversity of treatment is otherwise prohibited by the Commerce Clause of the Constitution, which has become an uneasy but strengthening counterweight to the Twenty-first Amendment in the jurisprudence of the Supreme Court. *Compare, e.g., State Bd. of Equalization of the State of Cal. v. Young's Mkt. Co.*, 299 U.S. 59 (1936), with *Granholm v. Heald*, 544 U.S. 460 (2005).

5. A Review of Tied-House Laws That Impinge on the State's Wine Industry and the Status of Direct Shipment Regulations Nationwide: Joint Hearing Before the S.Comm on Governmental Affairs and the S. Select Comm. on California's Wine Industry, 1999 Leg., App. B, "Tied-House Law" History (Cal. 1999) (testimony of John Peirce, Staff Counsel of the California Department of Alcoholic Beverage Control).

6. *Cal Beer Wholesalers Ass'n v. Alcoholic Beverage Control Appeals Board*, 5 Cal. 3d 402, 407 (1971).

7. Alabama, Idaho, Iowa, Maine, Michigan, Mississippi, Montana, New Hampshire, North Carolina, Ohio, Oregon, Pennsylvania, Utah, Vermont, Virginia, Washington, West Virginia, Wyoming, and Montgomery and Worcester Counties, Maryland.

8. Many control states occupy one or more of the three distribution tiers, and some are control states for distilled spirits only, leaving wine to be distributed through the three-tier system. Washington is one example.

9. *But see* note 93, *infra*.

10. Hence the admonition, still in use today, "There is no such thing as a free lunch!"

11. *National Distrib. Co., Inc. v. U.S. Treasury Dep't, Bureau of Alcohol, Tobacco and Firearms*, 626 F.2d 997, 1010 (D.C. Cir. 1980).

and horizontal integration and the excessive sales of licensed beverages produced by the overly aggressive marketing techniques of larger alcoholic beverage concerns."[12]

Most states saw the principal tied-house evil as *control* of retailers by suppliers. Tied-house statutes normally prohibit such control. However, California adopted what may have seemed at the time to be a more comprehensive nomenclature designed to prohibit control. In general, California's tied-house laws prohibit the *direct* or *indirect* ownership of *any interest* by a supplier in a retail license and the business or equipment used in the retail business.[13] These laws generally regulate two major categories: the ownership of interests the supplier may have in a retailer and the benefits a supplier may provide to a retailer.

California's tied-house scheme so severely restricted even benign marketing practices that it has now become riddled with statutory exceptions. Those exceptions, which we will examine shortly, come at a price; and while they are usually reasonable and designed to accommodate a modern world of international conglomerates the original drafters of the tied-house laws could not have foreseen, they have become increasingly difficult to secure. The resistance comes from wholesalers, who perceive any new tied-house exception as increasing the threat to the distribution monopoly that wholesalers still largely enjoy within their states.

Before examining the California tied-house scheme in detail, we shall address similar but, for reasons that will soon be obvious, much less effective federal tied-house laws.

B. FEDERAL TIED-HOUSE REGULATION

As the nation emerged from Prohibition, the federal government sought to safeguard the newly legal alcohol industry against the corruption that had become rampant during the ban.[14] As part of the New Deal, the Roosevelt administration established the Federal Alcohol Control Administration under the National Industrial Recovery Act (NIRA).[15] When the Supreme Court declared the NIRA unconstitutional in 1935, alcohol was again left unregulated. In the words of one court, the industry was "infested with bootleggers and racketeers anxious to continue their trade and willing to thwart tax and health laws."[16] Congress, which had sought to rely on the existing antitrust laws to regulate alcohol after the demise of the NIRA, acted quickly by adopting the Federal Alcohol Administration (FAA) Act of 1935.[17]

12. *Cal Beer Wholesalers Ass'n*, 5 Cal. 3d at 407.
13. Cal. Bus. & Prof. Code §§25500 (on-sale licensees), 25502 (off-sale licensees).
14. *Fedway Assocs., Inc. v. U.S. Treasury, Bureau of Alcohol, Tobacco and Firearms*, 976 F.2d 1416 (D.C. Cir. 1992).
15. *National Distrib.*, 626 F.2d at 1005.
16. *Id.*
17. *Fedway*, 976 F.2d at 1418.

1. FEDERAL ALCOHOL ADMINISTRATION ACT

Now codified at 27 U.S.C. §§201 *et seq.*, the FAA Act contains the federal tied-house restriction at §205(b). The tied-house provision of the FAA Act prohibits a supplier[18] from inducing a retailer to purchase its products to the "exclusion in whole or in part" of products from other suppliers[19] in a transaction that implicates interstate commerce.

Of the three necessary jurisdictional elements — (1) a sale in interstate or foreign commerce, (2) an unlawful inducement, and (3) exclusion of competitors' products — the first two are usually easiest to prove.

With respect to the second element, unlawful inducement, the regulation lists as means of inducement: owning any interest in the business, real, or personal property of a retailer; giving, selling, or renting any fixture or thing of value to a retailer (subject to exceptions); paying a retailer for advertising; guaranteeing a loan for a retailer or extending more than customary credit; requiring a retailer to buy a quota of products (including tie-in sales); and commercial bribery.[20]

The third element, exclusion, is not always so easy to analyze. The courts have read the exclusion requirement narrowly, so that it prevents the application of the federal tied-house laws in the majority of cases. The D.C. Circuit examined the exclusion criterion at great length in the leading case, *Fedway Associates, Inc. v. United States Treasury Department Bureau of Alcohol, Tobacco and Firearms.*[21]

Circuit Judge Ruth Bader Ginsberg provided the following summary of the case in her decision:

> Fedway's promotional campaign lasted for three months, during which retailers were offered — on a non-discriminatory basis — certain consumer electronic goods if they agreed to purchase designated quantities of Finlandia vodka or Captain Morgan spiced rum. As described by the Bureau of Alcohol, Tobacco and Firearms, retailers would get a microwave oven for purchasing five cases of liquor from Fedway; a thirteen-inch color television for ten cases; a compact disc player for fifteen cases; and a VCR for twenty-five cases. The wholesale value of these items ranged from $104 to $280. The retailers were under no obligation to participate. If they chose to participate, they would not be bound by contract to buy less vodka or rum from Fedway's rivals. The promotion placed no restrictions on how or where retailers used the incentive equipment; a TV or VCR could be used on the retailer's premises (a *popular* choice for bar owners) or given to an employee for use at home. The case against Fedway rests solely on this single campaign. No prior or subsequent Fedway promotion figures in the record we are called upon to review.

---

18. "[A]ny person engaged in business as a distiller, brewer, rectifier, blender, or other producer, or as an importer or wholesaler, of distilled spirits, wine, or malt beverages, or as a bottler, or warehouseman and bottler, of distilled spirits, directly or indirectly or through an affiliate." 27 U.S.C. §205 (2006).

19. 27 U.S.C. §205(b) (2006).

20. *Id.*

21. *Fedway*, 976 F.2d n.14.

The three-month promotion successfully boosted Fedway's sales of Finlandia vodka and Captain Morgan spiced rum. Several retailers testified that the promotion led them to buy more cases of Fedway's liquor than they otherwise would have; a few even bought enough cases to qualify for more than one electronic gadget. Most of these same retailers also testified that their increased purchases of Fedway liquor in turn led them to purchase less vodka and rum distributed by rival wholesalers.[22]

The court in *Fedway* determined that "Congress intended the 'exclusion' criterion to direct the regulator to determine something more" than merely leading a retailer to purchase less of a product than it would have otherwise.[23] Instead, "Congress used 'exclusion' to indicate placement of retailer independence at risk by means of a 'tie' or 'link' between the wholesaler and the retailer or by any other means of wholesaler control."[24]

Accordingly, an unlawful inducement in and of itself does not necessarily violate the FAA Act. The general rule is "that transactions between suppliers and retailers do not induce the 'exclusion in whole or in part' of competing suppliers unless their purpose or potential effect is to lead to supplier control over ostensibly independent purchasers."[25] Exclusion therefore requires more than the face of the statute suggests and is thus quite difficult to prove.

In fact, the courts have been reluctant to hold that a practice violates the FAA Act, short of "egregious violations" by a supplier that so dominate a retailer that the retailer is compelled to purchase substantially all of its beverage products from that wholesaler.[26]

2. CODE OF FEDERAL REGULATIONS

The Alcohol and Tobacco Tax and Trade Bureau (TTB) of the U.S. Department of the Treasury, formerly that portion of the Bureau of Alcohol, Tobacco, and Firearms that regulated licensed beverages,[27] is the agency charged with enforcing the federal tied-house laws and issuing the operative administrative regulations.[28] The TTB's regulations not only clarify the meaning of the statutory language but also provide exceptions to the general prohibitions contained in the FAA Act.[29] (Curiously, the regulations do not apply to any transaction between an industry member and a wholly owned retailer, a relationship that would be illegal under most state tied-house laws.[30])

22. *Id.* at 1418.
23. *Id.* at 1420.
24. *Id.* Although Fedway addressed a relationship between a wholesaler and a retailer, a similar analysis applies to relationships between other suppliers (a winery, distillery, or importer) and a retailer.
25. *Foremost Sales Promotions v. Dir., Bureau of Alcohol, Tobacco and Firearms*, 860 F.2d 229, 237 (7th Cir. 1998).
26. *Id.*
27. ATF is now the Bureau of Alcohol, Tobacco, Firearms, and Explosives and is part of the Department of Justice.
28. 27 C.F.R. §§6.1-6.153 (2010).
29. *Id.* §6.81.
30. *Id.* §6.3(a).

Federal regulations specifically identify certain acts that are violations (i.e., "red light" acts), certain acts that are not violations (i.e., "green light" acts), and certain acts that "put retailer independence at risk" and therefore may be deemed an unlawful inducement (i.e., "yellow light" acts).

Red light acts include, but are not limited to, renting of display space by an industry member at a retail establishment (§6.35); the act by an industry member of furnishing, giving, renting, lending, or selling any equipment, fixtures, signs, supplies, money, services, or other things of value to a retailer (§6.41); furnishing of free warehousing by delaying delivery of distilled spirits, wine, or malt beverages beyond the time that payment for the product is received (§6.44); paying or crediting a retailer for any advertising, display, or distribution service (§6.51); an arrangement in which an industry member participates with a retailer in paying for an advertisement placed by the retailer (§6.52); purchase, by an industry member, of advertising on signs, scoreboards, programs, scorecards, and the like at ballparks, racetracks, or stadiums from the retail concessionaire (§6.53); rental by an industry member of display space at a retail establishment (§6.56); and requiring a retailer to take and dispose of any quota of distilled spirits, wine, or malt beverages (§6.71).

Green light acts include, but are not limited to, giving or selling product displays so long as the total value of all product displays does not exceed $300 per brand at any one time in any one retail establishment, and the displays contain conspicuous and substantial advertising matter on the product (§6.83); point-of-sale advertising materials such as posters, placards, designs, inside signs (electric, mechanical, or otherwise), window decorations, trays, coasters, mats, menu cards, meal checks, paper napkins, foam scrapers, back bar mats, thermometers, clocks, calendars, and alcoholic beverage lists or menus (§6.84(1)); consumer advertising specialties such as trading stamps, non-alcoholic mixers, pouring racks, ashtrays, bottle or can openers, corkscrews, shopping bags, matches, printed recipes, pamphlets, cards, leaflets, blotters, postcards, pencils, shirts, caps, and visors (§6.84(2)); giving a sample of distilled spirits, wine, or malt beverages to a retailer who has not purchased the brand from that industry member within the last 12 months (§6.91);[31] packaging and distributing distilled spirits, wine, or malt beverages in combination with other, non-alcoholic items for sale to consumers (§6.93); and providing coupons and other direct offerings subject to certain limitations (§6.96).[32]

Yellow light acts, those that put retailer independence at risk, include, but are not limited to, the act by an industry member of resetting stock on a retailer's premises (other than stock offered for sale by the industry member);

31. For each retail establishment the industry member may give not more than 3 gallons of any brand of malt beverage, not more than 3 liters of any brand of wine, and not more than 3 liters of distilled spirits. If a particular product is not available in a size within the quantity limitations of this section, an industry member may furnish to a retailer the next larger size.

32. With respect to coupons, all retailers within the market where the coupon offer is made may redeem such coupons, and an industry member may not reimburse a retailer for more than the face value of all coupons redeemed, plus a usual and customary handling fee for the redemption of coupons. Direct offerings may be offered by industry members directly to consumers. Officers, employees, and representatives of wholesalers or retailers are excluded from participation.

purchasing or renting display, shelf, storage, or warehouse space (i.e., slotting allowance); ownership by an industry member of less than a 100 percent interest in a retailer, where such ownership is used to influence the purchases of the retailer; and requiring a retailer to purchase one alcoholic beverage product in order to be allowed to purchase another alcoholic beverage product at the same time (§6.152). An industry member should not engage in such acts without performing a careful analysis.

The exceptions do not entirely overwhelm the rule, but combined with the exclusion requirement they present a real impediment to federal tied-house enforcement.

3. PREEMPTION

The Twenty-first Amendment gives states broad powers to regulate the importation and use of licensed beverages within their borders.[33] As the Supreme Court has noted, "a state has virtually complete control only over interests that engage the core powers reserved to the states by the Twenty-first Amendment — that of exercising control over whether to permit importation or sale of liquor or how to structure the liquor distribution system."[34] The federal government, however, retains Commerce Clause authority to regulate licensed beverages as they affect interstate commerce.[35] Accordingly, activities relating to the sale and distribution of licensed beverages must be considered with both the state and federal rules in mind.

The issue of preemption and the relationship between federal and state laws was thoroughly analyzed by the Ninth Circuit in *Stein Distributing Company, Inc. v. Department of the Treasury Bureau of Alcohol, Tobacco & Firearms*.[36] In 1986 Stein Distributing was the largest beer and wine wholesaler in Boise, Idaho. Consistent with industry practice, Stein routinely prepared schematic diagrams depicting proposed product arrangements for its customers. In addition, Stein provided people to arrange or "reset" the beer and wine sections to conform to the schematics, which often included moving its competitors' products.[37] Stein argued that its actions were authorized by state law[38] and, therefore, could not violate federal tied-house laws.

After a complete hearing and ruling by an administrative law judge, the director of the Bureau (on a petition for review) determined that Stein's wine wholesaling activities violated federal tied-house prohibitions.[39] The Ninth

33. *Stein Distrib. Co. v. Dep't of the Treasury Bureau of Alcohol, Tobacco & Firearms*, 779 F.2d 1407, 1410 (9th Cir. 1986).

34. *Id.* (citing *Capital Cities, Inc. v. Crisp*, 467 U.S. 691 (1984)) (internal quotes omitted).

35. *Stein Distrib. Co.*, 779 F.2d at 1410.

36. *Id.*

37. *Id.* at 1409.

38. Idaho law allows "wholesalers, with the permission of the retailer, to reset all wine upon the retailers' shelves." *Id.* at 1410.

39. *Id.* at 1409. Notably, the director found that Stein Distributing's actions with respect to beer did not violate federal tied-house laws because there was no state law imposing a similar restriction, an enforcement requirement brewers inserted in the FAA Act's "penultimate clause" at the statute's adoption. *Id.*

Circuit upheld the director's ruling, finding that the state statute "permitting wholesalers to reset retailers' wine sections involves neither the state interest in controlling the importation of liquor into the state nor the state interest in structuring the liquor distribution system."[40] Moreover, the state and federal statutes were not in conflict and, therefore, the Twenty-first Amendment was not implicated. As the Ninth Circuit noted: "This is not, therefore, a case where state law compels conduct prohibited by federal law."[41]

As *Stein Distributing* clearly demonstrates, licensees must consider both state and federal rules when analyzing the legality of their actions with respect to the sale and distribution of licensed beverages.

C. CALIFORNIA TIED-HOUSE REGULATION

The California Constitution instructs the legislature to regulate the licensed beverage trade.[42] The Constitution authorizes the California Department of Alcoholic Beverage Control (ABC) to suspend or revoke any alcoholic beverage license inconsistent with the "public welfare and morals."[43] The California ABC Act,[44] including the tied-house laws,[45] is codified in the Business and Professions Code. The accompanying administrative regulations are in Title 4 of the California Code of Regulations.[46]

The California tied-house laws are both more comprehensive and more exception-filled than their federal counterparts, but still represent one of the strictest tied-house regulatory schemes in the country. Most significantly, while the federal laws require exclusion of a competitor's product to find a violation, the California law requires *only an unlawful interest or inducement leading to an unlawful act*. California ABC enforcement is therefore much easier and more vigorous than TTB activities against similar alleged abuses.

The California tied-house restrictions, unlike the federal ones, act against both suppliers (producers, importers, and wholesalers) and retailers. As noted, the laws address two major categories: the ownership interests a supplier may have in a retailer and the benefits a supplier may provide to a retailer.

1. RESTRICTED OWNERSHIP LAWS AND EXCEPTIONS

The most fundamental of the tied-house restrictions are those dealing with ownership. True to the historical purpose of the laws, California's tied-house regime begins by prohibiting a supplier from owning any interest in a retailer. Note how much further this restriction goes than simple prohibition of a brewer owning pubs in its local market. The formula appears to be

40. *Id.* at 1410.
41. *Id.* at 1411.
42. Cal. Const. art. XX, §22.
43. *Id.*
44. Cal. Bus. & Prof. Code §§23000 *et. seq.* (2009).
45. Cal. Bus. & Prof. Code §§23771-72, 25500-25512 (2009).
46. Cal. Code Regs., tit. 4, §§1-150 (2010).

all-inclusive: complete prohibition of a supplier[47] from holding "the ownership, directly or indirectly, of any interest in any" retailer, be it an on-sale[48] or off-sale[49] licensee.[50] The ban operates both ways, and retailers (both on- and off-sale) are similarly prohibited from owning any interests in suppliers.[51] California tied-house restrictions therefore do not prohibit just the traditional tied-house but *any* cross-ownership interest whatsoever between the supplier tiers and retail tier, no matter how small or attenuated, whether or not it might lead to actual control of a retailer.[52] For example, the California ABC recently informally stated that it would view the purchase of a Spanish winery by an investment group that owned a California retailer as a prohibited tied-house violation even though the putative owner offered to sign an undertaking that not one drop of the Spanish winery's products would be imported into the United States.

The breadth of the tied-house restrictions, combined with evolving economic realities and the acquisition of ever more retail licenses by persons with an interest, however slight, in a supplier, has given rise to an almost equally broad patchwork of exceptions.[53]

Nearly every modern exception is carefully tailored to apply only to the person who requested it, a political necessity to secure wholesaler neutrality or support. The exceptions include the ability of a supplier to lease space to a retailer at fair market value (with ABC approval);[54] to own a diminutive amount of stock and serve on the board of a publicly traded retailer (enacted to permit the president of Joseph E. Seagram, then a major spirits supplier, to serve on the board of Safeway Stores);[55] and to own hotels of a certain size (enacted to permit Grand Metropolitan, a British alcoholic beverage supplier, to own

---

47. A manufacturer, winegrower, manufacturer's or winegrower's agent, rectifier, distiller, bottler, importer, wholesaler, or officer or director or agent of one of the above. The California legislature adopted the term "winegrower" at the request of the California Wine Institute to emphasize wine's agricultural roots and to attempt to move it, at least to some degree, away from a manufactured product.

48. An entity, such as a bar or restaurant, that sells alcohol for consumption on the premises.

49. An entity, such as a grocery or liquor store, that sells alcohol for consumption off the premises.

50. Cal. Bus. & Prof. Code §§25500 (wine and spirits suppliers prohibited from owning on-sale licenses), 25501 (similar prohibitions for beer suppliers), 25502 (similar prohibitions for off-sale licenses) (2009).

51. *Id.* §§25505 (prohibiting on-sale licenses from owning any interest in a wine supplier), 25506 (prohibiting off-sale licenses from owning any interest in a spirits supplier); *see also Cal. Beer Wholesalers Ass'n, 5 Cal. 3d 402.*

52. Even stricter prohibitions apply to manufacturers of distilled spirits. The statute prohibits any person who manufactures distilled spirits anywhere (including locations outside California) from holding any distilled spirits license other than a manufacturing license. Cal. Bus. & Prof. Code §§23771-72 (2009). Specifically, manufacturers of distilled spirits are prohibited from holding any interest whatsoever in a wholesaler's, rectifier's, or retailer's license. *Id.* §23772.

53. These include permitting suppliers to own a single on-sale license provided it is for a club or on a vehicle such as a boat, train, or airplane, *id.* §25500(c); and to own a single on-sale license in a county with a population of less than 15,000, *id.* §25500(b), and an off-sale license in a county of similar size, if the license was held before September 19, 1947. *Id.* §25502(b). Winegrowers are allowed to hold off-sale licenses directly. *Id.* §25507.

54. *Id.* §25503.10.

55. *Id.* §25503.11. A parallel section, §25503.11, permits a retailer to own a diminutive amount of stock in a supplier.

the Intercontinental Hotel group, which in turn owned and operated the Mark Hopkins Hotel). The section was later amended to lower the number of required hotel rooms (to permit Bass Ale to own Holiday Inns)[56] and to allow a supplier to own marine parks (enacted to permit Anheuser-Busch to own SeaWorld in San Diego; Anheuser-Busch sold SeaWorld in 2009);[57] to own the premises of an on-sale[58] or off-sale[59] licensed cooking school (these sections permitted McKesson Corp., then an alcoholic beverage wholesaler, to own the California Culinary Academy in San Francisco); to own, serve on the board of, and promote a cooking school in Napa County (to permit vintners to participate in the Culinary Institute of America in St. Helena);[60] to own cruise ships (added at the request of a major brewer that was considering the purchase of a cruise line but later opted against it);[61] to own movie production theme parks (added at the request of Joseph E. Seagram when it purchased Universal Studios; Universal is now an asset of NBC Universal, in turn now owned 51 percent by Comcast and 49 percent by General Electric);[62] and to own an interactive entertainment facility.[63] A special section of the ABC Act was adopted to permit COPIA, a wine, food, and art cultural museum in Napa, to hold a special license that includes on- and off-sale privileges and also permits suppliers to own, serve on the board of, and promote the organization.[64]

Another special section permits winegrowers to own on-sale licenses if none of its products are sold by such licensees,[65] but this provides very limited help to winegrowers who want to participate in restaurant ownership. The legislature partially cured the problem first by permitting small winegrowers to own up to two on-sale licenses under highly restrictive conditions,[66] and then by permitting winegrowers of any size to own interests in any number of on-sale licenses, provided they sell their own wines in no more than two such licensed premises and that the number of wine items produced by the winegrower does not exceed 15 percent of the wines offered for sale by the retailer by brand.[67] (Microbreweries, on the other hand, can hold up to six on-sale licenses.[68]) Note that the tied-house laws do not apply to restaurants at winery premises that operate pursuant to the winegrower's production license.[69]

56. *Id.* §25503.16.
57. *Id.*
58. *Id.* §25503.17.
59. *Id.* §25503.18.
60. *Id.* §25503.20.
61. *Id.* §25503.19.
62. *Id.* §25503.29.
63. *Id.* §25503.37.
64. *Id.* §23396.2(g). Unfortunately, COPIA has ceased operations.
65. *Id.* §25503.15(a).
66. *Id.* §25503.15(b).
67. *Id.* §25503.30.
68. *Id.* §25503.28.
69. *See id.* §23358.

2. RESTRICTED BENEFITS LAWS AND EXCEPTIONS

The second branch of California tied-house regulations are those restricting the benefits a supplier may provide to a retailer. At the outset, the statute dictates that no supplier shall "furnish, give, or lend any money or other thing of value, directly or indirectly, to, or guarantee the repayment of any loan or the fulfillment of any financial obligation of, any [retailer]."[70] Further, suppliers are prohibited from engaging in consignment sales of licensed beverages, giving secret rebates or making secret concessions as part of a sale, engaging in price discrimination, paying a retailer for advertising space, or, subject to exceptions at §25611.1, giving signs and displays to retailers.[71] Finally, commercial bribery — giving anything of value to a retailer's employee in the hope of gaining customers — is prohibited.[72] This prohibition not only acts against suppliers, but also makes it a misdemeanor for retail employees to accept such a bribe.[73]

The tied-house restrictions on benefits are equally challenging in today's business environment. Like the restrictions on ownership, these are well tempered by exceptions, many of which are critical for the industry to function efficiently. Thus, suppliers can provide retailers with certain signs, displays, and promotional material,[74] and a wholesaler can sell or rent any lawful product to a retailer at the market price.[75] Brewers can provide wholesalers and retailers with specified tapping equipment.[76] Suppliers can provide shelf stocking services (but are permitted to touch only their own goods)[77] and free food, drink, and entertainment at meetings at the supplier's premises,[78] at retailers' conventions,[79] and to retailers and certain retailer employees at business meetings, along with surface transportation to and from the meetings and tickets for entertainment events, including food, beverages, and transportation.[80] However, the law does not permit winegrowers to fly retailers to the winery or provide lodging for them at winery guest houses. Certain suppliers can provide consumers with free entertainment, wine, and spirits (but not beer) at private parties under highly restricted conditions.[81]

An important and well-used exception permits suppliers to provide courses of instruction for licensees and, as part of those courses, to supply the products they are discussing.[82] Beer producers and wholesalers can provide similar instruction (with small tastes of beer) to consumers on or off retail

70. *Id.* §25500 (wine and spirits at on-sale premises). Similar prohibitions for beer suppliers are found at §25501 (with the exception of coasters and table tents) and for off-sale licenses at §25502.
71. *Id.* §25503.
72. *Id.* §25503(d).
73. *Id.*
74. *Id.* §25503.1.
75. *Id.*
76. *Id.* §25510.
77. *Id.* §25503.2.
78. *Id.* §25503.7
79. *Id.* §25503.3.
80. *Id.* §25503.27.
81. *Id.* §25600.5.
82. *Id.* §25503.5.

premises.[83] Winemakers' dinners can occur at a retailer's premises and include small free tastes of wine.[84] Like all tied-house exceptions, such events are subject to numerous restrictions.

Suppliers can pay retailers for market research data[85] and provide consumers, under certain conditions, with addresses of on-sale[86] and off-sale[87] retailers who sell their goods. Numerous exceptions permit suppliers to pay retailers for advertising space in specified venues, including stadiums and arenas,[88] zoos and aquariums,[89] racetracks,[90] and even water skiing arenas that meet certain specifications.[91]

Many other tied-house exceptions exist. And while the legislature has shown some willingness to create more as the need arises, it is now much harder, as previously noted, to obtain such exceptions than in the past, primarily due to wholesalers' concern that each exception further attenuates their statutory monopoly.

3. TIED-HOUSE CASE LAW

The California tied-house restrictions have been heavily litigated, in part because they prohibit practices commonplace in other industries. While the meaning of the law on its face seems relatively clear, the courts have added their own gloss to the statutory language. The tied-house jurisprudence provides useful examples of how the restrictions actually operate. In practice, the ABC often alleges violations of both the tied-house and the free goods laws in a single case. However, the following cases turn primarily on judicial interpretation of the tied-house laws. (For a discussion of the free goods law, see below.)

The leading tied-house case is *California Beer Wholesalers Assn., Inc. v. Alcoholic Bev. etc. Appeals Bd.*,[92] in which the ABC denied a retailer's application for a wholesale liquor license. The Court of Appeal stated what has become the controlling interpretation of the California tied-house laws:

> Following repeal of the Eighteenth Amendment, the vast majority of states, including California, enacted alcoholic beverage control laws. These statutes sought to forestall the generation of such evils and excesses as intemperance and disorderly marketing conditions that had plagued the public and the alcoholic beverage industry prior to prohibition [citations]. By enacting prohibitions against "tied-house" arrangements, state legislatures aimed to prevent two particular dangers: the ability and potentiality of large firms to dominate local markets through vertical and horizontal integration [citation] and the

83. *Id.* §25503.45. *See also infra* at 59 (text following note 119).
84. *Id.* §25503.4.
85. *Id.* §25503.24.
86. *Id.* §§25000.1, 25000.2.
87. *Id.* §25502.1.
88. *Id.* §§25503.6, 25503.8.
89. *Id.* §25503.85.
90. *Id.* §25503.26.
91. *Id.* §25503.23.
92. *Cal. Beer Wholesalers Ass'n*, 5 Cal. 3d 402.

excessive sales of alcoholic beverages produced by the overly aggressive marketing techniques of larger alcoholic beverage concerns [citations].

The principal method utilized by state legislatures to avoid these antisocial developments was the establishment of a triple-tiered distribution and licensing scheme [citations]. Manufacturing interests were to be separated from wholesale interests; wholesale interests were to be segregated from retail interests. In short, business endeavors engaged in the production, handling, and final sale of alcoholic beverages were to be kept "distinct and apart."[93]

The ABC has been especially vigilant against *indirect* inducements, where suppliers try to do indirectly what they cannot do directly. In *Department of Alcoholic Beverage Control v. Alcoholic Beverage Control Appeals Board (Deleuze)*,[94] the Court of Appeal reinstated the ABC's decision (previously reversed by the ABC Appeals Board) that an indirect tied-house violation existed where a winery purchased advertising space in a retailer's catalogue by paying the catalogue's printer, thereby reducing the cost of the catalogue to the retailer, who subsequently deposited the payment in the retailer's postal account. The court noted that §25502(a)(2) prohibits a winegrower from directly or indirectly giving money or other things of value to a retailer and deferred to the ABC's alcoholic beverage industry expertise.[95]

In *Department of Alcoholic Beverage Control v. Alcoholic Beverage Control Appeals Board (Schieffelin & Somerset Co.)*,[96] the court reinstated the ABC's decision (again, one the ABC Appeals Board had previously reversed) that payment by a distilled spirits supplier violated §§25502(a)(2) and 25503(h), which prohibit a wholesaler from directly or indirectly paying a retailer for placing advertising on or in a retailer's premises; the prohibited ads were logos on applications for the retailer's "fun run" event and on T-shirts distributed at the event. The court concluded that Schieffelin's payments to the event promoter (rather than the retailer) violated the indirect prohibitions of the tied-house law and were not saved by Rule 106(i)(2), which permits sponsorship of races, contests, and similar activities by payments to "bona fide amateur or professional organizations established [to encourage and promote] the activities involved" because the promoter's principal focus was operating professional marketing promotions rather than promoting the sport of running.[97]

But the prohibition on indirect inducements has its limits. Anheuser-Busch was one of three alcoholic beverage suppliers that signed contracts with Shecky's, a New York–based event promoter, to sponsor a series of "Girls Night Out" shopping events throughout the United States. The brewery's contract left virtually all event details to Shecky's, which agreed to conduct each

---

93. *Id.* at 407 (citing 25 Ops. Cal. Atty. Gen. 288, 289 (1955)). Note that while courts frequently cite this language as controlling, it is not, strictly speaking, accurate that California law requires the separation of manufacturing from wholesale interests. While most retailers are prohibited from owning wholesale licenses, a California beer and wine importer can own a wholesale and Type 20 (limited) retail license; in fact, a few California breweries and wineries own their own wholesale operations.

94. 100 Cal. App. 4th 1066 (2002).

95. *Id.* at 1080.

96. 128 Cal. App. 4th 1195 (2005).

97. *Id.* at 1209.

event in strict accord with local law. Shecky's was free to serve what beverages it wished and to hire a caterer of its choice, and it agreed to secure all necessary permits and licenses. Anheuser-Busch did give Shecky's logoed T-shirts to lend to caterers in those states (most states but not California) where this was legal. But, except for the payment of a sponsorship fee and the provision of point-of-sale material, the contract required Shecky's to handle all the details.

In 2007 Shecky's hired a retailer-concessionaire to obtain a license and serve licensed beverages at an event in San Francisco. The concessionaire failed to get a license but did not tell Shecky's, which, in violation of its contract with Anheuser-Busch, lent the retailer a logoed T-shirt. The ABC filed an accusation against Anheuser-Busch for sales without a license, unlawful inducements (lending a T-shirt to a retailer), and several other related claims.

In 2009 an ABC administrative law judge (ALJ) found in the brewery's favor on all counts, and the ABC adopted the ALJ's decision.[98] The case stands for the proposition that mere sponsorship of an event by a supplier does not subject the sponsor to ABC sanctions on an indirect theory of liability for unlawful activities that may occur at the event, such as the unlicensed sale of alcohol and lending a T-shirt to a retailer, but, more broadly, a minor's consumption of alcohol at a ball game, concert, or even a county fair event sponsored by a supplier. Had the ABC prevailed, it is possible that supplier sponsorships, including sponsorships of major league sports teams, would have disappeared from the California landscape. How such a result could benefit the "public welfare and morals" is a mystery of attempted regulatory enforcement perhaps only understood by the ABC.

While §25505 of the ABC Act clearly prohibits commercial bribery, not every payment to a retailer or its employees is prohibited. For example, the ABC held that prizes awarded in a supplier-sponsored contest in which bartenders raced up California Street in San Francisco carrying trays of mixed drinks did not violate the tied-house laws where the contest was not on a retailer's premises and there was no finding that the contest required the bartenders to promote or encourage the sale of the sponsor's products, and no such promotion or encouragement occurred.[99]

Although the ABC's rulemaking authority is broad, and courts usually defer to its expertise, the ABC cannot exceed statutory limits. Thus, tied-house exceptions are the province of the legislature, not the regulatory agency.[100]

---

98. *In the Matter of Anheuser-Busch, Inc., California Department of Alcoholic Beverage Control,* Reg. No. 08069642 (Nov. 12, 2009). Because the ABC director "adopted" the ALJ's decision, it is technically a decision by the ABC. And while such decisions do not constitute precedent, the present ABC administration, at least, is unlikely to take a contrary position.

99. *In the Matter of Allied Domecq Spirits and Wine, California Department of Alcoholic Beverage Control,* Reg. No. 02052713 (Nov, 21, 2002).

100. *Cal. Beer & Wine Wholesalers Ass'n v. Dep't of Alcoholic Beverage Control,* 201 Cal. App. 3d 100 (1988) (provision of ABC Department Rule 106 permitting certain gifts of supplies by beer wholesalers to on-sale retailers, where such gifts are prohibited by ABC Act §25501(a), is invalid). *See also People ex. rel. Dep't of Alcoholic Beverage Control v. Miller Brewing Co.,*104 Cal. App. 4th 1189 (2002). (ABC department rules cannot exceed statutory authority).

4. CALIFORNIA FREE GOODS LAW

a. Statute and Regulations

The basic free goods law is §25600 of the ABC Act,[101] but it is substantially augmented by ABC regulations in Rule 106.[102] Section 25600(a)(1) provides that "[n]o licensee shall, directly or indirectly, give any premium, gift, or free goods in connection with the sale or distribution of any alcoholic beverage, except as provided by rules that shall be adopted by the [ABC] department to implement this section or as authorized by this division." Rule 106(e) distinguishes between retailer and consumer advertising specialties (the latter may be furnished by a supplier to a retailer or directly to consumers) and imposes a limit of $1 on the original cost of such specialties furnished by a wine supplier, of $5 by a distilled spirits supplier, and of $3 by a beer supplier. The statute requires that, with respect to *beer*, a "premium, gift or free goods," including advertising specialties, may not cost more than $0.25 per unit or, when given by a single supplier to a single retailer, be worth more than $15 per year;[103] however, as noted, a recent amendment permits breweries, but not wholesalers, to give consumer advertising specialties worth up to $3 directly to the consumer provided the brewer itself makes the gift.[104] Several exceptions to the general statutory prohibitions exist, and it is important to examine the rule and the cases whenever a trade practice issue arises. For the practitioner, the most important exceptions permit

- Retailers to accept returns and make refunds or exchanges;[105]
- Winegrowers to make refunds to consumers no matter where the wine was purchased;[106]
- Samples to be given to licensees;[107]
- Gifts to be given to non-licensees;[108]
- Certain inside signs to be given to retailers;[109]
- Licensees to furnish certain services to specified communities and non-profit organizations;[110] and
- Licensees to sponsor certain contests on or off their premises.[111]

Creative use of these provisions will often make possible a promotion that appears at first blush to be unlawful. But in order to fully utilize these exceptions, it is critical to do so in light of the case law they have generated.

101. Cal. Bus. & Prof. Code §25600 (2009).
102. Cal. Code Regs., tit. 4, div. 1, §106 (2010).
103. Cal. Bus. & Prof. Code §25600(b)(1) (2009).
104. Cal. Bus. & Prof. Code §25600(b)(2)(A) (2009); Cal. Code Regs., tit. 4, §106(e) (2010).
105. Cal. Bus. & Prof. Code §25600(a)(2)(A) (2009).
106. *Id.* §25600(a)(2)(B).
107. Cal. Code Regs., tit. 4, div. 1, §52(a) (2010).
108. *Id.* §52(b).
109. *Id.* §106 (c)(1).
110. *Id.* §106(h).
111. *Id.* §106(i).

b. Free Goods Case Law

The leading case under §25600 *is Miller Brewing Co. v. Department of Alcoholic Beverage Control,*[112] in which the court addressed the definition of *distribution,* which the legislature added to the statutory prohibition against giving free goods in connection with the *sale* of licensed beverages. In 1983 Miller sponsored a national tour featuring comedian Joe Piscopo. To promote the tour, Miller placed its logo on concert tickets and on jackets, both of which were to be given away by co-sponsoring radio stations. The department contended that the logoed tickets and jackets were illegal "premium[s], gift[s] or free goods," in violation of the statute. In sustaining the ABC's position, the court held that "distribution" included "marketing or merchandising . . . sales promotion as a comprehensive function including market research . . . and effective advertising and selling" of alcoholic beverages.[113] This expansive definition of "distribution" has significantly restricted the promotion of wine and other licensed beverages in California.

There is interesting case law on the meaning of "premium, gift, or free goods," which §25600 now prohibits in connection with the sale or distribution of licensed beverages. In a significant win for the industry, the court in *Gonzales & Co., Inc., v. Department of Alcoholic Beverage Control*[114] held that wine rebate coupons were not premiums, gifts, or free goods in violation of §25600. Subsequently, the ABC took the aggressive (some might say bizarre) position that although rebates were legal on beer and, of course, on non-alcoholic beverage items, a cash rebate on such items that was contingent on buying a licensed beverage (e.g., $1 off the purchase of a Miller beer product if the consumer also bought specified non-alcoholic products such as ground beef, pickles, soda, or buns) violated §25600 and Rule 106(j) because the rebate was more than the $0.25 then permitted for *premiums* given in connection with beer. In *People ex rel. Department of Alcoholic Beverage Control v. Miller Brewing Co.,*[115] the court continued the ongoing judicial exercise involving the definition of "premium, gift, or free goods" and determined that the contingent promotions at issue were none of the above and were therefore permissible.[116]

Despite the coupon victory, the industry has not fared as well in other challenges to §25600. For example, in *Department of Alcoholic Beverage Control v. Alcoholic Beverage Control Appeals Bd. (Anheuser-Busch, Inc.),*[117] the court addressed the meaning of "gift" in an attempt to reconcile Rule 106 with Rule 52, which deals with both samples (Rule 52(a)) and gifts (Rule 52(b)) of licensed beverages.[118] Although the court ultimately decided that the practice of trade sampling, whereby wholesaler employees offered bar

---

112. 204 Cal. App. 3d. 5 (1988).
113. *Id.* at 15.
114. 151 Cal. App. 3d. 172 (1984).
115. 104 Cal. App. 4th 1189 (2002).
116. Rule 106(j) still prohibits most cross-merchandising promotions, at least presumably those that do not involve coupons.
117. 71 Cal. App. 4th 1518 (1999).
118. *See also* Rule 53.5, "Samples Used in Beer Tastings," adopted in 1994 after this case was decided.

patrons bottles or cans of the wholesaler's products, violated Rule 52(b)'s sampling requirements, it also urged "the Legislature, or the [ABC] Department, or both, to attempt a wholesale clarification of what items may be given away by licensees, to whom, and in what manner."[119] In 2010 the legislature partially addressed this issue by enacting §§25503.56 and 23396.6. These statutes permit retailers to obtain licenses that authorize suppliers to offer "instructional" tasting of beer, wine, and spirits to consumers at retail premises.

The court found no such ambiguity, however, in the case of sweepstakes where the prizes exceed the statutory minimums established in §25600 and Rule 106 ($0.25 (now $3) for beer, $1 for wine, and $5 for spirits) even when the ABC completely reversed a long-standing policy permitting sweepstakes. ABC decisions and policies are not precedent and are therefore subject to administrative amendment. Such a change occurred in 1999 when the ABC amended Rule 106(j) to no longer permit sweepstakes. In *Coors Brewing Co. v. Stroh,*[120] the court once again engaged in the judicial exercise of determining the meaning of "premium," this time concluding that a beer sweepstakes prize with a value greater than $0.25 is, in fact, a prohibited premium. By such exegesis, California is the only state in the union that prohibits sweepstakes promotions in connection with licensed beverages unless, as the ABC is quick to point out, the value of the prizes falls within the highly restrictive limits of §25600 and Rule 106.

D. WASHINGTON STATE TRADE PRACTICE LAW

In 1934, in response to the passage of the Twenty-first Amendment, the state of Washington passed the Steele Act, regulating the distribution and sale of licensed beverages.[121] Through the Steele Act, Washington, unlike many other states, elected to implement a "mixed" form of regulation in which the state retained control over the sale of distilled spirits (through state and contract stores) but implemented a three-tier distribution system for the sale of beer and wine.[122] The Steele Act also created the Washington State Liquor Control Board (WSLCB), consisting of three members appointed by the governor and confirmed by the senate to oversee the licensed beverage industry.[123]

Since the implementation of the three-tier system, the beer and wine industries have changed dramatically. In the last 30 years Washington has seen a huge increase in its wine industry. In 1981 Washington had 19 wineries; in 2001 it had 170 wineries. Today there are more than 600.

Washington's current primary tied-house statute contains two general prohibitions: manufacturers, importers, distributors, and their authorized agents are prohibited from (1) owning or having a financial interest in a retail license

119. *Anheuser-Busch,* 71 Cal. App. 4th at 1528-1529.

120. 86 Cal. App. 4th 768 (2001).

121. Codified as Title 66 of the Revised Code of Washington ("Wash. Rev. Code").

122. Wash. Rev. Code §66.16.010 (2009); Wash. Admin. Code §§314-01-005 to 314-76-035 (2010).

123. Wash. Rev. Code §66.08.012 (2009).

or owning property on which a retailer operates, and (2) providing "money or money's worth" to a retailer.[124] Of course, there are a number of exceptions to these general rules.

Many of the exceptions to the financial interest prohibition address the unique positioning of small wineries and breweries. For example, wineries and breweries may sell their wine and beer, as well as wine and beer produced by others, at retail on their premises.[125] A winery may hold a restaurant license on its premises or on contiguous property.[126] Similarly, a brewery may hold up to two licenses for a restaurant and/or tavern on its premises or at a separate location.[127] As in California, Washington wineries and breweries even have self-distribution rights from their licensed premises, permitting them to sell directly to retailers and consumers.[128]

The "money's worth" restriction also has many exceptions. For example, a winery may provide certain services for a retailer, such as pouring at a restaurant or at bottle signings.[129] A manufacturer or distributor may also provide a retailer with certain items, such as devices to mark beer or wine taps, can openers, bottle openers, and corkscrews; these items must be of nominal value or cost to the manufacturer or distributor.[130]

Over the years, Washington has modified its regulations on a piecemeal basis as various issues arose. But despite requests from various stakeholders, systematic changes to the system were slow in coming, primarily because while most stakeholders[131] agreed that changes were desirable, few could agree on what changes should be made.[132]

In 2004 Costco Wholesale Corporation intensified a push for comprehensive changes to the state's licensed beverage system. Costco filed an antitrust and Commerce Clause civil action against the WSLCB (and several other parties) in the Federal Court for the Western District of Washington alleging that Washington's laws and regulations, especially the trade practice laws, governing the sale of beer and wine

> restrict many of [Costco's] efficient and competitive practices as to wine and beer suppliers and create or facilitate agreement among distributors and among wineries and breweries ('manufactures') in restraint of competition. . . . [Therefore] the challenged laws and regulations were restraints of trade preempted by Section 1 of the Sherman Act, 15 U.S.C. §1.[133]

---

124. *Id.* §66.28.010(1)(a).
125. *Id.* §66.28.010.
126. *Id.*
127. *Id.*
128. *Id.* §§66.24.170(3), 66.24.240(2).
129. *Id.* §66.28.010(1)(h).
130. Wash. Admin. Code §314-16-020 (2009).
131. The stakeholders, which included manufacturers, distributors, and retailers, understandably have different priorities and concerns with respect to regulation of licensed beverages.
132. Washington State Liquor Control Board, Beer and Wine Three-Tier System Review Task Force Report, 1 (November 2006) (hereinafter Task Force Report), available at http://www.specialtywineretailers.org/members/documentary/WAstate-3TierReport.pdf.
133. *Costco Wholesale Corp. v. Maleng*, 522 F.3d 874, 882-883 (2008).

Costco specifically challenged nine restraints:

1. The "uniform pricing rule" requires breweries and wineries to sell a particular product at the same price to every distributor.[134] In turn, distributors must sell to all retailers at the same posted price.[135]
2. The "price posting" requirement compels beer and wine distributors to file with the WSLCB "a price posting showing the wholesale prices at which any and all brands of beer and wine sold by such beer and/or wine distributor shall be sold to retailers within the state."[136] The posted prices are made publicly available.[137]
3. Pursuant to the "hold" requirement, beer and wine manufacturers and distributors must "hold" their posted prices for at least 30 days.[138]
4. The "minimum mark up provisions" require distributors and suppliers, with limited exceptions, to price their products at no less than 10 percent above their acquisition costs.[139]
5. Quantity discounts, based on the volume of product purchased, are prohibited.[140]
6. No sales on credit; retailers must pay cash upon delivery.[141]
7. The "delivered price" requirement forces distributors to sell beer and wine at the same "delivered" price to all retailers, even if the retailer pays the freight and picks up the goods itself.[142]
8. The "central warehousing ban" prohibits retailers from storing or taking delivery of beer or wine at a central warehouse.[143]
9. Retailers may not sell beer or wine to other retailers, except under limited circumstances.[144]

The District Court upheld the retailer-to-retailer ban but found in Costco's favor with respect to all of the other statutes, holding that they irreconcilably conflicted with federal antitrust laws and, therefore, were invalid.[145] The state promptly appealed the decision to the Ninth Circuit Court of Appeals.

Upon receiving the District Court's ruling, the Washington state legislature directed the WSLCB to establish a task force to conduct a comprehensive review of the state's regulatory system for the distribution and sale of beer and

134. Wash. Rev. Code §66.28.180(3)(b) (2009).

135. *Id.* §66.28.180(2)(c).

136. *Id.* §66.28.180(2)(a).

137. In 2004, before the court issued its ruling, Washington actually amended the law to eliminate public access to posted prices.

138. Wash. Admin. Code §§314-20-100(2), (5), 314-24-190(2), (5) (2010).

139. Wash. Rev. Code §66.28.180(2)(d) (2009).

140. *Id.* §66.28.180(2)(d), (3)(b).

141. *Id.* §66.28.010(a); Wash. Admin. Code §§314-20-090, 314-13-015 (2010).

142. Wash. Rev. Code §66.28.180(2)(h)(ii) (2009).

143. *Id.* §66.28.185(4).

144. *Id.* §66.28.070(1).

145. *Costco*, 522 F.3d at 884-885. The court found that the state did not properly supervise its regulatory scheme because "it neither reviewed resulting prices for reasonableness nor monitored market conditions." The state's lack of involvement prohibited it from seeking protection under antitrust immunity laws. Accordingly, the district court ruled that the regulatory scheme was subject to federal preemption.

wine.[146] The task force comprised 20 individuals including local legislative representatives, the Seattle City Attorney, various retailers, out-of-state manufacturers, local distributors, local law enforcement, and prevention/treatment community members.[147]

Initially, an independent management consulting firm conducted over 100 interviews to identify issues relating to the current licensed beverage regulations. In addition, the WSLCB posted material on its website encouraging interested persons to submit written comments relating to the strengths and weaknesses of the current system. The consultant provided the task force members with information collected during the interviews and from public comments. It was clear from the beginning that most members agreed that changes to the current system should be made, but, as in the past, members often disagreed on what those changes should be and when they should occur.[148]

After months of intense effort, the task force ultimately made recommendations related to several issues, including the state's licensed beverage control policy,[149] tied-house prohibitions against providing money or money's worth to retailers, tied-house ownership and financial interests, price posting, mandatory minimum mark-ups, volume discounts, common carriers, credit, and enforcement resources.[150]

For example, the task force recommended continuing the current approach of adopting specific exceptions to the prohibitions against providing money or money's worth to retailers and urged the board to create a list of proposed exceptions to present to the legislature.[151] In creating the list, the task force directed the board to consider factors such as industry business needs, customer benefits, potential for improper inducements, potential for increased misuse of alcohol, and enforcement resources.[152] The task force also recommended liberalizing ownership restrictions.[153] At that time, the state did not allow any ownership interest between the tiers, and some task force members believed that allowing a manufacturer to hold an interest in a retailer would not necessarily lead to misuse of alcohol or product exclusion.[154]

While the task force was conducting its review, the Ninth Circuit Court of Appeals was conducting its own analysis of Washington's regulations. Ultimately, it reversed in part and affirmed in part the district court's ruling. The court upheld the ruling that the retailer-to-retailer sales ban constituted a unilateral restraint of trade that is not subject to preemption by the Sherman Act, because "the potential anti-competitive effect is not the result of private pricing or marketing decisions, but the logical and intended result of the

---

146. 2SSB 6823.PL, 59th Leg. Reg. Sess. (Wash. 2006), §13.

147. Task Force Report, *supra* note 132, app. Q.

148. *Id.* at 4-6.

149. To prevent the misuse of alcohol, promote the efficient collection of taxes, and promote the public interest in fostering the orderly and responsible distribution of malt beverages and wine toward the effective control of consumption.

150. Task Force Report, *supra* note 132 at 17-53.

151. *Id.* at 3, 21-23.

152. *Id.*

153. *Id.* at 3, 24-25.

154. *Id.*

statute itself."[155] With respect to the other regulations, however, the Ninth Circuit found that they were all valid restraints except for the post-and-hold pricing system.[156] Costco subsequently announced that it would not appeal to the United States Supreme Court.

In the spring of 2010, Initiative Measure No. 1100 was filed with the Washington Secretary of State's Office. Initiative 1100, if passed, would take distilled spirit sales out of the state's hands and turn Washington into a complete license state.[157] It would allow stores that now sell beer and wine to also sell distilled spirits, eliminate price controls, allow bulk discounts, and authorize retailers to buy distilled spirits directly from manufacturers.[158] If passed, Initiative 1100 would essentially eliminate the three-tier system and treat licensed beverages like any other product.[159]

Specifically, §25 of Initiative 1100 would delete and add language from and to the state's alcohol beverage code as follows:

> ~~The legislature recognizes that Washington's current three-tier system, where the functions of manufacturing, distributing, and retailing are distinct and the financial relationships and business transactions between entities in these tiers are regulated, is a valuable system for the distribution of beer and wine. The legislature further recognizes that~~ The historical total prohibition on ownership of an interest in one tier by a person with an ownership interest in another tier, as well as the historical restriction on financial incentives and business relationships between tiers, is unduly restrictive. The ~~legislature finds the modifications contained in chapter 506, Laws of 2009 are appropriate, because the modifications do~~ people find that liquor regulations should not impermissibly interfere with the goals of orderly marketing of alcohol in the state, encouraging moderation in consumption of alcohol by the citizens of the state, protecting the public interest and advancing public safety by preventing the use and consumption of alcohol by minors and other abusive consumption, and promoting the efficient collection of taxes by the state.

Eliminating the three-tier system may, on its face, look attractive in that it proposes to make purchasing licensed beverages more convenient and less

155. *Costco*, 522 F.3d at 889-890.

156. *Id.* at 896-900.

157. Costco Supports Initiative 1100, Privatizing Liquor Sales in Washington State, Costco Wholesaler (May 24, 2010), http://phx.corporate-ir.net/phoenix.zhtml?c=83830&p=irol-newsArticle_print&ID=1430618&highlight (accessed December 14, 2010).

158. Washington Initiative Measure No. 1100, filed April 27, 2010.

159. *Id.* §35. This would repeal the following sections of the state's alcoholic beverage law, which form an integral part of the three-tier system: (1) Wash. Rev. Code §66.28.010 (manufacturers, importers, distributors, and authorized representatives barred from interest in retail business or location; advances prohibited; "financial interest" defined; exceptions), 2009 ch. 373 §5, 2008 ch. 94 §5; (2) Wash. Rev. Code §66.28.285 (three-tier system; definitions), 2009 ch. 506 §2; (3) Wash. Rev. Code §66.28.290 (three-tier system; direct or indirect interests between industry members, affiliates, and retailers), 2009 ch. 506 §3; (4) Wash. Rev. Code §66.28.295 (three-tier system; direct or indirect interests; allowed activities), 2009 ch. 506 §4; (5) Wash. Rev. Code §66.28.300 (three-tier system; undue influence; determination by board), 2009 ch. 506 §5; (6) Wash. Rev. Code §66.28.305 (three-tier system; money advances; prohibition), 2009 ch. 506 §6; (7) Wash. Rev. Code §66.28.310 (three-tier system; promotional items), 2010 ch. 290 §3, 2010 ch. 141 §2, 2009 ch. 506 §7; (8) Wash. Rev. Code §66.28.315 (three-tier system; recordkeeping), 2009 ch. 506 §8; and (9) Wash. Rev. Code §66.28.320 (three-tier system; rule adoption), 2009 ch. 506 §9.

expensive. Under Washington's current regulatory system, consumers must purchase distilled spirits from a state-run licensed beverage store and licensees are not permitted volume discounts. One of the most significant impacts of the three-tier requirement and the volume discount ban is that they level the playing field for small businesses. Without price protection, Initiative 1100 would put many small business owners out of business.[160]

The principal sponsor of Initiative 1100 was Costco.[161] A couple of months before the 2010 election, Costco secured more than 300,000 signatures in support of Initiative 1100, thereby ensuring its presence on the November 2010 ballot.[162] But even before the election not everyone supported the total privatization of licensed beverage sales. For example, the Marin Institute, whose mission is to protect the public from the impact of the alcohol industries' negative practices, adamantly opposed Initiative 1100, claiming that control states experience lower alcohol consumption rates and lower instances of binge drinking than licensing states.[163]

According to Rick Garza, the WSLCB deputy administrative director, if Initiative 1100 passes, it will be the most dramatic change to the regulation of licensed beverages since the passage of the Twenty-first Amendment. And, undeniably, the passage of Initiative 1100 would affect more than just the state of Washington.

Initiative 1100 had some competition from Initiative 1105, which also aimed at privatizing liquor sales but seeks to maintain the three-tier system. Initiative 1105 was primarily sponsored by wholesale interests in an obvious attempt to maintain their businesses and their jobs. Although Initiative 1105 also secured enough signatures to be placed on the November ballot, reports stated, "Costco officials say they're not worried about the opposition. 'Judging by the way the signatures came in, this is going to be a very, very popular measure with the voters,' Costco spokesman Joel Benoliel said. 'We've got the better position going into this.'"[164]

On November 2, 2010, Washington voters rejected the privatization movement. Initiative 1100 failed 46.7 percent to 53.3 percent, and Initiative 1105 failed 35.2 percent to 64.8 percent.[165]

---

160. Whether it is the state's responsibility to provide economic protection to small licensed beverage businesses is another issue.

161. Jim Camden, Initiatives Would Close Washington State Liquor Stores, Spokesman-Review (June 23, 2010), http://www.spokesman.com/stories/2010/jun/23/initiatives-would-close-state-liquor-stores/ (accessed December 14, 2010).

162. *Id.*

163. Costco Infuses Alcohol Initiative with More Cash, Marin Institute Alcohol Advisory Watchdog (June 22, 2010), http://www.marininstitute.org/site/index.php?option=com_content&view=article&id=494:costco-infuses-alcohol-initiative-with-more-cash&catid-38&Itemid=9 (accessed December 14, 2010).

164. Amy Rolph, Costco Has a Big Stake in the Liquor Game, Seattle PI (August 8, 2010), http://www.seattlepi.com/local/424690_COSTCO.html (accessed December 14, 2010).

165. http://vote.wa.gov/Elections/WEI/Results.aspx?RaceTypeCode=M&JurisdictionTypeID=-2&ElectionID=37&ViewMode=Results (accessed December 14, 2010).

E. NEW YORK STATE TRADE PRACTICE LAW

New York's traditional trade practices statutory and regulatory scheme has been in place, in substantially the same form, since the Repeal of Prohibition. Following many other states, New York adopted a three-tier licensing system regulated by the State Liquor Authority (SLA).[166] The SLA is responsible for, among other things, regulating trade and credit practices related to the sale and distribution of licensed beverages at the wholesale and retail levels, ensuring compliance with the ABC laws, and bringing disciplinary action where appropriate.[167] New York, like Washington and California, has many laws prohibiting close relationships between manufacturers and wholesalers, on the one hand, and retailers on the other. The general rule is clear and prohibits manufacturers and wholesalers from having an interest in a retailer:[168]

> It shall be unlawful for a manufacturer or wholesaler licensed under this chapter to:
>
> (a) Be interested directly or indirectly in any premises where any alcoholic beverage is sold at retail; or in any business devoted wholly or partially to the sale of any alcoholic beverage at retail by stock ownership, interlocking directors, mortgage or lien or any personal or real property, or by any other means.[169]

Similarly, manufactures and wholesalers are prohibited from making a loan or gift to a retailer. They cannot:

> (b) Make, or cause to be made, any loan to any person engaged in the manufacture or sale of any alcoholic beverage at wholesale or retail.
>
> (c) Make any gift or render any service of any kind whatsoever, directly or indirectly, to any person licensed under this chapter which in the judgment of the liquor authority may tend to influence such licensee to purchase the product of such manufacturer or wholesaler. The provisions of this paragraph shall not be construed to prevent a manufacturer or wholesaler from entertaining a licensee at lunch or dinner, or to prevent a manufacturer or wholesaler from participating in or supporting bona fide retailer association activities such as, but not limited to, associate memberships, dinners, conventions, trade shows, product tastings and product education where such participation is in reasonable amounts and does not reach proportions that indicate attempts to influence the purchase of products of contributing manufacturers and wholesalers by the members of such retailer associations.[170]

Although the laws were essentially the same as those of many other states, corruption was rampant and trade practice laws went largely

166. History, New York State Liquor Authority: Division of Alcoholic Beverage Control, http://www.abc.state.ny.us/history (accessed December 14, 2010).

167. *Id.*

168. New York also has many exceptions to the general rule. *See, e.g.*, N.Y. Alcoholic Beverage Control Law §101 (2010). In fact, most manufacturers located in New York also hold a wholesaler's license. Thus, they may sell to traditional wholesalers (who then sell to retailers), but they may also sell directly to retailers.

169. N.Y. Alcoholic Beverage Control Law §101(1)(a) (2010).

170. *Id.* §101(1)(b), (c).

unenforced.[171] A report by the New York State Law Revision Commission noted that "[s]ince its inception, the SLA has been plagued with problems of licensing delays, inadequate enforcement, inefficient and ineffective administration and, indeed, bribery and corruption."[172]

This lack of enforcement provided ample opportunity for licensees to play fast and loose with the rules. Despite the enactment of price posting requirements and other trade practice laws, "[f]or decades, pay-to-play practices were rampant in the state's alcohol industry as retailers, wholesalers and suppliers used a variety of schemes to avoid the clear directive of the State's Alcohol Beverage Control Law. . . . The system benefitted a favored few, to the detriment of thousands of smaller stores, bars and restaurants."[173] Organized crime was prevalent and licensees commonly would operate a premises for six months to a year, "take whatever money they can out of it," and move the operation to another location once the license was revoked.[174]

Between 2005 and 2007 the Office of the Attorney General began an intense investigation into New York's licensed beverage industry and found many examples of violations against which the SLA was not taking action.[175] One example was the "game" licensees played in connection with price post-and-hold requirements.[176] The law is clear: manufacturers and wholesalers are prohibited from favoring select retailers with discounts, rebates, allowances, free goods, or other inducements.[177] The state's price posting system is designed to eliminate such favoritism.[178] The system requires wholesalers to send the SLA their current prices, which are then made available to retailers. Wholesalers are required to "hold" the published prices for a period of time, allowing all retailers to pay the same price, without any extra inducements, discounts, or rebates, for the same product.[179] Nevertheless, for many years, favored retailers were purchasing products at prices very different from those posted with the state.[180]

Wholesalers' ability to charge lower prices to favored retailers was a function of the SLA's unsophisticated price posting system. For many years, there was no easy way retailers could access the postings filed with the SLA. In fact, to view the postings, a retailer was required to physically go to SLA headquarters. Consequently, a publisher, working with wholesalers, published a book listing

171. New York State Law Revision Commission, The New York State Law Revision Commission Report on the Alcoholic Beverage Control Law and its Administration 56-67 (Dec. 15, 2009), http://www.lawrevision.state.ny.us/reports/12-15-09%20Report%20on%20ABC%20Law.pdf.

172. *Id.* at 5.

173. Agreement Is First in Ongoing Efforts to Remove Illegal Practices in State's Liquor Industry, Law Fuel (March 17, 2003), http://www.lawfuel.com/show-release.asp?ID=7601 (citing then attorney general Eliot Spitzer) (accessed December 13, 2010).

174. New York State Law Revision Commission, *supra* note 171 at 63.

175. *Id.* at 65-66.

176. Following the Repeal of Prohibition, price wars raged throughout New York. For example, before the price posting requirement was enacted, a four-day "price war" resulted in prices that were moving so quickly that stores posted hourly price changes on blackboards in the windows. *Id.* at 201-202. At the time, the State Liquor Authority claimed it had no jurisdiction over the price wars other than enforcing rules regarding signage. *Id.*

177. N.Y. Alcoholic Beverage Law §101(b) (2010).

178. *Id.*

179. *Id.*

180. New York State Law Revision Commission, *supra* note 171 at 201-221.

the prices at which retailers would purchase. Unfortunately, the prices listed in the book were not necessarily consistent with the postings filed with the state. Instead, the pricing book was based on verbal representations made by the wholesalers. This permitted wholesalers to provide favored retailers with illegal discounts without raising a red flag for the SLA.

Ultimately, in 2006, after more than a year of investigation, the state and several major manufacturers and wholesalers entered into a consent decree and judgment.[181] Among other things, the consent decree enjoined wholesalers and manufacturers from, directly or indirectly, providing retailers with things of value in connection with the sale of wine or distilled spirits and from discriminating between retailers. Specifically, the consent decree prohibited, subject to certain exceptions, payments or gifts to retailers, discrimination among retailers, discrimination in the distribution of limited items, tie-ins,[182] credits and rebates, payments to certain persons or entities that perform services for retailers,[183] payments for wine and drink menus, buy-back events, gifts of product, and payment for participation in retailer advertising. Although such practices were already generally prohibited by New York state law (again, subject to specified exceptions), the consent decree imposed substantial fines (ranging from $100,000 to $225,000) against several manufacturers and wholesalers for past practices and provided a vehicle for imposing similar fines upon a finding that the consent decree was violated.[184]

Most recently, New York's Law Revision Commission (which was created in 1934 and has undertaken numerous studies and made recommendations for change on a wide variety of subjects)[185] conducted an examination of New York's licensed beverage control laws and the state's administration of such laws.[186] In connection with its study, the Commission, among other things, studied historical documents (such as statutes, judicial opinions, and journals) and conducted hundreds of interviews with stakeholders (producers, wholesalers, and retailers), attorneys, state and local law enforcement, community members, SLA staff, and legislative staff.[187] The Commission essentially recommended a complete overhaul of the SLA — a process described by the Commission as "herculean."[188]

The Commission's recommendations were divided into two primary areas, the substantive law and the law's administration. As the Commission aptly

---

181. *People (New York) v. Bacardi U.S.A., et al.*, I.2006-9782, Consent Decree and Judgment, State of New York, Supreme Court, County of Erie, October 31, 2006.

182. Requiring or compelling retailers to purchase a particular brand in order to purchase another brand.

183. Prohibited if payment constitutes an incentive, award, or rebate, if the entity is owned or controlled by retailer(s) or if the principal, officer, or employee of a retailer is an officer or employee of the entity.

184. Bacardi, Consent Decree and Judgment, *supra* note 181. The current consent decree technically applies only to those companies that signed it. In 2010, however, the SLA made clear to all industry members that they were expected to abide by the same rules.

185. About the Commission, New York State Law Revision Commission, http://www.lawrevision.state.ny.us/index.php (accessed December 7, 2010).

186. New York State Law Revision Commission, *supra* note 171 at 1.

187. *Id.* at 2-4.

188. *Id.* at 5.

noted, "statutory overhaul would be futile unless and until the dysfunctional and programmatically-challenged SLA is rehabilitated so that it can fulfill the mission for which it was designed."[189]

The Commission recommended changes to several different substantive laws, including the tied-house laws. As noted above, manufacturers and wholesalers are prohibited from making any gift or rendering any service of any kind directly or indirectly to another licensee that "may tend to influence such licensee to purchase the product of such manufacturer or wholesaler."[190] Like California and Washington, New York law provides many exceptions to the general rule prohibiting tied-house acts. For example, manufacturers are allowed to give retailers certain items, such as wine racks, bins, barrels, casks, and various advertising merchandise.[191]

The Commission recommended a two-pronged approach to controlling and preventing tied-house abuse.[192] First, the state must "establish rules and regulations that clearly outline impermissible trade practices and permissible exceptions. . . ." Second, the state must enforce the rules and regulations by responding to complaints and conducting routine and random compliance audits.[193] The SLA recommended incorporating the consent decree into the state's statutes and amending the tied-house laws to apply uniformly to all licensed entities regardless of type of licensed beverage.[194]

Shortly before the Law Revision Commission published its findings, the governor appointed Dennis Rosen as the new SLA chairman. Notably, Mr. Rosen, a former assistant attorney general, had spearheaded the attorney general's 2005 investigation into the licensed beverage industry. Upon his appointment as chairman of the SLA, Mr. Rosen made many personnel changes throughout the agency.[195] The Commission commended this and other recent changes such as the reinstitution of basic administrative protocols and meetings with stakeholders and legal officials to discuss new policies and procedures.[196] The Law Revision Commission encouraged these efforts and expressed its hope that its report would help "facilitate [the SLA's] efforts and accelerate the much-needed reformation of the agency."[197]

In March 2010 SLA Chairman Rosen testified before the Senate Committee on Investigations and Government Operations.[198] He, too, recommended a complete overhaul of New York's licensed beverage law:

> One of the major hurdles facing the alcohol industry as well as the SLA is trying to do business in the 21st Century with a statute that was passed in 1934

---

189. *Id.*
190. N.Y. Alcoholic Beverage Control Law §101(1)(c) (2010).
191. N.Y. Alcoholic Beverage Control Law, Appendix §§86.1-86.17 (2010).
192. New York State Law Revision Commission, *supra* note 171 at 175.
193. *Id.* at 175-176.
194. *Id.* at 175-177.
195. *Id.* at 5-6.
196. *Id.*
197. *Id.* at 6.
198. New York State Liquor Authority, Division of Alcoholic Beverage Control, Media Advisory: Chairman Testifies Before Senate Committee on Investigations and Government Operations (March 24, 2010), http://www.abc.state.ny.us/newsletter/media-advisories/chairman-testifies-before-senate-committee-on-investigations-and-governm (accessed December 14, 2010).

> coming out of Prohibition. Since its inception, there have been various amendments to the ABC Law. While many of these amendments have been well-intentioned and indeed necessary, what I believe is needed today is a total overhaul of the statute. I recently told a reporter that what we have with the ABC Law is not what one would typically call a statute. A statute is logically written. What we have with the ABC Law is a collage. This is because it has persistently been jerry-rigged to suit the perceived needs of the moment without much deference to its overall structure or logic. Thus, it is difficult for even attorneys to understand, and almost impossible for the average licensee to know exactly what their responsibilities are under the statute.[199]

Chairman Rosen identified additional steps the SLA has recently taken to address the problems identified in the Law Revision Commission's report. The agency hired many new professionals, including an internal auditor. Enforcement priorities were refocused: "[w]e are getting away from counting fruit flies in bottles to cracking down on underage drinking, sales to intoxicated patrons, and the bars and nightclubs that wreak havoc on their neighborhoods."[200]

One component of the SLA's refocused enforcement priorities relates to the consent decree's prohibition against wholesalers/suppliers providing a thing of value to retailers. In the summer of 2010 a wholesaler invited several retailers to attend a professional baseball game at its expense. The wholesaler rented a bus to transport the retailers to the event; the retailers sat in the wholesaler's luxury box and, after the game, the bus took them home. After learning of the incident, the SLA filed an accusation against the wholesaler on the grounds that such conduct violated the consent decree and N.Y. CLS Al. Bev. §101(c). Ultimately, the wholesaler agreed to pay a $50,000 fine.

News of the $50,000 fine spread quickly throughout New York, and many in the industry expressed concern over the SLA's position that such activities were unlawful and over the gravity of the fine. In August 2010 Chairman Rosen called an industry meeting to discuss regulatory reform in New York. Over 75 people, representing diverse industry interests, including representatives from the various trade associations, general counsel for several distilled spirits organizations, large wholesalers, private attorneys, and miscellaneous small beer wholesalers, attended the meeting.

Among other things, Chairman Rosen expressed his personal views relating to retailer entertainment and its relationship with the prohibitions in the consent decree.[201] According to Chairman Rosen, although reasonable entertainment was permissible, wholesalers/suppliers are prohibited from taking retailers to expensive sporting events because such behavior constitutes an impermissible provision of a thing of value in violation of N.Y. CLS Al. Bev. §101. He explained that these trips were not generally available to the public or

---

199. *Id.* at 2.

200. *Id.* at 4.

201. *Id.* Chairman Rosen also explained that the SLA expected the industry to continue complying with the consent decree and all applicable laws. He stated that the SLA's resources are spread thin and that he fully expected the industry to engage in "self compliance." He noted that to the extent the SLA became aware of violations, the licensee should expect serious ramifications.

retailers and that suppliers typically invited only select retailers. Chairman Rosen took a literal and narrow reading of the statute and opined that wholesalers' provision of entertainment to retailers should be limited to a reasonable lunch or dinner.[202]

The vast majority of the industry members attending the meeting adamantly opposed Chairman Rosen's position. They claimed that attending events, including being provided with luxury transportation, was permissible entertainment (so long as the wholesaler/supplier also attended) and a key component of industry marketing.

Notably, shortly after the meeting, the industry was informed that the SLA, including Chairman Rosen, was reconsidering its position on entertainment and its relationship with the prohibitions against providing a thing of value to retailers. The SLA is currently considering the permissible boundaries of "entertainment."

Most in New York agree that the SLA and the laws it enforces require significant changes. But Chairman Rosen believed that "the legislature has a great opportunity this session to overhaul this anachronistic law and help us fix this agency,"[203] an opportunity of which the legislature has so far failed to avail itself.

F. CONCLUSION

Since the repeal of Prohibition, tied-house law has evolved from an apparently rational solution to a perceived social evil (the supplier-owned so-called open saloon) to something very different today. While in its pure form (prohibiting most suppliers from owning interests in most retailers) it restricts a supplier from forcing a retailer to buy the supplier's products, formulations like California's have given wholesalers a potent weapon to maintain their monopoly status as members of the middle tier in the three-tier distribution system.

Wholesalers play a critical role in the licensed beverage industry; they are indispensable, especially to large suppliers who sell throughout the country and must deliver product to thousands of separate retailers (including restaurants) in vastly different markets. But the law in every open (as distinguished from monopoly) state requires licensed beverage suppliers outside the state to sell only to in-state wholesalers, who, in turn, are the only licensees permitted to sell and deliver to retailers.[204] Wholesalers cherish and generally do everything possible to protect and maintain this favored monopoly position.

---

202. *Id. See also* N.Y. Alcoholic Beverage Control Law §101(c) (2010) ("The provisions of this paragraph shall not be construed to prevent a manufacture or wholesaler from entertaining a licensee at lunch or dinner. . . .").

203. New York State Liquor Authority, Division of Alcoholic Beverage Control, Media Advisory: Chairman Calls for Overhaul of the ABC Law (March 24, 2010), http://www.abc.state.ny.us/system/files/mediaadvisiory032510.pdf.

204. The most significant exception, of course, is the ability of out-of-state wineries to ship direct to consumers in other states whose laws permit such shipment by in-state wineries pursuant to the Supreme Court decision in *Granholm v. Heald*, 544 U.S. at 493 (2005).

And while there are many fewer wholesalers than in the past, those that have survived become increasingly powerful as they continue to grow through acquisition and consolidation. The chairman of one such wholesaler publicly favors a duopoly at the wholesale tier in every state. In practice, a duopoly already exists in California and several other states. In the 1960s, for example, nearly 35 full-service wholesalers sold wine and spirits in San Francisco; at the dawn of the twenty-first century that number had shrunk, effectively, to 2.[205]

Wholesalers often resist any regulatory or legislative initiative designed to promote programs to which they may be required to contribute money or effort, even when such programs are designed to increase their business. This attitude applies with special force to attempts to provide focused exemptions to the tied-house laws, which most wholesalers view as a bulwark against the weakening of their monopoly status. They have acquired legislative influence through close and continual cultivation and support of their elected representatives; as a result, in many states, passage of even the least controversial supplier-sponsored tied-house exceptions have become increasingly difficult to enact.

For example, in 2009 a large winery offered a generous gift of wine and cash to the San Francisco Symphony. But the Symphony held an on-sale general alcoholic beverage license for a small room in Davies Hall (its performance venue), in which it sold drinks and food to major contributors, and the winery conditioned the gift on the Symphony's finding its own solution to the resulting tied-house problem.[206] California law permits wineries (but not other licensed beverage suppliers) to give wine to bona fide charities,[207] but no law permits similar gifts of cash or other licensed beverages when the charity holds an on-sale license.

When the Symphony became aware that the tied-house law blocked its receipt of a substantial portion of the proffered gift, it sought a surgically targeted tied-house exception. The only opposition to the bill came from the beer and wine wholesalers association, which demanded several changes — including a requirement that the Symphony pay an annual fee of $750 before it accepted any gift and that the ABC report all such gifts in its annual report to the legislature. The Symphony resisted the requirement and was forced, instead, to accept a five-year sunset clause as a compromise in order for the proposal to become law.[208]

The tied-house and trade practice laws are difficult to amend. Amendments require substantial lawyer and registered lobbyist time and, as the

205. These are Southern Wine and Spirits of California and Young's Market Company. Other wholesalers carry both wine and spirits, but none rank close to the aforementioned in size, economic power, reach, brand selection ("book"), and "feet on the street."

206. Sales of licensed beverages to the general public before Symphony events and during intermission are handled by an outside caterer.

207. Cal. Bus. & Prof. Code §25503.9 (2009).

208. *Id.* §25503.31. The section applies only to a charitable, nonprofit symphony association that has operated in San Francisco for at least 99 years and produces not less than 175 public musical events per season, among other restrictions, but it does permit gifts from brewers, spirits producers, and retailers (but not wholesalers) as well as winegrowers.

preceding example illustrates, even the most benign proposals often face considerable political challenges.

Any lawyer who advises wineries must have at least a working knowledge of the trade practice laws. These laws are complex themselves and are also subject to changing regulatory interpretations. While the courts sometimes grant relief from overzealous enforcement, they are more inclined to defer to the administrative agency's regulatory expertise. Thus, open communication with state and federal licensed beverage regulators can greatly enhance a lawyer's understanding of the trade practice laws. But there are many gray areas in which the safest posture for a regulator is simply to deny permission to conduct the requested practice or promotion.[209] Lawyers must advise their clients when a given program falls into a gray area. If it does (and in trade practice and tied-house law it often will), a counselor must analyze and explain the risks, and the client must make its own business decision, after considering the risks and rewards, about whether to test the agency's interpretation of the law.

In the meantime, an enlightened interpretation, which considers modern business realities, can help. The tied-house laws, in particular, are vestigial remains of Repeal and now operate in and often control a commercial environment their drafters could never have imagined 75 years ago. They are mid-twentieth-century laws controlling an industry operating in a twenty-first-century environment.

Some have questioned the need for parallel state and federal regulation in the trade practices area. But neither the states nor Congress has shown interest in or appetite for relinquishing their power to control licensed beverages. In 2010 the wholesalers, frustrated by frequent legislative and litigation losses in the states with regard to wine direct shipping under the *Granholm* doctrine, introduced H.R. 5034 (amended and reintroduced in 2011 as H.R. 1161, the "Community Alcohol Regulatory Effectiveness" Act of 2011, or, for short, the "CARE" Act), a bill that would permit states, under certain circumstances, to pass laws discriminating against licensed beverages from out of state without regard to the Commerce Clause. At this writing the bill's fate is uncertain.

If tied-house laws are designed to prohibit manufacturers from controlling the purchasing practices of retailers, it would not be unreasonable for the ABC to interpret them to reach that result. However, so far, licensed beverage regulators in California and some other states have often taken a safer and less controversial route by expressing sympathy for those who need a legitimate exception but doing nothing to grant it, referring the issue to the legislature, where, as we have seen, politics often has more to do with protecting vested interests than with facilitating the original and rational intent of those who wrote the laws.

---

209. A sardonic adage holds that "No regulator ever got fired for saying 'No'!"

CHAPTER 3

LABELING AND ADVERTISING

Wendell Lee

A. INTRODUCTION

A little over 30 years ago, when I just started my job as a junior lawyer at Wine Institute, I was a dinner guest in a room full of mostly strangers. Claiming it was just for fun, the host, whom I had never met until that evening, first announced my position as the new wine lawyer to his other guests, then handed me a glass of wine and challenged me to tell him about it and to identify the wine. Ambush time, I thought, but I did what I thought was expected of me. I held the glass carefully at the stem, rotating my wrist so that the contents would swirl against the sides. I raised the glass toward the overhead light and peered intently at the wine as I let it settle down the sides of the glass, and then I covered the top of the glass with my nose and breathed in. I moved the glass up to my lips, took just a small sip along with some air, and let the wine rest on my tongue. After pausing several seconds for dramatic effect, I spoke to the group, accurately identifying not just the country of origin but the precise appellation, the vintage year, the brand name of the wine, and the New York importer.

The host, unable to embarrass me, was stunned at the uncanny accuracy of my guess. He gracefully turned to the guests. "Now, see here, that is why he got the job." He did not know that earlier in the evening, in my quest to find a good beer, I had seen the bottle of wine in the refrigerator. I had to remove the bottle to get my can of Coors and had shaken my head: "Oh God, not another Riesling fan." Sometimes you are just lucky that way, but to this day, whenever I cross paths with the host, which is not frequently, he thinks of me as nothing less than a wine god.

Every label tells a story about the pedigree of what is in the bottle. Depending on the winery as well as the reader, the story can be light and informative, ponderous and detailed, funny and entertaining. The story of this chapter, however, is about how that information has come to the consumer. This story goes beyond the label to the legal areas that push, twist, and pull the words, graphics, and messages that bring the American wine label and advertising to its final presentation to consumers.

This chapter attempts to cover some fundamentals of label regulation, legal requirements, design, advertising, and policy issues. It takes the reader through the process of creating a legal label and then provides a regulatory biography for each label element. In the end, I hope the reader will be a wine god as well, or at least be able to read a label while in search of a beer.

B. JURISDICTION: WHO GOVERNS WINE LABELS?

Any discussion of wine label forensics usually starts with a jurisdiction lesson. Knowing who is in control of the label information provides a context for the requirements that are imposed.

When a winery pulls its wine from its cellar and moves it out of its bonded facility for sale, the slim adhesive strips of paper that cling to the container have already gone through a very long journey of laws, regulations, and history. Wine labels have evolved over time, but most of this evolution has been buried in mounds of obscure public policy and regulatory rulemakings. Because these issues rarely make headlines, label rule development occurs virtually off the grid, in a world inhabited by compliance specialists, industry members (wineries, wholesalers, retailers), and trade associations.

Winery owners, when given any encouragement, will speak endlessly about the plethora of rules that they must follow. They use cryptic code terms like "TTB," "BATF," "Part 4," or "ABC." They tell stories of how certain marketing, advertising, or labeling efforts that sound seemingly innocuous were thwarted by this agency or that state. It will sound as if they are making things up just for the drama, but they probably are not too exaggerated in their descriptions.

Wine is regulated with a fierceness unseen in almost any other product. Its badge of courage is the U.S. Constitution and the two Amendments that began and ended national Prohibition. Since then, this country has gone through a long, strange road of post-Prohibition Repeal, with the federal government as well as the states enacting complex and often disparate rules for how to make, sell, import, and label wines. Alcohol regulation is a vast area of layered, multilevel control that shifts depending on the subject and the market. Is it unstable? Not really, but because of its sheer breadth, it has created its own economy and infrastructure of licensees, employees, regulators, trade associations, retail stores, lawyers, and end users, among many others. Is it treacherous? Wineries must walk very carefully at times to address all the layers of complexity. Often inefficient themselves, regulators arguably need to build in inefficiencies in order to address alcohol issues adequately. Even with wine labels, a very narrow and not frequently visited part of the universe of wine, there can be more layers than a wedding cake.

So who governs wine labels and advertising in the United States? This question was asked in a classroom filled with college students one day. The federal government? Yes. But which federal agencies? The Food and Drug

Administration (FDA)? Yes. The Bureau of Alcohol, Tobacco and Firearms (BATF)? Not so much after the Bureau was transferred to Homeland Security, but definitely the Treasury Department, through the Alcohol and Tobacco Tax and Trade Bureau (TTB). How about the Federal Trade Commission (FTC)? Yes, especially if the label or advertising is considered misleading or deceptive.[1] The state ABC? Yes, especially if there is a winery in the state. Everybody seems to want a role in the process.

For wineries, their labels are subject to review by three regulatory agencies. The TTB takes the lead, with less influence from state alcoholic beverage regulators, and even less from the FTC. Not that the FDA does not have jurisdiction (it does). However, for the sake of simplicity and efficient governance, one agency had to stand down.[2] Generally speaking, federal authorities control the results.

Most of this chapter addresses policy changes administered by the TTB[3] and its predecessor organization, the BATF,[4] prior to its transfer to the Department of Justice following the passage of the Homeland Security Act of 2003. The law enforcement functions of the BATF under the Department of the Treasury were transferred to the Department of Justice at that time, while the tax and trade functions of the BATF were retained in the Treasury Department with the newly formed TTB.[5]

C. FEDERAL LABELING REGULATIONS ARE DESIGNED TO PREVENT CONSUMER DECEPTION

Whenever label rules are challenged, claims of consumer deception are almost always at the center of the case. That is because the Federal Alcohol

1. The FTC is playing an increasingly larger role in recent years because of the increase in advertising-related issues. Social media, email, advertising, and the making of green and environmental claims all fall within the FTC's administrative net. *See, e.g.*, FTC, The FTC in 2009: Federal Trade Commission Annual Report (2009) (describing the FTC's activities regarding, *inter alia*, online behavioral advertising and green marketing claims), available at http://www.ftc.gov/os/2009/03/2009ftcrptsv.pdf (last visited Feb. 1, 2011).

2. On November 20, 1987, the FDA entered into a Memorandum of Understanding (MOU) with the then BATF, in which the respective responsibilities of the two agencies were delineated. FDA & BATF, MOU 225-88-2000, Memorandum of Understanding Between the Food and Drug Administration and the Bureau of Alcohol, Tobacco, and Firearms (1987), available at http://www.fda.gov/AboutFDA/PartnershipsCollaborations/MemorandaofUnderstandingMOUs/DomesticMOUs/ucm116370.htm (last visited Jan. 21, 2011). The MOU does not concede jurisdiction but recognizes that the primary labeling responsibility resides with the BATF. *Id.* §IIA. The MOU is still in effect today between the FDA and the TTB, the BATF's successor organization. *Id.* §V. The MOU is narrowly written but has played an important role in health-related issues such as the making of therapeutic claims, the disclosure of sulfur dioxide, allergen labeling of food products, and menu labeling. Wine is a "food" as defined by the FDA's Food, Drug and Cosmetic Act, and falls within the FDA's jurisdiction. Pub. L. No. 75-717, 52 Stat. 1040 (1938) (codified at 21 U.S.C. §§301-397 (2006)).

3. The Tax and Trade Bureau's website is at http://www.ttb.gov.

4. The Bureau of Alcohol, Tobacco and Firearms website is at http://atf.gov. Sometimes the acronym for this agency is ATF.

5. Homeland Security Act of 2002, Pub. L. No. 107-296, §1111(d), 116 Stat. 2135, 2274-2275 (2002) (codified at 6 U.S.C. §531 (2006)).

Administration (FAA) Act[6] authorizes the TTB to enact labeling regulations for two purposes: (1) to provide consumers with adequate product information and (2) to prevent consumer deception.[7] Not surprisingly, in label controversies both supporters and opponents often advance their positions based on these identical purposes. The TTB and its predecessor agency, the BATF, have used these same reasons to support their regulatory actions.

The case of Guns n' Roses lead singer Slash is instructive. His product endorsement of "Black Death" Vodka and his use of the bottle onstage may have prompted a review of the label after it entered commerce. "Black Death" Vodka's label was first approved, but then the BATF revoked the approval for two reasons: (1) the reference to the plague ("Black Death"), combined with the use of a skull image, created a misleading impression that the product was inherently unsafe for human consumption at any level; and (2) the label "mocked" the real health risks that may result from alcohol consumption by making an obviously false claim about the dangers.[8] These arguments, however, failed to convince a U.S. District Court judge that approval of the label should be revoked.[9]

Those seeking regulatory changes to labeling rules almost always claim that the existing regulations result in consumer confusion or deception. But another way to look at existing labeling regulations is that they are the result of a federal agency's exercise of authority to address the very same goals of preventing consumer confusion and deception, which are articulated in the FAA Act of 1935.

It is often too simplistic to challenge existing regulations based on absolute principles of consumer deception without first understanding the rulemaking history. The argument of consumer deception may seem convincing to consumers when it is found in newspaper and magazine articles, but this argument, while politically convenient, lacks sufficient context and ignores the extraordinary efforts that the rulemaking agencies take to address these very concerns during rule development. Rulemaking agencies such as the TTB do not develop regulations that purposely deceive consumers. Even in highly political situations, agencies cannot act arbitrarily or capriciously when establishing regulations. Although Wine Institute and other trade associations and industry organizations actively participate in the TTB's rulemaking efforts, the regulations themselves must embody and reflect the standards of the FAA Act.

In the 1981 case of *Wawszkiewicz v. Dep't of the Treasury*,[10] a group of consumers challenged the Treasury Department's varietal designation and appellation of origin labeling regulations, alleging that they failed to require

6. 27 U.S.C. §§201-219A (2006).

7. *Id.* §§113(1), 205(e); *see also* TTB, Industry Circular No. 2007-4, Pre-COLA Product Evaluation 1 (2007), available at www.ttb.gov/industry_circulars/archives/2007/07-04.html (last visited Jan. 31). Note the term "adequate" information, not "complete" information.

8. *See Cabo Distrib. Co. v. Brady*, 821 F. Supp. 601 (N.D. Cal. 1992).

9. *Id.*

10. 670 F.2d 296 (D.C. Cir. 1981).

accurate (that is, absolute) percentages for such information. The challenge was unsuccessful; the court refused to substitute its judgment for that of the rulemaking agency.[11]

Whenever a label issue involves a proposed rule that is less than absolute, purists will argue, as Wawszkiewicz did, that consumers have a right to know everything about the bottle's contents, down to exact percentages. Even a cursory analysis of the TTB's regulations reveals that labeling standards are not based on absolute or categorical standards but are rather the result, over the years, of reasoned analysis and a balancing of interests. Varietal designations do not call for 100 percent of a specific varietal;[12] the use of "produced and bottled by" does not require that the bottling winery ferment 100 percent of the grapes used to make the wine;[13] vintage dates are not required to reflect the harvest year for 100 percent of the grapes.[14] These regulations exist because they represent a reasoned approach to label information, responsibly balancing industry and non-industry viewpoints. The underpinnings of wine labeling regulations on the federal level are rarely measured in terms of absolutes.

D. WINE LABELS: PRIOR APPROVAL REQUIRED

Wine labeling regulations confront wineries with much more immediacy than other food products. Unlike labels for other food products, which are judged after entering the marketplace, every wine label must be approved by the TTB very early in the production cycle, before the bottled wine enters commerce.[15] Every wine bottle label has been reviewed by the federal government long before the consumer sees it.

Prior label approval means just that. A winery must submit its proposed label to the TTB before putting the label on a bottle.[16] The TTB reviews the label in detail and either approves or rejects it.[17] Fortunately for producers, a large and ever-growing body of publicly available examples of approved labels can

11. *Id.* at 303.
12. 27 C.F.R. §4.23(b) (2010).
13. *Id.* §4.35 (a)(2)(i)-(iii).
14. *Id.* §4.27(a).
15. Actually, TTB regulations require that labels be approved prior to bottling, which can really be a problem for production flow. 27 C.F.R. §4.50 (2010). Many wineries have not quite decided on a label and cannot really define the story they want to tell until after the wine is bottled. So how can a winery tell you that the wine was bottled on a certain date if the label has to be approved prior to bottling? The law requires that the bottling be covered by approval of a label but not necessarily the one that eventually ends up on the bottle. *See* Rachel Dumas Rey, eCompli: The Top Ten Common Compliance Errors 1 (2008), available at http://www.compli-beverage.com/pdf/Top_10_Compliance_Errors.pdf (last visited Jan. 31, 2011). Many wineries will have a few "red wine" or "white wine" generic labels that have been approved. These approvals are intended to cover a winery's entire range of products so that the winery can concentrate on production considerations and become concerned about label information when it is ready to do so.
16. 27 C.F.R. §4.50 (2010).
17. *Id.*

be found online. At the TTB's online Public COLA Registry,[18] users can enter a product name in the text box and see not only the approval history of the product's labels but also (in most cases) a digital image of the label itself.[19]

How long does the approval last? Does a winery need a new approval each year for the same wine from different vintages? For the most part, label approvals are good until they are not good. The third page of the TTB's Application for Certification/Exemption of Label/Bottle Approval[20] contains a table that lists the allowable revisions to approved labels that do not require resubmission to the TTB. Label approvals can have a very long life; if the only changes are, for example, the vintage year and the alcohol content within a tax class, the approval will cover labels year after year.

1. EXEMPTION FROM LABEL APPROVAL

Decisions rendered by the TTB's label approval staff have been the source of industry urban legend for years. When human beings are required to apply less than absolute rules to label content and design, questionable calls and outright mistakes will happen. Fortunately, they do not happen often, and fortunately as well, there is a review process. Close calls can be appealed, bad calls can be rescinded, and the TTB can change its mind over time.[21]

I believe that the TTB does a great job of label approval in almost every situation. One result of the "Black Death" Vodka decision was that the BATF realized that it had no clear procedures in place for "disapproving" a label that already had been approved. In order to address procedural due process issues, the BATF initiated and then finalized rulemaking that created procedures for appealing label decisions and for rescinding label approvals.[22] Although these regulations, found at 27 CFR Part 13, exist today, in practice they are rarely (if ever) used. Most label disputes are dealt with at the initial level of administration—with the label approval staff, known as the TTB's Alcohol Labeling and Formulation Division. But it is good to know that there is an authorized process in place for extraordinary label circumstances.

When a TTB label specialist is asked about bad calls, it becomes clear that the regulators have a large compilation of stories of outrage as well. The large body of label approval wine lore is not limited to the TTB's decisions but also includes industry actions. Whenever a winery may have slipped up, one

18. "COLA" is an acronym for "CERTIFICATE OF LABEL APPROVAL." The full name of the form, TTB F 5100.31, is Application for Certification/Exemption of Label/Bottle Approval. The Public COLA Registry can be found online at https://www.ttbonline.gov/colasonline/publicSearchColasBasic.do (last visited Jan. 21, 2011).

19. Users of the Public COLA Registry often do not take advantage of the advanced search interface, which opens up the world of wine labels dramatically.

20. Available currently at http://www.ttb.gov/forms/f510031.pdf (last visited Jan. 15, 2011).

21. The famous Kenwood label of the naked woman was first rejected by the BATF as obscene, then subsequently approved years later, when it presumably was no longer obscene. To view the label online, go to www.kenwoodvineyards.com/#/artistseries, select "Artist Series, 1975-2006, then click on the first link to the artist David Lance Goines.

22. Procedures for the Issuance, Denial, and Revocation of Certificates of Label Approval, Certificates of Exemption From Label Approval, and Distinctive Liquor Bottle Approvals, 64 Fed. Reg. 2122, 2131-32 (Jan. 13, 1999) (to be codified at 27 C.F.R. pt. 13).

approach that is available to every label practitioner is an exemption from the Certificate of Label Approval, described in the following paragraph.

The timetable for wine production is something that most consumers would never think about. Wine production cycles, storage space, and harvest schedules often do not help in label planning. For printing a new label, the lead time for a moderately sized winery is a little over two months.[23] Often a winery that is rushed for time will send out a label for printing before the label has been approved, only to discover, when it finally submits its COLA application, that the label is non-compliant for one reason or another. In such cases practitioners approach the TTB and attempt to obtain a variance to allow the use of the non-compliant label; this is called "use-up" permission. If that fails and the winery is able to sell the wine only within the state where the wine was produced, a COLA exemption could be considered. Because the wine will not be sold in interstate commerce, the FAA Act provisions do not apply. The exemption constitutes a promise by the winery that the mislabeled product will be sold only within that state and not within interstate commerce. The TTB generally will require a disclosure statement such as "FOR SALE IN CALIFORNIA ONLY" to ensure that the product stays within the state. This is not the best solution, but sometimes it is the only one.

E. BARE BONES WINE LABEL CONSTRUCTION

When my middle daughter was 18 and a fairly new driver, she got into her car, turned the key, but found that the car would not start. Because she was somewhere that she knew I would not have approved of, she attempted to solve the problem on her own. She walked four miles home, found some jumper cables in our garage, walked back to the car, and realized she needed another car to jump hers. She had her friend pull up to her car so that both cars were in the proper position, but because her friend was too embarrassed to admit that he did not know how to hook up the cables, he crossed the wires, which basically destroyed the alternator.

A person does not need to know how to put a car together to drive one. For the purposes of this chapter, however, it is helpful to know how to assemble a simple wine label. In this section, I first cover mandatory label information, then I present each mandatory element and expand on that element's regulatory and policy history. In that way, it is possible to get a short but useful background of label design.

The TTB makes readily available some consumer brochures on how to read wine, beer, and spirits labels.[24] Many very good books and articles also give

23. *See* Letter from Robert Koch, President, Wine Institute, to Francis W. Foote, Director, TTB Regulations and Rulings Division, 32, regarding TTB's 2007 proposal of nutrition labeling (Jan. 27, 2008), available at http://www.wineinstitute.org/files/SFLPC.pdf (last visited Jan. 31, 2011).

24. *See Labeling*, TTB, http://www.ttb.gov/labeling/index.shtml (last visited Jan. 15, 2011), and in particular, the links to "What You Should Know About Labeling" under the "Labeling

consumers a valuable perspective on how to interpret a wine label and understand label terms and their significance.

By the time a consumer is looking at a label, it has been likely months if not years since it was first designed and approved. From a winery's standpoint, the road to a TTB-approved label can be a very long one. Wineries must develop legitimate information that meets their production programs, grape sources, and marketing plans, as well as the TTB's labeling regulations.

Here are some label approval statistics from 2008. The TTB received 133,427 label applications in that year.[25] Wines composed 85 percent of those label applications, which are also required for beer and spirits.[26] In 2009 the Bureau processed nearly 125,000 COLAs, a decline of 6 percent from the prior year and the first reversal of the growth trend since the Bureau began tracking this metric.[27] The TTB surmises that the "decline is partly attributable to the economic downturn, as the cost of redesigning labels or introducing new products may have been prohibitive."[28] In FY 2009 the significant majority of label applications received were for wine products.[29] The wine industry submitted 84 percent of the label applications processed by the TTB.[30] In the world of label approvals, wine reigns supreme. Wine Institute has a full-time staff person in its Washington, D.C., office who handles paper label approval submissions for its members. The TTB also offers a "COLAS ONLINE" service where a winery may submit label approval applications online.[31] Processing time for electronic submissions (approximately 20 days) is now shorter than for paper submissions.

Assembling a label that will meet TTB approval is, in fact, relatively easy as long as one pays attention to the mandatory information. The purpose of this exercise is to illustrate that anyone can build a label that will be approved by the TTB. I do not go into type size or information placement (even though that is very attractive factual information for the obsessive-compulsive). The goal of this exercise is to provide a foundation for understanding the issues that have arisen with each of these pieces of mandatory information over the past 30 years or so.

Easy labels are not exciting labels. In fact, the bare-bones wine label is, frankly, very boring. In a sea of wine labels floating along the wine aisles, a

---

Information Resources" heading; *see also* the ALFD's Sample Wine Labels: A Bit Beyond the Basics, June 2008, available at www.ttb.gov/pdf/06-08-expo-sample-labels.pdf (ALFD is the acronym for TTB's Advertising, Labeling, and Formulation Division).

25. Sandi Sisler, Wine Labeling Specialist, TTB Advertising, Labeling, and Formulation Division, presentation at 2009 TTB Expo, Labeling Essentials for Domestic Wines 50 (June 24, 2009), available at http://www.ttb.gov/expo/presentations-black/w09-bw.pdf (last visited Jan. 31, 2011).

26. *Id.* at 51.

27. TTB, Annual Report 5 (2009), available at www.ttb.gov/foia/ttbar2009.pdf (last visited Jan. 31, 2011).

28. *Id.*

29. *Id.*

30. *Id.*

31. *TTB's COLAs Online Electronic Filing System*, TTB, http://www.ttb.gov/alfd/colasonline.shtml (last visited Jan. 21, 2011).

wine label is usually the first thing that "touches" a willing buyer. A bare-bones label will never do that.

The TTB requires that every wine label contain certain elements that are mostly listed at 27 CFR §4.32. The mandatory elements for a label are shown below.

The "brand label"[32] must include the following:[33]

- A brand name;
- The class, type, or other designation in accordance with 27 CFR 4.34;
- An alcoholic content statement (unless implied in the class/type designation); and
- If the wine is a blend of U.S. and foreign wine *and* if you make reference to the origin of this blend, the exact percentage by volume.

In addition, the following information must appear on "any" label:[34]

- Name and address of the bottler;
- Net contents of the container (unless blown into the bottle);
- If present, a statement that the product contains FD&C Yellow Dye Number 5; and
- A declaration of sulfites if detected at 10 parts per million (ppm) or more.

Finally, there is the government warning statement, shown in Figure 3-1. It is not required by 27 CFR §4.32 but by 27 CFR §16.21.[35]

---

32. Many wineries have learned to play with the "brand label." The term itself is somewhat imprecise, so a "brand label" is generally determined by finding the information that is required to be on it. If you have ever seen the wonderful "art" labels that consist of a main label panel that simply contains artwork, with the mandatory information on what one would call the "back" label, you know what I mean. In the industry, this is sometimes referred to as the "front label–back label game." The mandatory information appears on what consumers consider the back label, with the art label (front label) featured on the retail shelf. The TTB does not distinguish between front and back labels.

33. 27 C.F.R. §4.32(a) (2010).

34. *Id.* §4.32(b)-(e). The "Contains Sulfites" disclosure statement was required by the BATF in 1987, Labeling of Sulfites in Alcoholic Beverages, 51 Fed. Reg. 34706 (Sept. 30, 1986). Following a series of unfortunate instances where sulfites caused allergic reactions primarily at salad bars, the FDA cracked down on sulfite use and banned its use on fresh fish and on fruits and vegetables for human consumption. *See* Food Labeling: Declaration of Sulfating Agents: Final Rule, 51 Fed. Reg. 25,012-25,020 (1986); Chris W. Lecos, *Sulfites; FDA Limits Use, Broadens Labeling,* 20(8) FDA Consumer 10-13 (1986). Remember that MOU discussed earlier? This is a great example of the BATF following the wisdom and expertise of the FDA when it comes to food safety issues. There is one other important point about the "Contains Sulfites" disclosure statement: the trigger is a detection level, not a threshold level for adverse reactions, because the mechanism behind such reactions is not well understood. *See* M.A. Kantor, *Adverse Reactions to Food Additives, in* Food Chemical Safety: Additives 161 (David H. Watson ed., 2002). Basing label information on detection levels is the perfect example of the "precautionary principle." In the European Union, the precautionary principle is embedded in statute. The principle implies that there is a social responsibility to protect the public from exposure to harm when scientific investigation has found a plausible risk. These protections can be relaxed only if further scientific findings emerge that provide sound evidence that no harm will result. Technically, detection levels for sulfites are much lower than 10 parts per million (ppm), but thankfully the regulation has not been amended to reflect advances in detection technology.

35. Implemented pursuant to the Alcoholic Beverage Labeling Act of 1988, Pub. L. No. 100-690, 102 Stat. 4181 (1988) (codified at 27 U.S.C. §§213-19A).

Figure 3-1
Government Warning

GOVERNMENT WARNING: (1) According to the Surgeon General, women should not drink alcoholic beverages during pregnancy because of the risk of birth defects.

In real life a consumer will not find a wine that mentions FD&C Yellow Dye Number 5. Nor will any U.S.-foreign wine blend proudly state that claim. So there are really only six mandatory label elements for most wine labels.

In sum, for a wine made from grapes and a bottle with the net contents statement blown into the glass, a winery can have a perfectly approvable label with just five elements. The most bare-bones label would look something like Figure 3-2.

Easy? Yes. Pretty? No. But perhaps it illustrates that the basic building block for all labels is not appellation or vintage or varietal, but rather 27 CFR §4.32. All labels begin there. It is the essential DNA for every label that you see.

1. INITIAL GLOSSARY OF TERMS

If mandatory information is the DNA of wine labels, then the TTB's administrative rulemaking efforts are the evolutionary milestones. Each of the mandatory label elements comes with a regulatory history. They will be considered in random order.

Today's wine label has a birthday. It is September 22, 1978, the effective date of the final omnibus labeling reform regulation published by the BATF.[36] The final rule made wholesale and significant changes to wine labeling regulations, providing more specificity, meaning, and accuracy to wine labels. Every element of label design was scrutinized in the three-year effort that included four notices of proposed rulemaking, published on July 17, 1975; February 25, 1976; November 12, 1976; and June 15, 1977.[37] Public hearings, a rarity today in federal administrative rulemaking, were held in Washington, D.C., and San Francisco, California, during April 1976, February 1977, and September and November 1977.[38]

For much of this section, we begin with the regulations and standards established in the particular rulemaking. First, however, I want to arm you with a few definitions that you should insert in your glossary of wine terms. We will use these terms in later discussions.

---

36. Appellation of Origin, Grape-Type Designations, Etc., 43 Fed. Reg. 37672 (Aug. 23, 1978) (to be codified at 27 C.F.R. pt. 4).

37. "Appellation of Origin" and "Viticultural Area"; Proposed Definition, 40 Fed. Reg. 30117 (proposed July 17, 1975); "Appellation of Origin," "Viticultural Area," and "Estate Bottled"; Hearing, 41 Fed. Reg. 8188 (Feb. 25, 1976); "Appellation Of Origin," "Viticultural Area," "Estate Bottled," "Grape Type Designations," and Miscellaneous Amendments; Hearing; Withdrawal of Previous Notices, 41 Fed. Reg. 50004 (Nov. 12, 1976); Labeling and Advertising of Wine; Appellation of Origin, Grape Type Designations, Etc., 42 Fed. Reg. 30517 (proposed June 15, 1977).

38. Appellation of Origin, Grape-Type Designations, Etc., 43 Fed. Reg. at 37672.

Figure 3-2
Great Brand Name Label

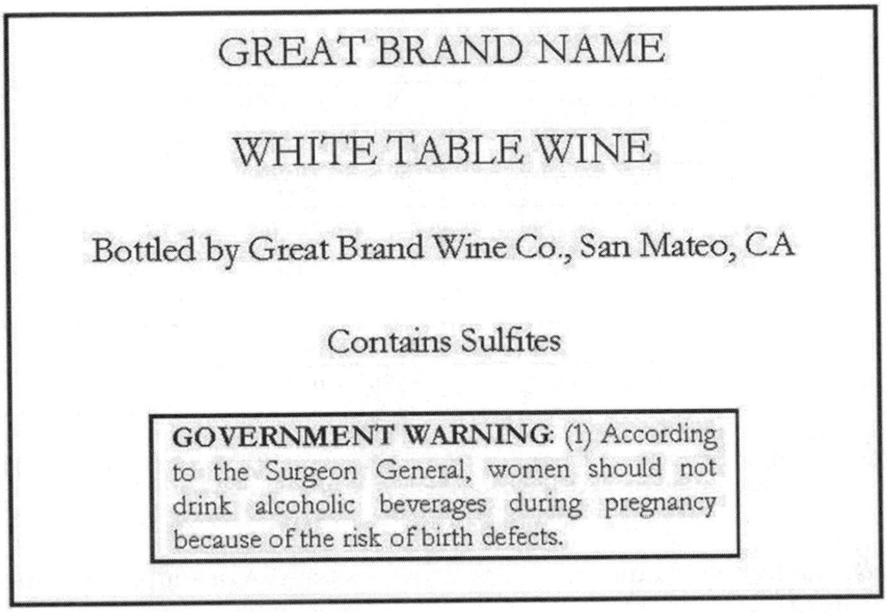

GREAT BRAND NAME

WHITE TABLE WINE

Bottled by Great Brand Wine Co., San Mateo, CA

Contains Sulfites

GOVERNMENT WARNING: (1) According to the Surgeon General, women should not drink alcoholic beverages during pregnancy because of the risk of birth defects.

When I speak with people who are looking to purchase wine, many of them talk about label terms from the consumer perspective and in a very general sense. "I would never buy a bottle of wine if it does not have a varietal and appellation" is a common refrain. It is not a snobby statement, but the line that many consumers use when they seek out quality wine. Wine labels, especially with respect to vintage-dated varietal wines, can say much about the quality of the product. Such information is accurate, although not necessarily precise, and the label allows a consumer to learn a lot about a wine without knowing very much about the winery. Label information and deductive reasoning will almost always lead to an impression of quality. The true anatomy of a wine label requires a deeper understanding of the following terms.

a. Appellations of Origin

The reason we start with a discussion of appellations of origin is that the regulations that address the use of vintage dates and varietal terms require that an appellation of origin accompany them, such as Cabernet Sauvignon Sonoma Valley or 2009 Paso Robles. Many consumers use "appellation" and "viticultural area" synonymously, but that is like saying that an orange is the same as a fruit. An appellation of origin conveys geographic information about the source of the grapes used to make the wine. Percentages of grape origin in the particular wine depend on the type of appellation used, as shown in Figure 3-3. In the United States, an appellation can be the United States or "American"; the name of a state or no more than three contiguous states; the name of a county or no more than three counties within the same state;

Figure 3-3
Appellations and Grape Origin Percentage Requirements

Appellation Used	FEDERAL Percentage of Grapes from Labeled Appellation
United States or "American"	75% from United States
Single State	75% from labeled state
Multi-state (must be contiguous*)	Must indicate % from each state
Single county	75% from labeled county
Multi-county (must be within same state)	Must indicate % from each county
Single viticultural area	85% from within viticultural area
Multiple viticultural areas	85% from the area of overlap

* BATF Ruling 91-1 held that three states "connected throughout in an unbroken sequence", such as Washington, Oregon, and California, are considered to be contiguous. Bureau of Alcohol, Tobacco and Firearms, BATF Ruling 91-1, 2 Quarterly Bulletin 3-5 (1991).

or an American viticultural area, also known as an AVA or simply as a viticultural area.[39]

For single country, state, and county appellations, 75 percent of the grapes must come from the labeled appellation.[40] For multi-state and multi-county designations, a winemaker must account for 100 percent of the grapes, denoting the percentage of grapes from each location with a 2 percent tolerance.[41]

VITICULTURAL AREA APPELLATIONS OF ORIGIN

Viticultural areas are a type of appellation of origin that differs from states, countries, or counties insofar as their boundaries are established by federal regulation, not by political authorities. In order to use a single AVA, 85 percent of the grapes used to produce the wine must come from within the boundaries of the named area.[42] A label can indicate more than one AVA only when at least 85 percent of the volume of the wine comes from grapes within the area of overlap of the named viticultural areas.[43]

AVAs are creatures of regulation. Every viticultural area is created in the same manner—by petition filed with the TTB providing evidence supporting the name, boundary, and viticultural distinctiveness of the area; the petition also must describe the boundaries of the area to be established.[44] The details of AVA establishment are covered in Chapter 6.

39. 27 C.F.R. §4.25 (2010).
40. *Id.* §4.25(b)(1)(i).
41. *Id.* §4.25(c), (d).
42. *Id.* §4.25(e)(3)(ii).
43. *Id.* §4.25(e)(4).
44. *Id.* §9.3(b).

Geography has long been a fundamental element of wine quality. A wine's geographic pedigree figures prominently and may greatly influence consumers' purchase decisions. The association between geography and quality is attributable in large part to the establishment, use, and promotion of AVAs. The efforts of wineries, grape growers, and their respective marketing and promotional organizations, coupled with the overall consumer experience of wines bearing these appellations, build value and quality and make AVAs increasingly significant.

The AVA regulations regarding AVA establishment reside at 27 CFR Part 9, and structurally all viticultural area regulations adhere to the same formula. The regulation will state the name of the viticultural area, the U.S.G.S. maps needed to plot the boundaries, and the point-to-point boundary descriptions. Every final rule that establishes an AVA will state the TTB's reasons for doing so in general terms: that the establishment of viticultural areas and the subsequent use of viticultural area names as appellations of origin in wine labeling and advertising will help consumers better identify the wines they may purchase and will help winemakers distinguish their products from wines made in other areas.

Can viticultural areas be too big? As a general policy, Wine Institute follows a "hands off" rule for AVA petitions because it believes that AVA development should be done at the local level in cooperation with growers and vintners in the area. Wine Institute has rarely participated in AVA rulemaking. One exception was the proposed "California Coast" viticultural area. Wine Institute opposed the "California Coast" area because the proposed area, spanning from northern California to the Mexican border, was considered too large and non-distinctive.

The "California Coast" saga began in 1997, when a small group of wineries submitted a request for establishment of a new AVA located along a portion of western California extending along the coastline from Mendocino to the Mexican border and inland from 2 to 60 miles.[45] The proposed area was to be designated the "California Coast."[46] This petition was withdrawn and a revised petition was submitted in 1998, renaming the proposed AVA "California Coastal."[47] The BATF received numerous comments objecting to this proposal and formally rejected it on December 1998.[48] On March 17, 2000, petitioners submitted a similar proposal with a slight boundary change, namely, the inclusion of the newly created San Francisco Bay AVA.[49] The BATF subsequently issued a notice of proposed rulemaking on September 26, 2000.[50]

---

45. *See* Daniel Sogg, *ATF Reconsiders Establishing New California Coast Appellation*, Wine Spectator (Oct. 9, 2000), http://www.winespectator.com/webfeature/show/id/ATF-Reconsiders-Establishing-New-California-Coast-Appellation_20810 (last visited Feb. 1, 2011).

46. *Id.*

47. *See* Nancy Sutton, ATF Response to the California Coast Viticultural Area Petition 11 (2002), available at www.ttb.gov/pdf/notices_alcohol/notice_951supprpt.pdf (last visited Feb. 1, 2011).

48. *Id.*

49. *Id.* at 12-13.

50. California Coast Viticultural Area, 65 Fed. Reg. 57763 (proposed Sept. 26, 2000) (to be codified at 27 C.F.R. pt. 9).

In response to formal objections from several organizations and individuals, the BATF extended the period for comments on this rulemaking until April 26, 2001.[51] Finally the BATF rejected the petition and brought an end to the effort to establish a "California Coast" or "California Coastal" AVA.[52]

In sum, appellations can be defined by political boundaries (state, county, country) or viticultural ones (AVAs). Appellations are geographic indicators that convey a sense of geography for consumers, but they also are required if the winery includes on the label a varietal name, vintage date, or the "estate bottled" designation.

THE "ESTATE BOTTLED" DESIGNATION

The term "estate bottled," although not an appellation, is recognized as a way to convey that the bottling winery controlled the grape growing, wine processing, and bottling of a particular wine. When the BATF was reviewing wine label regulations in 1977, it proposed that the term "estate bottled" not be used on wine labels.[53] The final regulations maintained the designation, but with very specific requirements that gave meaning to the term.

27 CFR §4.26 states:

> (a) Conditions for use. The term Estate bottled may be used by a bottling winery on a wine label only if the wine is labeled with a viticultural area appellation of origin and the bottling winery:
>
> (1) Is located in the labeled viticultural area; (2) grew all of the grapes used to make the wine on land owned or controlled by the winery within the boundaries of the labeled viticultural area; (3) crushed the grapes, fermented the resulting must, and finished, aged, and bottled the wine in a continuous process (the wine at no time having left the premises of the bottling winery).
>
> (b) Special rule for cooperatives. Grapes grown by members of a cooperative bottling winery are considered grown by the bottling winery.
>
> (c) Definition of "Controlled". For purposes of this section, Controlled by refers to property on which the bottling winery has the legal right to perform, and does perform, all of the acts common to viticulture under the terms of a lease or similar agreement of at least 3 years duration.
>
> (d) Use of other terms. No term other than Estate bottled may be used on a label to indicate combined growing and bottling conditions.

Four main points in the regulation stand out for the production winery. First, both the winery and the vineyards whose grapes are used to make the wine must reside in the same viticultural area. Second, the wine must be made in a single continuous process at the bottling winery. Transfer of the wine to a location off the bonded premises would disqualify the wine for the "estate bottled" designation. Third, "control" does not mean "ownership," so a winery

---

51. Extension of the Comment Period of the Proposed California Coast Viticultural Area, 65 Fed. Reg. 81455 (proposed Dec. 26, 2000).

52. Denial of the California Coast Viticultural Area Petition, 67 Fed. Reg. 51156 (proposed Aug. 7, 2002) (to be codified at 27 C.F.R. pt. 9).

53. *See* Appellation of Origin, Grape Type Designations, Etc., 42 Fed. Reg. 30517 (proposed June 15, 1977).

may lease vineyards in accordance with the regulation and use the grapes from the leased vineyards for their "estate bottled" program. Fourth, any use of the term "estate" on a wine label may trigger the provisions of the regulation.

In operation, if you can convince the TTB that the term "estate" (without the accompanying word "bottled") on your label does not convey combined growing and bottling conditions, you may be allowed to use it. For example, wineries commonly use the term "estate" in a brand name. A brand name such as "ABC Estate Vineyards" may be permissible because it does not lead the consumer to believe that the wine is "estate bottled." But any mention of "estate" rightfully sets off warning bells for the TTB's label specialists.[54]

There have been situations where a winery's vineyards are located in a different viticultural area than the winery, or where a winery is not in a viticultural area but its grapes are. In those situations, the winery has been allowed to use the term "Vintner Grown" or "Proprietor Grown" to convey growing conditions without the more rigid viticultural area requirements of 27 CFR §4.26.[55]

FOREIGN APPELLATIONS

Federal regulations address appellations for imported wines separately. An imported wine is entitled to an appellation of origin (specifically, a country, state, province, territory or similar political subdivision, but not cities and towns) if at least 75 percent of the wine is derived from fruit or agricultural products grown in the area indicated by the appellation of origin, and the wine conforms to the requirements of the foreign laws and regulations governing the composition, method of production, and designation of wines available for consumption within the country of origin.[56] Imported wines also can use a viticultural area, defined as a delimited place or region recognized and defined by the country of origin for use on wines available for consumption in that country, if 85 percent of the grapes used to make that wine are from the named area and the wine conforms to the requirements of the foreign laws and regulations governing the composition, method of production, and designation of wines available for consumption within the country of origin.[57]

Some labeling provisions are stuck in an infinite loop. With respect to foreign appellations, the TTB's provisions firmly require compliance with both U.S. laws and the laws in the country of origin.[58] The loopback to the foreign country's production standards and the validation of label claims for foreign wines imported into the United States have always been a concern for domestic wineries. The paucity of good forensic tools to certify label claims can lead to unequal enforcement, and the TTB has neither the budget nor resources to investigate questionable foreign label claims.

---

54. *See, e.g.*, Use of Various Winemaking Terms on Wine Labels and in Advertisements; Request for Public Comment, 75 Fed. Reg. 67666 at 67667-67668 (proposed Nov. 3, 2010).

55. *Id.* at 67668.

56. 27 C.F.R. §4.25(b)(2) (2010).

57. *Id.* §4.25(e)(1)(ii), (e)(3).

58. *Id.* §4.25(b)(2)(i); Miscellaneous Trade and Technical Corrections Act of 2004, Pub. L. No. 108-429, §2002 (2004).

b. Vintage Date

A vintage date can be used only for Class 1, 2, or 3 wines (grape wine, sparkling wine, and carbonated grape wine, respectively).[59] Additionally, a winery cannot use a vintage year on a wine label without also having an accompanying appellation or origin that is smaller than a country.[60] If the appellation is a state or county, 85 percent of the grapes used to produce the wine must have been harvested in the year stated.[61] If the appellation is a viticultural area, 95 percent of the grapes must have been harvested in the vintage year.[62] The very definition of "vintage" precludes the use of multiple vintages on a label. Specifically, vintage dating refers to the year in which the grapes were grown and harvested, not when the wine was bottled.[63]

c. Varietal Term

Labels often bear varietal terms. Names such as Cabernet Sauvignon, Merlot, and Chardonnay describe the variety of grapes from which a particular wine is made. Most wine labels bear a single varietal term, which must constitute at least 75 percent of the wine,[64] but the regulations allow a winemaker to use two or more varietals to compose a given wine as long as percentage of each varietal is shown.[65] In order to use a varietal term on a wine label, however, the label also must bear an appellation or origin.[66]

Now that these terms are defined, the label forensics lesson can begin.

2. MANDATORY LABEL INFORMATION

a. Brand Names

About a year ago, Wine Institute started a project to develop a new logo. The old logo had been used for about 15 years and seemed dated and old-fashioned, showing signs of wear. So some people within our organization were appointed to work with creative consultants to develop a logo design that would eventually be sent to me for trademark registration.

Logos are very subjective, but to come up with something that was unique and also communicated what the association did was a task so daunting that I was thankful not to have been involved in the creative process. My job was to wait dutifully for the final design so that I could take care of the trademark registration.

Months after the project began, the final design was sent to me for trademark application. As a first step, however, the trademark counsel

59. 27 C.F.R. §4.27(a) (2010).
60. *Id.*
61. *Id.* §4.27(a)(2).
62. *Id.* §4.27(a)(1).
63. *Id.* §4.27(a).
64. *Id.* §4.23(b).
65. *Id.* §4.23(d).
66. *Id.* §4.23(a).

performed a trademark search. Within days the association received the results. Months of work and hours of staff and consultant time were washed away when the search found a direct hit for an already registered trademark.

The moral of the story is that a company can never be too careful when selecting a trademark, whether it is a graphic symbol or a brand name. Brand names are trademarks. They are used to name a product so that it will convey a sense of quality and distinguish the brand name owner's product from all similar products in the marketplace. The other thing I learned from our logo experience is that it is not at all easy to come up with a mark that someone else has not already used in some form or fashion.

Nothing substitutes for competent trademark counsel and a trademark search by a reputable trademark search firm, but many online sources can help someone determine if a brand name is available. Even before a winery calls a lawyer, it is advisable to do three things: an Internet search with online search engines like Google and Bing, an International Class Code search at the United States Patent and Trademark Office (USPTO) website using its trademark search engine, and a search of the TTB's Public COLA registry.

Everybody with Internet access can use Google, and if a brand name is out there as text, generally Google will find it. Google is not as reliable with respect to graphic images, and there hiring good trademark counsel can be invaluable.

A common misunderstanding is that a COLA affords some degree of trademark protection. Many years ago, a winery member complained that someone was using its brand name on a label. The winery (the name has been changed to maintain confidentiality) was called Fox Vineyards. The owner reported that there was an imported brand being sold as Fox Winery. "How could the government approve such a label?"

Label approval does not equate to trademark protection. The COLA form expressly says so on its second page: "NOTE: This certificate does not constitute trademark protection."[67] Brand names are trademarks. A winery can have many brand names. Many wineries use multiple brands to produce various wine lines. Some wine brands are long-lived and well respected, with a large consumer following. Others are short-lived.

GEOGRAPHIC BRAND NAMES

Wineries often choose to use geographic terms in their brand names. "Sonoma Vineyards," "Napa Ridge," and "Kenwood" are some examples of brand names that utilize geography. Although this practice is not recommended among wine lawyers familiar with the issues surrounding geographic brand names, the practice continues non-stop. There is nothing that will start a quarrel among industry members faster than geographic brand names, and it is a great example of where public policy, law, and common sense (attempt to) intersect.

---

67. TTB, OMB No. 1513-0020, Form5100.31, Application for and Certificate/Exemption of Label/Bottle Approval 2, available at www.ttb.gov/forms/f510031.pdf (last visited Feb. 1, 2011).

There was a commercial for Pace Picante Sauce in which a group of ornery cowboys are sitting around a campfire at night, awaiting their meal and berating the cook for using salsa from New York City. The commercial's goal was to instill the idea that salsa from New York City is in some way inferior to salsa from Texas. One can only guess what the cowboys would think of salsa from Alaska.

Pace Picante Sauce uses geography in this commercial but not in its brand name. Many products are sold on the basis of their geographic origin, regardless of their brand. A consumer who purchases Kona coffee from his or her local Starbucks expects that the beans are from Kona. A consumer who purchases a Kona coffee "blend" expects something less. Maui onions are another example of goods sold on the basis of geography, and they are "brandless" by the time they are placed on the produce bin at the supermarket. But what would consumers think about purchasing Maui Coffee Company brand's 100 percent Kona coffee? Would they be deceived? Would they expect the caffeine police to impound all of that great coffee because Kona is not on Maui?

Geographic brand names on wine operate in much the same way, but the issue is even more complex because wine is sold in so many different ways. The core of the issue is that brand names as well as place names, when associated with goods or services, both have value.[68] The whole issue of geographic brand names pits intellectual property rights in a brand name against the interest of an appellation of origin to protect its integrity and consumer recognition. Both of these interests are legitimate, and both carry a certain degree of value.

Geography permeates the TTB wine labeling and advertising regulations in a confusing swirl of legal terminology. There are generic, nongeneric, and semigeneric designations of geographic significance (27 CFR §4.24), and if that is not enough, there is a regulation that addresses brand names generally (27 CFR §4.33), and a regulation that addresses "brand names of viticultural significance" (27 CFR §4.39(i)). An entire section of regulations at 27 CFR Part 12, completely separate from the labeling and advertising section, is solely devoted to addressing foreign names of geographic significance used in the designation of wines that are recognized as nongeneric, entitled "Foreign Nongeneric Names of Geographic Significance Used in the Designation of Wines."

BRAND NAMES OF VITICULTURAL SIGNIFICANCE

All of these regulations add to the confusion and contribute, rightly or wrongly, to the debate, but they illustrate one undeniable regulatory

68. An intellectual property lawyer once attempted to explain the two prevailing views on protecting geographic indicators—the "Old World" view and the "New World" view, with the main priority of the first being protection of the producer, and the main priority of the second being protecting the consumer. Law students and professionals take note: we would greatly appreciate your contributions to a better understanding of geographic indicators on a global level. Many WTO member countries continue to search for meaningful ways to implement protection for geographical indications. From country to country, there is a clear lack of consistency for the protection of geographical indications, while those very same countries may recognize long-established trademark rights.

concept—namely, that geography is important to wine. Of particular interest is 27 CFR §4.39(i), which is so important to our discussion that the subsection is copied in full below:

> (i) *Geographic brand names.* (1) Except as provided in subparagraph 2, a brand name of viticultural significance may not be used unless the wine meets the appellation of origin requirements for the geographic area named.
>
> (2) For brand names used in existing certificates of label approval issued prior to (July 7, 1986):
>
> (i) The wine shall meet the appellation of origin requirements for the geographic area named; or
>
> (ii) The wine shall be labeled with an appellation of origin in accordance with §4.34(b) as to location and size of type of either:
>
> (A) A county or a viticultural area, if the brand name bears the name of a geographic area smaller than a state, or;
>
> (B) A state, county or a viticultural area, if the brand name bears a state name; or
>
> (iii) The wine shall be labeled with some other statement which the appropriate TTB officer finds to be sufficient to dispel the impression that the geographic area suggested by the brand name is indicative of the origin of the wine.
>
> (3) A name has viticultural significance when it is the name of a state or county (or the foreign equivalents), when approved as a viticultural area in part 9 of this chapter, or by a foreign government, or when found to have viticultural significance by the appropriate TTB officer.

Brand names can be geographic yet not have any viticultural significance. A brand name has viticultural significance only when it has, as part of its name, the name of a state, county, or an approved viticultural area, or when the TTB finds it to be otherwise viticulturally significant.

Names like "Sonoma Vineyards" have viticultural significance because "Sonoma Valley" is a viticultural area;[69] Sonoma also is the name of a county. Another example of a brand name with viticultural significance, "Rutherford Hill," is shown in Figure 3-4. The brand name "Windsor Vineyards" may have geographic significance but not "viticultural significance" unless the TTB finds it so, because "Windsor" is not the name of a state, county, or approved viticultural area. In the end, the TTB determines whether a brand name has viticultural significance, regardless of whether there is an AVA by that name.

TTB regulations do not prohibit a winery from having a viticulturally significant brand name; they just require it to comply with certain provisions if it does. In operation, the TTB's regulations can have some interesting results. Assume that one morning (long after July 7, 1986) someone decides to create a new brand of wine called "Napa Time Winery" and that it does not infringe on someone's trademark. The TTB would have no problem with the brand name if and only if the wine meets the appellation of origin requirement (75 percent from Napa, the county appellation) or is labeled in some other

69. 27 C.F.R. §9.29 (2010).

Figure 3-4
Rutherford Hill Label

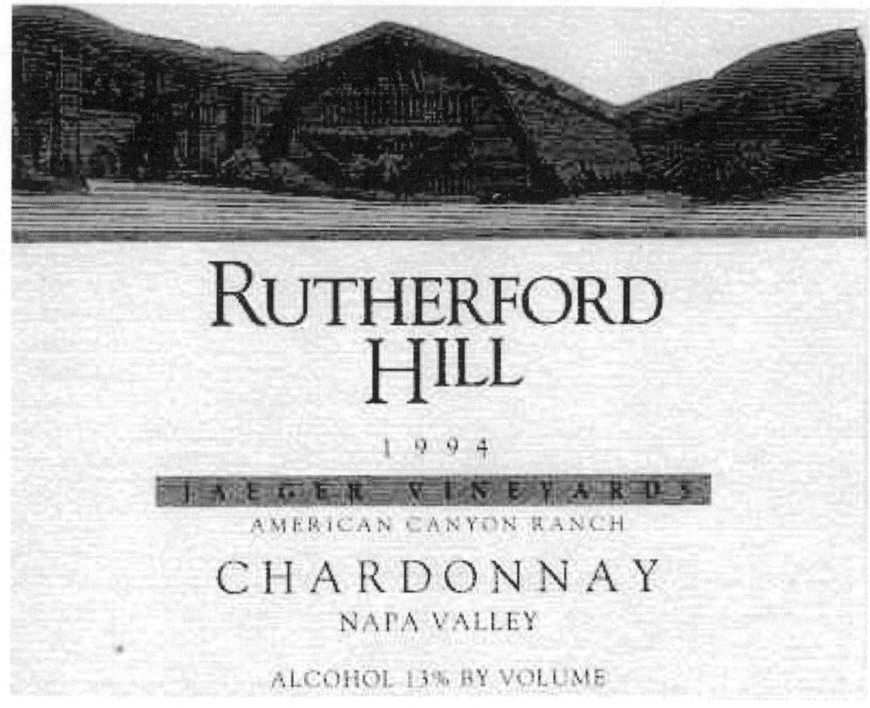

This brand name has viticultural significance because "Rutherford"is the name of an established viticultural area.

fashion to satisfy the TTB Director that the consumer will not be misled[70] as to the origin of the grapes from which the wine was made.[71]

The July 7, 1986, date is the temporal dividing line between those brand names with viticultural significance that *can* be used without having to conform to the appellation of origin requirement of the place named in the brand and those that *cannot.* Geographic brand names that predate July 7, 1986, are treated differently. If someone created "Napa Time Winery" on July 6, 1986, he or she could use the brand name under federal regulations as long as the winery also used an accurate county or viticultural area appellation of origin, e.g., "Napa Time Winery" Sonoma Valley Chardonnay or Napa Ridge North Coast Merlot, shown in Figure 3-5.

70. I cannot recall any TTB ruling on what a misleading brand name has to do to no longer be considered misleading. Although the regulation gives the TTB Director great discretion, it is not a power that has been used.

71. *See* 27 C.F.R. §4.33(b) (2010) (misleading brand names).

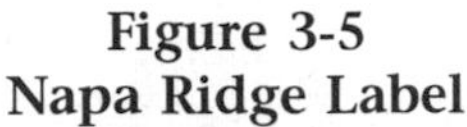
Figure 3-5
Napa Ridge Label

"Napa Ridge" is a pre-1986 brand name, in this label using the "North Coast" viticultural area as the required appellation of origin.

In use, brand names of viticultural significance do not show their age; they all look the same. A consumer cannot distinguish brand names that were created before or after July 7, 1986.

Grandfather dates are regulatory concessions. We know that brand names of viticultural significance, if they are misleading, are not any less misleading because they were created before July 7, 1986. The July 7, 1986, date is simply the effective date of the Treasury Decision that amended 4.39(i) into the version that we have today.[72] But the TTB had to draw a line somewhere, and it chose the effective date of the decision.

Foreign geographic terms are a further consideration in brand name selection. A brand name can acquire "viticultural significance" and trigger the requirements of 4.39(i), if it includes a foreign appellation name or if this country has recognized it as a foreign "term of geographic significance." Regardless of whether the burden of proof is the same as in this country for the establishment of a viticultural area (in many cases, it is not) and regardless of whether there is government control or just a loose recognition policy, the TTB's recognition of more geographic terms from foreign countries as being viticulturally significant in *this* country provides a medium for intellectual property mischief.

A review of the regulatory history of geographic brand names shows a federal administrative agency in some degree of turmoil over its control of

72. Wine Labeling and Advertising, Use of Geographic Brand Names, 51 Fed. Reg. 20480 (June 5, 1986) (to be codified at 27 C.F.R. pt. 4).

geographic brand names. The TTB's predecessor agency, the BATF, initially proposed in the 1978 label revisions that a brand owner could fix any inherent consumer deception by placing the term "brand" after the name ("Napa Time Winery Brand").[73] But the BATF even by this point already knew that it was being scrutinized by someone other than its director. In December of 1981, the BATF had been told by the federal District of Columbia Court of Appeals that something was not right with the agency's regulations.[74] Even after the establishment of the current version of 4.39(i), the BATF was still searching for a satisfactory solution to the geographic brand name quandary.[75]

Many wineries use place names as their brand names, real or fictitious. Some wineries are proud of their winery's location and use that location as part of their brand. Some wineries take the "Pepperidge Farm" approach and create a fictitious, place-sounding name to imply that they are located in some romantic location overlooking mystic cliffs in the cove of Monarch Bay.

At times these names are actual places that are not the names of states or counties but that are known to be places, because they can be found on a map. A brand name is considered to have viticultural significance when it bears the name of a state, county, or viticultural area, but it is often overlooked that other geographic references in brand names are as (or even more) recognizable to consumers than their viticultural area counterparts. While many consumers give a lot of legitimacy and authenticity to a viticultural area name, brand names that contain the name of towns and other geographic areas can be equally misleading or deceptive. Ventana Vineyards and Windsor Vineyards, for example, are places that are allowed as brand names because they are not the names of a state, county, or viticultural area.

---

73. Appellation of Origin, Grape-Type Designations, Etc., 43 Fed. Reg. 37672, 37678 (Aug. 23, 1978).

74. As was mentioned earlier, three sophisticated wine consumers brought suit challenging regulations promulgated by the BATF in an effort to set standards for labeling and advertising grape wine. *Wawszkiewicz v. Dep't of the Treasury,* 480 F. Supp. 739 (D.C. 1979). The United States District Court for the District of Columbia, Gerhard A. Gesell, J., entered a judgment from which both the consumers and the Treasury Department appealed. *Wawszkiewicz v. Dep't of the Treasury,* 670 F.2d 296 (D.C. Cir. 1981). The Court of Appeals held that the grape wine varietal labeling regulation promulgated by the BATF, allowing wine labels to carry the name of a single grape type or variety without disclosing that other possibly inferior grape varieties may compose up to 25 percent of the volume, was the product of a reasoned and amply elucidated process and would thus be upheld; however, those labeling regulations pertaining to the use of geographical terms and winemaking terms could not be upheld and would be sent back to the BATF to afford it an opportunity to show that such regulations meaningfully control misleading labeling and advertising. *Id.*

75. Long after the decision in *Wawszkiewicz,* the BATF issued another ambitious rulemaking covering several labeling aspects. In its 1992 publication of Notice No. 722, the BATF makes this statement: "Present regulations provide that a brand name of viticultural area significance, which cannot meet the appellation of origin requirements for the geographic area named, may not be used unless it was previously used in a certificate of label approval issued prior to July 7, 1986. Therefore, a viticultural area approved on or after July 7, 1986, would effectively cancel any certificates of label approval issued after this date with a brand name containing the name of that approved viticultural area. A proprietor with a geographical brand name approved after July 7, 1986, should not be penalized for any viticultural area established after the geographical brand name approval date. The proposed revision of 27 CFR §4.39 would correct this regulatory oversight." Wine Labeling Amendments, 57 Fed. Reg. 27401-27402, 27404 (proposed June 19, 1992). This proposal did not result in a final rule.

BRAND NAME CAN BE OVERTAKEN BY A VITICULTURAL AREA

This scenario occurs when a brand name acquires "viticultural significance" after an AVA has been established. Before that event, the brand name could be used without restriction. Once the brand name acquires "viticultural significance" (in this case, by the TTB's approval of a viticultural area), the provisions of §4.39(i) are triggered. Brand names in existence before July 7, 1986 can continue to be used as long as the label includes an appropriate appellation of origin. Brand names that were approved after that date are more severely restricted.

STATE APPELLATION CONTROLS

While the BATF and later the TTB were struggling to find viable solutions for the issues of trademarks and geography and while wine trade associations like Wine Institute were finding it difficult to achieve membership consensus on those issues, the momentum for changes to the regulations governing geographic brands became unstoppable. The Napa Valley Vintners took action to pass state protective legislation, and a few other California regions later followed their lead.

California already had enacted several state laws that imposed stricter requirements than their federal counterparts. For example, California regulations prohibit the use of sugar in wine production[76] even though federal winemaking regulations permit chaptalization and amelioration. California regulations also require that 100 percent of the grapes used to produce a wine must come from within the state of California if the California appellation or a county appellation is used on a wine label.[77] Federal law requires only 75 percent grapes to come from the area for state and county appellations. Oregon's labeling regulations go even further, requiring that all appellations within the state, including AVAs, be derived 100 percent from grapes grown within those areas.[78] State legislation may seem an inelegant solution to geographic area protection, but at the time it appeared to be the only option available.

---

76. Cal. Code Regs. tit. 17, §17010 (2009).

77. *Id.* §17015. This section, entitled "Wines Bearing the Appellation of Origin 'California' or a Geographical Subdivision Thereof," reads:

> (a) A grape wine shall be entitled to the appellation of origin "California" or a geographical subdivision thereof only if: (1) 100 percent of its volume is derived from fermented juice of fruit grown within California; except that wine spirits produced in California from residues of wines, which contain grapes grown outside of California, may be used in the production of wines bearing the appellation of origin "California" or subdivisions thereof, subject to all of the following limitations: (A) The wine shall not derive more than 1 percent of its volume from fruit grown outside California. (B) The non-California portion shall be derived solely from residue wine spirits. (C) Grapes, juice, concentrate, wine or other distilling material shall not be imported into California for distilling of wine spirits for use under this Section, and (2) It has been fully produced and finished within the State of California, and (3) It conforms to the requirements of these regulations; provided, that no wine shall be entitled to an appellation of origin in violation of Section 25236 or Section 25237 of the California Alcoholic Beverage Control Act.

Id.

78. Or. Admin. R. 845-010-0920 (2010).

The Napa Valley Vintners lobbied successfully for the passage of Assembly Bill 683 in 2000. The bill became California Business and Professions Code §25241, which provides generally that the term "Napa" can be used on brand names or anywhere else on wine labels or in advertising only if the wine qualifies under federal regulations for the "Napa County" appellation. The statute survived a constitutional challenge based on First Amendment and Commerce Clause grounds, among others, in a case that reached the California Supreme Court in 2005.[79] Sonoma followed shortly thereafter with Senate Bill 1380, which became effective on January 1, 2007.[80]

Napa, Sonoma, and other winegrowing regions have successfully sought legislation to add other appellation requirements onto the federal regulatory scheme. These statutes for specific appellations generally fall into the following categories: (1) sourcing/false advertising provisions (such as the ones described above), which prohibit the label usage of a term that is recognized by state statute as "viticulturally significant" unless the wine qualifies for the appellation; and (2) conjunctive labeling provisions, which require the mention of a larger viticultural area when using the viticultural area appellation of a smaller area that is wholly enclosed within the larger area.[81] The rules for Napa, Sonoma, Paso Robles, and Lodi are summarized in Figure 3-6.

"Conjunctive labeling" statutes have a purpose altogether apart from those that address misleading geographic terms. These statutes prevent the overall dilution of a larger viticultural area by requiring its mention on any label that uses an AVA that is wholly enclosed within the larger area.[82] These statutes take advantage of the TTB's regulation that allows the use of more than one viticultural area name as an appellation of origin if at least 85 percent of the

Figure 3-6
Region/Conjunctive Labeling/Source Table

Region	Conjunctive Labeling?	Sourcing / False Advertising?
Napa	Yes—CA Business and Professions Code (BP) §25240	Yes—BP §25241
Sonoma	No	Yes—BP §25242
Paso Robles	Yes—BP §25244 (for wine bottled after January 1, 2008)	No
Lodi	Yes—BP §25245 (for wine bottled after January 1, 2009)	No

79. *Bronco Wine Co. v. Jolly,* 29 Cal. Rptr. 3d 462 (2005), *on remand from* 95 P.3d 422 (Cal. 2004).

80. S.B. 1380, 2005-2006 Sess. (Cal. 2006) (codified at Cal. Bus. & Prof. Code §25242 (2009)).

81. *See* Cal. Bus. & Prof. Code §§25240 (Napa Valley), 25244 (Paso Robles), 25245 (Lodi).

82. Napa Valley Vintners, Issue Brief, Conjunctive Labeling in Napa Valley: It's the Law! (2009), available at www.napavintners.org/news/images/Feb09/law.pdf (last visited Feb. 1, 2011).

Figure 3-7
Groth Label

This label follows conjunctive labeling requirements, stating "Napa Valley" in addition to the smaller and wholly enclosed "Oakville" viticultural area.

grapes come from the area of overlap of the named AVAs.[83] An example of conjunctive labeling is presented in Figure 3-7.

---

83. 27 C.F.R. §4.25(e)(4). This subsection reads: "Overlap viticultural area appellations. An appellation of origin comprised of more than one viticultural area may be used

In conclusion, every wine label needs a brand name, but when choosing one a winery needs to know that geographic names, especially ones that might become viticulturally significant in the future, can seriously affect a brand's intellectual property value.

b. Standards of Identity

Around 2003 and 2004 there was a product on the market called "AWOL." The acronym stood for "alcohol without liquid." Originally created in Asia and Europe, the device vaporizes alcohol into a fine mist so that the user, instead of drinking a beverage, inhales it.[84] This interesting device did not meet any of the existing standards of identity for wine and was not easily defined. Regulators could not quite make the device fit into any beverage category, because it was more of an alcohol delivery system than a beverage. The TTB's label approval regulations thus did not apply to the device, but the FDA's regulations for drug delivery devices came into play, and states passed legislation to ban the product.

Fortunately for wine, most products do fit into a defined category. Under federal law and regulations, in order for wine to be called "wine," it must fall into one of the nine separate and distinct classes defined at 27 CFR §4.21. Most of the time, we see Class 1 grape wine labels that are further divided into table wine (up to 14 percent alcohol by volume)[85] and dessert wine (above 14 percent to 24 percent).[86] There also are standards of identity for sparkling wine,[87] champagne,[88] and fruit wine,[89] along with an "imitation" wine class.[90] Within each class of wines are various subclasses; occasionally there are also unique products that defy classification.[91]

Typical products fit typical classifications. The real issues involving the standards of identity occur when atypical products are presented to the TTB for label approval. Malt-based coolers, products like Mike's Hard Lemonade, and products that generally are referred to as "wine with natural flavors" or "OTS" (for "other than standard") wine[92] can raise problems for the TTB not only with respect to the standards of identity but also for taxation (for example, sake is a wine for labeling purposes but a beer for tax purposes).[93] Because every product needs to have a label approval, the TTB is the initial

---

in the case of overlapping viticultural areas if not less than 85 percent of the volume of the wine is derived from grapes grown in the overlapping area."

84. *See Alcohol without liquid*, Wikipedia, http://en.wikipedia.org/wiki/Alcohol_without_liquid (last visited Jan. 16, 2011) for a brief description.

85. 27 C.F.R. §4.21(a)(2) (2010).

86. *Id.* §4.21(a)(3).

87. *Id.* §4.21(b)(1).

88. *Id.* §4.21(b)(2).

89. *Id.* §4.21(e).

90. *Id.* §4.21(h).

91. Wine consumers from the mid-1980s probably remember the wine cooler craze. But wine coolers were concocted beverages made from wine, water, and flavorings with an alcohol content of approximately 5 percent. What standard of identity would a wine cooler fit in? How would someone label such a product?

92. 27 C.F.R. §4.21(h) (2010).

93. 26 U.S.C. §5052 (2006).

gatekeeper for new and novel products. The agency must determine whether products imagined by producers and manufacturers meet a specific standard of identity and whether the label is deceptive or misleading.

While not classified as wine products, flavored malt beverages and caffeinated alcoholic drinks have an important presence in the marketplace. Products like Four Loko and Jooce are problematic from a public policy standpoint, because they are unconventional and attract younger drinkers. The TTB struggles with these products; they are legitimate but not the best examples of social responsibility. When public health issues are raised, the FDA may become involved, as illustrated by its recent ongoing investigation into the safety of caffeinated alcoholic beverages.[94]

In the late 1990s new wine products were introduced in five-liter boxes. They were sold at very low prices and positioned in the wine section of off-sale retail stores. These products fell outside of any of the established standards of identity and were given the clinical name of "flavored wine products."[95] They are still in the marketplace today and generally are derived from grape wine or other wines, including citrus wine (e.g., orange wine, grapefruit wine), fruit wine (e.g., apple wine, berry wine, pear wine), and wine from other agricultural products (e.g., carrot wine, dandelion wine, honey wine).[96] They also may contain flavoring material, coloring material, sugar, and water in excess of what would be allowed in standard wine.[97]

Because flavored wine products do not fall within any of the current standards of identity, the brand label must contain a truthful and adequate statement of composition.[98] The labels have traditionally displayed statements of composition such as "Grape Wine with Natural Flavors." Almaden's "Chardonnary Wine with Natural Flavors" is shown in Figure 3-8.

A controversy arose in the wine industry when these products began to use varietal and semigeneric names as product descriptors on their labels. The products most often would have an appellation of origin, such as "California," in conjunction with the grape varietal or semigeneric name in the statement of composition, for example, "California Chardonnay (or Chablis) with Natural Flavors."

The BATF commenced rulemaking after receiving a petition to do so, but even earlier the agency had commissioned a survey to determine the extent to which consumers were confused by these labels. The petitioner, the California Association of Winegrape Growers, commissioned its own consumer survey. Both surveys are referenced in the BATF's final rule, issued in 2000.[99]

The public comments supported the BATF's conclusion that statements of composition on flavored wines that include a varietal or semigeneric name are

---

94. *See* Caffeinated Alcoholic Beverages, FDA, http://www.fda.gov/food/foodingredientspackaging/ucm190366.htm (last visited Jan. 16, 2011) for further information.

95. *See* Labeling of Flavored Wine Products, 65 Fed. Reg. 59718-59724, 59719 (Oct. 6, 2000) (to be codified at 27 C.F.R. pt. 4).

96. *Id.*

97. *Id.*

98. *Id.; see also* 27 C.F.R. §4.34(a) (2010).

99. Labeling of Flavored Wine Products, 65 Fed. Reg. at 59720.

Figure 3-8
Almaden Advertisement

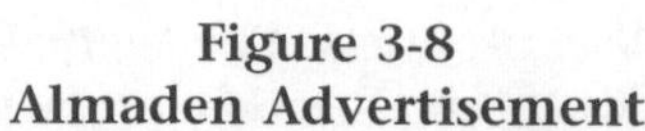

"Chardonnay Wine With Natural Flavors"

likely to mislead consumers and do not provide adequate information about the identity and quality of the product.[100] The BATF's proposed solution of creating a new class designation was not supported by most commenters, however.[101]

100. *Id.* at 59722.
101. *Id.*

In the end the final rule did not adopt the BATF's proposal to establish a new class designation, "Flavored Wine Products,"[102] but amended section §4.34(a) to prohibit the use of any varietal designation, type designation of varietal significance, semigeneric geographic type designation, or geographic distinctive designation in statements of composition for flavored wines and other wine specialty products.[103]

The existence of these products continues to breed discontent in the industry. California grape growers, among others, are not convinced that these products are properly labeled. In 2009 they petitioned the TTB to require that these products be called "Imitation Wine." The TTB has indicated that it will publish a Notice of Proposed Rulemaking in February of 2011.[104]

Further controversy has arisen over the distinction between "table wine" and "dessert wine." Table wine is defined as that containing up to 14 percent alcohol by volume and dessert wine as that containing greater than 14 percent to 24 percent.[105] But many traditional table wines, including vintage-dated varietal wines, often have alcohol levels in the dessert wine category. Although it may be difficult for the consumer to determine the correct class unless he or she looks at the alcohol content statement, the big difference is money. Tax rates for table wine are $1.07 per gallon on the federal level but jump to $1.57 per gallon for dessert wine of over 14 to 21 percent alcohol by volume.[106] Wineries follow trends and attempt to replicate wines that are successful in the market. Today the high-alcohol, high-extraction wines are rated highly by wine critics such as Robert Parker, but wineries also are frugal. To some extent technologies such as spinning cone and reverse osmosis along with blending have been employed to lower alcohol content while maintaining high quality. However, many wineries will accept the higher tax rate for the sake of what they consider to be a better-tasting wine.

GRAPE VARIETALS IN LIEU OF CLASS AND TYPE

According to urban legend, the Inuit have hundreds of different words for snow. Although not strictly accurate, the story keeps getting retold because of the lessons it embodies. Similarly, there are many words for wine varietals as well, far beyond the Chardonnay and Cabernet with which consumers are so familiar.

When the bare-bones label was assembled earlier in this chapter, I noted that one mandatory element for a valid wine label is a class and type designation. Federal label regulations allow wineries to use any varietal designation in

102. *Id.* at 59721, 59723.

103. *Id.* at 59723.

104. View Rule: Proposals Concerning Labeling of Imitation Wine (RIN No. 1513-AB76), Office of Information and Regulatory Affairs, www.reginfo.gov/public/do/eAgendaViewRule?pubid=201010&RIN=1513-AB76 (last visited Jan. 17, 2011).

105. 27 C.F.R. §4.21(a)(iv)(2)-(3) (2010).

106. 26 U.S.C. §5041(b)(1), (2) (2006).

lieu of the class and type designation, as long as it is accompanied by an appellation of origin showing the true place of origin of the wine.[107]

Wineries often enter into long-term grape purchase agreements with grape growers for specific grape varietals, often from specific appellations or specific vineyards. This practice assures wineries of an adequate supply of grapes for their various programs. How can the winery be assured that the grapes it purchases are indeed the correct varietal? A tool that would assist in the authentication of grape varieties would be useful within the industry and with regulators, but the issue of varietal authenticity and naming is still a shifting science that is anything but exact.

Federal administrative rulemaking is generally measured in terms of years, not months. For varietal names, federal rulemaking could have been measured in decades. On February 4, 1986, the BATF issued a Notice of Proposed Rulemaking in the Federal Register, proposing to establish a standardized list of varietal names.[108] That rulemaking was not completed until January 8, 1996 for the most part.[109] Ten years is a long time for any rulemaking, but it does not begin to explain the amount of work that the BATF devoted to varietal names from 1982 to 2002. Even before the 1986 rulemaking, the BATF assembled a group of experts in December, 1982, as part of the Varietal Names Advisory Committee.[110] Figure 3-9 presents a brief chronology of rulemaking activities with respect to varietal names.

Since 2002 the BATF and later the TTB have remained silent regarding varietal names. What caused the TTB to become silent, when its own regulations require it to publish an annual list of varietal names?[111] Have varietals been approved after 2002 but not yet announced?

The final rule on varietal names divides varietals into two lists. There is a list of prime varietal names[112] and a second list of alternative names permitted for temporary use.[113]

---

107. 27 C.F.R. §4.34(a) (2010). This subsection provides:

> In the case of still grape wine there may appear, in lieu of the class designation, any varietal (grape type) designation, type designation of varietal significance, semigeneric geographic type designation, or geographic distinctive designation, to which the wine may be entitled. . . . (b) An appellation of origin such as "American," "New York," "Napa Valley," or "Chilean," disclosing the true place of origin of the wine, shall appear in direct conjunction with and in lettering substantially as conspicuous as the class and type designation if: (1) A varietal (grape type) designation is used under the provisions of §4.23; (2) A type designation of varietal significance is used under the provisions of §4.28; (3) A semigeneric type designation is employed as the class and type designation of the wine pursuant to §4.24(b); (4) A product name is qualified with the word "Brand" under the requirements of §4.39 (j); or (5) The wine is labeled with the year of harvest of the grapes, and otherwise conforms with the provisions of §4.27. The appellation of origin for vintage wine shall be other than a country.

108. Grape Variety Names; Wine Labeling, 51 Fed. Reg. 4392 (proposed Feb. 4, 1986).

109. Grape Variety Names for American Wines, 61 Fed. Reg. 522 (Jan. 8, 1996) (to be codified at 27 C.F.R. pt. 4).

110. *Id.*

111. *See* 27 C.F.R. §4.93(e) (2010), which states: "(e) The Administrator shall publish the list of approved grape variety names at least annually in the Federal Register."

112. *Id.* §4.91.

113. *Id.* §4.92.

Figure 3-9
Chronology of Rulemaking Activities on Varietal Names

December 1982	BATF establishes Varietal Names Advisory Committee
February 4, 1986	First Notice of Proposed Rulemaking announcing the findings of the Advisory Committee and proposing a list of varietal names
April 8, 1986	Public comment period reopened
September 3, 1992	Notice of Proposed Rulemaking reissued
October 26, 1992	Public comment period reopened
January 8, 1996	Final Rule published
April 7, 1997	Final Rule published for Gamay Beaujolais
January 6, 1999	Final Rule published for Johannisberg Riesling
March 9, 2000	Notice of Proposed Rulemaking, Dornfelder
December 14, 2000	Final Rule, Dornfelder
April 17, 2001	Notice of Proposed Rulemaking, Counoise
July 19, 2001	Notice of Proposed Rulemaking, Albarino
September 27, 2001	Final Rule, Counoise
January 23, 2002	Notice of Proposed Rulemaking, Tannat
March 18, 2002	Final Rule, Albarino
April 10, 2002	Notice of Proposed Rulemaking, Petite Sirah, Zinfandel, Primitivo
June 6, 2002	Public comment period extended, Petite Sirah, Primitivo
September 4, 2002	Final Rule, Tannat
July 24, 2008	TTB withdraws Primitivo, Petite Sirah Proposed Rule

Wineries are required to maintain adequate records to substantiate all label claims.[114] Most wineries are able to provide invoices and weigh tags that indicate the varietals purchased. The ironic point is that the purchase documents only show that someone purchased grapes; they do not necessarily prove the varietal content in the finished wine. When purchase documents are all that a winery has, however, it can run into a situation like the one facing Petite Sirah producers.

What makes the Petite Sirah situation interesting is that it is a rulemaking that time forgot. Almost all people, from wineries to educators, believe that the TTB ruled that Durif and Petite Sirah are synonyms. In fact the rule was never completed. Wineries with invoices for Durif grapes are labeling the wine as Petite Sirah, but technically it is incorrect to do so without a finding that the two are synonyms. Here is a short regulatory history of that portion of the varietal rulemaking.

"Petite Sirah" was initially proposed as a synonym for Durif on September 3, 1992.[115] In 1996 the BATF concluded that not enough DNA evidence then existed to support the widely held belief that Petite Sirah and Durif are different names for the same grape variety and should be listed as synonyms rather than as separate prime names; however, the agency stated in its decision that it would remain open to future evidence regarding "the true identity of the grape called Petite Sirah."[116] The agency's 1996 conclusion was based largely on input from Dr. Carole Meredith, Professor Emerita at the Department of Viticulture and Enology, University of California at Davis (UC Davis).[117]

However, in 1999 Dr. Meredith completed a DNA study of California Petite Sirah vines, in which she confirmed that the approved variety known as "Durif" is a cross between Sirah and Peloursin.[118] After comparing California Petite Sirah plants to French Durif, Dr. Meredith concluded that a majority of the vines labeled as Petite Sirah were genetically identical to Durif.[119] DNA marker analysis of 13 Petite Sirah vines from the UC Davis private collection identified 9 of the vines as Durif.[120] In addition, DNA testing of 53 commercial Petite Sirah vines from 26 private California vineyards identified 49 of these vines as Durif.[121] The remaining vines were found to be Peloursin, Sirah, or Pinot Noir, which Dr. Meredith attributed to misidentification due to errors in labeling and planting.[122]

Primarily as a result of this research, the BATF again proposed on April 10, 2002,[123] that the varietal names regulation should be amended to recognize

114. *Id.* §24.314.

115. Grape Variety Names for American Wines, 57 Fed. Reg. 40380, 40383 (proposed Sept. 3, 1992).

116. Grape Variety Names for American Wines, 61 Fed. Reg. at 526 (Jan. 8, 1996).

117. *Id.*

118. Carole P. Meredith, et al., The Identity and Parentage of the Variety Known in California as Petite Sirah, 50 Am. J. Enol. Vitic. 236, 241 (1999).

119. *Id.*

120. *Id.*

121. *Id.*

122. *Id.* at 240.

123. Proposal To Recognize Synonyms for Petite Sirah and Zinfandel Grape Varieties, 67 Fed. Reg. 17312 (proposed Apr. 10, 2002).

Durif and Petite Sirah as synonyms. Of the 41 public comments the agency received in response to the proposed rule, only 2 specifically mentioned the issue of Durif and Petite Sirah. Wine Institute supported the proposal; the other comment came to no conclusions. The rulemaking was withdrawn on July 24, 2008[124] before the agency reached any conclusions. The TTB's withdrawal of the proposed rulemaking was not accompanied by any reasons to support its action. Currently 27 CFR §4.91 continues to list Durif and Petite Sirah separately as distinct varieties.

Based on the available scientific information, there is more than sufficient evidence to approve the name Petite Sirah as an acceptable synonym for the name Durif. As authorized by §4.93,[125] an association of Petite Sirah wineries and growers submitted a rulemaking petition in 2009 to support a proposal to find them synonymous.[126] On January 20, 2011, the TTB issued a long-awaited Notice of Proposed Rulemaking that would add a number of new names to the list of grape variety names approved for use in designating American wines. In that notice, TTB proposed to recognize Petite Sirah as a synonym for Durif.[127]

Perhaps one reason that the Petite Sirah rulemaking stalled was its association with Zinfandel/Primitivo, which were proposed as synonyms in the same 2002 rulemaking.[128] Zinfandel has been promoted as the "California" grape, but Primitivo, which is found in many parts of the world, does not produce

---

124. *See* Dep't of the Treasury, Semiannual Agenda and Fiscal Year 2009 Regulatory Plan 96 (RIN: 1513-AA32) (November 24, 2008), available at http://www.ttb.gov/pdf/treas-fincen-2008-0021-0001.pdf (last visited Feb. 1, 2011).

125. 27 C.F.R. §4.93 (2010) (Approval of grape variety names) reads in full as follows:

> (a) Any interested person may petition the Administrator for the approval of a grape variety name. The petition may be in the form of a letter and should provide evidence of the following—(1) acceptance of the new grape variety, (2) the validity of the name for identifying the grape variety, (3) that the variety is used or will be used in winemaking, and (4) that the variety is grown and used in the United States. (b) For the approval of names of new grape varieties, documentation submitted with the petition to establish the items in paragraph (a) of this section may include—(1) reference to the publication of the name of the variety in a scientific or professional journal of horticulture or a published report by a professional, scientific or winegrowers' organization, (2) reference to a plant patent, if so patented, and (3) information pertaining to the commercial potential of the variety, such as the acreage planted and its location or market studies. (c) The Administrator will not approve a grape variety name if: (1) The name has previously been used for a different grape variety; (2) The name contains a term or name found to be misleading under §4.39; or (3) The name of a new grape variety contains the term 'Riesling.' (d) For new grape varieties developed in the United States, the Director may determine if the use of names which contain words of geographical significance, place names, or foreign words are misleading under §4.39. The Administrator will not approve the use of a grape variety name found to be misleading. (e) The Administrator shall publish the list of approved grape variety names at least annually in the Federal Register.

126. *See* Proposed Addition of New Grape Variety Names for American Wines, 76 Fed. Reg. 3573, 3579-3580 (Jan. 20, 2011).

127. Proposed Addition of New Grape Variety Names for American Wines, 76 Fed. Reg. 3573, 3579-3580, 3583, 3584 (Jan. 20, 2011).

128. Proposal to Recognize Synonyms for Petite Sirah and Zinfandel Grape Varieties, 67 Fed. Reg. 17312 (proposed April 10, 2002).

wines of the quality claimed by California producers of Zinfandel wines.[129] It could do severe damage to the Zinfandel market to have a grape once thought exclusive to California suddenly become synonymous with pedestrian wines from Italy and to allow Primitivo wines to be labeled as Zinfandel. The TTB's reference to DNA evidence may be compelling, but at this point, there are no plans to advance the issue. Rulemaking on Zinfandel has officially ended.

Wine Institute also was actively involved with other varietal names and recently completed a successful petition for the recognition of Grenache Noir. Although Grenache Noir was authorized as a varietal name on March 12, 2007, there was no official notice of that authorization to the rest of the world.[130] This raised the question of how many other grape varietal names have traversed the path of petition and recognition without publication in an official regulation. That question was answered on January 20, 2011, with the TTB's publication of Notice No. 116.[131] In the same rulemaking that resurrected the proposal that Petite Sirah should be a synonym for Durif; 58 other varietal names were also included for public comment.[132] Of those 58 varietal names, 55 had previously been approved by the TTB.[133]

As with viticultural areas, new varietals are supposed to be recognized by regulation. The TTB provides a procedure for petitioning the Bureau to establish new varietal names and add them to the list of authorized names.[134] Those interested in how varieties come into commercial existence, however, need to look elsewhere. There are great web resources for grape varietals, and a great facility on the grounds of UC Davis assists the TTB in resolving varietal name issues.

The TTB and the wine industry are trying to find a reliable method to determine varietal content in other ways. Foundation Plant Services is a self-supporting service department in the College of Agricultural and Environmental Sciences at UC Davis that produces, tests, maintains, and distributes premium foundation-level virus and disease-tested plant materials for use by California nurseries.[135] Its National Grapevine Importation Program is the largest nationally recognized program for importing grape selections into the United States. Foundation Plant Services quarantines imports and uses an impressive laboratory to treat plants to ensure disease-free availability.[136] It works with the University of California, the U.S. Department of Agriculture,

---

129. *See* Letters from Bruce Cousins (May 24, 2002), E. Peter Seghesio (May 27, 2002), and John McClelland (July 2, 2002) to TTB in response to TTB Notice 941, 67 Fed. Reg. 17312 (Apr. 10, 2002), available at www.ttb.gov/nprm_comments/ttbnotice941_comments.shtml (comments 15, 16 and 34) (last visited Feb. 1, 2011).

130. The TTB stated in its letter to Wine Institute, dated March 12, 2007, "We will formally add this grape name ("Grenache Noir") to the list in Section 4.91 through the publication of a document in the Federal Register at a later date. In the interim, we have advised our Advertising, Labeling and Formulation Division that they may approve applications for certificates of label approval for American wines designated with this grape variety." Letter from Robert Koch, Wine Institute, to Francis Foote, TTB (March 12, 2007) (on file with the author).

131. Proposed Addition of New Grape Variety Names for American Wines, 76 Fed. Reg. 3573 (Jan. 20, 2011).

132. *Id.*

133. *Id.*

134. 27 CFR §4.93 (2010).

135. Foundation Plant Services, http://fpms.ucdavis.edu/ (last visited Jan. 21, 2011).

136. *Id.*

the California Department of Food and Agriculture, and the grape industry.[137] The program claims that, from 1995 through 2006, over 640 new selections have been imported, including new varieties, clones, and rootstocks, plus germplasm intended for research.[138]

Additionally, the National Grape Registry is an online database that, in a single comprehensive site, lists all grape plant material available within the United States.[139] Quarantine regulations and the high cost of bringing in new stock from abroad make it critical for growers and researchers to be able to locate existing material already in the United States. This site was created to help interested parties find domestic sources of diverse varieties and clones and identify material which has been tested and certified as clean in regard to certain grapevine diseases.[140]

Both the Foundation Plant Services and the National Grape Registry are invaluable resources for the industry.

VALIDATING FOREIGN VARIETAL AND GEOGRAPHIC LABEL CLAIMS

Previous sections have discussed the difficulty that regulators face in authenticating label claims for imported wine. How would a regulator ensure that label claims on imported wines are valid? In a recent case, the amount of wine imported into the United States from the Languedoc region of France appeared to exceed the acreage capacity of vineyards in the region. The TTB learned from French authorities that their investigation of wine producers and merchants in the Languedoc-Roussillon region of France had resulted in criminal convictions for fraud for selling wine as Pinot Noir when the wine was produced from Merlot and Sirah grapes.[141] The TTB then issued Industry Circular 2010-5 on May 5, 2010,[142] set forth in full below:

> To help ensure the integrity of imported wines in the U.S. marketplace, beginning on May 3, 2010, for all bottled or bulk wine from the Languedoc-Roussillon region of France covered by a Certificate of Label Approval (COLA) naming pinot noir as the single grape varietal and an appellation of origin in the Languedoc-Roussillon region of France, all proprietors importing such wine in bottles or bottling and labeling such wine which was imported in bulk must obtain a declaration from the Government of France which:
>
> 1. States that the wine was produced from at least the minimum percentage of wine derived from pinot noir grapes as required by French law for the labeled appellation of origin;

137. *Id.*
138. *Id.*
139. National Grape Registry, http://www.ngr.ucdavis.edu/ (last visited Jan. 21, 2011).
140. *Id.*
141. TTB, Industry Circular No. 2010-5, Pinot Noir from the Languedoc-Roussillon Region of France (2010), available at http://www.ttb.gov/industry_circulars/archives/2010/10-05.html (last visited Jan. 21, 2011).
142. *Id.* The complex industry circular was later accompanied by a FAQ document that can be found at Frequently Asked Questions on TTB Industry Circular 2010-5, TTB, http://www.ttb.gov/industry_circulars/archives/2010/10-05-faqs.html (last visited Jan. 21, 2011).

2. States that the wine was produced from at least the minimum percentage of wine derived from pinot noir grapes grown in the labeled appellation of origin as required by French law for the labeled appellation of origin;
3. States that the wine conforms to the requirements of the French laws and regulations governing its composition, method of production, and designation;
4. Provides the basis on which the certifying French Government agency is certifying the wine;
5. Includes the name and address of the producer;
6. Includes the brand name, appellation of origin name, and vintage date, if any;
7. Appears on French Government Agency letterhead;
8. Is signed and dated by a French Government official; and
9. Is in English, or, if in French, is accompanied by an English translation.

In the case of wine imported in bottles, proprietors must have the declaration in their possession at the time of release of any of these wines from United States Customs and Border Protection (CBP) custody. However, importers should note that they do not need to present the declaration as part of the CBP entry process. Importers in receipt of shipments on or after May 3, 2010, which were shipped to the United States prior to that date and for which documentary evidence of a shipping date before May 3, 2010, exists must obtain a declaration for the wine within 30 days from the date of release from customs custody.

In the case of wine imported in bulk, proprietors must have the declaration in their possession at the time of bottling and labeling the wine with a French appellation of origin. This includes wine that has already been imported into the United States, but has not yet been bottled. Proprietors are reminded that if imported bulk wine is to be blended after arrival in the United States, after blending, the wine must continue to meet French requirements including those for minimum percentage of pinot noir and wine derived from grapes grown in the labeled appellation of origin area if it is labeled with a French appellation of origin.

The TTB, in issuing this Industry Circular, took a strong position on fraudulent varietal and appellation claims, but it did so with little notice to the purchasers of those grapes and wine. The French government could not validate the Pinot Noir pedigree of the wines that were imported into the United States. This interrupted the bottling operations of these imported wines in California. Companies had no choice but to downgrade these wines on their labels, resubmitting the labels for approval under the class "Red Table Wine." Because the French government could not certify any appellation other than "France," the labels could not include a vintage date, which is allowed only when the label includes an appellation of origin smaller than a country.

c. Alcohol Content

Presumably alcohol content information should not pose many administrative issues, and that presumption is almost correct. Alcohol content information is an objective value. Wine Institute at one time wanted to create a label that would be accepted worldwide and, as a first step, successfully requested the TTB to permit the alcohol content to appear on the label in a type size ranging from one to three millimeters so as to be consistent with the regulations of the European Union and other countries.[143]

Alcohol levels for wine are generally stable once fermentation ends. Labeling regulations permit alcohol content to be expressed as a single number or as a bracketed value, with tolerances prescribed for each manner of expression.[144] The regulations recognize that the use of the "table wine" type designation for grape wine having between 7 and 14 percent alcohol by volume obviates the need to state the alcohol content by number.[145] The regulation itself is straightforward, but two areas of regulatory interpretation have presented problems.

First, wineries frequently misunderstand and misapply the tolerance range prescribed in the regulations. For example, it might appear that a wine that tests at 14.2 percent alcohol by volume could be labeled at 13.9 percent alcohol by volume, because 27 CFR §4.36(b)(1) permits a 1.5 percent tolerance for wine containing 14 percent or less of alcohol by volume. The TTB usually discovers such products in its random sampling of wine products at the consumer level. In almost every case, the wineries have misread the regulation. Subsection (c) of 27 CFR §4.36 states:

> (c) Regardless of the type of statement used and regardless of tolerances normally permitted in direct statements and ranges normally permitted in maximum and minimum statements, alcoholic content statements, whether required or optional, shall definitely and correctly indicate the class, type and taxable grade of the wine so labeled and nothing in this section shall be construed as authorizing the appearance upon the labels of any wine of an alcoholic content statement in terms of maximum and minimum percentages which overlaps a prescribed limitation on the alcoholic content of any class, type, or taxable grade of wine, or a direct statement of alcoholic content which indicates that the alcoholic content of the wine is within such a limitation when in fact it is not.

The 14.2 percent alcohol wine therefore cannot be labeled as 13.9 percent, because the tax class changes at 14 percent. The TTB has an obvious reason for

---

143. 27 C.F.R. §4.38(b) (2010). This subsection provides:

Size of type. (1) Containers of more than 187 milliliters. All mandatory information required on labels by this part, **except the alcoholic content statement**, shall be in script, type, or printing not smaller than 2 millimeters; except that if contained among other descriptive or explanatory information, the script, type, or printing of the mandatory information shall be of a size substantially more conspicuous than that of the descriptive or explanatory information. (2) Containers of 187 milliliters or less. All mandatory information required on labels by this part, except the alcoholic content statement, shall not be smaller than 1 millimeter, except that if contained among other descriptive or explanatory information, the script, type, or printing of the mandatory information shall be of a size substantially more conspicuous than that of the descriptive or explanatory information. (3) **Alcoholic content statements shall not appear in script, type, or printing larger or more conspicuous than 3 millimeters nor smaller than 1 millimeter on labels of containers having a capacity of 5 liters or less and shall not be set off with a border or otherwise accentuated.**

(Emphasis added.)

144. *Id.* §4.36(b).

145. *Id.* §4.36(a).

requiring an accurate depiction of alcohol content, because taxes are imposed based on the class and type of the wine. Short of a scientific test to determine alcohol content, the TTB must rely on a winery to represent the wine's tax class correctly.

The TTB is not usually merciful when it discovers that a winery has defrauded the government by misstating the alcohol content. This is particularly so if the government stands to lose tax revenue from each bottle sold. There also are situations where the reverse has happened, that is, where a winery misrepresented a wine to be a dessert wine (over 14 percent alcohol by volume) when the wine tested out to be a table wine. This is still a mislabeling offense, but the TTB refunds the overage of excise taxes paid.

The second problem area relates to testing and measurement. Occasionally, a winery's analysis of a wine's alcohol content is not consistent with the TTB's analysis, which may occur when the alcohol content is very close to either side of 14 percent alcohol by volume. For example, a winery may label a wine's alcohol content as 13.9, but the TTB's laboratory may show an alcohol by volume value of 14.3. In such cases, Wine Institute usually recommends a retesting of wine samples from the same lot of wine at a commercial laboratory and a resolution of the dispute based on those commercial tests.

d. Net Contents

The following saying has been attributed to Henry Ford: "Any customer can have a car painted any color that he wants so long as it is black."[146] Similarly, wine can actually come in more sizes than one, but each container must conform to the prescribed standards of fill found at 27 CFR §4.72. The authorized bottle sizes are shown in Figure 3-10.

A net contents statement is mandatory label information, unless the statement is blown into the glass bottle. Around 30 years ago, one would hear about problems with consistent fill, in which a wine bottle that claimed to contain 750 ml of wine contained a little less than 750 ml. These underfill/overfill

Figure 3-10
Authorized Bottle Sizes for Wine

3 liters	375 milliliters
1.5 liters	187 milliliters
1 liter	100 milliliters
750 milliliters	50 milliliters
500 milliliters	

146. Henry Ford, My Life and Work 71-72 (1922).

issues raised questions of consumer fraud and unfair business practices, but with the advent of the modern bottling line, there have not been many concerns regarding accurate fill levels.

The BATF had at one time issued an Advance Notice of Proposed Rulemaking on whether the standards of fill should be eliminated,[147] but it later aborted this proposal. Over the years, the TTB has eliminated the 500 ml size for distilled spirits.[148] But it also has added 100 ml and 375 ml sizes for distilled spirits,[149] a 355 ml container for distilled spirits in cans (the equivalent of 12 fluid ounces, as with beer),[150] and 50 ml and 500 ml container sizes for wine.[151]

The 500 ml container size was authorized in 1990, based on statements by proponents that such a wine bottle would be more appropriate than any currently authorized size for two people to enjoy with a meal.[152] Some participants in the public comment process specifically mentioned the appropriateness of this size in a restaurant setting.[153] A related reason was that the 500 ml size would promote moderation and hence reduce the hazard of driving while intoxicated.[154] Twenty years later, the 500 ml container has not lived up to this prediction at on-sale establishments, and wine is still most commonly sold in 750 ml containers.

One of the most interesting proposals on net contents came with the TTB's Notice No. 861, published in the Federal Register on May 15, 1998.[155] Based on a petition it had received, the BATF proposed an amendment to the labeling regulations to provide that the net contents statement for wine in containers of less than one liter may be expressed on the label in centiliters (cl) as an alternative to milliliters (ml).[156] The BATF stated in the notice that the proposed regulation would provide industry members with greater flexibility in labeling their wines while ensuring that the consumer is adequately informed as to the net contents of the product.[157]

The petition was filed by Banfi Vintners (Banfi) of Old Brookville, New York.[158] Banfi had asked that the regulations be amended to allow the net contents of wine bottled in a 750 milliliter (750 ml) bottle to be expressed in centiliters, as "75 cl."[159] Banfi stated that 75 centiliters is a universally recognized measurement equivalent to 750 milliliters (ml) in the metric system

147. Standards of Fill for Wine and Distilled Spirits, 52 Fed. Reg. 23685 (proposed June 24, 1987).

148. Elimination of the 500 Milliliter Metric Standard of Fill for Distilled Spirits, 51 Fed. Reg. 16167 (May 1, 1986) (to be codified at 27 C.F.R. pt. 5).

149. 100 Milliliter and 375 Milliliter Standards of Fill for Distilled Spirits, 48 Fed. Reg. 43319 (September 23, 1983) (to be codified at 27 C.F.R. pt. 5, 19).

150. Standards of Fill for Distilled Spirits, 57 Fed. Reg. 31126 (July 14, 1992) (to be codified at 27 C.F.R. pt. 5).

151. Standards of Fill for Wine, 46 Fed. Reg. 1725 (January 7, 1981) (to be codified at 27 C.F.R. pt. 4); Standards of Fill for Wine; New 500 Milliliter Size, 55 Fed. Reg. 42710 (October 23, 1990) (to be codified at 27 C.F.R. pt. 4).

152. Standards of Fill for Wine; New 500 Milliliter Size, 55 Fed. Reg. at 42711.

153. *Id.*

154. *Id.*

155. Net Contents Statement on Wine Labels, 63 Fed. Reg. 27017 (proposed May 15, 1998).

156. *Id.* at 27017.

157. *Id.*

158. *Id.*

159. *Id.*

and that authorizing this alternative net contents statement on wine labels "would simplify current regulations and allow for an easier flow of wines among Europe, the world markets and the United States."[160]

Another incentive for the rulemaking petition was that, at the time, there was a growing market for imported glass. Wineries would purchase imported glass at low prices, believing that such purchases would help to cut costs. Much of the glass had net contents embossed or blown into the glass, but with a "cl" net content statement rather than an "ml" statement.

Surprisingly, of the 95 comments the BATF received in response to its notice, 82 of them objected to the proposal.[161] Comments were submitted by consumers, industry members representing domestic and foreign interests, various organizations, and trade associations, e.g., the National Conference on Weights and Measures, the U.S. Metric Association, Inc., Wine Institute, the National Association of Beverage Importers, the Scotch Whisky Association, and one Federal agency (U.S. Department of Commerce–National Institute of Standards and Technology).[162]

The commenters, including Wine Institute, contended that the American consumer is not yet fully oriented to the metric system and that adopting the proposed regulations would result in consumer confusion.[163] Furthermore, they argued that the current regulations provide consumers with one standard of common measurement for wine bottled in containers of less than one liter, that is, milliliters; having net contents expressed in either milliliters or centiliters on bottles of the same size might lead consumers to assume the containers do not hold the same amount of wine.[164]

The National Conference on Weights and Measures (NCWM) is a standards-development organization whose members include representatives of federal, state, and local weights and measures groups and other government agencies; businesses; trade and professional organizations; consumers; and other interested groups.[165] The NCWM submitted the following comment:

> The proposed changes are in direct conflict with the metric provisions of the "Uniform Packaging and Labeling Regulation" adopted by the NCWM in 1993, the metric regulations adopted by the Federal Trade Commission (1994), and metric labeling regulations proposed by the Food and Drug Administration for foods, drugs and cosmetics (1993). . . . The labeling requirements for packaged goods adopted by the NCWM, other Federal Agencies, and OIML limit quantity declarations on consumer products to either milliliters or liters to reduce the possibility of consumer confusion. The Committee urges BATF to withdraw its proposal to permit centiliters because its adoption would result in a proliferation of net quantity declarations that may mislead consumers.[166]

160. *Id.* at 27018.
161. Net Contents Statement on Wine Labels, 64 Fed. Reg. 33448, 33449 (June 23, 1999).
162. *Id.*
163. *Id.*
164. *Id.*
165. *Id.*
166. *Id.*

Other commenters expressed the same views as the NCWM, including the National Institute of Standards and Technology (a federal agency within the Department of Commerce) and the U.S. Metric Association, Inc.[167] The U.S. Metric Association was established in 1916 for the purpose of assisting the United States in adopting the metric system and providing guidance for metric system usage to industry, business, education, and consumers.[168]

The BATF withdrew its proposal after the end of the public comment period.[169] Although this might appear to be an insignificant regulatory event, I learned more from this rulemaking than from many of the others in which I have been involved. At first the change seemed to be just simple math. It was like saying that the time was quarter to eight instead of seven forty-five or saying a distance was three feet instead of a yard. Yet the comments made me realize that much more than math was at stake and that sometimes consumer confusion can result from expressing an equivalent amount in a different measure.

Finally, the TTB permits, on a case-by-case basis, aggregate packaging.[170] One of Wine Institute's associate members that manufactures aseptic packaging approached Wine Institute to support an amendment to the standards of fill regulations that would add a 250 ml container size. This size, which is commonplace for juice and non-carbonated drinks, was not on the list of recognized container sizes. Because a one liter container had been recognized for quite some time, Wine Institute suggested that the winery seek a COLA for a bundled package of four 250 ml containers, with each 250 ml container bearing mandatory information, the Government Warning, and the statement "Not for Individual Sale in USA." The bundled four-container single unit sales packaging and label were approved by the TTB.

Are "standards of fill" necessary if net contents are properly stated on a label? Consumers already can purchase spirits in plastic pouches[171] and gel-shots.[172] Can containers be designed in a way that masks content or deceives the consumer? Should regulators give consumers more credit and conclude that an accurate net contents statement is all that is needed, regardless of container size? Every so often, we hear that the TTB is considering rescinding the standard of fill regulations for wine and spirits because they are unnecessary. There are no standards of fill for beer, yet the 12 ounce can has become the industry standard through market pressures. By removing standards of fill, wine could be sold in a container of any size and shape. Yet removing fill standards may lead to additional costs, as wineries adjust to a world where wine can be sold in everything from small plastic pouches to juice containers to bota bags and as wineries assess the social consequences that come along with that privilege.

167. *Id.*

168. *Id.*

169. *Id.* at 33449-33450.

170. *See* Prohibition of Certain Alcohol Beverage Containers and Standards of Fill for Distilled Spirits and Wine, 64 Fed. Reg. 6486 (proposed February 9, 1999). The BATF had proposed regulations that would have prohibited aggregate packaging, but the proposal did not result in a final rule.

171. *See* Pocket Shot, http://www.pocketshot.net (last visited Jan. 21, 2011).

172. *See* Gel Shots, http://www.gelshot.com/servlet/StoreFront (last visited Jan. 21, 2011).

e. Contains Sulfites

For a time after the first sulfite disclosure statements started appearing on wine labels, Wine Institute occasionally received letters from consumers stating that they would not be drinking California wine anymore now that wineries were using sulfites. Even after those consumers were contacted and informed that the wines had not been reformulated and that sulfites had always been present in wine, it was still very difficult to get them to believe it.

Sulfur dioxide in its many derivations has many uses at a winery and in wine. In wine it is used as an antioxidant. The maximum amount that can be present in wine is 350 parts per million;[173] a minimum amount of 10 parts per million will trigger the label disclosure requirement.[174] Sulfur dioxide, which can come in liquid and gaseous form, is used at the winery as a fumigant and antibacterial agent. For example, it is not uncommon for wineries to use sulfur dioxide to sterilize barrels and thus prevent the growth of bacteria. New industrial safety rules in California have interpreted federal Environmental Protection Agency regulations to categorize sulfur dioxide as a pesticide; the state now requires training and licensing for anyone intending to use sulfur dioxide as an antibacterial and antimicrobial agent.[175]

It is important to point out that the 10 parts per million threshold for sulfur dioxide disclosure is an analytical threshold and not a level at which adverse reactions will occur. Since sulfur dioxide is ubiquitous, present in so many substances, it is very difficult if not impossible to determine an exposure action level. The FDA chose to establish an analytical level to trigger disclosure in keeping with the precautionary principle. The BATF followed the FDA's lead.[176]

---

173. 27 C.F.R. §4.22(b) (2010). This subsection reads: "Alteration of class or type shall be deemed to result from any of the following occurring before, during, or after production. (1) Treatment of any class or type of wine with substances foreign to such wine which remain therein: *Provided*, That the presence in finished wine of not more than 350 parts per million of total sulfur dioxide, or sulphites expressed as sulfur dioxide, shall not be precluded under this paragraph."

174. *Id.* §4.32(e). This subsection provides:

> Declaration of sulfites. There shall be stated on a front label, back label, strip label or neck label, the statement "Contains sulfites" or "Contains (a) sulfiting agent(s)" or a statement identifying the specific sulfiting agent where sulfur dioxide or a sulfiting agent is detected at a level of 10 or more parts per million, measured as total sulfur dioxide. The provisions of this paragraph shall apply to: (1) Any certificate of label approval issued on or after January 9, 1987; (2) Any wine bottled on or after July 9, 1987, regardless of the date of issuance of the certificate of label approval; and, (3) Any wine removed on or after January 9, 1988.

175. California Department of Pesticide Regulation, Winery Use of Sulfur Dioxide (June 2009), available at www.cdpr.ca.gov/docs/dept/factshts/so2.pdf (last visited Feb. 1, 2011).

176. The TTB reasoned:

> Since FDA has determined that the presence of undeclared sulfites in foods and beverages poses a recognized health problem to a certain class of individuals, ATF believes that the declaration of sulfites in the labeling of alcoholic beverages is necessary in order to inform sulfite-sensitive individuals of the presence of sulfites in alcoholic beverages. A label declaration of sulfites in foods and beverages will enable persons who are aware of an intolerance to sulfites to minimize their exposure to these ingredients. This final rule requires the labeling of sulfites *present* in alcoholic beverages at a level of 10 or more parts per million (ppm), measured as total sulfur dioxide, by *any* method sanctioned by the Association of Official Analytical Chemists (AOAC). The mandatory sulfite declaration applies to alcoholic beverages which, at the time of bottling, contain

For wine label policy purposes, the BATF's deference to the FDA on sulfur dioxide should be contrasted with the TTB's approach to allergen labeling, which is discussed more fully later. Although in both situations the BATF/TTB commenced its own rulemaking, the BATF simply followed the FDA's lead when it came to determining threshold sulfur dioxide levels.[177] The TTB has yet to issue a final rule on allergen labeling, but its Notice of Proposed Rulemaking indicates it will follow a parallel course and defer to the FDA's requirements. The main difference is that the FDA and the BATF had much more administrative discretion to rule on sulfur dioxide, because the issue was not driven by a federal statute but was a perceived public health issue. With the passage of the Federal Allergen Labeling and Consumer Protection Act (FALCPA),[178] there is less administrative latitude. Regulations and requirements must be consistent with the FALCPA.

Finally, the sulfite label statement is not a warning statement but a disclosure statement. It requires the words "Contains Sulfites," not "WARNING: CONTAINS SULFITES." Generally, adverse sulfite reactions are dose-dependent phenomena that affect sensitive individuals and asthmatics. The disclosure statement is meant to notify those individuals that sulfites are present in wine, but it does not necessarily mean that adverse reactions will occur upon consumption.

In addition to added sulfites, sulfur dioxide can occur naturally in wine as a by-product of fermentation. This has led to some interesting and seemingly contradictory wine labels that make two claims: "No Sulfites Added" along with "Contains Sulfites." As an aside and a final comment, sulfites are allowed to be used in the production of organic wine.[179]

f. Government Warning

As with the FALCPA, the source of the "Government Warning" requirement found on all wine labels is federal statute. The Alcoholic Beverage Labeling Act (ABLA) of 1988 was spearheaded in Congress by South Carolina Senator Strom Thurmond.[180] After the bill was adopted, the TTB's charge was to

---

10 or more parts per million of sulfites measured as total sulfur dioxide. This final rule does not distinguish between the "free" and "bound" forms of sulfites.

Labeling of Sulfites in Alcoholic Beverages, 51 Fed. Reg. 34706, 34708 (Sept. 30, 1986) (to be codified at 27 C.F.R. pt. 4, 5, 7) (emphasis added).

177. The BATF's Notice of Proposed Rulemaking on sulfites disclosure regulations is at Disclosure of Sulfiting Agents in the Labeling of Wine, Distilled Spirits and Malt Beverages, 50 Fed. Reg. 26001 (proposed June 24, 1985). The BATF's Final Rule on sulfites disclosure can be found at Labeling of Sulfites in Alcoholic Beverages, 51 Fed. Reg. 34706 (September 30, 1986) (to be codified at 27 C.F.R. pt. 4, 5, 7).

178. On August 2, 2004, President Bush signed into law the Food Allergen Labeling and Consumer Protection Act of 2004 (FALCPA), Pub. L. No. 108–282, 118 Stat. 905, tit. II (2004) (enacting 21 U.S.C. §374a, 42 U.S.C. §242r, amending 21 U.S.C. §§321, 343, 343-1, and enacting provisions set out as notes under 21 U.S.C. §§321, 343, 42 U.S.C. §§243, 300d-2). The FALCPA amends portions of the Federal Food, Drug and Cosmetic Act (FD&C Act, 21 U.S.C. §§301-99 (2006)) to require a food that is, or contains an ingredient that bears or contains, a major food allergen to list this information on its label using plain, common language.

179. TTB, ALFD Guidance for Organic Labeling Applicants 5 (2010), available at www.ttb.gov/pdf/organic/alfd-guidance-for-organic-labeling-applicants.pdf (last visited Feb. 1, 2011).

180. 27 U.S.C. §§213 19 (2006).

implement the provisions of the Act with consistent regulations. The TTB could not exercise much discretion with the language of the warning, although the final regulations did impose requirements regarding placement, type size, and type compression.

The BATF first issued an interim regulation on February 16, 1989,[181] followed by a final rule a year later on February 14, 1990.[182] The Center for Science in the Public Interest subsequently attempted to amend the appearance of the warning statement,[183] but that effort failed. Since that time, there have been no further attempts to alter or modify the appearance of the warning.

The Government Warning regulations impose a maximum number of characters per inch, a requirement that does not exist for other mandatory information. In BATF's final rule implementing the provisions of ABLA, the agency states:[184]

> **No Compression/Maximum Characters per Inch**
> In its examination of alcoholic beverage labels bearing the health warning statement, the Bureau has observed that the statement is easier to read and more legible when the letters and words have sufficient space between them, i.e., they are not compressed. At the same time, the Bureau has observed that on containers required to display the warning statement in two millimeter size type, a statement that contains approximately 25 characters per inch tends not to exhibit compression of letters and/or words and is also easier to read. The same holds true for a statement in one millimeter type that contains approximately 40 characters per inch.
>
> The GAO made a similar observation in its June 1989 report, and thus recommended that ATF's final rule specify space and lettering requirements for the warning statement. As stated in their report, '[t]he readability of the warning statement could also be enhanced by setting a specific standard for the number of letters that can be used in a designated amount of space; for example, the number of letters per inch.'
>
> Accordingly, the Bureau is specifying in this final rule that the letters and/or words of the health warning statement may not be compressed in such a manner that the statement is not readily legible (i.e., touching, and/or overlapping to such a degree as to render the statement or particular words in the statement, not readily legible). . . .
>
> ATF believes that the above requirement will ensure that the health warning statement on each alcoholic beverage container is more easily read by the average consumer. In addition, the specification of maximum characters per inch provides the industry with a specific guideline which will assist them in designing labels to accommodate the health warning statement.

The Government Warning requirements are very strict.[185] In the early implementation stage, many wineries' efforts to comply met with label

---

181. Implementation of the Alcoholic Beverage Labeling Act of 1988 (Pub. L. No. 100-690); Health Warning Statement, 54 Fed. Reg. 7160 (proposed Feb. 16, 1989).

182. Implementation of Alcoholic Beverage Labeling Act of 1988; Health Warning Statement, 55 Fed. Reg. 5414 (Feb. 14, 1990) (to be codified at 27 C.F.R. 4, 5, 7, 16).

183. *See* Alcohol Beverage Health Warning Statement, 66 Fed. Reg. 28135 (proposed May 22, 2001).

184. Implementation of Alcoholic Beverage Labeling Act of 1988; Health Warning Statement, 55 Fed. Reg. 5414, 5417-5420 (Feb. 14, 1990) (to be codified at 27 C.F.R. 4, 5, 7, 16).

185. *See* 27 C.F.R. §16.22 (2010).

rejection. The wineries quickly learned that there are no variances from the stated regulatory requirements; every label must meet the literal requirements of the regulations. Today, very few wineries fail to obtain label approval because of a problem with the Government Warning statement.

g. Name and Address

The bare-bones wine label includes, and TTB regulations require, the name and address of the bottler. 27 CFR §4.35 sets forth the requirements for the name and address. Most wine labels include optional statements in addition to the name and address of the bottler. The TTB also imposes requirements for the use of these optional statements.

"Produced" or "Made" and bottled by—means that the winery fermented not less than 75 percent of the wine at the address stated, or changed the class or type of the wine by addition of alcohol, brandy, flavors, colors, or artificial carbonation, or produced sparkling wine by secondary fermentation at the stated address.[186]

"Blended" and bottled by—means that the winery mixed the wine with other wines of the same class and type at the address stated.[187]

"Cellared," "Vinted," or "Prepared" and bottled by—means that the named winery subjected the wine to cellar treatment in accordance with 27 CFR §4.22(c).[188] Cellar treatment includes many winemaking processes such as fining, filtering, and refrigeration. Almost any wine treatment will qualify for this designation.[189]

With respect to optional statements, the TTB rarely allows for variances. Terms like "Crafted and bottled by" or "Hand brewed and bottled by" or, in the case of a special bottling for a new birth in the family, "Conceived and bottled by" will probably not be approved.

h. Vintage Date

Vintage dates are not mandatory information, but if a winery chooses to include a vintage statement on its label, the wine must also be labeled with an appellation of origin smaller than a country.[190] Additionally, as noted previously, 85 percent of the wine must be derived from grapes harvested in the stated vintage year if the wine is labeled with an appellation other than a country or viticultural area; 95 percent of the wine must be derived from grapes harvested in the stated vintage year if labeled with a viticultural area.

Prior to Wine Institute's petitioning for a regulation change in 2005, the 95 percent requirement applied to all wines.[191] Wine Institute members requested the change because the labeling standards of other countries required

186. *Id.* §4.35(a)(2)(iii).
187. *Id.* §4.35(a)(2)(iv).
188. *Id.* §4.35(a)(2)(v).
189. *Id.* §4.22(c)(1)-(7).
190. *Id.* §4.27(a).
191. Change to Vintage Date Requirements, 70 Fed. Reg. 25748 (May 2, 2006).

only 85 percent.[192] Although U.S. regulations at the time required that wines entering the U.S. meet the 95 percent vintage date requirement,[193] this standard was not routinely adhered to by wineries in other countries. In briefly reviewing the TTB's regulatory actions over the past several years, Wine Institute was unaware of any enforcement action taken by the agency against a winery, domestic or foreign, for vintage date violations.

Wine Institute understood the enforcement difficulties and costs involved in a prosecution against foreign wineries for vintage date violations. Compared to the records maintained by basic permittees that are readily available to the TTB, evidence to validate label claims is not always as accessible or even procurable from foreign sources. These evidentiary difficulties, along with the lack of reliable scientific tests to determine vintage date percentage compliance, called into serious question the efficacy of the regulation. While basic permittees in the United States can have their records inspected at any time by TTB officials, the inspection of the records of a foreign winery is not within the enforcement purview or budget of the TTB. While the U.S. vintage date requirement has no effect outside the country, neither did it have much of an effect on wines entering the country from abroad. Wine Institute claimed in its rulemaking petition that this absence of enforcement presence with respect to vintage date percentage compliance for imported wines was inequitable.[194] The resulting market imbalance led to an uneven competitive environment, disadvantaging those winemakers in countries that have higher vintage date percentages, such as the United States.

Competitively, U.S. consumers were increasingly purchasing these imported wines over domestic wines.[195] While U.S. wineries had to adhere to a very strict 95 percent vintage date requirement, much of the rest of the world was producing and exporting to the United States vintage wine at the lower 85 percent standard, as shown in Figure 3-11.

Clearly the vintage date requirements in the United States were significantly stricter than those of all the other countries listed. Looking at the top 10 global producers of wine (based on 2001 data), at least 82 percent of the wine they produce (and probably more) was made under vintage date regulations that are less restrictive than those that apply in the United States.[196] And at least 90 percent of the wines exported from the top 10 exporters were made under less restrictive regulatory regimes.[197]

---

192. Letter from Robert Koch, President, Wine Institute, to John Manfreda, Administrator, TTB (Apr. 12, 2005), available at http://www.ttb.gov/announcements/vintagedatereg042705.pdf (last visited Jan. 21, 2011).

193. 27 C.F.R. §4.27(a)(1) (2010).

194. Letter from Robert Koch to John Manfreda, *supra* note 192.

195. In its Agricultural Import Commodity Aggregations report published by the United States Department of Agriculture's Foreign Agricultural Service, for example, Australia's wine imports into the United States increased 19.88 percent from calendar year 2003 to 2004. Cited without attribution in Letter from Robert Koch to John Manfreda, note 192 at 4, n.4. Australia's vintage date percentage is set at 85 percent. *Id.* Likewise, Spain's percent gain for the same period, according to the FAS, was 14.36. Spain's vintage date percentage is 85 percent. *Id.*

196. *Id.* at 4.

197. *Id.* at 4.

Figure 3-11
Vintage Date Percentages of Major Winemaking Countries

Country	Minimum quantity of grapes from a given vintage in order to be labeled with that vintage date	Reference
USA	95%	27 CFR Ch. 1 §4.27
Canada		No national wine standard, however, provincial Vintners' Quality Alliance regulations state 95%
Australia	85%	AWBC Act Sheet 40H (1) and Regulation 22.
New Zealand	85%	ANZFA Standard P5 and P6
European Union	85%	EU Regulation: 1493/99, Annex VIII, E.7
Chile	75%	Official Gazette of the Republic of Chile/Viñas De Chile: Decree 464, Article 5
South Africa	75%	Wines of South Africa: labeling requirements (South Africa) paragraph 14; Cape Wine and Spirits Institute

This figure is reprinted verbatim from the letter from Robert Koch, Wine Institute, to John Manfreda, TTB, *supra* note 192 at 4.

Wine Institute also argued that the vintage dating differences between the United States and other wine-producing countries with a lower percentage requirement placed U.S. wineries at a technological disadvantage. Wine Institute's rulemaking petition explained this in some detail:

> When making mid-range wines, where consistency of flavor and mouthfeel is desirable between years and where a large proportion of the global wine market exists, there is considerable winemaking advantage in being able to use either a younger or an older wine in a blend. For instance, 15 percent of a wine from an older riper vintage will help to achieve a desired style when the current vintage has produced thinner, more acid wines. An 85 percent vintage date regulation, as proposed, would lead to improved taste appeal and quality perception for many wines. Young red wines would be smoother and less "green" and would be more consistent across vintages. Older white wines would be fresher and fruitier and more consistent across vintages as well. In the end, consumers

> would benefit from the U.S. winemaker's ability to produce better quality wine at the same cost.
>
> Not only does the imbalance in vintage date percentage requirements directly impact the consumer's perception of price/value, it economically impedes the efficiency of those California wineries that maintain separate tanks for older vintages, increasing production costs for these wineries over those in other countries. Global competition need not invest in as much cooperage as these California wineries since they do not require as many additional tanks for older vintage inventory. This less efficient tank utilization could compel some California wineries to make greater capital investments in new storage. With a change in the regulation as proposed, better tank efficiency would lead to lower production costs for these wineries, which will support more competitive pricing. A sampling of major California Central Valley wineries indicates that tank utilization under an 85 percent vintage date rule would be improved by 6 percent.
>
> The regulatory change proposed would establish a needed and important baseline vintage date percentage requirement that is more consistent with world standards. It would allow California and other U.S. wineries to compete more openly and fairly because the economic and technological advantages of a lower percentage vintage date requirement will be neutralized, and will allow U.S. wineries to once again compete fairly based on price and quality. Wine Institute's proposal would not preclude wineries from producing vintage wine using higher percentages, and it would not prevent wineries that choose to do so from marketing their wines based on these higher percentages. What the change accomplishes is a leveling of the playing field with respect to vintage labeling standards, and the establishment of a vintage date percentage that is more in keeping with the world market.[198]

The TTB received 98 comments on its Notice of Proposed Rulemaking[199] from 37 growers, 33 wineries, and 9 industry associations.[200] The remaining commenters included two consumers, two brokers, a foreign government official, a journalist, and a retailer.[201] Of the total comments, 64 opposed the proposed change, 30 of which appeared to be from growers.[202] And there were 32 comments in support of the proposal.[203]

The TTB's final rule is a work of art, methodically addressing each of the issues raised in the public comments. The TTB's Final Rule, issued May 2, 2006, granted Wine Institute's request for a rule change.[204] The final regulation again uses geography as a key criterion, applying different percentages based on the kind of appellation used.[205]

---

198. *Id.*

199. Proposed Change to Vintage Date Requirements, 70 Fed. Reg. 38058 (proposed July 1, 2005).

200. Change to Vintage Date Requirements, 71 Fed. Reg. 25748, 25749 (May 2, 2006).

201. *Id.*

202. *Id.*

203. *Id.*

204. *Id.* at 25751.

205. *Id.*

F. PROHIBITED PRACTICES

Prohibited label practices[206] closely parallel the TTB's prohibited advertising practices;[207] in most instances, they are identical. This makes sense. If you are prohibited from making a statement on your label, the same should hold true for advertising. The major difference between statements made on a wine label and those made in advertising is that labels need to be preapproved, while advertising is not required to undergo a pre-review process with the TTB.

There is a long list of prohibited practices at 27 CFR §4.39, but the two main points are that labels as well as advertising should provide truthful, non-misleading, accurate, and specific information about the product that does not cause any consumer deception or confusion. A statement can be truthful yet misleading if it contains ambiguity, factual omission, or deceptive inferences. Some of the more interesting prohibited practices follow:

- A statement cannot be "disparaging" of a competitor's products. At one point, comparative advertising was thought to be de facto disparaging, but the current regulations recognize the legitimacy of comparative advertising for taste tests.[208]
- Statements that are obscene or indecent are prohibited. Today, there are relatively few examples of this on the TTB level. Some states still enforce their own community standard definition of obscenity. Hahn Family Wines' "Cycles Gladiator" label, shown in Figure 3-12, was banned in Alabama for being obscene.[209] The winery pulled out of the state, and the publicity caused sales of its product to soar. "Banned in Bama" T-shirts and other merchandise still can be purchased on Cycle Gladiator's website at http://www.cyclesgladiator.com.
- No use can be made of trade or brand names that are the names of living individuals of public prominence, or existing private or public organizations, or any representations of such thing, if intended to mislead the consumer to believe that the person or organization has endorsed the wine. For label approval purposes, at times the TTB will require that the organization or person being used on a label sign a release for the use of his or her name or image.
- Subsection (a)(7) of 27 CFR §4.39 prohibits statements that tend to create the impression that a wine has intoxicating qualities. "Fortified wine" is one such statement, although it is commonly used in the wine world to denote a wine to which grape spirits or brandy has been added.
- A label is prohibited from using flags, seals, coats of arms, crests, or insignia if the use is likely to lead the consumer to believe that the product has been endorsed by the U.S. government. "Flag" labels are commonly seen

---

206. 27 C.F.R. §4.39 (2010).

207. *Id.* §4.64.

208. *Id.* §4.65(b).

209. Lucy Shaw, Alabama Ban on Nude Nymph Wine Label, Decanter (July 31, 2009), http://www.decanter.com/news/wine-news/484381/alabama-ban-on-nude-nymph-wine-label (last visited Feb. 1, 2011).

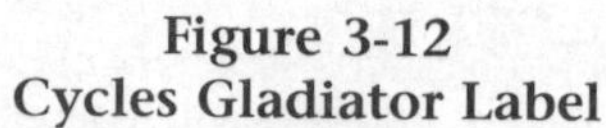

Figure 3-12
Cycles Gladiator Label

Cycles Gladiator label was banned in Alabama because it is considered to be obscene.

prior to the 4th of July or when wine is being produced for a presidential inauguration. In most cases, the labels are rejected.

Sometimes label practices border on the comedic. California Chardonnay producers are experimenting with wines that are not aged in barrels. Wineries have had labels approved that make a claim that the wine is "unoaked." In a recent label dispute with the TTB, the use of the term "oakless" was rejected on a label because the label reviewer did not know what the word meant, even though the reviewer knew perfectly well what the term "unoaked" meant, having approved labels using that term in the past.

a. Therapeutic Claims

By far the most common label offense is the making of improper therapeutic claims. After Morley Safer delivered his "French Paradox" segment on "60 Minutes" in November 1991, many wineries (and others) have attempted to channel its meaning to wine labels and advertising. Current regulations have evolved from a categorical prohibition against the making of therapeutic claims in labeling and advertising at the time of the broadcast to a more complex provision that draws distinctions between "specific health claims" and "health related statements."[210] Although most claims still fall into the "specific health claim" category and are generally prohibited unless truthful and non-misleading, the current regulation reflects an ironclad administrative position under the weight of evidence from science and industry and allows for "less than therapeutic" claims.

Five years after the "60 Minutes" segment, the Fourth Edition (1995) of the Dietary Guidelines for Americans was published by the U.S. Department of Agriculture and the U.S. Department of Health and Human Services.[211] This edition of the Guidelines contained a detailed discussion of the health consequences of alcohol consumption, recognizing that "[c]urrent evidence suggests that moderate drinking is associated with a lower risk of coronary heart disease in some individuals."[212] The Guidelines then went on to discuss the "serious health problems" caused by higher levels of alcohol consumption, including increased risk of high blood pressure, stroke, and heart disease. Nevertheless, the significance of a government agency that finally recognized that wine consumption might actually be healthful did not go unnoticed.

The 1995 Guidelines recommended that if adults choose to drink alcoholic beverages, they should consume them only in moderation.[213] The term "moderation" was defined as no more than one drink per day for women and no more than two drinks per day for men.[214] But the Guidelines provided additional and balanced information, emphasizing that many people should not drink alcoholic beverages at all, including children and adolescents, women who are trying to conceive or who are pregnant, individuals who plan to drive or take part in activities that require attention or skill, and individuals using prescription and over-the-counter medications.[215] Finally, the 1995 Guidelines suggested that individuals of any age who could not restrict their drinking to moderate levels should not drink at all.[216]

Trade associations, including Wine Institute, which closely monitored and provided public input into the Fourth Edition of the Guidelines, sought to capitalize on the first governmental acknowledgment that wine consumption may have some positive health benefits. Industry trade organizations adopted the following strategy: rather than making a therapeutic claim, the label could direct consumers to either their physician or the Dietary Guidelines to learn about the health effects of wine consumption. One such back label is shown in Figure 3-13. Labels along these lines eventually were approved, but with the conditions set forth in the current version of §4.39(h):

> iii) Health-related directional statements. A statement that directs consumers to a third party or other source for information regarding the effects on health of wine or alcohol consumption is presumed misleading unless it—

---

210. *See generally* 27 C.F.R. §4.39(h) regarding health-related statements.

211. USDA and U.S. Dep't of Health and Human Services, Dietary Guidelines for Americans (1995), available at http://www.health.gov/dietaryguidelines/dga95/pdf/DIETGUID.pdf (last visited October 30, 2010).

212. *Id.* at 40.

213. *Id.*

214. *Id.*

215. *Id.* at 41.

216. *Id.*

Figure 3-13
Directional Statement Submitted for Approval by Wine Institute

TO LEARN THE HEALTH EFFECTS OF WINE CONSUMPTION, SEND FOR THE FEDERAL GOVERNMENT'S *DIETARY GUIDELINES FOR AMERICANS*, CENTER FOR NUTRITION POLICY AND PROMOTION, USDA, 1120 20TH STREET, NW, WASHINGTON DC 20036 OR VISIT ITS WEB SITE: HTTP://WWW.USDA.GOV/FCS/CNPP.HTM

(A) Directs consumers in a neutral or other non-misleading manner to a third party or other source for balanced information regarding the effects on health of wine or alcohol consumption; and

(B) (1) Includes as part of the health-related directional statement the following disclaimer: "This statement should not encourage you to drink or to increase your alcohol consumption for health reasons;" or

(2) Includes as part of the health-related directional statement some other qualifying statement that the appropriate TTB officer finds is sufficient to dispel any misleading impression conveyed by the health-related directional statement.

Although the directional statement label approval was considered a significant development by the industry trade associations, no wineries currently take advantage of health-related directional statements. Nevertheless, the issuance of the Dietary Guidelines and the BATF's subsequent regulatory efforts to provide clarity to health claims were important steps for the industry and for the TTB. In the years following the final rule that amended the therapeutic claims provisions,[217] the TTB would have to face issues concerning "organic" wine[218] and the making of "green claims." The final rule on health claims compelled an approach to label claims generally that was vitally needed as the country began to focus on allergen, nutrition, and green claims.

217. Health Claims and Other Health-Related Statements in the Labeling and Advertising of Alcohol Beverages, 68 Fed. Reg. 10076 (March 3, 2003) (to be codified at 27 C.F.R. pt. 4, 5, 7). By then the BATF had been absorbed by Homeland Security, and the TTB published the final rule.

218. Organic Claims in Labeling and Advertising of Alcohol Beverages, 67 Fed. Reg. 62856 (Oct. 8, 2002); *see also* TTB, Guidelines for Labeling: Wine with Organic References (2009), available at http://www.ttb.gov/pdf/wine.pdf.

In practice, the general rule remains that making any health claim on a wine label or in advertising is a violation. In many situations, wineries are not aware that their label text might be interpreted as a prohibited therapeutic claim. From a label approval or advertising standpoint, it is not that easy to determine whether a statement is truthful as well as non-misleading. Consider the following:

- **Please Enjoy Our Wine in Moderation** was originally considered to be a prohibited therapeutic claim that was rejected on a submitted label. The TTB thought that the statement implied that consuming wine in moderation might have some therapeutic value. This claim is generally permissible today.
- **Wine Has Been Known Historically as a Family Beverage** was considered to be a therapeutic claim, and the COLA application was initially rejected. Today this and similar claims can be made.
- **Science Is Clear: Wine Can Be Good for You** is considered to be a therapeutic claim. While the statement is true, it is generally considered misleading on its own without further qualification or explanation.
- **"To Your Health" or the Italian "Salute!"** was initially considered to be a prohibited therapeutic claim, implying that consuming the product might lead to health benefits.
- **Refreshing and Lively When Served Cold** was never considered a therapeutic claim, but the term "lively" was considered to connote effervescence and was only allowed for sparkling wines. Today this and similar claims can generally be made.

And finally, in a position that continues to seem baffling, the TTB has asserted that caloric or carbohydrate statements are not nutritional claims but a statement on vitamin content is:

> The term [health-related statement] also includes statements and claims that imply that a physical or psychological sensation results from consuming wine, distilled spirits, or malt beverages, as well as statements and claims of nutritional value. Statements concerning caloric, carbohydrate, protein, and fat content of alcohol beverages are not considered nutritional claims about the product. However, statements of vitamin content are considered nutritional value claims, and *will be prohibited if presented in a fashion that tends to mislead consumers as to the nutritional value of the product.*[219]

Drawing a distinction between caloric or carbohydrate claims and vitamin claims makes no sense. Nutritional information, whether vitamin content, caloric content, or fat content, can provide important neutral information for a consumer's purchase decision. When the TTB eventually publishes its serving facts final rule, which will be discussed next, advertising standards will not be far behind. Many already are familiar with the advertisements for light beer that show two people arguing over whether the product tastes

219. 27 C.F.R. §7.54(e) (2010) (emphasis added).

Figure 3-14
Barcardi and Diet Cola Advertisement

great or is less filling. Prior to the publication of the last serving facts proposal, there were a few examples of distilled spirits nutrition value advertising. One of the most compelling was the Bacardi Rum advertisement (Figure 3-14) touting that the consumption of its product with diet cola would net zero carbohydrates and zero sugar, failing to disclose the number of calories that were in the mixed drink overall.

G. WHAT'S TO COME?

The outcome of two pending rulemakings will significantly change the way that wine labels appear. One rulemaking effort is the result of federal law; the other is the result of requests from organizations and some industry members to include nutritional information on their labels. From an implementation standpoint, a final rule on both topics is inevitable. Whatever the outcome, one hopes that the TTB will implement both rules at the same time, so that wineries will be required to change their labels only once.

1. SERVING FACTS

The July 31, 2007, issue of the Federal Register contained a Notice of Proposed Rulemaking to require mandatory serving facts on all alcoholic beverage labels.[220] The proposed regulations would generally require wine, beer, and spirits labels to include a "Serving Facts" panel (Figure 3-15) that would consist of a serving size statement, the number of servings per container, and values for

Figure 3-15
Proposed Serving Facts Panel

Serving Facts	
Serving Size	5 fl oz (148 ml)
Servings Per Container	2 ½
	Amt Per Serv.
Calories	120
Carbohydrate	3g
Fat	0g
Protein	0g

220. Labeling and Advertising of Wines, Distilled Spirits and Malt Beverages, 72 Fed. Reg. 41860 (proposed July 31, 2007).

calories, carbohydrates, fat, and protein.[221] The comment period for this proposal ended several years ago, on October 27, 2007.

The proposed rule is the result of several administrative efforts. The TTB's Initial Advance Notice of Proposed Rulemaking in 1993 to require mandatory nutritional labeling did not proceed beyond the initial comment stage.[222] However, in 2003 rulemaking petitions for allergen labeling, ingredient labeling, and alcohol facts labeling led the TTB to publish two "white papers"[223] and then to publish an Advance Notice of Proposed Rulemaking on many label issues.[224]

Many labeling schemes and issues were considered, including a voluntary rather than a mandatory label panel, a serving size statement, the number of servings per container, a "standard drink" definition, a statement of the amount of alcohol (in ounces) contained in a single serving, nutritional information, comparison graphics, the Dietary Guidelines statement on moderate drinking, and ingredient labeling.[225] Two such proposals are presented in Figures 3-16 and 3-17.

Figure 3-16
Serving Facts Proposal from Summer 2004 "White Paper"

221. *Id.*

222. Nutrition Labeling for Wine, Distilled Spirits, and Malt Beverages, 58 Fed. Reg. 42517 (proposed Aug. 10, 1993).

223. *See* Labeling and Advertising of Wines, Distilled Spirits and Malt Beverages; Request for Public Comment, 70 Fed. Reg. 22274, 22282 (proposed April 29, 2005).

224. *Id.*

225. *Id.*

Figure 3-17
Center for Science in the Public Interest's Alcohol Facts Proposal, Submitted to the TTB in 2003

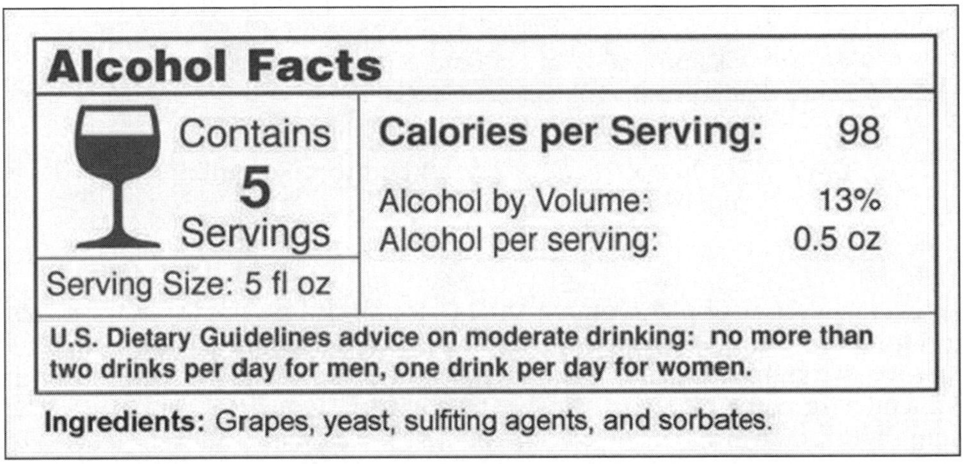

Alcohol Facts

Contains 5 Servings

Serving Size: 5 fl oz

Calories per Serving: 98

Alcohol by Volume: 13%

Alcohol per serving: 0.5 oz

U.S. Dietary Guidelines advice on moderate drinking: no more than two drinks per day for men, one drink per day for women.

Ingredients: Grapes, yeast, sulfiting agents, and sorbates.

The current "Serving Facts" proposal is the culmination of the many earlier label initiatives. The proposal either incorporates or dismisses all these labeling initiatives except for ingredient labeling, which may be part of a future rulemaking. Several contemplated label changes were not implemented in the current Serving Facts rulemaking. For example, the pending proposal does not include a standard drink definition. The TTB also dismissed efforts to include comparison graphics and the Dietary Guidelines statement on moderate drinking. The proposal, however, does require mandatory alcohol content statements expressed in terms of alcohol by volume.[226] Current wine regulations, by contrast, allow wines not in excess of 14 percent alcohol by volume to use the designation "table wine" in lieu of an alcohol by volume statement. The current proposal, however, will allow the alcohol content statement to appear anywhere on the label, unlike current regulations, which require alcohol content statements to appear on the brand label.[227] The proposal also mandates a Serving Facts panel that includes caloric, carbohydrate, fat, and protein statements.[228]

The mandatory Serving Facts panel will require wineries to state the number of servings per container. A "single serving" is based on what the TTB considers to be an amount of wine customarily consumed in a single serving. The TTB is proposing two "single serving" categories, as shown in Figure 3-18. For wine from 7 percent to no more than 14 percent alcohol by volume, the TTB is proposing a single serving size of 5 fluid ounces.[229] For wine

226. Labeling and Advertising of Wines, Distilled Spirits and Malt Beverages, 72 Fed. Reg. at 41866, 41876-7 (proposed July 31, 2007).

227. *Id.*

228. *Id.* at 41868, 41877-41879.

229. *Id.* at 41877.

Figure 3-18
Servings Per Container

For products containing	a single serving or serving size is:
At least 7% and not more then 14% alc/vol.	5 fliud ounces (148 milliliters).
Over 14% and not more then 24% alc/vol.	2.5 fliud ounces (74 milliliters).

over 14 percent alcohol by volume, the TTB is proposing a single serving size of 2.5 fluid ounces.[230] Interestingly, the TTB is not proposing a separate serving size for sparkling wines, nor is the agency proposing separate serving sizes for varietal wines over 14 percent alcohol by volume. These drinks are treated the same as dessert wines. The number of servings per container must be labeled to the nearest quarter serving.[231]

The proposed rule also allows, but does not mandate, a statement of alcohol expressed in fluid ounces per serving.[232] Although this is optional, if such a statement is made, the panel must include the alcohol content statement expressed in alcohol by volume, as shown in Figure 3-19.[233]

Generally, the Serving Facts panel must appear on all products in the format prescribed in the proposed rule—in a box in specific type not smaller than one millimeter for containers of 237 milliliters or less and not smaller than two millimeters for larger containers, as shown in Figure 3-20.[234] The proposed regulations establish uniform formatting and type styles to ensure that the Serving Facts panel appears the same for all products.[235]

The proposal makes one exception to the box format and allows for the Serving Facts information to be expressed in a linear fashion, but only for containers that are 50 milliliters (or smaller, but for wine 50 milliliters is the smallest authorized standard of fill).[236]

The proposed regulations set forth tolerance ranges for the various values that must be included in a Serving Facts panel. The tolerances for the respective values are shown in Figure 3-21.

With respect to nutritional advertising, the TTB is proposing to amend the mandatory information requirements for advertising generally by requiring

230. *Id.*
231. *Id.*
232. *Id.* at 41878.
233. *Id.*
234. *Id.* at 41877.
235. *Id.* at 41878.
236. *Id.* at 41873-41875, 41877, 41880, 41882.

Figure 3-19
Serving Facts and Alcohol Content Statement

Serving Facts	
Serving Size	5 fl oz (148 ml)
Servings Per Container	5
	Amount Per Serving
Alcohol by volume	14%
fl oz of alcohol	0.7
Calories	120
Carbohydrate	3g
Fat	0g
Protein	0g

When the Serving Facts panel includes a statement of the amount of fluid ounces of alcohol per serving, the panel must also include the alcohol by volume statement.

Figure 3-20
Serving Facts Box Format

Serving Facts: Serving size: 1.7 fl oz (50 ml); Servings per container: 1; **Alcohol by volume:** 14%; Fl oz of alcohol: 0.2; **Calories:** 41; **Carbohydrates:** 1g; **Fat:** 0g; **Protein:** 0g

that an advertisement contain a Serving Facts panel whenever the advertiser makes an explicit or implicit caloric or carbohydrate claim.[237]

Wine Institute submitted extensive comments during the rulemaking, but one of the organization's primary concerns was the cost of compliance for wineries. Most wine is inherently variable in composition; it is not made to a fixed recipe. Alcohol and residual sugar levels vary significantly among wine styles and also from year to year, region to region, and lot to lot. Winemakers adjust wine blends to meet stylistic targets, often right up to the time of bottling. Accordingly, mandatory Serving Facts labeling such as that proposed by the TTB would impose severe financial and logistical burdens on the industry. For example, wineries would be required to analyze each lot of wine just before

237. *Id.* at 41877.

Figure 3-21
Serving Facts Panel—Statement and Tolerance

Statement	Tolerance
Calorie content	+5 or −10 calories of the labeled amount (e.g., a label showing 96 calories is acceptable if TTB analysis shows the content to be between 86 and 101 calories)
Carbohydrate content	Within a "reasonable range"below the labeled amount and not more than 20 percent above the labeled amount (e.g., a label showing 4 grams of carbohydrates is acceptable if TTB analysis shows a carbohydrate content of not more than 4.8 grams)
Fat content	Within a "reasonable range"below the labeled amount and not more than 20 percent above the labeled amount (e.g., a label showing 4 grams of fat is acceptable if TTB analysis shows a fat content of not more than 4.8 grams)
Protein content	Within a reasonable range above the labeled amount and not more than 20 percent below the labeled amount
Alcohol content	The proposed rule does not modify current alcohol content tolerances (1.5 percent for wines containing 14 percent or less of alcohol by volume; 1 percent for wines containing more than 14 percent alcohol by volume)

bottling to ensure that the elements of the Serving Facts label fall within the tolerances specified. Assuming that the TTB's estimate of $250 per sample[238] represents what industry members would be charged, a medium-sized winery performing 500 pre-bottling analyses per year would incur an additional, ongoing annual cost of $125,000.

Whenever the analyses show that a blend's Serving Facts information is outside the tolerances for the information already printed on the label, the winery would have to delay bottling until the blend is adjusted to conform with the Serving Facts information on the label. This blend adjustment (along with its resulting delay) might have several adverse consequences. First, it could negatively impact the quality of the product. Winemakers go to great lengths to minimize the number of process steps employed in winemaking, because wine flavors and aromas suffer incrementally as processing increases. Second, it would result in additional analytical costs to verify that the adjusted blend is within the required tolerances. Third, it could increase overall bottling and cellar costs if there is a need to make unanticipated changes to bottling

238. *Id.* at 41873.

schedules. Finally, it could create the need for as much as 10 percent additional cooperage to store the wine during blend adjustment and repeat analysis.[239] Current cooperage costs are approximately $4 per gallon of wine.

Additionally, the analytical requirements and the blending considerations previously mentioned would significantly decrease the flexibility that wineries currently enjoy to use spot and/or bulk purchases of wine. Disruptions in the bottling cycle inevitably lead to similar disruptions in sales cycles, introducing uncertainty into the commonly accepted periods of time in which wine moves from production to bottling and from wholesaler to retailer. Thus, for example, white wines normally released in early spring following the harvest may not be available until summer.

Wine Institute also noted that the TTB's proposed rule allows a tolerance of + 5 and − 10 calories per serving versus what is shown in the Serving Facts disclosure.[240] However, the TTB's wine labeling rules currently allow a tolerance of 1.5 percent alcohol by volume from the value stated on the label. This alcohol tolerance range converts to a caloric variance of 12.5 calories per serving, significantly exceeding the tolerance for calories stated in the proposed rule, but taking no account of any additional variance in calories contributed by the carbohydrates that are present in the product. Thus the effect of the proposed rule would be to shrink substantially the alcohol by volume tolerance for wine and thus further reduce the winery's flexibility with regard to wine blends.

In Notice No. 73, the TTB responded to previous industry comments on the costs and burden of a mandatory Serving Facts requirement. The TTB believes that, after the phase-in period, the only significant burden of the rule would be the cost of analysis.[241] But costs would be much greater for the wine industry than for beer or spirits, because wine is inherently more variable in composition.

Regardless of the outcome of the proposal, will the eventual final rule achieve its public policy objectives and be worth the costs to consumers and industry? Consumers are deluged with nutritional claims. On any box of cereal, there are multiple claims about fiber content, calories, and fat. The television shows many direct-to-consumer pharmaceutical commercials for asthma, erectile dysfunction, and depression. The Nutrition Labeling and Education Act (NLEA)[242] has compelled nutrition panel information for almost all food products since 1990, but there has been a steady rise in obesity rates since that time.[243]

Advertising always closely follows mandatory nutrition panels. Since the NLEA's introduction in 1990, consumers have been worn down, and research shows a decline in consumer use of nutrition panels.[244] Advertising fills that

---

239. Letter from Robert Koch, Wine Institute, to Francis Foote, TTB, *supra* note 23, at 7.

240. *Id.* at 8.

241. Labeling and Advertising of Wines, Distilled Spirits and Malt Beverages, 72 Fed. Reg. at 41875-41876 (proposed July 31, 2007).

242. Pub. L. No. 101-535, 104 Stat. 2352 (1990) (codified at 21 U.S.C. §§301, 343, 337, 345, 321, 371).

243. *See* the Centers for Disease Control national map showing obesity trends state-by-state at U.S. Obesity Trends, CDC, http://www.cdc.gov/obesity/data/trends.html (last visited Jan. 21, 2011). The rise in these rates is both shocking and compelling.

244. As an example, *see* Jessica E. Todd & Jayachandran N. Variyam, USDA and Economic Research Service, Economic Research Report No. 63, The Decline in Consumer Use of Food Nutrition Labels, 1995-2006, (2008), available at http://www.ers.usda.gov/Publications/ERR63/ (last visited Jan. 21, 2011).

vacuum with front-of-container nutritional claims that attempt to influence consumer purchases. For alcoholic beverages the Serving Facts panel may simply be the foundation needed for diversionary advertising. Comparative advertising campaigns for alcoholic beverages based on caloric, fat, carbohydrate, and even alcohol content levels may not be far behind, and they will certainly be more influential than any Serving Facts panel.

Finally, although this will not modify wine labels directly, in the near future consumers will be able to garner caloric information when they visit their favorite restaurant chain with 20 or more locations doing business under the same name. On March 23, 2010, President Obama signed the health care reform legislation into law. Section 4205 of the Patient Protection and Affordable Care Act of 2010[245] requires restaurants and similar retail food establishments with 20 or more locations to list calorie content information for standard menu items on restaurant menus and menu boards, including drive-through menu boards.[246] Other nutrient information—total calories, fat, saturated fat, cholesterol, sodium, total carbohydrates, sugars, fiber and total protein—would have to be made available in writing upon request.

The FDA is required by law to issue proposed regulations to carry out these provisions by March 23, 2011.[247] The agency initiated rulemaking on July 7, 2010, to gather public comments.[248] Does the MOU between the FDA and the TTB apply in this situation? It probably does not, and the TTB will probably not engage in rulemaking on this effort as it has done on allergen labeling. The TTB would be hard-pressed to construe a menu at retail establishments as "labeling" under the MOU, and it would be a stretch for the TTB to consider a menu that contains caloric information as "advertising." Moreover, the TTB does not issue permits to, or otherwise regulate, alcoholic beverage retailers, including chain restaurants.

Fortunately, the statute permits the use of databases as a source of nutritional values:

> (iv) REASONABLE BASIS.—For the purposes of this clause, a restaurant or similar retail food establishment shall have a reasonable basis for its nutrient content disclosures, including nutrient databases, cookbooks, laboratory analyses, and other reasonable means, as described in section 101.10 of title 21, Code of Federal Regulations (or any successor regulation) or in a related guidance of the Food and Drug Administration.

Online databases allow anyone to obtain general nutritional values for various foods.[249] By entering the word "wine" in the keyword search criteria at the USDA National Nutrient Database (http://www.nal.usda.gov/fnic/foodcomp/search/), it is possible to obtain nutrition information for many categories of wine.

---

245. Pub. L. No. 111-148 (March 23, 2010) (codified at 21 U.S.C. §343(q)(5)(H)).
246. 21 U.S.C. §343(q)(5)(H)(i) (2006).
247. *Id.* §343(q)(5)(H)(x)(i).
248. *See* Disclosure of Nutrient Content Information for Standard Menu Items Offered for Sale at Chain Restaurants or Similar Retail Food Establishments and for Articles of Food Sold From Vending Machines, 75 Fed. Reg. 39026 (proposed July 7, 2010).
249. 21 U.S.C. §343(q)(5)(H)(iv) (2006).

Unfortunately, many retail operations are apparently dissatisfied with using database values and are requiring their vendors to submit their products for analytical testing. This increases the costs of compliance beyond those contemplated in the statute. For wineries, repeated testing of products from vintage to vintage and varietal to varietal will only add to their burdens.

One advantage of federal menu labeling is that it preempts state efforts to require the same. Various states or local municipalities within states have engaged in inconsistent and nonuniform menu labeling efforts. At least for chain restaurants, having one standard will help alleviate some of the state compliance costs involved with more localized menu labeling schemes. Regardless of how the final regulations turn out, consumers will be seeing more nutrition information on restaurant menus.

2. ALLERGEN LABELING

Unlike the Serving Facts rulemaking, which was the culmination of various forces at work over a period of time, the allergen labeling rulemaking is the result of a federal statute. On August 4, 2004, President George W. Bush signed into law the Food Allergen Labeling and Consumer Protection Act (FALCPA), a set of statutes requiring all food products sold in the United States to disclose the presence of allergens.[250] The Act took effect on January 1, 2006; it applies to any food labeled after that date.[251] Although the applicability of the FALCPA to wine, beer, and spirits is clear, its deployment is significantly different for wine, beer, and spirits, primarily because the TTB has principal jurisdiction over alcoholic beverage labeling.[252]

The law identifies eight "major food allergens": milk, egg, fish (e.g., bass, flounder, or cod), crustacean shellfish (e.g., crab, lobster, or shrimp), tree nuts (e.g., almonds, pecans, or walnuts), wheat, peanuts, and soybeans.[253]

The law generally requires that food labels disclose the presence of these allergens if they are used as ingredients or as parts of additives during processing. The label must disclose the presence of these allergens in its ingredient list, using the common or usual name of the allergen.

---

250. Pub. L. No. 108-282.

251. The FALCPA is self-executing and took effect for all food products under the FDA's jurisdiction on January 1, 2006. The FDA does not have, nor did it feel compelled to publish, implementing regulations. Instead, the FDA relied on the familiarity of its policies on ingredient labeling, its past policies and procedures, and a series of publications available online to provide compliance information to food producers subject to the agency's jurisdiction. The TTB, on the other hand, chose to take the administrative rulemaking route and published its Notice of Proposed Rulemaking at the same time it published voluntary allergen labeling regulations on July 26, 2006. Title, 71 Fed. Reg. 42260 (July 26, 2006). That is why foods under the FDA's jurisdiction already bear allergen statements, while alcoholic beverage producers await the outcome of rulemaking.

252. In 1987 a Memorandum of Understanding between the BATF and the FDA was signed, transferring the public safety of beverage alcohol product responsibilities to the BATF. *See* note 2, *supra*.

253. Of the "big eight" allergens, wine could contain six. Some wineries have been allowed to use chitosan, which is made from crustacean shellfish. Isinglass comes from fish. Soy flour is permissible as a yeast nutrient, as are albumen, or egg whites, and milk or milk products as fining agents. A paste of sawdust, wheat flour, and water is used in wine barrel production to seal the heads to the staves.

TTB regulations in Part 24 authorize specific materials to be used in wine production. For example, §§24.246 and 24.247 authorize the use of albumen or egg white (as a fining agent), isinglass (to clarify wine), and milk (also a fining agent).[254] When any of these processing aids is used in wine production, trace amounts may remain in the finished wine.

The law contains procedures for applying for an exemption either by petition or by notification,[255] but the earlier petitions that were submitted to the FDA, which is responsible for the enforcement of the FALCPA, suggest that the exemption procedures are empty and illusory. Every petition submitted to the FDA has been rejected.[256] The final result appears inevitable. Wineries that use such things as milk, isinglass, soy flour, and albumen or that use wine barrels to store their wines may be required to disclose that their products "contain" the allergens, which in fact may not be truthful, accurate, or specific.

One major problem with the FALCPA is that disclosure is based on use of an allergen during production, as opposed to its presence in the finished product. Fining agents are used in wine production, but they are not intended to remain in the finished product and are filtered out before bottling. That is not to say that there is absolutely no milk or fish protein left in wine when it ultimately reaches the consumer. But testing for these proteins is still far from perfect.

This leads to an interesting compliance and enforcement dilemma for the TTB. Wineries keep cellar records that indicate the addition of materials that may contain allergens.[257] Recording the use of milk, for example, is all the evidence the TTB needs to require that the wine label state, "Contains Milk."

Although cellar records can be used to trigger compliance, there are no reliable tests to show that allergens are present in the finished wine. Simply put, the TTB can only say this: "We know you used an allergen by your own admission, but we cannot prove that it is in your product by scientific means." The requirements of the FALCPA are a prime example of law racing ahead of the applicable science.

Enzyme-linked immunosorbent assay (ELISA) is a technique used to detect the presence of an antibody or antigen in a sample.[258] ELISA kits need to be product-specific to be accurate.[259] Unfortunately, there are no ELISA kits to detect any of the allergens in the presence of wine.[260] Early use of ELISA kits to detect egg in the presence of other material, when applied to wine, has rendered erratic results.[261]

---

254. 27 C.F.R. §§24.246, 247 (2010).

255. FDA allergen exemption petitions can be viewed at Exemptions from Food Allergen Labeling Petition & Notification Process: Industry/Regulator Information, FDA, http://www.fda.gov/Food/LabelingNutrition/FoodAllergensLabeling/ExemptionsfromFoodAllergenLabelingPetitionNotificationProcess/default.htm (last visited Jan. 21, 2011).

256. *Id.*

257. *See* 27 C.F.R. §24.315 (2010).

258. *See* Letter from Robert Koch, President, Wine Institute, to John Manfreda, Administrator, TTB 5(Dec. 26, 2006), submitted in connection with TTB Notice No. 62, 71 Fed. Reg. 42329 (July 26, 2006), available at www.ttb.gov/nprm_comments/ttbnotice62/0620039.pdf (last visited Feb. 1, 2011).

259. *Id.*

260. *Id.*

261. *Id.*

The following points were made by Wine Institute in its final comments to the TTB on the proposed regulations.[262] Only the presence, not the use, of a material containing an allergen should trigger disclosure. There should be a "cross-contact" exemption for the wheat paste used in wine barrels (although Wine Institute is working with barrel manufacturers to discourage the use of wheat flour). A "Processed With . . ." rather than "Contains [name of allergen]" statement would be more truthful. Finally, TTB regulations should establish a standard of proof and recognize the best and reasonably available scientific evidence and methods.

Food allergies are very serious, but is there a history of allergic reactions to wine? A significant body of data has been collected over the years by the Liquor Control Board of Ontario (LCBO). The LCBO is one of the world's largest retailers of alcoholic beverages and imports products from over 60 countries, supporting a retail network of more than 800 stores in the province of Ontario, Canada.[263] In 2005 its sales totaled approximately $3.68 billion Canadian.[264] The LCBO, as part of its operations, also receives and investigates consumer complaints.[265] Since 2000 the LCBO has recorded about 486,000 customer complaints.[266] The LCBO investigated about 1,300 of these complaints, and, of these, 337 reported an alleged illness.[267] Of the 337 investigated complaints, not one involved wine fining agents or production practices.[268]

When analyzing the costs and benefits of allergen disclosure, we must distinguish fact from fiction. In one account, it is stated that about 25 percent of the population believe that they are allergic to certain foods.[269] Still others estimate that about 33 percent of Americans believe that they have a food allergy.[270] Consequently, mislabeling wine as containing an allergen or allergens will have consequences beyond the very small number of wine-consuming adults who have genuine allergies to the allergens in wine fining agents.[271]

---

262. *Id.*

263. Letter from Dr. George J. Soleas, Vice President of Quality Assurance, LCBO, to John Manfreda, Administrator, TTB 2(Dec. 19, 2006), submitted in connection with TTB Notice 62, 71 Fed. Reg. 42329 (July 26, 2006), available at www.ttb.gov/nprm_comments/ttbnotice62_comments.shtml (comment 28) (last visited Feb. 1, 2011).

264. *Id.*

265. *Id.*

266. *Id.* at 3.

267. *Id.*

268. *Id.*

269. *See* Food Allergies: Just the Facts, Family Doctor, http://familydoctor.org/340.xml (last visited Jan. 21, 2011) ("FACT: Although 25 percent of people think they're allergic to certain foods, studies show that about only 8 percent of children and 2 percent of adults have a food allergy.").

270. International Food Information Council, IFIC Review: Understanding Food Allergy 1 (2001) ("Surveys show that about one-third of all adults believe they have food allergies. Yet true food allergy is estimated to affect less than two percent of the population."), available at http://www.foodinsight.org/Content/76/Understanding-Food-Allergy.pdf (last visited Jan. 21, 2011).

271. In Comment 22 to TTB Notice No. 62, Michael Muilenberg, an instructor and researcher for the Harvard School of Public Health, submits that "approximately 2 % of the population . . . has verified food allergies." *See* TTB Notice No. 62 Comments, TTB, http://www.ttb.gov/nprm_comments/ttbnotice62_comments.shtml (last visited Jan. 21, 2011). But Mr. Muilenberg's general figure includes the entire population and all food allergies. The more relevant data indicate

It may perpetuate the misunderstanding of food allergies rather than helping to convey useful information to those that need it. While it is convenient to suggest that wineries label their products with allergen disclosure statements so that those with allergies can make informed decisions, inaccurate information may unreasonably and unnecessarily restrict the already limited choices available to the allergenic individual, causing relatively large numbers of consumers who are at no risk to shy away from wine.

H. ADVERTISING

Labeling practices and advertising practices on the federal label do not substantially differ. What is prohibited on a label is prohibited in advertising. In many cases, a winery could use a label approved by the TTB to "clear" advertising statements that it wishes to use in the marketplace.

There are, however, major differences in the advertising practices across product categories. Malt beverage and spirits producers generally spend much more money advertising than wineries. Here is a simple test: Try to remember your favorite television commercial for beer. Did it make you laugh? Now, do the same for wine. Did any brand come to mind? Television is not the medium of choice for wine products because of cost and effectiveness. Wine advertising is generally confined to print, radio, and new or social media outlets. But when the public looks at alcoholic beverage advertising, it does not make distinctions between wine, beer, and spirits advertising. Every industry segment is painted with the same brush.

Wine advertising is limited in great part not by medium but by content. State and federal trade practice laws, discussed in Chapter 2 of this book, often frustrate a winery's advertising plans, regardless of the medium chosen. For example, in California a strict interpretation of Business and Professions Code §25600 prohibits wineries from engaging in contests within the state.

Content is also regulated in large part by industry advertising codes. In 1978 Wine Institute was the first trade association to publish a formal Code of Advertising Standards (the "Code"). Before that time industry codes were informal and overly general, although the wine, beer, and spirits sectors had each adopted general advertising practices and codes beginning in the 1940s. Before the launch of Wine Institute's Code of Advertising Standards in 1978, the FTC had to determine whether a trade association like Wine Institute could require adherence to the Code provisions by its members. The FTC's opinion required that Code compliance remain voluntary, but since then the FTC has retreated somewhat from that position. Today Wine Institute requires compliance with the Code by all its members as a condition of membership, and although the consequences of noncompliance hardly constitute punishment (violations are published on the Wine Institute website), as we discuss later, that is more than adequate.

---

that milk allergenic consumers represent about 0.3 percent of the adult population, egg allergy about 0.2 percent, and fish allergy about 0.4 percent. *See* Letter from Robert Koch, Wine Institute, to John Manfreda, TTB, *supra* note 258, at 14.

Since 1978 both the Beer Institute and the Distilled Spirits Council of the United States (DISCUS) have launched their own self-regulation programs, surpassing in many ways the provisions of Wine Institute's Code.[272] Both organizations implemented third-party review of advertising before Wine Institute did, for example; this relates primarily to the differences in advertising pervasiveness and content among the various industry sectors.

Since 1999 the FTC has reviewed self-regulation in the alcohol industry. In response to a request from the Congressional Committees on Appropriations, the FTC examined the effectiveness of the alcohol industry's voluntary guidelines on advertising and marketing to underage audiences. The 1999 report[273] includes company-specific information supplied in response to orders by the Commission.

The FTC reviewed the industry again in September 2003 and in June 2008. In all these reviews, industry advertising guidelines and industry self-regulation were shown to reduce the likelihood that such marketing will, by its content or placement, target those under the legal drinking age:[274]

> A well-constructed self-regulatory regime has advantages over government regulation. It conserves limited government resources and is more prompt and flexible than government regulation, given the substantial time required to complete an investigation or to adopt and enforce a regulation. Finally, self-regulation is an appropriate response to concerns about the impact of alcohol advertising on youth, in light of protections provided by the First Amendment to the U.S. Constitution. The Commission continues to believe, therefore, that alcohol industry self- regulation must play a prominent role in addressing concerns about alcohol marketing and youth. The Commission looks forward to the industry's adoption of its recommendations.[275]

The Center for Alcohol Marketing and Youth (www.camy.org) has been on the front line of advocacy for close federal monitoring of alcoholic beverage advertising. Its database of advertisements, including video, is thought-provoking, but the organization's bias for greater control is very clear.

Wine advertisements are rarely controversial. Wine Institute's third-party review procedure has never been used, and there is on average one complaint every two years. In every complaint to Wine Institute to date, the cited issues have been resolved quickly, effectively, and without incident. Here is one example:

---

272. Wine Institute's Code can be found at Code of Advertising Standards, Wine Institute, http://www.wineinstitute.org/initiatives/issuesandpolicy/adcode/details (last visited Jan. 21, 2011). The Beer Institute Code can be found at Advertising and Marketing Code, Beer Institute, http://www.beerinstitute.org/tier.asp?bid=249 (last visited Jan. 21, 2011). The Distilled Spirits Council of the United States Code can be found at Code of Responsible Practices for Beverage Alcohol Advertising and Marketing, DISCUS, http://www.discus.org/responsibility/code.asp (last visited Jan. 21, 2011). The DISCUS code is especially impressive, with institutionalized publication of a semi-annual Code Report that documents all complaints and resolutions.

273. FTC, Self Regulation in the Alcohol Industry: A Review of Industry Efforts to Avoid Promoting Alcohol to Underage Consumers (1999), available at http://www.ftc.gov/reports/alcohol/alcoholreport.shtm (last visited Jan. 21, 2011).

274. FTC, Self-Regulation in the Alcohol Industry (2008), available at http://www.ftc.gov/os/2008/06/080626alcoholreport.pdf (last visited Jan. 21, 2011).

275. *Id.* at 25.

Wine Institute's Advertising Code Prohibits the Use of Santa Claus[276]

3. Any advertisement which has particular appeal to persons below the legal drinking age is unacceptable, even if it also appeals to adults. Therefore, wine and wine cooler advertising by code subscribers shall not: . . .

b. Use music, language, gestures, cartoon characters, or depictions, images, figures, or objects that are popular predominantly with children or otherwise specifically associated with or directed toward those below the legal drinking age, including the use of Santa Claus or the Easter Bunny.

A few years ago, Wine Institute received a complaint from one of its members that another member was using a Santa Claus plush toy in its product displays in a national program. After one call to the member, the "Bad Santa" was removed from product displays in more than 20 states within two weeks.

Two complaints involved the labels of non-members. Following the movie release of Disney's "Ratatouille" in 2007, the company planned to sell a "Ratatouille" branded wine as part of its marketing plan. After a letter was sent to Disney explaining the Wine Institute Advertising Code, the plan to market the wine was scrapped. Wine Institute, however, could not replicate that result with the "Hello Kitty" wine labels that are currently being imported from Italy. After licensing "Hello Kitty" images from Sanrio, an Italian wine producer launched a product line consisting of four labels utilizing four "Hello Kitty" images.[277] After coming across a number of press accounts of the products, Wine Institute has located all of the label approvals in the TTB Public COLA Registry and sent a letter similar to the one that was sent to Disney to both the Italian producer and the New York importer. Wine Institute has not received a response, and the product, to best of its knowledge, is still being sold in various states. The "Hello Kitty" label is shown in Figure 3-22.

But nothing illustrates the interconnection of the industry codes with government sanctions better than the "Wide Eye" schnapps and caffeine product. When Wine Institute was discussing the impact of industry advertising codes, many critics complained that the codes needed to go further in terms of punishment. In other words, self-regulation should also include harsh provisions for punishing an offender.

"Wide Eye" was marketed both on the Internet and in print advertising.[278] Because this was a distilled spirits–based product, DISCUS reviewed the product advertising following a competitor's complaint.[279] The complaint alleged that the advertising for "Wide Eye" violated the DISCUS code provision that prohibits the promotion of the potency of an alcoholic beverage product.[280]

276. Code of Advertising Standards, *supra* note 272.

277. *See* Maggie Rosen, First Hello Kitty Wine on the Market, Decanter (June 4, 2009), http://www.decanter.com/news/wine-news/484739/first-hello-kitty-wine-on-the-market (last visited Jan. 21, 2011).

278. Constellations Brands, Inc.: Analysis of Proposed Consent Order to Aid Public Comment, 74 Fed. Reg. 31442, 31444 (July 1, 2009).

279. DISCUS, Semi-Annual Code Report: Code of Responsible Practices for Beverage Alcohol Advertising and Marketing 16 (Nov. 2008), available at http://www.discus.org/pdf/61367_DISCUS_WEB.pdf (Feb. 1, 2011).

280. *Id.*

Figure 3-22
Hello Kitty Sparkling Wine Label

Disney's plans to market a "Ratatouille"wine were canceled, while "Hello Kitty" wine continues to be imported.

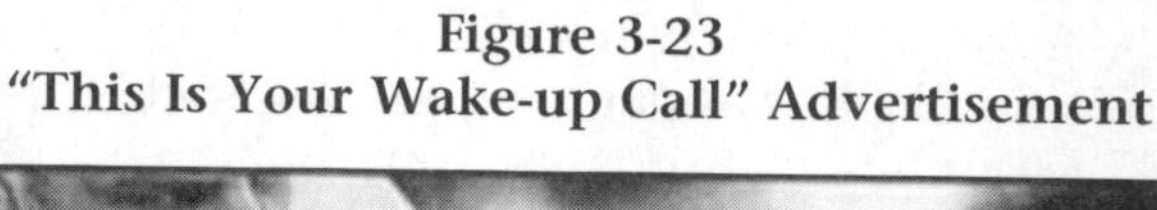

Figure 3-23
"This Is Your Wake-up Call" Advertisement

The DISCUS Code Review Board held that there was no violation regarding the "Wide Eye" brand name and that there was no violation of the Code for the tagline "This is your wake-up call." The tagline is shown in Figure 3-23.[281]

In the "Wide Eye" case, one consequence of failing to move fast enough following the finding of an Advertising Code violation was an action initiated by the FTC for making deceptive claims. The FTC decided to move ahead with its complaint despite the fact that the manufacturer of the product already had

281. *Id.*

decided to discontinue it.[282] Specifically, the FTC alleged that the manufacturer represented, expressly or implicitly, that consumers who drink "Wide Eye" will remain alert when consuming alcohol but had no reasonable basis to substantiate that representation when it was made.[283] A consent decree to prevent the manufacturer from engaging in similar practices in the future was issued following a public comment period.[284] But "Wide Eye" serves another purpose, one that illustrates the gauntlet that a winery's advertising must safely pass through. Notwithstanding label approvals, a winery's labels and advertising must comply with industry and agency standards that go beyond the immediate reach of the TTB.

Today's food packaging seems to overwhelm consumers with specific nutrition information. Figure 3-24 is an example. Low fat, low sodium, whole grains, fruit, nut, multigrain, fiber—consumers are misdirected to these claims rather than the information on the nutrition panel. Whether selling alcohol based on its caffeine content, its resveratrol levels, its carbohydrate or caloric content, or its alcoholic strength, these advertising claims all run the risk of exposing the products to closer scrutiny not only from the TTB and the FTC, but also from the very consumers who purchase these products.

1. NEW MEDIA

Wineries are rapidly utilizing social media websites to advertise their products. Social media websites can reach millions of users, and many sites provide tools that allow wineries to exclude underage viewers from entering their web areas. These gateways are, for the most part, effective in excluding underage visitors from the winery's social community. Social media sites bring with them the interesting phenomenon of social "policing," which, by all reports, appears to work quite effectively.

Although winery websites generally employ a mechanism that requires a visitor to affirm that he or she is over the legal drinking age before being able to view the rest of the content, these gateways are easy to foil by simply saying one was born in 1900 or thereabouts. Social media websites such as Facebook, on the other hand, do not rely on such age affirmation devices, but rather on gateways that wineries can raise to prevent underage viewers from joining the community. However, the social media sites generally do require users to post a profile that includes the user's age. It is the user's personal community that monitors the veracity of the user's profile. In other words, someone who says she is 16 years of age on Facebook, for example, is probably 16 years of age. Someone who says she is 21 when she is actually 16 will be pressured by her Facebook friends to come clean. This is not true in all instances, but so far advertising of alcoholic beverages on social media websites has not raised issues with the FTC so long as these gateways are deployed.

---

282. *See* In the Matter of Constellation Brands, Inc., a Corporation: FTC File No. 092 3035, FTC, http://www.ftc.gov/os/caselist/0923035/index.shtm (last visited Jan. 21, 2011).

283. Constellations Brands, Inc.; Analysis of Proposed Consent Order to Aid Public Comment, 74 Fed. Reg. at 31443.

284. *Id.*

Figure 3-24
Trader Joe's High Fiber Cereal

All of the industry advertising codes apply to electronic media but not with any great precision. Wine Institute will be reviewing its Advertising Code and updating it with new media provisions throughout the 2010–2011 fiscal year, but it has been encouraging an opt-in approach for social media sites, advising its members to require that visitors affirmatively grant permission before being connected to winery social media areas and receiving e-mails that may be generated by the social media site itself. Requiring visitors to opt in has additional advantages. Many social media sites will generate e-mails automatically based on some event that occurs on the site; for example, someone adds a winery event to a social media site and the site itself generates e-mails to the winery community, or someone adds a comment in a discussion thread and the site generates e-mails to all members of the community that have requested e-mail notification.

2. "DO NOT E-MAIL" LAWS

Most computer users hate spam, yet all accept the massive amounts of unsolicited e-mail as a necessary although an unwelcome part of being online, and they buy into services and software to manage it. Although the "do not call" registry that the FTC launched has worked well to prevent those telemarketer phone calls, attempts to control spam on a national level have not met with great success.[285] Yet today's electronic media and automatic e-mail generation features raise special issues with wineries because of the "do not e-mail" laws in Michigan and Utah. If winery e-mail marketers and social media users send advertising messages (or cause them to be sent) to e-mail addresses or domains listed in either state's child protection registry, they may face stiff penalties.

In 2005 Michigan and Utah enacted laws that create a children's protection registry in each state.[286] The purpose of both laws is to prohibit certain vendors from sending (and thereby prevent minors from receiving) electronic messages that advertise a product or service that a minor is prohibited by law from purchasing, viewing, possessing, or participating in. These communications include those for wine and other alcoholic beverages, tobacco products, and pornographic materials. The registries in Michigan and Utah allow parents and guardians in those states to register "contact points," including e-mail addresses, mobile phone numbers, fax numbers, and instant messaging user names, for inclusion in the registry. Once entered, these contact points are deemed protected and are thus off limits to such communications.

The Michigan and Utah laws apply to any communications made after August 1, 2005, and August 15, 2005, respectively. It does not matter if the mailing was previously requested or if users had previously opted in to receive future e-mails. Wineries are considered "senders," and in order to comply with the law, they must match their mailing lists against the registries on a monthly basis, for which they must pay both Michigan and Utah a per-e-mail-address

285. *See* FTC, National Do Not Email Registry: A Report to Congress, at i (2004), available at http://www.ftc.gov/reports/dneregistry/report.pdf (last visited Jan. 21, 2011).

286. *See What You Need To Know About The Michigan Children's Protection Registry*, Project MI Child, https://www.protectmichild.com/ (last visited Jan. 21, 2011); *Protect Your Family's Addresses*, Utah Kids Registry, https://www.utahkidsregistry.com (last visited Jan. 21, 2011).

fee. Violations can be costly; both states prescribe both civil and criminal penalties. Wineries can pay a fee to have their e-mail lists "scrubbed" by third-party providers.

E-mail addresses are, by nature, portable and not geographic (for example, a person may have moved from California to Michigan but kept the same e-mail address), so a winery utilizing an online service that features automatic e-mail generation must exercise caution if e-mail addresses are not kept up to date or have not been validated.

3. GREEN CLAIMS

The FTC's Green Claims Guide at 16 CFR §260, issued in 1992 and updated in 1998, has guided advertisers for many years, but advertisers increasingly have been making environmental claims. Wineries are claiming their own stake in the environmental movement and have advertised their investments in the environment. If wineries claim to be "carbon neutral" (see Figure 3-25), "sustainable," or "biodynamic," they must be able to substantiate those claims with competent and reliable evidence. Like other claims, green claims must be factually correct and supported by sound evidence.

Figure 3-25
Parducci Advertisement

Guidelines for the making of specific green claims — "compostable," "biodegradable," "recycled," "ozone safe," and other general claims — can be found in the FTC's Green Claims Guide.[287] These guidelines are currently under review. The making of unsubstantiated environmental claims is an increasingly relevant issue, as producers and retailers reposition their products to consumers as environmentally friendly. Although wineries have not yet been the subject of such action, the Sigg water container/BPA debacle[288] from 2009 illustrates that few things will destroy a company's reputation faster than a green misstep.

I. CONCLUSION

I am a wine label junkie and a Part 4 addict. It started out innocently enough, with forms to review, and class and type designations to determine; then, when I got to varietals and appellations, I was hooked. It is shameful, I know, but I must admit that I am totally in awe when I see a good wine label or advertisement. The goal of this chapter is to get you to say to yourself, "Gee, I did not know that!" If I have done that, I have accomplished my task. As should now be clear, every element of a wine's label has been scrutinized and been the subject of at least one federal rulemaking. Wine labels and the information on them are also part of a larger universe of regulations and laws than you might have first imagined. Indeed, label design is not only about art, but law as well.

I leave you with my favorite wine label, one from a bottle that was purchased at a local retail store when Wine Institute was investigating Moldovan wine. It is shown in Figure 3-26. On the brand label, it is a Pinot Noir. Turn the bottle around, and it is a Cabernet Sauvignon!

There are countless examples of beautiful wine labels, dramatically telling of the land that claims it and the people who bring it to you. Wine labels are a reflection not only of the wine and its geography, but also of the people behind the label. I have been blessed with a job that puts me in contact with winery owners and staff who have proven to me time and again that the quality of their products is surpassed only by the quality of their character.

---

287. Guides for the Use of Environmental Marketing Claims, FTC, http://www.ftc.gov/bcp/grnrule/guides980427.htm (last visited Jan. 21, 2011).

288. Sigg manufactures aluminum bottles. During the bisphenol A (BPA) controversy in 2008 and 2009, consumers abandoned plastic water bottles in favor of reusable metal bottles to reduce waste and their exposure to BPA. Sigg took advantage of this and strongly implied that its bottles were BPA-free, even though the liner for the bottles contained small amounts of BPA. Sigg eventually confirmed that BPA was used in the production of its bottle liners. Consumers reacted strongly, and Sigg eventually offered bottle replacements for all customers that purchased bottles with the BPA liners. Sigg still faces a number of lawsuits. *See* Bonnie Rochman, How Green Is Your SIGG Water Bottle?, Time, Oct. 27, 2009, available at http://www.time.com/time/health/article/0,8599,1932826,00.html (last visited Jan. 21, 2011).

Figure 3-26
Belle Terre Label

More and more, labeling and advertising are being influenced by large retailers, eager marketers, and consumer trends. Yet when winery members meet at Wine Institute to discuss label rules, it is clear to me that their goal is to establish reasonable label and advertising standards that embody the ethics of the wine industry and reflect their commitment as individuals and as businessmen to responsibility and quality.

CHAPTER 4

BUSINESS MODELS FOR MAKING WINE AND GROWING GRAPES

James W. Terry and Erik W. Lawrence

The traditional view of the wine business is that wine is produced at a winery estate complete with on-site vineyards and winery facilities. While this romantic image is still common in the modern winemaking world, it is only one of several ways to make and market wine. A prospective winemaker faces a myriad of choices for entering the industry, including whether to grow or buy grapes and whether to produce the wine independently, to have it custom made by a third party, or to buy and blend bulk wine.

This chapter begins with an examination of the most popular business models for wine production, including the purchase of an existing winery, the development of a traditional bricks-and-mortar winery, operation as an alternating proprietor or as a négociant, and producing wine through the use of a custom crush wine company. Whatever choice is made, the winemaker must comply with a unique set of local, state, and federal regulations and must obtain all required licenses and permits to produce and sell the wine.

The discussion then turns to the vineyard side of the winery equation; without grapes, wine cannot be made. As in the case of wine production, there are many options for obtaining grapes, including vineyard ownership (and possibly outside farm management), vineyard leasing, and the purchase of grapes. It is not unusual for a wine company to use all of these methods concurrently. We explore each of these options in turn, focusing on the large number of specific laws that make the wine sector different from other industries that also must acquire raw materials.

Because 90 percent of domestic wine is made in California, this chapter focuses on California law and applicable federal law. Although state requirements for vintners and grape growers vary, many of the key concepts are similar throughout the wine-producing regions of the country.

A. THE TRADITIONAL MODEL: BRICKS-AND-MORTAR WINERIES

There are many reasons an aspiring vintner might want to own and operate its own production facility, including tradition, quality control, the opportunity to conduct on-site sales, and even ego gratification. A key threshold decision for a vintner is whether to purchase raw land and build a new winery, purchase an existing winery, or lease an existing winery. While the development of a new winery may seem appealing, the process is almost always complicated and expensive as a result of local and state land use and environmental laws and regulations. Although purchasing an existing winery is generally more costly, it provides more certainty to a prospective purchaser because most of the groundwork with respect to regulatory compliance and local permitting has been completed. No aspiring vintner, however, should acquire a property, even an agricultural property, without first assessing its general suitability for winery development and the likelihood of obtaining local, state, and federal approvals, licenses, and permits for the development of the property and the production of wine.

1. DEVELOPING A NEW WINERY FACILITY

Following is a brief summary of the process of acquiring land to be used for the construction of a new winery facility.

a. The Acquisition Process

The first phase of developing a traditional bricks-and-mortar winery is the purchase of unimproved land. After identifying a target property for development, the vintner will negotiate the key terms of the purchase transaction with the seller (ultimately captured in a definitive purchase and sale agreement) and investigate the property to ensure that it is both legally and practically suited for its intended purpose.

NEGOTIATING THE SALE

Term Sheet or Letter of Intent. Rather than immediately negotiating a definitive purchase and sale agreement, which can be a lengthy and costly process, many parties choose to first negotiate and come to agreement on the material terms of the transaction (including price, payment terms, and due diligence period) with the use of either a term sheet or letter of intent (LOI). A term sheet is merely a summary of key terms with no commitment by either party to take further action. By contrast, an LOI typically contains an agreement between the parties to prepare and enter into a final, binding purchase and sale agreement according to the terms outlined in the LOI.

Purchase and Sale Agreement. The purchase and sale agreement (PSA) is the definitive document binding the parties to their respective obligations to purchase and sell the specific real property. The PSA describes every facet of the transaction, including the parties involved (i.e., the buyer and seller), the property being acquired, the purchase price, and the payment terms. The PSA also includes representations and warranties by both parties, which are statements of fact that the parties explicitly rely upon in carrying out the various terms of the transaction. The buyer often will seek representations and warranties from the seller about the property's condition and suitability for the buyer's intended use, while the seller will typically seek to make as few representations as possible, preferring to sell the property "as is."[1] The PSA should contain provisions establishing pre-closing conditions that must be satisfied before the purchaser is obligated to buy the property, including satisfactory completion of the due diligence review by the buyer. Counsel for either party must be extremely careful in drafting the PSA because its provisions can be the focus of litigation resulting from a broken transaction.

INVESTIGATING THE PROPERTY: DUE DILIGENCE AND TITLE REVIEW

The PSA should provide a time frame and process for the buyer and the buyer's attorney and consultants to investigate the property being acquired (the "due diligence period"). The purpose of the due diligence period is to enable the buyer to determine whether the property is compatible with the buyer's intended uses, discover any problems that warrant a price reduction or rejection of the purchase, and identify any warranties with respect to the property or conditions to closing that should be included in the final transaction.

Due diligence can be divided into two categories, legal due diligence and non-legal due diligence. Legal due diligence requires a review of applicable land use laws and zoning ordinances, which may require, among other things, compliance with a county-supervised process for obtaining a use permit to develop and operate the property as a winery. The buyer will be able to assess the project's feasibility after a thorough review of all local restrictions affecting not only the development of the property, but also the operation of the business on the property. In Napa County, for example, the Winery Definition Ordinance[2] regulates many aspects of winery operations, including grape sourcing, tours, tastings, special events, facilities size, facilities locations in relation to roads and streams, sales of non-wine items, and many other matters that are key to generating income. These types of land use restrictions vary widely from county to county in California, as discussed in Chapter 7.

Legal due diligence also includes a review of all matters affecting the title (i.e., legal right to possess the property) as revealed by all documents in the

---

1. Under California law, an "as is" provision puts the burden on the buyer to ascertain the condition of the property. Nevertheless, the seller must disclose all hidden material defects of which the seller has knowledge. Failure to do so constitutes fraud. *See, e.g. Lingsch v. Savage*, 213 Cal. App. 2d 729 (1963). Additionally, notwithstanding an "as is" provision, the seller must comply with other disclosure obligations imposed by statute. *See, e.g.*, Cal. Civ. Code §§1102-1102.17 (2009); Cal. Health & Safety Code §25359.7 (2009).

2. Napa County, Cal., Ordinance 947 (Jan. 23, 1990) (as amended by Napa County, Cal., Ordinance 1340 (May 11, 2010)) (codified at Napa County, Cal., Code §§12069-12072, 12418-12420, 12420.1, 12421-12422, 12602.3 (1993)).

public record affecting the property. Recorded restrictions and encumbrances may affect the use of or access to the property to the same degree as local ordinances. For instance, title research will uncover all easements (i.e., rights concerning use of or access to the property by another) that benefit the property, including access and utility easements that are necessary to fully utilize the property. The scope of the access easements that benefit the subject real property over the lands of another must be sufficiently broad to include winery uses, and any described roadways that are part of an easement must be wide enough to meet local standards for roadways serving winery production facilities.[3]

The reviewing lawyer must ensure that the parcel or parcels constituting the targeted property have been legally created under state law. A legal parcel is one that has been created in compliance with the requirements of the California Subdivision Map Act or other county-level ordinances predating the Subdivision Map Act.[4] In many instances, a legal parcel is a requirement for obtaining development rights for the property. Proof that the parcel was legally created also is typically required by a lender, which may be relying on the property as collateral. Finally, proper title review will expose any burdens or encumbrances on the property, such as conservation easements, view easements held by others over the subject property, rights of first refusal, and, if the property is surveyed, encroachments of structures and fences on the property. Each of these burdens or encumbrances can threaten the intended use of the property or adversely affect the property's marketability.[5]

Non-legal due diligence similarly requires an assessment of the property's basic compatibility with its intended uses. In a land acquisition for purposes of winery development, this process includes, among other things, an evaluation of access to public roads, site suitability for the construction of a processing facility, and access to a suitable and sufficient water source.

b. The Development Process

After completing due diligence and acquiring the property pursuant to the terms of the PSA, the prospective vintner faces new challenges in developing and building a suitable winery facility. For example, a vintner seeking to construct a traditional stand-alone winery must do so in a manner that complies with local zoning and land use laws.

---

3. For example, in Napa County, access driveways to off-site parking lots for wineries must be maintained at 18 feet for two-way traffic. *See* Napa County, Cal., Code §18.104.130(D)(12) (1993), available at http://library.municode.com.

4. *See generally*, Cal. Govt. Code §§66410-66499.37 (2009). In California, buyer's counsel should always ensure that the title policy includes a CLTA 116.7 endorsement, which establishes that the subject parcel was legally created under the Subdivision Map Act.

5. In California there are two basic types of title insurance: California Land Title Association (CLTA) basic coverage and American Land Title Association (ALTA) extended coverage. The primary distinction is that a CLTA policy is based only on a search of public records that affect the property. An ALTA policy is based on public records and a physical survey of the property, which will be used to evaluate the boundaries and any easements burdening or benefiting the property that only a physical inspection would reveal, and any interests in the property that may arise by adverse possession. For a more detailed discussion of title insurance policies, *see* CEB, California Title Insurance Practice (2d ed. 1999).

2. ACQUIRING AN EXISTING WINERY FACILITY

Many vintners choose to forgo the cost, uncertainty, and delays associated with building a new winery and instead purchase an existing winery facility. Frequently, the vintner who purchases a winery facility also purchases an established business with wine inventory, brands, other intellectual property, and ongoing liabilities, although this is not required. This section discusses some of the key business issues to be addressed in such acquisitions.

STRUCTURING THE ACQUISITION

There are several ways to acquire an existing winery business. The three most common methods are an asset purchase, an equity purchase, and a merger.

Asset Purchase. In an asset purchase, the buyer acquires some or all of the seller's assets, typically including real estate, and assumes none of the seller's liabilities (except those that the buyer chooses to accept). The aspiring vintner who wishes to acquire only a winery facility and not an ongoing business would purchase just the real estate assets, including the winery buildings and improvements. A buyer acquiring an entire bricks-and-mortar winery, including the business, typically would purchase the following assets: (1) real estate and improvements (i.e., the winery building); (2) equipment, including barrels and tanks, presses, crusher-destemmers, bottling equipment, pumps, hoses, and equipment and furniture in the tasting room and offices; (3) inventory, including bottled wine, bulk wine in tanks or barrels, bottles, corks, labels, and packaging materials; and (4) intellectual property, including trademarks, brands, and trade names used in the business and the associated goodwill of the enterprise.[6] The buyer also may choose to assume certain contracts, such as the winery's existing grape purchase agreements, distribution agreements, and winemaker consulting agreements.

An asset purchase is the most common structure for acquisitions in the wine industry today because buyers prefer the ability to carefully select which assets and which liabilities they will acquire and assume. The seller will remain responsible for all non-assumed liabilities. In addition to the control afforded the buyer in an asset purchase, this structure provides the buyer with the opportunity for advantageous tax treatment: the buyer's tax basis in many assets will "step up" to the allocated purchase price,[7] leading to higher depreciation and lower income taxes and lower capital gains taxes in the future.[8] The disadvantages associated with an asset purchase include a complicated

---

6. Often a winery's intellectual property is its most valuable asset.

7. In an asset sale, both the buyer and seller are required to file a Form 8594 with the IRS allocating the purchase price to seven separate asset classes. 26 U.S.C. §1060 (2006); 26 C.F.R. §1.1060-1(e)(1)(ii)(A) (2010). The allocation has real economic consequences to buyer and seller. For example, amounts allocated to a seller's covenant not to compete are taxed as ordinary income to the seller and are amortizable, intangible assets to the buyer.

8. Both buyer and seller should seek tax advice concerning the purchase price allocation. One common problem occurs when the amount allocated to accounts receivable and inventory (referred to as "hot" or "fast pay" assets) is less than those assets' fair market value. In such cases, the buyer may be forced to realize accelerated taxable income.

transaction structure requiring separate documentation for conveyance and assignment of various assets and obligations, the potential for application of the bulk sales law (which may be triggered by the sale of inventory),[9] and the seller's payment of sales tax.

Equity Purchase. In an equity purchase, the buyer purchases some or all of the current owner's interest in the winery, and the winery operations continue uninterrupted, with all existing assets and liabilities remaining in place. An equity purchase is the simplest acquisition structure because there is generally no separate documentation required to transfer assets and all contracts continue in effect (unless they contain a change-in-control provision, in which event the parties must obtain consent from the counterparty to the applicable contracts). The primary disadvantage of an equity purchase for the buyer is that all of the winery's liabilities continue in place, even those not disclosed to the buyer, which could result in some surprises for the new owners. In addition, if the buyer desires to acquire 100 percent of the winery's equity, a small minority shareholder could prevent the sale.[10] Finally, equity purchases, with limited exceptions, do not receive the same favorable tax treatment as asset purchases.

Merger. Mergers are extremely rare in the wine business. In a merger, one company, including all of its assets and liabilities, is merged into a surviving company, and the merged company ceases to exist. Depending on the facts and circumstances, mergers can be structured in many ways: a buyer may merge into the target company, the target company can be merged into the buyer, a buyer can form a subsidiary into which the target is merged ("forward triangular merger"), or the buyer can form a subsidiary that is merged into the target company ("reverse triangular merger"). The advantages of a merger are that it is simpler than an asset purchase, it is easier to structure as a "tax-free" transaction, and unanimous approval of the owners typically is not required (unless the owners of the target company are subject to an agreement that states otherwise, such as a shareholders' agreement, limited liability company operating agreement, or partnership agreement). As in the case of an equity purchase, the buyer will assume all unknown or undisclosed obligations of the merged company, and dissenting owners are afforded "dissenters' rights" by which they are permitted to protest the merger and demand payment in cash for their shares.[11]

THE ACQUISITION PROCESS

After the vintner has identified a target winery and determined the preferred acquisition structure, the acquisition process is quite similar to the raw

---

9. Cal. Comm. Code §§6101-6111 (2009).

10. Unless a shareholder is subject to a shareholders' agreement requiring him to sell under certain circumstances, he cannot be compelled to sell his shares. Therefore, a holdout shareholder can refuse to sell and prevent the buyer from acquiring 100 percent of the company's equity.

11. Cal. Corp. Code §§1300-13 (2009).

land acquisition process described above. However, a vintner acquiring a stand-alone winery often is acquiring an ongoing business in addition to real estate. The additional due diligence required in investigating the ongoing winery business will make the process longer and more complicated compared to a land-only transaction. If structured as an asset purchase, the vintner should closely examine all assets, contracts (e.g., grape purchase agreements, equipment leases, and distributor agreements) and liabilities in order to determine which assets to purchase and which contracts and liabilities to assume, and what third-party consents, if any, must be obtained. In equity purchases and mergers, the vintner should use the due diligence period to fully evaluate the winery's business operations, which may lead to a renegotiation of the purchase price.

Regardless of the structure, the buyer must comply with local, state and federal regulations governing the production and sale of alcoholic beverages in order to operate the winery. This involves applications for state licenses and federal permits. The process can be lengthy, so it should be started as early as possible. However, there also are some important ways to close a purchase and sale transaction while the license and permit applications are pending.

For example, in California, if the acquisition is structured as an asset purchase, the existing winery may transfer its state alcohol beverage licenses via a "person-to-person" transfer to the new winery owner. When the buyer files the application for a person-to-person transfer of the existing winegrower's license at that location, the California Department of Alcoholic Beverage Control (ABC) will issue a temporary permit upon request, allowing the new vintner to operate the acquired winery on an interim basis until the ABC formally approves the license transfer to the new owner.[12] On the federal side, the new vintner in an asset purchase must apply for and obtain a new federal basic permit. However, the new vintner will be permitted, following timely notice to the federal Alcohol and Tobacco Tax and Trade Bureau (TTB),[13] to operate under the prior owner's permit until the new permit issues, usually pursuant to the terms of a management agreement that will terminate when the TTB issues the new federal basic permit. If the acquisition is structured as an equity purchase, the licensed entity remains unchanged; only the underlying ownership changes. In such cases, the vintner must notify the state and federal agencies of the change in control, and the new control group must be qualified following the filing of appropriate applications.[14]

In addition to the notifications and applications that must be filed with the alcoholic beverage regulators in the state where the winery is located and at the federal level, wineries must notify state agencies in other states to which the existing winery ships its wines. Some states permit a simple name change on the license held by the existing winery in the case of an acquisition or change in control, but other states require a brand new application, complete

12. Cal. Bus. & Prof. Code §24045.5 (2009).

13. *See* 27 C.F.R. §1.44 (2010). New owners must file an application for a new basic permit with the TTB within 30 days after the transaction closes.

14. *Id.*

with personal affidavits from the company owners and supporting entity documentation. A state-by-state analysis of the applicable rules and regulations, along with discussions with state agency personnel, typically are required to determine the appropriate steps to ensure the winery's continued operation.

3. LEASING AN EXISTING WINERY FACILITY

An excellent choice for a vintner seeking to operate a traditional winery without expending the capital necessary to build or acquire a winery facility is to lease an existing winery. Most provisions of a winery lease are identical to those in standard commercial leases and are not discussed here. However, one important consideration for a vintner relates to the winery's tasting room. A tenant winery that builds a strong tasting room presence becomes well known for that specific location and typically generates significant retail sales. If the tenant winery must relocate after lease maturity, consumers may be confused or have difficulty finding the new location, which could adversely affect retail sales and the winery's brand equity both in the short and long term. In order to ensure long-term occupancy of the winery facility, winery tenants often will negotiate for an option to purchase the property. Such options can be part of the lease (a "lease option"). Although leasing may be highly desirable to vintners because of the cost savings involved, there are, in fact, very few winery facilities available for lease, so these opportunities are few and far between.

A vintner leasing a winery will be required to obtain its own federal and state licenses to produce wine on the leased premises and will have to confirm that the landlord has a use permit authorizing the winery use.[15]

4. LICENSES AND PERMITS FOR TRADITIONAL BRICKS-AND-MORTAR WINERIES

Regardless of whether a vintner develops a new winery or acquires or leases an existing winery, it will have to comply with the rules and regulations governing the production, sale, and distribution of alcoholic beverages imposed by state and federal agencies.

a. State Regulation

A vintner operating a traditional winery must comply with the home state's alcoholic beverage laws as well as rules and regulations imposed by other agencies within the state.

---

15. In California, use permits run with the land by operation of law. *See County of Imperial v. McDougal*, 19 Cal. 3d 505, 510 (1977); *Cohn v. County Bd. of Supervisors of L.A.*, 135 Cal. App. 2d 180 (1955). Thus, the tenant will benefit from the landlord's use permit. Obtaining the use permit in the first place typically is the landlord's responsibility.

CALIFORNIA DEPARTMENT OF ALCOHOLIC BEVERAGE CONTROL

In California any person desiring to produce and sell wine must apply for a Type 02 winegrower's license from the ABC.[16] Under the California Constitution and California's Alcoholic Beverage Control Act (ABC Act), power is vested in the state, through the ABC, to license the manufacture, importation, distribution, and sale of alcoholic beverages.[17] The winery's operations and activities must be specifically permitted by the ABC Act or its implementing rules and must be conducted by a licensed individual or entity unless a specific exemption applies.[18] A license issued under the ABC Act is a permit to do that which would otherwise be unlawful. Such a license is not a right but a privilege that can be suspended or revoked by administrative action (e.g., because of a violation of the ABC Act).

To obtain a Type 02 winegrower's license, the vintner must submit an application to the ABC including information regarding, among other things, the type of business entity that owns the winery; the amount and source of funds invested in the business; the personal and financial qualifications, along with fingerprints, of the officers, directors, managers, and persons holding a 10 percent or greater interest in the business, including their spouses; the tied-house interests of the owners, directors, and managers, regardless of the amount of their ownership interest; and the location, layout, and proposed uses of the subject premises.[19] The personal affidavits must include a statement that the affiant has not been convicted of a felony or, if such a statement cannot be made, an explanation of the facts and circumstances surrounding the felony conviction.[20] Before ABC will issue the Type 02 license, the applicant must show that it has complied with local permitting requirements and that the federal basic permit has been issued.

The privileges of a Type 02 winegrower license include the ability to (1) conduct wine tastings under certain specified conditions;[21] (2) sell wine to any person holding a license authorizing the sale of wine;[22] (3) sell wine to consumers for consumption off the premises, provided that at least 50 percent

16. Cal. Bus. & Prof. Code §23356 (2009); see list of common licenses and associated privileges available at http://www.abc.ca.gov/forms/abc616.pdf (last visited Jan. 17, 2011).

17. Cal. Const. art. XX, §22.

18. Cal. Bus. & Prof. Code §23300 (2009).

19. The ABC application package includes some or all of the following ABC forms, depending on the ownership structure: Form ABC-217, Application Questionnaire, disclosing, among other things, sources of funds and felony convictions; Forms ABC-208A and ABC-208B, Individual Personal Affidavit and Individual Financial Affidavit, respectively; Form ABC-253, Supplemental Diagram, with a drawing of the real property and an exterior view of the premises and surrounding area; Form ABC-257, Licensed Premises Diagram/Planned Operation, showing the floor plan, including overall dimensions of the licensed premises and description of proposed operations; Form ABC-069, Statement of Citizenship, Alienage, and Immigration Status for State Public Benefits and supporting documents; Form ABC-255, Zoning Affidavit, confirming compliance with local zoning; Form ABC-247, Statement Re: Residences, disclosing any residences within 100 feet of the proposed licensed premises; and Form ABC-251, Statement Re: Consideration Points, including nearby schools, hospital, churches, public playgrounds, parks, and youth facilities.

20. Cal. Bus. & Prof. Code §23952 (2009).

21. *Id.* §23356.1.

22. *Id.* §23356.

of the wine sold is produced on the winery's premises;[23] (4) operate a public eating place on the licensed premises and sell beers, wines, and brandies, regardless of source, in that eating place for consumption on the premises;[24] (5) manufacture grape brandy for fortification purposes only;[25] (6) provide samples to retailers in certain circumstances;[26] and (7) sell wines for export.[27]

The ABC requires a license at each location where the winery accepts orders. Therefore, if the winery will use a separate or additional office location for accepting and processing orders, or if a winery has an off-site retail room, a separate application for a duplicate winegrower license is required for each of these locations. Although there is no limit to the number of duplicate winegrower licenses that a winery may obtain for additional office locations, wineries may only have one duplicate winegrower premise where wine tastings occur and/or where wine is sold to consumers for consumption off the premises.[28]

Other wine-producing states, including Oregon[29] and Washington,[30] have laws and regulations covering the same subject matter that are similar to California's laws and regulations.

CALIFORNIA DEPARTMENT OF FOOD AND AGRICULTURE

In addition to the licensing requirements imposed by the ABC, a traditional bricks-and-mortar winery that purchases and crushes wine grapes, even if the grapes are from related entities,[31] for the purpose of making

23. *Id.* §23358.

24. *Id.*

25. *Id.* §23359. Note that a winegrower licensee must obtain a separate license if manufacturing grape brandy for any purpose other than fortification.

26. *Id.* §23386.

27. *Id.* §23356.

28. *Id.* §23390.

29. In Oregon, the Oregon Liquor Control Commission (OLCC) regulates the production and sale of wine. The stated mission of the OLCC is to promote the public interest through the responsible sale and service of alcoholic beverages. The OLCC derives its authority from Oregon's Liquor Control Act. To operate a winery in Oregon, the vintner must apply for and obtain a Winery License. The application process is similar to that of California and can take two to four months to complete. The Winery License allows an Oregon vintner to import, bottle, produce, store, transport, and export wines. Additionally, the Winery License allows vintners to sell wine at wholesale to the OLCC, licensees of the OLCC, and consumers at retail. *See* About the OLCC, http://oregon.gov/OLCC/about_us.shtml (last visited Jan. 17, 2011); Or. Rev. Stat. §§471.223, 311, 313 (2009).

30. In Washington, the Washington State Liquor Control Board (WSLCB) regulates the production and sale of wine under Washington's Alcoholic Beverage Control Law. The stated role of the WSLCB is to contribute to the safety and financial stability of local communities by ensuring the responsible sale, and preventing the misuse, of alcohol and tobacco. To operate a winery in Washington, the vintner must apply for and obtain a Domestic Winery License. The application process is similar to that of California and can take up to 90 days to complete. The Domestic Winery License allows a Washington vintner to produce wine and sell it directly to consumers and to retail and wholesale licensees. Additionally, the Domestic Winery License allows a Washington vintner to operate up to two off-site tasting rooms. *See* Washington State Liquor Control Board, Board Information, http://liq.wa.gov/general.aspx (last visited Jan. 17, 2011); Wash. Rev. Code §66.24.170 (2009).

31. For example, sometimes a vintner owns a vineyard and sells those grapes to a separate winery entity that it also owns.

wine must register as a processor with the California Department of Food and Agriculture (CDFA) and annually renew the processor's license.[32] Because processor license fees are based on the volume of grapes purchased, a winery that crushes grapes must provide a report to the CDFA by January 10 of each year describing the total tons of grapes purchased during the preceding harvest, broken down by reporting district, tons harvested, variety, and price paid per ton.[33] Failure to comply with the reporting requirement could lead to investigation and audit by the CDFA and, potentially, fines, suspension, or revocation of the processor's license. This information is also used annually to produce the CDFA Final Grape Crush Report, discussed in more detail below.

CALIFORNIA STATE BOARD OF EQUALIZATION

A winery, like any other California business that sells tangible personal property, must register for a seller's permit and pay sales tax to the California State Board of Equalization (BOE) on a quarterly basis.[34] Wineries also must pay an excise tax on wine that varies depending on the wine's percentage of alcohol.[35] However, as a result of a surtax that was imposed in California, the state excise tax rate for all still wines is $0.20 per gallon.[36] The BOE may require a winery to post some collateral, such as cash or a bond, to secure its excise tax payments, although this is not always required.[37]

b. Federal Regulation

A vintner operating a bricks-and-mortar winery must comply with federal laws governing the production, sale, and distribution of alcoholic beverages, including federal tied-house laws. The applicable federal permits must be issued by the TTB before winery operations can begin.

ALCOHOL AND TOBACCO TAX AND TRADE BUREAU

The TTB is charged with regulating the production and sale of alcoholic beverages under the Internal Revenue Code (IRC),[38] the Webb-Kenyon Act,[39] the Federal Alcohol Administration (FAA) Act,[40] and the Alcoholic Beverage Labeling Act.[41] The TTB's stated mission is to qualify and issue operating

---

32. Cal. Food & Agric. Code §§55521, 55861-55862 (2009).
33. *Id.* §55601.5.
34. Cal. Rev. & Tax. Code §§6051, 6066, 6452 (2009).
35. *See, e.g.*, Cal. Rev. & Tax. Code §32151 (2009). In other wine-producing states, the excise taxes are typically much higher. For example, in Oregon, for wines with less than 14 percent alcohol the tax rate is $0.67 per gallon, and for wines over 14 percent alcohol the tax rate is $0.77 per gallon. Or. Rev. Stat. §473.030 (2009). In Washington, for wines with less than 14 percent alcohol the tax rate is $0.87 per gallon, and for wines over 14 percent alcohol the tax rate is $1.72 per gallon. Wash. Rev. Stat. 66.24.210 (2009). *See also* State Taxes on Wine, available at http://www.taxadmin.org/fta/rate/wine.pdf (last visited Jan. 17, 2011).
36. *See* Cal. Rev. & Tax. Code §32220 (2009).
37. *Id.* §32102.
38. 26 U.S.C. §§5001-5008, 5010-5011, 5041-5045, 5051-5056, 5061-5062, 5064-5067 (2006).
39. 27 U.S.C. §122 (2006).
40. *Id.* §§201-208, 211 (2006).
41. *Id.* §§213-219(a) (2006).

permits, known as basic permits, to wineries, importers, and wholesalers of wine; secure and collect revenue from winery operations; protect consumers by ensuring that alcohol products are labeled, advertised, and marketed in accordance with applicable laws; and ensure fair trade practices in the wine industry.

A bricks-and-mortar winery that will be producing or blending wine is required to apply for and hold a federal basic permit under the FAA Act to produce and blend wine[42] and also to register as a Bonded Wine Cellar (BWC) under the IRC to operate the winery premises.[43] To obtain the BWC approval, a vintner must have a secure winery premise to protect the wine (and thereby preserve the government's revenue source) and obtain a wine bond from either an insurance company or some other surety, which acts as collateral to secure payment of the winery's estimated tax liability.[44] This is the derivation of the term "bonded wine premise." The applicant's excise tax liability is calculated based on the estimated number of gallons of wine produced and the particular types of wine produced.

As with the state licensing process, the vintner's applications to the TTB for a basic permit and a BWC registration must describe in detail the people who own, manage, and control the business, the premises, and the proposed operations. More specifically, the application provides the TTB with information regarding the personal and financial qualifications of the owners and various aspects of the operation such as the amount, source, and disposal of garbage and liquid waste; the source of power; operational noise sources; and discharges into navigable waters. Once the application is filed, the review and investigation process, which is run out of the TTB's National Revenue Center in Cincinnati, Ohio, can take two to four months. The TTB will conduct a telephone interview with the applicant and may conduct a field investigation to verify that (1) there is no hidden ownership of the applicant, a process that includes verification of the applicant's sources of funds; (2) the applicant is not prohibited from obtaining a permit;[45] (3) the applicant is likely to commence operations and comply with state and federal law;[46] (4) the government's source of revenue will be protected by adequately secured premises; and (5) the information contained in the application is accurate. When the TTB approves the applications, the vintner will receive a unique federal basic permit number and a unique IRC registry number.

After a winery begins operating, it must pay federal excise taxes on wine in accordance with, and at the times prescribed by, federal regulations.[47] A winery's federal excise tax is calculated based on wine type and alcohol

42. *Id.* §§203, 204.
43. 26 U.S.C. §5351 (2006).
44. *Id.* §5551.
45. A person is prohibited from obtaining a permit if such person (or in case of a corporation, any of its officers, directors, or principal stockholders), within five years prior to the date of application, has been convicted of a felony under federal or state law or, within three years prior to date of application, has been convicted of a misdemeanor under any federal law relating to liquor, including the taxation thereof. 27 C.F.R. §1.24(a) (2010).
46. *Id.* §1.24(b).
47. 26 U.S.C. §§5041-5045 (2006).

content.[48] A domestic winery that produces fewer than 250,000 gallons of wine may qualify for the Small Producer's Wine Tax Credit, which can reduce the excise taxes owed by as much as $0.90 per gallon.[49]

FOOD AND DRUG ADMINISTRATION

A new winery must register with the Food and Drug Administration (FDA) as a "food facility" pursuant to the Public Health Security and Bioterrorism Preparedness and Response Act of 2002 ("Bioterrorism Act")[50] before commencing wine production activities.[51] Congress passed the Bioterrorism Act following September 11, 2001, to enhance the security of the nation's food supply. The Bioterrorism Act imposes an ongoing recordkeeping obligation on food producers, including wineries. Wineries must establish and maintain, for two years, records that allow the FDA to identify the sources and recipients of their products to allow it to address credible threats to public health.[52]

B. "NON-TRADITIONAL" WINERIES

The acquisition and operation of a fully licensed and permitted bricks-and-mortar winery can be complicated, expensive, and time consuming. Two basic structures have evolved to allow new vintners to enter the wine industry without incurring these hefty acquisition and development expenses: the custom crush arrangement and the alternating proprietorship.

1. CUSTOM CRUSH

In a custom crush arrangement, an aspiring vintner (the client) hires a host winery to produce wine, from grapes provided by the client, to the client's specifications. The host winery, which holds a basic permit as a bonded winery, will handle all production, recordkeeping, and reporting to the TTB, with limited client oversight. In this arrangement, the client is not a bonded winery, does not own or lease a facility or equipment, and is not subject to any regulatory reporting requirements with respect to the winery premises. The client merely buys or grows grapes, delivers the crop to the host winery, and provides general instructions to the host winery for producing and bottling wine. In many cases, the client or a consulting winemaker hired by the client will closely supervise, and sometimes direct, production, but the client has no right

48. *Id.* §5041. The tax rate is calculated as follows: from 0.5 percent but not more than 14 percent alcohol, $1.07 per gallon; from 14 percent but not more than 21 percent, $1.57 per gallon; from 21 percent but not more than 24 percent, $3.40 per gallon; artificially carbonated, $3.30 per gallon; and sparkling, $3.40 per gallon. *Id.*

49. *Id.* §5041(c).

50. Pub. L. No. 107-188, 116 Stat. 594 (2002).

51. 21 U.S.C. §350d (2006).

52. 21 U.S.C. §350c (2006).

to make its own wine at the host winery; that has to be done by the host winery itself.

No fermentation or production licenses are required of the client, and it has no bonded premises. The client relies upon the production permits and bond of the host winery until the wine is bottled, labeled, and released by the host winery as "tax paid" (meaning that the federal excise tax on that wine has been paid, and the wine has been removed from the bonded premise) or the wine is transferred in bond to another bonded premise such as a warehouse.

A vintner may not bottle or sell wine until the TTB has approved the label for that wine by issuing a Certificate of Label Approval (COLA). Only the host winery as the bonded winery can apply for and obtain a COLA for the client's brands. Because the client is not a winery, the TTB will not allow the word "winery" as part of the client's brand or trade name (e.g., Client's Winery); this is considered misleading. The client can select some other brand or trade name, such as Client's Cellar.

In the custom crush model, before bottling and labeling the client's wine, the host winery will adopt the client's trade name by adding it to the host winery's federal basic permit.[53] The host winery first files and publishes a Fictitious Business Name Statement in the county in which it does business[54] and then files that statement with the TTB along with a written authorization from the client to the host winery to add the client's trade name as an "additional bottling trade name" on the host winery's basic permit. The label will reflect that the wine is "Produced and Bottled by [*Trade Name*]." For example, if the client intends to market wine under the brand Escalier Wines, the host winery will file and publish a Fictitious Business Name Statement indicating that the host winery is doing business as Escalier Wines. The host winery then will amend its federal basic permit to reflect Escalier Wines as one of its additional bottling trade names, specifying that it is for the account of the client. At that point, the wine label may report that the wine is "Produced and Bottled by Escalier Wines." Although the TTB could track the custom-produced wine back to the client, a consumer would find it difficult, if not impossible, to know that Escalier Wines is something other than a producing winery.

The custom crush arrangement allows aspiring vintners to enter the wine business and build a brand and distribution network with little capital investment and limited regulatory complications and responsibilities compared to brick-and-mortar wineries. The client has no need to purchase or lease property, facilities, and equipment. The client has no reporting responsibility to the TTB regarding the wine made for it and has no direct responsibility to pay wine excise taxes to the TTB upon release of the wine from the host winery's bonded premises. The client need not engage a winemaker, although many do so for purposes of quality control.

The custom crush model is commonly used in the industry. The Napa Valley Vintners Association reports that in 2010, 140 of its 400 vintner

53. Under 27 C.F.R. §4.35 (2010), the wine label must include the name of the entity bottling the wine, and that name must be identical to the name that appears on the producer's basic permit.

54. Cal. Bus. & Prof. Code §17915 (2009).

members practiced custom crush at a host winery.[55] While custom crush is often associated with small companies and new entrants into the industry, there are numerous large and very profitable companies that operate under the custom crush model. Those companies are most likely perceived by consumers as being traditional bricks-and-mortar wineries.

a. Federal and State Regulation of Custom Crush Arrangements

The state licensing sought by a client will vary depending on the client's marketing plan as well as its state of domicile. In California a client typically will obtain both a Type 17 Beer and Wine Wholesaler's License, which allows sales of wine to other licensees in the state for the purpose of resale, and a Type 20 Off-Sale Beer & Wine License, which, when held in conjunction with a Type 17 license, allows the sale of wine directly to California consumers in a retail sales outlet and/or by telephone, Internet, and mail order.[56] A client also must obtain a wholesaler's basic permit from the TTB, which authorizes the client to sell wine that has been made for it to other wholesalers and retailers. Finally, clients must comply with state and federal tied-house regulations.

Although a custom crush arrangement provides an easy entry into the wine business, it has several limitations. The holder of a Type 17 wholesaler's license in California may not conduct wine tastings.[57] The client has limited rights to sell wines direct to consumers in other states compared to licensed producers.[58] Additionally, many state tied-house exceptions are available only to licensed winegrowers and not wholesalers or retailers.

b. Custom Crush Agreements

Although the ABC and TTB do not typically scrutinize custom crush arrangements, the custom crush contract should reflect the regulatory underpinnings of the relationship. Because the client has no licenses or permits for producing, fermenting, processing, storing, bottling, or packaging wine, those activities must be performed by the host winery. It is the obligation of the host winery to store the wine in bond, maintain all required licenses, comply with all reporting requirements, and comply with applicable labeling requirements.

---

55. Author's conversation with Napa Valley Vintners, St. Helena, California (October 13, 2010).

56. The licensing required in a custom crush arrangement differs based on the state in which the host winery is located. For example, in Washington clients can obtain a Wine Distributor/Importer License, which allows for the sale of wine to other licensees for resale but does not allow for sales directly to consumers. *See* Wash. Rev. Code. §66.24.170 (2009). In Oregon clients can obtain a Winery License, exactly as if they operated stand-alone wineries. *See* Or. Rev. Stat. §471.223 (2009).

57. This is one of the privileges conferred on the holder of a Type 02 winegrower's license but not on the holder of a Type 17 Beer and Wine Wholesaler's License or a Type 20 Off-Sale Beer & Wine License. Cal. Bus. & Prof. Code §23356.1. A wholesaler may pour wine in certain limited circumstances where the client donates wine to a qualified charitable organization. *Id.* §24045.18.

58. Many states only allow wineries, not custom crush clients who are licensed as wholesalers and/or as retailers, to ship their wines directly to in-state consumers. *See, e.g.*, Tex. Alco. Bev. Code Ann. §§54.01, 54.03 (2010).

The contract should reflect that all of these responsibilities fall squarely on the host winery.

Custom crush contracts may allow a client to provide winemaking specifications to the host winery. Typically, title to the wine remains with the client at all times. The host winery then returns the finished wine to the client. The host winery is responsible for paying excise taxes upon release of the wine from the bonded premises, although contracts typically require the client to reimburse the host winery for the taxes paid. A host winery contracting with multiple custom crush clients must include all wine produced for all of its custom crush clients, as well as its own production, for purposes of calculating the federal excise tax and determining eligibility for the Small Producer's Wine Tax Credit.[59]

Because the winemaking responsibility necessarily falls on the host winery, which is required to produce wine according to the client's specifications, the custom crush contract tends to focus on risk allocation and liability protection for both parties. The host winery may seek broad indemnifications for its winemaking activities, coupled with releases of liability. Contracts generally recognize that a host winery may be liable for negligence, but the host winery often seeks to cap its liability in the amount of the bulk value of the wine, not its ultimate resale value. The host winery generally requests disclaimers of express and implied warranties of fitness, quality, and character of the wine; waivers of consequential damages; and disclaimers of responsibility for shrinkage and breakage, subject to negotiated limitations. Dispute resolution, arbitration, and mediation provisions are common.

Custom crush contracts generally provide that fees charged by the host winery are based on volume of production measured by tons, gallons, or cases. For example, a custom crush agreement might provide for specific services such as crushing, fermenting, and pressing at a fixed price per ton of fruit processed. Additional services typically are charged on a volume basis, such as barrel or cased goods storage for a monthly fee per barrel or case.

The host winery should obtain a security interest in the customer's wine under the California Commercial Code to secure the customer's payment obligations and should file a financing statement. The host winery also should conduct a UCC search and, at a minimum, obtain warranties and representations from the client with respect to competing liens such as grower's liens and liens of lenders, along with a representation by the client that its grapes and wine are free of encumbrances.

c. The Négociant Model

The term "négociant" generally refers to a producer who purchases bulk wine from different sources, blends that wine, and bottles the blend under its own label. The practice originated in the Burgundy region of France and now serves as the business model for many producers in the United States.[60]

---

59. The host winery's total production also is relevant to compliance with any production (gallonage) limitations in the host winery's use permit.

60. Karen Macneil, The Wine Bible 196-197 (2001).

Most négociants obtain licensing identical to that required for custom crush clients. Vintners are attracted to the négociant model for good reason. It requires little to no investment in facilities and equipment. Particularly in bad economic times, the négociant can obtain high-quality wine at low prices and react quickly to changing market conditions. On the other hand, the négociant may find it difficult to make (blend) a consistent product from vintage to vintage without a secure long-term grape source.

Wineries choose to sell bulk wine for many different reasons. In some cases, the winery holds more wine in inventory than it can sell at acceptable prices. In other cases, the bulk wine being sold does not meet the winery's quality standards. Therefore, wineries that sell bulk wine to négociants should ensure that the bulk wine sales agreement includes a confidentiality provision ensuring that the wine sold is never identified as that of the seller, as well as a liquidated damages provision quantifying the measure of damages in the event of breach by the buyer.[61]

2. ALTERNATING PROPRIETORSHIP

In an alternating proprietorship arrangement, an existing operating winery with excess production capacity (the "host winery") allows another wine producer (the "alternating proprietor"), and sometimes several other producers, to produce wine at the facility. This model is also commonly known as a "winery within a winery." The alternating proprietorship model is essentially a collaboration of independent bonded wineries, including the host winery, operating under one roof. The host winery and all alternating proprietors are separately bonded wineries, each responsible for its own production, recordkeeping, excise tax payments, and label approvals.

The alternating proprietorship model is conceptually similar to a residential condominium development consisting of commonly owned areas for the enjoyment of all condominium owners as well as separate, independently owned living spaces. In an alternating proprietorship, each bonded winery may have a designated area dedicated to the exclusive use of the winery for storage of its wine. The host winery and each alternating proprietor will also share the production facilities and winemaking equipment of the host winery. Since only one winery may use a particular tank or bottling line at any given time, the use of the facilities alternates between the host winery and the alternating proprietor. The shared production facilities and dedicated areas together comprise the bonded wine premises of the alternating proprietor, separate and distinct from the bonded wine premises of the host winery and those of other alternating proprietors.

61. If a winery sells bulk wine without a written agreement, it is not without recourse if the buyer discloses the winery's identity. Common law and federal trademark rules prevent unlicensed use of the winery's trade name. In California and many other states, the right to publicity prevents the unauthorized commercial use of a winery's name. *See, e.g.*, Cal. Civ. Code §3344(a) (2009).

a. Federal and State Regulation of Alternating Proprietorships

In states that allow alternating proprietorships, such as California, Oregon, Washington, and Colorado, the alternating proprietor is required to obtain its own state licenses for the production and sale of wine. For example, in California, an alternating proprietor is required to obtain a Type 02 winegrower license. An alternating proprietor also must obtain its own federal basic permit and is solely responsible for its own winemaking, recordkeeping, and reporting to the ABC, TTB, and other governmental agencies, including the payment of excise taxes.

New vintners are attracted to the alternating proprietorship for a variety of reasons. If the alternating proprietor's production is less than 250,000 gallons, it will qualify for the Small Producer's Wine Tax Credit.[62] Additionally, as the holder of a winegrower's license in California, the alternating proprietor enjoys the same rights and privileges as the bricks-and-mortar winery holding the same license, including the right to conduct wine tastings and operate an off-site tasting room. Consumers looking at an alternating proprietor's wine label typically would not know that the winery is anything other than a stand-alone, traditional winery. Finally, the alternating proprietor has no obligation to comply with burdensome and expensive local regulations and use permit processes, that being the responsibility of the host winery.

TTB SCRUTINY

Alternating proprietorship arrangements are specifically permitted by federal regulations.[63] However, because alternating proprietors as independent producers are eligible for the Small Producer's Wine Tax Credit, which has the potential of reducing revenue to the government, the TTB will carefully scrutinize an alternating proprietorship arrangement to verify that the alternating proprietor is truly acting as a separately bonded winery rather than as a client of the host winery under a custom crush arrangement.[64] In the custom crush situation, the excise tax is paid by the host winery, which, when it combines its own production with that of all its clients, might not qualify for the credit.

The TTB also wants to ensure that the alternating proprietor will itself engage in wine production. The TTB will consider the alternating proprietor's business history and development plans to demonstrate that commitment. If the alternating proprietor intends to rely on the host winery to make its wines and run its winery operations, the TTB will refuse to issue a bonded winery basic permit to that person or entity.

---

62. 27 C.F.R. §24.278 (2010).
63. *Id.* §§24.135, 24.136.
64. TTB, Alternating Proprietors at Bonded Wine Premises, TTB Industry Circular No. 2008-4 (Aug. 18, 2008), §6(a), available at http://www.ttb.gov/industry_circulars/archives/2008/08-04.html. TTB Industry Circular No. 2008-4 entirely supersedes TTB Industry Circular No. 2003-7.

SCOPE OF THE BONDED PREMISES

Central to its function of securing and collecting revenue from winery operations, the TTB carefully regulates the definition and delineation of the bonded premises of each alternating proprietor. As noted above, an alternating proprietor's bonded premises must include the alternating production areas where the wine is produced by each proprietor and typically also a dedicated area where the alternating proprietor stores its wine in barrels, bottles, or finished cases. The shared and dedicated areas together constitute the bonded premises of each alternating proprietor.

The alternating proprietor must report the movement of the wine into and out of its bonded premises, even if the transfer is from one alternating proprietor to the host winery or between alternating proprietors. In order to facilitate such reporting and enable the TTB to locate and identify the wines of each alternating proprietor, the TTB may require visual or structural delineation of the dedicated premises of the alternating proprietor(s) and the host winery. This can involve signage or even lines on the ground or, depending on the design of the facility, fencing or other physical separation between the dedicated areas.

b. The Alternating Proprietorship Agreement

During its investigation and analysis of an alternating proprietor's application for a federal basic permit, the TTB will pay close attention to the written agreement between the alternating proprietor and the host winery. The alternating proprietorship agreement should expressly state that the alternating proprietor is responsible for its own production, recordkeeping, reporting, labeling, and payment of taxes, independent of the host winery.[65] The agreement should provide that the alternating proprietor will pay the host winery directly for its floor space, equipment use, and, where applicable, personnel time and material consumed if the host winery is to provide services or materials. Pricing should be structured around rental of space and rates for specific services rendered.[66] Payment to the host winery should not be based on volume rates (tons, gallons, or cases), a method of charging more appropriate for custom crush agreements.[67] The TTB reviews all of these factors to determine if the arrangement is a true alternating proprietorship and not a custom winemaking relationship in disguise.

Although it is acceptable for the alternating proprietorship agreement to provide for the use of the host winery's employees for certain services, it must be clear that such employees will be acting solely at the alternating proprietor's direction or be hired directly by the alternating proprietor.[68] The contract should clearly state that the alternating proprietor is in control of, and responsible for, bottling under its permit, storing of bulk wine in its premises, and

65. *See* Industry Circular No. 2008-4, §6(a), *supra* note 64.
66. *Id.*
67. *Id.*
68. *See* Industry Circular No. 2008-4, §6(c), *supra* note 64.

removal of wine from the bonded premises.[69] The alternating proprietor must have absolute access to its bonded premises and its wine at all times.[70] The agreement also must allow the TTB unfettered right of access to the bonded premises.[71]

3. THE UNINTENTIONAL VINTNER: GROWER CUSTOM CRUSH

When grapes are in over-supply (or under-demand), many growers with unsold grapes choose to convert those grapes to wine to preserve their economic value. A grower without winery facilities must make arrangements with a winery to process its fruit. Commonly, the grower will deliver grapes to the winery, the winery will process and market the resulting bulk wine, and the grower and winery will split the profits, if any, when the wine sells. The legal issues arising out of this structure depend on whether the arrangement is characterized as a sale of wine or a sale of grapes.

a. Sale of Wine?

In some instances, the parties intend that the winery merely act as a processor and never take title to the grapes or bulk wine. Yet sharing profits implies that the winery and the grower share ownership of the wine, and growers that do not regularly produce and sell wine typically do not hold the requisite state licenses and federal permits to sell wine.

Recognizing how common this situation is, the California legislature in 1983 created the Type 29 Winegrower's Storage license specifically to address this circumstance.[72] The Type 29 license allows a grower to hire a winery to ferment its grapes and store the resulting bulk wine at the winery, and it also allows that grower to sell the bulk wine in California to wineries and blenders, but not to wholesalers or retailers. Under the Type 29 license, the grower may sell only wine produced from grapes that he has grown. With respect to federal permits, if the grower is engaged in the business of purchasing wine for resale at wholesale and if the grower has control over activities normally associated with wholesaling (price determination, buyer selection, and marketing), the grower may be required to obtain a wholesaler's basic permit.

b. Sale of Grapes?

If the transaction is not characterized as a sale of wine, it may constitute a sale of grapes by the grower to the winery. This poses a legal problem because the grape prices to be paid by the winery generally will not be determined until the wine is sold — many months, if not years, after the grape harvest. The Clare Berryhill Grape Crush Report Act of 1976 (the "Berryhill Act")[73] requires

---

69. *Id.*
70. *See* Industry Circular No. 2008-4, §6(d), *supra* note 64.
71. *Id.*
72. Cal. Bus. & Prof. Code §23358.3 (2009).
73. Codified at Cal. Food & Agric. Code §55601.5 (2009).

every processor who crushes grapes to deliver a report to the Secretary of Food and Agriculture by January 10 following harvest indicating the total number of tons of grapes purchased in California during the preceding harvest and the final prices of those grapes.[74] A violation of these provisions is a crime. Unless the grower and the winery can agree on the price of the grower's grapes before January 10 following harvest, the grower should obtain a Type 29 license.

C. GRAPE SOURCING

It is obvious that a winery must obtain grapes before it can produce wine.[75] What is not obvious are the many available choices. A winery may buy raw land and develop a vineyard, buy an existing vineyard, lease raw land and develop a vineyard, lease an existing vineyard, or buy grapes from a grower. Each of these options is discussed below.

1. PURCHASING RAW LAND OR AN EXISTING VINEYARD

a. Raw Land

Developing a vineyard from raw land allows the winery ultimate control over varietal selection and viticultural techniques. The winery will have a long-term stable source of fruit perfectly suited to its chosen wine style and marketing plan. There are many downsides to this approach, however. First, the winery must devote significant financial resources to acquiring, developing, and maintaining land and improvements. Second, it usually takes three to four years before a vineyard produces a commercially viable crop. Add this to the one to four years it takes to convert grapes into finished product, and the winery clearly may have to wait up to eight years before it realizes any cash return on its investment. Finally, wine is a consumer product, and tastes change rapidly. The winery runs the risk that whatever variety it plants now will fall out of favor in the future. Nevertheless, many wineries choose this alternative.

b. Existing Vineyard

To save time and avoid the expense of developing a vineyard (development costs range from $30,000 to $250,000 per acre),[76] a winery may choose to

74. *Id.* §55601.5(g) provides that "all grape purchase contracts entered into on or after January 1, 1977, shall provide for a final price, including any bonuses or allowances, to be set on or before the January 10 following delivery of the grapes purchased. Any grape purchase contract entered into in violation of this subdivision is illegal and unenforceable." The Berryhill Act defines "purchase" as "the taking by sale, discount, negotiation, mortgage, pledge lien, issue or reissue, gift or any other voluntary transaction creating an interest in property." *Id.* §55601.5(i)(6). The Berryhill Act further defines "sale" as the passing of title from the seller to the buyer for a price. *Id.*

75. Alternatively, the winery can purchase bulk or bottled wine.

76. A number of variables affect the cost of development, including the location of the vineyard (flat valley floor vs. steep hillside), the availability of water (development of a reservoir may be required), and the desired viticultural practices.

purchase a mature vineyard. The winery will gain immediate possession of a crop that it can use to produce wine and will have control over farming practices. The downside is that a mature vineyard will cost more per acre than raw land and typically will have a shorter useful life than a newly developed vineyard. Additionally, the buyer is limited to the grape varietals and vineyard design (including, for instance, orientation of and spacing between the vines) that the seller selected.

c. Acquisition Process

The process of acquiring raw land or an existing vineyard is quite similar to acquiring land for winery development. The parties typically negotiate the key terms in a term sheet or LOI, which the parties will incorporate into a definitive purchase and sale agreement. The buyer, together with his advisors and counsel, will conduct a due diligence review of the property.

There are also several issues the buyer must focus on during due diligence that are unique to vineyard (or future vineyard) acquisitions.

d. Legal Due Diligence Concerns

ZONING

Counsel for the buyer should determine how the subject parcel is zoned. Zoning restricts the uses of a parcel and places other restrictions on the property, which may include minimum setbacks, water and septic requirements, and height restrictions for structures. In Napa County, California, for example, vineyard property is most frequently located in areas zoned as either Agricultural Preserve (AP)[77] or Agricultural Watershed (AW).[78] Each zoning district imposes unique restrictions on the uses to which a property may be put.

MATERIAL CONTRACTS AND WATER RIGHTS

The buyer's attorney should review material contracts that affect the land, particularly if the buyer is acquiring an existing vineyard. Material contracts include, but are not limited to, loan documents, grape purchase agreements, farming agreements, and equipment leases. The buyer should determine whether it wants to assume any of the existing contracts. The buyer's attorney should review the desirable contracts to determine whether the seller can assign its rights and obligations under those contracts to the buyer and, if so, whether the seller must consent to the assignment. The buyer's attorney must provide in the PSA that the seller's written consent to assignment of all contracts to be assumed is a condition to closing the transaction. Buyer's counsel also should obtain documents related to water rights, which are particularly important to agricultural operations in California. These rights are reflected in

---

77. Napa County, Cal., Code §§18.16.010-18.16.040 (1993).
78. *Id.* §§18.20.010-18.20.040.

state permits granting appropriative water rights,[79] reservoir permits, common law riparian rights,[80] and water pipeline and sharing agreements.[81]

NEIGHBORS

In agricultural areas, an experienced local land use attorney should know or ascertain the attitude and demeanor of the owners of neighboring parcels. This knowledge will be very useful if the buyer intends to seek approval to develop the property in the future and if the approval process will involve a public hearing and comment.

TITLE ISSUES

Buyer and buyer's counsel should examine whether the property is subject to any so-called Williamson Act contract or conservation easements during the title review process.

Williamson Act Contracts. It is very common for agricultural land in California to be subject to a Williamson Act contract.[82] In a Williamson Act contract between a property owner and the county, the property owner agrees to devote the property to agricultural use in exchange for lower property taxes. Typically, cancellation of such contracts requires 10 years' notice. Material breach of a Williamson Act contract could lead to stiff penalties, including a fine of up to 25 percent of the fair market value of the land and improvements.[83] Williamson Act contracts are recorded against the subject property and should therefore be discovered during title review.

Conservation Easements. The title review may reveal a conservation easement against the subject property. A conservation easement is created when a property owner donates or sells an easement, typically to a local nonprofit land trust, pursuant to which the landowner agrees to limit development on some

---

79. The California Water Resources Control Board was created in 1967 to oversee water allocation and water quality protection. Cal. Water Code §§13100-13197.5 (2009).

80. *See, e.g., In re Determination of Rights to Water of Hallett Creek Stream Sys.*, 44 Cal. 3d 448, 464 (1988) (citing *Lux v. Haggin*, 69 Cal. 255 (1886)).

81. These agreements generally are recorded and are discovered in connection with title review.

82. The California Land Conservation Act of 1965 (Cal. Gov't Code §§51200-51297.5 (2009)), commonly referred to as the Williamson Act, enables local governments to enter into contracts with private landowners for the purpose of restricting specific parcels of land to agricultural or related open-space use. In return, landowners receive property tax assessments that are much lower than normal because they are based upon farming and open-space values as opposed to full market value. Local governments receive an annual subvention of forgone property tax revenues from the state via the Open Space Subvention Act of 1971. As of 2005 more than half of California's 30 million acres of agricultural lands and open space was protected under the Williamson Act, including over 70 percent of the state's prime farmland. See California Dep't of Conservation, California Department of Conservation Celebrates 40 Years of the Williamson Act (2005), NR 2005-12, available at http://www.consrv.ca.gov/index/news/2005%20News%20Releases/NR2005-12_Williamson_Act_at_40.htm.

83. Cal. Gov't Code §51250 (2009). Williamson Act amendments enacted in 2003 (A.B. 1492, Cal. Assemb. (Cal. 2003)) provide for enhanced penalties for material breach of a Williamson Act contract.

or all of a particular parcel.[84] Limitations imposed by conservation easements bind the landowner and its successors in interest in perpetuity so long as the land is in private hands. Buyer's counsel should review conservation easements of record carefully to evaluate compatibility with the client's intended uses and development plans, including future land divisions or lot line adjustments. Buyer's counsel should pay special attention to the rights of any third-party land trusts to inspect, police, and enforce the terms of the easement.

e. Non-Legal Due Diligence Concerns

When evaluating an existing or potential vineyard property, the buyer should investigate, among other things, the site's soil quality, slope (particularly if excessive slope is a hindrance to development),[85] access roads, reservoirs and other water sources, and visible environmental hazards. The buyer should engage experts to evaluate the quality of the water source, the site's drainage, and the potential for discharge of waste and storm water.

The buyer who is acquiring an existing vineyard should obtain very detailed information about the property prior to closing the transaction. Specifically, the buyer should identify the vineyard developer, current farming company, and any viticultural consultants and, if possible, interview those people to learn about the vineyard. Additionally, the buyer should obtain an accurate count of producing and missing vines, vineyard maps, viticultural reports, and climate logs along with information such as the year the vineyard was planted or replanted, the varietal clone and rootstock, vine spacing, trellis system, irrigation system and schedule, soil preparation and amendments, ongoing soil or drainage issues, nutritional inputs, pest and disease issues, pesticide use reports, annual petiole analysis, harvest dates, yield history, and grape juice analysis. All of this information will provide the buyer with a realistic picture of the vineyard's health and performance and, depending on what is discovered, may result in a renegotiation of the purchase price.

2. LEASING RAW LAND OR AN EXISTING VINEYARD

Many vintners lease raw land for vineyard development or lease an existing vineyard rather than purchase vineyard property. Vintners and landowners have unique motivations for entering a lease, which become relevant when they negotiate the lease terms.

---

84. In addition to an altruistic desire to preserve agricultural and open space, a property owner may be motivated to grant a conservation easement by various tax benefits. For instance, the taxpayer may claim an immediate federal income tax deduction based on various factors, including a decrease in the property's value resulting from the imposition of restrictions (26 U.S.C. §170 (2006)), save substantially on federal estate taxes (*id.* §2031(c)), claim an immediate deduction against California income taxes (Cal. Rev. & Tax. Code §24357 (2009)), and receive California income tax credits (Cal. Pub. Res. Code §§37000-37042 (2009))

85. *See* Napa County, Cal., Code §18.108.060 (1993).

a. Vintner's Motivation to Lease

Purchasing raw land or an existing vineyard requires a large amount of capital. To obtain this capital, a buyer must either use its own cash, borrow, take on equity investors, or implement some combination of the above. Most vintners do not have enough cash to purchase land without outside financing, and may be adverse to the liability associated with borrowing money and the lack of control associated with additional equity investors. When capital limitations make acquiring a vineyard unattractive, a vintner who wants to control how his grapes are farmed should consider a vineyard lease. Importantly, a vintner who leases a vineyard is allowed to use the term "Estate Bottled" on his wine label, a benefit not allowed if the vintner were to purchase grapes under a typical grape purchase agreement.[86] Many vintners believe that the term "Estate Bottled" can increase the prestige and bottle price of wine.

b. Landowner's Motivation to Lease

An owner of raw land may lack the capital to develop the land into a vineyard. In a vineyard development lease, it is the vintner/tenant that pays the development costs and ongoing farming costs as well as other expenses typically associated with land ownership such as real property taxes, assessments, and insurance.

The landowner may be motivated by the opportunity to convert nonproductive raw land into income-producing property. During the lease term, the vintner/tenant will pay the landowner rent in the form of fixed annual payments or a certain percentage of the crop proceeds. At the end of the lease term, ownership of the developed vineyard and related improvements typically reverts to the landlord.

c. A Side Note on Sale-Leaseback Transactions

A common real estate transaction that is relatively new to the wine industry is the "sale-leaseback."[87] In these transactions, a real estate owner sells property to a buyer and immediately leases the property back for its own use. This option is attractive to vineyard and winery owners that need cash now, which they receive in the form of the purchase price, but who want to continue using the real estate for their vineyard and/or winery operations. While property owners can obtain bank loans for needed capital, banks will lend only up to a certain percentage of the property's value (60-65 percent is typical). A sale-leaseback is sometimes viewed as a method for obtaining

---

86. A winery may use the term "Estate Bottled" on its label if 100 percent of the wine came from grapes grown on land either owned or controlled by the winery, which must be located in a viticultural area that is identified on the label. 27 C.F.R. §4.26(a) (2010). "Controlled by" refers to property on which the winery has the legal right to perform, and does perform, all of the acts common to viticulture under the terms of a lease or similar agreement of at least three years duration. Id. §4.26(c).

87. See, e.g., Lilly Vitorovich, Diageo Signs Sale, Leaseback Wine Deal in US, Dow Jones Newswire, June 24, 2010, available at http://www.advfn.com/news_Diageo-Signs-Sale-Leaseback-Wine-Deal-In-US_43355949.html.

100 percent financing. In most sale-leaseback transactions, the seller/tenant will retain an option to purchase the property at the end of the lease term at a predetermined price or according to a pricing formula.

d. Process

Most vineyard leases are long-term commitments and are entered only after long periods of investigation and negotiation. Therefore, the process is very similar to a purchase. Often the parties will negotiate a term sheet or LOI to agree upon the material terms before negotiating all the details of the vineyard lease.

e. Unique Vineyard Development Lease Elements

Although a vineyard development lease and a lease of an existing vineyard are structured similarly, there are key distinctions between them. A development lease requires the tenant to spend significant sums early in the lease term to develop the vineyard. Additionally, the newly developed vineyard will not produce a commercially viable crop for several years. Accordingly, a development lease will generally have a longer term than an existing vineyard lease, allowing the tenant to recoup his investment over time. Often, in the first three to five years of a development lease, rent will be reduced or abated because of the development expenses and negative cash flow that the tenant experiences. Commonly, a development lease is contingent on the tenant's ability to obtain proper permits for the intended use. A development lease ordinarily will include additional provisions describing the construction plans and costs.

f. Subdivision Map Act Concerns (California Only)

In many cases, the landowner will continue living in a residence on the leased parcel while leasing the vineyard portion. In California, leasing a parcel of real property while retaining a portion of that parcel is considered a "subdivision" of the parcel, in violation of California's Subdivision Map Act.[88] If the lease is for "agricultural purposes," however, the Subdivision Map Act does not apply, and the landlord may retain an interest in a homesite on the leased premises.[89] Counsel for the landlord, therefore, should ensure that the tenant will use the leased premises only for agricultural purposes. If the landlord will retain a homesite, the lease should describe the method of allocating water between the residential and agricultural areas and provide for access to the home without interfering with farming activities.

g. Lease Term Issues

Vineyard leases, especially vineyard development leases, have lengthy terms. In California, the term of the lease can have adverse property tax consequences. If the lease term is 35 years or more, including options to extend the

88. Cal. Gov't Code §66424 (2009).
89. *Id.* §66412(k).

term, the lease transaction will constitute a "change in ownership," triggering a reassessment of the property by the county assessor and a resulting increase in real property taxes.[90] Leases often allocate property tax payment responsibilities between the vineyard and residential areas, or they may allocate any increase in property taxes to the tenant.

h. Rent Issues

Vineyard lease rates are often calculated as a fixed amount per acre, paid annually. Because the leases often are for long terms, the landowner typically will require adjustments to the rental amount over time to protect against inflation. Some vineyard leases include a standard adjustment based on changes in the consumer price index (CPI). More specific to vineyard leases are adjustments based on changes in average grape prices as published in the annual California Grape Crush Report.[91]

Vineyard leases also may involve the calculation of rental payments as a percentage of the proceeds of the crop plus a minimum fixed payment per acre. Such a lease, generally known as a "crop share," allows the landlord to enjoy a greater return in productive years while accepting reduced payments in years during which grape prices are down or yields are low. The sharing of the risk in the context of a material participation lease may enable the landlord to take advantage of special use valuations of the property, resulting in reduced estate taxes after death.[92]

i. Vineyard Improvements

Most often, vineyard improvements such as vines, stakes, trellising, and irrigation systems remain with the landlord at the end of the lease term. In vineyard development leases, the tenant may seek some compensation at the end of the lease term for the capital invested in these improvements, depending upon the length of the term and whether the tenant has the continuing obligation to maintain the vineyard in good condition, including vine replacement obligations through the end of the lease.

3. PURCHASING GRAPES

For some vintners, purchasing grapes is their only means of supply. Other vintners rely on purchased grapes to supplement the harvest from the

---

90. Cal. Rev. & Tax Code §61(c) (2009).

91. The California Grape Crush Report is published annually by the USDA National Agricultural Statistical Service, California Field Office. The report publishes results from the prior harvest, including total tons harvested and price per ton, by district and grape varietal. The report is available at http://www.nass.usda.gov.

92. Under 26 U.S.C. §2032A (2006), taxpayers may lower the value of agricultural property by up to 75 percent for estate planning purposes. As one of several qualification tests, the taxpayer transfering the property at his or her death must have "materially" participated in operating the farm. The taxpayer can satisfy this test if he or she substantially participates in management decisions relating to production. A properly drafted material participation lease agreement should provide for the landlord's material participation in such decisions.

vineyards that they own or lease. Grape purchase agreements vary from simple one-year agreements intended to fill a temporary need to multi-year contracts intended to create a lasting bond between grower and vintner.

As with many farmers, a culture exists among some grape growers, especially old-timers, to do business "on a handshake," dispensing with written agreements and avoiding the cost of engaging legal counsel. These trusting growers should be aware, however, that in most wine-producing states, a contract for the sale of goods, including grapes, for $500 or more is unenforceable unless it's in writing.[93] In bad economic times, wineries seeking to cut costs may seize the opportunity to terminate an oral agreement that is unenforceable. Although a grower with an oral grape contract is at risk, the parties may have exchanged sufficient writings such as e-mails and letters to establish a written contract, leaving certain provisions unstated. In most states, the law will impose material provisions such as price and timing of payment even without a written contract.[94] If the parties desire certainty or wish to avoid litigation, they should enter into a formal written grape purchase agreement.

a. Grape Purchase Agreement

A written grape purchase agreement (GPA) is uniquely interconnected; almost every material provision affects other provisions. For example, the provision that states which party controls farming practices will affect the pricing mechanism, grape quantity, grape quality, term, and harvest provisions. Counsel for either party to a grape contract must be acutely aware of this interconnectedness and negotiate and draft the contract accordingly. The material provisions in a grape purchase agreement are described next.

PREAMBLE AND RECITALS

Like a PSA and a vineyard lease, the GPA generally begins with a preamble that describes the agreement and the parties, followed by recitals. It is critical to specify the source vineyard. Often a vintner will purchase only a portion of a vineyard's production. In such cases, the parties typically identify specific vineyard blocks or rows as the source of fruit; the rootstock and varietal clone also might be specified.

TERM AND TERMINATION

A GPA's term is determined primarily from the vintner's goals. In some cases, the vintner is seeking a short-term source of grapes to fill a temporary need. Here the GPA's term might be as short as one year or one harvest, with no automatic renewal provision. In other cases, the vintner might seek a long-term source of fruit for its most stable brands. The relationship between vintner and grower in a longer-term contract is closer to a partnership than an ordinary vendor relationship. A typical term for such a contract is five to seven years.

---

93. *See* Cal. Comm. Code §2201 (2009); N.Y. U.C.C. Law §2-201 (2010); Or. Rev. Stat. §72.2010 (2009); Va. Code Ann. §8.2-201 (2010); Wash. Rev. Code §62A.2-201 (2009).

94. *See, e.g.,* Cal. Food & Agric. Code §§55601.3(c) (2009).

Longer-term contracts often contain a so-called evergreen provision where the final term is perpetually extended unless either party notifies the other of its intent to terminate the agreement. Usually after the notice of termination is given, the contract will continue for an additional one to five years, during which time the grower will seek a new buyer and the vintner will find replacement fruit.

Because long-term contracts create substantial financial obligations, vintners will not enter such contracts without ample due diligence. Often a vintner seeking a long-term source of grapes from a new grower will negotiate for an initial short-term "look-see" period. During this period, usually one to three years, the vintner has an opportunity to evaluate the quality of the grower's vineyard, viticultural practices, and grapes. At the end of the look-see period, the vintner will have the option to extend the term of the GPA, in which case it will convert to a longer-term GPA with an evergreen provision. If the vintner elects to not continue, the GPA will terminate at the end of the look-see period.

QUANTITY

Historically, vintners typically purchased a fixed tonnage of grapes in each harvest year. Today, fixed-tonnage contracts are more common in short-term contracts in which the vintner has little input into farming practices. It is now common for vintners to purchase all the grapes produced from a specified vineyard or portion of a vineyard. Such "all-production" arrangements are often found in long-term contracts where the vintner has considerable, if not total, control over farming decisions. An all-production contract ensures that the grower will be adequately compensated if farming practices directed by the vintner lower the yield in the vineyard.

QUALITY

Almost all GPAs contain a provision describing the required quality of grapes that the grower will deliver. In addition to generally requiring the grapes to be sound, merchantable, and suitable for making a particular quality of wine, the GPA may include specific standards. For example, the GPA may set a cap on the amount of grape defects (for example, mold or rot) and material other than grapes (MOG) as a percentage of the grapes delivered. A typical cap is 1 percent. In most cases, if the defects or MOG exceed the cap, the vintner will be allowed to reject the load of grapes. Less frequently, if defects or MOG exceed a certain percentage of all grapes delivered, the vintner will have the ability to reject all the grapes. To resolve disputes over grape quality, including MOG, the parties may appoint a third party, such as an inspector from the Grape Inspection Service of the California Department of Food and Agriculture, to referee.[95]

95. *See* Cal. Code. Regs., tit. 3 §§1650.15, 1658.3, 1661, 1661.1, 1661.2, 1661.4 (1993). *See also* California Winegrape Inspection Advisory Board, Defect Inspection Information, available at http://www.cwiab.org/pdf/Defect-Inspection-Information.pdf.

PRICING AND PAYMENT

There are many different methods used to determine grape prices. Some GPAs use a fixed price per ton of grapes delivered; others use a fixed price per acre harvested; still others employ a pricing mechanism tying grape prices through a formula to the bottle price of the wine produced from the grapes purchased under the GPA. California, as previously noted, requires final grape prices to be determined on or before January 10 in the year following harvest.[96] If a vintner fails to comply with the Berryhill Act, the grower has the option of terminating the GPA, and the vintner may be investigated by the California Department of Agriculture.[97]

Price per Ton. This is the most common pricing mechanism in GPAs. In most cases, the price per ton is a fixed dollar amount. If the contract is longer term, there typically is a pricing adjustment mechanism tied to an outside index. Although the CPI is used frequently, it is not directly tied to grape prices and thus can lead to odd results. In California, a common alternative to the CPI is the annual percentage change in the weighted average price per ton of grapes paid for the given varietal in the local reporting district, as published in the Grape Crush Report. A downside to relying on the Grape Crush Report for adjusting pricing is the lag effect: pricing adjustments in a given year are based on changes in the prior year's Grape Crush Report.

The price per ton itself may be calculated by reference to the Grape Crush Report — for example, by setting the price per ton at the price corresponding to a particular level of cumulative tonnage for a specific varietal in a certain district. As an illustration, the price for Cabernet Sauvignon grapes may be set at the per-ton price corresponding to the 95th percentile of the total tonnage of Cabernet Sauvignon grapes sold in Napa County.

Per-Acre Pricing. In situations where the vintner controls farming practices, the grower may be concerned that the vintner could manage the farming in a manner that will reduce the crop yields, thereby reducing the price the grower will receive in a price-per-ton contract. An alternative is a fixed price per acre; under this formulation, annual yield fluctuations will not affect the amount the grower receives. It is common for the parties to adjust the price per acre by reference to an outside index such as the CPI or Grape Crush Report. Additionally, the parties should consider price adjustments for replanted or diseased vines or other natural factors that could reduce the crop yield. If the vintner resists per-acre pricing, the grower might consider a price-per-ton formula with a per-acre floor; the floor (minimum price) should be set at a level sufficient to cover the grower's farming costs plus a reasonable return on the grower's investment.

---

96. Cal. Food & Agric. Code §55601.5(g) (2009).
97. *Id.* §55601.5(g), (h).

Bottle Pricing. In premium wine production, a grower may seek to share in the profit that the vintner earns from wine produced from the grower's grapes. One method to achieve this goal is to include a bonus pricing mechanism that is based on the bottle price of wine produced from the grower's grapes. In California, a significant obstacle to bottle pricing is the Berryhill Act. Converting grapes to finished, saleable wine takes between one and four years following harvest, making it impossible to know the price of the bottle of wine made from the grower's grapes by January 10 following harvest. Some GPAs include a bottle pricing payment that ties the price of the current year's grapes to the most recent vintage of wine being sold by the winery that was made from the grower's grapes. This approach, however, does not work for new wine offerings.

Other Price Adjustments. Price adjustments can be used to protect both grower and vintner from various risks depending on the context. In some cases, a GPA will include pricing adjustments based on certain qualities of the grapes delivered. For example, many vintners prefer grapes to have a higher sugar content, measured in degrees Brix. However, to achieve higher sugar content, the grower must delay harvest until later in the season, known as a long "hang time," when the risk of crop loss or weight loss is greater. If price were calculated on a per-ton basis, the grower would realize less revenue absent a price adjustment. To compensate the grower for the higher risk of loss and lower yield, the grower may insist that the vintner make increasing bonus payments as the Brix level rises above a threshold stated in the contract. In a per-acre contract, the vintner may require a downward price adjustment in the event of low yields resulting from acts of God or blight. In other cases, the vintner might require a downward price adjustment if the percentage of grapes with defects or MOG is too high. There are many variations on this theme.

Timing of Payment. Although the Berryhill Act requires that the price paid for grapes be determined by January 10 following harvest, there is no requirement that payment be made by that date or any other specific date. If the GPA does not include a provision regarding the timing of payments, however, the vintner must pay the grower within 30 days after taking delivery or possession of the grapes.[98] Ordinarily the parties will include a provision regarding the timing of payment(s). For tax purposes, the grower may desire to defer some or all of the payment until after December 31 of the harvest year. A common payment schedule is for 50 percent of the price to be paid within 30 days after harvest, with the balance due by January 15 of the year following harvest.

98. Cal. Food & Agric. Code §55601 (2009).

VINEYARD DESIGNATION

Many vintners use a vineyard designation on the label to identify the vineyard from which the vintner's wine was produced.[99] Under TTB regulations, a vintner may not use a vineyard designation on its label unless 95 percent of the wine in the bottle was produced from fruit grown in the named vineyard.[100]

It is the grower, not the winery, that possesses rights in the vineyard name. However, according to the doctrine of "fair use," if a grower sells wine grapes under a vineyard name, the winery may fairly use that name, even without the grower's consent, on the wine produced from those grapes to designate origin so long as such use complies with TTB vineyard designation labeling requirements. A grower that wishes to control the winery's ability to use the vineyard name on wine should include language in the grape purchase agreement prohibiting the use of the vineyard name without the grower's prior consent.

If the parties envision the winery's use of a vineyard designation at the time of the contract negotiation, the contract should explicitly authorize that use and specify that, upon termination of the contract, the winery shall cease use of the vineyard name (except on wines already produced from the grower's grapes). A grower holding a trademark registration for a vineyard name might consider licensing the name to the winery for use as a vineyard designation on the winery's label.[101] Such an arrangement is more typical in a long-term relationship and provides the winery with clear rights to use the name and the grower with an additional economic return in the form of a royalty and additional goodwill value in the vineyard.[102]

FARMING PRACTICE AND VITICULTURAL CONTROL

The description of farming practices can be quite basic ("consistent with viticultural practices in Santa Barbara County") or quite detailed, with reference to a farming plan. Traditionally, the grower will control farming practices, but in some premium wine programs, the GPA gives that control to the vintner. Growers are understandably hesitant to cede control over farming, particularly when the grape price is set on a per-ton basis.[103] For that reason, if

---

99. Two well-known examples of vineyard designation are Martha's Vineyard in Napa and the Sangiacamo Vineyard in Sonoma. See Heitz Cellar, Martha's Vineyard, http://www.heitzcellar.com/vineyards/marthas.cfm (last visited Jan. 7, 2011); Sangiacamo Family Vineyards, Our Clients, http://www.sangiacomo-vineyards.com/wines/clients (last visited Jan. 7, 2011).

100. 27 C.F.R. §4.39(m) (2010).

101. The owner of a new vineyard may file for an "intent to use" trademark application, which will reserve the grower's rights in the name pending maturation of the vineyard and sufficient use of the name in interstate commerce to qualify for trademark status. See 15 U.S.C. §1051(b)(1) (2010).

102. *See* J. Scott Gerien, The Vineyard Designation: Branding & Trademark Issues for Wineries & Vineyard Owners, Wine Business Monthly, Apr. 15, 2003, available at http://www.winebusiness.com/wbm/?go=getArticle&dataId=23622 (last visited Jan. 7, 2011). In some cases, the vintner and grower will jointly apply for and hold a trademark for a specific vineyard. This aligns the parties' interests and in some cases allows the vintner to continue using the mark after the GPA and license agreement have been canceled.

103. The concern is that a vintner might intentionally reduce crop yield to improve grape quality or for some nefarious purpose, thereby reducing the overall payment under the GPA.

the GPA allows the vintner to control farming practices, the grower should negotiate for a per-acre price so that the grower will be unaffected by reduced yields. A compromise is to provide for cooperative control over farming, requiring consensus between grower and vintner for certain farming decisions. This approach may prove difficult in practice, however. Other provisions that should be negotiated in tandem with farming practices include risk-of-loss provisions and quality standards; greater vintner control makes it less fair for the grower to be forced to bear the risk of loss or meet rigid quality standards.

HARVEST, DELIVERY, AND RISK OF LOSS

Traditionally, the vintner instructs the grower when to harvest grapes. In most cases, the vintner will want the grapes to mature on the vine as long as possible to increase sugars and enhance flavor profiles. The grower, on the other hand, will be eager to harvest sooner rather than later because of the risk that late fall rains could cause mold or other damage. Additionally, the longer the grapes hang on the vine, the more water weight they lose, which affects price in a GPA with per-ton pricing. The grower should consider a "harvest notice" provision whereby the grower will notify the vintner that the grapes are ready for harvest as soon as they reach pre-determined Brix and pH levels. If the vintner elects to delay harvest beyond this point, the risk of loss passes to the vintner.

The harvest provision often describes the manner of harvest (e.g., manual or machine harvesting) and might even require a specific size of picking bin (e.g., a half-ton bin). The contract should address delivery scheduling. Harvest is a hectic time at a winery because grapes arrive throughout the day, often from multiple vineyard sources. The grower should provide a minimum notice time (24 or 48 hours, for example) before delivering grapes.

The parties should determine when the risk of loss passes. Typically, the risk of loss passes to the winery when the grapes are off-loaded at the crush pad, but the grower might request that risk of loss pass when the truck enters the winery's premises. The reason for such a provision is that the grower should not be held accountable if the grapes are damaged because of a delay at the winery's crush pad.

A BRIEF NOTE ON GROWER'S LIENS

In California, any farmer, including a grape grower, who delivers a crop to an agricultural processor,[104] including a winery, automatically obtains a lien on the crop and products made from the crop by operation of law until the

104. "Processor" means

> any person that is engaged in the business of processing or manufacturing any farm product, that solicits, buys, contracts to buy, or otherwise takes title to, or possession or control of, any farm product from the producer of the farm product for the purpose of processing or manufacturing it and selling, reselling, or redelivering it in any dried, canned, extracted, fermented, distilled, frozen, eviscerated, or other preserved or processed form. It does not, however, include any retail merchant that has a fixed or

grower is paid in full. Although the statute refers to this as the producer's lien, it is commonly known in industry vernacular as the "grower's lien."[105] This lien is superior to a secured lender's interest.

While a powerful remedy for the grower, the grower's lien has limitations in practice. A grower may enforce a grower's lien only through judicial action, which can be very costly, especially if the GPA does not allow the prevailing party to recoup its attorney's fees. Additionally, many wine companies operate under a custom crush model and hold no processor's license.[106] If a grower sells grapes to such a buyer, the grower's lien will not apply by operation of law and, after delivering the grapes, the grower will simply be an unsecured creditor.

To enhance its position, particularly if it sells to a wine company that holds no processor's license, the grower should consider negotiating a provision allowing it to file a UCC-1 financing statement. By filing a UCC-1 financing statement, the grower could pursue non-judicial foreclosure or self-help repossession to enforce its security interest.[107] A vintner likely will resist granting the grower this right, particularly if doing so would violate the loan agreement between the vintner and its bank.

D. CONCLUSION

The American wine industry has evolved beyond a collection of traditional winery estates to a sophisticated modern industry with many options available for entering the industry. In view of the complicated and highly regulated nature of the wine business, the wine industry lawyer has an important role to play in advising vintners and growers about the various models for producing and selling wine and growing grapes.

---

established place of business in this state and does not sell at wholesale any farm product which is processed or manufactured by him.

Cal. Food & Agric. Code §55407 (2009).

105. *Id.* §§55631-55653. In 2006 the grower's lien was greatly increased by California's Fifth District Court of Appeal in the case of *Frazier Nuts, Inc. v. American Ag Credit*, 141 Cal. App. 4th 1263 (2006). In this case, the court expanded the grower's lien to cover cash proceeds and accounts receivable arising from the sale of agricultural products, including wine.

106. Unless they also hold a CDFA processor's license, these companies are not considered "processors" under the California Food & Agriculture Code. *See* Cal. Food & Agric. Code §§55407, 55521 (2010)

107. *See* Cal. Comm. Code §§9601, 9609 (2010).

CHAPTER 5

THE COMMERCE CLAUSE AND THE TWENTY-FIRST AMENDMENT: AN EVOLVING CONSTITUTIONAL PUZZLE

Margot Mendelson[1]

A. INTRODUCTION

In 2005, the Supreme Court's decision in *Granholm v. Heald* made waves among court watchers and wine lovers alike.[2] The case challenged the authority of Michigan and New York to regulate wine distribution in their states by permitting in-state wineries to ship directly to consumers while denying direct shipment privileges to out-of-state wineries. More broadly, the case pitted the protective language of the Twenty-first Amendment of the Constitution, which expressly recognizes a role for states in regulating the liquor market, against the principles of economic unity among states espoused by the Commerce Clause of the Constitution.

Although *Granholm* represents the most visible contemporary example of the unique application of the Commerce Clause to alcoholic beverages, the case constitutes just part of a complex jurisprudence that predates the Twenty-first Amendment and continues to develop today. Indeed, the shipment of alcoholic beverages between states has been a subject of active constitutional debate since well before Prohibition, and there is reason to suspect that the

1. I would like to thank Professor Heather Gerken of Yale Law School for her support of my early research on this subject. I am enormously grateful to my father for his tremendous inspiration and assistance with this project. I would also like to thank my patient mother and brother, who have endured many a dinner conversation about the contours of the Twenty-first Amendment.

2. 544 U.S. 460 (2005).

debates working their way through the courts since *Granholm* may be ripening toward a future Supreme Court cases.

The earliest U.S. regimes for controlling alcoholic beverages were highly local, and legislators tended to avoid the difficult questions of alcohol control by delegating them to ever smaller political units — whenever possible letting towns and counties decide who could purchase, sell, and consume alcohol and where and when they could do so. State level prohibition laws were enacted beginning in the 1850s, and they produced controversy from the start. Creating a dry state required closing that state's borders to imports of alcoholic beverages from sister states and abroad — and such protectionism offended the principles of economic unity among the several states enshrined in the Commerce Clause of the U.S. Constitution.

The Commerce Clause itself provides that "[t]he Congress shall have power . . . [t]o regulate commerce with foreign nations, and among the several states, and with the Indian tribes."[3] According to interpretations by the courts dating back to 1824, the Commerce Clause possesses a negative corollary, known as the dormant Commerce Clause. The dormant Commerce Clause addresses the authority of the states to regulate or affect interstate commerce, given the Constitution's explicit grant of Commerce Clause authority to Congress. As interpreted by the Court, the dormant Commerce Clause expresses the notion that "[s]tates may not enact laws that burden out-of-state producers or shippers simply to give a competitive advantage to in-state businesses."[4] As the Court explained in *Hughes v. Oklahoma*, "[t]his mandate reflect[s] a central concern of the Framers that was an immediate reason for calling the Constitutional Convention: the conviction that in order to succeed, the new Union would have to avoid the tendencies toward economic Balkanization that had plagued relations among the Colonies and later among the States under the Articles of Confederation."[5] As early as 1876, the Court held that the Commerce Clause was intended to "insure . . . against discriminating State legislation."[6]

The Court's jurisprudence with respect to state action under the dormant Commerce Clause has shifted over time. In one reading, states have a free hand to regulate whenever Congress has not explicitly done so. At the other extreme, matters of interstate commerce are reserved for federal action, so that states are barred from legislating even where Congress has taken no action. Over time the Court has focused on at least five separate factors to resolve conflicts between state and federal authority under the Commerce Clause: whether Congress has acted on or delegated its authority in the particular field or been silent; whether the subject matter of the state or federal law or regulation is national or local; whether the state action imposes direct or indirect burdens on interstate commerce; whether the state law or regulation is discriminatory or protectionist; and whether the interstate burdens of the state action outweigh the local benefits.[7]

---

3. U.S. Const. art. I, §8, cl. 3.
4. *Hughes v. Oklahoma*, 441 U.S. 322, 325 (1979).
5. *Id.* (internal quotations omitted).
6. *Welton v. Missouri*, 91 U.S. 275, 280 (1876).
7. *See generally* Boris I. Bittker, Bittker on the Regulation of Interstate and Foreign Commerce §6.02, at 6-14 (1999).

Alcoholic beverages have long played an important role in the development of dormant Commerce Clause doctrine. Alcoholic beverage cases came before the Court frequently prior to National Prohibition — particularly in the context of persistent efforts by the states to control or ban alcohol. Courts were called upon to determine the point at which the regulation of the so-called liquor trade constituted an impermissible burden on interstate commerce. In making those determinations, the Court considered everything from the origin of the alcoholic beverage (foreign or domestic), to the purpose of its importation (personal use or resale), and even to its packaging (whether the wine bottles had been removed from the case in which they were received and then repackaged for sale). In the decades leading up to National Prohibition, the Court articulated a broad conception of the dormant Commerce Clause as limiting state action — largely through a series of decisions that invalidated state prohibition laws on the grounds that they discriminated against interstate commerce.

The ratification of the Twenty-first Amendment repealing National Prohibition gave rise to a new field of constitutional analysis specific to "intoxicating liquors." Section 2 of the Twenty-first Amendment explicitly recognized a role for the states in regulating alcoholic beverages, thus creating tension with the principle in the dormant Commerce Clause that forbids states from discriminating against interstate commerce. The two constitutional provisions seemed to envision contrary roles for the states in regulating alcoholic beverages: the Commerce Clause had long been interpreted as imposing limits on any state action that affected interstate commerce, but the Twenty-first Amendment appeared to give states the freedom to regulate alcoholic beverages, even when those regulations clearly discriminated against interstate commerce, such as by imposing costly license fees or taxes on alcoholic beverages from out of state.

Courts have been called in to referee the interplay between the dormant Commerce Clause and the Twenty-first Amendment since the ratification of Repeal. Over time, courts have moved from a highly deferential reading of the Twenty-first Amendment, in which they permitted virtually unlimited state action under Twenty-first Amendment authority, to a much greater reluctance to allow states to discriminate against interstate commerce. In striking down Michigan's and New York's protective direct shipment laws on the grounds that they discriminated against interstate commerce and were not saved by the Twenty-first Amendment, *Granholm v. Heald* reflected a broader trend in Twenty-first Amendment jurisprudence away from viewing Repeal as a free pass for discriminatory state regulation and toward more rigorous judicial scrutiny of state regulation of interstate commerce.

Granholm, however, does not represent the last word on the matter. To the contrary, the opinion appears to have stirred up as many questions as it answered. *Granholm* demonstrated that the Court would not accept facially discriminatory laws, but it left open questions about how courts would rule on an ever-growing number of laws regulating the wine industry that are facially neutral but discriminate against interstate commerce in effect or purpose. As the wine industry grows and more dollars are at stake, states are scrambling to craft laws around *Granholm*'s dictates, and the focus of the cases has spread from direct shipping by producers to direct shipping by retailers. It remains to be seen how far the courts will go under the dormant Commerce Clause in striking down or upholding laws that protect states' alcoholic beverage distribution systems. Likewise, whether the Twenty-first Amendment will "save" this new crop of more subtly discriminatory laws has yet to be determined.

The story of the dormant Commerce Clause and its relationship to alcoholic beverages, particularly after the Twenty-first Amendment, involves an actively developing area of constitutional jurisprudence. It invokes complex textual tensions between distinct constitutional provisions, with dramatically changing interpretations over time. This story is also inextricably tangled with our nation's idiosyncratic history with alcohol and alcohol control; it reflects the legacy of our unique experience with National Prohibition and the lasting legal impact of Repeal. The subject raises fundamental questions about local control, free markets, and the underpinnings of our economic union.

Furthermore, wine occupies an increasingly central role in this jurisprudence. Whereas beer and spirits dominated early cases, wine is the focal point of recent considerations and is likely to continue in that role. Not only is wine shaping the dormant Commerce Clause jurisprudence, but the jurisprudence, in turn, is shaping the wine industry. Indeed, in the coming years and decades the courts will resolve many critical questions about how wine will be ordered, delivered, and consumed.

This chapter explores the nature of the dormant Commerce Clause, both philosophical and doctrinal, and the development of the jurisprudence since the early days of the United States.[8] The chapter then considers the specific application of the dormant Commerce Clause to alcoholic beverages before Prohibition, after Prohibition, during the time leading up to *Granholm v. Heald*, and since *Granholm*.

B. THE DORMANT COMMERCE CLAUSE: HISTORY AND DOCTRINE BEFORE THE EIGHTEENTH AMENDMENT

The Supreme Court first interpreted the Commerce Clause in 1824 — 35 years after the Constitution was ratified. In the earliest Commerce Clause cases, the Court navigated among broadly divergent interpretations of the clause and its implications. By one account, the clause granted the federal government complete authority over interstate commerce to the exclusion of state legislative authority. By another account, the clause required deference to states in

---

8. This chapter is limited to dormant Commerce Clause jurisprudence and does not consider all Twenty-first Amendment jurisprudence. The Court has balanced the Twenty-first Amendment with other provisions of the Constitution, including the First Amendment, *44 Liquormart, Inc. v. Rhode Island*, 517 U.S. 484 (1996); the Establishment Clause, *Larkin v. Grendel's Den, Inc.*, 459 U.S. 116 (1982); the Equal Protection Clause, *Craig v. Boren*, 429 U.S. 190 (1976), and *California v. LaRue*, 409 U.S. 109 (1972); *N.Y. State Liquor Auth. v. Bellanca*, 452 U.S. 714 (1981); the Due Process Clause, *Wisconsin v. Constantineau*, 400 U.S. 433 (1971); the Import-Export Clause, *Dep't of Revenue v. James B. Beam Distilling Co.*, 377 U.S. 341 (1964); and the Supremacy Clause, *Capital Cities Cable, Inc. v. Crisp*, 467 U.S. 691 (1984).

all matters about which Congress had not explicitly legislated. Although the Court wavered about the extent of permissible state authority over interstate commerce, the early cases paved a tentative middle path between extreme interpretations of the clause. Through these cases, the Court adopted a doctrine of partial federal exclusivity and recognized concurrent powers of state and federal legislation.

In its earliest interpretation of the Commerce Clause, the Supreme Court invalidated a New York state law that granted private individuals the exclusive right to operate in interstate waterways.[9] Although the case, *Gibbons v. Ogden*, turned on the Supremacy Clause, in which the Court construed a 1793 law as authorizing American vessels to engage in interstate trade,[10] it also raised critical questions about the relationship of state police power to federal commerce power. The opinion is considered an early articulation of the dormant Commerce Clause because it indicated that the constitutional grant of power to the federal government significantly limited state legislative authority over interstate commerce: "Few things were better known, than the immediate causes which led to the adoption of the present constitution . . . that the prevailing motive was *to regulate commerce*; to rescue it from the embarrassing and destructive consequences, resulting from the legislation of so many different States, and to place it under the protection of a uniform law."[11] *Gibbons* was a forceful assertion of exclusive federal power over interstate commerce. Indeed, *Gibbons* gave rise to the term "dormant Commerce Clause," in addition to articulating the logic of the concept. In dicta, Chief Justice John Marshall referred to a power to regulate interstate commerce "which . . . can never be exercised by the people themselves, but must be placed in the hands of agents or lie dormant."[12]

Three years later in *Brown v. Maryland*, Chief Justice Marshall again considered the scope of the Commerce Clause, this time in a case involving the states' power to regulate imported goods.[13] In this early liquor law case, the Court held that a state could not levy a license fee on foreign importers until the import had "become incorporated and mixed up with the mass of property in the country."[14] In reaching its decision, the Court had to define "commerce" and determine its scope. The Chief Justice built upon the expansive conception of "commerce . . . among the several States" that the Court had announced in *Gibbons*, defining commerce not just as traffic, but as "commercial intercourse" that necessarily extends beyond the external boundaries of each state and reaches from one state into another.[15] In the context of foreign trade, which Congress had explicitly authorized, the Court concluded that the state had no ability to impose a fee on an imported alcoholic beverage until the

9. *Gibbons v. Ogden*, 22 U.S. 1 (1824).

10. Act of February 18, 1793, 1 Stat. 305 ("An Act for enrolling and licensing ships or vessels to be employed in the coasting trade and fisheries, and for regulating the same").

11. *Gibbons*, 22 U.S. at 11.

12. *Id.* at 189. The Chief Justice again referred to the federal "power to regulate commerce in its dormant State" in dicta in *Willson v. Black Bird Creek Marsh Co.*, 27 U.S. 245, 252 (1829).

13. 25 U.S. 419 (1827).

14. *Id.* at 441-442.

15. *Id.* at 451.

product "has become incorporated and mixed up with the mass of property in the country, . . . [and] lost its distinctive character as an import, and has become subject to the taxing power of the State; but while remaining the property of the importer, in his warehouse, in the original form or package in which it was imported, a tax upon it is too plainly a duty on imports to escape the prohibition in the constitution."[16] This theory came to be known as the "original packages doctrine."

The following year, in *Willson v. Black Bird Creek Marsh Co.*, Chief Justice Marshall produced his third opinion involving the Commerce Clause, which departed somewhat from *Gibbons* in upholding a Delaware state law authorizing the construction of a dam that blocked passage through a navigable stream.[17] The Court found no conflict between the Delaware act and any federal law and concluded that the construction of the dam constituted a legitimate exercise of state police power, not "repugnant to the [federal] power to regulate commerce in its dormant state."[18] Thus, the Court afforded the states some measure of authority to legislate on matters that affect interstate commerce.[19]

Eighteen years later, with Marshall no longer presiding, the Court returned to the subject of the states' ability to regulate trade in alcoholic beverages. In 1847 the Court considered three consolidated cases challenging the alcoholic beverage laws of Massachusetts, Rhode Island, and New Hampshire, known as *The License Cases*.[20] The Court issued a unanimous decision with six separate opinions that share little, if any, common ground. Nonetheless, the Court made two separate and important holdings. First, the Court upheld the Massachusetts and Rhode Island licensing requirements for alcoholic beverage retailers because, as applied to imported liquors, those licensing laws "act upon the article *after* it has passed the line of foreign commerce and become a part of the general mass of property in the state."[21] Second, with respect to interstate commerce, the Court upheld a New Hampshire licensing requirement for purveyors of distilled spirits and wines. The case involved an unlicensed importer of a barrel of gin from another state. The Court upheld the state's licensing law because Congress had not exercised its Commerce Clause authority by passing any law on the subject of interstate trade in liquor. The holding echoed the Marshall Court's approach in *Willson v. Black Bird Creek Marsh Co.* in its deference to the states' rights to regulate in matters involving

16. *Id.* at 441-442.

17. 27 U.S. 245 (1829).

18. *Id.* at 252.

19. Bittker has suggested that the Court's conclusion in *Willson Creek* can be explained in part by the purely intrastate nature of the creek in question as well as the fact that the creek was "a 'sluggish' stream rather than a river like the lordly Hudson" Bittker, *supra* note 7, at §1.02, 1-19. "A state-authorized dam blocking navigation in such a major waterway would surely have required the Court to devote more time to the claim . . . that the Commerce Clause sometimes bars state legislation even if Congress has failed to act." *Id.* More fundamentally, however, Bittker points out that the Marshall Court's Commerce Clause jurisprudence was marked by ambivalence in which the "forceful assertions of the power of Congress . . . were coupled, more than once, with equally extravagant testimonials to the powers retained by states." *Id.* at 1-20.

20. 46 U.S. 504 (1847).

21. *Id.* at 577 (emphasis added).

interstate commerce in the absence of federal action. As Chief Justice Taney wrote in the *License Cases*, "it appears . . . to be very clear that the mere grant of power to the general government cannot, upon any just principles of construction, be construed to be an absolute prohibition to the exercise of any power over the same subject by the states. . . . [T]he state may . . . for the safety or convenience of trade, or for the protection of the health of its citizens, make regulations of commerce for its own ports and harbors, and for its own territory; and such regulations are valid unless they come in conflict with a law of Congress."[22]

Lest the evolution of Commerce Clause jurisprudence seem too straightforward, it should be noted that this was only one approach that the Court would employ in deciding when the Commerce Clause deprives the states of their regulatory authority. In an 1851 case, *Cooley v. Board of Wardens*, the Court upheld a state law that required ships entering and leaving the port of Philadelphia to hire local pilots.[23] In this ruling the Court articulated an altogether different test for the application of Commerce Clause principles. The Court reached its holding in *Cooley* on the basis of the subject matter of the challenged law — concluding that local subject matter could appropriately be legislated by states, and national subject matter was reserved exclusively for uniform federal legislation. "[T]he nature of this subject is such, that until Congress should find it necessary to exert its power, it should be left to the legislation of the states; that it is local and not national; that it is likely to be the best provided for, not by one system, or plan of regulations, but by as many as the legislative discretion of the several states should deem applicable to the local peculiarities of the ports within their limits."[24]

The Court adopted yet another approach just over 10 years later, when it attempted to distinguish between *direct* and *indirect* burdens on interstate commerce in determining which laws to uphold. In *Smith v. Alabama*, the Court upheld state licensing of locomotive engineers on the grounds that it affected interstate commerce "only indirectly, incidentally, and remotely."[25]

C. ALCOHOLIC BEVERAGES AND THE COMMERCE CLAUSE IN YOUNG AMERICA

Although early Commerce Clause cases covered a wide range of subject matter, the liquor trade cropped up time and again in the developing jurisprudence. That was never truer than in the years before the ratification of National Prohibition. In those decades, judicial interpretations of the Commerce Clause shaped the way Americans bought, sold, and consumed alcohol. Likewise, the constant march of liquor cases through the courts, as well as the interplay

22. *Id.* at 579.
23. 53 U.S. 299 (1851).
24. *Id.* at 319.
25. 124 U.S. 465, 482 (1888).

between Congress and the Courts over liquor laws, left an indelible mark on Commerce Clause jurisprudence.

Chief Justice Marshall's enunciation in 1824 of the "original packages doctrine," for example, had a direct effect on the growing temperance movement in the United States. As the states began to adopt laws curtailing the sale of alcoholic beverages, the doctrine prevented them from banning the importation of wines, beers, and spirits from abroad that remained in their original packages. For that reason, the Maine Law of 1851, which spawned a wave of prohibitory laws across the United States, expressly exempted alcoholic beverages "of foreign production . . . imported under the laws of the United States . . . contained in the original packages."[26]

To be sure, not all constitutional issues affecting the liquor trade pertained to the Commerce Clause. After the Fourteenth Amendment was ratified in 1868, the Court had to decide whether states could constitutionally ban the production and sales of alcoholic beverages and whether they would have to compensate existing manufacturers for their losses.[27] Ultimately, the Court upheld state laws prohibiting both the production and sale of alcoholic beverages.[28]

At the same time it upheld these prohibitory laws under the Fourteenth Amendment, the Court struck down restrictive state laws that discriminated against out-of-state or foreign interests. In *Walling v. Michigan*, the Court overturned a state tax imposed on persons residing outside the state who sold liquor to be shipped into the state; again, no such tax was imposed on in-state sellers of alcoholic beverages produced in the state.[29] In *Walling*, the Court specifically distinguished Michigan's tax from the occupational taxes on liquor purveyors that had been upheld in *The License Cases*, noting that unlike the tax at issue in *Walling*, those taxes did not "operate as a discriminative burden against the introduction and sale of the products of another state, or against the citizens of another state."[30]

In the last two decades of the nineteenth century, the Court affirmed increasingly robust understandings of the dormant Commerce Clause's limitations on the states. The Court moved beyond the discriminatory laws like those at issue in *Walling* and overturned prohibitory laws that, although not overtly discriminatory, restricted interstate and foreign commerce. In the eyes of temperance crusaders, the Court's opinions demonstrated its preference for interstate commerce over in-state interests. With each decision, they became more incensed.

The dry state of Iowa, surrounded by wet states like Illinois, provided the setting for several of the most significant cases in the period leading up to

26. 1851 Me. Acts 211, §11.

27. *Bartmeyer v. Ohio*, 85 U.S. 129 (1873); *Boston Beer Co. v. Massachusetts*, 97 U.S. 25 (1877); *Mugler v. Kansas*, 123 U.S. 623 (1887).

28. *Mugler*, 123 U.S. 623.

29. 116 U.S. 446 (1886).

30. *Id.* at 461. The Court also overturned a state law that imposed a "peddler's license tax" on persons selling various goods not manufactured or grown in the state when there was no such tax on peddlers selling in-state goods. *Welton v. Missouri*, 91 U.S. 275 (1875). The goods at issue in that case were sewing machines, not liquor.

National Prohibition. In an 1888 case, *Bowman v. Chicago and Northwestern Railroad*, the Court overturned Iowa's prohibitory law because it banned the importation of alcoholic beverages from other states.[31] The Bowman brothers had sued the Chicago and Northwestern Railroad for refusing to ship 5,000 barrels of beer from a location in Chicago to a location in Iowa, where they intended to sell the beer. The railroad company sought to defend the law as a quarantine regulation or a sanitary measure. The Court acknowledged the defendant's argument that States possessed the power to prohibit the introduction of articles of trade that "would bring in and spread disease, pestilence and death, such as rags or other substances infected with the germs of yellow fever, or the virus of small-pox, or cattle or meat or other provisions that are diseased or decayed, or otherwise, from their condition and quality, unfit for human use or consumption."[32] Indeed, the Court declared that such articles "are not legitimate subjects of trade and commerce. . . . The self-protecting power of each state, therefore, may be rightfully exerted against their introduction, and such exercises of power cannot be considered regulations of commerce prohibited by the constitution."[33]

Nonetheless, in its *Bowman* decision the Court rejected the argument that alcoholic beverages are inherently deleterious to human health and safety. The Court warned of the dangers of permitting states to prohibit the importation of "*any* . . . article, the use or abuse of which it may deem deleterious" and decried the confusion and protectionism that would result if each state could make its own determination about which commercial products could be outlawed: "[A state] may choose to establish a system directed to the promotion and benefit of its own agriculture, manufactures or arts of any description, and prevent the introduction and sale within its limits of any or of all articles that it may select as coming into competition with those which it seeks to protect. . . . In view of the commercial anarchy and confusion that would result from the diverse exertions of power by the several states of the Union, it cannot be supposed that the constitution or congress has intended to limit the freedom of commercial intercourse among the people of the several states."[34]

Ultimately the *Bowman* Court held that the states did not have the "right and power to prevent [the] introduction [of intoxicating liquors] by transportation from another State."[35] As the Court stated, "[t]he absence of any law of Congress on the subject is equivalent to its declaration that commerce in that matter shall be free."[36] The Court, however, did not decide at what point in the stream of commerce the state could permissibly regulate the liquor in question.

---

31. 125 U.S. 465 (1888).
32. *Id.* at 489.
33. *Id.*
34. *Id.* at 494 (emphasis added).
35. *Id.* at 500.
36. *Id.* at 508.

For the growing number of temperance activists in the country, the Court's robust defense of open state borders meant that the "very existence of wet states" posed a "constant and insidious threat . . . to the order and security of dry states."[37] Not only could imported alcoholic beverages in their original packages enter a dry state (following the Court's decision in *Brown v. Maryland*), but now also alcoholic beverages from other states. What began as judicial quibbling over a puzzling clause of the Constitution had arrived at the saloon, the church, the dinner table, and city hall.

The Court took one step further toward dismantling state prohibition measures in the name of Commerce Clause principles two years later in *Leisy v. Hardin*, a decision that all but ushered in Congressional legislation to facilitate statewide prohibition.[38] Leisy Brewery, located in Illinois, shipped its packaged beer to an Iowa retailer who sold it in its original package, in violation of Iowa's prohibitory law.[39] Leisy challenged the law, and the Supreme Court struck it down as a violation of the Commerce Clause. In overturning the state law, the Court for the first time established the point at which interstate commerce protection ended and the state's police power attached, holding that the plaintiffs "had the right to import this beer into [Iowa], and in the view which we have expressed they had the right to sell it, by which act alone it would become mingled in the common mass of property within the state. Up to that point of time, we hold that, in the absence of congressional permission to do so, the state had no power to interfere by seizure, or any other action, in prohibition of importation and sale."[40] Congressional silence no longer would be interpreted as an authorization of state action. After *Leisy*, which effectively overturned *The License Cases* of 1847, states could no longer bar out-of-state liquor from sale in its original package, notwithstanding congressional silence.

The Court's *Leisy* ruling confirmed temperance activists' worst fears. "The *Leisy* ruling," according to historian Richard Hamm, "flooded the dry states with liquor."[41] "Within a month of the ruling, 'original packages houses' . . . had sprung up in every prohibition state."[42] Suddenly, dry states that had been waging war against the saloon for decades confronted a new and apparently lawful incarnation of their old foe.

The language of the *Bowman* and *Leisy* decisions suggests that the Court may have been pressing Congress to act. Both decisions are relatively deferential to the goals of temperance ideology, and they specifically point to the absence of congressional direction as the critical factor in their conclusions. In *Bowman*, the Court explained that it was legally bound to strike down the state's alcohol regulations "however desirable such [] regulation[s] might be,"

---

37. Norman H. Clark, Deliver Us from Evil: An Interpretation of American Prohibition 118 (1976).

38. 135 U.S. 100 (1890).

39. After *Bowman* Iowa repealed its nuisance law and provided that no intoxicating liquor, domestic or foreign, could be sold in Iowa except for pharmaceutical and medical purposes or, in the case of wines, for sacramental use. 22d General Ass., Iowa Acts 91, ch. 71. It was this new law that *Leisy* challenged.

40. *Leisy*, 135 U.S. at 124.

41. Richard F. Hamm, Shaping the Eighteenth Amendment 70 (1995).

42. *Id.* at 69.

and that only the "consent of congress, express or implied" could enable such laws to advance.[43] The *Leisy* decision referred specifically to "the absence of legislation on the part of congress" and pointed out that the outcome was unrelated to the Justices' "individual views" about "the deleterious or dangerous qualities" of the regulated items.[44]

Under intense pressure from temperance advocates across the country, Congress passed the Original Packages Act, commonly known as the Wilson Act, in the summer of 1890. The Wilson Act provided that "all . . . intoxicating liquors . . . transported into any State or Territory . . . for use, consumption, sale or storage therein, shall upon arrival in such State or Territory be subject to the operation and effect of the laws of such State or Territory enacted in the exercise of its police powers, to the same extent and in the same manner as though such . . . liquors had been produced in such State . . . and shall not be exempt therefrom by reason of being introduced therein in original packages or otherwise."[45] The Act was intended not to implement prohibition at a national level but rather to overcome the constitutional barriers to state prohibitory laws. Simply stated, the law "empowered the States to regulate imported liquor on the same terms as domestic liquor."[46] If a state prohibited the sale of alcoholic beverages within its borders, it no longer would have to allow out-of-state and out-of-country imports of the prohibited goods. In this way, a dry state could seal its borders without running afoul of the law or exposing itself to costly constitutional litigation.

Although the Act survived an initial challenge in which the Court held that it did not constitute an impermissible delegation of Congress's commerce power to the states,[47] it soon fell to the same Commerce Clause challenges that had laid waste to so many of its state law antecedents. In *Rhodes v. Iowa*, a railway station agent in the state had been charged and convicted under an amended version of the state's prohibitory law for having received a wooden box containing liquor shipped from Illinois directly to an Iowa resident.[48] The railway company appealed the conviction, arguing that neither the Wilson Act nor Iowa's prohibitory law could lawfully apply to consumer-direct interstate liquor sales. The Court agreed with the railway company, holding that the state law could not attach to imports before they reached their point of destination within the state. Acknowledging that the Wilson Act "undoubtedly" was intended "to enable the laws of the several states to control the character of merchandise therein

---

43. *Bowman*, 125 U.S. at 493.

44. *Leisy*, 135 U.S. at 110, 125.

45. Original Packages (Wilson) Act, ch. 728, 26 Stat. 313 (1890).

46. *Granholm*, 544 U.S. at 461. In *Scott v. Donald*, 165 U.S. 58, 100 (1897), the Court held that under the Wilson Act, a "[s]tate cannot . . . establish a system which, in effect, discriminates between interstate and domestic commerce in commodities to make and use which are admitted to be lawful."

47. *Wilkerson v. Rahrer*, 140 U.S. 545 (1891). The Court found that Congress had not "attempted to delegate the power to regulate commerce, or to exercise any power reserved to the states, or to grant a power not possessed by the states, or to adopt state laws." Rather, Congress had "taken its own course, and made its own regulation, applying to these subjects of interstate commerce one common rule, whose uniformity is not affected by variations in state laws." *Id.* at 561.

48. 170 U.S. 412 (1898).

enumerated" at an earlier date than would have been otherwise the case, the Court nonetheless interpreted the statutory language "upon arrival in such state" to mean following delivery to the consignee rather than upon crossing the state line as a matter of constitutional avoidance: "The right to contract for the transportation of merchandise from one state into or across another involved interstate commerce in its fundamental aspect, and . . . necessarily must be governed by laws apart from the laws of the several states."[49]

In so holding, the Court in *Rhodes* carved out yet another loophole for the entry of liquor into dry states. Although a drinker might be prohibited from purchasing liquor in a dry state, he could order it from out-of-state dealers without unreasonable state interference. Once again, Congress was called into action to fix an intolerable outcome. In 1913, it passed the Webb-Kenyon Act, which prohibits the interstate shipment of "spirituous, vinous, malted, fermented, or other intoxicating liquor [which] is intended, by any person interested therein, to be received, possessed, sold, or in any manner used, either in the original package or otherwise," in violation of any law of the state into which they are shipped.[50] In passing the Act, Congress expressed its unambiguous intent to allow dry states to stop direct-to-consumer interstate liquor shipments.[51]

The Webb-Kenyon Act, however, did not allay prohibitionists' fears that a future Congress or Supreme Court would reverse course. To protect their cause from wavering political and jurisprudential tides, they pressed for a constitutional amendment that, they hoped, would resolve the matter forever. Led by the politically powerful and astute Anti-Saloon League and bolstered by the Women's Christian Temperance Union, as well as church and business leaders, the prohibition movement propelled Congress to adopt the Eighteenth Amendment in December 1917. Thirty-six states ratified the amendment by 1919. The Amendment provides:

> Section 1. After one year from the ratification of this article the manufacture, sale, or transportation of intoxicating liquors within, the importation thereof into, or the exportation thereof from the United States and all territory subject to the jurisdiction thereof for beverage purposes is hereby prohibited.
>
> Section 2. The Congress and the several States shall have concurrent power to enforce this article by appropriate legislation.

---

49. *Id.* at 424.

50. Webb-Kenyon Act, ch. 90, 37 Stat. 699 (1913) (codified at 27 U.S.C. §122 (2006)). The Webb-Kenyon Act carried no specific provisions for federal enforcement and included no penalties; that was left to the states. Prosecutions for violation of the state prohibitory laws were to be in state courts. Interestingly, that issue was addressed 87 years after the enactment of the Webb-Kenyon Act, with the passage of the Twenty-first Amendment Enforcement Act, Pub. L. No. 106-386, 114 Stat. 1547 (2000) (codified at 27 U.S.C. §122a (2006)). That law for the first time granted state attorneys general federal court jurisdiction to pursue potential civil injunctive relief for alleged violations of state law regulating the importation or transportation of alcohol.

51. The Webb-Kenyon Act was challenged on constitutional grounds in *James Clark Distilling Co. v. Western Maryland Railway Co.*, 242 U.S. 311 (1917). There the plaintiff railway company that had transported liquor interstate for personal use argued that the Act was an impermissible delegation of Congress's Commerce Clause authority and also was not uniform in its state-by-state application. The Supreme Court upheld the law, just as it had upheld the Wilson Act in *Wilkerson v. Rahrer*, 140 U.S. 545.

The efforts of the federal and state governments to enforce National Prohibition are beyond the scope of this chapter. Suffice it to say that the liquor trade, which the Amendment banned with few exceptions, never really died; it simply went underground, with criminal syndicates, local gangsters, and even heretofore law-abiding citizens partaking in illegal liquor production and sale.[52]

Just as the onset of World War I had prepared the nation for the sacrifices that National Prohibition entailed, the Great Depression of 1929 advanced the cause of Repeal of the Eighteenth Amendment. Among the groups advocating Repeal were the Association Against the Prohibition Amendment, the Voluntary Committee of Lawyers, the Women's Organization for National Prohibition Reform, labor unions, medical societies, and business leaders. Ultimately they succeeded, and Congress and the states for a second time enshrined "intoxicating liquors" in the U.S. Constitution.

D. PROHIBITION, REPEAL, AND THE JUDICIAL AFTERMATH: THE COMMERCE CLAUSE AND THE TWENTY-FIRST AMENDMENT

Repeal happened quickly. Congress passed the resolution proposing the Twenty-first Amendment on February 20, 1933. For the first time, Congress called for the Amendment to be ratified by state conventions under Article V of the Constitution rather than state legislatures.[53] Prohibition officially ended when Utah became the thirty-sixth state to ratify Repeal on December 5, 1933.

With the passage of Repeal a new set of tensions arose surrounding the regulation of alcohol. The purposes of the Twenty-first Amendment were to repeal Prohibition (§1) and to restore to the states the ability to regulate their own liquor markets — even to the point of forbidding alcoholic beverage sales altogether (§2). Wisconsin Senator John Blaine, a member of the drafting committee, stated that the purpose of §2 was "to assure the so-called dry States against the importation of intoxicating liquor into those States."[54] Virginia Senator Carter Glass added, "Liquors may be shipped across a State in interstate commerce from one wet State to another wet State, but [§2] as I have drafted it prohibits the shipment of intoxicating liquors into a State whose laws prohibit the manufacture, sale, or transportation of liquors."[55] Thus §2 (reproduced in full below) allowed states to remain dry after Prohibition ended, and many states did so.

52. *See* Richard Mendelson, From Demon to Darling: A Legal History of Wine in America 78-85 (2009).

53. State conventions as a means of ratification were proposed largely in order "to circumvent the various state legislatures, where, it [was] feared, dry legislators from rural districts (because rural districts were represented with a strength so inconsistent with their actual population) might present a serious barrier to ratification." Clark, *supra* note 37, at 205.

54. 76 Cong. Rec. 4141 (1933).

55. *Id.* at 4219.

> Section 2. The transportation or importation into any State, Territory, or possession of the United States for delivery or use therein of intoxicating liquors, in violation of the laws thereof, is hereby prohibited.

The challenge of interpreting this sentence and reconciling it with disparate sections of the Constitution has plagued courts since the passage of Repeal and continues to confront courts today.

Of course, the right of states to regulate the passage of alcohol into and through their borders was a subject of controversy well before Prohibition or Repeal, by virtue of the unique moral, religious, and social issues surrounding the consumption and distribution of alcohol. To suggest that the regulation of alcohol was ever a subject of scrutiny equivalent to the regulation of milk or other commonplace goods would vastly overlook the passions on all sides of the issue from the early days of the Union.[56] Nonetheless, the passage of Repeal set the stage for the particular battles waged in the courts today. These battles are not just philosophical and cannot be understood simply as functions of the evolution of Commerce Clause jurisprudence. Instead, they revolve around tensions between the language of the Twenty-first Amendment and the strictures of the dormant Commerce Clause.

In the immediate aftermath of Repeal, the Court expressed the view that state action with regard to alcohol, even if discriminatory, would be upheld on account of the Twenty-first Amendment's explicit grant of authority to the states. This position was set forth in a series of opinions written by Justice Brandeis, which vigorously defended the absolute nature of states' authority to regulate alcohol. Principal among those opinions was the 1936 case of *State Board of Equalization v. Young's Market Company*, in which the Court upheld a California law requiring a beer wholesaler there to obtain a $500 importer's license in addition to a $50 wholesaler's license for the privilege of importing beer and then selling it in the state while wholesalers of beer produced in California needed only a wholesaler's license.[57] The Court held that the second section of the Twenty-first Amendment plainly "confer[s] upon the State the power to forbid all importations which do not comply with the conditions which it prescribes" — whether or not the regulations are reasonable.

Another Brandeis opinion three years later, *Indianapolis Brewing Company v. Liquor Control Commission*, went even further.[58] In this case the Court upheld a Michigan law that prohibited dealers in that state from purchasing, selling, receiving, or possessing beer manufactured in any state that discriminated against beer manufactured in Michigan — a total of 10 states at

---

56. As Justice Stevens stated in his dissent in *Brown-Forman Distillers Corp. v. New York State Liquor Auth.*, 476 U.S. 573, 590 (1986), "[f]or some of us who were 'present at the creation' of the Twenty-first Amendment, there is an aura of unreality in [the] assumption that we must examine the validity of New York's Alcoholic Beverage Control Law (ABC Law) just as we would examine the constitutionality of a state statute governing the sale of gasoline' — or, I would add, of milk" (alterations in original). In this passage, Justice Stevens quotes Judge Friendly's statement in *Battipaglia v. New York State Liquor Auth.*, 745 F.2d 166, 168 (2d Cir. 1984), but Judge Friendly refers only to gasoline; Justice Stevens added the comparison to milk.

57. 299 U.S. 59 (1936).

58. 305 U.S. 391 (1939).

the time the Court considered the case. The Court dismissed the plaintiff's challenges to the law despite claims that the law was retaliatory and patently violated the Commerce Clause, stating that "[f]or *whatever its character*, the law is valid. Since the Twenty-first Amendment, as held in the *Young* Case, the right of a state to prohibit or regulate the importation of intoxicating liquor *is not limited by the commerce clause. . . .*"[59]

The Brandeis opinions do not reveal the precise analysis that led the Court to its conclusion that the Twenty-first Amendment trumped the Commerce Clause. Perhaps the Court was following the logic that the more precise provision of the Constitution, namely the Twenty-first Amendment with respect to intoxicating liquor, prevailed over the more general provision — the Commerce Clause. The Court's decisions also could be rationalized on the basis of plain meaning; certainly, the language of §2 of the Twenty-first Amendment includes no limitation on state regulatory authority over the transportation or importation of alcoholic beverages for delivery or use in the state. The legislative history offers some support for the Court's holdings.[60] Proponents of absolute state control over the delivery and use of alcoholic beverages within state borders pointed to the initial inclusion of §3 in the Twenty-first Amendment, which gave Congress and the states concurrent power over alcoholic beverage sales at on-site retail establishments like bars and restaurants. That section provided that "Congress shall have concurrent power to regulate or prohibit the sale of intoxicating liquors to be drunk on the premises where sold."[61] Congress later deleted the provision because of concerns about federal jurisdiction over purely intrastate businesses. Nonetheless, proponents of the Brandeis approach argue that the deletion of §3 and the absence of any discussion of concurrent powers in §2 suggest that the grant of state authority is exclusive and absolute.

Over time, however, the absolutist tone of the Brandeis opinions yielded to a more flexible interpretation of the competing concerns of the Twenty-first Amendment and the Commerce Clause. The Supreme Court's 1964 decision in *Hostetter v. Idlewild Bon Voyage Liquor Corporation* marked a significant retreat from its hard-line approach following Repeal.[62] There the Court examined the case of a company engaged in the business of selling duty-free alcoholic beverages to departing international airline travelers at a New York airport, for delivery upon arrival at their foreign destinations. The New York State Liquor Authority sought to halt the business and to prohibit the passage of liquor through New York State territory to the airport liquor store. In examining the case, the Court considered "whether the Twenty-first Amendment so far obliterates the Commerce Clause as to empower New York to prohibit absolutely the passage of liquor through its territory, . . . acting under federal law, for delivery to consumers in foreign countries. For it is not disputed that, if

59. *Id.* at 394 (citation omitted) (emphasis added).

60. *See generally* Todd Zywicki & Asheesh Agarwal, *Wine, Commerce, and the Constitution*, 1 N.Y.U. J. L. & Liberty 609, 625-639 (2005)

61. Bittker, *supra* note 7, at §13.02, 13-15.

62. 377 U.S. 324 (1964).

the commodity involved here were not liquor, but grain or lumber, the Commerce Clause would clearly deprive New York of any such power."[63]

The *Hostetter* Court enjoined New York from interfering with Idlewild's business and, in so doing, rejected the complete subordination of the Commerce Clause to the Twenty-first Amendment in no uncertain terms: "To draw a conclusion from this line of decisions that the Twenty-first Amendment has somehow operated to 'repeal' the Commerce Clause wherever regulation of intoxicating liquors is concerned would, however, be an absurd oversimplification. If the Commerce Clause had been pro tanto 'repealed,' then Congress would be left with no regulatory power over interstate or foreign commerce in intoxicating liquor. Such a conclusion would be patently bizarre and is demonstrably incorrect."[64] Rather, the Court implemented a balancing test that, though vague, reflected the complexity of the question that confronted it: "Both the Twenty-first Amendment and the Commerce Clause are parts of the same Constitution. Like other provisions of the Constitution, each must be considered in the light of the other, and in the context of the issues and interests at stake in any concrete case."[65]

1. DORMANT COMMERCE CLAUSE JURISPRUDENCE

Hostetter can be understood in part as a reflection of the broader developments taking place in dormant Commerce Clause jurisprudence in the decades following Repeal. Many of the cases that have come to define the modern approach to the dormant Commerce Clause arose during the 1960s, like *Hostetter*, as well as during the 1970s. Although these cases do not raise the unique concerns about alcohol that are at issue in the Brandeis cases and *Hostetter* — in which courts were charged with balancing the principles of the Commerce Clause and the scope of the Twenty-first Amendment's delegation of authority to the states — they nonetheless demonstrate the Court's changing perspectives on the power of states to regulate matters affecting interstate commerce in the absence of federal legislation.

Modern approaches to the dormant Commerce Clause have long discarded *Cooley*'s subject matter-based inquiry and no longer distinguish between direct and indirect burdens on interstate commerce, as did *Smith v. Alabama*.[66] Instead, the Court has adopted a two-step inquiry to determine whether laws that burden interstate commerce are nonetheless permissible. Courts first consider whether a challenged law or ordinance discriminates against

63. *Id.* at 329. Arguably, *Hostetter* did not actually invoke the Twenty-first Amendment because the liquor was not destined for "delivery or use" within the state. However, because the state of New York had an interest in ensuring that alcoholic beverage imports destined for the retailer, Idlewild, were not diverted en route, the Twenty-first Amendment was implicated. Concerns about the diversion of alcohol constitute an important state interest that is directly related to the delivery and use of alcohol in the state. *See, e.g., North Dakota v. United States*, 495 U.S. 423 (1990) (alcoholic beverages destined for federal lands within the state fall under the Twenty-first Amendment because of the states' interest in prohibiting diversion of alcohol).

64. *Hostetter*, 377 U.S. at 331-332.

65. *Id.* at 332.

66. *Cooley*, 53 U.S. 299; *Smith v. Alabama*, 124 U.S. 465, 482 (1888).

interstate commerce. Then, if a court determines that the law regulates in a neutral manner (that is, it does not discriminate), the court assesses whether the ordinance imposes a burden on interstate commerce that is clearly excessive in relation to the putative local benefits.

This modern approach to Commerce Clause jurisprudence was crystallized in 1970 in the oft-cited case of *Pike v. Bruce Church, Inc.*[67] In this case the Court considered the Arizona Fruit and Vegetable Standardization Act, which required that all cantaloupes grown in Arizona and offered for sale be packed in closed standard containers approved by government officials. The state had issued an order under the Act prohibiting the plaintiff, a cantaloupe farming company, from transporting uncrated cantaloupes from its Arizona ranch to its California packing plant. Consequently, the plaintiff's only option was to build a packing plant within the Arizona state limits, at an estimated cost of $200,000, to duplicate the function of its existing packing facility, which was located about 30 miles across the border. The Court determined that the "purpose and design" of the Act — namely, to "protect and enhance the reputation of growers within the State" — were "surely legitimate."[68] Nonetheless, the Court concluded that "the State's tenuous interest in having the company's cantaloupes identified as originating in Arizona [could not] constitutionally justify the requirement that the company build and operate an unneeded $200,000 packing plant in the State."[69] Because the state's interest was "minimal at best," it could not justify imposing "a straitjacket on the . . . company with respect to the allocation of its interstate resources."[70] Therefore the Court invalidated the law as an impermissible burden on interstate commerce, in violation of the dormant Commerce Clause.

In reaching its holding, the *Pike* Court enunciated a balancing approach that continues to govern in cases where laws affect interstate commerce but do so in a nondiscriminatory manner:

> Where the statute regulates evenhandedly to effectuate a legitimate local public interest, and its effects on interstate commerce are only incidental, it will be upheld unless the burden imposed on such commerce is clearly excessive in relation to the putative local benefits. If a legitimate local purpose is found, then the question becomes one of degree. And the extent of the burden that will be tolerated will, of course, depend on the nature of the local interest involved, and on whether it could be promoted as well with a lesser impact on interstate activities.[71]

The Court has continued to apply the *Pike* balancing test. In *Kassel v. Consolidated Freightways*, for example, it invalidated an Iowa law limiting truck lengths on the grounds that the state had failed to present sufficient evidence of the safety value of the law, the law was out of step with other states' regulations, and the requirements "substantially burden[ed] the

67. 397 U.S. 137 (1970).
68. *Id.* at 143.
69. *Id.* at 145.
70. *Id.* at 146.
71. *Id.* at 142 (citation omitted).

interstate flow of goods by truck."[72] That same year, in *Minnesota v. Clover Leaf Creamery Co.*, the Court upheld a Minnesota law that prohibited the sale of milk in plastic nonreturnable, nonrefillable containers but permitted sales in paperboard cartons.[73] After concluding that the state statute regulated even-handedly "without regard to whether the milk, the containers, or the sellers are from outside the State," Justice Brennan, writing for the majority, held that the law passed the *Pike* test because it imposed "relatively minor" burdens on interstate commerce in relation to the substantial state interest "in promoting conservation of energy and other natural resources and in easing solid waste disposal problems."[74]

Central to the modern approach to the Commerce Clause is the determination as to whether a law discriminates — that is, whether it is "basically a protectionist measure" or whether "it can fairly be viewed as a law directed to legitimate local concerns, with effects upon interstate commerce that are only incidental" (in which case the *Pike* test applies).[75] In a classic case, *City of Philadelphia v. New Jersey*, the Supreme Court determined in 1978 that a law prohibiting importation of waste from out of state was discriminatory.[76] The Court determined that the law violated the principle of nondiscrimination "on its face," holding that "whatever New Jersey's ultimate purpose, it may not be accomplished by discriminating against articles of commerce coming from outside the State unless there is some reason, apart from their origin, to treat them differently."[77]

Decades later, the Court struck down another state statute as nakedly discriminatory, irrespective of the magnitude or impact of the discrimination. In *Wyoming v. Oklahoma*, the Court invalidated an Oklahoma law that required local coal-fired electric generating plants to burn a mixture containing at least 10 percent Oklahoma-mined coal.[78] In reaching its conclusion, the Court rejected the state's rationale for the law — that it "conserves Wyoming's cleaner coal for future use" — and found that the real reason "cannot be characterized as anything other than protectionist and discriminatory."[79] With that finding, the Court saw no need to analyze the scope of the interstate burden, which Oklahoma had argued was negligible.

> Our cases . . . indicate that where discrimination is patent, as it is here, neither a widespread advantage to in-state interests nor a widespread disadvantage to out-of-state competitors need be shown. . . . Varying the strength of the bar against economic protectionism according to the size and number of in-state and out-of-state firms affected would serve no purpose except the creation of new uncertainties in an already complex field.[80]

72. *Kassel v. Consol. Freightways Corp. of Del.*, 450 U.S. 662, 671 (1981).
73. *Minnesota v. Clover Leaf Creamery Co.*, 449 U.S. 456 (1981).
74. *Id.* at 457, 472-473.
75. *City of Phila. v. New Jersey*, 437 U.S. 617, 624 (1978).
76. *Id.* at 626-627.
77. *Id.*
78. *Wyoming v. Oklahoma*, 502 U.S. 437 (1992).
79. *Id.* at 455, 457.
80. *Id.* at 456 (quoting *New Energy Co. of Ind. v. Limbach*, 486 U. S. 269, 276-277 (1988)).

Even if a court determines that a state law does not discriminate on its face, it may nonetheless find that the law discriminates in effect or has a protectionist purpose. In 1977, for example, the Supreme Court struck down a North Carolina law requiring the use of U.S. Department of Agriculture grades and forbidding state grades on imported apples. The Court in *Hunt v. Washington State Apple* found that the law discriminated in *impact* because it raised the cost of doing business and stripped away the competitive advantage for certain out-of-state apple growers, particularly Washington growers, while leaving in-state growers unaffected.[81] As the Court explained, "[t]his discrimination resulted from the fact that North Carolina, unlike Washington, had never established a grading and inspection system. Hence, the statute had no effect on the existing practices of North Carolina producers. . . . Washington growers and dealers, on the other hand, were forced to alter their long-established procedures, at substantial cost, or abandon the North Carolina market."[82] Finding that impact to constitute discrimination against interstate commerce, the Court invalidated the North Carolina law.

In 1994 the Court overturned a Massachusetts law that it determined to be protectionist in *purpose*. In *West Lynn Creamery v. Healy*, the Court considered a state law requiring all milk dealers operating in-state to make monthly premium payments based on their milk sales; money from that fund was then distributed to local dairy farmers.[83] The Court found that while pure subsidies are permissible exercises of state power, a subsidy to in-state dealers that comes directly from a tax on all dealers is discriminatory and therefore impermissible because "the purpose and effect of the pricing order are to divert market share to Massachusetts dairy farmers."[84]

If a law discriminates, whether facially or otherwise, it "invokes the strictest scrutiny of any purported legitimate local purpose and of the absence of nondiscriminatory alternatives."[85] As the Court set forth in *Maine v. Taylor*, "once a state law is shown to discriminate against interstate commerce . . . the burden falls on the State to demonstrate both that the statute 'serves a legitimate local purpose,' and that this purpose could not be served as well by available nondiscriminatory means."[86] As such, courts typically strike down discriminatory laws, as the Supreme Court has done in several cases involving local processing requirements — from the more recent *C & A Carbone, Inc. v. Clarkstown*, where the Court overturned a municipal ordinance that required all solid waste to be processed initially at a local site, after which it would be shipped to elsewhere for further processing,[87] to the older case, *Dean Milk Co. v. Madison, Wisconsin*, where the Court invalidated a municipal ordinance requiring that all milk sold in Madison be pasteurized within five miles of the city on

81. *Hunt v. Washington State Apple Advertising Comm'n*, 432 U.S. 333 (1977).
82. *Id.* at 340.
83. *West Lynn Creamery, Inc. v. Healy*, 512 U.S. 186 (1994).
84. *Id.* at 203.
85. *Hughes*, 441 U.S. at 337 (1979). State laws found to discriminate are held to "a virtually *per se* rule of invalidity." *City of Phila. v. New Jersey*, 437 U.S. at 624.
86. 477 U.S. 131, 138 (1986) (citing *Hughes*, 441 U.S. at 336).
87. 511 U.S. 383 (1994).

the grounds that "reasonable and adequate alternatives are available" to meet the city's professed concerns about ensuring that milk sold within its borders was properly pasteurized.[88]

In fact, *Maine v. Taylor* is a rare case in which the Court found a law to be facially discriminatory but upheld it nonetheless.[89] In that 1986 case, the Court decided that Maine's prohibition on the importation of baitfish discriminated against interstate commerce on its face, but upheld the law because Maine demonstrated both that the statute served a legitimate local purpose — namely, protecting its unique population of wild fish from nonnative species — and that the purpose could not be served as well by available nondiscriminatory means.[90] Given the rigor of the test to which discriminatory laws are held, cases like *Maine v. Taylor* are uncommon.

Although the Court has developed a number of exceptions to its dormant Commerce Clause jurisprudence, most notably for a state that enters a market itself and becomes a so-called "market participant,"[91] the approach that has emerged from the last several decades of Commerce Clause litigation is now widely applied.

2. THE DORMANT COMMERCE CLAUSE AND TWENTY-FIRST AMENDMENT JURISPRUDENCE

Recent cases involving the states' regulation of the liquor trade under the Twenty-first Amendment draw heavily on developments in the area of dormant Commerce Clause analysis. Indeed, as courts have shifted away from the absolutist interpretations of the Twenty-first Amendment that were advanced shortly after its passage, these cases increasingly follow the analytical framework of *Pike* and its brethren. The evolving jurisprudence still takes the states' Twenty-first Amendment concerns into account, but the judicial inquiry tends to be limited to whether those interests can tip the balance or even "save" a law that could otherwise not withstand dormant Commerce Clause scrutiny.

Bacchus Imports, Ltd. v. Dias, for example, is widely viewed as a decisive step in Twenty-first Amendment jurisprudence toward a more vigorous defense of the principles underlying the dormant Commerce Clause.[92] The case involved a 20 percent excise tax on alcoholic beverages that exempted certain locally produced products such as okolehao (a brandy distilled from the root of an indigenous plant) and pineapple wine. There, referencing classic dormant

88. 340 U.S. 349 (1951).

89. *Taylor*, 477 U.S. 131.

90. *Id.* at 142, 151.

91. The classic examples of the market participant exception are in the fields of public utilities and state-owned natural resources, but one recent case involved wine. In *Brooks v. Vassar*, 462 F.3d 341 (4th Cir. 2006), Virginia's decision to sell only wines produced in-state in its state-owned retail stores was upheld under the market participation exception. The court wrote that "just as the Commonwealth has elected not to sell every brand of liquor manufactured, it has elected not to sell out-of-state wines, choosing instead to sell only Virginia-produced wines. In doing so it competes as a participant in the Virginia wine market with the thousands — more than 10,000, according to Virginia — of other private wine retailers who sell both Virginia wines and out-of-state wines in Virginia." *Id.* at 357.

92. 468 U.S. 263 (1984).

Commerce Clause cases such as *Hunt v. Washington State Apple* and *Philadelphia v. New Jersey*, the Court concluded that the liquor tax exemption "violated the Commerce Clause because it had both the purpose and effect of discriminating in favor of local products."[93] The Court then embarked on a second analytical step that has come to characterize many cases that simultaneously consider dormant Commerce Clause principles and Twenty-first Amendment concerns. After determining that the challenged statute violates the dormant Commerce Clause, the Court inquired whether the Twenty-first Amendment "saves" the measure. With respect to the second inquiry, the Court in *Bacchus* developed a "core interests" analysis, holding that the law "is not saved by the Twenty-first Amendment" because it "violates a central tenet of the Commerce Clause but is not supported by any clear concern of the Amendment in combating the evils of an unrestricted traffic in liquor."[94] The Court explained:

> [O]ne thing is certain: The central purpose of [§2 of the Twenty-first Amendment] was not to empower States to favor local liquor industries by erecting barriers to competition. . . . State laws that constitute mere economic protectionism are therefore not entitled to the same deference as laws enacted to combat the perceived evils of an unrestricted traffic in liquor. Here, the State does not seek to justify its tax on the ground that it was designed to promote temperance or to carry out any other purpose of the Twenty-first Amendment, but instead acknowledges that the purpose was 'to promote a local industry.'[95]

In other words, the Court determined that the interests advanced by Hawaii's legislation fell outside the "core interests" of the Twenty-first Amendment and therefore did not warrant protection from invalidation by the Commerce Clause.

Because the core interests of the Twenty-first Amendment are not stated in the Amendment itself, their scope is imprecise. In a 1990 case, *North Dakota v. United States*, the Court upheld two North Dakota regulations requiring out-of-state shippers of alcoholic beverages to affix a label to each bottle of alcoholic beverage sold to in-state military bases and to file monthly shipping reports identifying the particular products and quantities of alcoholic beverages shipped into the state.[96] The state's declared interest was to prevent liquor moving in transit through the state from being diverted for unauthorized uses within the state. The Court found that "[t]he risk of diversion into the retail market and disruption of the liquor distribution system is thus both substantial and real."[97] On that basis, the Court concluded that the North Dakota regulations were consistent with "the core of the State's power under the Twenty-first Amendment. . . . In the interest of promoting temperance, ensuring orderly market conditions, and raising revenue, the State has established a comprehensive system for the distribution of liquor within its borders. That system is unquestionably legitimate."[98]

---

93. *Id.* at 273.
94. *Id.* at 264.
95. *Id.* at 276.
96. 495 U.S. 423.
97. *Id.* at 433.
98. *Id.* at 432.

The Court emphasized in both the *Bacchus* and *North Dakota* cases that states can organize their alcoholic beverage markets as they wish in order to promote temperance. The states also may take steps to prevent the diversion of alcoholic beverages in order to combat the "social evils" that occurred during Prohibition and to ensure an orderly market. Generally, when a state law is challenged, the state articulates the purpose of its alcoholic beverage regulations, and the courts then endeavor to decide "whether the interests implicated by a state regulation are so closely related to the powers reserved by the Twenty-first Amendment that the regulation may prevail, notwithstanding that its requirements directly conflict with express federal policies."[99]

In the years following *Bacchus*, the Court continued to affirm that the Twenty-first Amendment would not "save" measures that otherwise offended the dormant Commerce Clause. In *Brown-Forman Distillers Corporation v. New York State Liquor Authority*, for example, the Court maintained the principle that states are prohibited from regulating interstate commerce by restricting commerce in other states.[100] The New York law in question stated that distillers could not sell liquor to New York distributors at a price higher than that charged anywhere else in the nation for that product for a prescribed period of time. Confusingly, several other states had similar "price affirmation" laws, so the practical result was that no distiller could sell its liquor anywhere at a discount. The Court held that "[w]hen a state statute directly regulates . . . interstate commerce, or when its effect is to favor in-state economic interests over out-of-state interests, we have generally struck down the statute without further inquiry" on the grounds that it violates the Commerce Clause.[101] The Court did not stray from that approach, despite the argument that the Twenty-first Amendment should dictate a contrary outcome.

Similarly, in *Healy v. Beer Institute*, the Court struck down a Connecticut price affirmation law dealing with the prices of beer.[102] Unlike the prospective price affirmation law at issue in *Brown-Forman*, Connecticut's law was contemporaneous, meaning that the price affirmation only applied at the moment when the seller posted its prices. The Court analyzed the effects of the statute on interstate commerce and concluded that, like the price affirmation law at issue in *Brown-Forman*, the Connecticut's contemporaneous price affirmation law had an impermissible extraterritorial effect. The Court also concluded that the law was discriminatory:[103]

> Connecticut has claimed throughout this litigation that its price-affirmation laws are designed to ensure the lowest possible prices for Connecticut consumers. While this may be a legitimate justification for the statute, it is not advanced by, in effect, exempting brewers and shippers engaging in solely

99. *Bacchus Imports*, 468 U.S. at 275-276 (citing *Capital Cities Cable*, 467 U.S. at 714).

100. 476 U.S. 573.

101. *Id.* at 579. Likewise, the Court in *324 Liquor Corp. v. Duffy*, 479 U.S. 335 (1987), decisively "rejected the view 'that the Twenty-first Amendment has somehow operated to 'repeal' the Commerce Clause wherever regulation of intoxicating liquors is concerned'" (quoting *Hostetter*, 377 U.S. at 331-332).

102. 491 U.S. 324 (1989).

103. *Id.* at 339-341.

domestic sales from the price regulations imposed on brewers and shippers who engage in sales throughout the region.[104]

Not surprisingly, price controls for alcoholic beverages, which are a favored means of controlling consumption and achieving temperance, have taken other forms, and those too have been challenged. In a 1980 case, *California Retail Liquor Dealers Association v. Midcal Aluminum, Inc.*, the Court invalidated California's pricing law, under which wholesalers could not sell their wines to retailers at any prices other than the ones set forth in a so-called fair trade contract or in a price schedule posted with the state.[105] The Court found that California's pricing scheme constituted resale price maintenance in violation of the federal Sherman Antitrust Act.[106] This case, of course, did not revolve around the dormant Commerce Clause but rather the Sherman Antitrust Act. Nonetheless, the Court's approach in discerning and balancing the interests of the Twenty-first Amendment are instructive. California asserted that the Twenty-first Amendment protected the price controls because they functioned to promote temperance and preserve an orderly market — therefore advancing the core concerns of the Amendment. In its analysis the Court specifically cited a study that found little correlation between resale price maintenance and temperance.[107] It also found the asserted state interests to be less substantial than the national policy in favor of competition. For these reasons, the Court held that "the Twenty-first Amendment provides no shelter for the violation of the Sherman Act caused by the State's wine pricing program" and struck down the law.[108]

In a more recent case, *Costco Wholesale Corp. v. Maleng*, the U.S. Court of Appeals for the Ninth Circuit considered a variety of price and non-price restraints on the sale of beer and wine imposed by the state of Washington that were also challenged as violations of the Sherman Act.[109] These restraints included requirements that manufacturers and distributors of wine and beer post their prices with the state liquor board and hold them for one month (a practice known as a "post and hold"), that distributors charge every retailer the same price for their products, that distributors sell at a "delivered price" even if the retailer picked up the product or paid freight costs, and that manufacturers and distributors mark up their wine and beer prices by at least 10 percent.[110] Additionally, Washington prohibited distributor sales to retailers on credit, volume sales discounts, retailers storing beer and wine at a central warehouse, and retailer sales to other retailers.[111] The district court found that all these restraints, other than the ban on retailer sales of beer and wine to other retailers, violated the Sherman Act. The Ninth Circuit upheld the district

---

104. *Id.* at 341.
105. 445 U.S. 97 (1980).
106. *Id.* at 102-103. Today, resale price maintenance is no longer a per se violation of the Sherman Act and is judged under the rule of reason. *See Leegin Creative Leather Products, Inc. v. PSKS, Inc.*, 551 U.S. 877 (2007).
107. *Cal. Retail Liquor Dealers Ass'n*, 445 U.S. at 112.
108. *Id.* at 114.
109. *Costco Wholesale Corp. v. Maleng* (*Maleng II*), 522 F.3d 874 (9th Cir. 2008).
110. *Id.* at 883-884.
111. *Id.*

court with respect to the retailer-to-retailer sales ban, but otherwise reversed the district court, validating all the restraints except post and hold.[112]

Again, the specific antitrust issues involved in the case are beyond the scope of this chapter, but the way in which the court addressed Washington's defense under the Twenty-first Amendment is instructive. The court reached its decision regarding the saving aspect of the Twenty-first Amendment through a three-step process. First, it examined the expressed state interests and their proximity to the "core concerns" that are protected by the Twenty-first Amendment, including promoting temperance, ensuring orderly market conditions, and raising revenue. Second, the court examined whether, and to what extent, the regulatory scheme served its stated purposes. Third, the court balanced the state's interest against the federal interest in promoting competition. The court acknowledged that temperance is a valid and important state interest under the Twenty-first Amendment.[113] But it found that the state "failed to demonstrate that its restraints are effective in promoting temperance," and therefore the asserted state interest did not outweigh the federal interest in promoting competition.[114]

E. GRANHOLM v. HEALD AND BEYOND

That wine should be the subject of the next seminal Supreme Court case involving the dormant Commerce Clause and the Twenty-first Amendment was in many ways predictable. Beginning in the 1970s, the U.S. wine industry experienced a renaissance, with both wine production and consumption soaring.[115] The number of wineries in the United States grew from 441 in 1970 to over 4,929 in 2005, when *Granholm* was decided.[116] Furthermore, wine purchasing patterns were shifting. The rise of the Internet beginning in the 1990s led to an explosion of online commerce and greater familiarity among consumers with direct shipment as a way to buy and receive goods. Because consumers now expected to be able to access goods despite geographical barriers, they clamored for direct access to out-of-state wines.

Following Repeal, most states adopted rigid and carefully prescribed systems of distribution for wine and other alcoholic beverages in order to achieve

---

112. *Id.* at 884, 889. The court concluded that Washington's ban on retailers selling to other retailers is a unilateral restraint that does not conflict with the Sherman Act and upheld it. A "unilateral restraint" is one that is imposed unilaterally by the state and does not grant a degree of private regulatory power to private concerns.

113. *Id.* at 902. The district court discovered that Washington law does not define temperance, so the court used the definition in *Black's Law Dictionary* — the restrained or moderate indulgence in alcohol. *Costco Wholesale Corp. v. Hoen* (*Hoen II*), No. C04-360P, 2006 WL 1075218, at *4 (W.D. Wash. Apr. 21, 2006).

114. *Maleng II*, 522 F.3d at 903. The district court investigated the state's interests in promoting an orderly market and raising revenue and determined that the restraints served neither interest and, even if they did, the state's interests were outweighed by the federal interest in promoting competition. *Hoen II*, No. C04-360P, 2006 WL 1075218, at *7-10 (W.D. Wash. Apr. 21, 2006).

115. *See supra* Chapter 1, Table 1.

116. Wine Institute, Number of California Wineries (Apr. 1, 2010), http://www.wineinstitute.org/resources/statistics/article124.

an orderly market and to avoid the social evils that plagued the pre-Prohibition and Prohibition eras. Each state made its own decision in this regard, exercising its authority under the Twenty-first Amendment. However, broadly speaking, 18 states decided to become direct market participants, serving as wholesalers and/or retailers of alcoholic beverages in these so-called control states.[117] The remaining states relied on the licensure of private parties as producers, importers, wholesalers, and retailers of alcoholic beverages. Their distribution systems often took the form of a "three-tier system of distribution," under which wine and other alcoholic beverages pass from the producer or importer to a separately licensed wholesaler who, in turn, sells to retailers for resale to consumers. Not surprisingly, there are many variations on this theme, with strict regulations governing the marketing, sales, and distribution of alcoholic beverages between each tier. In a strict three-tier distribution system, only in-state retailers are allowed to sell and ship wine directly to in-state consumers. Out-of-state wineries have to sell and ship their wines to an in-state importer or wholesaler (depending on the laws of the particular state), which in turn sells them to a retailer for resale to in-state consumers.

Of course, this labyrinthine structure was of little concern to the growing numbers of Internet consumers in the burgeoning world of e-commerce. And, in fact, long before the Internet took hold, many states had authorized local wineries to sell their wines directly to consumers, typically when those consumers visited the winery, as legislative exceptions to the three-tier system. This concept of a "farm winery," first introduced in the 1970s, was intended to promote tourism and boost the local agricultural economy.[118]

As the Internet increased the demand from both consumers and wineries to allow interstate direct shipping, states expanded the wineries' direct shipping privileges — often in ways that directly discriminated against other states. By 2003, 30 states permitted winery direct-to-consumer shipments within the state.[119] Of this number, 24 states also allowed some form of direct interstate shipping.[120] Thirteen of these 24 passed "reciprocity" laws that granted out-of-state wineries the right to ship a certain amount of wine per month to an in-state consumer on the express condition that the winery's home state must afford wineries in the destination state a similar direct-to-consumer privilege.[121] Some of the remaining 11 states allowed direct shipping by out-of-state wineries, but placed restrictions on their interstate shipments

117. *See* Chapter 1 for more information about control states and license states, which are the two main approaches the states used after Repeal to organize and regulate their alcoholic beverage markets.

118. See Chapter 7 for a discussion of the history of "farm wineries" in the United States. These wineries were allowed to sell wines produced from local grapes directly to consumers inside the state.

119. Fed. Trade Comm'n, Possible Anticompetitive Barriers to E-Commerce: Wine 7 (July 2003), available at http://www.ftc.gov/us/2003/07/winereport2.pdf.

120. *Id.*

121. *Id.* at 7-8; *see also* Iowa Code §123.187(2) (2003) (repealed 2010) ("A winery licensed or permitted pursuant to laws regulating alcoholic beverages in a state which affords this state an equal reciprocal shipping privilege may ship into this state by private common carrier, to a person twenty-one years of age or older, not more than eighteen liters of wine per month, for consumption or use by the person"). These laws were not unlike the law at issue in the famous case of *Indianapolis*

that were not imposed on intrastate shipments.[122] Still, approximately half the states allowed no direct interstate shipments at all, and some of these states made it a felony for out-of-state wineries to ship wine to in-state consumers.[123] The states made these decisions under the authority of the Twenty-first Amendment, presumably without considering the requirements of the dormant Commerce Clause.

Given the distance, both temporally and doctrinally, from the ratification of the Twenty-first Amendment and the absolutist interpretation of the scope of the Amendment advanced by the Brandeis opinions, the stage was set for a new round of Commerce Clause litigation. Indeed, by the time *Granholm v. Heald* came before the Supreme Court, a circuit split had developed with respect to states' measures to foster their own wine industries through limitations on out-of-state direct shipping. In 2003 the Fourth Circuit invalidated a North Carolina law that required out-of-state manufacturers to use the three-tier distribution system while allowing in-state manufacturers to ship directly to consumers on the grounds that it violated the Commerce Clause and was not saved by the Twenty-first Amendment.[124] One year later the Second Circuit upheld a New York law restricting direct shipment of out-of-state wine to New York consumers on the ground that it *was* protected by the state's Twenty-first Amendment powers — recognizing the additional costs imposed on out-of-state manufacturers, but finding that "New York's regulatory regime falls squarely within the ambit of section 2's grant of authority."[125] The Seventh Circuit, in reasoning that echoed that of the Second Circuit, held in *Bridenbaugh v. Freeman-Wilson* that an Indiana statute prohibiting direct shipments from out-of-state producers to Indiana consumers was saved by the Twenty-first Amendment.[126] The Fifth and Sixth Circuits, by contrast, adopted logic similar to the Fourth Circuit in finding that the direct shipping laws of Texas and Michigan violated Commerce Clause principles; accordingly, the courts invalidated these laws notwithstanding the Twenty-first Amendment.[127]

Brewing Co. v. Liquor Control Comm'n, 305 U.S. 391, in which Justice Brandeis upheld a law prohibiting dealers in Michigan from purchasing, selling, receiving, or possessing beer manufactured in any state that discriminated against beer manufactured in Michigan. As discussed above, Justice Brandeis upheld that law based on an extremely broad reading of the Twenty-first Amendment that was repudiated by subsequent case law. *See infra* text surrounding note 58.

122. Fed. Trade Comm'n, *supra* note 119, at 8. In 2002, following the ban imposed by the Transportation Security Administration on passengers carrying onto airplanes liquids in containers larger than three ounces (*see* Transp. Sec. Admin., 3-1-1 for Carry-ons, http://www.tsa.gov/assets/pdf/311_brochure.pdf (last visited Feb. 2, 2011)), Congress passed a federal direct shipment law, 27 U.S.C. §124, that allows a consumer who has purchased wine "while the purchaser was physically present at the winery" to ship it to her home in accordance with her state's rules on personal importation. This exception is in effect only so long as the Federal Aviation Administration's security restrictions on air travel remain in place.

123. Fed. Trade Comm'n, *supra* note 119 at 8.

124. *Beskind v. Easley*, 325 F.3d 506, 519-520 (4th Cir. 2003).

125. *Swedenburg v. Kelly*, 358 F.3d 223, 227 (2d Cir. 2004).

126. 227 F.3d 848, 854 (7th Cir. 2000).

127. *Dickerson v. Bailey*, 336 F.3d 388, 410 (5th Cir. 2003); *Heald v. Engler*, 342 F.3d 517, 527 (6th Cir. 2003). Interestingly, the Eleventh Circuit's decision on this issue relied on *Bacchus*'s language with respect to the core concerns of the Twenty-first Amendment. In *Bainbridge v. Turner*, 311 F.3d 1104, 1106, 1114 (11th Cir. 2002), the court noted that Florida's prohibition against out-of-state wineries shipping directly to consumers could be upheld against a dormant Commerce

Broadly speaking, the Court took up the same issue in *Granholm*, considering the constitutionality of laws in Michigan and New York that allowed in-state wineries, but not out-of-state ones, to circumvent the three-tier distribution system, thereby giving the in-state wineries a competitive advantage. Although the Michigan statute required out-of-state wineries to channel their sales through wholesalers and the New York statute permitted out-of-state wineries either to do likewise or to establish a physical presence as a so-called "branch winery" in the state, both states allowed in-state wineries to obtain licenses for direct sales to consumers without additional steps.[128] Considering whether "a State's regulatory scheme that permits in-state wineries directly to ship alcohol to consumers but restricts the ability of out-of-state wineries to do so violate[s] the dormant Commerce Clause in light of §2 of the Twenty-first Amendment," the Court invalidated both statutes on the grounds that they discriminated facially against interstate commerce.[129] In other words, the "object and design" of both statutes was "to grant in-state wineries a competitive advantage over wineries located beyond the states' borders."[130] The Court held, in a 5-to-4 decision, that such favoritism violates the Commerce Clause's implied restriction on state protectionism.

Granholm clarified that neither the Constitution nor Congress had authorized states to discriminate against interstate commerce. The Court rejected the argument that the Twenty-first Amendment permits states to legislate in ways that would otherwise be precluded under the dormant Commerce Clause doctrine, rejecting, as had *Bacchus*, the idea that the Twenty-first Amendment would "save" or "supersede" state laws that violate other provisions of the Constitution.[131] Instead, in *Granholm* the Court held that "state regulation of alcohol is limited by the nondiscrimination principle of the Commerce Clause."[132]

In reaching its holding, the Court rejected the argument that the Webb-Kenyon Act, still in effect today, had "removed any barrier to discriminatory state liquor regulations."[133] Instead, the Court interpreted the Webb-Kenyon Act as an extension of the Wilson Act, which also remains in effect and explicitly prohibits discrimination against interstate commerce by the states.[134]

Clause challenge if Florida could prove that the statute was closely related to a core concern of the Twenty-first Amendment and that the state's statutory scheme is "genuinely needed to effectuate the proffered core concern."

128. *Granholm*, 544 U.S. at 468-471.

129. *Id.* at 471. With respect to New York's in-state presence requirement, the Court found that it "runs contrary to our admonition that States cannot require an out-of-state firm 'to become a resident in order to compete on equal terms.'" *Id.* at 475 (quoting *Halliburton Oil Well Cementing Co. v. Reily*, 373 U.S. 64, 72 (1963)).

130. *Id.* at 466.

131. *Granholm*, 544 U.S. at 486, 489.

132. *Id.* at 487.

133. *Id.* at 482.

134. Justice Kennedy authored the *Granholm* opinion and Justices Scalia, Souter, Ginsburg, and Breyer joined. Justices Stevens and Thomas both wrote dissenting opinions, in which Justice O'Connor and Chief Justice Rehnquist joined. Chief Justice Rehnquist and Justices Stevens and O'Connor were widely expected to vote to uphold the laws because they had dissented in *Bacchus*, in a clear case of a protective tariff — expressing their view that the liquor tax exemption for locally produced Hawaiian alcoholic beverages at issue in that case "plainly" constituted "an exercise of a

In keeping with the *Pike* test, the Court examined whether there was any reasonable, nondiscriminatory means to accomplish the states' legitimate objectives after it concluded that the New York and Michigan laws discriminated against interstate commerce on their faces. The states argued that their laws were necessary to prevent youth access to alcoholic beverages, to ensure the collection of the states' tax revenue, to hold out-of-state wineries accountable, and to maintain an orderly market. The Court rejected each claim, noting that either there was no evidence of a problem (for example, in the case of youth access to alcohol or failure to collect taxes) or there were nondiscriminatory means to address the problem (for example, licensing schemes and self-reporting requirements for all direct shipments).[135]

Importantly the Court fashioned no remedy in *Granholm*. The states were free to "level up" (allowing in-state and out-of-state wineries alike to ship directly to in-state consumers) or "level down" (allowing states to prohibit *all* wineries from shipping directly to consumers) in order to end discrimination. *Granholm* also left open a series of questions that would arise in its wake.

Granholm required all the state legislatures that discriminated in their direct shipping laws against out-of-state wineries to revisit and revise those laws. As they did so, the rules of the game changed for interstate direct shipping. After *Granholm*, most states decided to level up. Today 37 states allow both in-state and out-of-state wineries to ship to in-state consumers. All but one reciprocal shipment law has been repealed following the Court's pronouncement in dicta in *Granholm* that "the perceived necessity for reciprocal sale privileges risks generating the trade rivalries and animosities, the alliances and exclusivity, that the Constitution and, in particular, the Commerce Clause were designed to avoid."[136] Several states leveled down, including New Jersey, Maryland, Mississippi, Alabama, and Kentucky.[137] Combined with the states that never allowed direct shipping (in-state or out-of-state), there are a total of 13 states that prohibit direct shipping: New Jersey, Massachusetts, Pennsylvania, Maryland, Alabama, Kentucky, Oklahoma, Delaware, Arkansas, Utah,

---

power expressly conferred upon the States by the Constitution," *Bacchus Imports*, 468 U.S. at 287, and that the "wholesalers' Commerce Clause claim is squarely foreclosed by the Twenty-first Amendment," *Id.* at 279. Justice Stevens' dissent in *Granholm* was particularly interesting, as it was largely grounded in his historical experience — thus lending strength to the notion of Twenty-first Amendment and Commerce Clause jurisprudence as a product of time:

> Today many Americans, particularly those members of the younger generations who make policy decisions, regard alcohol as an ordinary article of commerce, subject to substantially the same market and legal controls as other consumer products. That was definitely not the view of the generations that made policy in 1919 when the Eighteenth Amendment was ratified or in 1933 when it was repealed by the Twenty-first Amendment. . . . My understanding (and recollection) of the historical context reinforces my conviction that the text of §2 should be 'broadly and colloquially interpreted.'

Granholm, 544 U.S. at 494, 496 (quoting *Carter v. Virginia*, 321 U.S. 131, 141 (1944) (Frankfurter, J., concurring)).

135. *Granholm*, 544 U.S. at 490-492.

136. *Id.* at 472.

137. Steve Gross, Dir. of State Relations, Wine Inst., Presentation at the Ship Compliant Users Conference & Direct Shipping Seminar: State by State Update (June 10, 2010) (on file with author).

Montana, Mississippi, and South Dakota.[138] As this book goes to press, wineries can ship their wines directly to 83 percent of adult Americans.[139]

The laws in the 50 states, however, are far from settled when it comes to direct shipping and regulation of the liquor trade. *Granholm* sent states scrambling to legislate around the dictates of the Court's holding. In the last several years, states have adopted new laws, tried new approaches, and then amended those laws and approaches. Among the more novel responses are the leveling up laws that seem to constitute discrimination in *effect*. Although their laws are not facially discriminatory like the laws considered by the *Granholm* Court, they include criteria that burden out-of-state producers. The criteria fall into three general categories: volume caps, wholesaler exclusion, and face-to-face sales.

Volume or capacity caps eliminate the direct shipping privilege for wineries, in-state or out-of-state, that produce more than a stated number of gallons of wine per year. Although the laws are facially neutral as to the citizenship of the wineries they regulate, capacity cap laws draw suspicion when the effect of the gallonage cap set by the particular state is to allow all in-state wineries to engage in direct shipping but exclude a large percentage of out-of-state wineries. In such cases, there is a reasonable suspicion of a discriminatory purpose or effect. This was the finding of the U.S. Court of Appeals for the First Circuit in the 2010 case, *Family Winemakers of California v. Jenkins*,[140] which overturned a Massachusetts law that made a "small winery shipment license" available to any winery that produces less than 30,000 gallons annually.[141] In 2006, when the law was enacted, 98 percent of domestic wine was produced by "large" wineries.[142] The remaining two percent of domestic wine was produced by the thousands of "small" wineries located in the United States, 31 of which were located in Massachusetts.[143] Importantly, all of the Massachusetts-based wineries fell within the "small" winery category, each producing between 200 and 24,000 gallons of wine per year.[144] Consequently, the impact of the law was to preserve the direct shipping privilege for in-state wineries but to eliminate it for wineries responsible for 98 percent of the nation's wine supply. The court found the Massachusetts law to be discriminatory in both purpose and effect, the latter as a result of "the statutory context, legislative history, and other factors."[145]

The second type of law, known as wholesaler exclusion, eliminates the direct shipping privilege for wineries that sell their wines to a wholesaler in the destination state. The logic underlying the exclusion is that only those

138. Free the Grapes!, Reflecting on the 5th Anniversary of *Granholm v. Heald* 1 (Apr. 19, 2010), available at http://www.freethegrapes.org/sites/default/files/FTG_Backgrounder_on_USSC_5.pdf. The laws change sufficiently swiftly from state to state that this list no doubt will be out of date by the time this book is in print.
139. *Id.*
140. 592 F.3d 1, 9-10 (1st Cir. 2010).
141. Mass. Gen. Laws ch. 138, §19F(b) (2009).
142. *Family Winemakers*, 592 F.3d at 8, 11-12.
143. *Id.* at 8.
144. *Id.* at 8-9.
145. *Id.* at 5.

wineries whose wines are not otherwise available in the state through the three-tier distribution system should be allowed to ship wines directly to in-state consumers. Because this criterion applies to both in-state and out-of-state wineries, it is facially neutral. Interestingly, Massachusetts combined the 30,000-gallon capacity cap with the wholesaler exclusion in the law at issue in *Family Winemakers*. Together, these two criteria, according to the First Circuit, forced large wineries to choose their distribution method.

> If ["large" wineries] choose direct shipping, . . . they are *forced* to terminate their existing wholesaler relationships, which also means that they lose all access to retailers in Massachusetts. Since this is a crucial way for a winery to build consumer awareness for the brand in Massachusetts, its unavailability means that these wineries are not able to compete on the same footing as §19F(b) "small" wineries.[146]

Because the Massachusetts law "change[d] the competitive balance between in-state and out-of-state wineries in a way that benefits Massachusetts's wineries and significantly burdens out-of-state competitors," the First Circuit ruled it to be discriminatory in effect. No balancing under *Pike* was required in light of the discriminatory purpose and effect of the statute.[147]

The court's concern about the forced termination of wholesaler relationships echoes *Pike* itself, which struck down the Arizona Fruit and Vegetable Standardization Act on the grounds that it imposed a "straight jacket on the . . . company with respect to the allocation of its interstate resources."[148] Courts have shown a consistent aversion to laws that so burden interstate commerce that businesses are forced to make specific choices about the allocation of their resources.

Courts, however, have not marched in lockstep with respect to their holdings on these post-*Granholm* laws. Arizona, for example, imposed a 20,000-gallon capacity cap, maintaining direct shipment privileges for all but one Arizona winery. The state also restricted direct-to-consumer shipments to wineries, in-state or out-of-state, large or small, that sold their wines to consumers in a face-to-face transaction at the winery.[149] This is the third type of facially neutral direct shipping law that burdens out-of-state wineries. These laws, which allow direct shipment only after a mandatory trip to the winery, come in various forms. Some states require only an initial visit, after which consumers can make subsequent remote orders; others require that every shipment be the culmination of an on-premises purchase.

In contrast to the First Circuit's treatment of the Massachusetts law, the Ninth Circuit in *Black Star Farms v. Oliver* upheld the Arizona law — largely on

---

146. *Id.* at 12 (emphasis added).

147. *Id.* at 10.

148. *Pike*, 397 U.S. at 146.

149. Ariz. Rev. Stat. §4-203.04(J) (2010). The legislature created the gallonage cap and face-to-face sales regulations in direct response to *Granholm*. The statement of purpose for the bill included the following language: "The purpose of this act is to conform Arizona laws regarding the intrastate and interstate sales and deliveries of wine to . . . the requirements of the decision of the United States Supreme Court in *Granholm v. Heald*, 544 U.S. 460, 125 S. Ct. 1885 (2005). . . ." S.B. 1276, 47th Leg., 2d Reg. Sess. (Ariz. 2006).

the ground that the plaintiff offered inadequate evidence of the law's alleged discriminatory effect.[150] The plaintiff in the case argued that the face-to-face requirement, also known as the "in person" exception, favored in-state interests because most Arizona consumers were likely to buy wine directly from Arizona wineries that were closer than out-of-state wineries.[151] Hence, out-of-state wineries would be disadvantaged by the "in person" requirement.[152] The court rejected the argument because there was no differential treatment between in-state and out-of-state wineries, and the "geographical proximity" of in-state wineries to Arizona consumers is a "natural condition" not amounting to a discriminatory effect under the Commerce Clause.[153] The court held in no uncertain terms that "[a]n effect is not discriminatory . . . if it results from natural conditions."[154]

In reaching its conclusion, the court in *Black Star Farms* emphasized that Arizona's law, unlike the Massachusetts law at issue in *the Family Winemakers* case, did not force "large" wineries to choose between distribution methods. Arizona's law permitted all large wineries to distribute their wine through the three-tier system and through direct shipping.[155] To the contrary, Massachusetts required all large wineries to distribute their wine either through the three-tier system or through direct shipping.[156] The Court concluded that "[the p]laintiffs proffer no evidence to suggest that such a limited [direct shipment] exception, applicable to both in-state and out-of-state wineries, erects a barrier to Arizona's wine market that in effect creates a burden that alters the proportional share of the wine market in favor of in-state wineries, such that out-of-state wineries are unable to effectively compete in the Arizona market."[157]

The post-*Granholm* litigation concerning these and other state liquor laws has produced divergent results. Recently, for example, a circuit split has begun to develop with respect to laws requiring in-person transactions as a precondition for direct shipment privileges. The Sixth Circuit invalidated a Kentucky law requiring in-person transactions because the evidence showed that the law was discriminatory in effect, favoring in-state wineries and wholesalers over

150. *Black Star Farms LLC v. Oliver*, 600 F.3d 1225, 1231 (9th Cir. 2010). As an evidentiary matter, the court noted that merely demonstrating that a law grants a "de minimis benefit to instate wineries is . . . insufficient" to warrant its invalidation.

151. *See id.* at 1234-1235 (discussing the plaintiff's challenge to Arizona's "in person" exception).

152. *Id.* at 1229 ("Black Star Farms filed an action under 42 U.S.C. [§] 1983 on the ground that the small winery and in-person exceptions to the three-tier distribution system violate the dormant [Commerce Clause] because, in practical effect, the two exceptions to the three-tier system discriminate against out-of-state wineries.").

153. *See id.* at 1234-1235. Both of these are relevant to the "in person" exception since Arizona's consumers are most likely to visit and make in-person purchases from in-state wineries, therefore allowing in-state wineries to take advantage of the benefits of shipping directly to consumers. *See id.*

154. *Id.* at 1234 (citing *Cherry Hill Vineyard, LLC v. Baldacci*, 505 F.3d 28, 38 n.7 (1st Cir. 2007)).

155. *See* Ariz. Rev. Stat. §§4-243.01, 4-244(6)-(7) (2010) (codifying the three-tier system); Ariz. Rev. Stat. §4-203.04(J) (2010) (codifying the "in person" exception permitting all wineries to ship directly to consumers, with some conditions).

156. Mass. Gen. Laws ch. 138, §19F(a) (2010).

157. *Black Star Farms*, 600 F.3d at 1231 (alteration in original).

out-of-state wineries.[158] However, the First and Seventh Circuits reached the contrary conclusion, sustaining state laws requiring in-person transactions because the evidence in those cases did not prove a discriminatory effect that altered the market share of in-state wineries.[159] Given the various combinations of provisions that can be included in these state laws and the complicated evidentiary issues related to market impact, such divergent results are likely to continue.

F. IS THE THREE-TIER DISTRIBUTION SYSTEM CRUMBLING?

Granholm's effects have spread not only to other state laws, but also to other tiers of the alcoholic beverage distribution channel. Although *Granholm* concerned only wineries' direct-to-consumer sales, post-*Granholm* litigation has involved liquor sales to and by retailers. In Washington State, Costco, the largest retailer of wine in the United States, was authorized to purchase wine directly from Washington state wineries but not from out-of-state wineries. Following the Supreme Court's nondiscrimination principle in *Granholm*, Costco sued the state to invalidate this facial discrimination.[160] In December 2005 the district court, in ruling on a motion for partial summary judgment, found that the Washington law discriminates against out-of-state producers and thus violates the dormant Commerce Clause because the law permits in-state wine and beer producers to distribute their products directly to retailers while withholding the same privileges from out-of-state wine and beer producers. The Court-ordered remedy was to eliminate this so-called "self-distribution" privilege for in-state wineries and breweries; however, the Court stayed the entry of judgment until April 2006 in order to provide a sufficient period of time for the Washington State legislature to determine whether to extend the self-distribution privilege to out-of-state beer and wine producers. The legislature responded by passing a measure that extends the self-distribution privilege to out-of-state manufacturers, effectively "leveling up" so that producers in any state can distribute directly to Washington retailers.[161]

Retailers were the next tier of the three-tier system to join the post-*Granholm* litigation. They sought the right to ship their wines to consumers around the country, challenging state laws that prohibit out-of-state retailers, including auction houses, from shipping their wines directly to in-state consumers while authorizing such shipments by in-state retailers. Many of these retailers banded together to form the Specialty Wine Retailers Association (SWRA),

---

158. *Cherry Hill Vineyards, LLC v. Lilly*, 553 F.3d 423, 432-434 (6th Cir. 2008).

159. *See Baldacci*, 505 F.3d at 36-38; *Baude v. Heath*, 538 F.3d 608, 613-615 (7th Cir. 2008); *Black Star Farms*, 600 F.3d at 1231; *see also Kleinsmith v. Shurtleff*, 571 F.3d 1033, 1042 (10th Cir. 2009) (distinguishing *Lilly* on the ground that the plaintiffs in *Lilly* had presented sufficient evidence to establish a discriminatory effect).

160. *Costco Wholesale Corp. v. Hoen* (*Hoen I*), 407 F. Supp. 2d 1247 (W.D. Wash. 2005), *rev'd on other grounds, Costco Wholesale Corp. v. Maleng* (*Maleng I*), 514 F.3d 915 (9th Cir. 2008).

161. 2006 Wash. Legis. Serv. 302, §4 (codified at Wash. Rev. Code §66.24.206 (2009)).

whose mission is broader than the guarantee of nondiscrimination and seeks "a free market in wine," in which "any adult consumer in any state should be allowed to legally purchase and have shipped to them any wine from any retailer in America."[162]

Despite the boldness of the SWRA's mission, the litigation results to date have not been particularly encouraging. Because *Granholm* concerned only producers, courts have not felt compelled to follow the nondiscrimination principle when it comes to retailers' sales and shipments to consumers. Even when a state law facially discriminates against out-of-state retailers, the law frequently has been upheld on the ground that such preferential treatment is within the state's prerogative of defining who is a retailer and what the retailer's privileges are within the three-tier system.[163] As the Fifth Circuit said in the 2010 case *Wine Country Gift Baskets.com v. Steen*, the in-state retailers' shipment right is inherent in the concept of retailing and does not constitute discrimination.[164] As of January 2011, only one district court has reached the opposite conclusion, and the appeal in that case was rendered moot when the legislature amended the statute.[165]

Perhaps it is too soon to proclaim the end of the three-tier system of distribution in the United States, as the *Wall Street Journal* did in 2006.[166] The litigation is not likely to end anytime soon, because the large economic stakes continue to compel actors at every level to bring their claims to the courts. Furthermore, these same actors can seek, and already have sought, legislative intervention. In 2010 Representative Bill Delahunt of Massachusetts introduced House Resolution 5034, known as the Comprehensive Alcohol Regulatory Act of 2010, to give states the power to regulate alcohol in ways that favor in-state interests over out-of-state companies.[167] The bill was reintroduced in identical form in the House of Representatives in March 2011.[168] Like the Wilson Act and the Webb-Kenyon Act, this bill would alter the landscape for state regulation of the liquor trade through Congress's exercise of its Commerce Clause authority. As of March 2011, Congress had not adopted that Act.

Perhaps the most likely scenario, as circuit courts continue to part ways with respect to post-*Granholm* dormant Commerce Clause issues, is that the Supreme Court will revisit these issues in the future. After all, the Supreme Court has been the arbiter of competing interpretations and applications of the dormant Commerce Clause since the early days of the union. That history is likely to be repeated, with wine as the focus of the Court's attention yet again.

---

162. Specialty Wine Retailers Ass'n, What We Stand For, http://specialtywineretailers.org/standfor.html (last visited Feb. 2, 2011).

163. *Wine Country Gift Baskets.com v. Steen*, 612 F.3d 809, 815-821 (5th Cir. 2010); *Arnold's Wines, Inc. v. Boyle*, 571 F.3d 185, 188-191 (2d Cir. 2009); *Brooks*, 462 F.3d at 351-352.

164. *Wine Country Gift Baskets.com*, 612 F.3d at 819-820.

165. *Siesta Vill. Mkt., LLC v. Granholm*, 596 F. Supp. 2d 1035, 1039-1045 (E.D. Mich. 2008), *vacated as moot*, Order Dismissing Action, July 17, 2009; *see also Wine Country Gift Baskets.com*, 612 F.3d at 817 n.5 (noting that the *Siesta Village Market* appeal was rendered moot by a change in statute).

166. Vanessa O'Connell, Wine Sales Thrive as Old Barriers Start to Crumble, Wall St. J., Aug. 25, 2006, at A1.

167. H.R. 5034, 111th Cong. (2010).

168. H.R. 1161, 112th Cong. (2011).

CHAPTER 6

WINE BRANDS AND APPELLATIONS OF ORIGIN

Richard Mendelson and Scott Gerien

The World Trade Organization (WTO) Agreement on Trade-Related Aspects of Intellectual Property Rights (TRIPS)[1] establishes the types of intellectual property rights that must be recognized by WTO members. The United States is a WTO member. Under TRIPS, intellectual property rights are generally divided into two areas: (1) industrial property, such as patents and distinctive signs and, in particular, trademarks and geographical indications;[2] and (2) copyright and related rights.

According to TRIPS, all intellectual property rights have equal stature. By and large, there is no conflict among the various types of intellectual property. The best-known and frequently used intellectual properties—copyright, trademark, and patent—rarely overlap. When multiple intellectual properties coincide, they usually coexist harmoniously because they serve distinct purposes.

Trademarks and geographical indications, however, are distinctive signs that serve different purposes and often do come into conflict. In the wine industry, the same term may be utilized as a trademark (a wine brand) to designate the producer of a product and as a geographical indication (an appellation of origin) to designate the geographical origin of the product. This dual usage can result in thorny questions about priority of rights, possible coexistence, and possible consumer confusion.

In the United States, the potential for conflict is exacerbated by the U.S. government, which acknowledges geographical indications as intellectual

1. TRIPS: Agreement on Trade-Related Aspects of Intellectual Property Rights, Apr. 15, 1994, Marrakesh Agreement Establishing the World Trade Organization, Annex 1C, 1869 U.N.T.S. 299, 33 I.L.M. 1197 (1994) (hereinafter TRIPS Agreement).

2. TRIPS Article 22(i) defines geographical indications as "indications which identify a good as originating in the territory of a Member, or a region or locality in that territory, where a given quality, reputation or other characteristic of the good is essentially attributable to its geographical origin."

property pursuant to TRIPS but has failed to fully define what constitutes a geographical indication under U.S. law. Neither statute nor case law clearly states whether geographical indications in the United States are geographical certification marks under the federal Lanham Act, appellations of origin for wine under the Federal Alcohol Administration (FAA) Act, or something else entirely.[3]

What is clear, however, is that in the United States one federal law protects trademarks as distinctive signs, and a separate body of federal law and a separate enforcement authority protect appellations of origins for wines as distinctive signs. The conflicts, inconsistencies, and commonalities between the rights offered under these laws, the procedures for obtaining these rights, and the forums for seeking redress for infringement of these rights make this area of law difficult to navigate. For that reason, a clear understanding of the laws governing brands and appellations of origin is of great value to members of the wine industry.

In Sections A and B, which follow, Scott Gerien addresses trademarks and copyrights, respectively. In Section C, Richard Mendelson discusses appellations of origin. The authors note at the outset that it is beyond the scope of this chapter to analyze TRIPS itself or the case law thereunder. We confine our discussion to U.S. law.

A. TRADEMARK LAW

The wine industry is one of the most fragmented industries for consumer goods in the United States. No individual wine brand accounts for more than 4 percent of the total wine market.[4] In 2009 the U.S. Patent and Trademark Office (USPTO) received 3,128 applications to register trademarks for wine and issued 2,295 trademark registrations for wine. The Alcohol and Tobacco Tax and Trade Bureau (TTB) issued 87,016 Certificates of Label Approval (COLAs) for wine products in 2009.[5] In this market, crowded with wine brands, a foundational understanding of trademark law is critical.

In the United States, the Lanham Act defines trademark law at the federal level. Most states also have statutory provisions in addition to the common law that govern the protection of marks.[6] In terms of the scope of protection, federal trademark registration is more advantageous than state registration because federal trademark rights extend to the entire United States. Registration under state law only confers rights in the particular state in which

---

3. The Lanham Act is at U.S. Code, Title 15, Chapter 22. The FAA Act is at U.S. Code, Title 27, Chapter 8.

4. IRI Report, 52 weeks ending on 10/4/2009.

5. *See* USPTO, Department of Commerce, Trademark Electronic Search System, http://tess2.uspto.gov/bin/gate.exe?f=tess&state=4006:qhrt91.1.1 (accessed December 16, 2010); Alcohol and Tobacco Tax and Trade Bureau, U.S. Department of the Treasury, COLA Registry.

6. *See, e.g.*, Cal. Bus. & Prof. Code §§14200-14272, 17200-17210 (2009); N.Y. Gen. Bus. Law §§360-360-R (2010); Or. Rev. Statutes §§647.005-647.155 (2009); Wash. Rev. Code §§19.77.010-19.77.040 (2009).

the registration is obtained. In situations involving alleged trademark infringement or dilution, a party often seeks protection under both federal and state law; the legal analysis in either jurisdiction is generally the same.[7]

As defined by the Lanham Act, a mark is a designation used to identify the goods and/or services of a party and to distinguish them from the goods and services of others.[8] A designation must be used in some prominent, distinctive manner in association with the particular product or service in order to communicate the mark's source-identifying purpose. The mark's use must communicate to the consumer that the designation is a brand identifying the particular producer of the product.[9] Using a designation in a manner that does not communicate its source-identifying function (e.g., as an aesthetic embellishment on packaging) will not establish the designation as a mark.

In the wine industry, the designation identifying the source of the goods is typically a word or group of words. Most commonly, the designation is the brand name of the wine, which is usually the most prominent term on the wine label. This designation is sometimes referred to as the "house mark." Brand names for wine include ROBERT MONDAVI, SUTTER HOME, and YELLOWTAIL, among many others with varying degrees of consumer recognition.

Other words on a label, which may serve as marks due to their source-designating symbolism, may be referred to as sub-brands. These label designations are usually subordinate in appearance or importance to the main brand, but they still assist the consumer in associating the particular wine with a particular producer. Sub-brands may be names of special proprietary wine blends or simply names used to differentiate various wines under the same house mark. For example, D'ARENBERG is a well-known Australian brand that features different wines under the D'ARENBERG house mark, all with unique names such as LAUGHING MAGPIE, THE FOOTBOLT, and DEAD ARM. All of these terms may be legally categorized as trademarks.

A "vineyard designation" also may appear on wine labels.[10] A vineyard designation functions like a sub-brand in that it usually appears on a wine label subordinate to the main brand; more specifically, it informs consumers about the source of the wine or, more particularly, the source of the wine grapes. A well-known vineyard designation is MARTHA'S VINEYARD, found on Heitz Cellars wine. This designation under TTB labeling regulations informs consumers that at least 95 percent of the wine is made from wine grapes grown on the vineyard property known as Martha's Vineyard. Section C below will cover this point in more depth.

Another example of a word mark is a tag line—a phrase used in the marketing and promotion of wine associated in the minds of consumers with a

---

7. *One Industries v. Jim O'Neal Distrib., Inc.*, 578 F.3d 1154, 1166 n.5 (9th Cir. 2009) (California trademark claims congruent to claims under Lanham Act) (citing *Acad. of Motion Picture Arts & Scis. v. Creative House Promotions, Inc.*, 944 F.2d 1446, 1457 (9th Cir. 1991).

8. 15 U.S.C. §1127 (2006).

9. Patent and Trademark Office, U.S. Department of Commerce, Trademark Manual of Examining Procedure (hereinafter TMEP) §1202 (6th ed. May 2010).

10. *See* J. Scott Gerien, The Vineyard Designation: Branding and Trademark Issues for Wineries and Vineyard Owners, Wine Business Monthly, April 15, 2003.

particular wine or producer. An early, classic example of a tag line in the wine industry was WE SHALL SELL NO WINE BEFORE ITS TIME, which consumers recognized as representing PAUL MASSON wine.

Logos, graphic presentations on a label, packaging elements, or even catalog covers, besides words, may also serve as symbols designating the source of particular own commercial impression; the logo may have independent significance as a mark. Figures 6-1 and 6-2 are two examples of wine logos with independent trademark significance.

Figure 6-1
Barefoot Logo (Registration No. 3,780,742)

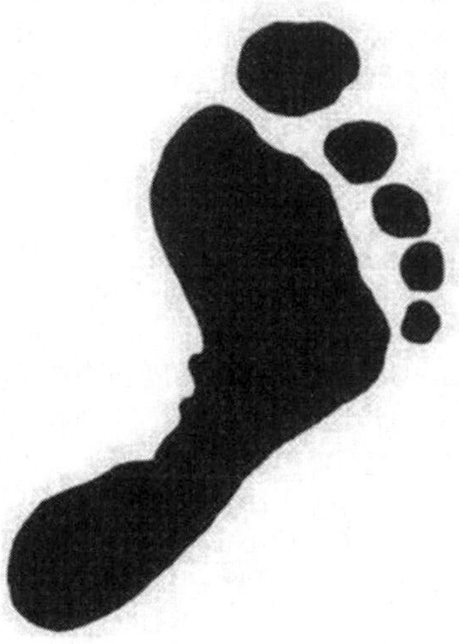

Figure 6-2
Ravenswood Logo (Registration No. 2,130,653)

The overall graphic representation of a label design also can have trademark significance. This is sometimes referred to as trade dress. Trade dress is the overall look and feel created by the packaging. Figures 6-3 and 6-4 are two examples of wine label designs protected as trademarks.

Figure 6-3
Vistamar Label (Registration No. 3,809,013)

Figure 6-4
Clancy's Label (Registration No. 3,712,315)

One of the most notable wine industry trademark cases involving trade dress is *Kendall-Jackson v. E. & J. Gallo.*[11] This case involved a dispute over the trade dress of two wine bottles, shown in Figure 6-5. Kendall-Jackson claimed that Gallo infringed its trade dress, consisting of a Bordeaux or Burgundy style wine bottle with a flanged lip, exposed cork, neck label, and a cream-colored rectangular main label with a multi-colored grape leaf bordered by gold

Figure 6-5
KENDALL-JACKSON and TURNING LEAF Bottles

11. *Kendall-Jackson Winery, Ltd. v. E. & J. Gallo Winery,* 150 F.3d 1042 (9th Cir. 1998).

bands.[12] Ultimately, the jury found that Gallo's trade dress for its TURNING LEAF product did not create a likelihood of consumer confusion, and on that basis no infringement was found.

As with logos, particular design elements of product packaging that create a distinctive commercial impression may be protected as marks. As shown in Figure 6-6, a striped capsule design for the top of a wine bottle has been registered as a trademark in and of itself, apart from other elements of the packaging. Similarly, a unique presentation of swirls forming the background design for a label and the exterior and interior of a wine shipper (Figure 6-7) have been registered.

Also the exterior of a wine catalog (Figure 6-8) may carry a distinctive design and be protectable as a mark. While simple design elements that are common in catalogs may not make any impact on consumers, more unique catalog designs can create the necessary commercial impression such that consumers recognize these designs as a particular producer's products.[13]

Figure 6-6
Terra D'Oro Striped Capsule (Registration No. 3,122,409)

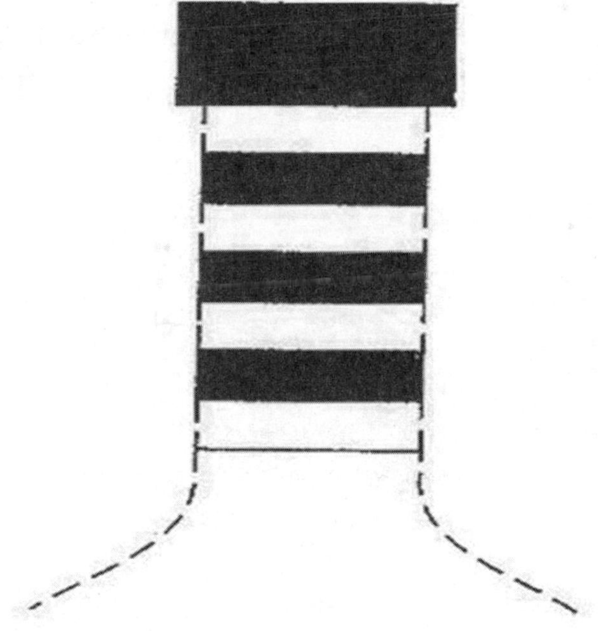

12. *Id.* The black-and-white bottle images reproduced here do not reveal the similar colors of the leaves on the two bottles.

13. Catalog covers are also usually protectable by copyright as creative works of graphic authorship.

Figure 6-7
Clos Du Val Swirl Designs (Registration No. 3,066,515)

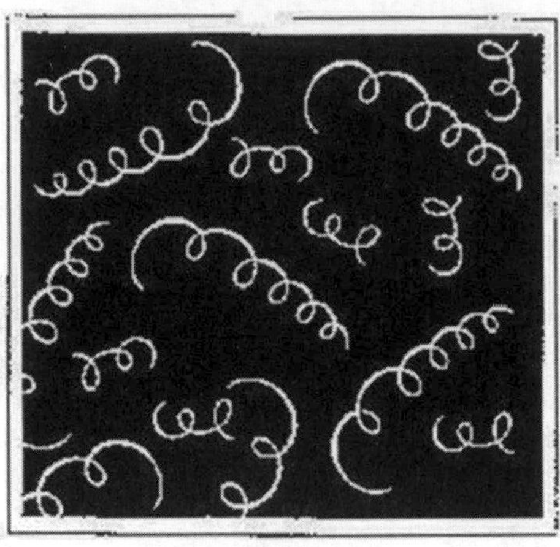

Figure 6-8
Bounty Hunter Catalog Cover (Registration No. 3,559,989)

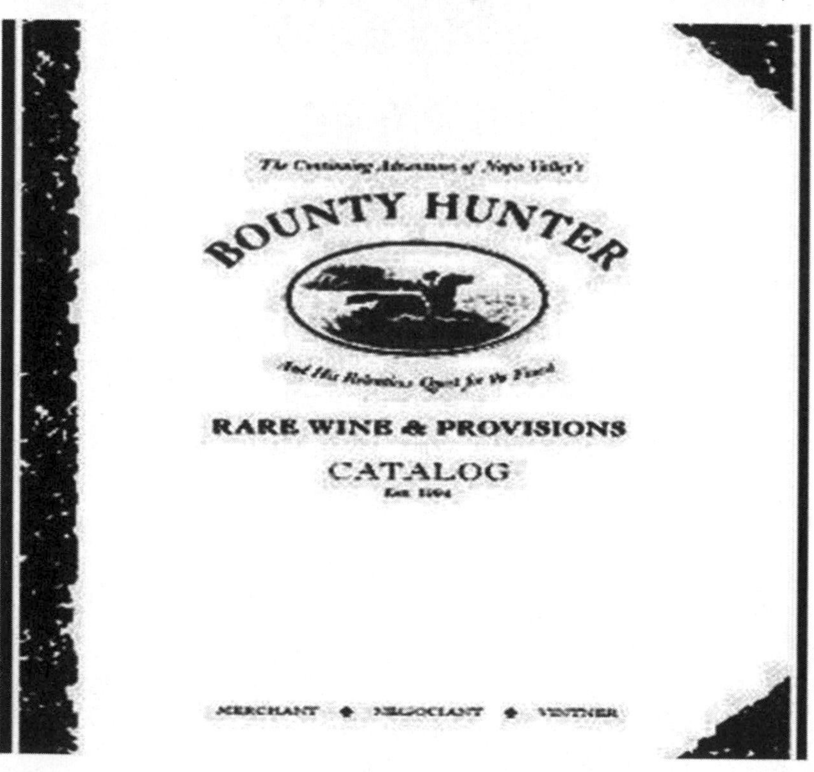

A single color may be protectable as a trademark although color alone is not inherently distinctive.[14] For a color to be protectable, it must acquire "secondary meaning" as a mark in the minds of consumers.[15] In the wine industry, producers have attempted to protect bottle color[16] and the color of labels[17] with mixed results. Even where color can be protected, the level of protection for such a mark may be diminished because, when evaluating the likelihood of confusion, the marks must be considered in the context of the entire packaging on which they appear. Often, the entire package has elements in addition to color that reduce any likelihood of confusion.

Although there do not appear to be any sound or smell marks in the wine industry, sound and smell also may function as symbols creating trademark significance. The distinctive sound of NBC's chime of the notes G, E, and C is protected,[18] as is the smell of cherry associated with synthetic lubricants for high-performance racing and recreational vehicles.[19] While particular wines are known for having distinctive aromas, such smells likely would be categorized as descriptive of the goods rather than distinctive, in which case they would not be protectable as marks.

1. CLASSIFICATION OF MARKS

This section explains how marks are defined as trademarks, service marks, certification marks, or collective marks based on their function. Any of the types of symbols identified in the previous section, including words, designs, and trade dress, can serve as any of the mark types discussed below.

The term "trademark" is commonly used to refer to the entire area of law dealing with marks as defined and protected under the Lanham Act. Technically, however, "trademark" only refers to marks used in association with goods as a means of designating the producer of the goods.

Service marks are marks used in association with services to designate the source of the services. Wine industry services include the retail sale of wine, wine club services, the production of wine for others, and vineyard management services.

Certification marks are terms or symbols that certify the quality and/or origin of a particular good or service. Some certification marks are intended solely to indicate that a product or service has met certain quality requirements. For instance, Underwriters Laboratories' "UL" certification mark indicates and certifies that products bearing that mark have met certain safety

---

14. *Qualitex Co. v. Jacobson Prods. Co.*, 514 U.S. 159 (1995).

15. *Wal-Mart Stores v. Samara Bros.*, 529 U.S. 205 (2000).

16. *See Freixenet v. Admiral Wine*, 731 F.2d 148 (3d Cir. 1984) (black bottle protectable as part of overall trade dress, but no confusing similarity found due to label differences); *see also Sazerac Co. v. Skyy Spirits*, 95 F.3d 53 (5th Cir. 1996) (cobalt blue bottle used by Skyy Spirits not protectable due to numerous examples of third-party use of cobalt blue bottles for alcoholic beverages).

17. Veuve Clicquot Ponsardin Maison Fondee En 1772 is the owner of U.S. Trademark Registration No. 2,052,302 for the color "orangish-yellow" used on labels for wine.

18. Registration No. 916,522.

19. Registration No. 2,463,044.

standards.[20] As another example, the Demeter Association certifies that certain goods produced from agricultural products, including wine, use agricultural ingredients that are grown with sustainable farming practices and produced with sustainable manufacturing processes. The certified goods are allowed to use the DEMETER certification mark.[21]

Geographical certification marks certify the origin of goods. They also may, but do not necessarily, certify the quality of the goods.[22] Examples in the wine industry include ASTI,[23] BADEN,[24] and LODI RULES.[25]

Unlike a trademark owner, the owner of a certification mark *cannot* use the certification mark; the mark may only be used to certify the goods of other parties who are entitled to use the mark.[26] This restriction is intended to maintain the integrity of the certification process. Additionally, any party whose products meet the certification standards may apply for certification and thereby be entitled to use the mark. The standards must be applied to all parties equally.[27] Finally, the certifier, not the government (unless the government is the owner of the certification mark), polices the users of the certification mark to ensure that the certification standards are being met.[28] However, an action to cancel a certification mark may be filed by any party with the USPTO.[29]

For geographical certification marks, the certifier must demonstrate that it has the authority to control the geographical term that is the subject of the certification mark. The certifier may be a government agency; if not, the certifier typically should be able to show that it is acting with the authority of a government agency.[30]

Geographical certification marks are an important way to protect the names of geographical regions known for the production of certain types of goods. In practice, however, the use of certification marks in the wine industry has been minimal. The main reason is that the TTB's wine appellation program has made geographical certification marks for the wine industry superfluous. Nevertheless, geographical certification marks still may play an important role in protecting wine appellations at home and abroad.

Finally, collective marks are used on goods or services exclusively by members of an association or organization.[31] A certification process or standard is not required for a collective mark, although the organization may elect to set standards for its members. Compared to certification marks, the rules related to the use and availability of collective marks are less strict, making collective

---

20. Registration No. 782,589.
21. Registration No. 2,097,857.
22. 15 U.S.C. §1127 (2006); TMEP §1306.02 (6th ed., May 2010).
23. Registration No. 3,369,276.
24. Registration No. 1,187,234.
25. Registration No. 3,736,971. *See* Section C for a discussion of the LODI RULES certification mark.
26. 15 U.S.C. §1127 (2006).
27. *Id.*
28. *Id.*
29. 15 U.S.C. §1064 (2006).
30. TMEP §1306.2(b) (6th ed. May 2010).
31. 15 U.S.C. §1127 (2006).

marks easier to maintain. In the wine industry, an example of a collective mark is WINE AND SPIRITS GUILD OF AMERICA.[32]

2. PROTECTABILITY AND THE SPECTRUM OF MARKS

All marks can be placed on a spectrum based on their degree of inherent distinctiveness and the protectability of the mark. Marks that are inherently distinctive and protectable upon their adoption are at one end of the spectrum. These marks are characterized as fanciful, arbitrary, or suggestive. At the other end of the spectrum are marks that are not inherently distinctive and either not protectable at the time of their adoption but capable of acquiring distinctiveness through use (i.e., descriptive marks) or not ever protectable, being non-exclusively used by all (i.e., generic marks).[33]

Fanciful marks consist of those terms or symbols that have no meaning and are completely original, the product of the imagination of their creators. An abstract design such as that found on the Meridian Vineyards label (Figure 6-9) or wine brands such as CAMIANA[34] and RAMIAN,[35] which have no known meaning, are fanciful marks. Because the meaning of these marks is unknown, consumers will associate them exclusively with the producer owning the particular mark. For this reason, fanciful marks are inherently distinctive and are considered the most distinctive of all marks.[36]

Arbitrary marks are next on the spectrum of inherent distinctiveness. An arbitrary mark is a term or design that already exists in the consumer's consciousness but not in association with the product or service with which it is used. Arbitrary marks include a wine label featuring the image of a red truck and such wine brand names as FAT BASTARD,[37] MAYA,[38] and BANDIT.[39] Although these designations mean something to consumers, the meaning is not associated with wine. As a result, the apparently arbitrary use of the mark in association with an unexpected product may make a strong and distinctive impression on consumers.[40]

Situated near the dividing line between distinctive and non-distinctive marks are those that suggest, but do not describe, a quality or characteristic of the product. The consumer must go through a multi-step thought process to associate the suggestive mark with the quality or characteristic of the good or service on which it is used. For example, the process of "veraison" occurs when grapes mature and change color during the growing season.[41] Consumers

32. Registration No. 2,277,008.
33. *See Kendall-Jackson*, 150 F.3d at 1047.
34. Registration No. 3,674,558.
35. Registration No. 3,088,347.
36. *Kendall-Jackson*, 150 F.3d at 1047 note 8.
37. Registration No. 2,230,941.
38. Registration No. 2,508,401.
39. Registration No. 3,311,926.
40. *Id.*
41. According to Jancis Robinson, veraison is the "intermediate stage of grape berry development which marks the beginning of ripening, when the grapes change from the hard, green state to their softened and coloured form." The Oxford Companion to Wine 1017 (Jancis Robinson ed., 1st ed. 1994).

Figure 6-9
Meridian Vineyards Label

seeing the brand VERAISON on a wine bottle will not immediately understand if the brand name relates to wine; they will follow a multi-part reasoning process: veraison is a stage of the grape growing process; grapes are used to make wine; therefore, VERAISON is suggestive of wine.[42] A suggestive mark such as VERAISON is distinctive upon adoption and immediately registerable.[43]

Certain suggestive marks are less distinctive than others. The less distinctive marks may be described as "highly suggestive." Such marks are protectable; however, they are harder to protect than marks that are arbitrary or fanciful.[44]

---

42. *See Kendall Jackson*, 150 F.3d at 1048-1049 ("The use of a grape leaf as a mark for wine would normally be inherently distinctive because it suggests, rather than describes, the product. One has to go through two or three steps to associate the leaf with the product—i.e., a grape leaf comes from a grapevine, which has grapes from which wine is produced. Under the standard test, a grape leaf could be suggestive and thus inherently distinctive.")

43. Registration No. 2,753,822.

44. *See Minnesota Mining & Mfg. Co. v. Johnson & Johnson*, 454 F.2d 1179, 1180 (C.C.P.A. 1972) ("Often the best trademarks are highly suggestive, and it is well settled that a valid trademark may be highly suggestive.").

Descriptive marks describe a quality or characteristic of the product or services on which the marks are used. Descriptive marks are not protectable upon their adoption but may acquire distinctiveness through use as a brand in association with a product or service. Descriptive marks are said to acquire a secondary meaning in the minds of consumers over time.

Descriptive wine industry marks that have acquired the distinctiveness required for protection include DOUBLE BARREL AGED[45] and CUVEE ROUGE.[46] The USPTO often will find terms descriptive that are actually suggestive of wine, such as "barrel," "plump," and "oak." In these instances, practitioners in the wine industry should consider taking steps to challenge the USPTO's determination.

Another form of descriptive mark is the surname of the wine producer. More than in any other industry, surnames are commonly used as trademarks for wine. On adoption, surnames are not protectable because a person should not be able to claim exclusivity in a name shared by others absent a showing of acquired distinctiveness. Indeed, even some of the best-known surname brands coexist, such as ROBERT MONDAVI and CK MONDAVI, as a result of the strong judicial tendency in the common law to allow an individual to use her surname in association with the product she produces.[47] Therefore, while Georgina Gerien might be the first to use Gerien as a trademark for wine, her brother Cameron Gerien would not be precluded from using Cameron Gerien as his brand of wine absent some showing of strength and acquired distinctiveness of the Gerien mark. That being said, some of the best-known marks in the wine industry are surnames that have acquired distinctiveness as wine brands: WENTE,[48] ANTINORI,[49] and TAITTINGER,[50] for example.[51]

Because wine is a product of place, geographical terms are almost as commonly used as surnames in wine marks. Typically, geographical terms in trademarks are either "primarily geographically descriptive,"[52] in which case they are not protectable, or they are misdescriptive of the wine's origin. But there are many exceptions. Some terms may have both geographical significance and non-geographical significance, but the overall significance is not primarily geographical. Even a term that is solely geographical may not be *primarily* geographically descriptive or misdescriptive if there is no goods-place

45. Registration No. 3,802,353.

46. Registration No. 3,374,998.

47. *See Friend v. H.A. Friend & Co.*, 416 F.2d 526, 531 (9th Cir. 1969), *cert. denied* 397 U.S. 914 (1970) ("the law is reluctant to preclude an individual's business use of his own name when no attempt to confuse the public has been made").

48. Registration No. 1,535,670.

49. Registration No. 1,155,028.

50. Registration No. 1,420,365.

51. *See, e.g., E. & J. Gallo Winery v. Gallo Cattle Co.*, 967 F.2d 1280 (9th Cir. 1992) (despite judicial reluctance to preclude one from using his own name, the court upheld injunction restricting brother of winery's principals from using GALLO as trademark on cheese due to strength of mark and consumer confusion).

52. A mark is primarily geographically descriptive if (1) the primary significance of the mark is geographic; (2) purchasers would likely think that the goods originate in the place identified in the mark (i.e., there is a place-goods association); and (3) the mark identifies the geographic origin of the goods. *See* 15 U.S.C. §1052(e)(2).

association in the minds of consumers between the geographical term and the goods on which it is used.[53] For instance, San Lorenzo is the name of an Italian saint as well as a city in California that has no association with the cultivation or production of wine. Therefore, the mark SAN LORENZO is neither primarily geographically descriptive nor misdescriptive of wine and is protectable as a trademark for wine.[54] As another example, there is an area in California called Jamieson Canyon, where grapes are grown. Despite the descriptiveness of the name, JAMIESON CANYON was found to be protectable as a trademark for wine because the area is not known to consumers and, therefore, is not primarily geographically descriptive.[55]

An important distinction between geographically descriptive and misdescriptive marks is that the former are not protectable absent acquired distinctiveness, but they still may be used on products so long as they are not misleading. Wine trademarks often include the name of the geographical area in which the grapes are grown in an effort to take advantage of the recognition of the particular region. Yet these brand owners know, or should know, that they cannot prevent others from using the same geographical term in their own marks.[56]

By contrast, trademarks that are primarily geographically misdescriptive and may deceptively influence consumer purchasing decisions violate the trademark laws and may not be used by anyone.[57]

Following the U.S. adoption of TRIPS, the use of a non-generic geographical indication on wine not from the place identified by the geographical indication is strictly prohibited for all wine brands adopted after 1996, regardless of whether the consumer is misled by the use of the geographical indication.[58] Thus, pursuant to Article 23 of TRIPS, the name of an obscure geographical area that produces a wine with particular characteristics may not be used or registered as part of a trademark for wine not from that area even if consumers in the United States have no familiarity with this geographical area. Presently, the USPTO appears to take a different approach to obscure geographical names. The use or registration of a geographical term on wine or spirits not from the identified area will only be prohibited if the name has developed a reputation

---

53. *See In re Brouwerij Nacional Balashi NV*, 80 USPQ 2d 1820 (TTAB 2006) (Balashi, Aruba is obscure to U.S. consumers and therefore registerable as a trademark for beer from that place).

54. Registration No. 3,003,575.

55. Registration No. 2,634,043.

56. Examples include the marks RUTHERFORD RIDGE, RUTHERFORD HILL, and RUTHERFORD RANCH, each of which refers to the Rutherford AVA situated inside the Napa Valley AVA. None of the owners of these marks has exclusive rights to the term "Rutherford," but each owner has exclusive rights in its own composite mark and benefits from the association of the brand with the AVA.

57. *See, e.g., Bronco Wine Co. v. Jolly*, 33 Cal. 4th 943 (2004) (upholding state consumer protection law requiring wine labels using "Napa" to qualify for the Napa County or Napa Valley appellation because consumers otherwise would be deceived).

58. 15 U.S.C. §1052(a); *see* TRIPS, *supra* note 1, at art. 22 and 23; Uruguay Round Agreements Act (URAA), Pub. L. No. 103-465, 103 Stat. 4809. The 1996 grandfather date, set forth in TRIPS, is distinct from the TTB's grandfather date for geographical brands, 1986, which is discussed in detail below.

among U.S. consumers. The USPTO's focus on whether the mark, in fact, misleads consumers is not required under Article 23 of TRIPS.[59]

Descriptive marks, including geographically descriptive marks and surnames, can cross the divide from non-distinctive to distinctive if they establish over time secondary meaning as brand names in the minds of consumers. Descriptive marks with secondary meaning are fully protectable in the same way as suggestive, arbitrary, or fanciful marks. The owner of the descriptive mark carries the burden of demonstrating acquired distinctiveness. In the context of trademark registration, this burden may be met by continuous exclusive use of the mark in U.S. commerce for a period of five years.[60] Secondary meaning also may be demonstrated by a significant sale of the product or significant advertising featuring the mark.[61] However, the best evidence of acquired distinctiveness, especially in an infringement action in federal court, is a consumer survey demonstrating consumer recognition of the mark as a brand.[62]

Different rules regarding the distinctiveness and exclusive use of geographical names apply to certification marks and collective marks. A geographical certification mark may be registered by the certifier under the name of the specific geographical area, and that name will receive instant protection and exclusivity without a showing that consumers have come to recognize the term as a distinctive geographical identifier. Thus, if the city of Chattanooga, Tennessee, wishes to obtain the certification mark CHATTANOOGA for wine made from grapes grown in Chattanooga, it would be able to claim exclusive rights in the trademark use of that term in association with wine even though the term is descriptive of a geographical place and has not acquired distinctiveness with consumers as a geographical indication. Once such a certification mark is registered, a winery in Chattanooga that makes wine from grapes grown there could not call itself Chattanooga Winery without the permission of the city of Chattanooga, the owner of the certification mark, to use the name Chattanooga.

On the other hand, the owner of a collective mark with geographical significance, for example, a regional trade association, may not claim exclusive use in the geographical term absent some evidence of fame or acquired distinctiveness. Thus, if a group of winegrowers from Lodi, California, wished to register LODI WINEGROWERS as a collective mark, it would have to disclaim exclusive rights to the term "LODI," and others would be allowed to use that name as part of competing collective marks (e.g., LODI WINERY ASSOCIATION) or as trademarks (e.g., LODI CELLARS). Put another way, the winegrowers' collective mark would not give them exclusivity in the use of the term "LODI."

Generic marks lie at the far end of non-distinctiveness. Under trademark law, a mark is generic if it functions to identify the product itself or has been

59. TMEP §1210.08(a) (6th ed. May 2010).

60. 15 U.S.C. §1052(f) (2006).

61. *See In re Uncle Sam Chemical Co.*, 229 USPQ 233, 235 (TTAB 1986) ("over eighteen years of substantially exclusive and continuous use of the term together with evidence of considerable sales of products sold under the mark is sufficient to support a claim of acquired distinctiveness").

62. *See Yankee Candle Co. v. Bridgewater Candle Co.*, 259 F.3d 25, 43 (1st Cir. 2001).

used in such a way so as to become an identifier of the product type in the minds of consumers. "Wine" is and always has been the generic term for wine, as it identifies the product. The court in the *Kendall-Jackson v. Gallo* case found that grape leaves, although originally suggestive of wine, had become generic symbols due to their prevalent use on wine labels in the marketplace.[63] Similarly, the term "champagne" has come to be recognized as a generic term for sparkling wine in the United States despite the fact that it is also a winegrowing region in France and is recognized outside the United States as a geographical indication for sparkling wine from that region.[64]

Unlike descriptive marks, generic terms or symbols may not acquire distinctiveness through use. Therefore, to the extent that a mark encompasses a term that conceivably could be defined as generic or descriptive, a party hoping to claim exclusivity in that term through use must not allow it to be classified as generic by the USPTO or otherwise.

In conclusion, the most distinctive brands are the easiest to register as trademarks. They also receive the highest level of protection against any confusingly similar brands. The distinctiveness of a brand, however, does not imply the successful marketing of the brand. Brands resonate with consumers for different reasons; brands with strong impact are not always distinctive. If a brand resonates with consumers because it describes some characteristic of the wine, for example, its geographical origin or the family producing the wine, the brand owner may find it difficult to prevent others from capitalizing on that same point of appeal in their own brand names.

3. ADOPTION AND REGISTRATION OF MARKS

In the United States marks can only be protected if they are used in commerce. Under common law, once a mark is used in commerce, rights in the mark are established in association with the particular goods and services. However, common law rights are limited to the geographical area in which the mark is actually used.[65] For example, if a California wine brand is not federally registered as a trademark and is only sold in California, the California winery cannot stop a New York winery from subsequently using the same brand name for its wine sold only in New York. Furthermore, if the California brand wine were ever sold in New York, the California winery would be infringing on the New York winery's common law rights despite the California winery's earlier common law use of the brand name in California.

63. *Kendall-Jackson*, 150 F.3d at 1048-1049.

64. *See, e.g., Door Systems, Inc. v. Pro-Line Door Systems, Inc.*, 83 F.3d 169, 170-171 (7th Cir. 1996) (dictum that "champagne" is a generic term identifying the product). The TTB classifies "champagne" as semi-generic for reasons explained in Section C.

65. *See Hanover Star Milling Co. v. Metcalf*, 240 U.S. 403 (1916); *see also Grupo Gigane SA De CV v. Dallo & Co., Inc.*, 391 F.3d 1088 (9th Cir. 2004) (priority of use in one area of the United States does not necessarily suffice to establish priority in another area).

a. Use in Commerce Requirement for Federal Registration

Federal registration of trademarks avoids the confusion and conflicts caused by ambiguous or overlapping markets by granting rights throughout the United States and in all of its territories.[66] Like common law rights, federal trademark rights cannot be secured unless or until the mark is used in commerce.[67] The Lanham Act defines commerce as "all commerce which may be lawfully regulated by Congress."[68] According to the Commerce Clause of the U.S. Constitution, use in commerce means the sale or transport of marked goods across state lines or between the United States and a foreign nation.[69] However, because Congress regulates the production and sale of wine in the United States,[70] it can be argued that even the intrastate sale of wine is commerce regulated by Congress and, therefore, sufficient to meet the "use in commerce" requirement for federal registration of a mark. However, there is no direct case law on point.

Use in commerce to support federal registration must be a "legal" use.[71] This means that the sale or shipment of any product that is the subject of an act of Congress, such as the Food, Drug and Cosmetic Act or the Meat Inspection Act, must comply with the applicable federal law to be considered a "legal" use for purposes of registration under the Lanham Act.[72] In the wine industry, the FAA Act requires all wineries to be qualified and permitted by the TTB; wineries also must obtain a COLA, or COLA exemption, for their wine labels before those wines are released from bond for sale.[73] The shipment or sale of wine that has not complied with these requirements arguably would not be a "legal" use sufficient to support a federal trademark registration.

A sale of goods to support federal registration is also inadequate if the goods themselves do not exist at the time of the sale.[74] Entering into a contract to buy goods that are not yet available does not constitute a use in commerce for purposes of federal registration.[75] Thus, where a winery has wine aging in barrel that has been advertised and sold on a "pre-release" basis, the sale of the pre-release wine is inadequate to demonstrate use of the mark in commerce.

Federal registration gives the registrant the right to stop any infringing activity by junior users anywhere in the United States. Because most wineries

---

66. *See Giant Foods, Inc. v. Nation's Foodservice, Inc.*, 710 F.2d 1565, 1568 (Fed. Cir. 1983).

67. 15 U.S.C. §1127 (2006).

68. *Id.*

69. U.S. Const., art. I, §8, cl. 3.

70. *See* Federal Alcohol Administration Act, 27 U.S.C. §202.

71. *See* C.F.R. §2.69 (2010).

72. *Id.; see also In re Stellar Int'l Inc.*, 159 USPQ 48 (TTAB 1968) (requiring compliance with Food, Drug and Cosmetic Act for registration); *In re Cook United, Inc.*, 188 USPQ 284 (TTAB 1975) (requiring compliance with Meat Inspection Act for registration).

73. 27 U.S.C. §204 (2006); 27 C.F.R. §13.21 (2010).

74. *See Richardson-Vicks, Inc. v. Franklin Mint Corp.*, 216 USPQ 989 (TTAB 1982) (where the goods that are the subject of the trademark registration application have been sold but have not yet been created and marked, such sale is inadequate to prove the use of the mark on the goods in commerce).

75. *See Geovision, Inc. v. Geovision Corp.*, 928 F.2d 387 (11th Cir. 1991) (an as-yet unperformed contract of sale does not result in goods being "sold or transported" in interstate commerce; the term "sold" contemplates a product with the mark on it).

do not sell their wine in most, or even many, states when they commence operations, especially where distribution or direct sales may not be legally or economically feasible, federal trademark registration allows them to protect their rights to a brand before they expand into new markets. However, a mark holder's ability to enforce trademark rights against another winery located in a different market is contingent on the two products entering the same market.[76] Once there is such a product overlap, the federal registration allows the registrant to stop the junior user's use of the mark, regardless of how long the junior user has been using the mark prior to the registrant's entry into the market.

b. Trademark Screening

Prior to adopting a new brand, a party seeking to protect its brand and avoid trademark infringement liability should conduct a trademark clearance search. An experienced trademark attorney is the most qualified advisor to evaluate the nuances related to the risks of infringement and the availability of marks; however, parties can conduct their own searches to generally evaluate availability.

The Internet has increased access to information previously unavailable to those without specialized databases and other resources. Public information is readily available about products offered for sale in the marketplace. Any lawyer or non-lawyer evaluating the availability of a new name as a trademark for wine need only fire up her computer, select her favorite search engine, and input the proposed brand name in combination with generic terms such as "wine," "vineyard," and "cellars." Internet research is a good tool for making a preliminary evaluation of the marketplace; however, it is not determinative of the availability or protectability of a potential brand name.

The TTB's online COLA database is another excellent resource for evaluating the availability of a potential wine brand.[77] COLAs do not provide a brand owner with any statutory trademark rights, and the COLA database is sometimes incomplete or incorrect, but the existence of a COLA indicates that a brand name likely has been used in commerce. The COLA database is a valuable resource for discovering more obscure brands that may not be located easily through an Internet search. A discovery of a potentially conflicting brand on the COLA database should be followed up with research concerning the actual use of the brand to determine if a conflict does, in fact, exist. The COLA database is also a valuable resource for a brand owner policing infringing uses by others once trademark rights have been established.

The USPTO Trademark Electronic Search System is possibly the most important resource for locating potentially conflicting marks.[78] This resource

---

76. *See Dawn Donut Co. v. Hart's Food Stores, Inc.*, 267 F.2d 358 (2d Cir. 1959) (where the parties' goods or services are not yet offered to the same geographical markets, there can be no harm and no infringement).

77. *See* Alcohol and Tobacco Tax and Trade Bureau, U.S. Department of the Treasury, COLA Registry, https://www.ttbonline.gov/colasonline/publicSearchColasBasic.do (accessed December 14, 2010).

78. *See* USPTO, Department of Commerce, Trademark Electronic Search System, http://tess2.uspto.gov/bin/gate.exe?f=tess&state=4007:q58rp2.1.1 (accessed December 14, 2010).

is available to the public on the USPTO website; however, the database is not user friendly. Many trademark practitioners subscribe to proprietary search systems that simplify and improve searches of the USPTO Register database. A USPTO search can be simplified by restricting search results to international Class 33 for wine and alcoholic beverages other than beer. Although difficult to navigate, the USPTO Register must be searched to identify marks that are the subject of pending applications and not yet in use. If pending marks are eventually used and the applications mature to registration, these marks could preempt the intervening use of a similar mark initiated after the trademark application date. Given the investment required to establish a new wine brand and the potential liability for infringing on the trademark rights of another brand owner, the cost of hiring experienced trademark counsel to perform a USPTO search and analyze potential likelihood of confusion with the proposed brand name may be money well spent.

Wine marks with geographical significance require particular attention. A trademark for wine should not include a geographical term associated with a particular wine region unless the wine is from that region. Use of a geographical reference on wine not from the identified region violates TRIPS Article 23, as recognized by the United States in the Lanham Act, even if the region is not well known in the United States so long as it is a region in which wine with a given quality, reputation, or other characteristic is produced.[79] In addition to violating TRIPS Article 23, labeling wine with the name of a winemaking region in which the subject wine was not produced would give rise to claims of consumer deception and false designation of origin under the Lanham Act.[80]

The use of wine brands that include geographical names is also regulated by the TTB, as discussed in more detail in Section C. A brand name featuring a recognized American viticultural area (AVA) or any other "name of viticultural significance"[81] can only be used on wines that meet the AVA requirements, namely, that at least 85 percent of the wine be made from grapes grown in that AVA.[82] Although not all geographical names used or locally recognized in winemaking areas are, or will become, names of viticultural significance, a brand owner runs the risk that a brand name that includes a known, or

79. While the United States indicated that it did not need to amend the Lanham Act to enact TRIPS Article 23 with respect to the improper *use* of geographical indications on wine because the TRIPS Article 23 protections already are encompassed within the Lanham Act, this interpretation of U.S. law is questionable. Because no case has been brought in a U.S. court attempting to enforce an Article 23 violation through a Lanham Act claim, one cannot say for certain whether such a claim would be recognized by a U.S. court.

80. If a mark encompasses the name of a wine region and the wine is from that region, the use of the mark is permissible unless the region also owns a certification mark that controls the use of the regional name on wine and that requires compliance with certain production guidelines. Nevertheless, the rights in a descriptive mark are fairly limited, and the use of the regional name by others in marks for wine from the region usually is allowed.

81. 27 C.F.R. 4.39(i)(3) (2010) provides that "a name has viticultural significance when it is the name of a state or county (or the foreign equivalents), when approved as a viticultural area in Part 9 of this chapter, or by a foreign government, or when found to have viticultural significance by the appropriate TTB officer."

82. *Id.* §4.25. There is a grandfather exception to this rule, at 27 C.F.R. §4.39(i) (2010), which is discussed in Section C below.

even a relatively obscure, geographical name could become the subject of a future AVA petition. If that AVA were established, the brand could only be used on wines that comply with the 85 percent grape source requirement for that AVA.

Brands encompassing the term "CALISTOGA" faced this problem when the TTB commenced rulemaking on a 2003 petition to establish the Calistoga AVA, situated in the northern part of the Napa Valley AVA. Wine grapes had been grown in the Calistoga area since the 1800s.[83] During the administrative comment period, Calistoga Cellars, which began using the mark CALISTOGA CELLARS in 1998 on wine *not* made 85 percent or more from grapes grown inside the proposed AVA, objected to the new AVA on the ground that it would restrict the winery's trademark rights.[84] After an extensive rulemaking, the TTB established the Calistoga AVA and required the CALISTOGA CELLARS label, among other impacted labels, to come into compliance with the 85 percent content requirement following a three-year phase-in period.[85] While the law in this area might change in the future, the TTB's willingness to establish AVAs with geographical names already in use as trademarks should be carefully considered by brand owners before they adopt a geographical mark.

At times, the USPTO is overly aggressive in rejecting trademarks for wine on the basis of geographical descriptiveness or deceptiveness when, in fact, the primary significance of the marks is not geographical. For example, marks that reference the name of a road located in a wine region are not necessarily geographically descriptive or deceptive because most consumers would not recognize the road name or know that it is located in that wine region. Nevertheless, the USPTO routinely refuses applications to register marks on the basis of geographical distinctiveness or deceptiveness. Applicants should be prepared to challenge the USPTO on such refusals.

c. The Application Process for a Federal Trademark Registration

Once a party has determined that a mark is available for use, the brand owner must consider whether the mark should be protected, and if so, to what degree. A brand owner is not obligated to protect its mark through registration of the trademark.[86] A party develops common law rights in a mark just by using it. However, as we have seen, a registered mark carries more benefits than a mark protected by common law principles. Contrary to some popular misconceptions, trademark registration is the only way to obtain statutory protection for a mark. This section discusses the application process for a federal trademark registration.

83. *See* Proposed Revision of American Viticultural Area Regulations, 72 Fed. Reg. 65261 (Nov. 20, 2007) (to be codified at 37 C.F.R. pts. 4, 9, and 70).

84. *Id.*

85. TTB Final Rule (T.D. TTB-83), 74 Fed. Reg. 64602 (Dec. 8, 2009).

86. While certain states require that a winery "register" its brand with the state's alcoholic beverage regulatory agency, this does not constitute registration of the trademark for protection purposes; that information is provided to the state for the state's own regulatory purposes, similar to the application for a COLA from the TTB.

A federal trademark registration will only issue after a mark has been used in commerce in association with the goods or services identified in the application. However, a mark need not be used in commerce before the mark holder initiates the trademark application process. A U.S. trademark application may be filed on three bases: (1) use of the mark in commerce;[87] (2) intended use of the mark in commerce;[88] and (3) ownership of a foreign application or registration by a foreign applicant intended for use in commerce.[89]

When a mark is already in legal use in commerce on wine, a trademark application may be filed based on such use. A "use-based" application may proceed immediately to registration after it has been examined and published for opposition.

Use-based applications often present practical problems for winery owners. The one-to-three-year production process for wine means that a wine brand may be developed many years before the wine is slated for release. Fortunately, the Lanham Act allows a trademark registration application to be filed where there is intent to use the mark on the particular goods or services. An "intent-to-use" (ITU) application need only include a verified statement that the applicant has a bona fide intent to use the mark on wine in the future,[90] as opposed to a verified statement and evidence that the mark is in use in commerce as required for a use-based application.[91]

An ITU application is examined and published for opposition in the same manner as a use-based application. However, once the application has successfully proceeded through the opposition period, a "notice of allowance" is issued against the ITU application.[92] To obtain registration, the applicant then must use the mark in commerce and submit an allegation of use within six months of issuance of the notice of allowance.[93] An ITU applicant may obtain one six-month extension to allege use and, upon a simple showing of good cause, an additional four six-month extensions to allege use before an application will be abandoned.[94] An ITU applicant may take up to three years in total after the issuance of a notice of allowance to use the mark in commerce and file a statement of use to perfect the registration.

Once an allegation of use is submitted and the registration issues, the registrant's rights in the mark are effective as of the original filing date of the application. The registrant may rely on registration to stop any party who adopted a confusingly similar mark after the registrant's trademark application filing date.[95] An ITU application can give a wine brand owner peace of mind that, once his wine is ready for release, he can use the brand name selected years earlier and stop any winery that adopted a similar mark in the intervening years.

---

87. 15 U.S.C. §1051(a) (2006).
88. *Id.* §1051(b).
89. *Id.* §1051(d)-(e).
90. *Id.* §1051(b).
91. *Id.* §1051(a).
92. *Id.* §1063(b)(2).
93. *Id.* §1051(d)(1).
94. *Id.* §1051(d)(2).
95. *Id.* §1057(c).

Pursuant to the U.S. accession to the Paris Convention, which is an international treaty, a person whose country of origin is a Paris Convention signatory[96] may seek registration of her mark in the United States based upon her trademark registration in her country of origin.[97] Under the Paris Convention, that party also may file a "priority application" in the United States based upon the first trademark application she filed for the mark in another Paris Convention country, provided the U.S. application is filed within six months after the filing date of the foreign application.[98] Upon filing, the U.S. application will be given the same effective date as the previously filed foreign application.[99]

A Paris Convention application requires a statement of intended use of the mark in the United States, but the foreign applicant need not actually use the mark in U.S. or foreign commerce or submit any statement for the registration to issue once examination and publication for opposition have been completed.[100] This relief from the use-in-commerce requirement allows foreign wineries to gain a foothold for their brands in the United States before they export any goods here. However, registrations without proof of use in commerce are susceptible to attack on the basis of abandonment after three years of non-use following registration or upon a showing of registrant's intent not to use the mark in the United States.[101] To maintain the validity of the registration, the foreign registrant must use the mark in U.S. commerce and submit a statement of such use between the fifth and sixth anniversaries of the registration.[102] Use in commerce is also a prerequisite to proving likelihood of confusion under the Lanham Act; a registrant cannot rely on a Paris Convention—based U.S. registration to bring an infringement action absent proof of use of its mark in U.S. commerce.[103]

A person who is not a citizen of the United States and whose domicile or residence is in a country that is a signatory to the Madrid Protocol, another international treaty, may obtain a U.S. registration based on a foreign registration by filing an International Registration application through its home country with a request for extension of protection to the United States. As with a Paris Convention application, the foreign applicant need only submit a declaration of a bona fide intent to use the mark in the United States; no actual use of the mark in U.S. or foreign commerce is required prior to obtaining registration.[104] Madrid Protocol registrations also are susceptible to

96. *See* WIPO, Contracting Parties: Paris Convention, http://www.wipo.int/treaties/en/ShowResults.jsp?lang=en&treaty_id=2 (accessed December 16, 2010).

97. 15 U.S.C. §1126(c), (e) (2006).

98. *See id.* §1126(c)-(d); *In re Fisons, Ltd.*, 197 USPQ 888 (TTAB 1978) (a claim of priority must be based on the first application filed in a Paris Convention country, not on any application filed in any Paris Convention country).

99. 15 U.S.C. §1126(d) (2006).

100. *Id.* §1126(e).

101. *See Oromeccanica, Inc. v. Ottmar Botzenhardt GmbH & Co. KG*, 223 USPQ 59 (TTAB 1983).

102. 15 U.S.C. §1058 (2006).

103. *See* 3 J. Thomas McCarthy, McCarthy on Trademarks and Unfair Competition §19:27 (4th ed. 2010).

104. 15 U.S.C. §1141(f) (2006).

cancellation and abandonment based on non-use; they cannot be invoked in infringement proceedings absent actual use of the mark in commerce.

Procedurally, a U.S. trademark or service mark application may be filed with the USPTO at the USPTO website through the Trademark Electronic Application System. Within four to six months after the filing, a USPTO trademark examining attorney will review the application for registrability. If the application is deemed not registerable, the USPTO issues an "office action" outlining the problems with the application. The applicant has six months to respond to the office action by either correcting the problems or contesting the examining attorney's assessment. The examining attorney may either accept the corrections and contentions or issue a final office action. An applicant has a right to respond to the final office action or to appeal the decision to the Trademark Trial and Appeal Board (TTAB) of the USPTO. If an applicant fails to timely respond to an office action, the application is deemed abandoned. If the applicant inadvertently fails to respond, the applicant may revive the application within two months after the issuance of the notice of abandonment by paying an additional fee.

Within three to four months after the examining attorney's approval of an application, the application is published for a 30-day period in the USPTO *Official Gazette* to allow possible third-party opposition. A third party may file a request with TTAB for a 30-day extension to oppose the application without cause and an additional 60-day extension upon a showing of cause, such as the need to investigate the applicant and its mark. An interested third party may oppose registration on any grounds on which the application could have been refused initially. Most often, applications are opposed on alleged likelihood of confusion with the opposer's mark. A claim of likelihood of confusion may be based on registered or common law trademark, or service mark rights or trade name rights.

If no opposition is filed and the application was based on use of the mark in commerce or on a foreign registration under the Paris Convention or Madrid Protocol, the USPTO normally will issue a registration certificate within three to four months following the end of the opposition period. If the application was based on intended use of the mark, a registrant must file a statement of use within six months following the issuance of the notice of allowance or during an extension period in order to perfect the registration. The USPTO will issue a registration certificate upon receipt of an acceptable statement of use. If the USPTO deems the statement of use insufficient, it will issue an office action, similar to the procedure used during the examination period.

During the first five years after registration, a third party may seek cancellation of a trademark registration based on likelihood of confusion with another's mark. After the fifth anniversary of the registration, the registration may only be canceled under limited circumstances, including deceptive use or genericness; the registration cannot be canceled based on likelihood of confusion with another's mark even if the other mark was used in commerce before the registrant's mark. The five-year period thus serves as a type of statute of limitations that gives registrants security in their registrations.

To maintain the registration, a registrant must file a declaration of current use of the mark between the fifth and sixth anniversaries of the registration.[105] The declaration must include a specimen of current use of the mark in commerce and be accompanied by a filing fee.[106] The USPTO will abandon a registration if the owner fails to file the current use declaration before the sixth anniversary of registration. Abandonment can be cured in the six-month period following the sixth anniversary if the registrant files the declaration of current use and pays a surcharge.[107]

Together with the registrant's filing of a declaration of current use or at any time after the fifth anniversary of the registration, a registrant may file a declaration of *continuous* use of the mark in commerce for the preceding five years.[108] After the USPTO accepts the registrant's declaration of continuous use and the accompanying filing fee, the registration becomes incontestable, and the registrant may claim an exclusive right to use the registered mark for the registered goods or services and assert exclusivity without challenge, except on limited statutory bases.[109]

The USPTO also requires that trademark registrants file a declaration of current use and a declaration of renewal in the year preceding the ten-year anniversary of the registration.[110] The declaration of use must include a specimen of current use of the mark in commerce, and both the use and renewal declarations must be accompanied by a filing fee.[111] A registrant's failure to file the current use declaration in the year preceding the tenth anniversary of the registration will result in abandonment of the registration. A registrant can cure the abandonment in the six-month period after the tenth anniversary for an additional charge.[112]

d. State Trademark Registration

All U.S. states and Puerto Rico have trademark registration systems independent of the federal system. State trademark registration only applies within the boundaries of the state in which registration is obtained. State trademark registration is superfluous if the registrant has obtained a federal registration because federal registration rights apply in all U.S. states and territories. However, a small winery or other wine business that conducts business exclusively in one state may prefer state registration as a less expensive alternative to federal registration. State registration also may be an alternative means of protection if prior use or registration of the mark by someone else is blocking a federal registration but does not conflict with the winery's intended use of the mark.[113]

---

105. 15 U.S.C. §1058 (2006).
106. *Id.*
107. T.M.R.P. 2.182.
108. 15 U.S.C. §1065 (2006).
109. *Id.* §1065; *see also Park N' Fly, Inc. v. Dollar Park and Fly, Inc.*, 469 U.S. 189 (1985).
110. 15 U.S.C. §§1058-1059 (2006).
111. *Id.*
112. T.M.R.P. 2.182.
113. For instance, the USPTO may refuse a registration for wine based on the use of the same mark for restaurant services. If the owner of the registration for restaurant services does business only in a state in which the winery does not intend to sell its wines, the winery might decide to register its mark in those other states.

e. Legal Systems That Provide No Statutory Trademark Protection

Not all registration systems for wine brands provide statutory protection against trademark infringement. In the wine industry, many brand owners mistakenly believe that obtaining a COLA for their wine label guarantees their right to use the brand name or a fanciful name identified on the COLA. In fact, the COLA application form expressly states: "This certificate does not constitute trademark protection."[114]

Registering a company name with the state in which a winery conducts business, receiving a certificate of incorporation from a state, or filing a fictitious business name statement with a state or county does not provide any statutory protection for a brand name. These types of filings are not intended to create rights in names, but rather to identify the business entity to the government and third parties for purposes of taxation, accountability for legal actions, and the like.

As a final example, the registration of an Internet domain name does not create any legal name rights. While the registration of an Internet domain name may create value in a marketing sense by securing a party's address in cyberspace, registration does not give the owner standing to take legal action against those who use terms similar to the domain name as a trademark.

4. ENFORCEMENT OF MARKS

Although some brand owners obtain trademark registration solely for the defensive purpose of preempting an infringement action against them, the business value of a mark is its exclusivity and its role in directing consumers to the owner of the mark or the goods or services on which the mark is used in the marketplace. To retain the trademark's value, the trademark owner must enforce his trademark rights against infringement by others. If a trademark owner does not stop others from using similar marks, the owner must live with the confusing or infringing uses.

In the case of *Russell v. Caesar*, the owner of the mark RABBIT RIDGE for wine obtained an injunction against the owner of the mark RABBIT HILL for wine. In that case, the judge noted,

> Because "Rabbit" is the single dominant or substantive term used by Rabbit Ridge on all of its products—including the 14.4 million bottles of wine already sold—Rabbit Hill's use of the term "Rabbit" even on a facially distinctive label or in conjunction with other terms cannot dissuade this Court from concluding that the marks are significantly similar for purposes of a finding of a likelihood of confusion.[115]

The court essentially acknowledged that the owner of RABBIT RIDGE had a monopoly in the term "RABBIT" in association with wine.

---

114. Alcohol and Tobacco Tax and Trade Bureau, Department of the Treasury, Application for and Certification/Exemption of Label/Bottle Approval Form 5100.31 (2009).

115. *Russell v. Caesar*, 62 USPQ 2d 1125, 1129 (N.D. Cal. 2001).

Interestingly, after the RABBIT HILL litigation, the RABBIT RIDGE owner ceased enforcing its judicially decreed right to the term "RABBIT." There are now several subsequent trademark registrations for wine encompassing the term "RABBIT."[116] The continuous enforcement of exclusive trademarks rights is difficult and costly, but the consequences of failing to enforce those rights can be the weakening of a mark's exclusivity.

Once a party has demonstrated a senior right in a trademark, the test for infringement is whether there is a likelihood of consumer confusion between the marks at issue. In determining likelihood of confusion, each federal circuit uses a different list of foundational factors.[117] As noted by Professor Thomas McCarthy, the eight basic factors are: (1) similarity between the marks at issue; (2) similarity of marketing methods and channels of distribution; (3) characteristics of prospective purchasers and degree of care; (4) degree of distinctiveness in the senior user's mark; (5) whether the goods or services at issue are competitive; (6) where the goods are sold in different territories and, if so, whether the senior user's mark is known in the junior user's territory; (7) the intent of the junior user; and (8) evidence of actual confusion.[118]

While these factors apply regardless of the nature of the goods or services at issue, many courts have applied these factors specifically to cases involving the alleged infringement of wine brands, sometimes with inconsistent results. These courts have found the following:

1. Generally, wine consumers tend to exercise less care when purchasing wine because of the lower cost of the goods.[119]
2. Champagne and sparkling wines are not necessarily expensive goods that are always purchased by sophisticated purchasers, and even sophisticated purchasers might be aware that Champagne houses

---

116. *See, e.g.*, FRENCH RABBIT, Registration No. 3,298,908; RABBIT RANCH, Registration No. 3,350,161; and RABBIT ISLAND, Registration No. 3,798,617.

117. *See Pignons S.A. de Mecanique de Precision v. Polaroid Corp.*, 657 F.2d 482 (1st Cir. 1981); *Polaroid Corp. v. Polaroid Electronics Corp.*, 287 F.2d 492 (2d Cir. 1961), *cert. denied*, 368 U.S. 820 (1961); *Interpace Corp. v. Lapp, Inc.*, 721 F.2d 460 (3d Cir. 1983); *Pizzeria Uno Corp. v. Temple*, 747 F.2d 1522 (4th Cir. 1984); *Roto-Rooter Corp. v. O'Neal*, 513 F.2d 44 (5th Cir. 1975); *Frisch's Rests v. Elby's Big Boy*, 670 F.2d 642 (6th Cir. 1982); *Helene Curtis Indus., Inc. v. Church & Dwight Co.*, 560 F.2d 1325 (7th Cir. 1977), *cert. denied*, 434 U.S. 1070 (1978); *SquirtCo v. Seven-Up Co.*, 628 F.2d 1086 (9th Cir. 1980); *AMF, Inc. v. Sleekcraft Boats*, 599 F.2d 341 (9th Cir. 1979); *Team Tires Plus, Ltd. v. Tires Plus, Inc.*, 394 F.3d 831 (10th Cir. 2005); *Frehling Enterprises, Inc. v. Int'l Select Group, Inc.*, 192 F.3d 1330 (11th Cir. 1999); *Am. Ass'n for Advancement of Sci. v. Hearts Corp.*, 498 F. Supp. 244 (D.D.C. 1980); *In re E.I. Du Pont Nemours & Co.*, 476 F.2d 1357 (C.C.P.A. 1973).

118. *See* 4 J. Thomas McCarthy, McCarthy on Trademarks and Unfair Competition §24:29 (4th ed. 2010).

119. *E. & J. Gallo Winery v. Gallo Cattle Co.*, 967 F.2d at 1293; *see also Taylor Wine Co. v. Bully Hill Vineyards, Inc.*, 569 F.2d 731, 734 (2d Cir. 1978) (the average American who drinks wine on occasion can hardly pass for a connoisseur of wines and remains an easy mark for an infringer); *E. & J. Gallo Winery v. Consorzio del Gallo Nero*, 782 F. Supp. 457, 465 (N.D. Cal. 1991) (there is little doubt that wine purchasers typically fall into the category of unsophisticated impulse buyers where confusion is more likely); *Nova Wines, Inc. v. Adler Fels Winery LLC*, 467 F. Supp. 2d 965, 981 (N.D. Cal. 2006) (same); *In re Vina Lo Miranda Limitada*, 2002 WL 732146 at *3 (TTAB 2002) (many purchasers of wine are members of the general public who would not necessarily exercise the high degree of care necessary to prevent confusion).

offer both expensive and less expensive sparkling wine products under similar marks.[120]

3. It is difficult to generalize about the degree of care that consumers of wine are likely to exercise in making their wine selections because the standard for the reasonable consumer includes the ignorant and credulous and must include as well the portion of wine consumers who are not especially savvy.[121]
4. Even at $30 a bottle, a wine could be an impulse purchase made by an ordinary consumer without a great deal of care.[122]
5. The wine-buying public, insofar as their selection and purchase of wine is concerned, is a highly discriminating group.[123]
6. The fact that the TTB requires source-identifying information on a wine label does not diminish the likelihood of confusion because consumers are more interested in the distinctive label design than in textual information regarding geographical origin, the dangers of alcohol to pregnant women, the presence of sulfites, or any other legally required verbiage that appears on the less interesting side of the bottle.[124]
7. If both parties laying claim to a trademark market their products through retail establishments such as wine shops and liquor stores and utilize magazines for advertising purposes, they use similar marketing channels for their wine as a matter of law.[125]
8. The fact that one wine is sold through mass market channels and the other is sold only through the defendant winery's tasting room weighs against a finding of likelihood of confusion.[126]
9. If the wines at issue are different in price, varietal, and origin, they still can be found to be similar due to the common practice in the wine industry of using the same brand for different wine varieties sold at different price points.[127]
10. Differences in varietal, price, and origin of wines diminish the likelihood of confusion.[128]
11. Differences in trade dress and differences in brand cannot be relied upon to distinguish the parties' products in an "on-premise" setting

120. *Palm Bay Imps., Inc. v. Veuve Clicquot Ponsardin Maison Fondee en 1772*, 396 F.3d 1369, 1376 (Fed. Cir. 2005).

121. *Vigneron Partners, LLC v. Woop Woop Wines Pty. Ltd.*, 2006 WL 1214859 at *8 (N.D. Cal. 2006)

122. *In re Saviah Rose Winery, LLC*, 2006 WL 2414518 *4 (TTAB 2006).

123. *E. & J. Gallo Winery v. Ben R. Goltsman & Co.*, 172 F. Supp. 826, 830 (M.D. Ala. 1959), criticized by *Gallo Nero*, 782 F. Supp. at 465; *see also Banfi Products Corp. v. Kendall-Jackson Winery, Ltd.*, 74 F. Supp. 2d 188, 199 (E.D.N.Y. 1999).

124. *Nova Wines*, 467 F. Supp. 2d at 981-982.

125. *Gallo Nero*, 782 F. Supp. at 464.

126. *Sutter Home Winery, Inc. v. Madrona Vineyards, L.P.*, 2005 WL 701599 at *7 (N.D. Cal. 2005); *see also Banfi Products*, 74 F. Supp. 2d. at 197 (where one wine is sold in discount drugstores, supermarkets, and mid-range Italian restaurants, and another is sold exclusively in fine restaurants and retail wine stores, there is a lower likelihood of confusion).

127. *Vigneron Partners*, 2006 WL 1214859 at *5; *see also Gallo Nero*, 782 F. Supp. at 464 (wines of all types constitute a single class of goods).

128. *Banfi Products*, 74 F. Supp. 2d at 197.

> in which consumers may order a glass of wine at a bar or make their purchasing decisions based on a restaurant wine list, although it is worth noting that wine lists usually include the source of the wine.[129]

As these cases demonstrate, there are no hard-and-fast rules concerning the foundational factors for trademark infringement claims related to the sale of wine. Therefore, a claim of infringement should be based, to the extent possible, on all of Professor McCarthy's eight factors.

Another means of protecting a select subset of trademarks is an action for trademark dilution. Trademark dilution is distinct from trademark infringement and is reserved for marks that can be shown to be famous among the general consuming public of the United States.[130] In a claim of dilution, the goods or services on which the parties' marks appear need not be competitive, nor do consumers need to be confused by the similarity of the marks.[131] A claim of trademark dilution alleges that a junior mark somehow dilutes a famous senior mark by blurring or tarnishing it.[132] Dilution can make a mark less distinctive or bring the mark into disrepute.[133]

To prevail in a dilution action, the diluted trademark owner must prove that the mark is famous. Proving fame within a particular market segment is not sufficient to invoke the protection of the federal dilution laws.[134] Nationwide fame is the required showing. In the wine sector, because a large percentage of the American public does not drink wine and the wine market is highly fragmented, fame and dilution of a wine trademark are difficult to prove.[135] Wineries, however, are susceptible to claims of trademark dilution from non-wine producers if their wine brand is too similar to a famous mark outside of the wine sector.[136]

5. LICENSING OF MARKS

While the uncontrolled use of an identical or similar mark on wine by a third party will jeopardize a winery's legal exclusivity in its mark, use of an identical or similar mark on wine by a third party subject to the control of the

---

129. *Sutter Home*, 2005 WL 701599 at *11.

130. 15 U.S.C. §1125(c) (2006).

131. 15 U.S.C. §1127 (2006).

132. *Id.* §1125(c).

133. *See Nike, Inc. v. Nikepal Int'l, Inc.*, 85 USPQ 2d 1820 (E.D. Cal. 2007) (distinctiveness of NIKE mark for apparel and footwear diluted by NIKEPAL for medical laboratory syringes); *Pepsico, Inc. v. #1 Wholesale, LLC*, 84 USPQ 2d 1040 (N.D. Ga. 2007) (using PEPSI cans to manufacture "stash can" storage containers for concealing illegal drugs tarnishes the PEPSI mark).

134. *See Bd. of Regents, Univ. of Texas Sys. ex rel. Univ. of Texas at Austin v. KST Elec., Ltd.*, 550 F. Supp. 2d 657, 675 (W.D. Tex. 2008) (fame of longhorn design among college football fans is insufficient to establish fame under federal dilution statute).

135. *See Maker's Mark Distillery, Inc. v. Diageo N. Am., Inc.*, 2010 WL 1407325 at *16 (W.D. Ky. 2010) (Maker's Mark dripping red wax top not famous: "While annual sales of 800,000 cases is somewhat significant, Maker's Mark is not the nation's largest whisky producer and its sales do not make it a behemoth in the distilled spirits world.").

136. *See Chanel Inc. v. Savannah-Chanel*, C-99-1790 (N.D. Cal. 1999) (dilution claim based on use of SAVANNAH-CHANEL as a mark for wine; case settled with change of brand to SAVANNAH-CHANELLE).

senior trademark owner will preserve the senior trademark owner's exclusivity. This arrangement is referred to as a trademark license.

A license agreement need not be in writing to be legally effective, but preparing a written license agreement is good business practice. Specific monetary consideration for the grant of a trademark license, known as a royalty, also is not a legal requirement of a license agreement. The licensor receives consideration when the licensee uses the licensed mark, which use inures to the benefit of the licensor and strengthens the protection of the licensed mark. The single critical element to make any license arrangement enforceable is the licensor's control over the quality of the licensed goods being sold under the licensed mark. A licensor's failure to exert or impose quality control on the licensee's use of a mark is a "naked license," which puts the licensor's trademark rights at risk.[137] Examples of licensed marks are NEWMAN'S OWN[138] and ARNOLD PALMER[139] for wines sold under these brand names.

A licensor can exert control over the quality of the licensed goods simply by asserting that the licensor is relying on the reputation of the licensee as a producer of high-quality wine.[140] However, to ensure that there is no challenge to the quality control mechanism, a written license should include a more specific provision for quality standards and control, for example, requiring the licensee to provide the licensed product to the licensor before the product is released. If the license agreement requires the licensee to provide product samples, the licensor should test the product and keep internal records concerning the inspection. The licensed goods do not need to be of superior quality, but rather have consistent quality. To further define consistency, license agreements often specify a standard such as a quality similar to that of licensee's other wine products or similar to that of other wine on the market at a similar price point.

In the fractured and highly competitive wine market, license arrangements allow a trademark owner to legally control its mark by licensing a use that may not present any true threat of diluting the licensor's brand in the market. For instance, if a large winery finds a small winery using its mark on a limited production run of wine sold only in a tasting room, the large winery may elect to license its name to the small winery rather than initiate federal infringement proceedings, which can be costly and generate negative publicity.

---

137. *See Barcamerica Int'l USA Trust v. Tyfield Imps., Inc.*, 289 F.3d 589 (9th Cir. 2002). In *Barcamerica*, plaintiff accused defendant of infringement of its LEONARDO DA VINCI mark on wine and alleged rights in the LEONARDO DA VINCI mark based on licensed use by a third party. Defendant attacked such rights on the grounds that the license agreement failed to include a quality control provision and plaintiff failed to produce any evidence that it actually exerted any control over the quality of the licensed wine on which the mark was used. Plaintiff was found to have abandoned its rights in the mark based on the naked license and the failure to exert control over the use of the mark.

138. Registration No. 3,679,763.

139. Registration No. 3,113,028.

140. Reliance on the reputation of the licensee was rejected as sufficient exercise of quality control in the *Barcamerica* case but was accepted in other cases. *See, e.g., Embedded Moments, Inc. v. Int'l Silver Co.*, 648 F. Supp. 187 (E.D.N.Y. 1986) (quality control satisfied where there is evidence that the licensor relied on the integrity of the licensee based on their prior relationship).

In the wine industry, license arrangements are frequently a part of grower and producer relationships. Wineries often purchase grapes from vineyards with particular vineyard names and use the vineyard name on the wine as a vineyard designation.[141] Does the producer need a license from the grower to use his vineyard name as a vineyard designation? The legal concept of "fair use"[142] suggests not; the producer is merely identifying the place from which the grapes originated. However, the "fairness" of the use also depends on the way in which the vineyard name actually appears on the label. If the winery uses the vineyard name prominently on the label, so that it looks like an independent brand, the use may not be deemed fair.

A grower should establish limits on the use of his vineyard name at the outset of a grape purchasing relationship, preferably in a written grape purchase agreement. By taking the position that the producer may *not* use the vineyard name on the wine absent permission from the grower, the grower can ensure that the vineyard name is not used on wine that the grower finds to be of substandard quality.

The use and establishment of vineyard designations can impact the bargaining power of grower and winery. A grower may be desperate for a winery to use his vineyard name so that he can establish a reputation for his vineyard. Alternatively, a new winery anxious to establish the quality of its brands may seek out vineyards with established reputations for growing quality grapes. In terms of compensation, the license royalty payment can serve as a pricing variable apart from the commodity value of the grapes. A well-drafted license agreement can address all these issues and assist the grower and the winery in establishing their respective rights relative to the use of the vineyard name.

B. COPYRIGHT

A trademark is a business symbol with an attached legal right that promotes the trademark owner's business and that protects consumers. By contrast, copyright is a distinct intellectual property that protects creative works and promotes and encourages the authorship of creative works. Copyright protects literary works; pictorial, graphic, and sculptural works; musical works and dramatic works; and others. Titles, names, short phrases, and taglines are not protectable by copyright, nor are ingredient lists and recipe instructions. Generally, trademarks offer more protections to wine brand owners and wine industry participants than copyright. However, copyright is an important overlay to trademark as well as an independent right that can benefit wineries, particularly in the context of retail sales. For example, logos and label designs are often pictorial and graphic works protected by copyright as well as trademark law. Similarly, advertising and promotional materials, including

141. *See* 27 C.F.R. §4.39(m) (2010).

142. Fair use occurs when a term is used in a non-trademark manner to provide descriptive information about the product.

websites, can be protected by copyright as pictorial, graphic, and literary works.

A copyright attaches upon the creation of the work, when pen is put to paper.[143] Registration is not required.[144] The author or creator of the work owns the copyright. A work created by a salaried employee of a winery in the context of the employee's job responsibilities, for example, the text for a tasting sheet created by the winemaker or the director of marketing, is a "work for hire," and the copyright in the work is owned by the winery.[145] However, an independent contractor or outside design company owns the copyright in a work created at the instruction of a winery (for example, a label design).[146]

Absent a work-for-hire arrangement or assignment of the copyright, the author of the work retains all copyright in it even if the work was created at the direction of, or commissioned by, a winery. However, a winery has the right to use the commissioned work. The winery paid for the work, and the work was created at the direction of the winery with the understanding that it would be used for a specific purpose—for example, a label design for bottles of wine. There is an implied license to use commissioned work based on the specific facts of the relationship.[147]

The implied license, however, only extends to the use of the work as the parties clearly understood in their contractual relationship. If the agreement between the winery and the label designer is unclear (for example, whether the label design can be used on promotional items such as posters, postcards, or coasters), the winery could find itself defending a copyright infringement claim. The author is aware of an incident in which a producer retained a famous label designer to design its label; when the producer used the label design on promotional items beyond the product itself, the label designer did not hesitate and, in fact, felt an obligation to assert his copyright in the design to extract further payment from the producer for the use of the design on promotional goods.

Wineries must take great care in using art on labels when the art was not directly commissioned for that use. If a winery owner purchases a piece of fine art for his art collection, he merely takes title to the physical piece of art. Absent an express written assignment from the artist, the artist retains all copyright in the art. The winery owner has no right to use an image of the artwork he purchased on his wine label simply because he bought the work of art. While the winery can request that the artist permit the use of that artwork on wine labels, permission should be expressly obtained in writing from the artist to avoid ambiguity. Copyright law presumes that the copyright belongs to the artist.

---

143. This is true of works created after January 1, 1978. Prior to 1978, works were not protected by copyright unless copyright registration was obtained.

144. While copyright registration is not required for protection, it is available, provides certain benefits such as statutory damages, and is a prerequisite to filing a copyright infringement lawsuit.

145. *Cmty. for Creative Non-Violence v. Reid,* 490 U.S. 730 (1989).

146. *Id.*

147. *See Effects Assocs., Inc. v. Cohen,* 908 F.2d 555 (9th Cir. 1990).

Finally, an image or text that appears on the Internet is not free for third-party use.[148] The author of the image or text, or some other party, likely owns a copyright in that image or text, and use of the copyrighted material without the permission of the copyright owner may constitute blatant copyright infringement. Stock image companies allow use of images for a set fee. Wineries are advised to pay for photographs from stock image companies rather than copy them from the Internet.

C. APPELLATIONS OF ORIGIN

We now turn from trademarks and copyrights and the federal and state laws governing them to wine appellations and the separate and distinct laws concerning their establishment and use. Appellations of origin are not a new concept,[149] nor are they restricted to wines. But wine labels in the United States for well over a century have routinely referred to the wine's appellation of origin, just as they have included wine brand names.[150]

After Repeal, American wine producers once again were allowed to state the geographical origin of the wine's grapes on their labels.[151] However, many of these place names were undefined in terms of their precise location. In 1978 the TTB's predecessor agency, the Bureau of Alcohol, Tobacco and Firearms (ATF),[152] adopted a formal wine appellation system in the United States. The structure of this appellation system, the various appellations established to date, the use of other geographical terms on wine labels and in wine advertising, and the future of American appellations are the subjects of this section.

---

148. Older works for which there is no copyright or for which the copyright has expired are free for use as they are considered to be in the public domain. However, works that are not at least a few hundred years old may be subject to a variety of copyright laws, depending upon the creation of the work and the term of protection, which could be from 28 years, the life of the author plus 70 years, or 120 years from the date of creation. It is also very difficult to research the existence of copyright registrations.

149. The Paris Convention for the Protection of Industrial Property, adopted in 1883, applies to industrial property in the widest sense, indications of source and appellations of origin. Last Revised July 14, 1967, 21 U.S.T. 1583, 828 U.N.T.S. 305; http://www.wipo.int/treaties/en/ip/paris/trtdocs_wo020.html (accessed December 8, 2010).

150. According to 27 C.F.R. §4.32 (2010), "[t]he [wine] product shall bear a brand name, except that if not sold under a brand name, then the name of the person required to appear on the brand label shall be deemed a brand name for the purpose of this part." The person referenced above is the bottler, who perhaps also is the producer, of the wine. *Id.* §4.35. Appellations of origin, unlike brand names, are not mandatory information on wine labels.

151. Amending Certain Provisions of the Wine Labeling and Advertising Regulation Relative to Standards of Identity and Other Matters, 3 Fed. Reg. 2093 (Aug. 26, 1938) (defining an "appellation of origin" for the first time as a "place or region of origin").

152. The Homeland Security Act of 2002 transferred responsibility from the ATF to the TTB. *See* Reorganization of Title 27, Code of Federal Regulations, 68 Fed. Reg. 3744 (Jan. 24, 2003) (to be codified at C.F.R. pts. 447, 448, 479, 555, and 646). The ATF was, and the TTB now is, part of the U.S. Treasury Department. For consistency, we use the term "TTB" to refer to both the ATF and the TTB.

1. DEFINING WINE APPELLATIONS

One of the fundamental tenets of the FAA Act, which was adopted by the U.S. Congress in 1935, is to protect consumers and ensure that they get accurate and meaningful information to guide their purchase decisions. From the 1930s to the 1960s, as the U.S. wine industry gradually reestablished itself after Prohibition, vintners did not make widespread use of wine appellations on their labels. The references that they did use typically were states and counties that had pre-established boundaries.

During the Wine Renaissance of the 1970s, this practice changed, and wineries increasingly referred to places and regions that had no clear boundaries. Examples include Northern California (Figure 6-10), California Mountain (Figure 6-11), Napa Valley, Howell Mountain, and North Coast.[153]

To prevent consumers from being misled by these references and to prevent unfair competition among wine producers, in 1978 the TTB adopted a formal framework for wine appellations in the United States. That multi-tiered framework consists of various types of appellations, each of which can be used on a wine label if the prescribed percentage of grapes from that area is used to make the particular wine.

Figure 6-10
J. Lohr Label

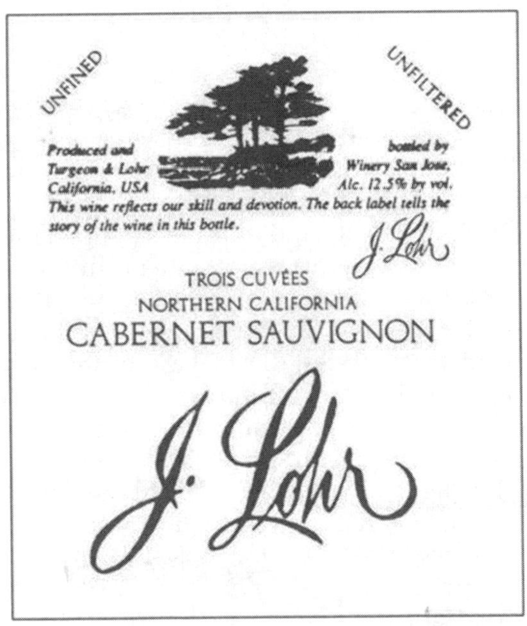

153. For the record, the Lohr's Northern California non-vintage wine had a handwritten back label describing the counties in which the grapes were grown.

Figure 6-11
Louis M. Martini Label

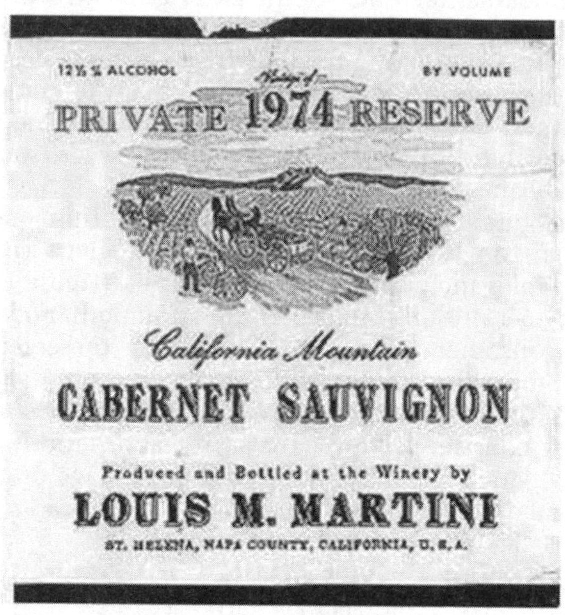

The TTB's practice of allowing the use of state and county names as appellations continued. As before, 75 percent of the wine bearing such an appellation has to be derived from grapes grown in the named state or county, and the wine has to be fully finished within the named state or an adjacent state in the case of a state appellation or within the state in which the named county is located.[154] Multi-county and multi-state appellations are authorized as long as no more than three counties in a state or three contiguous states are listed on the label and the percentage of grapes from each county or state is shown, adding up to 100 percent (with a tolerance of 2 percent).[155]

For previously undefined places, the TTB established a new type of appellation known as the "American viticultural area," or AVA. AVAs are defined as "delimited grape growing regions distinguished by geographical features, the boundaries of which have been recognized and defined" by the TTB.[156] An AVA can be used on a wine label if at least 85 percent of the wine is made from grapes grown inside that AVA and the wine is fully finished in the state, or one of the states, in which the AVA is located.

If a winery also includes a vineyard designation on its label, the TTB requires that 95 percent of the grapes used to make that wine be grown in

154. 27 C.F.R. §4.25(b)(1)(i) (2010).
155. *Id.* §4.25(c), (d).
156. 27 C.F.R. §4.25(a)(1)(vi), (e) (2010).

the named vineyard. However, the TTB did not establish formal vineyard appellations in the same way it did for AVAs. The location of the vineyard is left to the discretion of the vineyard owner.[157]

Foreign wine appellations can be used on labels of wine imported into the United States. They consist of two types. First, foreign political appellations include a country, state, province, territory, or other political subdivision of a country equivalent to a state or county. A foreign political appellation can be used on labels of wine sold in the United States if at least 75 percent of the wine is derived from grapes grown in the named appellation, and the wine conforms to the requirements for the use of that appellation in the country of origin. The second type of foreign appellation is a viticultural area, defined as a "delimited place or region, the boundaries of which have been recognized and defined by the country of origin for use on labels of wine available for consumption within the country of origin."[158] Like a domestic AVA, a foreign viticultural area can be used if at least 85 percent of the wine is made from grapes grown in that area and the wine conforms to the production, composition, and designation requirements of the country of origin.

a. American Viticultural Areas

As a part of the TTB's 1978 rulemaking process, the agency set up a procedure to establish AVAs. Any interested party may petition the TTB to establish an AVA, and a petition must contain the following information:

1. Evidence that the name of the viticultural area is locally and/or nationally known as referring to the proposed area;
2. Historical or current evidence in support of the boundaries of the viticultural area;
3. Evidence relating to the geographical features, such as climate, soil, and topography, which distinguish the viticultural area from surrounding areas; and
4. The specific boundaries of the area based on features found on the topographic maps of the U.S. Geological Survey.[159]

---

157. The dispute between Robert Mondavi Winery and grapegrower Andy Beckstoffer over the To-Kalon Vineyard designation is one of the consequences of the TTB's decision not to establish formal vineyard designations. H. W. Crabb had established the 359-acre To-Kalon vineyard in 1868. Around a century later, Mondavi acquired 250 of those acres and registered To-Kalon Vineyard as a federal trademark for wine. Mondavi later acquired some adjoining vineyards and called its entire 550-acre vineyard holding To-Kalon Vineyard. In 2000 Beckstoffer, who had previously purchased 89 acres of Crabb's original vineyard not owned by Mondavi, sold those grapes to Schrader Winery, which used the vineyard designation, Original Tokalon Vineyard. Mondavi sent Schrader a cease and desist letter for infringing its mark, after which the litigation commenced. Beckstoffer and Schrader argued that Mondavi's mark was deceptive and should be canceled. The case ultimately settled, and both parties now use the Tokalon name. In November 2010 the TTB issued an Advance Notice of Proposed Rulemaking seeking input on whether and how to define certain winemaking terms, including "Single Vineyard." TTB Advance Notice of Proposed Rulemaking (Notice No. 109), 75 Fed. Reg. 67666, 67668 (Nov. 3, 2010). The TTB specifically asked whether that term should be defined to mean that 100 percent of the grapes used to make the wine came from one vineyard. *Id.*

158. 27 C.F.R. §4.25a(e)(1)(ii) (2010).

159. *Id.* §9.3(b).

Upon receipt of a complete petition from any person — grower, vintner, or other — the TTB commences a public rulemaking process under the Federal Administrative Procedure Act.[160] Typically, the process includes at least one Notice of Proposed Rulemaking (NPRM), a public comment period of between 30 and 90 days, and a Final Rule, each of which is announced in the Federal Register. In controversial cases, the TTB may hold a public hearing, generally at the site of the proposed AVA.

As of January 2011, 197 viticultural areas had been established in 33 states. There is no prescribed size of a viticultural area. Consequently, they range from the very large (e.g., the over 16-million-acre (6.7 million hectare) Ohio River Valley, spanning parts of four states) to the very small (e.g., the 160-acre (64.7 hectare) Cole Ranch viticultural area in California).

There also is no prescribed order for the creation of AVAs. Some larger viticultural areas have been carved into smaller, "nested" AVAs, often referred to by the trade and consumers as sub-appellations or sub-AVAs. Examples include Napa Valley (Figure 6-12), which now consists of 13 nested appellations;[161] Lodi (Figure 6-13), consisting of 7 sub-appellations; Willamette Valley (6 sub-appellations); and Paso Robles (Figure 6-14), with its 11 proposed sub-appellations. This process of subdividing AVAs is partially the result of the early tendency to create very large AVAs that included any outlying property with roughly similar viticultural characteristics; it also is a natural evolution as vintners and growers come to better understand their terroir and desire to express the differences in growing conditions and wine characteristics within those larger AVAs. Less frequently, large viticultural areas have been formed around preexisting smaller AVAs, as with the San Benito viticultural area in California.

In Sonoma County, which is home to 13 AVAs, there is layer upon layer of AVAs, which can be confusing. For example, the 15,400-acre Rock Pile AVA in northern Sonoma County is partly in the Dry Creek Valley AVA. Dry Creek Valley is inside the larger Northern Sonoma AVA, but the portion of Rock Pile that is outside of Dry Creek Valley is also outside of the Northern Sonoma AVA. Russian River Valley, consisting of 154,984 acres, entirely encompasses two smaller AVAs — the Chalk Hill AVA, in the northeastern corner, and the Green Valley of Russian River Valley AVA (formerly known as Sonoma County Green Valley), in the southwest. The Russian River Valley, with the exception of its southern tip, lies within the Northern Sonoma AVA.[162] Russian River Valley also is largely but not entirely within the Sonoma Coast AVA.

---

160. 5 U.S.C. §§551-559 (2006).

161. The sub-appellations, also known as "nested" AVAs of Napa Valley are, in order of their establishment, Carneros (1983), Howell Mountain (1984), Wild Horse Valley (1988), Stags Leap District (1989), Mt. Veeder (1990), Atlas Peak (1992), Spring Mountain District (1993), Rutherford (1993), Oakville (1993), St. Helena (1995), Chiles Valley (1999), Yountville (1999), Diamond Mountain District (2001), Oak Knoll District of Napa Valley (2004), and Calistoga (2010). Carneros and Wild Horse Valley AVAs lie partially inside and partially outside of the Napa Valley AVA.

162. The TTB proposed in Notice of Proposed Rulemaking No. 90, 79 Fed. Reg. 49123, 49127-49128 (Aug. 20, 2008), a southern and southeastern extension of the Northern Sonoma AVA to encompass all of the Russian River Valley AVA, including the southern expansion of that AVA proposed in the same NRPM. This rulemaking is pending as this book goes to press.

Figure 6-12
Napa Valley and Its Sub-AVAs[163]

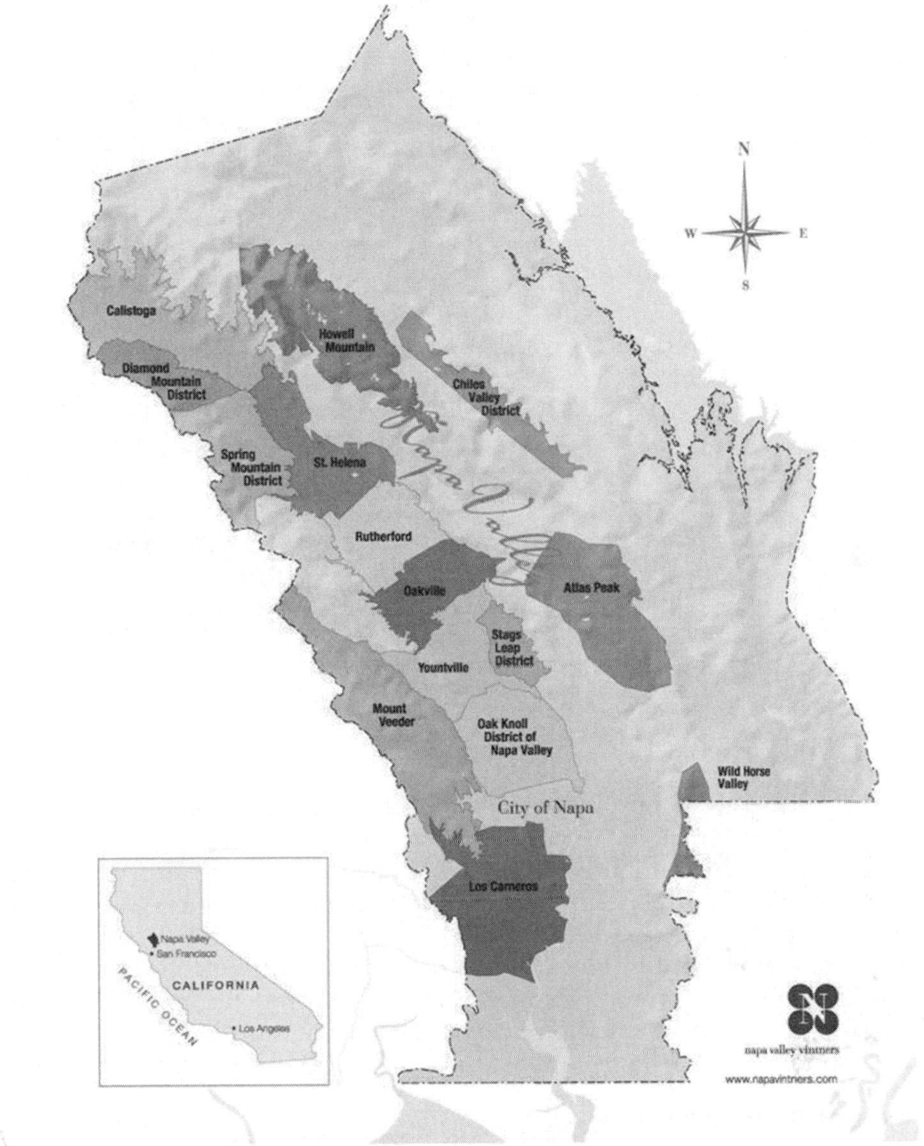

The Northern Sonoma and Sonoma Coast AVAs partially overlap. The order of establishment of these AVAs followed no particular rhyme or reason.

163. Courtesy of Napa Valley Vintners, http://www.napavintners.com/downloads/Napa_Valley_Appellation_map.pdf.

Figure 6-13
Lodi and Its Sub-AVAs[164]

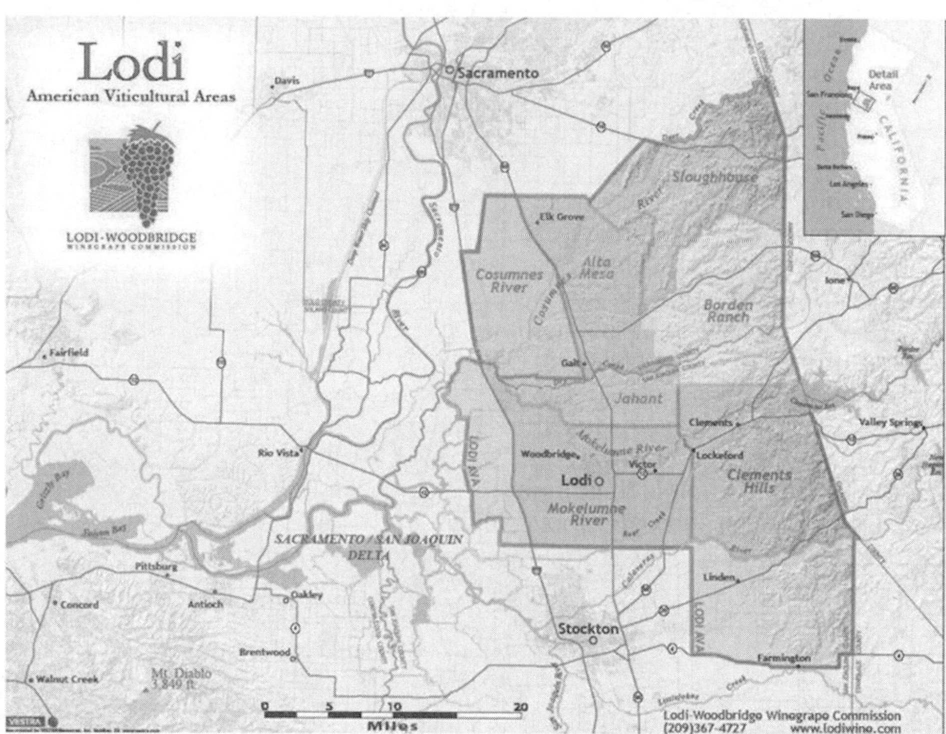

Early on, the TTB determined that one AVA can partially overlap another. The Carneros AVA is situated in part in the Sonoma Valley AVA and in part in the Napa Valley AVA. Initially, Carneros was envisioned as a sub-AVA of the Napa Valley, but after the petition was filed, neighboring owners in Sonoma Valley west of the proposed AVA petitioned for inclusion. The TTB stated in the Final Rule establishing the Carneros AVA: "Based on written comments submitted and oral testimony from the hearing, ATF determined that the boundaries of Los Carneros should extend into Sonoma County."[165] The agency pointed to climate and soils as the key physical features distinguishing the Carneros AVA.

Unlike the traditional European appellation systems, U.S. wine appellations indicate grape origin only and do not involve or imply any quality controls. None of the criteria for establishing an AVA refers to the taste, character, or quality of the wine, and there is no organoleptic aspect to the

164. Courtesy of Lodi Winegrape Commission, http://www.lodiwine.com/wp-content/uploads/2010/04/appellation_2010.jpg.
165. 48 Fed. Reg. 37366 (Aug. 18, 1983).

Figure 6-14
Paso Robles and Its Proposed Sub-AVAs[166]

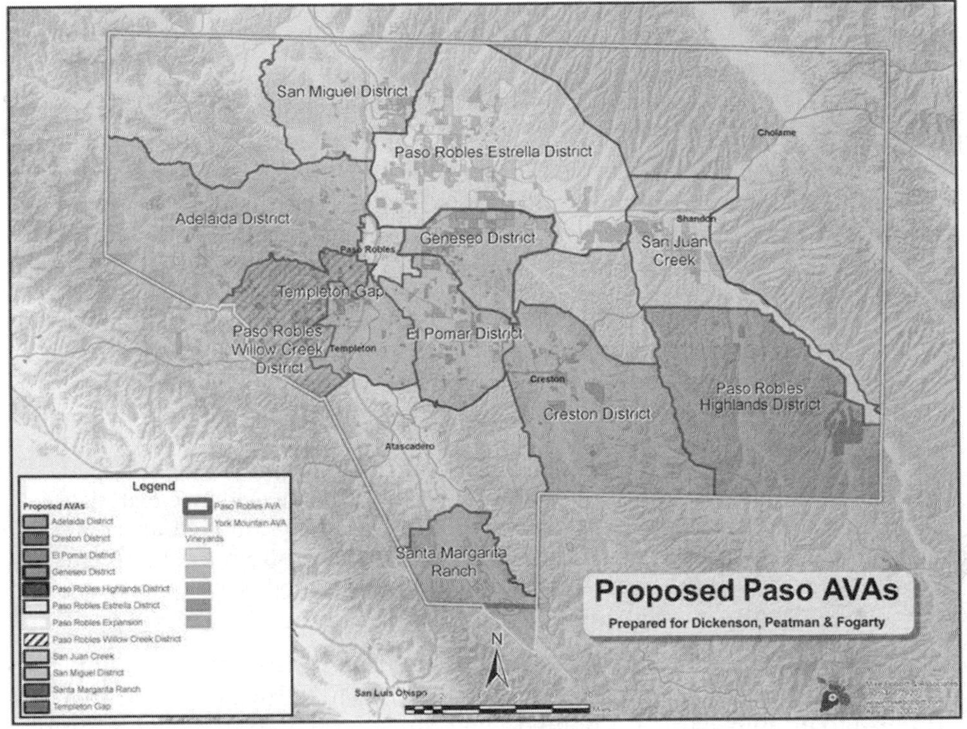

U.S. appellation system.[167] The TTB makes no endorsement of the wine made from an AVA. The TTB's standard approval language follows:

> The establishment of viticultural areas allows vintners to describe more specifically the origin of their wines to consumers and allows consumers to attribute a given quality, reputation, or other characteristic of a wine made from grapes grown in an area to its geographical origin. Establishment of a viticultural area is neither an approval nor an endorsement by TTB of the wine produced in that area.[168]

Although the TTB requires evidence of viticultural distinctiveness, it makes no attempt to control grape varieties or viticultural practices through the appellation system.[169] AVAs, in this sense, are analogous to the original French

166. The Paso Robles sub-AVA petitions were filed in 2007.

167. Under the FAA Act, 27 USC §205(e), (f) (2006), and its implementing regulations, 27 C.F.R. §§4.39, 4.64 (2010), government endorsement of wine, organoleptic or otherwise, in labeling or in any other manner is specifically prohibited.

168. 74 Fed. Reg. 64602 (Dec. 8, 2009) (establishing the Calistoga AVA).

169. It is not clear that the FAA Act confers sufficient authority for the TTB to dictate which grape varieties may be grown in which locations. In all likelihood, it would take an Act of Congress to implement such a program, and Congress is not likely to require a farmer to replant a vineyard in view of the expenses involved.

appellations simples established prior to 1935. They are provenances of origin, without associated, appellation-specific viticultural or enological controls.

i. AVA NAMING

The proposed AVA name need not have any specific wine meaning or following in the wine industry or among wine consumers. Any name that has local or national recognition will suffice, including Native American names (Napa was named by the Wappo tribe of Native Americans), Mexican land grants (Carneros derives its name from Rancho El Rincon de los Carneros), and surnames of individuals that are now attached to particular places (the town and AVA of Rutherford were named after Thomas Rutherford). The TTB, in its recent revisions to the AVA regulations, discussed in detail below, states:

> The name and the evidence in support of [an AVA] must come from sources independent of the petitioner. Appropriate name evidence sources include, but are not limited to, historical and modern government or commercial maps, books, newspapers, magazines, tourist and other promotional materials, local business or school names, and road names. Whenever practicable, the petitioner must include with the petition copies of the name evidence materials, appropriately cross-referenced in the petition narrative. Although anecdotal information by itself is not sufficient, statements taken from local residents with knowledge of the name and its use may also be included to support other name evidence.[170]

The TTB expresses concern over any name that is misdescriptive and confusing to consumers. In 1981, Paul Masson Vineyards, Inc., objected to a TTB proposal to establish an AVA named The Pinnacles, which had been proposed by vintner Chalone Vineyard.[171] Paul Masson Vineyards objected on the basis that it had acquired trademark protection for the terms "Pinnacle" and "Pinnacles" and for the phrase "A Pinnacles Selection." Paul Masson Vineyards argued that consumers who recognized those terms in connection with Paul Masson wines would be confused and misled because Paul Masson's Pinnacles brand wine was not made from grapes grown in the proposed AVA; in fact, its vineyard sources were located nearby and had been excluded from the AVA. The TTB agreed with Paul Masson Vineyards and asked Chalone if it would accept a different name for the AVA. Chalone agreed to use its own Native American name, and the TTB established the Chalone AVA.[172]

In the petition for the Temecula AVA, the TTB refused to include vineyards within the neighboring city of Murrieta because of possible consumer confusion.[173] The TTB reasoned that grapes grown in the city of Murrieta were never

170. 76 Fed. Reg. 3501 (Jan. 20, 2011).

171. ATF Notice of proposed rulemaking (Notice No. 386), 46 Fed. Reg. 49600 (Oct. 7, 1981).

172. ATF Final Rule (T.D. ATF-107), 47 Fed. Reg. 25517 (June 14, 1982) (to be codified at 27 C.F.R. pt. 9). It is somewhat surprising that Chalone agreed to call the AVA by its own brand name, which is also a registered trademark. This solution worked only because Chalone owned or controlled, and intended to use, all the grapes in the Chalone AVA. In this sense, the Chalone AVA is a monopoly like the Condrieu appellation in France, with all the grapes in that appellation owned by a single winery, Château-Grillet.

173. ATF Final Rule (T.D. ATF-188), 49 Fed. Reg. 42563 (Oct. 23, 1984).

known by the name of Temecula, which is a separate city. Although the Temecula AVA is not confined to the city of Temecula, the TTB modified the proposed boundary to exclude the neighboring town. Otherwise, the TTB reasoned, consumers might be misled as to the origin of the grapes.

One of the more recent and novel efforts to create name evidence is the proposed "Alexander Mountain" AVA. After the TTB rejected a petition to establish "Alexander Mountain" as an AVA for lack of name evidence, a winery petitioned the U.S.G.S. to change the name of the land that it owns, which is identified as "Black Mountain" on current U.S.G.S. maps, to "Alexander Mountain," some say to take advantage of the reputation of the nearby Alexander Valley viticultural area. If successful, the name change would provide important evidence that the name "Alexander Mountain" is locally and/or nationally known as referring to the proposed AVA.

ii. AVA BOUNDARIES

The TTB requires historical or current evidence that the boundaries of the proposed AVA match the name. This requirement is deceptively complicated. Petitioners have pointed to a variety of types of evidence to make their case, from phone directories (in the case of the Napa Valley AVA) to school districts (e.g., the Yamhill-Carlton Union High School and the Yamhill-Carlton School District in support of the Yamhill-Carlton AVA) to historical maps (Stags Leap, for example, is printed on the same U.S.G.S. topographical map on which the TTB requires AVA boundaries to be plotted).

Rarely do the boundaries of an AVA match exactly those of the cited examples. From the TTB's perspective, the problem is greater when a portion of the proposed AVA has never been known by the proposed name than when the name has applied historically to an area larger than that of the proposed AVA. In other words, from an evidentiary perspective, over-inclusiveness is more acceptable than under-inclusiveness.

Unlike in France and other countries of the Old World, the boundaries of AVAs are mostly geographical features (roads, rivers, elevation contours, mountain peaks), not property lines. It is not uncommon for an AVA boundary to divide a property, in which case the grower must separate the grapes from different parts of the vineyard and indicate the correct AVA on each load of grapes. This is especially important if the AVA wine made from those grapes is blended very close to the 85 percent grape source standard. As noted below, the burden of proof is on the bottling winery, which obtained the COLA but may not have grown the grapes, to justify any and all label claims.

iii. VITICULTURAL DISTINCTIVENESS

Although the regulatory definition of an AVA as a geographically distinctive grape-growing region would suggest that viticultural distinctiveness is the most important AVA criterion, the TTB has not accepted that argument. All of the regulatory criteria for AVA establishment are weighted equally. The failure to prove any one criterion will prove fatal to an AVA petition. More importantly, when the evidence in support of a particular AVA criterion (e.g., name or boundary) fails to coincide on the ground with evidence of viticultural distinctiveness (e.g., distinguishing geography, geology, or soils), the TTB has to exercise its discretion in establishing, modifying, or rejecting the particular proposal.

Over time, AVA petitioners have become increasingly sophisticated in their assertions and preparation of supporting data concerning viticultural distinctiveness, as seen quite clearly in the field of climate and its effects on the grapes grown inside and outside of a proposed AVA. In the first decade of the AVA program, most climate discussions focused on degree days, which is a measurement of the heat available for vine development during the growing season.[174] Although the degree day classification scheme proposed by Professor Albert Winkler of the University of California—Davis was widely accepted, data often were sparse, making it difficult to compare areas inside and outside of a proposed AVA boundary.

Today, climate data are more readily available, with many growers owning their own weather-monitoring stations that collect measures of temperature, humidity, precipitation, wind direction, and speed every 15 minutes. This abundance of data allows for more detailed analysis of microclimates within a proposed AVA. Recently, these data were used to help defeat the proposed Paso Robles Westside AVA. The opponents hired a meteorologist to analyze the long-term data from a multitude of monitored stations inside and outside of the proposed AVA. The TTB summarized these data as follows:

> Mr. Donald Schucraft, a certified consulting meteorologist with the Western Weather Group, explains in his opposing comment (comment 122) that in the mid-1990's he led a team of meteorologists and physical scientists that established a network of automated weather stations in the Paso Robles region, and that these stations continue to provide key information for localized Paso Robles weather forecasts. Based on the data from these stations, Mr. Schucraft states that the Salinas River does not provide a suitable boundary line for the many different microclimates found in the Paso Robles viticultural area. He notes that there are distinct microclimates to the west of the Salinas River within the proposed Paso Robles Westside viticultural area, and that these microclimates change from north to south as well as east to west.[175]

iv. AMENDING AVA NAMES OR BOUNDARIES

The TTB will consider petitions to amend the name or boundaries of existing AVAs. In the first two decades after the AVA system took effect, such petitions were routinely granted. For a boundary expansion, the petitioner had to present evidence showing that the added acreage shares the

174. Professor Winkler first advanced the concept of growing degree days (GDD) in his seminal book, A. J. Winkler et al., General Viticulture 61 (2d ed. 1975). By convention, grape degree days are tallied between April 1 and October 31, and a base temperature of 50° Fahrenheit is used. *Id.* Winkler's formula for calculating degree days follows: GDD = Sum of ([(Daily Maximum Temperature—Minimum Temperature) ÷ 2]—50) for all days from April 1 to October 31. Winkler established five grape-growing regions based on seasonal degree day accumulations: Region I, less than 2,500 degree days; Region II, 2,501-3,000 degree days; Region III, 3,001-3,500 degree days; Region IV, 3,501-4,000 degree days; and Region V, above 4,000 degree days. *Id.* at 61-64.

175. TTB Notice of Proposed Rulemaking (Notice No. 94), 74 Fed. Reg. 19917, 19920 (April 30, 2009) (to be codified at 27 C.F.R. pt. 9).

same viticultural characteristics as the rest of the AVA.[176] Generally, the enlargement area was not planted to vines or not considered plantable at the time of the AVA establishment, and the Final Rule did not specifically address that area. This gave the TTB some leeway in altering the boundaries.

The TTB, however, was and still is reluctant to expand an AVA that was controversial at the time of its original establishment. For example, the bureau carefully scrutinized and rejected the petition of Sonoma-Cutrer Winery to expand the Carneros AVA. The TTB generally contacts the petitioners for the existing AVA to ensure that they have an opportunity to comment on the proposed expansion.

Today, the TTB, following the 2011 revisions to its AVA regulations, scrutinizes AVA expansion petitions more carefully. The agency requires, among other things, detailed evidence of the distinguishing features of the expansion area that justify its inclusion in the existing AVA. The petitioner must show that these same features are not found in the surrounding, excluded areas.

The TTB also will amend an AVA name so long as there is national or local recognition of that name in relationship to the proposed area. Temecula was later renamed Temecula Valley,[177] and Yamhill-Carlton District became Yamhill-Carlton.[178] The TTB also will modify AVA names to avoid a fight between brand owners and AVA proponents over a particular geographical name so long as the modified name meets the AVA regulatory criteria. An example is the name change from Santa Rita Hills to Sta Rita Hills, which is discussed more fully below.

2. PROTECTING WINE APPELLATIONS

The TTB enforces its appellation requirements through the federal label review process and audits of winery production records. No wine, domestic or foreign, can be sold in the United States without a COLA.[179] The TTB issues a COLA following a review of the proposed label to ensure compliance with federal law. The TTB also has a list of prohibited labeling practices. Any label information that is false or misleading or tends to create a misleading impression, including as to origin, is prohibited.[180] The TTB has the right to conduct an inspection of the bonded winery and its required recordkeeping to verify any winery's labeling claims.

---

176. Almost all amendments have sought to enlarge, not contract, AVAs. The exception is when boundaries of adjacent AVAs are being realigned; an example is Santa Lucia Highlands and Arroyo Seco AVAs (moving approximately 200 acres from Arroyo Seco to Santa Lucia Highlands). TTB Final Rule (T.D. TTB-49), 71 Fed. Reg. 34525 (June 15, 2006).

177. The Temecula Valley Winegrowers Association, which petitioned for the change, argued that the new name would provide a more accurate description of the region's geography and "provide greater clarity as to the area's location for wine consumers and the public." The new name also distinguished the winegrowing area from the City of Temecula. TTB Final Rule (T.D. TTB-10), 67 Fed. Reg. 64573 (Oct. 21, 2002).

178. TTB Final Rule (T.D. TTB-87), 75 Fed. Reg. 67616-67618 (Nov. 3, 2010). The petitioners for the name change said that the AVA name was too long to use on wine labels. They argued that Yamhill-Carlton was locally recognized as referring to the AVA, and the TTB agreed.

179. 27 C.F.R. §4.50 (2010).

180. *Id.* §4.39(a)(1).

If a label claim cannot be justified, the COLA will be rejected or revoked, the wine may be seized, and/or the winery's or importer's federal operating permit can be suspended or revoked.

3. OTHER GEOGRAPHICAL DESIGNATIONS ON WINE LABELS

Appellations are not the only geographical references that are authorized on wine labels in the United States. Other approved uses include brand names of geographical significance; generic, semi-generic, or non-generic classes or types of wine with geographical significance; and varietal names with geographical significance. Each of these uses is discussed below.

a. Brand Names of Geographical Significance

Just as Chateau Margaux in France incorporates the name of the appellation in which it is located, there are numerous U.S. wineries whose brand names have viticultural significance. Examples include Napa Wine Company in the Napa Valley viticultural area, Carneros Creek Winery in the Carneros viticultural area, and Santa Cruz Mountain Vineyard in the Santa Cruz Mountain viticultural area.

In many of these cases, the wineries have selected these brand names because of their geographical significance. At the same time, as noted in Section B, wineries typically wish to protect these brand names as trademarks to prevent others from adopting and using similar brand names to identify their wines. Under U.S. trademark law, there is no inherent inconsistency in claiming trademark rights in a term that has geographical significance. However, to the extent that a geographical term describes the location from which a product originates, it cannot function as a trademark because it does not operate to distinguish products of multiple manufacturers located in the region to which the term applies.[181]

As previously noted, the Lanham Act provides that a geographically descriptive trademark may not be registered as an inherently distinctive trademark.[182] However, such a mark may be entitled to registration and the associated protections if it can be shown that the mark "has become distinctive of the applicant's goods in commerce."[183] Thus, for example, "Chalone Vineyard" is registered as a trademark with the U.S. Patent and Trademark Office despite the TTB's designation of "Chalone" as a viticultural area. Misdescriptive geographical trademarks, however, cannot be registered if they were first used after January 1, 1996.[184]

Geographical terms, we know, also can function as certification marks. The TTB, however, does not defer to certification marks in defining wine

181. *See* 1 J. Thomas McCarthy, McCarthy on Trademarks and Unfair Competition, §14.1 (4th ed. 2010).

182. 15 USC §1052(e) (2006).

183. *Id.* 1052(f).

184. *Id.* §1052(a).

appellations. The TTB stated its position on this subject very clearly in the case of the North Coast AVA in California. The California North Coast Grape Growers Association (CNCGGA) relied on its existing North Coast certification mark for grapes to justify its position on the proposed boundaries of the North Coast AVA. The TTB was not persuaded:

> CNCGGA claims that use of the "North Coast" appellation by wineries using grapes from outside of Napa, Sonoma, and Mendocino Counties constitute infringement of the mark under the Lanham Act, 15 USC Chapter 22. In the event a direct conflict arises between some or all of the rights granted by a registered certification mark under the Lanham Act and the right to use the name of a viticultural area established under the FAA Act, it is the position of [TTB] that the rights applicable to the viticultural area should control. Since the evidence shows that portions of Napa, Sonoma, Mendocino, Solano, Lake, and Marin Counties meet the requirements for a viticultural area as set forth in 27 CFR 4.25a(e), the North Coast viticultural area includes portions of all six counties.[185]

Even if a winery were to acquire trademark rights in a geographical term, it could not prevent certain uses of the term by others. In particular, the owner of rights in a geographically descriptive term cannot prevent others from making non-trademark uses of that term to describe the geographical origin of their products.[186] Such use of a term, referred to as a "fair use," provides an outer limit on the trademark monopoly that one may acquire in a geographical term.

In its early AVA rulings, the TTB often ignored claims by the owners of registered trademarks that their names were being infringed and diluted by the government's establishment of AVAs by the same or similar names. In 1985, the TTB approved the petition of Chicama Vineyards of West Tisbury, Massachusetts, for an AVA known as Martha's Vineyard.[187] The TTB established the AVA over objections of the much better-known Heitz Wine Cellars of Napa Valley, which claimed that approval of the AVA would undermine its common law trademark rights in the name of its most famous wine, Martha's Vineyard Cabernet Sauvignon, named after the grower's wife, Martha May.

In 1988, the TTB issued a very clearly worded position statement on the issue of conflicts between geographical brands (in TTB parlance, "brand names of viticultural significance") and AVAs. The statement is included in the Final Rule establishing the Wild Horse Valley viticultural area over the objection of the owner of the Wild Horse brand, whose wine was not made from grapes grown in the proposed AVA:

> It is not the policy of ATF to become involved in purely private disputes involving proprietary rights, such as trademark infringement suits. However, in the event a direct conflict arises between some or all of the rights granted by a registered trademark under the Lanham Act and the right to use the name of a

185. ATF Final Rule (T.D. ATF-145), 48 Fed. Reg. 42973, 42976 (Sept. 21, 1983).

186. 15 U.S.C. §1115(b)(4) (2006); *see also In Re Nantucket*, 677 F.2d 95, 102-103 (C.C.P.A. 1982) (Nies, J.,concurring).

187. ATF Final Rule (T.D. ATF-193), 50 Fed. Reg. 255 (Jan. 3, 1985).

> viticultural area established under the FAA Act, it is the position of ATF that the rights applicable to the viticultural area should control.[188]

More recently, the TTB followed the same logic in the battle involving the Santa Rita Hills AVA and the Santa Rita trademark held by Santa Rita Winery in Chile. The TTB established the Santa Rita Hills AVA in 2001 over the objection of the Chilean winery, which feared infringement, tarnishment, and dilution if the Santa Rita name were used by other wineries.[189] The Chilean winery responded by commencing a legal action against the TTB in federal district court. The TTB prevailed, largely because the court determined that legal redress could not be sought from the TTB, which established the AVA, but from users of the AVA in commerce.[190] The outcome of such an action no doubt would depend on the way in which the AVA name appeared on the subject label. For example, if the AVA name were prominently displayed and led consumers to believe that the wine was the product of the Santa Rita Winery, a trademark infringement action might be appropriate.

Santa Rita Winery has never filed such an action. Instead, the Chilean winery and other wineries in the Santa Rita Hills AVA agreed to change the name of the AVA to "Sta Rita Hills" to avoid consumer confusion between the brand and the appellation. The TTB consented, and the name change was approved in 2005.[191]

The TTB has wrestled with conflicts between brand names and AVA names since the passage of the FAA Act. It has adopted and then abandoned a series of solutions. For example, the TTB once required wineries to modify their geographic brand names with the word "brand," or with ™ or ®, to indicate to consumers that this is only a brand name and does not imply the geographical origin of the fruit. In 1986, after a lengthy rulemaking, the TTB adopted what appeared to be its final regulatory solution. In that rulemaking, the TTB concluded that brand names of viticultural significance, which typically are the most prominent feature on a wine label, can mislead consumers about the origin of the grapes used to make the wine.[192] For that reason, the bureau decided that if a brand name incorporates the name of a state, county, or viticultural area or is otherwise found to have viticultural significance by the TTB, the wine must comply with the appellation requirements for the named area.

The discretion afforded the TTB allows the agency to determine whether the full AVA name or any part thereof has viticultural significance (known as a "term of viticultural significance"). For example, the TTB has stated that "Napa" alone, instead of the full AVA name Napa Valley, has viticultural significance. Because "Napa" is so distinctive, unlike "Green" in the AVA Green Valley of Solano County, "Napa" alone cannot be used in a brand unless the

---

188. ATF Final Rule (T.D. ATF-278), 53 Fed. Reg. 48244 at 48246 (Nov. 30, 1988).
189. ATF Final Rule (T.D. ATF-454), 66 Fed. Reg. 29476-29480 (May 31, 2001).
190. *Sociedad Anomina Vina Santa Rita v. U.S. Treasury Dep't,* 193 F. Supp. 2d 6 (D.D.C. 2001).
191. TTB Final Rule (T.D. TTB-37), 70 Fed. Reg. 72710-72713 (Dec. 7, 2005).
192. 27 C.F.R. §4.39(i) (2010), which is set forth in full in Chapter 3; *see also* Wine Labeling and Advertising; Use of Geographic Brand Names, T.D. ATF-229 (May 16, 1986).

wine qualifies for the Napa Valley AVA or Napa County appellation, or is otherwise grandfathered, as explained below.

In its 1986 ruling, the TTB also established an exception for preexisting brand names of viticultural significance. Under this grandfather provision, wineries that obtained label approval from the TTB for a brand name of viticultural significance prior to July 7, 1986, are allowed to continue to use that brand name, and even to sell it to other proprietors who could use it, so long as the label includes an appropriate appellation of origin for the wine or a label disclaimer.[193] An appropriate appellation or disclaimer is defined as follows:

> A county or a viticultural area, if the brand name bears the name of a geographical area smaller than a state, or . . . [a] state, county or a viticultural area, if the brand name bears a state name; or . . . [t]he wine shall be labeled with some other statement which the appropriate TTB officer finds to be sufficient to dispel the impression that the geographical area suggested by the brand name is indicative of the origin of the wine.[194]

As an example, the brand Napa Ridge was first used in a COLA approved by the TTB before 1986, so the winery can continue to use that name, including for wines that are not made from Napa Valley grapes, so long as the label includes an appropriate appellation of origin. An example of such a grandfathered label would be Napa Ridge Central Coast Cabernet Sauvignon. (Napa Valley is not a part of the Central Coast AVA.) By contrast, a hypothetical new wine sold under the brand Napa Valley Oaks would have to include at least 85 percent Napa Valley grapes, or that brand name could not be used.

The TTB's grandfather exception provided an opportunity for the owners of pre-1986 brands to profit by sourcing lower-cost grapes for wines labeled with a well-known geographical brand name that would fetch a higher price. Bronco Wine Company (Bronco) purchased three such brands: Napa Ridge, Rutherford Vintners, and Napa Creek Winery, sample labels of which are shown in Figure 6-15.

Figure 6-15
"Napa" Labels

193. 27 C.F.R. §4.39(i) (2010).
194. *Id.*

Because these brands were grandfathered, Bronco could use the names and source grapes from any AVA as long as an appropriate appellation was identified on the label. Recognizing the potential for confusion and damage to the reputation and economy of Napa Valley, the California legislature passed Business and Professions Code §25241, which prohibits the use of a brand name with the word Napa, or any federally recognized viticultural area wholly within Napa County, or any confusingly similar name on the label, packaging material, or advertising of wine produced, bottled, labeled, offered for sale, or sold in California, unless at least 75 percent of the grapes used to make the wine are from Napa County. The legislature adopted the following findings in support of the bill:

> (1) The Legislature finds and declares that for more than a century, Napa Valley and Napa County have been widely recognized for producing grapes and wine of the highest quality. Both consumers and the wine industry understand the name Napa County and the viticultural area appellations of origin contained within Napa County (collectively "Napa appellations") as denoting that the wine was created with the distinctive grapes grown in Napa County.
>
> (2) The Legislature finds, however, that certain producers are using Napa appellations on labels, on packaging materials, and in advertising for wines that are not made from grapes grown in Napa County, and that consumers are confused and deceived by these practices.
>
> (3) The Legislature further finds that legislation is necessary to eliminate these misleading practices. It is the intent of the Legislature to assure consumers that the wines produced or sold in the state with brand names, packaging materials, or advertising referring to Napa appellations in fact qualify for the Napa County appellation of origin.[195]

Bronco challenged the state law, claiming, among other things, that federal law preempted the more restrictive California legislation and that the Court "should find implied preemption . . . because section 25241 stands as an obstacle to the accomplishment and execution of the full purposes and objectives of Congress."[196]

The Court found that

> nothing in the history of the underlying federal statute or the federal regulations suggest[s] that, although the [ATF] may have determined that as a *general matter* its grandfather clause was appropriate so as to avoid destroying an "entire class" of brand-name labels, states would or should be precluded from adopting more stringent brand-name labeling requirements as necessary to address local concerns.[197] [Emphasis in original.]

California's labeling rule therefore was not preempted by federal law and did not "frustrate Congress's intent or stand as an obstacle to the accomplishment

195. Cal. Bus. & Prof. Code §25241(a) (2009).

196. *Bronco*, 33 Cal. 4th at 956. In addition to its preemption cause of action, Bronco claimed that the California law violated the First Amendment, the Commerce Clause, and the Takings Clause of the U.S. Constitution. *Id.* at 955.

197. *Id.* at 994.

and execution of the full purposes and objectives of Congress." In conclusion, the Court ruled without dissent as follows:

> Bronco has failed to carry its burden of demonstrating federal preemption of a long-established and legitimate exercise of state police power with respect to the subject regulated by section 25241. As we have seen, there is no express preemption in the present context, and Bronco's assertions of implied preemption are contradicted by the long history we have described of concurrent state and federal regulation of wine labels including, historically, the representations appearing on labels suggesting the place of origin of the grapes used to make wine. Nor has Bronco succeeded in providing any persuasive indication that this long-standing concurrent regulatory scheme no longer is compatible with Congress's overall purposes which have been to support the states' efforts to protect consumers from misleading labeling, not to permit the type of labeling at issue here. Finally, Bronco has not established that, by purchasing a brand name that had been used prior to 1986, it acquired a federally recognized right or license exempting it from stricter state regulation.
>
> California is recognized as a preeminent producer of wine, and the geographical source of its wines—reflecting the attributes of distinctive locales, particularly the Napa Valley—forms a very significant basis upon which consumers worldwide evaluate expected quality when making a purchase. We do not find it surprising that Congress, in its effort to provide minimum standards for wine labels, would not foreclose a state with particular expertise and interest from providing stricter protection for consumers in order to ensure the integrity of its wine industry.[198]

Both before and after the *Bronco* case, the TTB has tried to avoid conflicts between brand names and AVA names in a number of ways. Perhaps the most common solution mentioned above is to modify the name of the AVA, such as Diamond Mountain District or Eola-Amity Hills, to differentiate those AVAs from the brands Diamond Mountain and Eola Hills. The full name of the AVA is then established by the TTB as the name of viticultural significance so that the brand names are unaffected by the provisions of 27 C.F.R. 4.39(i). But sometimes this solution has not worked.

The most recent contentious battle, described briefly in Section B, was fought over the name Calistoga.[199] Although the TTB found a "substantial

---

198. *Id.* at 997. California's action to codify Business & Professions Code §25241 was not the first time that the Napa Valley wine industry had turned to the state to protect the Napa Valley brand. In 1989 California adopted a law requiring "conjunctive labeling" for Napa Valley wines. Cal. Bus. & Prof. Code §25240 provides that any wine labeled with a Napa Valley sub-AVA must also say "Napa Valley" on the label. Oregon also has adopted wine labeling standards that are stricter than the federal labeling regulations—for example, for varietal wines (Oregon Administrative Rules (OAR) 845-010-0915 requires 90 percent varietal content for some varietals and 75 percent for others compared to the federal requirement of 75 percent) and appellations of origin (OAR 845-010-0920 requires 95 percent grape sourcing from Oregon appellations, including Oregon AVAs, counties, and the state, compared to the federal requirement of 85 percent).

199. Given the role that Calistoga played in Napa Valley's rise to prominence in the wine world, it is surprising that it was not a recognized AVA sooner. Chateau Montelena's 1973 Chardonnay, produced in Calistoga, took first prize for white wine in the Paris Tasting of 1976. George M. Taber, Judgment of Paris: California vs. France and the Historic 1976 Paris Tasting 201-202 (New York: Simon & Schuster 2005).

basis for the establishment of the viticultural area"[200] under the Calistoga name in the northern part of the Napa Valley AVA and no evidence was presented to contradict the petitioners' evidence of viticultural distinctiveness, the TTB was troubled by the claims of Calistoga Partners, L.P., doing business as Calistoga Cellars (its brand name), and Chateau Calistoga (Calistoga Estates brand name) that their brands would be adversely impacted or eliminated altogether by the TTB's action. Calistoga Cellars and Calistoga Estate did not source enough grapes from the proposed Calistoga AVA to meet the 85 percent grape sourcing requirement. In its rulemaking notice, the TTB made it clear that it "do[es] not believe that, in the context of the labeling provisions of the FAA Act, it is an appropriate government role to make choices between competing commercial interests, if such choices can be avoided."[201] That is, the TTB would be hard-pressed to establish an AVA that would cause an existing winery to "forfeit" its trademark rights and invested capital in its brand name.

The preferred resolution of revising the AVA name was unavailable; petitioner Chateau Montelena would not accept Calistoga District as the AVA name and as the name of viticultural significance. After the Bronco saga, Chateau Montelena feared that there would be a variety of brands with Calistoga name variations (Calistoga Caves, Calistoga Hills, Calistoga Wine Cellars), none of which would have to use Calistoga AVA grapes because the brands did not include the precise words "Calistoga District."

Although the TTB might have solved the problem by denying the petition altogether, the agency proposed a new compromise and, in doing so, sparked a hotly contested and heavily politicized AVA rulemaking proceeding. The agency's proposal, in the form of Notice of Proposed Rulemaking No. 77, published in the Federal Register on November 20, 2007, was to expand grandfather protection beyond the pre-1986 limit to include brands that had been in actual commercial use for a "significant period" prior to the filing of the AVA petition and to require additional information on the allowed labels sufficient to dispel the impression that the wines qualified as Calistoga AVA wines.[202] The solution was essentially a one-brand fix for Calistoga Cellars. Calistoga Estates would be left out because its first COLA was approved after the TTB issued the first Notice of Proposed Rulemaking for the Calistoga AVA in March 2005.

The TTB received over 1,350 comments in response to Notice No. 77. Of the comments received, over 1,160 were in the form of letters and postcards championing "the little guy" brand owners being denied their "due process right."[203] Most of these comments were form letters submitted by "Stand Up for the Little Guy," a group supporting Calistoga Cellars.[204]

---

200. TTB Final Rule (T.D. TTB-83) at 64605.
201. *Id.*
202. TTB Notice of Proposed Rulemaking (Notice No. 77), 72 Fed. Reg. 65257-65261 (Nov. 20, 2007).
203. TTB Final Rule (T.D. TTB-83) at 64606.
204. *Id.*

In forming its response to the debate, the TTB stated that many commentators got it wrong. The issue was not about large versus small wineries:

> The present rulemaking raised the question of what to do about viticultural area petitions that are received long after the issuance in 1986 of §4.39(i) on the use of geographical brand names of viticultural significance where the petition proposes a name that results in a conflict with a brand name first used on an approved COLA not covered by the grandfather provision in §4.39(i). Such a circumstance may occur for legitimate reasons because exact terms of viticultural significance are not always universally agreed upon, and relevant facts and issues regarding terms and areas of viticultural significance are not always brought forward until a petition is published for rulemaking.[205]

The TTB concluded in December 2009 that the "adoption of a specific, limited grandfather provision would not be appropriate in this case."[206] The TTB also abandoned the notion that a back label disclaimer could adequately dispel consumer confusion. The TTB's ultimate compromise was to create a three-year "use up period," during which the Calistoga-named brands could be transitioned to new names or brought into compliance with the AVA grape-sourcing requirements.[207]

b. Generic, Semi-generic and Non-generic Names of Geographical Significance

The same distinction between generic and geographically descriptive designations under the Lanham Act discussed in Section A is recognized by the TTB. Under the FAA Act, the TTB has the authority to establish "Standards of Identity for Wine," which include various classes of wine (e.g., grape wine, sparkling grape wine, fruit wine) and types of wine within each class (e.g., table or dessert wine, champagne, berry wine as well as varietal types).[208] A generic wine name is a designation for a particular class or type of wine. Generic names also can have geographical significance. In the United States, vermouth and sake now are considered to be generic names that have lost their original geographical significance. These terms may be used on wine labels without any indication of origin.

Other names retain their original geographical reference but also indicate a type of wine under U.S. law.[209] There are 16 authorized semi-generic names—generic as to product characteristics but not as to origin—that may be used to designate wines from the original source or, when modified by an appropriate appellation of origin displayed in direct conjunction with the name, from some other source (e.g., California Sherry).[210] The 16 semi-generics are Angelica, Burgundy, Claret, Chablis, Champagne, Chianti, Malaga, Marsala,

205. *Id.* at 64610.
206. *Id.* at 64611.
207. *Id.*
208. 27 U.S.C. §205(e); 27 C.F.R. §§4.20-4.23 (2010).
209. 27 C.F.R. §4.21 (2010).
210. 26 U.S.C. §5388(c) (2006); 27 C.F.R. §4.24(b) (2010).

Madeira, Moselle, Port, Rhine Wine, Sauterne, Haut Sauterne, Sherry, and Tokay.

Finally, names deemed non-generic may be used only to designate wines of the origin indicated by such names.[211] Non-generic status under the TTB regulations is of two sorts. First, certain non-generic designations are deemed to be "distinctive designations" of particular wine types and suffice as class and type designations in their own right. These designations include Chateau Margaux, Graves, Medoc, Rhone, and over 100 other names listed in 27 C.F.R. Part 12, Subpart D. To be so classified, the names must be found by the director of the TTB to be known to the U.S. consumer and trade as designating a specific wine from a particular place and distinguishable from all other wines.[212]

The second type of non-generic name can be used only to designate wine of the origin indicated by such name but is not sufficiently well recognized to serve as a class and type designation under U.S. law. Such wine names, including Bandol, Piemonte, Rheinfalz, and others listed in Part 12, Subpart C, still must be accompanied by an acceptable class or type designation on the label.

The difference between these categories of non-generic names is not well understood. Although both are non-generic, the second category seems to imply a lesser degree of protection. Additionally, those foreign wine names not entered on either list appear to be unprotected. In fact, Subpart C of Part 12 lists only "examples" of foreign non-generic names rather than a comprehensive list (as is the case for Subpart D, concerning foreign distinctive designations), further confusing the status, use, and protection afforded non-generic names.

c. Varietal Names with Geographical Significance

Another possible geographical reference on a U.S. wine label is as part of a varietal name. The TTB initiated rulemaking in 1986, and completed it in 1995, establishing an approved list of wine grape varietal names.[213] Certain contentious varietal names such as Johannisberg Riesling and Gamay Beaujolais were phased out.

4. THE FUTURE OF WINE APPELLATIONS IN THE UNITED STATES

The wine appellation system in the United States is now over 30 years old. Its future will be shaped by two separate and independent processes. The first is governmental; the TTB has recently completed a comprehensive review of the appellation rules and regulations and amended certain of the AVA regulations. The second is private; various vintner-grower groups are taking steps on their own to give their appellation wines added meaning and value.

211. 27 C.F.R. §4.24(c) (2010).
212. *Id.* §4.24(c).
213. Grape Variety Names for American Wines, 61 Fed. Reg. 522 (Feb. 13, 1996).

a. Revisiting the Regulations

In 2007 the TTB decided that it was time for a comprehensive review of the appellation system. On its own initiative, the bureau issued Notice of Proposed Rulemaking No. 78, with a series of questions and reform proposals.[214] Not surprisingly, disputes between brand names and AVAs were first on the list. The TTB described the problem as follows:

> Since July 1986, more than 100 AVAs have been established in response to petitions from industry members and grape growers, reflecting the increased interest in, and spread of, viticulture throughout the United States. In addition, in recent years an increasing number of petitions have been submitted that, if the AVA were to be established with the petitioned-for name, would affect established brand names. As noted above, our intent in administering the AVA program, consistent with the intent behind the original grandfather approach, is to recognize established grape-growing regions while avoiding interference with established brand names.
>
> While TTB will continue to work with future AVA petitioners to limit the adverse impact on established brand names, we recognize that sometimes it will not be possible to amend a petition to achieve this result. In such cases, we believe that application of a new prospective grandfather approach would achieve the most balanced result. Accordingly, we are proposing to amend §4.39(i) by adding a new grandfathering standard that would apply in the case of AVAs established after adoption of the final rule in this matter and that would be based on a specified number of years that a COLA was issued, and whether the brand label was in actual commercial use, before receipt by TTB of a perfected AVA petition. This approach would permit the establishment of the AVA and at the same time afford appropriate protection of existing labels.[215]

The TTB's specific proposal provided that, for a post-1986 geographical brand to be grandfathered, it must be used in a COLA issued at least five years before the establishment of an AVA bearing that geographical name and that wine brand must have been commercially sold for at least three of those five years. Further, a geographical brand, if used on a wine that does not qualify for the named AVA, must include a label disclaimer.[216] Although no particular disclaimer language was proposed, presumably it would be something like "This ABC brand wine is not from the ABC appellation." This is commonly referred to as a rolling grandfather rule because the precise grandfathering date would be decided on a case-by-case basis, depending on the date of "perfection" of the AVA petition.

In Notice 78 the TTB also addressed the issue of AVAs that are nested inside of other AVAs and AVA expansions. Regarding the former, the bureau described its concerns as follows:

> TTB has come to recognize that [petitions for AVAs that would be entirely or partially within the boundaries of existing AVAs] can create the appearance of a

214. TTB Notice of proposed rulemaking (Notice No. 78), 72 Fed. Reg. 65261-65275 (Nov. 20, 2007).

215. *Id.* at 65263.

216. *Id.* at 65267.

> conflict or inconsistency because, with reference to the criteria set forth in §9.3(b), the new petition might draw into question the accuracy and validity of the evidence presented in support of the establishment of the existing AVA or the legitimacy of the justification for establishing the AVA.[217]

For that reason, the TTB proposed to reserve the right, when establishing an AVA within an AVA, to carve it out of the larger area of which it is part.[218] For example, a future "Coombsville" AVA in the southeastern portion of Napa Valley might be considered so distinct that it would no longer be considered part of the Napa Valley AVA. If that were to happen, grapes grown there would not count toward the 85 percent grape source requirement for Napa Valley wines.

The TTB also proposed to clarify in Notice 78 that amendments to existing AVAs will only be approved if the expansion area shares "essentially the same" distinguishing viticultural features as the rest of the AVA and the petitioner can show that the area outside the expanded AVA has different features.[219] Additionally, "[t]he petition must explain how the boundary of the existing AVA was incorrectly or incompletely drafted or is no longer accurate due to new evidence or changed circumstances with reference to the name evidence and distinguishing features" of the AVA.[220]

Finally, the TTB sought to clarify the grounds upon which an AVA petition can be rejected and to more completely describe the submission and review processes, including the actions that the TTB is empowered to take at each stage of the process.[221]

TTB's Final Rule on Notice 78 was published on January 20, 2011, just as this book was being sent to the publisher.[222] The TTB carefully analyzed the 191 comments that it received from U.S. senators and representatives, state government representatives, local government officials, wine industry members, trade associations, interest groups, and others. The large majority of the comments opposed part or all of the TTB's proposed changes; some commenters recommended their own changes to the AVA regulations.[223]

In the Final Rule, the TTB amended Part 9 of 27 C.F.R. in the following areas: the submission of AVA petitions (§9.11), AVA petition requirements (§9.12), initial processing of AVA petitions (§9.13), and the AVA rulemaking

217. *Id.* at 65262.
218. *Id.* at 65268.
219. *Id.*
220. *Id.*
221. *Id.* at 65269.
222. TTB Final Rule (T.D. TTB-90), 76 Fed. Reg. 3489 (Jan. 20, 2011).
223. Jess Jackson, owner of Kendall-Jackson and many other wine brands, recommended that the TTB classify appellations based on their size, viticultural distinctiveness, and homogeneity in grape growing attributes; specifically, he recommended the establishment of AVA zones, regions and districts. Comment from Jess S. Jackson, March 19, 2008; http://www.regulations.gov/search/Regs/home.html#docketDetail?R=TTB-2007-0068 (accessed December 8, 2010). The ID number of Mr. Jackson's comment is TTB-2007-0068-0106.1. This scheme harkens back to a proposal made earlier by geographer Harm Jan de Blij who recommended the establishment in the U.S. of regional appellations (e.g., Ohio River Valley, Pacific Northwest), state and county appellations, and smaller AVAs. Harm Jan De Blij, *Viticultural Areas and Mental Maps,* 21 East Lake Geographer, Sept. 1, 1986.

process (§9.14). The new regulations take effect on February 22, 2011. Petitions received prior to that date are processed under the pre-existing rules.

The TTB decided to abandon its proposal for a rolling grandfather rule to resolve conflicts between brand names and appellations. This was not surprising in light of the TTB's earlier decision on the Calistoga AVA brand name conflict and the fact that 105 of 107 comments that the bureau received on this issue opposed the TTB's proposal. The TTB noted in the Final Rule that in almost all instances of name conflicts, the parties have been able to reach a satisfactory compromise. It cited specific examples involving AVA name modifiers like "District" (e.g., Diamond Mountain District AVA), the consent of the affected brand owners to comply with the AVA's grape sourcing requirement (e.g., Lake Chelan), the change of an AVA's name (e.g., Chalone AVA), and the rejection of an AVA petition (e.g., the Tulocay AVA in Napa Valley). The TTB then referred to the transitional three-year period that it adopted in the Calistoga situation, which gave the affected brand owners time to modify their grape sourcing or adopt a new brand name. And the bureau added that "we continue to believe that dispelling information [a disclaimer] is appropriate in certain situations."[224] With all these tools at its disposal, the TTB decided that future brand name—appellation conflicts can be resolved on a case-by-case basis without a "new grandfather provision as a default resolution."[225] The bureau reserved the right to revisit the issue in the future should circumstances warrant and, in the meantime, encouraged all concerned parties, including consumers, to resolve any name conflicts on their own rather than rely on rulemaking.

On a related issue, the TTB chose not to adopt any new regulation about "terms of viticultural significance" but instead will continue to rely on 27 C.F.R. §4.39(i)(3) to make those determinations. That subsection reads: "A name has viticultural significance when it is the name of a state or county (or the foreign equivalents), when approved as a viticultural area in part 9 of this chapter, or by a foreign government, or when found to have viticultural significance by the appropriate TTB officer." The bureau cited a comment that it received on this subject stating that no rule on "terms of viticultural significance" should be promulgated by the TTB "without explaining the criteria for the selection so that the industry can provide meaningful comments."[226] Since December 2005 the TTB has stated the "terms of viticultural significance" in each of its Final Rules establishing AVAs.[227]

With respect to nested AVAs, the TTB received strong opposition to its stated concerns and proposal. The TTB agree with the commenters that "consumer interests are served by greater specificity within a hierarchy, where a true hierarchy exists."[228] But the TTB restated its belief that some AVAs formed within larger, existing AVAs might be so distinct as to confuse consumers if

---

224. *Id.* at 3499.
225. *Id.* at 3498.
226. *Id.* at 3499.
227. *See, e.g.*, 27 C.F.R. §9.185 (Texoma AVA), established by T.D. TTB-38, 70 Fed. Reg. 72716 (Dec. 7, 2005).
228. TTB Final Rule (T.D. TTB-90) at 3499.

both AVA names could be used on wine labels. The TTB gave the following example:

> [I]f an existing AVA is defined as being a large valley and its distinguishing geographical features are those that are found on the valley floor, it may be appropriate to approve a proposed AVA described as being situated in whole or in part on the same valley floor within the existing AVA if the proposed AVA shares some of the geographical features with the existing AVA but at the same time has other geographical features that are sufficiently distinctive as to warrant its own AVA designation. On the other hand, if within that large valley AVA there is a mountain on which a petitioner proposes to establish a new AVA above the 500-foot elevation line, the evidence provided in the petition might demonstrate that the distinguishing features of the proposed AVA bear no relationship to those of the valley floor. In the latter case, the new petition has demonstrated that this is not a hierarchical situation involving some sharing of common features but rather is a proposal to establish an entirely distinctive AVA. In such a case, TTB believes it may be inappropriate to take a regulatory action that could cause consumers mistakenly to conclude that wine produced from grapes grown within the petitioned-for AVA has the same characteristics as wine produced from grapes grown in the existing AVA.[229]

This prompts the question of how TTB might react to a future petition for a high-elevation, mountain-named AVA that is entirely within a low-lying, valley-named AVA. Many such AVAs already exist, such as Sonoma Mountain in Sonoma Valley and Diamond Mountain District or Howell Mountain in Napa Valley. Fortunately, the TTB stated in the Final Rule that carving out a nested AVA from the larger AVA of which it is part is likely to occur only in "very rare instances in which no notable common geographical features between the two AVAs can be found."[230]

In the Final Rule, the TTB modified the evidentiary requirements for an AVA petition, although in practice these requirements have been in effect for several years.[231] The requirements vary with the three different types of AVA petitions: those seeking to establish new AVAs that do not overlap or lie wholly within an existing AVA, those seeking to establish AVAs that are partially or wholly within another AVA, and those that modify the boundaries or name of existing AVAs. For a new, free-standing AVA, the petition must still provide evidence of the name, boundary, and viticultural distinctiveness of the area, but the regulations now provide more detail on the types of information that are required or disallowed. The petition must contain sufficient information, data, and evidence so that the TTB does not need to conduct any independent verification or research. With respect to the proposed AVA name, "[t]he name . . . must be currently and directly associated with an area in which viticulture exists. All of the area within the proposed AVA

229. *Id.* at 3496.

230. *Id.*

231. The TTB itself stated that the new requirements do not impose new standards but "represent a codification of longstanding administrative authority and practice and address a need for greater transparency." TTB Final Rule (T.D.-90) at 3499.

boundary must be nationally or locally known by the name specified in the petition, although the use of that name may extend beyond the proposed AVA boundary."[232] The petition must completely explain the manner in which the name is used for the proposed area. That evidence must come from sources independent of the petitioner. Statements from local residents may be included, although they are not sufficient in and of themselves.

With respect to the proposed boundary, the new regulation, 27 C.F.R. §9.12. states, "The petition must explain in detail the basis for defining the boundary. . . . In support of the proposed boundary, the petition must outline the commonalities or similarities within that boundary and must explain with specificity how those elements are different in the adjacent areas outside that boundary."[233]

Finally, the petition for a new AVA must explain the viticultural distinctiveness of the area compared to the adjacent areas. Distinguishing features affecting viticulture are defined to include (1) climate, including temperature, precipitation, wind, fog, solar orientation and radiation, and other information; (2) geology, including the underlying geologic formations, landforms, and geophysical events such as earthquakes, eruptions, and major floods; (3) soils, including the soils series denoting parent material, texture, slope, permeability, soil reaction, drainage, and fertility; (4) physical features such as flat, hilly, or mountainous topography, geographical formations, bodies of water, watersheds, irrigations resources, and other features; and (5) elevation. As always, the petition must include the boundaries on U.S.G.S. maps; the boundaries also must be described in narrative.

For petitions proposing to establish an AVA entirely within or partially overlapping an existing AVA, the same evidence is required as for a new AVA, as described above, but it must be supplemented by evidence identifying the attributes of the proposed AVA that are "consistent with" and "sufficiently distinct from" the existing AVA so as to justify separate recognition of the proposed AVA.[234] As noted previously, when a smaller AVA has name recognition and features that clearly distinguish it from a larger AVA of which it is part, the TTB may determine in the course of the rulemaking that the new AVA is not a part of the larger AVA.

The third type of AVA petition seeks to modify an existing AVA boundary or name. With respect to the former, the petitioner must include all of the evidence required for a new AVA along with the following additional information: (1) name evidence showing that the name applies to the new area, whether expanded or reduced in size; (2) distinguishing features affecting viticulture that are essentially the same as those of the existing AVA and different from those outside the proposed boundary; and (3) boundary evidence and description, including an explanation of how the boundary of the existing AVA was incorrectly or incompletely defined or is no longer accurate due to new evidence or changed circumstances. For petitions that seek to change the

232. *Id.* at 3500-3501.
233. *Id.* at 3501.
234. *Id.*

name of an existing AVA, the petition must establish the suitability of the new name by providing the name evidence required for a new AVA petition.

Finally, the TTB has spelled out in more detail its AVA procedures. After a petition is filed, the TTB will notify the petitioner of receipt within 30 days. The TTB then will review the petition to determine whether or not it is a "perfected petition," defined as "a petition containing all of the evidence meeting the requirements of §9.12 and containing sufficient supporting information for TTB to decide whether or not to proceed with rulemaking to establish a new AVA or to change an existing AVA."[235] The TTB will return petitions that are not perfected without prejudice to the later filing of a revised petition. If a petition is perfected, the TTB will decide whether to proceed with rulemaking and advise the petitioner of its decision in writing. The TTB will place a notice on its website when a perfected petition has been accepted for rulemaking.

If the TTB determines that rulemaking is appropriate, it will prepare and publish a NPRM to solicit public comment. After receiving comments, the TTB can prepare a Final Rule, adopting the proposed AVA with or without changes, withdraw the proposal, prepare a new Notice of Proposed Rulemaking, or take any other action it deems appropriate as authorized by law. The TTB must cite the reasons for withdrawing an AVA petition, which must include at least one of the following: (1) insufficient viticulture within the proposed AVA, with no objective standard to determine that in terms of the number of planted vineyard acres or the percentage of the AVA land mass planted to vines (the TTB, however, did provide one example in the Final Rule: five acres of grapes in a 10,000-square-mile AVA will not suffice to designate a new AVA[236]); (2) insufficient evidence of name, boundary, or distinguishing features; or (3) inconsistency with one of the purposes of the Federal Alcohol Administration Act or other federal statute, or a decision that the proposal is contrary to the public interest, which is a nebulous grab bag of potential grounds for withdrawal.

Although it is impossible to know how these changes will affect future AVA petitions, three things seem fairly certain. First, petitions for nested or overlapping AVAs will be scrutinized more closely and will have to meet a higher burden of proof than in the past. That being said, the movement to establish nested AVAs will not be stymied by the increased governmental scrutiny. Second, the TTB will look to the concerned parties in most instances to resolve disputes between brands and appellation names. Clearly, the bureau does not want to become embroiled in another multi-year Calistoga-style dispute. Third, AVA petitions will become increasingly detailed and sophisticated. This is a welcome development.

b. Privatization

Separate and apart from these regulatory reforms, grower-vintner groups in numerous appellations are taking private steps to promote the particular

235. *Id.* at 3500.
236. *Id.* at 3494.

characteristics and qualities of their wines to the wine trade and consumers. Several examples follow.

In the viticultural area of Augusta in the state of Missouri, the local town council has awarded a special town seal, the Owl Seal, for those wines that abide by the city's viticultural and enological controls and have passed the required organoleptic evaluation. The Montelle label shown in Figure 6-16 includes the Owl Seal. The required taste test was largely designed to weed out defective wines. The program is now defunct.

For many years in the viticultural area of Carneros in southern Napa and Sonoma counties, the local vintners produced a cooperative, master blend of Pinot Noir and Chardonnay, marketed by the local trade association previously known as Carneros Quality Alliance (CQA), and today as Carneros Wine Alliance, under the association's label (Figure 6-17). The purpose of the joint undertaking was to showcase the unique characteristics and quality of the appellation's two most distinctive varietals.

The Napa Valley Vintners (NVV), a trade association with over 400 vintner members located in that appellation, registered a certification mark in the form of a logo that can be used only on wines that are entirely produced and bottled in the Napa Valley AVA and made from 100 percent Napa Valley grapes, not 85 percent as federal law requires.[237] The mark is shown in Figure 6-18. The use of the certification mark is voluntary. Any winery whose wines meet the certification criteria can use the mark on those wines, whether or not that person or entity is a member of NVV.

In Mendocino County, the group Coro Mendocino created a protocol for the production of wine distinctive to that appellation. Coro Mendocino's mission is to "increase the awareness and value of Mendocino wine and winegrape products through the production of Coro Mendocino, a controlled, ultra

Figure 6-16
Montelle Label

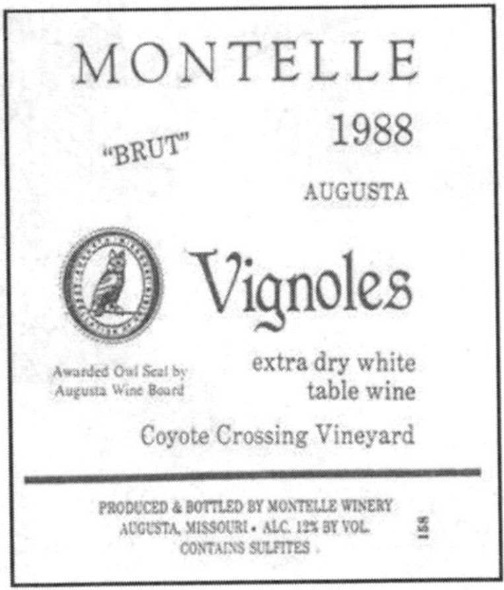

237. Registration No. 3232326.

Figure 6-17
Carneros Label

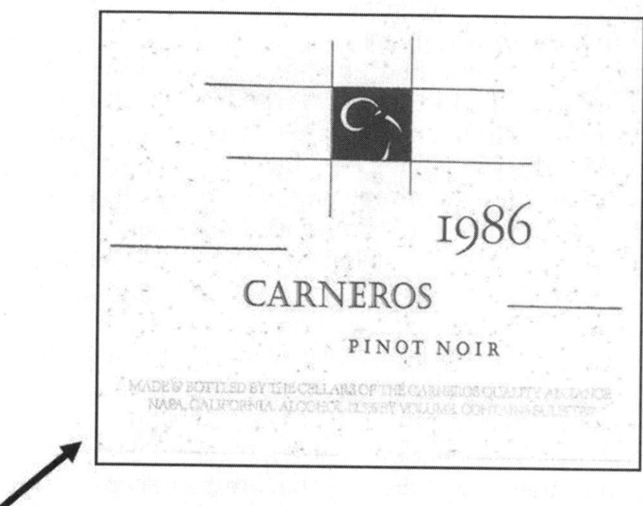

"MADE & BOTTLED BY THE CELLARS OF THE CARNEROS QUALITY ALLIANCE"

Figure 6-18
100% Napa Valley Mark

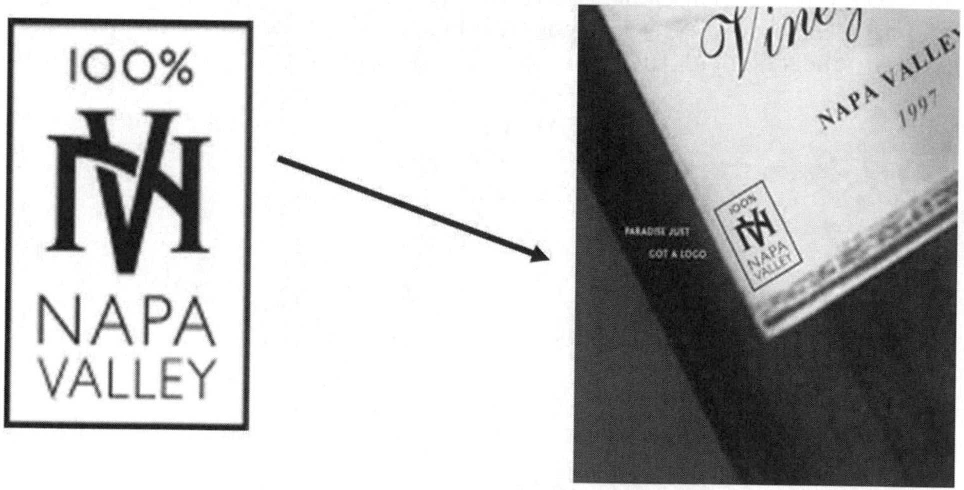

premium blended wine that reflects the quality and commitment of the Mendocino County wine industry."[238] Coro Mendocino requires wine to be

---

238. Consortium Mendocino By-Laws as amended August 2005, http://www.coromendocino.com/img/CoroBylaws.pdf.

produced according to specific winemaking parameters and to be submitted to a blind tasting panel.[239] If the wine passes, it is then packaged in uniform bottles with labels bearing the individual brand in conjunction with the Coro Mendocino trademark and trade dress. The Coro Mendocino protocol requires Zinfandel to be the dominant varietal in the wine, comprising a minimum percentage of 40 percent and a maximum of 70 percent. There are nine allowed second-tier varietals, but any one of the second-tier varietals cannot exceed the quantity of Zinfandel. An additional 10 percent of the wine can be made from any varietal. Coro Mendocino also designates basic chemistry and sensory limits and prescribes the details of both cooperage and aging. The group does not place any restrictions on viticultural practices. The Coro Mendocino bottles and mark are shown in Figures 6-19 and 6-20.

The Lodi Winegrape Commission's "Lodi Rules for Sustainable Winegrowing" have become a benchmark for sustainable or "green" viticultural practices.[240] The project began in the early 1990s in an effort to increase and encourage sustainability in winegrowing. At the time, the term "green" had not become a marketing buzzword for pro-environment products and processes. The program, which was developed with extensive input from growers, vintners, scientists, academics, and environmentalists, has culminated in the publication of the nearly 300-page *Lodi Winegrower's Workbook*.[241]

Figure 6-19
Coro Mendocino Bottles

239. *See* http://www.coromendocino.com/ProductionProtocol.htm (accessed December 8, 2010).

240. *See* http://www.lodiwine.com/lodirules_home1.shtml (accessed December 8, 2010).

241. Chris Storm, Clifford Ohmart & Steve Matthiasson, Lodi Winegrowers' Workbook, 2d ed. (San Francisco: Wine Appreciation Guild 2010).

Figure 6-20
Coro "Mark"

The *Workbook* serves as a guide for vintners and growers to make measurable improvements in the health of their property's ecosystem and society at large and to improve wine quality and purity.

The Lodi Rules program has two components: sustainable winegrowing standards and pesticide assessment that measures the impact of all pesticides, both organic and synthetic, used in a vineyard. In order to qualify for certification and earn the right to place the "Lodi Rules" certification mark on wine labels, the winery or vineyard must achieve a minimum number of sustainable farming points, as defined in the *Workbook*, and must not exceed a maximum number of pesticide impact points. The Lodi Rules mark and sample labels are shown in Figures 6-21, 6-22, and 6-23.

Figure 6-21
Lodi Rules Mark

Figure 6-22
Lobo Loco Label

Figure 6-23
Mohr-Fry Ranches Back Label

Lodi Rules has led numerous growers to adopt more sustainable and eco-friendly farming practices, but the Lodi Rules program is also a marketing effort to re-brand the Lodi AVA as a winegrowing region that values sustainable farming. The Lodi Rules program is not touted as creating qualitative sensory differences in wine produced under the standards. The Lodi Rules also do not define the characteristics of wine produced from Lodi grapes. Instead, the Lodi Rules promote Lodi as a region distinctive for its farming and values.

D. CONCLUSION

The United States is a brand-driven market economy that does not have the same tradition as, say, Europe with respect to products of place. Wine is the exception, but even then wine appellations are less important to most consumers than wine brands. The United States embarked more than 30 years ago on the path of defining its wine appellations. That evolution has had noticeable successes and failures.

Interestingly, some of the most prestigious wine appellations, such as Napa Valley, today have to protect their good names from impostors at home and abroad who seek to profit from consumer confusion.[242] For example, the NVV has fought against the following Napa-named brands around the world: Ca' de Napa (Italy), Varon de Napa (Spain), Napa Crest (United Kingdom), Napatina (Argentina), Napa (Taiwan and Vietnam), and Valley Napa (China). None of the wines sold under these brand names is made from Napa Valley grapes.

In its present form, TRIPS does not provide any form of automatic international protection for geographical indications. The holder of these intellectual property rights must establish the existence of, and protect, the geographical indication in each country based on the particular uses of that name there (as a brand, generic name, wine appellation, or otherwise), all in keeping with the laws of that particular country, in accordance with the principle of territoriality. This rule respects all intellectual property rights, including brands (trademarks) and appellations (geographical indications). But it also means that the tensions between brands and appellations are not likely to be resolved in the near term. Each name and each situation will present unique facts, and each country will have its own legal regime to resolve conflicts. As domestic wine production and wine exports continue to expand in the United States, the role of intellectual property lawyers is secure.

---

242. Author Richard Mendelson should and could have predicted this evolution based on the following personal observation: "When I first worked in the wine industry in Burgundy, France, in the late 1970s, before Napa Valley began its meteoric rise, I visited the Comité Interprofessionel du Vin de Champagne and met with the chief counsel of that organization. As I walked into his office, I saw a slew of Champagne-designated non-Champagne products, including Spanish Champagne, Champagne toothpaste, Champagne cigars, and Champagne cookies. When I asked the chief counsel to explain what he did, those imposter Champagne-named products figured prominently in his response."

CHAPTER 7

LAND USE: RURAL WINERIES AND URBAN BARS

Richard Mendelson[1] *and Lynne Carmichael*[2]

Wine is directly tied to the soil and grape growing, so it should come as little surprise that land use law is important to the wine industry. However, the myriad ways in which land use controls affect the wine industry may not be obvious to even an industry veteran. Let us recite some simple examples. Wine appellations would not mean much if the zoning of an area prohibited agricultural uses, namely the growing of grapes. If wineries could be located only in industrial zones or if winery tasting rooms could be established only in commercial areas, much of the mystique of wine country would be lost.

Land uses are regulated by states and their political subdivisions—cities, counties, wards, parishes, and the like—in the exercise of their police powers. This typically takes the form of specific land use laws. But land use controls also may be embodied in other laws, including specific alcoholic beverage control laws. This assortment of laws and regulations determines where bars and liquor

1. Richard Mendelson authored the section on rural wineries, with contributions by Terri Cofer Beirne (Virginia), Jesse Lyon and Michael Gelardi (Oregon), and Hillary Gitelman (Napa County, California). Ms. Beirne is Eastern Counsel of Wine Institute. Before that, she was a private attorney in Virginia and specialized in alcoholic beverage matters. Messrs. Lyon and Gelardi are at the law firm of Davis Wright Tremaine in Portland. Mr. Lyon serves as General Counsel to the Oregon Winegrowers Association and is Coordinating Chair of his firm's Food and Agriculture Practice. Ms. Gitelman is the director of the Napa County Department of Conservation, Development and Planning.

2. Lynne Carmichael wrote the section on urban retailers, with contributions by Susan Johnson (Washington), Jack Martin (Texas), and Leonard Fogelman (New York). Ms. Johnson is a partner in the law firm Stoel Rives, LLP, in Seattle. She practices solely in the area of alcoholic beverage law. Mr. Martin, principal of the law firm Jack Martin & Associates in Austin, represents alcoholic beverage retailers, marketers, distributors, and manufacturers in all matters related to their regulated operations in Texas. Mr. Fogelman, of Fogelman & Fogelman, LLC, practices alcoholic beverage law in New York and Massachusetts.

stores are located, their hours of opening and other aspects of their operations, and what constitutes a "disorderly house" and what can be done about it.

This chapter focuses on the particular land use issues involved with wineries situated in agricultural settings, and bars and bottle shops located in urban areas. Although rural wineries and urban liquor retailers are commonplace, the ways in which states and cities control their establishment and operations vary considerably.

A. RURAL WINERIES

The quintessential image of a winery is an agricultural estate in the middle of farm country, with a vineyard, winery, and estate home. Although there are numerous exceptions to this rule in the form of urban and suburban wineries, the tie to the land remains a distinguishing feature of wine and the wine industry, setting it apart from beer and spirits. This special place-goods association is captured in the concepts of *terroir*, defined as the natural features of the vineyard, and *goût de terroir*, the effects of *terroir* on the characteristics of the grapes and the resulting wine. These concepts underscore the fact that grape growing is an agricultural use.[3]

To survive and prosper in a rural setting, wineries typically do more than grow grapes.[4] They also make wine (an industrial operation) and engage in a variety of marketing and sales activities (commercial operations), all of which are critical to their success.

After Repeal, the wine industry had to completely retool, in the vineyards as well as the wineries, in terms of both physical and human capital. State and local governments in the wine-producing regions of the United States were hopeful that wine would become an engine of economic development, leading to higher land values, spurring agri-tourism, and generally helping states to revive their lagging post-Depression economies. It was not until the 1960s that this dream began to be realized.

By the 1970s, as the Wine Revolution took hold across the United States, many states established "farm wineries," emphasizing the local agricultural roots of grape growers and wine producers. Farm wineries were allowed to sell to consumers at the winery premises wines made from local grapes, however "local" might be defined under the applicable local or state law. For example, New York's 1976 Farm Winery Law authorized farmers to make wine from the grapes grown on their own properties and to sell those wines directly to the public from tasting rooms at the winery. As Jim Trezise, president of the New York Wine and Grape Foundation, explains: "The concept [of a farm winery] was derived from the commonly understood view that

3. *See, e.g.*, Sarah Bradshaw, Winery, Town Battle over Meaning of "Agricultural," Poughkeepsie J., Feb. 27, 2010, at BPJ.1.

4. As Jim Terry points out in Chapter 4, some wineries do not grow their own grapes but purchase grapes or bulk wine from independent grape growers or wineries, respectively, as the raw material for their own branded wines.

winemaking was a natural extension of the grape growing process, and that the production of grapes into wine was a value-added process that a grower could utilize for his crop."[5] In 1978, the New York law was amended to allow farm wineries to sell at their premises wines made from grapes grown anywhere in New York State.

While this rooting in agriculture is a distinguishing feature of wineries, rural wineries present complicated land use issues because they are mixed uses, often combining farming, winemaking, marketing, and retail sales at a single location on agricultural land. The following sections review the basic precepts of land use law and address the various approaches adopted by several states and localities to regulate rural wineries.

1. LAND USE BASICS

The Tenth Amendment to the U.S. Constitution reserves to the states all powers not delegated to the federal government.[6] This "police power" affords states the authority to regulate land uses within their jurisdictions to promote the health, safety, and welfare of their residents.[7]

Many states delegate the police power to local governments by state constitution, state law, or charter.[8] Early jurisprudence in the United States held that, absent an express or implied delegation, the states alone retain the police power. This is known as Dillon's rule, after the judge who formulated the doctrine in 1865.[9]

Subsequently, many states established what is known as "home rule" whereby a city or county government is allowed to exercise any function reserved to the state, including land use planning, so long as it is not prohibited under the state constitution or by state statute. Home rule may be established legislatively or constitutionally.

---

5. Letter from Jim Trezise, president, New York Wine and Grape Foundation,, to Town of New Paltz Zoning Board of Appeals (Oct. 15, 2007), available at http://www.rivendellwine.com/Lawsuit%20Files/Support%20Letters/nywgf10.15.07.pdf.

6. The Tenth Amendment reads, "The powers not delegated to the United States by the Constitution, nor prohibited by it to the States, are reserved to the States respectively, or to the people." U.S. Const. amend. X.

7. A land use regulation lies within the police power if it is reasonably related to the public welfare. *Associated Home Builders Inc. v. City of Livermore*, 557 P.2d 473, 485 (Cal. 1976) (quoting *Miller v. Bd. of Pub. Works*, 234 P. 381, 385 (Cal. 1925)). Justice Douglas in *Berman v. Parker*, 348 U.S. 26, 33 (1954), elaborated on the concept of public welfare, stating that it "is broad and inclusive. The values it represents are spiritual as well as physical, aesthetic as well as monetary" (citation omitted). In a later case, *Village of Belle Terre v. Boraas*, 416 U.S. 1, 9, (1974), Justice Douglas added: "The police power is not confined to elimination of filth, stench, and unhealthy places. It is ample to lay out zones where family values, youth values, and the blessings of quiet seclusion and clean air make the area a sanctuary for people."

8. Municipalities are creatures of the state, and the states grant them their legal existence, typically in the form of a charter. The charter grants certain powers to the municipality, places limits on its powers, and sets forth its boundaries.

9. "It is a familiar and elementary principle that municipal corporations have and can exercise such powers, and *such* only, as are expressly granted, and such incidental ones as are necessary to make those powers available and essential to effectuate the purposes of the corporation; and these powers are strictly construed." *Clark v. City of Des Moines*, 19 Iowa 199, *7 (1865) (opinion by J. John Dillon).

By far the majority of states today adhere to home rule. One wine-producing state, Virginia, strictly follows Dillon's rule. California, by contrast, expressly allows its cities to regulate land uses to benefit the public health and welfare. The California constitution specifically provides, "A county or city may make and enforce within its limits all local, police, sanitary, and other ordinances and regulations not in conflict with general laws."[10]

Zoning is the primary, though not the only, means by which governments control land uses. Most jurisdictions establish zoning districts to regulate the location, type and intensity of land use and land development.[11] In any given county, one may find residential (single-family or multi-family), commercial, industrial, and agricultural zoning districts. Zoning ordinances allow some uses in each district and prohibit others; the regulations often vary significantly from one district to the next. For example, bars serving alcohol may be excluded from certain zoning districts inside a city. Or a county might establish an agricultural zoning district to preserve and protect valuable farmland, prohibiting non-agricultural uses there. Mixed-use zones allow a variety of activities to occur in the same zoning district.

Most jurisdictions also allow certain uses by conditional use permit or by special exception. The conditional use permit (CUP) allows a local government to make an individualized determination about the suitability of a proposed use in a particular location. The local government, generally in the form of an appointed planning commission or elected council or board of supervisors, decides on a case-by-case basis whether a particular use is detrimental to the public health, safety, or general welfare and whether it is compatible with existing, neighboring uses. The government can impose particular conditions to mitigate any potential adverse impacts. With respect to grape growing and winemaking, agricultural zones typically allow vineyards as a matter of right, and wineries often require a CUP, perhaps because they themselves are mixed uses.

Another form of special exception to zoning regulations is a variance.[12] By granting a variance, the decision maker(s) can waive or modify quantitative standards such as setbacks to avoid hardships.

---

10. Cal. Const. art. XI, §7. The court in *Candid Enterprises, Inc. v. Grossmont Union High School District*, 39 Cal. 3d 878, 885 (1985), elaborated on just how broad this delegated authority is.

> Under the police power granted by the Constitution, counties and cities have plenary authority to govern, subject only to the limitation that they exercise this power within their territorial limits and subordinate to state law. Apart from this limitation, the "police power [of a county or a city] under this provision . . . is as broad as the police power exercisable by the Legislature itself" (alterations in original) (citations omitted).

11. The U.S. Supreme Court validated zoning in *Village of Euclid v. Amber Realty Co.*, 272 U.S. 365 (1926). Amber Realty claimed that the restricted uses under the zoning ordinance of Euclid, Ohio, substantially reduced the value of its property. Its suit was denied and the zoning ordinance was upheld based on the court's finding of a valid governmental interest in maintaining the community's character in the face of burgeoning industrial growth in Cleveland, which threatened to subsume Euclid.

12. A variance is a permit issued to a landowner to build a structure or engage in a use not otherwise permitted under the current zoning regulations. Typically, the landowner must prove that he or she would suffer unique hardship under the zoning regulations because the parcel in question is different from others to which the regulations apply because of its size, shape, topography, location, or other special circumstances. *See, e.g.*, Cal. Gov't Code §65906 (2009).

There are constitutional limits to a state's or municipality's land use authority. These include the takings provision of the Fifth Amendment to the U.S. Constitution, the Due Process and Equal Protection Clauses of the Fourteenth Amendment, and the First Amendment guarantee of free speech and freedom of religion. Each area has spawned significant jurisprudence seeking to balance private property rights and other basic rights of individual landowners against the public good as expressed by the state or local government.

2. CALIFORNIA

California, as a home rule state, delegates a large portion, but not all, of its police powers to local agencies to protect the public health, safety, and welfare. Municipalities oversee the uses of land within their boundaries—the cities within city limits and the counties in the remaining, "unincorporated" lands.

Local government avails itself of a wide variety of land use planning and development controls. For example, elected municipal council members and elected members of county boards of supervisors adopt a general plan (the equivalent of a local constitution), pass zoning ordinances, issue CUPs, and create parcels (legal lots of record), typically by subdividing existing parcels. As we shall see, each locality can chart its own course in this regard; some might decide to facilitate growth, whereas others might stifle it.

In California, voters wield power in the land use arena in several ways. First, they elect government officials who, in turn, vote to approve or reject particular development projects, public infrastructure projects, and land use ordinances. Second, they can comment directly on particular development proposals. Finally, they can submit initiatives or referenda affecting particular development projects or policies in the form of a petition signed by a required number of voters.[13] If passed in a local election, these initiatives and referenda bind local elected bodies.

Normally, changes to land use regulations and specific development projects are proposed by the local agency (often, the local planning department) and/or by private parties. These changes and proposals are reviewed by the professional staffs of the various local agencies. The planners, engineers, and environmental experts ensure that the proposal meets the jurisdiction's general plan and zoning requirements as well as applicable state laws and local ordinances. If public notice and a public hearing are required, the planning department staff prepare and present a report on the proposed project to the elected officials and the public prior to holding the hearing on the project.

In the case of an initiative or referendum that qualifies for the ballot, staff review is limited to the potential consequences of the ballot measure, if passed.[14] This report, prepared at the discretion of the local board of supervisors, is presented to the elected body and to the public to help voters understand the issue at election time.

13. Cal. Const. art. II, §§8-9.
14. Cal. Elec. Code §9111 (2009).

California law mandates that any governmental action that is discretionary be taken in full public view. Thus, general plan adoption and amendment, zoning ordinance changes, use permit issuance, and parcel creation, among other actions, can occur only after public notice through a published agenda, a public hearing, and deliberation by the elected officials in open session. The issuance of a building permit, by contrast, is generally a ministerial action rather than a discretionary one. If the jurisdiction's building code requirements are met, the building permit will issue without need of a public hearing.

The distinction between ministerial and discretionary actions also is important in determining the extent of environmental review appropriate for any proposed project. The California Environmental Quality Act (CEQA)[15] requires that every discretionary project be analyzed in terms of its direct, indirect, and cumulative environmental effects. The project cannot be approved until all significant adverse effects that are likely to result from the project are reduced to less than significant levels. The mitigation measures that serve to eliminate or reduce the project's significant adverse impacts are included as conditions for the project's approval. Alternatively, the governing body may lawfully approve the project notwithstanding the identification of unmitigatable impacts by adopting "findings of overriding consideration"; through such findings, the agency determines that the economic, legal, social, technological, or other benefits outweigh the significant environmental impacts.

a. Napa County, California

Napa County, one of California's original counties (established in 1850), has a land area of 754 square miles (1,953 square kilometers) and a population of approximately 140,000. Within the county are five municipalities: Napa, Yountville, St. Helena, Calistoga, and American Canyon. The county is governed by a five-member board of supervisors and the municipalities by their respective city or town councils. Land use planning and development controls were not established in the county until the mid-1900s. The first building permits were issued by the county in 1955, and the first general plan was adopted in 1969. That first general plan, and every general plan since then, has recognized agriculture as the highest and best use of land in Napa County.

As the San Francisco Bay Area expanded in the latter half of the twentieth century, the recognition of Napa's unique value as a grape-growing and wine-producing area took on added importance. Other parts of the region, such as Santa Clara County, long known as a fertile agricultural area, were gradually overtaken by urban sprawl. As former Santa Clara County planner Karl Belser said of the decade of the 1960s, "Wild urban growth attacked the [Santa Clara] valley. . . . What so recently had been a beautiful, productive garden was suddenly transformed into an urban anthill."[16] Napans had the foresight and courage to take bold steps to avoid the same fate.

---

15. Cal. Pub. Res. Code §§21000-21177 (2009).

16. Leonard Downie Jr., The Santa Clara Valley's "Appointment with Destiny," APF Newsletter (Alicia Patterson Foundation) (October 1971), available at http://aliciapatterson.org/APF001971/Downie/Downie02/Downie02.html.

In 1968, after heated debate among vineyard and winery owners, the Napa County Board of Supervisors by unanimous vote approved an Agricultural Preserve (AP) zoning district[17] covering 25,950 acres (10,768 hectares) on the floor of the Napa Valley. The new zoning district established a minimum parcel size for a legal lot of 20 acres (8.3 hectares), which was a substantial increase over the 1 acre (0.4 hectare) minimum that applied before AP zoning was established. This "large-lot" zoning was the first in the United States. designed to protect a specific agricultural resource.[18]

AP zoning was highly controversial. Many property owners believed their property rights and their economic value were being taken by the government without compensation. Proponents, by contrast, argued that large-lot zoning was the only way to prevent Napa County from being overtaken by urban sprawl, as had occurred in Santa Clara Valley. Joseph Peatman, who served as Napa County Supervisor from 1969 to 1973 and supported the Agricultural Preserve, recalls: "The opponents didn't want anyone telling them what they could or couldn't do with their land. They wanted to be able to subdivide their land into several one acre parcels, each with the right to have a single family home. The proponents were not flaming liberals, but they didn't want to repeat the Santa Clara Valley story. They argued that development should occur in the cities and in the hills, not on the valley floor."[19]

Not surprisingly, AP zoning was challenged in court, but it was upheld.[20] In the 42 years since the Agricultural Preserve was established, the only changes have been to add vineyard land to the AP zone; in 1979, to raise the minimum parcel size within the zone to 40 acres (16.6 hectares); and more recently to permit new uses in the AP zone, including farm management and farmworker housing.

Since 1968 the county has adopted other important land use regulations designed to preserve Napa Valley's agricultural heritage and to avoid urban sprawl. The county subjected wineries to using permit control beginning in 1974, following a controversy over the construction of a modern barrel storage building that blocked the view of the historic 1879 Inglenook Winery. The requirement for a CUP allows the county to deny any given project if required findings cannot be made or to impose conditions of approval and mitigation measures.

---

17. Napa County, Cal., Ordinance 274 §1 (Apr. 9, 1968) (amending Ordinance 186 of Jan. 25, 1955) (codified as amended at Napa County, Cal., Code §§18.16.010-.040''' (1993), available at http://library.municode.com/HTML/16513/book.html.

18. Tax incentives offered by the state of California through the California Land Conservation (Williamson) Act, 1965 Cal. Stat. 3377 (codified as amended at Cal. Gov't Code §§51200-51297.4 (2009)), also helped to keep land in agriculture. Under its provisions, counties may enter into 10-year continuously renewable contracts with landowners under which the landowners agree to retain their land in agricultural and compatible uses for 10 years and in return pay property taxes based on the value of the land as farmland rather than as land available for subdivision and urban development.

19. Telephone interview with Joseph Peatman, former supervisor, Napa County, Cal. (July 29, 2010).

20. *Napa Valley United Farmers v. County Bd. of Supervisors* (Napa County Super. Ct. 1971); *see* judgment at Official Records of Napa County, Book 15, p. 574 (1971).

To ensure that farming would continue unabated, the county adopted the Right to Farm Act in 1990 whereby each person buying property or building in or near an agricultural zone would receive a notice about the possible negative impacts of agricultural activities (spraying, noise, odors, etc.). The Act prohibits a nuisance finding as long as the agricultural operation is conducted according to "proper and accepted customs and standards" and has existed at the same location for more than three years.[21]

In 1973 the minimum parcel size in the remaining unincorporated area outside of the Agricultural Preserve, largely in the hills and mountains surrounding the valley floor (known as the Agricultural Watershed (AW) zoning district), was raised from 1 acre (0.4 hectare) to 40 acres (16.6 hectares) in order to protect the county's watersheds. Over two decades later, in 1994, the minimum parcel size of the then 450,000 acres (186,722 hectares) of Agricultural Watershed zoned lands was raised from 40 acres to 160 acres (66.4 hectares).[22]

In 1983 Napa County adopted urban growth boundaries for the City of Napa, which limit the development of urban infrastructure outside established municipal boundaries.[23] This serves to limit the development potential in those areas. In a related move in 1990, the voters of the county adopted, by initiative, restrictions on the conversion of agricultural land for urban uses, requiring until the year 2020 a county-wide vote on any proposal to redesignate agricultural lands to non-agricultural purposes or to change the building intensity of such lands.[24] That deadline has since been extended to 2058, at which time the original Agricultural Preserve zoning will have had a 90-year history.[25]

Also in 1990 county government began to regulate more closely the establishment of new wineries and the expansion of existing wineries, restricting their commercial and industrial operations on agriculturally zoned lands and further protecting the valley from encroaching urbanization and the pressures of tourism.[26] The impetus for the restrictions was the existence of several wineries in Napa County that made wine from grapes grown outside the county and engaged in extensive marketing and sales activities with only limited winemaking facilities (essentially, a few outdoor tanks). In the county zoning ordinance, these kinds of winery activities were unregulated. Grapes could be sourced from anywhere, and the winery's accessory uses such as marketing, wine tastings, and sales were largely unregulated.

---

21. Napa County, Cal., Code §2.94.020 (1993).

22. Napa County, Cal., Ordinance 1058 §2 (Jan. 11, 1994) (increased minimum parcel size from 40 to 160 acres) (codified at Napa County, Cal., Code §18.104.010 (1993).

23. Napa County Dep't. Conservation, Dev. & Planning, Napa County General Plan 243-44 (Conservation and Open Space Element) (1983).

24. Agricultural Lands Preservation Initiative ("Measure J") (amending Napa County General Plan Land Use Element).

25. Agricultural Lands Preservation Initiative ("Measure P") (1990), Napa County, Cal., Ordinance 08-03 (Nov. 4, 2008).

26. Winery Definition Ordinance, Napa County, Cal., Ordinance 947 (1990) (codified as amended in scattered sections of Napa County, Cal., Code tit. 18 (1993).

The county decided to impose new, more restrictive rules in the newly enacted Winery Definition Ordinance (WDO).[27] The WDO, which applies in the county's AP and AW zoning districts but not in the cities or in the other zoning districts of the county, first defines what a winery is and does as its primary activity, namely, fermenting grapes into wine.[28] But no longer would it be just any grapes; 75 percent of the wine produced at a new winery located in the county's agricultural zoning districts would now have to be derived from Napa County grapes.[29] Existing wineries were exempted from this grape source rule for the production levels authorized in their pre-WDO use permits.[30] However, for those wineries that later expand their footprint (known as the "winery development area") in order to increase production capacity beyond the originally approved annual gallonage, the increased production is subject to the 75 percent grape source rule.[31]

The WDO also spells out the specific "accessory uses" that are allowed at wineries; all other accessory uses are prohibited.[32] This supplanted the pre-existing rule, which allowed any accessory use, whether or not enumerated in the county code, that was "incidental or subordinate to the principal use."[33] The accessory uses allowed in the WDO include tours, wine tastings, the display but not the sale of art and items of ecological or viticultural significance, and child care centers to care for the children of winery employees.[34] Within each category of approved use, there may be additional restrictions. For example, the WDO for the first time prohibited drop-in public tours and tastings at any newly approved winery. Pre-existing wineries with approved public tasting privileges are unaffected, but they cannot increase the size of their

27. *Id.*

28. Napa County, Cal., Code §18.08.640 (1993).

29. *Id.* at §18.104.250(B).

30. Other California counties have adopted similar grape sourcing rules to tie the industrial operation (winemaking) to the local land (grapes). Santa Barbara County has a 50 percent local grape sourcing requirement for its wineries but defines local to include both Santa Barbara County and San Luis Obispo County. *See* Santa Barbara County, Cal., Code §35-42.280(D) (1985), available at http://search.municode.com/html/16322/book.html. Santa Barbara County is presently considering new Agricultural Preserve rules, including a new grape sourcing requirement that 51 percent of the winery's case production derive from grapes grown on the premises and/or from other contracted land *under the same ownership* in Santa Barbara County, provided that at least 20 percent of the case production comes from grapes grown on the parcel where the winery is situated. In Sonoma County certain land use categories refer to agricultural processing facilities as those facilities used for the processing of agricultural products "of a type grown or produced primarily on site or in the local area." *See, e.g.*, Sonoma County, Cal., Code §26-04-020(g) (1996), available at http://search.municode.comhtml/16331/book.html (permitted uses in Land Intensive Agriculture zoning district). Typically, this would mean that a winery must source grapes primarily from Sonoma County, although this is subject to interpretation on any given project. Finally, Riverside County followed Napa County's lead in adopting a 75 percent local grape source rule with certain exceptions. Riverside County, Cal., Code §17.136.040(D)(3)(a) (2000) (effective Jan. 24, 2011), available at http://search.municode.com/html/16320/book.html.

31. Napa County, Cal., Code §18.104.250(C) (1993); *see also id.* §18.104.210. Although never challenged in court, the local grape source requirement might violate the dormant Commerce Clause, just as the local milk bottling requirement did in *Dean Milk Co. v. City of Madison, Wis.*, 340 U.S. 349 (1951).

32. Napa County, Cal., Code §§18.16.030(H) (AP zone), 18.20.030(J) (AW zone) (1993); *see also id.* §18.08.020 (defining "accessory use").

33. Napa County, Cal., Code §4.03 (1963).

34. Napa County, Cal., Code §§18.16.030(H) (AP zone), 18.20.030(J) (AW zone) (1993).

pre-WDO tasting room. New wineries have to engage in by-appointment-only, private tours and tastings.[35] This visitation restriction is designed to control traffic congestion on local roads.[36] New wineries also have to be located on parcels of at least 10 acres,[37] must observe expanded setbacks from public roads and private roads used by the public,[38] and must meet strict accessory-to-production square footage ratios.[39]

As another example of Napa County's strict controls over winery operations, retail sales are now limited to wine fermented and bottled at the winery, wine produced by or for the winery from grapes grown in Napa County, and wine-related items.[40] Authorized marketing activities specifically exclude commercial food service (restaurants) and social events that are not directly related to consumer education and development.[41] Weddings, for example, are not allowed to be conducted at rural Napa Valley wineries; the only exceptions involve non-commercial weddings of the winery owners' immediate families. Even when winery marketing rights under the WDO were slightly expanded in 2010 as part of an economic stimulus package, these marketing restrictions remained, as did the 75 percent grape source rule.

Wine tastings, wine sales, and even food service at wineries are also regulated by the California Alcoholic Beverage Control Act. Wineries are allowed under state law to conduct tastings of wine produced or bottled by, or produced and packaged for, the licensee.[42] They can sell wine and brandy to customers to be consumed off-site, and they also can sell beers, wines, and brandies, regardless of source, for consumption at a restaurant on the winery premises.[43]

Do these more liberal provisions of state law trump the restrictive, locally adopted WDO? While a preemption argument might be asserted, it would not prevail in California because of Business and Professions Code §23790, under which the state defers to a valid zoning ordinance of a county or city.[44]

In 1991 agriculturalists and environmentalists worked together to put in place regulations designed to minimize the environmental impacts of vineyard development. Concerned about the continuing development of hillside vineyards, these local regulations, known as the Conservation Regulations, supplement state and federal environmental laws and mandate the inclusion of erosion control measures, riparian and wildlife corridors, protections for streams and wetlands, and other environmental controls in vineyard development and

---

35. *Id.* §18.08.620 (defining "tours and tastings").

36. Use permit conditions typically limit the hours and visitor numbers for private tours and tastings. The hours are set so as to avoid the peak travel time on the nearby roadways.

37. Napa County, Cal., Code §18.104.240(B) (1993). Prior to this change, the minimum parcel size for a winery was 1 acre. *Id.* §18.104.240(A).

38. *Id.* §18.104.230; *but see* exceptions at *id.* §§18.104.235, .245.

39. *Id.* §18.104.200.

40. *Id.* §§18.16.030(G)(5)(c), (H)(4) (AP zone), 18.20.030(I)(5)(c), (J)(4) (AW zone).

41. *Id.* at §18.08.370 (defining "marketing of wine").

42. Cal. Bus. & Prof. Code §23356.1(a) (2009).

43. *Id.* §23358(a)(2), (4).

44. The deference to local law is explicit with respect to retail licenses but is also applied in practice by the California Department of Alcoholic Beverage Control to manufacturer licenses.

farming operations.[45] The regulations apply to any new or redeveloped site with a slope of more than 5 percent. Because the regulations make the planting of a vineyard on other than flat land a discretionary action, CEQA also applies.

It is worth noting that not all California counties share Napa's concerns about protecting agricultural lands from urban sprawl. In some cases, the counties simply do not have the same development pressures caused by proximity to a large metropolitan area. For example, Mendocino County, located northwest of Napa County on the California coast, has an active wine production industry but does not impose the same level of restrictions on wineries or their operations. Wineries are classified as "packing and processing facilities" and are a permitted use in most of the county's agricultural and rural areas, without the requirement that a CUP be obtained.[46] As such, there is no public hearing or CEQA environmental review; all that is needed is a building permit for the winery structure. The only limitation on accessory uses is that the tasting room cannot exceed 25 percent of the total floor area of the production building. There is no requirement that the grapes be grown in Mendocino County, no restrictions on the type or number of wine tastings and marketing events, and no visitor limitations. This tendency to welcome and stimulate winery development with attendant commercial uses is a rural economic development strategy that is prevalent in many newer "wine countries" across the United States.

In southern California, where viticultural areas such as Temecula Valley are situated in close proximity to urban areas, counties have attempted to protect the wine industry from incompatible development. For example, in Riverside County, where Temecula is situated, regulations similar to those of Napa County establish minimum parcel sizes for wineries and require that 75 percent of the local winery's grapes be sourced from the winery property or elsewhere in the county. Unlike Napa County, however, Riverside County allows a winery to incorporate non-agricultural commercial facilities such as a delicatessen, restaurant, bed and breakfast inn, special-occasion facility for weddings and similar social events, and even a hotel. This allows Temecula Valley wineries to sell most of their wines directly to visitors from the large, surrounding metropolitan area. As journalist Cary Ordway wrote in a recent online article entitled "Wineries: Visitors Find Temecula Offers a Unique Getaway":

> With its location between Los Angeles and San Diego, its inland balmy weather and its impressive group of first-class wineries, it's no wonder the Temecula Valley has become a major weekend destination for SoCal leisure travelers.
>
> There are 35 wineries in Temecula, most of them conveniently located along a few major thoroughfares that stretch several miles eastward from Temecula's more densely populated areas. The city itself has expanded in

45. Napa County, Cal., Ordinance 991 (1991) (codified at Napa County, Cal., Code §§18.108.010-18.108.140 (1993)).

46. All development proposals in coastal areas require special review for compliance with the California Coastal Act of 1976, Cal. Pub. Res. Code §§30000-30900 (2009).

> recent years to the point that more than 300,000 people live in the Temecula Valley.
>
> Along with that expansion has come several big-time wineries that have built tasting rooms, restaurants and other tourist-friendly facilities right alongside their wine-making operations.[47]

A study commissioned in 2007 by the Temecula Valley Convention and Visitors Bureau concluded that the Temecula wine country can achieve its tourism potential only if it can master the tricky combination of supporting wine-related growth that maintains the rural character of the area and resisting residential and strip mall development.

3. VIRGINIA

Agriculture has been the backbone of the Virginia economy for four centuries, generating $55 billion per year and providing at least 35,000 jobs in 2009. More than 47,000 farms in Virginia cover 8.1 million acres or 32 percent of the total land area. The Virginia General Assembly promotes and protects Virginia's agrarian history and agricultural investment with numerous laws and policies to conserve, protect, and encourage the development and improvement of land for the production of food and other agricultural products. Accordingly, the popularity of growing grapes and making wine as an agricultural pursuit in Virginia has exploded in recent years, with the commonwealth's farm wineries growing in number and consistently improving the reputation of their wines.

When the Virginia General Assembly initially passed the law defining a farm winery in 1980, there were six wineries and merely 286 acres of vineyards in Virginia. In 2005 the Virginia Wine Board estimated that Virginia's then 120 farm wineries and 2,000 acres of vineyards had an in-state economic impact of $362 million. Today there are 180 licensed farm wineries sprinkled across 45 of Virginia's 95 counties with a concentration of farm wineries in the rural counties of Albemarle, Loudoun, and Nelson. There are also nearly 3,000 acres of vines found in more than 270 vineyards statewide. Grapes rank twentieth on the list of Virginia farm commodities with cash receipts of more than $10 million. In 2007 Virginia ranked eighth nationally in commercial grape production; today it ranks fifth. In calendar year 2009, Virginia's wineries and farm wineries sold 399,745 cases of wine. The sale of Virginia wine within Virginia in fiscal year 2010 generated more than $1.6 million in wine liter (excise) taxes, representing 4.4 percent of all wine sold in Virginia. From all estimates, the industry will continue to grow so long as state or local governments do not create barriers to entry or further complicate the channels of wine distribution.

Distinct from commercial wineries, Virginia's farm wineries are agricultural operations that produce wine from grapes that they must partially cultivate; they may also sell their wines at rural state-licensed facilities and special

47. Cary Ordway, Wineries: Visitors Find Temecula Offers a Unique Getaway, http://www.californiaweekend.com/california-vacation/temecula-wineries.html (last visited Dec. 22, 2010).

events open to the general public. This complex blend of agricultural activity, wine production, and commercial sales in a rural locality makes farm wineries a challenge for Virginia's rural counties to govern. A shifting line between where state regulation of Virginia farm wineries stops and local regulation starts is at the core of most disputes. While the production of any alcohol is strictly controlled statewide by the Virginia Department of Alcoholic Beverage Control (ABC) under the guidance of the ABC Board, the agricultural and land use controls associated with the siting and operation of wineries are delegated to county governments operating under local ordinances. Such ordinances are uniquely crafted by each county's governing board of supervisors and reflect the distinct public goals for the wine industry within each particular county.

a. Source of Authority for Virginia Localities

Virginia localities are expressly granted power by the General Assembly to regulate territorial land use, with the option and the right to divide jurisdictions into zoning districts with differing uses, including agriculture. Farming and agriculture are permitted by right in agricultural districts and occasionally within more intense land use categories depending on the county. Within each district, a locality may regulate the use of land as well as the size, height, location, removal, and maintenance of structures; the area and dimensions of land, water, and air space occupied by various structures and uses; open space; and the size of lots based upon the availability of public utilities.[48] Farm wineries benefit immensely from zoning restrictions on agricultural lands that encourage grape growing as an agricultural enterprise and protect the rural character and scenic views that often draw visitors to wineries. At the same time, farm wineries have clashed with local ordinances that restrict on-site sales and marketing activities.

Dillon's rule of construction, discussed previously, is rigorously applied in evaluating the effect of Virginia local governmental action upon farm wineries. Under that rule, a locality may exercise those powers expressly granted to it by statute or charter but no other powers unless necessarily implied in or incident to the powers expressly granted or essential to the declared purposes. Once the grant of authority is affirmed, the question becomes whether the local ordinance is consistent with it. An ordinance is inconsistent with state law when state law preempts such local regulation either expressly by prohibiting local regulations or by enacting state regulations so comprehensive that the state may be considered to occupy the entire field.[49]

Where the Virginia General Assembly has enacted comprehensive legislation in a particular field, namely alcoholic beverage control law, local government legislation is preempted. Such preemption is based on legislative intent. In *Board of Supervisors v. Pumphrey*,[50] a county ordinance dealing with beer container returns was held to be invalid because state statutes regulating alcoholic beverages preempt the field. Narrowing that opinion with regard

48. Va. Code §15.2-2280(2)-(3) (2010).
49. *King v. County of Arlington*, 81 S.E.2d 587, 590 (Va. 1954).
50. 269 S.E.2d 361 (Va. 1980).

to preemption of local decisions by the ABC Board, the Virginia Supreme Court in *City of Norfolk v. Tiny House, Inc.*,[51] and later in *County of Chesterfield v. Windy Hill, Ltd.*,[52] ruled that local zoning ordinances may regulate the *location* of businesses selling alcoholic beverages and that the legislature did not intend for the ABC to preempt the field in this regard.

Beyond case law, the General Assembly has passed several statutes that greatly benefit farm wineries and that cannot be limited by localities under their land use or zoning powers. Although statewide in effect, these laws often are enforced by local governments during the zoning approval or building construction process. The privileges granted by these statutes, coupled with the statewide benefits of an ABC license, preclude local involvement in most aspects of wine production, distribution, and sales. The particular statutes, each of which is discussed below, include the definition of and privileges afforded to farm winery licensees, the Virginia Right to Farm Law, a 2007 statutory change codifying local regulation of farm wineries, an exemption from Uniform Statewide Building Code requirements, and limits on liability under the Virginia Agritourism Liability Act. Together these laws guide much of the interaction between farm wineries and their rural county homes.

b. Statutory Benefits of Licensed Farm Wineries in Virginia

Virginia Code §4.1-100 defines a farm winery as "an establishment located on a farm in the state with a producing vineyard and facilities for fermenting and bottling wine containing less than 18 percent alcohol." What constitutes a "producing vineyard" is not set out in statute or regulation.[53] Licensed farm wineries may buy grapes from other agricultural growers in the state; they also may manufacture, sell, deliver, or ship wine to the ABC (Virginia is a control state that operates 332 government ABC stores that are the only retail outlets for spirits but that also sell Virginia wine), to wine wholesalers and to consumers within and without the state.[54] Unlike a commercial winery license, a farm winery license authorizes the giving away of samples and the sale of wine at a retail tasting room on the farm winery premises as well as at five additional retail outlets at any given time.[55] Wineries commonly use these remote licenses to participate in wine festivals across the state throughout the year.

With regard to siting and initial licensure, the ABC provides notice to localities when applications for facilities within their jurisdiction are filed, which offers localities an opportunity to submit objections.[56] As a result of such objections, the ABC Board may hold a public hearing about issuance of the license. In addition, Virginia Code §4.1-222(2) outlines the conditions

---

51. 281 S.E.2d 836 (Va. 1981).
52. 559 S.E.2d 627 (Va. 2002).
53. Terri Cofer Beirne, however, recalls that, while representing a client in a hearing when this subject was at issue, a member of the ABC Board verbally suggested that six vines old enough to produce grapes were insufficient to be considered a producing vineyard.
54. Va. Code §4.1-207(5) (2010). Although Virginia may allow farm winery sales to consumers out of state, the laws of the destination state determine whether such sales are lawful.
55. 3 Va. Code §4.1-207(5) (2010).
56. Va. Code §4.1-230(B) (2010).

under which the ABC Board may refuse to grant a license, namely that the place to be occupied by the licensee is so located that it will interfere with the normal conduct of affairs at public facilities such as churches or schools, or is so located with respect to a residential area that operation of the license will "adversely affect real property values or substantially interfere with the usual quietude and tranquility of such . . . residential area." In practice, unless one of these statutory conditions is proven, the ABC generally takes note of local objections based on land use considerations but issues the license without condition.

Virginia farm wineries are designated as either Class A or Class B licensees. For both classes, no more than 25 percent of the fruits, juices, or wine used in the total production may be grown or produced outside Virginia. For the Class A designation, at least 51 percent of the grapes, juice, or wine used to manufacture the farm wine must be grown or produced on the farm. Generally, Class B wineries are "mature" wineries in existence for more than seven years and must use 75 percent of Virginia-grown or -made products to make their wine.

c. Right to Farm

In 1993 the General Assembly expressly recognized that "[w]hen nonagricultural land uses extend into agricultural areas, agricultural operations often become the subject of nuisance suits."[57] Pressure on rural land triggered the General Assembly in 1995 to protect agriculture from encroachment by residential and commercial development through the passage of the Virginia Right to Farm Act.[58] The Act prohibits localities from adopting any ordinance requiring a special-exception or special-use permit for agriculture or forestry activity in an agricultural zoning district. It further prohibits localities from enacting zoning ordinances that would "unreasonably restrict or regulate farm structures or farming and forestry practices" in an agricultural district unless they bear a relationship to the health, safety, and general welfare of its citizenry. Notably, the Act protects only the actual production or harvesting of agricultural or silvicultural products, not the *processing* of agricultural products. It does, however, permit counties to adopt setback, minimum area, and similar requirements for farmland in agricultural districts.

As applied to Virginia farm wineries, the Right to Farm Act protects the planting, spraying, tending, and harvesting of grapes. It also spares a winery from nuisance claims or unreasonable limits on noise or lighting from harvesting, temporary labor activity, or farm vehicle traffic, among other things. These are state statutory protections that localities cannot reduce or eliminate. However, the Act stops far short of defending farm wineries against claims arising from the important tasks of crushing, bottling, and storing. Ask a farm winery proprietor with an unhappy neighbor how much time and

57. Va. Code §3.1-22.28 (1993) (repealed 1994).
58. Virginia Right to Farm Act, 1994 Va. Acts 779 (codified as amended at Va. Code §§3.2-300 to -3.2-302 (2010)).

money he or she has spent defending against allegations of trespass from the drifting of dust off a gravel driveway to the tasting room, a noise ordinance violation from a summer evening concert, or the lack of a Virginia Department of Transportation—approved turning lane, for example. While the Virginia Right to Farm Act provides valuable protection against complaints about growing and harvest activities, it leaves many farm wineries far short of the protections they need to process, market, and sell their agricultural products.

d. Statutory Protection for On-Site Marketing and Sales

Like other wineries across the country, Virginia farm wineries generate wine sales by publicizing unique events in their tasting rooms or renting space within the winery for weddings or community meetings. And, as noted above, the Virginia Right to Farm Act fails to prevent challenges to such marketing and sales activities. Virginia localities are expressly granted the power to protect the health, safety, and welfare of their inhabitants by controlling activities open to the public within their borders. In recent years certain counties have attempted to characterize these advertised activities as "special events" requiring advance notice to the locality and/or special-use permits. Some counties also have begun to use local ordinances to micro-manage wineries, similar to the approach in Napa County: limiting the production capacity of a winery facility, limiting the size of tasting rooms, establishing hours of operation, capping the number of people that can visit wineries, and regulating commercial vehicle access to wineries, among other things. This growing tension between wineries and counties prompted the Virginia wine industry to appeal to the General Assembly for relief from local management of their affairs.

In 2006 one winery engaging in large-scale marking activities in a county resistant to growth introduced an aggressive bill before the General Assembly to exempt it from any local control. The Virginia Association of Counties jumped into the debate and significantly altered the law that eventually passed that year. In its adopted form, the bill saved farm wineries from having to get special-exception or -use permits for processing activity. It also froze all counties' special-use/condition permit requirements to those existing on January 1, 2006, and prohibited a locality from banning music that was not audible at the property line, from regulating private family events hosted by winery owners, and from adopting requirements for the construction or expansion of facilities.

The 2006 legislation also required the Virginia Secretary of Agriculture and Forestry to convene a study group to examine the wine industry and "develop recommendations, including legislative, administrative or other recommendations as appropriate for how the state can better foster the economic viability of Virginia farm wineries." Such recommendations were to "address the relationship between farm wineries and the communities in which they operate, including an assessment of local land use regulations as they relate to efforts to market Virginia wines through activities, whether held inside or outside farm winery structures, such as wine tastings, special events such as wine festivals, or other promotional activities held at farm wineries, and the potential for a more efficient and streamlined permitting process for such activities."[59]

The Virginia wine industry, the Virginia Association of Counties, and numerous other stakeholders spent much of 2006 negotiating the language of another bill that was considered by the 2007 General Assembly. That bill, now codified as Virginia Code §15.2-2288.3, lists specific farm winery activities that a locality may not regulate under any circumstances. Those include the production and harvesting of fruit; the on-premises sale, tasting, or consumption of wine *during regular business hours*; the direct sale and shipment of wine; the sale and shipment of wine to the ABC, wholesalers, and out-of-state purchasers; the storage, warehousing, and wholesaling of wine; and the sale of wine-related items incidental to the sale of wine. Further, the new law exempts from regulation private personal gatherings at the winery but permits local regulation of outdoor amplified music equal to that in the jurisdiction's general noise ordinance.[60]

Despite hours of searching for a compromise, the new law does not directly address how localities may regulate special events that happen outside of regular business hours. A policy statement in the law posits that local restriction of events "shall be reasonable and shall take into account the economic impact on the farm winery of such restriction, ['the agricultural nature of such activities and events' was added in 2008] and whether such activities and events are usual and customary for farm wineries throughout the Commonwealth. Usual and customary activities and events at farm wineries shall be permitted without local regulation unless there is a substantial impact on the health, safety, or welfare of the public."[61] There is no definition of what constitutes "reasonable" local restrictions or "usual and customary," but clearly it must be evaluated statewide. This law was hard fought by all interested parties, and the result is far from precise in specifying local controls over farm wineries. However, its passage appears to have slowed the county-by-county development of farm winery ordinances with ever greater restrictions. Provisions in this law will need to be litigated to firm up its boundaries, but to date wineries in the more experienced rural counties have achieved a healthy balance over what can and cannot be regulated by county governments.

e. Building Code Exemption and Ancillary Uses

Another important statutory exemption benefits farm wineries, but always shocks the building inspector charged with approving the winery construction. Pursuant to Virginia Code §36-99, "farm buildings and structures shall be exempt from the provisions of the Uniform Statewide Building Code ("Code"), except for a building or portion of a building located on a farm that is operated

59. 2006 Va. Acts 794 (codified as amended at Va. Code Ann. §15.2-2288.3 (2010)).
60. 2007 Va. Acts 657 (codified as amended at Va. Code §15.2-2288.3 (2010)).
61. Va. Code §15.2-2288.3(A) (2010).

as a restaurant. . . ." Virginia Code §36-97 defines "farm building or structure" as follows:

> [A building or structure] not used for residential purposes, located on property where farming operations take place, and used primarily for any of the following uses or combination thereof: 1. Storage, handling, production, display, sampling or sale of agricultural, horticultural, floricultural or silvicultural products produced in the farm; 2. Sheltering, raising, handling, processing or sale of agricultural animals or agricultural animal products; 3. Business or office uses relating to the farm operations; 4. Use of farm machinery or equipment or maintenance or storage of vehicles, machinery or equipment on the farm; 5. Storage or use of supplies and materials used on the farm; or 6. Implementation of best management practices associated with farm operations."

Without question, a licensed farm winery satisfies the definition of a farm building or structure and is, therefore, exempt from the Code requirements. It is easy to envision the legislature's intention in adopting the exemption when imagining existing farm buildings being refurbished or expanded into a farm winery tasting room, for example. However, the often massive and elaborate structures resulting from new construction of a production facility or tasting room to accommodate thousands of visitors a year are difficult projects for a county building inspector to ignore. Farm winery proprietors spend an inordinate amount of time educating local officials about this exemption, yet they still meet with resistance.

Rather than litigating the matter or drawing attention to the law and being accused of compromising visitor safety, several winery proprietors have voluntarily complied with the Code. Their reasons are varied, but include perceived liability for injuries from non-compliant buildings, builders that are more comfortable building to Code specification, or a willingness to cooperate with resistant counties for gains on other issues. While farm wineries are exempt from design criteria under the Code, their proprietors still must secure a county building permit and pay the permit fees before any construction may begin.

Nothing in state law other than this Code exemption addresses the lawfulness of a farm winery serving food or opening a restaurant. The decision to allow a winery such an ancillary use is a purely local one; often only an invisible county line separates those wineries that may and may not serve food. A handful of counties have permitted restaurants associated with wineries, with the largest one located adjacent to a farm winery and its affiliated country inn; another is associated with a winery in a very rural county without any zoning. At the other extreme, the mere service of prepared food such as cheese and crackers has provoked inquiries from some county health inspectors. The state law definition of a restaurant is vague,[62] and counties are given discretion to sweep certain activities under the umbrella of a "restaurant." This issue remains unsettled and will likely be the subject of legislative clarification

62. *See* Va. Code §35.1-1(9) (2010).

in the future, particularly since the Virginia industry is well aware that the 2010 Maryland General Assembly expressly permitted the service of certain prepared food at that state's wineries to support a public policy of encouraging patrons to eat while consuming alcoholic beverages.

f. Virginia Agritourism Liability Act

In 2006 the General Assembly passed another law designed to benefit agricultural activities, expressly including wineries and vineyards. It was the first time Virginia defined the term "agritourism" in statute and represents a significant development for Virginia's agricultural pursuits. Virginia law now limits the liability of proprietors for death or injury to anyone engaged in agritourism, defined as "any activity carried out on a farm or ranch that allows members of the general public, for recreational, entertainment, or educational purposes, to view or enjoy rural activities, including farming, wineries, ranching, historical, cultural, harvest-your-own activities. . . ."[63] By posting the statutorily prescribed warning, proprietors may assert an affirmative defense of assumption of the risk. They are not liable for injury or death of a participant resulting from the inherent risks of these agritourism activities unless there is negligence or willful or wanton disregard for safety, actual or reasonable knowledge of a dangerous condition, or intentional injury to the participant. No suits have been brought under this Act to date.

g. Case Study: Paradise Springs Winery in Fairfax County

The interplay between state law and county control over farm wineries, as well as the effect of the recent law governing local control of wineries in Virginia, is beautifully summarized by the recent opening of the Paradise Springs Winery in Fairfax County, a heavily populated suburb of Washington, DC. One family in the relatively rural southern corner of the county, filled with horse farms on large residential parcels, was determined to pay off $750,000 in estate taxes and retain ownership of a 37-acre tract that was part of a land grant from Lord Fairfax in 1716. The family's July 2008 request to build a winery on the agriculturally zoned site was opposed by neighbors and denied by Fairfax zoning officials, who argued that the winery was an industrial use because of its need to purchase grapes from elsewhere that would be delivered by trucks. The Fairfax Board of Zoning Appeals agreed. Despite this refusal, the family filed an application for a farm winery license from the Virginia ABC.

A Deputy County Attorney testified at the ABC hearing on the license that Fairfax County would likely sue to stop the winery if the ABC granted the license. However, in September 2009, the ABC granted the family a farm winery license, dismissing objections from neighbors and county zoning officials. The ABC Hearing Officer ruled that the winery's reliance on grapes purchased off site was permitted under the ABC license so long as the requirement was met that 51 percent of the grapes used be grown on that farm, as mandated by

63. Va. Code §3.2-6400 (2010).

Virginia Code §4.1-219. Further, she ruled, ABC law trumped the local zoning code.

In a related action, a Fairfax state delegate introduced a bill in the 2009 General Assembly to exempt only Fairfax County from the provisions of Virginia Code §15.2-2288.3 and impose reasonable conditions upon a farm winery. The bill was defeated in House committee by voice vote.[64] Paradise Springs Winery opened for business in January 2010, to newspaper coverage of the Deputy County Attorney's opinion that the County did not expect to intercede further and the Chairman of the Board of Supervisors' statement that "[w]e don't have the authority to restrict the kinds of events."[65]

4. OREGON

In 1972 Oregon passed Senate Bill 100 mandating visionary statewide land use planning.[66] The foundation of the state's land use program is a set of 19 statewide planning goals. The goals express the state's policies on land use and related topics, including housing, natural resources, recreation, and transportation. The goals are accompanied by guidelines, which are suggestions, not mandates, on how each goal should be applied.

The state goals are implemented and achieved through local comprehensive planning. Oregon law requires each city and county to adopt a comprehensive plan, similar to California's General Plans.[67] The local comprehensive plans must be consistent with the statewide planning goals. They are reviewed for consistency by the Oregon Land Conservation and Development Commission (OLCDC). After OLCDC approval, the plan is said to be *acknowledged* and becomes the controlling document for land uses in the area covered by the plan. The local jurisdiction then adopts various land use ordinances to put the plan into effect.

The wine industry actively supported Senate Bill 100. That law, through the use of such mechanisms as exclusive farm use (EFU) zoning and urban growth boundaries, set aside hillside land that had been designated as "view property" for agricultural development. At the time of the law's passage in 1972, there were only seven wineries in the state.

Oregon land use laws, at the state level, divide the state into commercial, residential, industrial, institutional, agricultural, forest, and recreational zones. Wineries typically are located in EFU and other agricultural zones. However, wineries (not vineyards) also may be located in commercial or industrial zones, often without any land use approvals other than an approved site plan and various ministerial permits such as building and septic permits.

---

64. H.D. 2606, 2009 Gen. Assem., Reg. Sess. (Va. 2009).

65. Derek Kravitz, Fairfax Winery Opens after Long Battle, Wash. Post, Jan. 12, 2010, at B1; *see also* Fredrick Kunkle, No One's Breaking Bread with This Wine, Wash. Post, Aug. 31, 2009, at A1; Fredrick Kunkle, Farm Winery Squeezes by Fairfax Zoning Law, Wash. Post, Sept. 4, 2009, at A20.

66. 1973 Or. Laws ch. 80.

67. Or. Rev. Stat. §197.175 (2009).

In an EFU zone, a winery is regarded as a permitted use if certain statutory requirements are met.[68] If the winery's maximum annual production is less than 50,000 gallons, the winery must have an on-site or contiguous vineyard of at least 15 acres, a long-term contract to purchase grapes from at least 15 acres of vineyards contiguous to the winery, or some combination of these sources totaling at least 15 acres. If the winery's maximum annual production is between 50,000 and 100,000 gallons, the minimum vineyard size is increased from 15 to 40 acres. If the winery can meet these criteria, the development can proceed, subject only to site plan approval and the issuance of any required ministerial permits.

Even if a proposed winery cannot meet these statutory requirements, it still may be allowed as a "commercial activity in conjunction with farm use," subject to review by the local government as a conditional use.[69] This applies to wineries in EFU and other agricultural zones such as the farm-forest or agriculture-forest zones. This process involves an application to the local planning department, public notice of the proposed development, and, in some cases, a public hearing. The project proponents must demonstrate that the development meets specific criteria such as consistency with the jurisdiction's comprehensive plan, enhancement of farming enterprises in the local agricultural community, and lack of adverse impact on farming and other approved uses on adjacent lands.[70]

Interestingly, there is a third way to establish a winery in Oregon under state land use law. "Farm processing facilities" are permitted if the farm provides at least 25 percent of the crops (grapes) processed and consists of no more than 10,000 square feet used for processing.[71] There is no proscribed production limit for farm processing facilities. These are permitted, not conditional, uses.

The subject of accessory activities allowed at the various categories of wineries is as complicated as in California and Virginia. Wineries in an EFU zone are closely regulated in terms of their on-site sales activities. Wineries can operate tasting rooms, retail rooms, souvenir shops, and restaurants so long as the wines sold there are those "produced in conjunction with the winery."[72] The non-wine items sold at the retail room must be directly related to wine and incidental to the on-site retail sale of wine. Finally, wineries in EFU zones can establish and operate "limited-service restaurants" on the winery premises.[73] Limited-service restaurants are defined as restaurants "serving only individually portioned prepackaged foods prepared from an approved source by a commercial processor and nonperishable beverages." Following passage of Senate Bill 1055 in 2010, the income from the sale of *incidental items and services*

68. Or. Rev. Stat. §215.452(1) (2009).

69. *Id.* §§15.213(2), 15.283(2).

70. Or. Rev. Stat. §215.296(1); *see, e.g.*, Marion County, Or., Zoning Code §§17.136.050(D)(2), 17.136.060(A), (D) (2009).

71. Or. Rev. Stat. §215.283(1)(r) (2009); Or. Admin. R. 660-033-0130(28) (2010).

72. Local governments have interpreted this requirement to allow sales of wines made off site for the winery under the winery's own brands.

73. Or. Rev. Stat. 624.010(4) (2009).

at wineries must not exceed 25 percent of the income from the retail sale of wine on site.[74]

The mention of services in the state law presumably includes activities such as weddings, bicycle races, rock festivals, and other special events that may occur at wineries. The counties in which those events occur have adopted different regulatory criteria and approval mechanisms for them, ranging from conditional uses to administrative approvals to permitted uses. Washington County, for example, has been fairly inflexible in its opposition to such events while Yamhill County has adopted more objective rules; specifically, Yamhill County allows every winery three events per year and requires a conditional use permit for any additional events. This lack of consistency from county to county has itself become a cause of concern. The 25 percent limitation on incidental services in Senate Bill 1055 was designed as a temporary solution to this problem. This legislation sunsets in 2013, inviting further legislation to define more specifically the range of permissible activities at permitted-use wineries.

The state does regulate one particular type of special event: outdoor gatherings of 3,000 or more people on a winery property for at least 24 hours.[75] Regardless of the zone, the county can issue a permit for such events only if the applicant demonstrates that there will be adequate water supply, drainage and sewage facilities, toilet facilities, refuse storage and disposal facilities, emergency medical facilities, communication systems, fire protection, security personnel, traffic control, and sanitary food service (if food is offered). The applicant also must have casualty insurance, and the county may require whatever plans, specifications, or reports are necessary to properly review the event and facilities.[76]

Wineries approved as commercial activities in connection with farm uses, in contrast to those permitted in EFU zones, can conduct only those accessory activities authorized by the particular county in which they are located as part of the conditional use permit.

Farm processing facilities cannot conduct any accessory activities, but state law does recognize "farm stands" as a permitted use in all agricultural zones.[77] Although farm stands cannot engage in winemaking, they can and do conduct many of the same accessory activities as wineries in the same zones. Specifically, the farm stand structure must be designed and used for the sale of crops grown on the farm and other farms in the local agricultural area. "Farm crops" include the processed form of the crops (e.g., wine from grapes) but not prepared food items. "Local agricultural area" is defined to include the entire state."[78] Farm stands can sell incidental retail items; they also can collect a fee for activities to promote their products, although they cannot include

74. *Id.* §215.452(3).

75. *Id.* §§433.735-433.770.

76. Note that a mass gathering permit for an activity lasting less than 120 hours in any three-month period is not a land use decision. Local governments may not regulate these gatherings except to ensure adequate health and safety precautions. *See* Landsem Farms, LP, 44 Or. Land Use Bd. App. 611, 617 (2003). Napa County has a similar approval process for so-called temporary events that involve the exercise of First Amendment rights (singing, music, etc.) to the public.

77. Or. Admin. R. 660-033-0120, tbl.1 (2010).

78. Or. Rev. Stat. §215.283(1)(o) (2009); Or. Admin. R. 660-033-0130(23) (2010).

structures intended for banquets, public gatherings, or public entertainment. As with wineries in EFU zones, farm stands' annual sales of incidental items plus their fees from promotional activities cannot exceed 25 percent of their total annual sales.

In addition to these controls on accessory uses, Oregon regulates land divisions in an effort to control urban and suburban sprawl. In 1993 the state legislature restricted the ability of landowners to subdivide lands in the EFU zones by requiring that newly created parcels be at least 80 acres in size.[79] The law included important grandfather exceptions, including the ability to sell any EFU-zoned land that existed as a legal "lot of record" before 1993 for winery or vineyard use, no matter how small the lot is.

Even with these exceptions, the restrictions were regarded by many as too stringent and resulted in a ballot initiative in 2004 known as Measure 37.[80] This measure, which the voters passed, allowed landowners to seek compensation from the state or local government or, if the government is unwilling to pay such compensation, to obtain a waiver of land use restrictions that had been imposed since the time the land was acquired and that resulted in a diminution of the value of the land. Over 7,000 claims had been filed for compensation or waiver by 2010, mostly for developments outside of cities and urban growth boundaries. The claims range from a timber company that wants to build homes on 32,000 acres of coastal timberland it recently acquired through a merger, to a developer seeking to build a casino resort on Marion County farmland.

Many wine industry veterans supported efforts to unwind the measure. This took the form of another ballot initiative, Measure 49, adopted by voters in 2007.[81] Measure 49 "modif[ies] Ballot Measure 37 (2004) to ensure that Oregon law provides just compensation for unfair burdens while retaining Oregon's protections for farm and forest uses and the state's water resources."[82] More specifically with respect to farmland, Measure 49 modified Measure 37 by providing for relief in two ways: a so-called express option that may allow up to three home sites on a given parcel,[83] and a "conditional option" that may

---

79. 1983 Or. Laws ch. 792 (codified as amended at Or. Rev. Stat. §215.780 (2010)).

80. Ballot Measure 37 (Or. 2004) (codified as amended at Or. Rev. Stat. §§195.300-195.336 (2010)).

81. Ballot Measure 49 (Or. 2007) (codified as amended at Or. Rev. Stat. §§195.300-195.336 (2010)).

82. *Id.*

83. The details of the express option are extremely complicated. Consider this explanation in the Oregon Department of Land Conservation and Development's Measure 49 Guide, at 4 (Mar. 7, 2008), available at http://www.oregon.gov/LCD/MEASURE49/docs/general/m49_guide.pdf:

> The number of lots, parcels or dwellings that may be approved under the Express option is limited to three. In addition, the number cannot exceed the number in the claimant's Measure 37 claim or waiver, if one was issued. If the property already contains one or more dwellings or more than one parcel, then neither the total number of dwellings nor parcels can exceed three. However, if a claimant's property already contains three or more parcels and three or more dwellings, the claimant may receive one more parcel and one more dwelling if the claimant otherwise qualifies under Measure 49. If a claimant's property already contains three parcels and has two or fewer dwellings, the claimant can receive only additional dwellings.

allow up to 10 home sites. The conditional option requires proof that the value of the claimant's property was reduced by the government's land use restrictions. To qualify for either option, the claimant must have had the right to develop the additional home sites when the property was acquired.

David Adelsheim, of Adelsheim Winery and former president of the Oregon Winegrowers Association, supported Measure 49, stating,

> Oregon winegrowers know the importance of preserving prime agricultural land. Oregon's land use laws are the reason our industry exists today. Without the establishment of Exclusive Farm Use zoning and Oregon's comprehensive land use system, the hillsides our industry needs to produce the best grapes would have been dotted with housing developments instead of rows of Pinot Noir vines. No visitor would want to come to a wine country filled with rural subdivisions. We need to be able to count on the same protections going forward, to ensure that Oregon's wines will continue to flourish.[84]

Since Measure 49 was adopted, the courts have been trying to reconcile the two ballot measures.

B. URBAN RETAILERS

Liquor stores and bars comprise the third tier of the three-tier system: the retail tier. Of course, retailers, like wine producers, can be found in both urban and rural settings, but urban bars and bottle shops pose particular land use problems that are the topic of this part of the chapter.

Retail licensees sell beer, wine, and spirits to consumers for drinking on or off the licensed premises. Most states have different classifications of alcoholic beverage licenses for on-sale consumption (restaurants, bars, clubs, and hotels) and off-sale consumption (wine shops, liquor stores, package stores, and, in some states, grocery stores and state liquor stores). Most states also distinguish between on-sale premises where minors are allowed because meals are served (restaurants, cafes, hotels), and bars and nightclubs where no or only minimal food is served and no one under 21 may be present. In this section, unless otherwise specified, "bars" refers to on-sale premises, including both bars and restaurants, and "liquor stores" refers to all off-sale premises selling alcoholic beverages in closed containers for consumption off the licensed premises. These may be liquor stores, wine shops, grocery stores, or even department stores.

As described previously, most states give wineries, particularly farm wineries or small wineries producing less than a specific number of gallons annually, on-sale privileges (tasting rooms) and off-sale privileges to sell directly to consumers from winery premises, through face-to-face transactions or deliveries in response to Internet, mail, or phone orders. This is a common exception to the normal tied-house prohibition against manufacturers also having

84. Jane Firstenfeld, Oregon Vineyards Protected From Developers, Wines & Vines, Sept. 2, 2010, http://www.winesandvines.com/template.cfm?section=news&content=78177.

an interest in retail outlets or exercising retail privileges. It is generally meant to address the problems that small wineries may have finding a wholesale distributor to handle their limited-production wines and to encourage local businesses and tourism. But in some cases, the exception has been expanded to include restaurants at the winery where wines and/or brandies produced by that winery or anyone else can be sold.[85]

In addition, some states allow wineries to exercise retail privileges from retail rooms not on the winery premises. New Jersey's wineries, for example, may have up to six retail outlets, apart from winery premises, from which to sell closed bottles to consumers.[86] California allows one[87] and Washington allows two additional locations away from the winery premises,[88] from which the winery can exercise off-sale, closed bottle privileges and on-sale tasting room privileges, excluding restaurants.

Some smaller wineries may be able to sell their entire production through tasting room sales and other direct sales to consumers, for example, via the Internet. Most wineries, however, rely on independent and economically viable retail outlets to achieve necessary sales volumes. Land use controls in urban settings, particularly those that make it more difficult for a bar or liquor store to start and stay in business, can adversely affect a winery's bottom line.

The discussion below is divided into two main parts: the controls and requirements for establishing a business in a new location, with separate sections on the laws of Washington State, Texas, New York, and California; and the increased restrictions on and changes to operating conditions that can be imposed on existing businesses in certain situations, using California as the example.

1. NEW LOCATIONS

The steps required for alcoholic beverage licensing vary depending on the locality. Some states delegate retail licensing approvals to county and city governments. The federal Alcohol and Tobacco Tax and Trade Bureau (TTB) licenses wineries and wholesalers, but it does not license retail establishments.[89]

85. *See, e.g.* Cal. Bus. & Prof. Code §23358(a)(4) (2009). A similar tied-house exception exists in Texas. A Texas winery has the ability not only to produce and blend wine at its production facility, but also to sell wine to, and purchase wine from, other permit holders "authorized to purchase and sell wine." Tex. Alco. Bev. Code §16.01(a) (2009). The winery is granted the authority to sell wine at retail for consumption either on or off the winery premises and to ship wine directly to consumers. Therefore, a Texas winery can be the manufacturer of its own wines as well as a wholesaler and, to a limited extent, a retailer of not only its own wines, but also the wines of other producers. There is at least one winery in Texas that has taken advantage of these provisions to establish a full-scale manufacturing facility, along with restaurants, at which it can sell wine (but not beer or distilled spirits) at retail.

86. New Jersey wineries may not ship wine ordered by phone, mail, or Internet. All winery retail transactions in New Jersey must be in person.

87. Cal. Bus. & Prof. Code §23390.5 (2009).

88. Wash. Rev. Code §66.24.170(4)(b) (2009).

89. The TTB does require special occupational tax registration, without payment of any tax, upon start-up of a retail alcoholic beverage business. 26 U.S.C. §§5122, 5124 (2006)).

While the principal focus of the following discussion of controls on the issuance of retail alcoholic beverage licenses in new locations is California, the first part includes descriptions of the licensing process applicable to retailers in Washington, Texas, and New York. Washington is a state that entirely controls the sale of spirits; Texas has wet and dry areas through the exercise of local control over sales of alcoholic beverages; and New York restricts the off-sale of wine to package liquor stores only, not convenience stores or grocery stores. The urban retail licensing requirements in these states are generally similar, but they differ with respect to local controls and ease of issuance.

a. Washington

In Washington State, the Liquor Control Board (WSLCB) is charged with protecting the "welfare, health, peace, morals, and safety" of the public and is the sole governmental body that holds the power to license and tax the sale and distribution of alcohol.[90] In addition, Washington is a control state, which means that the WSLCB is the only authorized wholesaler and operator of liquor stores that sell spirits. As such, the WSLCB issues retail licenses to bars for the sale of beer, wine, and spirits for on-sale consumption; issues beer- and/or wine-only licenses to private liquor stores; and operates, or contracts for the operation of, state liquor stores that predominantly sell spirits but also often carry beer and wine. By and large, the licensing process as it relates to zoning and land use issues is fairly straightforward. As in all states, the local zoning ordinances govern the use of the premises; in Washington there are generally no complex roadblocks to operating an on- or off-sale retail business.

Washington differs from California and the handful of other states that treat bar licenses as personal property that can be bought and sold. In addition, there is a statutory cap on the number of bar licenses that may be issued by the WSLCB. At the time of writing, the aggregate number of spirits, beer, and wine nightclub and restaurant licenses cannot exceed "one license for each one thousand two hundred of population in the state."[91] Historically, however, each time the existing statutory limit has been approached, the legislature has amended the statute to make more licenses available. There is no statutorily imposed limit on the number of beer and wine bar licenses that may be issued by the WSLCB.

Even though an applicant for a bar license will likely not face an obstacle due to the statutory cap, other potential hurdles could arise. The WSLCB is directed to refuse to issue a bar license to an applicant "if in the opinion of the board the spirits, beer, and wine restaurant licenses already granted for the particular locality are adequate for the reasonable needs of the community."[92] The WSLCB is also directed to, "so far as in its judgment is reasonably possible," confine bar licenses to business districts and not approve such licenses in residential districts.[93]

90. Wash. Rev. Code §66.08.010, 66.08.120 (2009).
91. *Id.* §66.24.420(4).
92. *Id.* §66.24.420(5).
93. *Id.* §66.24.420(2).

During the licensing process, retail applicants submit a license application packet, after which the WSLCB posts a public notice at the premises naming the interested parties and the license type and sends notice of the application to the local authority, be it a city or county.[94] The WSLCB also will notify public institutions, churches, and schools that are within 500 feet of the proposed premises.[95] The local authority has 20 days to object to, or request additional time to evaluate, the application. At this stage, the local authority generally circulates the application to various departments, including the law enforcement and zoning departments. Typical land use issues that may arise include building occupancy and zoning issues, which can cause a delay in the application process.

Along with the public notice posted at the premises, the process allows interested parties to comment on and object to the application. Objections usually are based on land use issues or public safety concerns.[96] Based on the response to the notices, a physical inspection of the premises, and investigation of the applicant, the WSLCB will grant or deny the application. Either an objecting party or the applicant can request a hearing to appeal the decision. In general, licenses are not subject to special conditions or restrictions, but there are two interesting exceptions.

The first exception applies to those off-sale beer and wine retail premises that are located within an alcohol impact area (AIA). There are currently only three AIAs, located in Seattle, Tacoma, and Spokane. An AIA is an area within a municipality or county where chronic inebriation or illegal activity connected with alcohol consumption has been determined by the locality to require special treatment. The WSLCB's purpose in adopting AIA rules was to "establish a framework under which the board, in partnership with local government and community organizations, may act to mitigate negative impacts on a community's welfare, health, peace, or safety that result from the presence of chronic public inebriation."[97] After the local government has created the AIA and the WSLCB has recognized it, an "enhanced" licensing procedure goes into effect for all new and renewal applications. The local authority notice period is extended from 20 days to 60 days, and the WSLCB is permitted to place restrictions on the license, such as limiting hours of operations and banning the sale of certain products.[98] For example, the most recent AIA—approved on April 7, 2010, for Spokane—included a list of 32 banned malt beverage products, such as Keystone Ice, Sparks, and Red Bull Malt Liquor.[99] The WSLCB notifies licensed distributors of the banned products and actively enforces the AIA restrictions.

---

94. How to Apply for a Liquor License, available at http://liq.wa.gov/licensing/license-how-to-apply.aspx; *see also id.* §66.24.010(8)(a).

95. Wash. Rev. Code §66.24.010(9)(a) (2009).

96. *Id.* §66.24.010(8)(c), (9)(a), (c), (12).

97. Wash. Admin. Code §314-12-210(1)(c) (2010).

98. *Id.* §314-12-215(3), (6)(a).

99. Recognizing the City of Spokane's Proposed Downtown Core Mandatory Alcohol Impact Area, Wash. State Liquor Control Bd. Res. No. BR-01-2010, at 4 (Apr. 7, 2010), available at http://www.liq.wa.gov/releases/2010-04-07-Spokane2010resolution.pdf.

The second exception is a relatively new development and not so clearly developed as the AIA. In 2009 the legislature approved a new nightclub license that allows a business primarily open between 9 p.m. and 2 a.m. to hold a spirits, beer, and wine on-sale license.[100] Previously, these businesses typically held a spirits, beer, and wine restaurant license, which had more stringent food service and operational requirements. Although the new nightclub license does not create a business model that was not previously allowed — nightclubs existed before, and there is no indication that their numbers will significantly increase due to this new license type — the legislature did build in a mechanism for the local authority to request that the WSLCB impose additional restrictions on the license.[101] Seattle, for example, requires nightclub applicants to submit safety plans and employ security personnel;[102] they must also participate in police training. The city will request these restrictions in response to the notice of a nightclub application; if the WSLCB approves them, the applicant is required to comply. There is, however, no clear indication whether the restrictions are conditions that have to be satisfied before the WSLCB will issue the license, or if the WSLCB will enforce these restrictions at all. These uncertainties are still being worked out between the city of Seattle and the WSLCB, but the outcome could have significant implications for nightclub applicants.

b. Texas

Following the Repeal of Prohibition, the Texas Constitution was amended to allow the residents of each city, justice precinct, and county to determine whether and to what extent alcoholic beverages should be made available for sale within its jurisdiction. The range of possible local options includes 10 categories, primarily determined by the range of beverages to be made available (i.e., beer, wine, and/or distilled spirits) and whether on-premises consumption will be allowed.[103] In fact, while much of Texas remains largely dry in aerial extent, all of the major population areas are "damp" to some degree. In any case, the possession of alcoholic beverages for personal consumption in the home is legal everywhere, as are private clubs that make alcoholic beverages available to their members for consumption on the club's licensed premises.

The manufacture, importation, distribution, marketing, and sale of alcoholic beverages are governed by the Texas Alcoholic Beverage Code (TAB Code), which is administered by the Texas Alcoholic Beverage Commission (TABC). Under the TAB Code, local control is limited to determination of local option, whether late-hours sales for on-premises consumption will be allowed (i.e., past midnight Sunday through Friday and past 1 a.m. on Sunday

100. Wash. Rev. Code §66.24.600 (2009).
101. *Id.* §66.24.600(5).
102. Seattle, Wash., Mun. Code §§10.11.010(E), 10.11.015 (2010).
103. *See* Tex. Elec. Code §501.035 (2009). The right to manufacture or distribute alcoholic beverages is determined by whether the class of beverages can be sold at retail there. Tex. Alco. Bev. Code §§11.01, 251.71(a) (2009).

mornings),[104] and the adoption of prohibitions on (i) the issuance of permits in residential areas or to locations within prescribed distances from schools, child care facilities, churches, and hospitals; or (ii) the possession of open containers of alcohol within a "central business district"[105] or within 1,000 feet of homeless shelters or substance abuse treatment centers located outside of a central business district. Cities and counties are expressly prohibited from imposing stricter regulatory standards upon the holders of alcoholic beverage permits than other businesses unless the permit holder derives in excess of 75 percent of its gross revenues from the sale of alcoholic beverages for on-premises consumption or is operating a sexually oriented business.[106] Nonetheless, cities and counties occasionally adopt ordinances or require specific use permits that impose restrictions in excess of those seemingly allowed by the TAB Code. This can be quite problematic for the applicants because the TABC has been increasingly reluctant in recent years to get involved in licensing disputes with cities and counties.

The number of permits that can be issued by the TABC is not restricted under the TAB Code. The initial step of the application process is to obtain certification by the local city and county that operations of the type applied for are authorized at that location by the local option, that the issuance of the permit is not prohibited by the jurisdiction's charter or ordinance (to the extent such charter or ordinance is authorized by the TAB Code), and that late hours are authorized if a Late Hours Permit is being sought. While this certification should be a straightforward determination based upon the location of the proposed business, cities and counties often use this process as leverage to ensure that the applicant has obtained any other licenses and certifications that may be required in its business, including its certificate of occupancy. This can create unwarranted delay in the licensing process.

Notice of the filing of an application must be published in two consecutive issues of a newspaper of general circulation published in the city where the proposed site is located or, if it is not located in a city, a newspaper published in the county.[107] A sign must be posted at all locations where a permit authorizing the sale of wine for on-premises consumption is being sought, giving notice of the application to the public, unless a permit authorizing the on-premises consumption of alcohol had been active at that location in the last 24 months. This sign must be posted for 60 days before the TABC will accept the application for processing. Finally, if a permit authorizing the on-premises consumption of wine is being sought, notice of the application must be mailed

---

104. Late hours are specifically authorized in cities or counties that had populations in excess of 500,000 at the time of the 2001 federal census or 800,000 or more at the time of the last preceding federal census (i.e., this will be a moving target in the future). Tex. Alco. Bev. Code §§105.03(c), 1105.04, 1105.05(c) (2009).

105. A "central business district" is defined as "a compact and contiguous geographical area of a municipality in which at least 90 percent of the land is used or zoned for commercial purposes and that is the area that has historically been the primary location in the municipality where business has been transacted." Tex. Alco. Bev. Code §109.35(d) (2009).

106. *Id.* §109.57(a)-(b), (d).

107. In the case of Wine & Beer Retailer's Permits and Wine & Beer Retailer's Off-Premise Permits, publication is left to the discretion of the County Clerk.

to every resident and neighborhood association located within 300 feet of the proposed location unless the applicant is also seeking a Food and Beverage Certificate.[108]

The issuance of most permits authorizing the manufacture, distribution, or sale of wine does not require a public hearing. The exceptions are applications for Wine and Beer Off-Premises Permits and Wine and Beer Retailer's Permits (authorizing the sale of wine and beer for on- or off-premises consumption.) In this case, the County Judge is required to call a hearing and to take into account the recommendations of the TABC, the local state senator and representative, the applicable county commissioner, the county sheriff, the district attorney, the mayor, the city council, and the local police chief.[109] The grounds for denial must be among those set forth in TAB Code §§61.42 and 61.43; these include refusal "based on the general welfare, health, peace, morals, safety, and sense of decency of the people,"[110] which establishes a wide range of grounds for denial. Nonetheless, most applications for Wine and Beer Off-Premises Permits and Wine and Beer Retailer's Permits proceed without protest or even any formal hearing.

c. New York

In New York State, there are three types of on-premises liquor licenses: On-Premises Liquor (for the sale of liquor, wine, and beer), Restaurant Wine (for the sale of wine and beer), and Eating Place Beer (for the sale of beer). Prior to filing an application with the New York State Liquor Authority ("Liquor Authority"), the Original Notice Application Form must be mailed to the Town Clerk of the municipality of the proposed premises or, in New York City, to the appropriate community board. There generally is no response from the local authorities, except in certain parts of New York City, where a community board may require the applicant to fill out a questionnaire and perhaps attend a community board meeting to describe the type of premises and the proposed method of operation.

Thirty days after the mailing of the Original Notice form, the license application can be filed with the Liquor Authority. The application is filed with one of the zone offices, in New York City, Albany, or Buffalo. The multi-page application describes in great detail all aspects of the proposed licensed premises and includes personal questionnaires for the principals of the applicant. An applicant also must provide adequate "source-of-funds" documentation. If the principals have borrowed money, loan agreements, personal questionnaires, and source-of-funds declarations from the lenders must be submitted to the Liquor Authority.

---

108. Food and Beverage Certificates are intended to prove that a business is operating as a restaurant and require that (i) revenues from food and non-alcoholic beverage sales exceed revenues from alcoholic beverage sales, (ii) at least eight entrees are made available for sale, and (iii) food and non-alcoholic beverages are available at all times that alcoholic beverages are available.

109. *See* Tex. Alco. Bev. Code §§61.3(b) (2009), in conjunction with 25.04 (Wine & Beer Retailer's Permit), 26.03 (Wine & Beer Retailer's Off-Premise Permit), and 61.32(c).

110. *Id.* §61.42(a)(3).

For On-Premises Liquor license applicants, if there are three or more similarly licensed premises within 500 feet of the proposed premises, the applicant must attend a "500 Foot Hearing" at the Liquor Authority. At such hearing, testimony is presented advising the Authority of the names and addresses of any other licensed premises within 500 feet. The applicant must convince the Liquor Authority that the "public convenience and advantage" will be served by the granting of a license for the location. Although there are no restrictions on the number of on-premises licenses the Authority can issue, if the applicant cannot make this showing, the Liquor Authority has the discretion to reject the application.

An application for an on-premises or off-premises license can be filed in the regular course or, if time is of the essence, via "Self-Certification." Under the latter option, adopted in 2009, if an applicant has an attorney file the application, the attorney can "self-certify." The attorney is basically advising the Liquor Authority that he or she has fully reviewed all aspects of the application, including the source of funds, and has made an on-site visit to the premises. The attorney signs the Self-Certification form and attests to the Liquor Authority that the application is meritorious and worthy of approval. When this process is used, the application is "looked at" by an investigator, but it is not thoroughly reviewed as is the case with a non-self-certified application. When the application has been reviewed and approved, the applicant receives a Conditional Letter of Approval. After satisfying the requested "subject to" conditions (such as a Certificate of Occupancy and "finished" photographs), the Liquor Authority will issue the license.

In New York State, unlike the practice in about 35 other states, liquor and wine for off-premises consumption are sold in "package-stores," and beer is sold in grocery stores, drug stores, and convenience stores. In nearly every annual legislative session, attempts are made to allow grocery stores with an off-premises license to sell wine, but, year after year, these attempts have failed. Beer also can be sold in a "beer & soda" store that has a Wholesale "C" license (a wholesale license with a retail privilege). By statute, the Liquor Authority cannot issue any new "C" licenses; if one wants a "C" license, it must be purchased from an existing licensee, and the license then can be transferred to a new buyer and/or a new location.

Although there are no restrictions on the number of off-premises liquor or wine stores, the Liquor Authority considers applications on a case-by-case basis. The applicant, who cannot have any interest in any other liquor or wine store and cannot have any interest in a wholesale or production license, must provide the Liquor Authority with the names, addresses, and distances of the four "closest" liquor stores. The Liquor Authority then writes to the four stores and asks them to provide their gross sales for the previous three years. If, in the opinion of the Liquor Authority, the proposed store is too close (not defined) to the other stores and/or if the other stores' gross sales are too low (not defined), or perchance are diminishing over those three years, the members will reject the application. The applicant generally attempts — by submitting as part of the application demographic material, including photos of new construction, census data, and supporting petitions — to convince the members that the "public convenience and advantage" would be served by the addition of a new liquor or wine store in the neighborhood. Commonly, at a meeting of the Liquor Authority, the nearby liquor store owners appear and present their case to try to convince the Liquor Authority that the neighborhood is currently well served by the existing stores and that the public convenience and advantage will not be served by the issuance of a new liquor/wine store license to a prospective competitor.

d. California

The California Department of Alcoholic Beverage Control (ABC) issues all alcoholic beverage licenses in the state. An amendment to the California Constitution, effective 1955, created the ABC as the state's sole license-issuing entity, replacing the Board of Equalization, the state agency that collects excise and sales taxes.[111] The ABC's mission is to ensure "strict, honest, impartial, and uniform administration and enforcement of the liquor laws throughout the State."[112] Applications for all new liquor licenses, and transfers of existing licenses, in the state are submitted to the ABC. By contrast, in some states, city government agencies issue retail licenses. In Chicago, for example, the Department of Business Affairs and Licensing is the agency responsible for license issuance.[113]

NEW ESTABLISHMENTS

To examine the controls on the establishment of new bar and liquor store businesses in California, this discussion focuses on San Francisco. There are many hurdles for a new business to surmount and, depending on the type of business proposed, many opportunities for neighbors to protest and delays to ensue.

Limits on the Number of Licenses Issued. Licenses allowing the sale of beer, wine, and spirits ("general" licenses), for both bars and liquor stores, are limited in number based on county population.[114] In San Francisco, the number of issued general licenses exceeds the statutory limit, based on the current city population; therefore, no new licenses can be issued. In order to start a new business with a general alcoholic beverage license, the business owner must purchase an existing license from a closed (or about to be closed) business. In counties where the limitation on the number of licenses is severe (e.g., because of a small population relative to the demand for licensed premises or resorts), the legislature has authorized new restaurant licenses to encourage economic development.[115]

---

111. Cal. Const. art. XX, §22 note (1954 amendment).

112. Cal. Bus. & Prof. Code §23049 (2009).

113. Mun. Code of Chi., Ill., §4-60-040(a) (2010); *see also* Chi. Bus. Affairs & Consumer Prot. Dep't, Chicago's Quick Guide to Liquor Licensing, available at http://www.cityofchicago.org/content/dam/city/depts/bacp/general/Liquor%20License%20Guide.pdf (last visited Dec. 30, 2010).

114. Cal. Bus. & Prof. Code §§23816, 23817 (2009).

115. 2007 Cal. Stat. 193 (Mono County), 2008 Cal. Stat. 130 (Napa County) (codified at Cal. Bus. & Prof. Code §§23826.9, 23826.10 (2009)); *see also* Cal. Gov't Code §§28020, 28050, 28077 (2009).

Until 1994 original beer and wine off-sale licenses were freely issued by the ABC in most counties without regard to the population of the county. One exception to this was Los Angeles County, which had restricted the issuance of new beer and wine off-sale licenses beginning in 1985, except for operations in which the annual sale of products other than beer and wine would exceed the annual sales of beer and wine.[116] The basis for this statutory restriction was a growing number of studies showing the relationship between high-crime neighborhoods, a lack of grocery stores, and an over-concentration of liquor stores selling beer, wine, and spirits and convenience stores selling beer and wine. While there are population restrictions on the number of off-sale general licenses, the lack of any ABC restrictions on off-sale beer and wine licenses had allowed the proliferation of convenience stores selling beer and wine, cigarettes, and a few relatively expensive grocery items in the impacted areas of Los Angeles. Large supermarkets were scarce. Proponents of the new law believed it would encourage the opening of grocery stores and reduce the number of beer and wine convenience stores in blighted areas of Los Angeles County.

The issuance of new beer and wine off-sale licenses was curtailed in 1994, when the state legislature imposed a moratorium on any new beer and wine off-sale licenses in any city or county where the number of off-sale beer and wine licenses exceeds one for each 2,500 residents.[117] In San Francisco, however, the computation combines off-sale beer and wine licenses with off-sale general licenses and imposes a moratorium on the issuance of new off-sale beer and wine licenses if the combined total exceeds one off-sale license for every 1,250 inhabitants.[118]

The proponents of the moratorium on off-sale beer and wine licenses believed that, by reducing the number of off-sale beer and wine outlets, "community problems associated with the sale of alcoholic beverages" would be ameliorated.[119]

> It is widely believed by local government officials, law enforcement and neighborhood activists, that the over-concentration of off-sale retail establishments selling low cost, high alcohol content malt liquor and fortified wine products, significantly contribute to the decay of neighborhoods and the proliferation of crimes. In many instances, liquor stores and convenience stores licensed to sell beer and wine located in specific areas are focal points for loitering, drug dealing, and other criminal and public nuisance activities.[120]

---

116. Cal. Bus. & Prof. Code §23826.2 (2009) provides: "No new off-sale beer and wine license shall be issued in a county of the first class, as specified in Section 28022 of the Government Code, unless it is issued with conditions, pursuant to Sections 23800 and 23801, which provide that the sale of products other than beer and wine on an annual basis, measured by gross receipts, shall exceed the annual sales of beer and wine products measured by the same basis."

117. *Id.* §23817.5(a)(1).

118. *Id.* §23817.5(a)(2).

119. Assem. B. 463, 1993-1994 Leg., Reg. Sess. (Cal. 1994) (B. Analysis—Concurrence in S. Amendments, at 2), available at http://www.leginfo.ca.gov/pub/93-94/bill/asm/ab_0451-0500/ab_463_cfa_940830_025953_asm_floor.

120. Assem. B. 960, 2007-2008 Leg., Reg. Sess. (Cal. 2007) (B. Analysis—Assem. Comm. on Gov't Org., at 4), available at ftp://www.leginfo.ca.gov/pub/07-08/bill/asm/ab_0951-1000/ab_960_cfa_20070424_122831_asm_comm.html.

The same law that restricted the issuance of licenses also increased police and ABC powers to deal with outlets that caused or supported "public nuisance activities" as discussed in more detail below.

In contrast to the restrictions on the issuance of beer and wine off-sale licenses, the issuance of new beer and wine on-sale licenses, whether for bars or restaurants, is not restricted by population, a reflection of reduced public health, safety, and welfare concerns at establishments where spirits are neither sold nor served. However, in many areas beer and fortified malt liquor may be equally, if not more, subject to abuse because they are widely available and inexpensive; in those areas, local forces may seek to impose conditions eliminating high-alcohol malt beverages or oversized containers or both.

In areas with a high concentration of on-sale licenses,[121] a "finding of public convenience or necessity" is required for the granting of bar licenses if meals are not served. In addition, minors may not enter these premises. For restaurant licenses, the applicant need only describe how the restaurant license will serve the public convenience or necessity; no governmental finding is required.

Even if the ABC can issue a license or the applicant can find a license to purchase and move to its new business location, there are many other opportunities for the application to be denied or for the operations of the business to be restricted, as described next.

Zoning. What is the zoning district? Do the zoning regulations permit the use? Is a conditional use permit needed? All states require that the local city or county zoning be appropriate for a business selling alcoholic beverages. As a practical matter, local zoning and other ordinances negate the uniformity in licensing that was one of the reasons for establishing the California ABC as the statewide agency for alcoholic beverage licensing. The ABC Act itself restricts the ABC's ability to issue new licenses in contravention of a valid zoning ordinance of the city or county where the premises are to be located.[122]

San Francisco's Planning Code divides the city into more than 50 use districts in the basic categories of residential, commercial, and industrial uses, with many variations based on neighborhood characteristics and mixed-use districts.[123] In most commercial districts, bars and liquor stores are permitted uses "as of right," without need of a conditional use permit. In other mixed residential-commercial districts, a conditional use permit is required for liquor stores or bars. In some districts, particularly districts zoned for predominantly residential uses, new bars and liquor stores are not permitted at all.

In addition to the zoning controls, some San Francisco areas have designated special overlay districts that conform to the neighborhood's official or

---

121. *See infra*, "Public Convenience or Necessity."

122. "No retail license shall be issued for any premises which are located in any territory where the exercise of the rights and privileges conferred by the license is contrary to a valid zoning ordinance of any county or city." Cal. Bus. & Prof. Code §23790 (2009).

123. City and County of S.F., Cal., Mun. Code, Planning Code §201 (2006) available at http://search.municode/html/14139/book.html.

unofficial boundaries in order to limit the number of bars or liquor stores, even in commercial districts. Some neighborhoods prohibit additional eating and drinking establishments in order to maintain convenient access to other types of neighborhood-serving businesses such as gyms, dry cleaning establishments, small markets, and other retail shops.[124] Other neighborhoods prohibit the establishment of any new liquor stores because of the perceived problems they cause. An example follows:

> There are an unusually large number of establishments dispensing alcoholic beverages, including beer and wine, for off-site consumption in the Neighborhood. . . . The existence of this many off-sale alcoholic beverage establishments appears to contribute directly to numerous peace, health, safety, and general welfare problems in the area, including loitering, littering, public drunkenness, defacement and damaging of structures, pedestrian obstructions, as well as traffic circulation, parking and noise problems on public streets and neighborhood lots. The existence of such problems creates serious impacts on the health, safety, and welfare of residents of nearby single- and multiple-family areas, including fear for the safety of children, elderly residents and visitors to the area. The problems also contribute to the deterioration of the neighborhood and concomitant devaluation of property and destruction of community values and quality of life. The number of establishments selling alcoholic beverages for off-site consumption and the associated problems discourage more desirable and needed commercial uses in the area.[125]

Use Permits and Conditions. While zoning or designation as an overlay district may prevent the establishment of any new liquor stores or bars in some areas, zoning in other areas may permit the use but require that a new business apply for a conditional use permit. CUPs for urban bars and liquor stores typically involve the same steps as a rural winery: (1) submission of an application to the Planning Commission describing the proposed use and (2) a staff investigation and report recommending denial or issuance with conditions, based on an assessment of the requirements of the general plan, the planning ordinance, and the potential for negative impacts on the surrounding neighborhood.[126] A notice of the public hearing is mailed to property owners within 300 feet, and a notice is posted on the property. Property owners, residential and business neighbors, and other interested persons are informed of the time and place of the hearing and invited to appear. Based on the recommendations of the staff report and on testimony from the applicant and the public at the public hearing, the Planning Commission may "condition" the use by imposing operational conditions aimed at mitigating neighborhood concerns (hours of operation, security, noise controls) as well as other conditions that may be required by the planning ordinance or building code, such as sufficient parking or landscaping and sign controls.[127] As with rural winery use permits, either

124. *See, e.g., id.* §718.1 (Upper Fillmore Street Neighborhood Commercial District).
125. *Id.* §784(a) (Lower Haight Street Alcohol Restricted Use District).
126. *Id.* §303.
127. S.F. Planning Dep't, Application Packet for Conditional Use Authorization (Oct. 6, 2010), available at http://www.sf-planning.org/Modules/ShowDocument.aspx?documentid=481.

the applicant or members of the public may appeal the Planning Commission's determination to the elected governing body, which is the Board of Supervisors in San Francisco.[128]

In some jurisdictions, the CUP process, even for an application that is not protested, can take up to a year, although there may be provisions for shortening the process by payment of an expediting fee.[129] Persons wishing to establish a new business may apply for a liquor license before any necessary CUP is obtained, but the license cannot issue until the use permit is approved.

Public Convenience or Necessity. In addition to the restrictions that may be imposed by the zoning ordinance, the ABC Act itself restricts the ABC's ability to approve a new retail alcoholic beverage business in a particular area. The ABC is required to deny a license application if issuance "would tend to create a law enforcement problem" or "result in or add to an undue concentration of licenses."[130] An area of undue concentration is defined as (1) a crime-reporting district where the number of reported crimes is 20 percent greater than the average of all crime-reporting districts of the local law enforcement agency, or (2) a census tract with a ratio of off-sale or on-sale retail licenses to the population in that census tract that exceeds the ratio of off-sale or on-sale retail licenses to the population in the county as a whole.[131]

Census tracts are small, relatively permanent statistical subdivisions of a county, outlined by local committees for the purpose of presenting data.[132] The boundaries normally are based on visible features but may follow the government's jurisdictional boundaries or other non-physical features. They never cross county lines. Designed to be relatively homogeneous units with respect to population characteristics, economic status, and living conditions, census tracts average about 4,000 inhabitants but may have as few as 2,500 or as many as 8,000 inhabitants.[133] Census tracts with predominantly commercial zoning and fewer residents tend to be "over-concentrated" because of zoning policies that encourage business development outside residential areas. There are, by design, fewer residents in most commercial areas, so the census tracts are generally larger and include more businesses.

If an undue concentration exists and the application is for a restaurant or a hotel, the ABC can issue the license if the applicant presents a letter describing its planned operations, including the type of food it intends to serve and the clientele it hopes to reach, and showing how the public convenience or necessity would be served by the issuance of the liquor license. The burden is on the applicant to show how public convenience will be served, but typically for new restaurants and hotels, if the police and the neighbors do not object, the ABC will act positively on the applicant's letter describing the proposed operations,

---

128. City and County of S.F., Cal., Mun. Code, Planning Code §308.1 (2006).
129. *See, e.g.*, City of L.A., Cal., Mun. Code §19.01(W) (2010).
130. Cal. Bus. & Prof. Code §23958 (2009).
131. *Id.* §23958.4(a).
132. U.S. Census Bureau, Census Tracts and Block Numbering Areas (Apr. 19, 2000), http://www.census.gov/geo/www/cen_tract.html.
133. *Id.*

the number of jobs created, perhaps the particular food philosophy or specific food that will be served, and the sales tax revenues to be generated for the local jurisdiction.

For bars (without meal service) and liquor stores, the governing body or its designee must make a determination within 90 days of notification of a completed application that public convenience or necessity would be served by the license issuance.[134] There are no specific statutory standards to guide the governing body in this determination. Again, the applicant has the burden of establishing that public convenience or necessity will be served.

In some jurisdictions, the governing body has designated the planning commission or the police department to make the public convenience or necessity finding. In some jurisdictions, notice and a public hearing are not required, and the determination is made by a zoning administrator or a police representative. When the planning commission has been designated, if a CUP is required, findings from the conditional use hearing can include a determination that the public convenience or necessity would be served by the issuance of the ABC license. In San Francisco, the board of supervisors has not delegated such responsibility. The board asks the Police Department and the Planning Department to make findings of public convenience or necessity, but all such requests are first heard in committee (City Operations and Neighborhood Services) and then by the full board. Applicants and those opposed to the issuance of the license may appear at the committee hearing and at the full board hearing. In San Francisco, determinations of public convenience or necessity may be issued with conditions on operations if so requested by the Planning Department or the Police Department.

In other local jurisdictions—for example, the City of Los Angeles—different public bodies are involved in issuing the use permit (the Planning Commission) and making the public convenience or necessity finding (the City Council), so it is not possible to combine the two functions or even obtain them at the same time. In Los Angeles, an applicant is required first to go through the use permit process and then ask for a finding of public convenience or necessity. The entire process in Los Angeles takes a year or more, even if no one is protesting.

ABC Notifications: Mailing, Posting, and Publication. When an application is filed with the ABC for a retail license at a location that is not currently licensed or is not currently licensed with the same type of license, the applicant must mail a Notice of Intention to Sell Alcoholic Beverages to all residential addresses within 500 feet of the new premises.[135] If the city or county provides free lists of names and addresses, the applicant also must mail the notice to all owners of property within 500 feet, whether or not they reside on the premises.[136] A large poster announcing the applicant's intention to engage in the

134. If the governing body does not make the determination within 90 days, the ABC may still issue the license if the applicant shows that the public convenience or necessity would be served.

135. Cal. Bus. & Prof. Code §23985.5(a) (2009).

136. *Id.* §23985.5(b).

sale of alcoholic beverages is posted near the entrance to the premises for 30 days,[137] and a notice is published in a local newspaper of general circulation.[138] In addition, upon receipt of the application, the ABC mails a notice of the application to the sheriff, chief of police, and district attorney of the locality in which the premises are situated; to the city or county planning director, as appropriate; to the county board of supervisors if the premises are in an unincorporated area; and to the city council or other governing body if the premises are in an incorporated area.[139] The public officials have up to 30 days to respond and can request an additional 20 days if they are preparing a protest or proposing conditions to be placed on the license.[140]

Neighborhood Groups. In some local jurisdictions, both the licensing and conditional use approval processes include a requirement that the applicant meet with neighborhood groups and obtain their approval of the proposed operations. In New York City, as described previously, an applicant for certain types of on-sale licenses must give notice to the relevant community board at least 30 days before filing the license application with the Liquor Authority.[141] In Los Angeles, the city has established a list of neighborhood groups that must receive notice of projects in their respective areas. Applicants for CUPs are encouraged to meet with the neighborhood council as part of the application process and to address the neighbors' concerns.[142] Even if there is no formal process for involving them, neighborhood groups, if they exist, can be a powerful force for organizing the neighborhood to support or protest a liquor license application.

Protests and Protest Hearings. Any person—not just public officials, residential neighbors, and property owners who receive the public notices—can protest the issuance of a license to the new business by lodging a written protest with the ABC within 30 days of the license posting or mailing, whichever is later.[143] While the ABC can reject a protest as "false, vexatious, frivolous, or without reasonable or probable cause,"[144] in practice it rarely does. Once any protests are accepted, the ABC investigator responsible for the application conducts an investigation, interviews the protestors, proposes possible measures to mitigate the objections, and recommends either denial or issuance, typically with conditions aimed at addressing the protestors' concerns.[145]

After the investigation is complete, if the ABC is recommending license issuance, with or without conditions, it mails a notice to every protestor with

137. *Id.* §23985; Cal. Code Regs. tit. 4, §109 (2010).
138. Cal. Bus. & Prof. Code §23986(a) (2009).
139. *Id.* §23987.
140. Id.
141. N.Y. Alco. Bev. Cont. Law §64(2-a) (2010).
142. L.A. Dep't of Reg'l Planning, Conditional Use Permit (CUP) FAQ, available at http://planning.lacounty.gov/faq/cup/ (last visited Jan. 5, 2011).
143. Cal. Bus. & Prof. Code §24013(a) (2009).
144. *Id.* §24013(b).
145. *Id.* §23800(a).

information about the conditions and its recommendation.[146] If it is recommending issuance in spite of a protest by a public agency that received notice by post of the application, the ABC also must provide that agency with a written notice of its determination, including the reasons for the recommendation to issue the license.[147] Persons who have protested the issuance of the license, including any public agency protestors, may withdraw their protests if they are satisfied that the conditions imposed address their concerns. Again, in practice, the ABC rarely if ever issues a recommendation for issuance when a public agency, particularly the police department or sheriff, has objected to the issuance. More commonly, if the decision is to recommend issuance, the ABC and the police will have agreed upon conditions in advance, and the public agency will have withdrawn its protest.

Each protestor has up to 15 days to request a hearing, and if any protestor does so, a hearing is scheduled. The complaint of any protestor who does not respond within the required amount of time is deemed withdrawn. If the ABC is recommending denial because of protests, the applicant can request a hearing to appeal the denial. At the hearing, with an administrative law judge presiding, the ABC attorney and investigator present the scope and results of the investigation if issuance is recommended, along with the ABC's basis for the recommendation at the hearing. The applicant presents its case for issuance of the license, and the protestors present their objections; the judge provides a written ruling after the hearing.

The delays involved with scheduling a hearing, plus the additional time required for any appeals from the administrative law judge's ruling, can add significantly to the time it takes for the ABC to process an application. It may be possible for the applicant to obtain an interim permit while waiting for the hearing,[148] but some applicants will not want to expend the money to start the business or make tenant improvements if there is a chance that the protest hearing will result in denial of the license or will impose conditions that would make the operations uneconomical.

ABC- and Police-Imposed Conditions. Even if no protests are filed against the issuance of a license by the neighbors or other interested citizens, the ABC and the police department are allowed separate and independent grounds for imposing conditions by the ABC Act. The ABC can impose conditions if grounds exist for denial of an application.[149] Significantly, applying for a license for an operation that will be located within 100 feet of a residence is grounds for denial.[150] In an urban setting, many if not most commercial properties are within 100 feet of residential properties. Further, the ABC can deny a license if issuance would tend to create a law enforcement problem.[151] The ABC and the local police often work together to impose "standard" conditions

146. *Id.* §24015(a).
147. *Id.* §24013(b).
148. *Id.* §24044.5.
149. *Id.* §23800(a).
150. Cal. Code Regs. tit. 4, §61.4(a) (2010).
151. Cal. Bus. & Prof. Code §23958 (2009).

for a city in an effort to mitigate such law enforcement problems. These conditions can include restrictions on hours of operations, on sales of single bottles of beer or high-alcohol wine, and on noise, signs, and lighting.

Standard conditions imposed on liquor stores in urban areas include the following:

(1) Sales and service of alcoholic beverages shall be permitted only between the hours of 7:00 a.m. and 12:00 midnight each day of the week.
(2) No distilled spirits shall be sold in bottles or containers of one-half pint or smaller.
(3) No wine shall be sold with an alcoholic content greater than 15 percent by volume.
(4) No malt beverage shall be sold with an alcoholic content greater than 5.7 percent by volume.
(5) Wine shall not be sold in bottles or containers smaller than 750 milliliters, and wine coolers must be sold in manufacturers' pre-packaged multi-unit quantities.
(6) No pay telephone shall be maintained on the exterior of the premises.

For bars and restaurants, typical conditions include:

(1) The licensee shall be responsible for maintaining free of litter the area adjacent to the premises over which it has control.
(2) The licensee shall not permit its patrons or the general public to loiter or congregate on the sidewalks adjacent to the licensed premises.

These conditions track very closely restrictions proposed in a publication titled "How to Use Local Regulatory and Land Use Powers to Prevent Underage Drinking."[152] This publication proposes restricting the number and location of commercial alcohol outlets, keeping them away from schools and other youth facilities, and restricting the hours of operation, container sizes, and types of products available. Does the imposition of these conditions actually result in a decrease in underage drinking or drinking in general? As discussed more fully in Chapter 8, jurisdictions throughout California and elsewhere in the country impose virtually identical conditions on liquor outlets in the belief that they are effective.

Entertainment Commission. The San Francisco Entertainment Commission was established to regulate, promote, and enhance the field of entertainment in San Francisco. The seven-member commission has the power to gather, accept, and review information and to conduct hearings for entertainment-related permit applications.[153] If a bar or club intends to provide live music or patron dancing or be open after hours (after 2:00 a.m.), its owners must

---

152. James F. Mosher & Bob Reynolds, How to Use Local Regulatory and Land Use Powers to Prevent Underage Drinking, Pacific Institute for Research and Evaluation (January 2000), available at http://www.udetc.org/documents/LocalRegulLandUse.pdf. *See also* Chapter 9, *infra.*

153. City and County of S.F., Cal., Mun. Code, Admin. Code §§90.3(a), 90.4(a) (2006).

apply to the Entertainment Commission for an Entertainment Permit and/or an After Hours Permit, respectively. The applications are considered in a hearing at which members of the public may voice their support or opposition. The Commission may issue one or both permits with Commission-drafted conditions on operations, including conditions for noise control, patron supervision, and security. The police may also contribute conditions, and if the business requires a CUP, those conditions will be imposed as well. There is no requirement that only one set of conditions be imposed by only one agency. Typically, the police, ABC, and Entertainment Commission will attempt to avoid imposing conflicting conditions on a business. More stringent requirements are usually the result of escalating protests, particularly involving clubs and other entertainment venues, as the applications move through the Planning Commission to the ABC protest procedures to the Entertainment Commission hearing.

Entertainment Zones. Not all land use controls focus on prohibiting or regulating urban bars and liquor stores. Some jurisdictions have established particular areas of a city that are dedicated to restaurants, music clubs, bars, sports arenas, and other entertainment venues. Entertainment zones include organized redevelopment projects such as LA Live,[154] San Diego's Gaslamp District,[155] and other urban areas "occupying the margins of downtowns in former commercial and industrial areas, underutilized retail corridors or underdeveloped waterfronts."[156] The French Quarter in New Orleans is one of the oldest entertainment zones. For older, more established entertainment zones such as the French Quarter, the interface (and interference) with residential neighbors may be less contentious, but in areas where the proliferation of clubs and bars is relatively new and the established residents must adapt to late-night hours, crowds, and noise in previously quiet areas, community opposition can be substantial.[157]

Summary: California's Controls on New Establishments. Although a new business rarely requires a conditional use permit, public convenience or necessity finding, *and* an entertainment permit, a bar or club without food and with entertainment will require the latter two and may also face neighbor protests to the issuance of the liquor license and entertainment permit. If persons or groups are determined to prevent or restrict the operation of a new urban bar or liquor store, they may have as many as four formal

---

154. L.A. Cmty. Redev. Agency CRA/LA Activity Report: Downtown Region City Center 5 (July 29, 2010), information available at http://www.crala.lacity.org/quarterly_reports/downtown/City_Center.pdf.

155. San Diego Centre City Dev. Corp., Downtown San Diego Neighborhoods 1, available at http://www.ccdc.com/images/stories/downloads/media-and-publications/Publications/11-602_neighborhood_map_082610_final_no_crop.pdf.

156. Daniel Campo & Brent D. Ryan, The Entertainment Zone: Unplanned Nightlife and the Revitalization of the American Downtown, 13 J. Urb. Design, 291, 292 (October 2008).

157. *See, e.g.*, Dan Levy, SOMA WARS: As More Residents Move to Neighborhood, the Battle with Nightclub Owners is Escalating, S.F. Chron., Apr. 14, 1998, available at http://articles.sfgate.com/1998-04-14/entertainment/17718928_1_after-hours-noise-11th-and-folsom-loft.

opportunities to object and appeal in San Francisco: at the conditional use permit hearing, at the public convenience or necessity hearing, at the ABC protest hearing, and at the Entertainment Commission hearing. Each of these hearings provides an opportunity for concerned citizens to appear, be heard, and potentially prevent the opening of the business. In addition to the formal opportunities to protest, neighborhood groups opposing a particular licensed business can apply pressure on the individual members of the board of supervisors and the police personnel responsible for the neighborhood. This array of opportunities can result in substantial delays for the developer of a new bar or restaurant, particularly one that does not want to incur costs until it becomes clear that the license will be issued. But it also offers residents the opportunity to demonstrate how crowds, noise, late hours, and extra traffic can disturb their quiet enjoyment.

2. CONTROLS ON EXISTING BUSINESSES IN CALIFORNIA

Although the applicant proprietor of a bar or liquor store may have satisfied all the requirements for beginning a licensed business and dealt with any protests, resulting in the issuance of all licenses and permits necessary to commence operations, the applicant may still face land use restrictions on the business. In addition to an ABC action to close a disorderly house or impose conditions on a business that has violated the ABC Act, several jurisdictions have enacted alcohol-specific ordinances that examine the operations of existing businesses and provide the community with options to close or restrict those operations to mitigate any disturbances they may cause.

a. Non-Conforming Uses

Depending on their age and when their zoning ordinances were adopted, many liquor stores and bars will not conform to the current requirements of a zoning ordinance, either because the use is not permitted under the new ordinance or because a CUP is now required. These are "grandfathered" or "non-conforming" uses. Generally, as long as the use continues without change or interruption, it will be allowed to continue in spite of its non-compliance with current ordinances. However, if there is a change of ownership, a transfer of the license for any reason, an interruption in the operation of the business, or a material change in operations (for example, from a restaurant to a bar, from a bar to a club with entertainment, or from a beer and wine liquor store to a beer, wine, and spirits store), the requirement for a use permit modification may be triggered.

In addition, the ABC Act allows the ABC to impose "reasonable" conditions on an existing business, whether it is a non-conforming use or not, upon a transfer of 50 percent or more of the ownership of a licensed entity.[158] The conditions may be based on the ABC's own investigation or they may be requested by the local governing body or its designated officer or agency,

158. Cal. Bus. & Prof. Code §23800 (2009) provides:

such as the police department, within 40 days of the filing of an application to transfer the license. The request for the imposition of conditions must be supported by substantial evidence that the problems on the premises or in the immediate vicinity, which have been identified by the governing body or its designated agency, will be mitigated by the imposition of the conditions. The statute provides a mechanism for the ABC to deny the imposition of conditions if it determines that there is not substantial evidence of a problem or that the conditions would not mitigate the problems,[159] but generally ABC defers to the requests from elected bodies or police departments for the imposition of conditions. The conditions imposed could substantially reduce the value of the business being transferred by, for example, imposing an earlier closing time or eliminating the sale of single containers of beer or fortified wines.[160]

b. Disorderly House Action

The ABC Act provides that keeping a disorderly house or allowing a disorderly house to exist is a misdemeanor and can subject the liquor license to revocation. A disorderly house is defined as a "place in which people abide or to which people resort, to the disturbance of the neighborhood, or . . . for purposes which are injurious to the public morals, health, convenience, or safety."[161] Any liquor store or bar that is characterized by loitering, noise, or petty crimes, or that exists in a neighborhood in which such behaviors cause more police action than other parts of the city, is at risk for a revocation action against its license. A substantial number of police calls to the vicinity, even if not pertaining to the liquor store or bar itself, can be grounds for a revocation action against the license on the grounds that the business is creating a police problem, even if the problem is with the neighborhood generally.

Studies of poor neighborhoods with an over-concentration of liquor outlets suggest that if the liquor outlets were closed or reduced in number, issues of

The department may place reasonable conditions upon retail licensees or upon any licensee in the exercise of retail privileges in the following situations: . . . (e) (1) At the time of transfer of a license pursuant to Section 24071.1, 24071.2, or 24072 and upon written notice to the licensee, the department may adopt conditions that the department determines are reasonable pursuant to its investigation or that are requested by the local governing body, or its designated subordinate officer or agency, in whose jurisdiction the license is located. The request for conditions shall be supported by substantial evidence that the problems either on the premises or in the immediate vicinity identified by the local governing body or its designated subordinate officer or agency will be mitigated by the conditions. Upon receipt of the request for conditions, the department shall either adopt the conditions requested or notify the local governing body, or its designated subordinate officer or agency, in writing of its determination that there is not substantial evidence that the problem exists or that the conditions would not mitigate the problems identified. The department may adopt conditions only when the request is filed. Any request for conditions from the local governing body or its designated subordinate officer or agency pursuant to this provision shall be filed with the department within the time authorized for a local law enforcement agency to file a protest or proposed conditions pursuant to Section 23987.

159. *Id.*
160. *Id.* at §23801.
161. *Id.* at §25601.

crime, drunkenness, loitering, noise, and perhaps even poverty would be eliminated. In fact, these may be neighborhood issues, not caused or even exacerbated by the liquor outlet. Supermarkets may have closed in poor neighborhoods; the residents may not have cars or adequate public transportation to travel to full-service grocery stores; and the corner store may be the only source, or at least the most convenient source, of groceries.[162] Of course, for residential neighbors of a liquor store that is a magnet for crime and loitering, the inconvenience of a longer trip to purchase groceries would probably be a welcome trade-off for the noise and disorder next door. Alternative places to gather and engage in healthful and constructive activities are often lacking in poor communities, and strategies for providing other activities may be just as effective as closing neighborhood liquor outlets.

Typical conditions on convenience store operations in a poor neighborhood require the proprietor to prevent loitering and noise, remove graffiti and trash, and not be a magnet for criminal activity. The responsibility for solving problems of unemployment, alcohol abuse, crime, violence—even graffiti, loitering, and litter—may impose an impossible burden on a neighborhood grocery and liquor store.

c. Deemed Approved Ordinances

Several cities in California and other states have adopted "deemed approved" ordinances to regulate bars and liquor stores by imposing a uniform set of conditions on the operations of non-conforming uses. The deemed approved ordinance in Oakland, California,[163] was adopted in 1993 and upheld by the courts.[164] It requires "Alcoholic Beverage Sales Commercial Activities that were Legal Nonconforming Activities immediately prior to the effective date of the Deemed Approved Alcoholic Beverage Sale regulations [to] comply with the Deemed Approved performance standards"[165] and to pay an annual fee to support the City's enforcement of the ordinance.

Under the ordinance, an activity shall retain its Deemed Approved status only if it conforms with all of the following Deemed Approved performance standards.

(1) It does not result in adverse effects to the health, peace, or safety of persons residing or working in the surrounding area;
(2) It does not result in jeopardizing or endangering the pubic health or safety of persons residing or working in the surrounding area;
(3) It does not result in repeated nuisance activities within the premises or in close proximity of the premises, including but not limited to disturbance of the peace, illegal drug activity, public drunkenness, drinking in public, harassment of passersby, gambling, prostitution, sale of stolen

162. Alameda County Pub. Health Dep't, Life and Death from Unnatural Causes: Health and Social Inequity in Alameda County 98 (August 2008), available at http://www.acphd.org/user/data/DataRep_ListbyCat.asp?DataRepdivId=2&DataRepdivcatid=62.
163. Oakland, Cal., Code of Ordinances, §§17.156.010-17.156.240 (2010).
164. *City of Oakland v. Superior Court*, 45 Cal. App. 4th 740 (1996).
165. Oakland, Cal., Code of Ordinances §17.156.030 (2010).

goods, public urination, theft, assaults, batteries, acts of vandalism, excessive littering, loitering, graffiti, illegal parking, excessive loud noises (especially in the late night or early morning hours), traffic violations, curfew violations, lewd conduct, or police detentions and arrests;

(4) It does not result in violations to any applicable provision of any other city, state, or federal regulation, ordinance or statute; and

(5) Its upkeep and operating characteristics are compatible with and will not adversely affect the livability or appropriate development of abutting properties and the surrounding neighborhood.[166]

The "repeated nuisance activities" described in the Oakland ordinance also can be evidence of, and grounds for, eliminating a disorderly house. But one of the main reasons Oakland and other cities have adopted deemed approved ordinances is that an alleged violation of the deemed approved ordinance can be prosecuted at the city level under the local land use laws, without having to rely on the ABC to take action against the license or a criminal court to find the business owner guilty of a disorderly house misdemeanor.[167]

Oakland's Deemed Approved ordinance has been in place for 16 years, yet the problems it was designed to address continue. As the City Attorney reported in 2009:

> While the City's efforts have yielded good results, problems at liquor stores continue. Oakland is still over-concentrated by 54 stores. Every City Council district has an over-concentration except [two largely residential districts out of seven]. One out of every three stores in Oakland has some recent disciplinary record with ABC. Overall, 106 stores have received 152 suspensions by ABC. Of those suspensions 126 were given for selling alcohol to a minor. The City Attorney's Office and [the Police Department] continue to work on problem outlets.[168]

d. Alcohol Impact Fees

When economic times are tough, cities, counties, and states look for revenue sources other than property or sales taxes. "Sin taxes" are particularly enticing because they not only raise revenues but also may reduce "bad behavior" and the societal costs of that behavior. A sin tax is an excise tax on substances that are considered harmful imposed in order to discourage their use and raise money for government. These taxes are imposed on cigarettes, alcohol, and even sodas.[169] "Deemed approved" fees that are used to fund enforcement of such an ordinance are a kind of sin tax.

---

166. *Id.* §17.156.090.

167. *Id.* §17.156.220.

168. Alexander Nguyen, Oakland Office of the City Attorney, City Attorney Report on the Status of Liquor Stores in Oakland 2 (Nov. 18, 2009), available at http://www.oaklandcityattorney.org/PDFS/Council%20Reports/Liquor%20Stores%202009.pdf.

169. One of the first sin taxes in the United States, imposed on distillers, was proposed by Alexander Hamilton, Secretary of the Treasury, in 1791 to retire Revolutionary War debts. The tax resulted in the Whiskey Rebellion in 1794.

In California the difference between a tax and a fee is significant. The imposition of a tax requires a two-thirds vote of the legislature or the voters. Once the measure is passed, however, revenues from taxes may be used for general governmental purposes. A fee, on the other hand, must be related to the costs and adverse effects of the fee payers' operations.[170] California state law provides that only the state may impose a tax on the production or sale of alcoholic beverages. Because of this preemption by the state, any revenue-raising efforts by California cities or counties must properly be characterized as a fee for services or a fee to mitigate harm caused by the activity upon which the fee is imposed.

In June 2010 one of the members of the San Francisco Board of Supervisors proposed an alcohol mitigation fee to be imposed on wholesale distributors and "other persons who distribute or sell alcoholic beverages in San Francisco" to recover part of the alcohol-attributable unreimbursed health care expenses and pay for the costs of collecting the fee.[171] On the basis of a nexus study of the police and health programs in San Francisco that deal with "alcohol-attributable conditions," the Alcohol Mitigation Fee was set at $0.035 per gallon of beer, $1.00 per gallon of wine, and $3.20 per gallon of spirits "sold within the geographic limits" of San Francisco.[172]

The purpose of the nexus study[173] was "to estimate a portion of the health-related economic costs of the measurable, direct effects of alcohol consumption to the City and County of San Francisco." The City and County used these estimates to assess the public health impact of alcohol and determine the appropriate fee to mitigate those effects.[174] The study found $17.7 million in unreimbursed costs attributable to alcohol consumption, including Department of Public Health detoxification centers and substance abuse programs and Fire Department emergency transportation services. The study also determined that there would be about $462,000 in administrative costs to impose the mitigation fee. To establish the fee, the authors divided the total costs by the estimated number of drinks consumed in San Francisco annually. They used national figures to estimate the average number of drinks consumed in California, divided by California's population and multiplied by San Francisco's population. Using an average drink size, they calculated the fee to be about a nickel a drink or 8.5 cents per fluid ounce of alcohol.[175]

---

170. Marin Institute, Local Alcohol Fees in California: Why Not Charge for Harm? 1 (June 2010), available at https://www.marininstitute.org/site/images/stories/pdfs/local_fee_fact_sheet.pdf.

171. Establishing an Alcohol Cost Recovery Fee, Ordinance 100865, 2010 S.F. Bd. of Supervisors (as passed Sept. 21, 2010), available at https://www.marininstitute.org/site/images/stories/pdfs/ordinance_sf_fee.pdf; John Avalos, Supervisor, San Francisco Board of Supervisors, "Ordinance ____ [Establishing an Alcohol Mitigation Fee]" (June 30, 2010), available at www.marininstitute.org.

172. *Id.*

173. Lewin Group, Inc., The Cost of Alcohol to San Francisco: Analyses Supporting an Alcohol Mitigation Fee 1 (June 30, 2010), available at https://www.marininstitute.org/site/images/stories/pdfs/sanfrancisco_fee_final_report.pdf.

174. *Id.*

175. *Id.* at 2-3.

The study focused on the costs directly attributable to alcohol, costs that "in the absence of alcohol use . . . would not be incurred."[176] The study consistently refers to alcohol "use" rather than "abuse," though there are a few references to "excessive" alcohol consumption. It did not account for positive contributions made by alcohol use, such as sales tax revenues, jobs, and tourism revenues.

At the time it was proposed, the San Francisco Alcohol Mitigation Fee ordinance was the first and only proposal in California for a mitigation fee measured by alcohol sales. It was passed by the board of supervisors but vetoed by the mayor. Whether it will become a popular city revenue-raising tool remains to be seen. Proposition 26 on the 2010 California state ballot, which passed with 52.9 percent of the vote, prohibits the levying of a fee for mitigation of adverse impacts without a two-thirds majority vote by the legislature or the voters.

C. CONCLUSION

Land use clearly affects the wine business in more ways than even an industry veteran might imagine. From the establishment and operations of a rural winery to the location and activities of an urban retailer, land use laws delve into the nuts and bolts of these businesses. The adoption and implementation of land use laws involve many groups and many interests. Complying with the laws is both time-consuming and complicated, but often land use policy will determine whether a rural winery or an urban bar can be started and can succeed.

176. *Id.* at 7.

CHAPTER 8

LITIGATING A CASE OF COUNTERFEIT WINE

William J. Casey and Andrew G. Wanger

A. INTRODUCTION

Is there a counterfeit wine problem today? If so, how long has the problem existed? Is the problem limited to old and rare "trophy" wines, or does the problem pervade every level of wine production and sale? Is the problem worldwide? What is the source of the counterfeiting problem? Would it be possible for one individual to create a counterfeit wine market? Does the principle of "caveat emptor" control a dispute between a buyer and seller regarding a claim for counterfeit wine? What evidence exists to prove that a wine is counterfeit, and how is a counterfeit wine demonstrated? Who will decide whether a wine is counterfeit? And what is the remedy to compensate the buyer of a counterfeit wine?

Counterfeit wine knows no price boundaries. From mass-produced Pinot Noir sold by Gallo Winery to first-growth Bordeaux from the world's most elite producers, all types of wine have been counterfeited. This chapter will largely focus on the issues raised by efforts to introduce counterfeit versions of rare Bordeaux wines into the secondary markets created by auction houses, retailers, brokers, and private collectors.

Counterfeit wine undoubtedly exists in great wine cellars or on the open market. In March 2007 the *Wall Street Journal* reported on a governmental investigation regarding the counterfeiting of rare wines, reporting, "[T]he inquiry comes as wine sales are booming amid a broader surge in the market for luxury goods. Backed in part by robust profits on Wall Street, collectors and speculators increasingly are paying $1,000 or more per bottle, especially for the rare Bordeaux vintages of France."[1] The most expensive 750 ml bottle of wine was sold in November 2010 at auction in Hong Kong: an 1869 Chateau Lafite

1. John R. Wilke, U.S. Investigates Counterfeiting of Rare Wines, Wall St. J., Mar. 6, 2007, at A1.

sold for $233,972.[2] Major auction houses reported that worldwide auctions of fine and rare wines produced sales revenue of more than $408 million in 2010.[3] Claims asserted in recent lawsuits suggest strongly that the number of old and rare wines being offered for sale, primarily French Bordeaux wines of historical significance from acclaimed vintage years, exceeds the production of these wines, particularly in large bottle formats that have appeared at auction or through international distributors. However, merely circumstantial evidence of historical anomalies or inconsistencies is insufficient to establish that a wine is not authentic or, more specifically, is a counterfeit.

Proving or establishing the lack of authenticity of any bottle of wine is a difficult task. Lawsuits challenging the authenticity of wine obtained through retailers, intermediaries, brokers, auction houses, and private collectors ultimately will turn on a party's ability to convince a judge or jury that the wine is not what it was purported to be. To overcome claims of counterfeit wine sales, the sellers will respond by demonstrating the provenance of the wine if any clear evidence is available. However, debates or disputes over the authenticity of a particular wine will end abruptly if either party is presented with good evidence of a wine's provenance, particularly if the bottle in question can be connected to the chateau responsible for producing the wine. But this rarely is the outcome of a dispute over authenticity. Secondary sources of a wine's past ownership cloud the provenance issues, as old and rare wines often are traded through reputable wine intermediaries and auction houses, and the records of these old transactions are incomplete at best. The most ardent collectors actively seek out, at any cost, fabled wine collections (including that of Czar Nicolas II of Russia before the 1917 Revolution[4]), and exciting wine discoveries (such as a bricked wall in Paris hiding eighteenth-century Bordeaux wines linked to Thomas Jefferson before the French Revolution[5]) lead the most ardent collectors to actively seek to obtain these trophies at any cost to complete their carefully developed cellars and collections. And if the source or provenance of a wine is questioned, today's purveyor and host of the greatest wine tasting spectacles in the world may become tomorrow's target of a counterfeit wine investigation.

Efforts to produce counterfeit wines have taken several forms. First, counterfeiters have simply affixed labels of more expensive wines to bottles of inferior wine. Others have refilled bottles of fine wine that have been consumed with something other than the wine represented on the label. This method has been facilitated with the advent of eBay and other Internet sites that traffic in all manner of goods. Recent searches of eBay turned up several empty bottles of fine wine, including Petrus, Chateau Margaux, and Chateau Latour. The process of counterfeiting a bottle of rare and fine wine often

2. Suzanne Mustacich, The Most Expensive Bottle of Wine in the World (for Now), Wine Spectator.com, Nov. 22, 2010.

3. Peter D. Meltzer, Global Wine Auctions Hit Record $408 Million in 2010, Winespectator.com, Dec. 29, 2010.

4. Molly O'Neill, Czar's Wines to Be Auctioned at Sotheby's, N.Y. Times, July 22, 1989, available at http://query.nytimes.com/gst/fullpage.html?res=950DE0DF143FF931A15754C0A96F948260.

5. Benjamin Wallace, The Billionaire's Vinegar 3-4 (2008).

involves replicating the capsule, the cork, the bottle, the label, and most important, the wine found in the bottle. In the context of larger frauds on the market, there have been several instances of wines by the case or pallet having been found to be something other than what was represented on the bottles' labels. Recently, E & J Gallo Wine, Inc. was found to have been the victim of fraud when several producers in France sold grapes marketed as 100 percent Pinot Noir for Gallo's Red Bicyclette label that, in fact, were the cheaper Syrah and Merlot grapes.[6] Several French wine producers were convicted in France of fraudulently supplying Gallo with the inferior grapes. The producers were alleged to have reaped roughly 7 million euros in profit from the tainted sales to Gallo.[7]

Counterfeit issues have been discreetly resolved in the past, and most likely continue to be settled quietly today. There has been no incentive for this issue to be resolved publicly as it negatively impacts all of the parties affected regardless of their respective roles or innocence in the debate. The great chateaus of Bordeaux have impeccable reputations and no motivation to produce "fake" wine. However, the discussion itself creates a level of public doubt about the product. Auction houses certainly do not wish to create any questions regarding the legitimacy of the rare wines they offer for sale in exchange for significant commissions. Private collectors are not pleased when someone calls into question the legitimacy and value of the collections that they carefully have assembled, and which include the exact same bottles as those claimed to be fake. Selfishly, even journalists and writers covering wine may hesitate to join this debate for fear that they could fall off the list of invitees to grandiose wine tastings and other events.

Nevertheless, the counterfeit wine discussion and debate entered the public sector during the last decade. Since 2006 at least six lawsuits have been filed by one person, William ("Bill") I. Koch, who has litigated and investigated the issue of counterfeit wine on a public stage, with much of his investigative research and findings now available to view and analyze. Bill Koch is an avid wine collector who launched a crusade to establish that the source and production of counterfeit wine can be tied directly to a German national, Hardy Rodenstock, who gained credibility in wine circles by holding lavish wine tastings in the 1980s and 1990s that gained the attention of prominent wine critics and experts, including the famed auction house Christie's and its director of wine, Michael Broadbent. In 1988 Koch purchased four bottles of wine that once were owned purportedly by Thomas Jefferson, but subsequently he could not authenticate his new trophies. Monticello (Jefferson's historical foundation) cast doubt on their authenticity, and Koch discovered possible misrepresentations by the auction house regarding the provenance of the wines and hard evidentiary pronouncements disputing the empirical history of the wine and its connection to Jefferson.[8]

---

6. Diana Macle & Tim Fish, Red Bicyclette Suppliers Convicted, Wine Spectator, Feb. 17, 2010, http://www.winespectator.com/webfeature/show/id/42200.

7. *Id.*

8. *See generally* Wallace, *supra* note 3, at 225-250.

As discussed in detail below, Mr. Koch has sued Rodenstock; the wine intermediaries from England and the United States (Illinois) from whom he purchased the four "Jefferson" bottles of wine; auctioneers and individuals in New York and California from whom he claims to have purchased other wine that purportedly is counterfeit; and finally, the fabled auction house of Christie's, against whom he levels claims of misrepresentation and fraud regarding Mr. Rodenstock's discovery and sale of the "Jefferson" bottles along with countless other sales of old and rare wines that were advertised as being authentic when, Koch claims, Christie's had no evidence that they were real.

These lawsuits have spawned a moot court professor's ultimate paradigm: a previously unsolved problem without case law or stare decisis as a guide; procedural issues of jurisdiction and venue; substantive common law issues of fraud, misrepresentation, negligence, breach of contract, and warranties; federal and state statutory claims of unfair business practices and interstate commerce violations; personal jurisdiction challenges; statute of limitation defenses; attacks on the claimed duty or fiduciary relationships between buyer and seller; factual disputes regarding actual and constructive knowledge claims to overcome the fraud and misrepresentation claims; proof and evidentiary issues and challenges; and the creation of a new cottage industry of wine experts, which will lead courts to determine the standards that will be employed to determine how and from whom expert testimony will be admitted.

B. RECENT HISTORY

The debate described above prompts the question of whether Hardy Rodenstock is the purveyor and creator of the majority of counterfeit Bordeaux wines from renowned vintages predating 1961. This is not a new question, but it has not previously been the subject of a public debate. Wine enthusiasts and insiders previously have pointed to the absence of evidence "to disqualify" the authenticity of any wine supplied by Mr. Rodenstock, however extraordinary. Yet, according to Bill Koch, the answer is unequivocally yes. Bill Koch is the most public protagonist in the search for the holy grail of wine counterfeiters. Mr. Koch thought himself lucky to have purchased four bottles of late-eighteenth-century Bordeaux wine that he believed once was owned by Thomas Jefferson, the third president of the United States. Mr. Jefferson assumed the duties of Minister of France from Benjamin Franklin in 1784 and held this post until 1789. Living in Paris, Mr. Jefferson purportedly developed quite a fancy for wine produced in Bordeaux and also purportedly acted as an informal purchasing agent of wine for his friend and colleague George Washington, who remained engaged in other duties in the newly formed United States. To ensure accountability and proper delivery, Mr. Jefferson purportedly identified his wine by etching his initials on a number of the wine bottles that he purchased in order to keep his lot and deliveries distinguishable from others earmarked for Mr. Washington and possibly other clients.

Fast-forward 200 years to 1985. Hardy Rodenstock, a German national with a penchant for fine wine and elaborate tastings and gatherings, announced that he had come upon an incredible discovery of wine that he announced had been hidden behind a false brick wall in the cellar of a Paris apartment. The wine was old, from 1784 and 1787, and it bore the remarkable inscription of the initials of our third president, Mr. Jefferson. Although his source was not revealed, the excitement of this discovery led Mr. Rodenstock to consign a bottle to the London auction house Christie's; it was a 1787 Chateau Lafite. Rodenstock never has revealed the source of his discovery in Paris.

Christie's was (and is) a world leader of fine wine auctions, and its former head of wine auctions, Michael Broadbent, offered the "Jefferson" bottle in a well-publicized auction. On December 5, 1985, Mr. Christopher Forbes, an art collector and vice chairman of the Forbes Publishing Company, obtained the right to purchase this bottle at a Christie's auction for the gavel price of 105,000 pounds (or $150,000). On December 4, 1986, Christie's auctioned another of Rodenstock's consigned "Jefferson" bottles, a 1787 Branne-Mouton for 36,000 pounds, and in 1987, at Vinexpo in Bordeaux, a 1784 Chateau Margaux.

In 1988 Mr. Koch purchased four of these "Jefferson" bottles through wine intermediaries Farr Vintners in London and The Chicago Wine Company in Illinois. Specifically, Mr. Koch purchased a 1787 Branne-Mouton for $100,000 and a 1784 Lafite, a 1787 Lafite, and a 1784 Branne-Mouton for an additional $211,804.40. All of these bottles bore the "Th.J." inscription.

After more than 15 years of showcasing his prized antiquities, Mr. Koch planned to include his "Jefferson" bottles in an exhibition of his collections at the Boston Museum of Fine Art. Spurred by the forthcoming public exhibition, Mr. Koch sought to secure the provenance of his "Jefferson" bottles with the Thomas Jefferson Memorial Foundation in Monticello, Virginia.[9] To his dismay, the Foundation refused to authenticate the collection. During this same time period, Mr. Rodenstock continued to hold his annual wine tastings in Germany and attracted the most notable names in the wine world, including Robert Parker, who declared at a 1995 tasting that the 1921 Chateau Petrus was "out of this universe" and awarded the wine a top score of 100 points under his own famous and influential wine rating system. Bill Koch does not appear to have been invited to any of the Rodenstock tastings. An interesting dichotomy had developed: the wine world considered Mr. Rodenstock's collection to be celebrated and unparalleled, and at the same time, Mr. Koch began to build his case against Mr. Rodenstock as a fraudster.

Christie's was next in line for Mr. Koch's inquiries. Unsatisfied by the responses provided by Christie's and Michael Broadbent, its head of wine auctions, Mr. Koch convened a private investigative team, engaged former FBI and Scotland Yard employees, re-engaged the Jefferson Memorial Foundation staff, and notified the FBI and local police authorities to further explore the authenticity questions that shrouded his four bottles.

At the time of the 1985 auction of the first "Jefferson" bottle, Christie's disclosed that it was not aware of the specific facts surrounding Mr. Rodenstock's

9. The Jefferson Memorial Foundation was founded in 1923 and operates the Thomas Jefferson Visitor Center and Smith Education Center, the Jefferson Library, and the Smith International Center for Jefferson Studies.

Parisian discovery—how the wine happened to be there, whether it was a Jefferson residence, or any other history regarding the wine. However, Christie's (through Mr. Broadbent) confirmed that "[a]ll we can say with certainty is that the bottle is of the correct date, the lettering and the wheel engraving are absolutely right for the period."[10]

Mr. Koch's private team determined that the bottles were not authentic, the provenance of the bottles could not be determined, and the inscriptions on the bottles could not be real. In fact, his investigative team determined that the etchings appeared to be inscribed with a dentist's drill from the twentieth century. The path led back to Hardy Rodenstock, and Mr. Koch filed a series of lawsuits in his crusade against counterfeit wine but, primarily, against Mr. Rodenstock.

Koch's investigation and discovery in litigation reveal that Rodenstock had supplied over 800 bottles of rare Bordeaux wines to New York wine distributor Royal Wine Merchants, and over 90 percent of the bottles were in large-format size.[11] The high incidence of these large-format bottles has increased doubt regarding the authenticity of these wines and has also drawn criticism in wine circles (along with legal claims of fraud in the Koch lawsuits).

C. LAWSUITS

Mr. Koch has filed the six lawsuits, each of which is summarized next.

1. KOCH v. RODENSTOCK[12]

Koch's lawsuit against Rodenstock stemmed from the events described above. In short, Koch alleged that Rodenstock's "discoveries" were fraudulent and that Rodenstock's misrepresentations led Koch to purchase fake bottles of wine.[13] Accordingly, Koch brought claims of common law fraud and declaratory relief, the latter to prove that the wines "discovered" by Rodenstock were fake.[14]

On May 18, 2010, the court entered an order for a default judgment against Rodenstock based on his failure to defend against Koch's allegations.[15]

2. KOCH v. GREENBERG[16]

Koch sued Eric Greenberg, the owner of one of the largest cellars in the United States, for knowingly consigning counterfeit wine to Zachys Wine

10. News From Christie's Wine Department, Season 1985/6: Sale Memorandum 314, at 2 (Dec. 5, 1985) (on file with author).
11. Complaint at 38, *Koch v. Christie's Int'l PLC*, No. 10 CIV 2804 (S.D.N.Y. Mar. 30, 2010).
12. Complaint, *Koch v. Rodenstock*, No. 06 CIV 6586 (S.D.N.Y. Aug. 31. 2006).
13. *Id.* at 5-7.
14. *Id.* at 12-13.
15. *Koch v. Rodenstock*, No. 06 CIV 6586, 2010 WL 2010900 (S.D.N.Y. May 18, 2010).
16. Complaint, *Koch v. Greenberg*, No. 07 CIV 9600 (S.D.N.Y. Oct. 26, 2007).

Auctions, and he also sued Zachys for knowingly, recklessly, or negligently auctioning the fake wine to Koch. To support his claim, Koch alleged that Greenberg first tried to consign his wine to Sotheby's, which, after examining Greenberg's cellar, concluded that a significant number of his wines were fake and therefore declined to auction the wine.[17] As a result, Greenberg sued and ultimately settled his claims against Royal Wine Merchants, Ltd., the company that helped him locate the wine.[18] Greenberg then consigned some of this wine to Zachys, who sold it at auction to Koch. Although both defendants blame one another,[19] Koch nonetheless brought a negligent misrepresentation claim against Zachys and the following claims against both Greenberg and Zachys: common law fraud and violation of sections 349 and 350 of the New York General Business Law,[20] which generally prohibit persons or businesses from engaging in deceptive business practices and false advertising.[21]

Interestingly, Greenberg attempted to resolve the case against him by tendering a check for the purchase price paid by Koch plus interest.[22] The court rejected this effort and allowed Koch to pursue his claimed damages.[23] Zachys and Koch agreed to settle their dispute on a confidential basis. The only details of the settlement disclosed to the public were that Zachys agreed to amend the "Conditions of Sale" in its auction catalogue. According to a statement from Mr. Koch, Zachys agreed to insert language into the "Conditions of Sale" that reflects Zachys's agreement to provide refunds of the purchase price to a buyer whose bottle of wine is later found to be counterfeit or has indicia of not being authentic. This new language in Zachys's "Conditions of Sale" will obviously weaken the impact of the "as is" clause utilized by the auction house. "As is" clauses are discussed below at page 341.

3. KOCH v. CHICAGO WINE COMPANY[24]

In suing the Chicago Wine Company, a wine retailer and auctioneer, and the Julienne Importing Company, an importer of fine wines, Koch alleged that he reasonably relied on the auctioneer's statements of authenticity before buying numerous bottles of wine that were later found to be counterfeit, including those purportedly once owned by Thomas Jefferson. To support his allegations, Koch noted that the auctioneer provided copies of materials authored by Christie's and its former wine department head, Michael Broadbent, to bolster the wine's authenticity.[25] Koch bought the wine, only to have experts question its authenticity several years later. Koch contended that, unlike laymen such as himself, auctioneers specializing in selling fine wines, including

17. *Id.* at 2, 4.
18. *Id.* at 4-5.
19. *Id.* at 6-7.
20. *Id.* at 11-15.
21. N.Y. Gen. Bus. Law §§349, 350 (2010).
22. Peter Hellman & Mitch Frank, The Crusade Against Counterfeits, Wine Spectator, Dec. 15, 2009, at 56.
23. *See Koch v. Greenberg*, No. 07 CIV 9600, 2008 WL 4778813, at *2 (S.D.N.Y. Oct. 31, 2008).
24. Complaint, *Koch v. Chicago Wine Co.*, No. 08L 003458 (Ill. Cir. Ct. Mar. 28, 2008).
25. *Id.* at 5.

the Chicago Wine Company, should have easily recognized that the wine they sold was counterfeit.[26] Instead, Chicago Wine Company knowingly or negligently misstated the authenticity of the wine it sold at auction.[27] Accordingly, Koch brought a multitude of claims against both defendants: common law fraud and breach of contract against the Chicago Wine Company, and violations of the Illinois Consumer Fraud and Deceptive Practices Act, the Illinois Uniform Deceptive Trade Practices Act, and the Massachusetts Unfair Business Practices Act against both parties.[28]

The Chicago Wine Company and Julienne Importing Company filed motions for summary judgment challenging the legal foundation of Koch's lawsuit. The case was settled on a confidential basis before the court ruled on the motions. As a result, Koch's lawsuit was voluntarily dismissed in October 2010.

4. KOCH v. ACKER MERRALL & CONDIT COMPANY[29]

In this complaint, Koch sued Acker Merrall & Conduit, another retailer and auctioneer of fine wines, for fraud, breach of contract, and violations of New York's and Florida's consumer protection statutes for materially misleading statements and unlawful conduct in connection with its sale of counterfeit wine to Koch. In support of his lawsuit, Koch alleged that experts hired to assess wine purchased from Acker Merrall concluded that the wines were fake.[30] Koch contended that, unlike laymen such as himself, auctioneers that are experts in wine, including Acker Merrall, should have easily distinguished authentic wines from the ones they sold to Koch.[31] Instead, he alleged, Acker Merrall knowingly or negligently misstated the authenticity of the wine.[32]

In May 2010 a New York appellate court dismissed Koch's claims that were based on New York's consumer protection statutes, holding that the "as is" language in Acker Merrall's catalogue would have alerted a reasonable consumer not to rely on the catalogue.[33]

5. KOCH v. RUDY KURNIAWAN[34]

Koch sued a young collector, Rudy Kurniawan, who had gained recognition for amassing a large wine collection before the age of 30. In his complaint, Koch alleges that Kurniawan took the wine scene by storm around 2005 when the young collector allegedly spent a million dollars a month at various wine auctions around the United States.[35] Koch purchased several bottles at auction in 2005 and 2006 that are alleged to have come from Kurniawan and also to be

26. *Id.* at 7.
27. *See id.* at 8-24.
28. *Id.* at 24-37.
29. Complaint, *Koch v. Acker, Merrall & Condit Co.*, No. 08601220 (N.Y. Sup. Ct. Apr. 23, 2008).
30. *Id.* at 2.
31. *Id.* at 3.
32. *Id.* at 9.
33. *Koch v. Acker, Merrall & Condit Co.*, 901 N.Y.S.2d 271, 272 (App. Div. 2010).
34. Complaint, *Koch v. Kurniawan*, Case No. BC421581 (Cal. Super. Ct. Sept. 10, 2009).
35. *Id.* at 1.

counterfeit.[36] In support of his contentions, Koch alleged that Kurniawan made two separate attempts to sell counterfeit wine at auction and was rebuffed. First, there was an attempt to auction Le Pin wine through Christie's in April 2007, which was allegedly thwarted by the chateau.[37] Next Kurniawan allegedly tried to sell counterfeit Ponsot wine through the auction house Acker Merrall in April 2008.[38] Laurent Ponsot challenged the veracity of the bottles bearing his name, and the auction was canceled.[39]

Relying on representations in auction catalogues prepared by Acker Merrall in 2005 and 2006, Koch purchased certain bottles of rare wine that were consigned by Kurniawan. Koch now alleges these bottles were counterfeit. As a result, he brought claims for fraud, negligent misrepresentation, and violation of California Business & Professions Code §§17200 and 17500.[40]

The case was referred to private arbitration.

6. KOCH v. CHRISTIE'S INTERNATIONAL PLC[41]

Koch sued Christie's, an international auction house describing itself as "firmly at the front of the international wine auction market,"[42] for allegedly colluding with wine sellers (including Hardy Rodenstock) and others (including Michael Broadbent) to sell him counterfeit wines, including those they claimed were formerly owned by Thomas Jefferson. To support his claim, Koch used expert and confidential witnesses to assert that Christie's knowingly auctioned wines that it knew were counterfeit or likely to be counterfeit without disclosing in its catalogue that the wines may be fake.[43] As a result, Koch brought claims for civil racketeering (RICO), conspiracy to defraud, aiding and abetting fraud, and violating §349 of the New York General Business Law.[44] In March 2011, the trial court granted Christie's motion to dismiss Koch's complaint.[45] Christie's asserted that Koch knew in the early 1990s that potential authenticity issues existed with the Jefferson bottles given his review of multiple press articles detailing the controversy, his retention of counsel in 1993 to investigate a lawsuit field in Germany against Mr. Rodenstock, and Koch's testing of his bottle in 2000.[46] Koch did not file the lawsuit against Christie's until March 2010.[47] The trial court agreed with Christie's finding that Koch was on notice no later than 2000 when he tested the bottle that "storm warnings" as to the authenticity of the Jefferson bottle were readily

36. *Id.* at 5.
37. *Id.* at 10.
38. *Id.* at 11-12.
39. *Id.* at 11-13.
40. *Id.* at 15-18; Cal. Bus. & Prof. Code §§17200, 17500 (2009).
41. Complaint, *Christie's*, No. 10 CIV 2804.
42. *Id.* at 3.
43. *Id.* at 6-7, 24-28.
44. *Id.* at 71-79; 18 U.S.C. §1964 (2006); N.Y. Gen. Bus. Law §349 (2010).
45. Memorandum & Order, *Christie's*, No. 10 CIV 2804.
46. *Id.* at 7-13.
47. Complaint, *Christie's*, No. 10 CIV 2804.

apparent.[48] Accordingly, the trial court dismissed Koch's lawsuit as time-barred. Koch has the right to fie an appeal of this decision.

In addition to Mr. Koch's numerous lawsuits, a class action complaint was filed in February 2010 against E & J Gallo Winery, Inc. for its alleged role in the marketing and sale of Pinot Noir wine through its Red Bicyclette.[49] The plaintiffs claim violation of California Business & Professions Code §§17200 and 17500, fraud, negligent misrepresentation, breach of the implied covenant of good faith and fair dealing, and money had and received.[50]

Another collector from the East Coast, Russell Frye, sued The Wine Library, a broker of fine wine from California, in August 2006.[51] The case was filed in federal court in the Northern District of California and confidentially settled in 2007.[52]

To date, none of these cases involving allegations of counterfeit wine has proceeded to trial.

D. INDUSTRY TECHNIQUES TO RESPOND AND PROTECT AGAINST COUNTERFEIT WINE

As with any luxury goods business, fine wine producers have a vested interest in protecting their brands and reputations. In the French wine industry, this effort has a long history. Napoleon, as part of the Exposition Universelle de Paris of 1855, requested that the brokers of fine wine in Bordeaux develop a qualitative ranking system to classify the various wines of Bordeaux. The Classification of 1855 proved extremely valuable for those select few wines deemed *premier crus*, or first growth: Chateaux Lafite, Latour, Margaux, Haut Brion, and Mouton.

Recently, chateaus in Bordeaux have been asked to verify the authenticity of bottles at issue in civil lawsuits filed in the United States. The authors are aware of at least one chateau that respectfully declined to take a definitive position as to whether bottles purportedly from it were authentic. This is not surprising, given the age of many of the bottles at issue and the lack of records—photographic or documentary—dating back more than a century that might aid efforts to prove whether a particular bottle is or is not authentic. The chateaus must balance their interest in preserving and protecting their brands with the potential of exposing themselves to warranty claims. The scenario is not inconceivable whereby a chateau offers an opinion as to the veracity of a questioned bottle that is later decided by a trier of fact in court to be of a character other than that opined by the chateau. In such case, the

---

48. Memorandum & Order, *Christie's*, No. 10 CIV 2804 at 18.

49. Complaint, *Zeller v. E & J Gallo Winery, Inc.*, No. BC432711 (Cal. Super. Ct. Feb. 25, 2010).

50. *Id.* at 8-13; Cal. Bus. & Prof. Code §§17200, 17500 (2009); Cal. Civ. Code §§1572(2), 1709, 1710 (2009).

51. Complaint, *Frye v. The Wine Library, Inc.*, No. C-06-5399 (N.D. Cal. Aug. 31, 2006). The defendant is "The Wine Library," not "Wine Library," and the complaint states as much.

52. Stipulation and Order Dismissing Case, *Frye, v. The Wine Library, Inc.*, No. C-06-5399 (N.D. Cal. Jan. 10, 2008).

aggrieved party at trial will already have displayed a willingness to litigate against all perceived wrongdoers and might view the chateau as yet another deep pocket to be used to right a "wrong."

Notwithstanding the natural reluctance to involve themselves in litigation, producers of fine wine have taken serious steps to protect their wines from counterfeiters. Indeed, substantial sums of capital have been invested to develop new technologies that will offer some protection to buyers who purchase these wines in the secondary market. Wineries are concerned with damage to their brands and reputations among collectors, many of whom are willing to expend large sums for their products. By investing in preventive measures, wineries create the impression that their products are trustworthy and, most importantly, are what the label on the bottle purports them to be.

These security measures include label watermarks, bottle engraving or etching, serial numbers on labels, placement of a microchip in the label, a proof tag made of gel that runs over the capsule onto the bottle neck, invisible ink detectable with a handheld scanner, multi-colored codes and graphics for the label, DNA marking of grapes used in the wine, bottle dating via ion beams, and RFID (radiofrequency identification) corks that have embedded chips containing unique identification numbers.

Employment of these security measures will obviously add to the overall cost of the bottle. As long as the economic incentive exists for the fraudster, these techniques will undoubtedly be tested and circumvented in an effort to capitalize on the high prices paid for trophy bottles of wine.

E. LEGAL ISSUES AND LITIGATION OF A COUNTERFEIT WINE CASE

Imagine that you are the proud new owner of a bottle of first-growth Bordeaux wine that was bottled before your grandparents were born. Undoubtedly, the price for this bottle is in five or six figures. In all likelihood it was purchased from a secondary source, that is, not the chateau whose label graces the bottle. As previously discussed, these sources commonly include auction houses, retailers, private collectors, and brokers. If a question arises regarding the authenticity of the bottle of wine, the seller is the obvious target for any litigated claim. The focus of such a claim could expand to those related parties that previously owned or sold the bottle of wine at issue. All participants in this chain of commerce face potential liability for a counterfeit bottle of wine brokered, auctioned, or sold to a buyer.

Bill Koch provides an excellent template for how to pursue a counterfeit wine claim. He is uniquely positioned as a litigant with sufficient financial resources to leave no stone unturned in the search for the truth—or, at least, victory in court. Attorneys preparing a legal complaint based on the purchase of counterfeit wine are obliged under Federal Rule of Civil Procedure 11 to conduct a reasonable inquiry into the factual contentions asserted in the complaint and confirm that the contentions have evidentiary support or will likely gain such support after a reasonable opportunity for further investigation or discovery. In the case of Mr. Koch, his efforts to shine a light on the issue of counterfeit wine have uncovered fascinating pieces of evidence that more than satisfy the liberal pleading standards in state and federal courts.

To investigate your particular claim concerning the potentially counterfeit first-growth Bordeaux wine in your possession, you likely will require the services of an expert, who will evaluate the bottle and determine if there are any indicia of fraud or counterfeit.

After conducting a preliminary investigation into the bottle at issue, the plaintiff's attorney will proceed to draft a complaint. This complaint will contain the factual allegations supporting the lawsuit, the legal theories under which the plaintiff is suing, and the damages sought through the litigation. The litigation attorney will face an interesting decision as to where the complaint should be filed—federal or state court. Typically, cases may be filed in federal court if the parties are citizens of different states (diversity jurisdiction) or claims are asserted under federal law. The plaintiff may also choose to file in state court. Factors to consider in selecting the venue for one's lawsuit include the locations of the witnesses, documents, and other evidence needed for trial.

1. WHO IS AN EXPERT IN COUNTERFEIT WINE?

Who is an appropriate expert to opine on the authenticity of a particular bottle of wine? A collector? An auctioneer? A wine critic and renowned taster? A producer or winemaker? A scientist? This question has yet to be answered in a court of law, but each of these individuals would likely qualify to offer an opinion as to the veracity of a bottle in question.

The expert witness will probably offer the most compelling and persuasive evidence in the counterfeit wine case. While expert witnesses are critical components to most litigated cases, their importance in a counterfeit wine claim is paramount. How many jurors will have purchased, tasted, or even seen a bottle of wine from the eighteenth or nineteenth century? As discussed earlier, there are several physical characteristics that experts will look to when inspecting and evaluating a bottle of rare wine. These include the shape of the bottle and the type or age of the glass used; the size of the bottle; qualities of the capsule covering the cork, including color, material, length, and wear; the cork and its wear and whether it is date-stamped; the label, including the paper on which it is printed, the glue with which it was affixed to bottle, the printing font, the artwork depicted on the label, and any appearance of artificial wear; the punt (the indentation at the bottom of the bottle); the fill level of the wine; the color of the wine; and, in certain rare circumstances where the wine is removed from the bottle, testing of the wine in an effort to date it.

To say that subjectivity pervades this analysis would understate the issue. Each potential expert will bring his or her own education, life experience, and point of view to the task at hand. For purposes of presenting a claim to a jury or defending against such a claim, the expert will need to provide opinions rooted in fact, buttressed with experience, and presented in a credible fashion. Under federal law, expert testimony is admissible at trial to aid the trier of fact.

> If scientific, technical, or other specialized knowledge will assist the trier of fact to understand the evidence or to determine a fact in issue, a witness qualified as

an expert by knowledge, skill, experience, training, or education, may testify thereto in the form of an opinion or otherwise, if (1) the testimony is based upon sufficient facts or data, (2) the testimony is the product of reliable principles and methods, and (3) the witness has applied the principles and methods reliably to the facts of the case.[53]

Challenges to a purported expert's testimony will likely focus on the following areas: the expert's qualifications, experience, background, education, or training; absence of a factual foundation for the proffered opinion; uncertainty regarding facts essential to the opinion; bias or self-interest; and lack of reliability of the theory or methodology of the opinion. Given the subjective nature of the exercise of evaluating bottles of wine, the court likely will be able to exercise its substantial discretion in determining both whether to allow an expert to testify and the extent to which that expert can offer opinions for the trier of fact.

2. LEGAL CLAIMS ASSOCIATED WITH COUNTERFEIT WINE

a. Breach of Contract

The parties to the sale of a bottle of rare wine likely entered into a written agreement for the purchase. The contract, even if a simple invoice or purchase order, will contain a description of the bottle(s) sold, the number of bottles, and the agreed-upon price. If the bottle is proven to be something other than what is represented in the invoice or contract, the buyer will establish a breach of the parties' agreement. Under California law, an aggrieved party has four years to file a claim for breach of a written contract[54] and two years to file a claim arising out of an oral contract.[55]

b. Breach of Warranty

A seller faces potential liability when representations are made regarding the quality or type of goods sold and the goods fail to match these representations. In the sale of wines, it is common for sellers to describe bottles as in "excellent condition" or to have been procured from a trusted source. Such representations open the seller up to warranty claims should the bottle turn out to be a counterfeit. Auction houses regularly employ a written contract for the sale of wines that includes a "sold as is" clause and affirmatively states that the seller (i.e., the auction house) "makes no express or implied representation, warranty, or guarantee regarding the origin, physical condition, quality, rarity, authenticity, value or estimated value of" the wines.[56] These clauses have been enforced by different courts.[57]

53. Fed. R. Evid. 702.
54. Cal. Civ. Proc. Code §337 (2009).
55. *Id.* §339.
56. *See, e.g., Acker, Merrall*, 901 N.Y.S.2d at 272.
57. *Id.*

c. Negligence

Typically, the counterfeit wine plaintiff alleges that the seller breached a duty of care to the buyer in selling a bottle that was fake. The seller is alleged to be in a position of greater knowledge than the buyer regarding the bottle, its provenance, condition, and authenticity and to owe the buyer a duty of care in marketing and selling the bottle. The buyer will need to prove that such a duty existed and that a breach of the duty occurred that resulted in damage to the buyer. Under California law, the plaintiff has two years to file a claim for negligence against the seller.[58]

d. Fraud

Under California Civil Code §§1572 and 1710, a claim for fraud may be pleaded when a party suggests as fact that which is not true when that party knows it not to be true.[59] For example, were a seller of counterfeit wine, having knowledge of the bottle's counterfeit nature, to market a bottle of the fake wine to an unsuspecting buyer, that seller could be held liable for fraud. The buyer will then need to establish that he would not have purchased the bottle but for the representations of the seller as to the authenticity of the bottle and that he has been damaged by the purchase. Should a trier of fact find the seller liable for fraud, in addition to compensatory damages the buyer will be able to seek punitive damages as punishment for the intentional conduct of the seller.

e. Negligent Misrepresentation

Negligent misrepresentation occurs if a party makes a positive assertion of fact without a reasonable basis for believing the fact to be true. Punitive damages are not recoverable under this legal theory.[60]

f. Unfair Business Practices

California Business and Professions Code §17200 prevents unlawful, unfair, or fraudulent business practices.[61] Section 17500 prevents acts of untrue and misleading advertising.[62]

3. DISCOVERY

The life of a litigated dispute relating to counterfeit wine will travel the normal course through the court system. The aggrieved party, the plaintiff, will file a complaint in either state or federal court. The defendant will then have the opportunity to challenge the complaint or to file an answer and assert various defenses to the claim. Discovery ensues, which in the counterfeit

58. Cal. Civ. Proc. Code §335.1 (2009).
59. Cal. Civ. Code §§1572, 1710 (2009).
60. Cal. Civ. Code §3294 (2009).
61. Cal. Bus. & Prof. Code §17200 (2009).
62. *Id.* §17500.

wine case will involve the normal methods used by lawyers to uncover the relevant evidence needed to support or defend against the claims asserted. These methods include written interrogatories,[63] requests for production of documents,[64] requests for admissions,[65] depositions,[66] and physical inspection of the wine.[67]

The plaintiff likely will focus on issues surrounding provenance and the genesis of the bottle(s) at issue. The specific representations made by the seller regarding the quality, condition, and source of the wine will play a major role in the plaintiff's discovery efforts. Documentation can be obtained in the form of written marketing materials that promoted the bottles for sale, such as e-mails, auction catalogues, or other advertisements. The oral representations a seller made to the buyer can be obtained through deposition testimony. Each of these pieces of discovery will aid the plaintiff in proving the counterfeit wine claim. The plaintiff will also seek to establish the chain of custody for the bottle—or, more accurately, the lack of a reputable chain of ownership. If the buyer can show that the seller had no good information on which to base the representations made during the marketing of the bottle (e.g., "excellent provenance"), the buyer will reinforce his effort to establish liability against the seller.

An interesting issue arises based upon a party's right to "inspect . . . test, or sample the following items in the responding party's possession, custody or control: . . . any designated tangible things. . . ."[68] A literal interpretation of this federal rule would allow a defendant to force a plaintiff to "test" or "sample" the bottle in question. The plaintiff, however, may not want to alter or otherwise taint the bottle through such invasive discovery procedures. But the plaintiff will face the argument from the defendant that if the bottle is a fake and otherwise worthless, the plaintiff should have no issue with such testing or sampling of the wine.

Discovery is often expensive and arduous for the parties. The process of collecting all relevant documents, deposing witnesses with knowledge of the facts surrounding the dispute, and preparing written responses to discovery requests can take months, if not years, to complete.

4. CASE LAW IMPACTING THE COUNTERFEIT WINE CLAIM

The lack of reported decisions from U.S. appellate courts forces a party involved in a counterfeit wine law claim to look to case law arising in other areas analogous to fine wine collecting. Logical comparisons can be drawn between fine wine and fine art or other collectibles routinely marketed and sold at auction.

63. Fed. R. Civ. P. 33.
64. *Id.* 34.
65. *Id.* 36.
66. *Id.* 30.
67. *See Id.* 34(a)(1)(B).
68. *Id.*

In *Weisz v. Parke-Bernet Galleries, Inc.*,[69] a New York appellate court held that where an art gallery's catalogue listing contains a clear disclaimer of any express or implied warranty or representation of the genuineness of any paintings, in the absence of the art gallery's willful intent to deceive, buyers who fail to assess the authenticity of a painting are precluded from recovering under a breach of warranty claim. This finding is consistent with the New York appellate court's affirmance of the dismissal of Bill Koch's claims against Acker Merrall arising under New York General Business Law §§349 and 350 (governing consumer fraud and false advertising).

In 2009 another New York appellate court seemed to further protect the auctioneer when it held that even though the auction house did not make any alleged false representations about a collectible, the buyer was nonetheless limited to a refund of the sales price because the buyer had accepted an order declaring that the item was sold "as is" and without any representation or warranty of any kind by the auctioneer.[70]

In 1995 a New York federal district court applying New York law held that where the facts represented by an auctioneer are not within its peculiar knowledge and the buyer has means available of knowing matters represented by the exercise of ordinary intelligence, the buyer must make use of those means and will not be able to recover under a misrepresentation claim.[71] The court further held that even if the provenance of the painting was misrepresented, the auctioneer's disclaimer, which expressly made no warranties or representations of the correctness of the catalogue, including provenance, precluded the auctioneer from being sued for fraud.[72] Finally, despite the buyer's significant interactions with the auctioneer, the court held that the buyer could not seek relief upon a negligent misrepresentation claim because the auctioneer owed no fiduciary duty to him.[73]

Finally, in *La Trace v. Webster*, an Alabama appellate court held that an auction owner who expressly makes false statements as to the authenticity of an item is liable for breach of warranty, breach of contract, and fraudulent misrepresentation, even if a buyer signs its agreement disclaiming any express or implied warranties.[74]

5. DAMAGES

Under California law, there are defined categories of damages available to a plaintiff. In the context of counterfeit wine claims, the primary damages recoverable include compensatory damages, restitution and disgorgement, punitive damages, prejudgment interest, and attorney's fees.

69. 351 N.Y.S.2d 911 (App. Div. 1974).
70. *Moustakis v. Christie's, Inc.*, 892 N.Y.S.2d 83, 83-84 (App. Div. 2009).
71. *Foxley v. Sotheby's Inc.*, 893 F. Supp. 1224, 1229 (S.D.N.Y. 1995) (a sophisticated buyer had access to an expert's discussion of a painting but failed to review it before purchasing the item) (citing *Danann Realty Corp. v. Harris*, 157 N.E.2d 597 (N.Y. 1959)).
72. *Foxley*, 893 F. Supp. at 1230-1231.
73. *Id.* at 1232.
74. 17 So. 3d 1210, 1217-1219 (Ala. Civ. App. 2008).

a. Negligence and Negligent Misrepresentation

Compensatory damages are awarded to compensate the aggrieved party for the actual losses suffered as a result of the defendant's negligence. This would include the purchase price of the bottle at issue and other reasonably foreseeable amounts. Economic damages could include objectively verifiable monetary losses, including loss of use of property, replacement costs, and loss of business opportunities.[75] Non-economic losses are classified as subjective, non-monetary losses, including emotional distress and injury to reputation.[76]

b. Breach of Contract

The California Civil Code sets forth the standard for breach of contract damages. Section 3300 states, "For the breach of an obligation arising from contract, the measure of damages, except where otherwise expressly provided by this code, is the amount which will compensate the party aggrieved for all the detriment proximately caused thereby, or which, in the ordinary course of things, would be likely to result therefrom."[77] Aggrieved buyers have sought to recover not only the purchase price for the alleged counterfeit bottle(s), but also a multiplier in recognition of the appreciation of the bottle's value during the time that the buyer held it. The theory behind this prayer for relief is that the buyer would have been able to sell the bottle for some amount greater than the amount for which it was purchased based on the historical performance of fine and rare wines on the open market. This theory has yet to be tested in a court of law.

c. Fraud

Pursuant to California Civil Code §3343, a party defrauded in the purchase of property is entitled to recover the difference between the purchase price and the value received from the seller and any additional damages arising from the transaction.[78] In the case of a counterfeit bottle of wine, the buyer likely would contend that the bottle is worthless, so at a minimum the purchase price would be sought. Then the aggrieved buyer would likely seek to recover lost profits from the potential resale of the bottle, lost appreciation, or lost opportunity to use the funds otherwise invested in the fake bottle.

d. Punitive or Exemplary Damages

California Civil Code §3294 provides: "In an action for the breach of an obligation not arising from contract, where it is proven by clear and convincing evidence that the defendant has been guilty of oppression, fraud, or malice, the plaintiff, in addition to the actual damages, may recover damages for the sake of example and by way of punishing the defendant."[79] Generally, these

---

75. Cal. Civ. Code §1431.2(b)(1) (2009).
76. *Id.* §1431.2(b)(2).
77. *Id.* §3300.
78. *Id.* §3343.
79. *Id.* §3294(a).

damages are difficult to recover and require a strong showing by the plaintiff that the defendant acted intentionally in injuring the plaintiff. A showing of mere negligence by the defendant will not result in recovery of these exemplary damages.

e. Interest

California Civil Code §§3287 and 3288 provide for the award of interest on damages awarded depending on whether the obligation was liquidated or not. The current rate of interest under California law is 10 percent.[80]

6. TRIAL

a. Jury selection

Jury selection for trial of a counterfeit wine claim has yet to occur in the U.S. court system. Often, trial lawyers retain jury selection consultants to assist in the process. These consultants often bring sociology or psychology backgrounds to the exercise. The goal is to find the panel of jurors that is most receptive to the theme of a party's case with the ability to reach a verdict.

Trial of a counterfeit wine claim could raise interesting jury selection issues for both sides. For example, the plaintiff will likely be a wealthy collector of fine wines. Presumably, this wealth was accumulated either through successful business pursuits of the plaintiff or at least through the protection of inherited assets. Such a plaintiff will have trouble engendering sympathy from a jury of individuals who have little connection to a world where one purchases a $25,000 bottle of wine or amasses a collection of 30,000 bottles of wine. For the common juror, such extravagance may give rise to feelings of resentment or a general attitude that someone traveling in circles where bottles of wine to be purchased or consumed run into the thousands of dollars should know better than to blithely rely upon the representations of a seller. In such a case, one would expect the defense to employ the phrase "caveat emptor" regularly and often.

Despite the potential for negative reactions to the buyer of luxury items such as a bottle of wine dating back to the 1800s, the aggrieved buyer will be able to present a simple and understandable message to the jury that she, as a consumer, should be able to rely upon the representations of the seller. Further, the seller will likely be portrayed as an "expert" in the field of sourcing, inspecting, and marketing such fine wine. This likely will create a heightened standard—if not legally imposed, psychologically imprinted on the jury—that the defendant-seller must deal with during the trial in order to establish that reasonable steps were taken to ensure that the bottle was as it appeared. Every juror has bought something of value and can easily understand the concept of relying on the seller for an accurate description of the item purchased. It is this personal connection that the litigator will try to establish

80. *Id.* at §§3287, 3288; *see also id.* §3289(b).

during trial, putting the jurors in the shoes of the purchaser of a bottle of wine that was not what the seller represented it to be.

The jury trial represents the next frontier for the counterfeit wine claim and should present a compelling drama for the trier of fact—whether that trier of fact is a jury, a panel of arbitrators, or a judge. Will corks be pulled? Will tastes be had by the jury? Would a jury know a Chateau Lafite from a Petrus? Who will qualify as experts, and what will they say about the bottle at issue?

F. CONCLUSION

While some of the questions posed at the outset and throughout this chapter remain unanswered as of the date of this writing, Bill Koch will likely have his day in court. Whether others will choose to embark on the expensive and long path that any litigated claim over counterfeit wine will present remains to be seen. But there can be no dispute that Mr. Koch has pulled back the curtain on an issue that provides a glimpse into world history, the lifestyles of the rich and famous, and the age-old question, what will they think of next?

CHAPTER 9

PUBLIC HEALTH AND SOCIAL RESPONSIBILITY

Richard Mendelson

> Wine [provides] cheerfulness, strength and nourishment, when taken only at meals, and in moderate quantities.
>
> Dr. Benjamin Rush, 1790[1]

> What do we know today about the risks and benefits of moderate alcohol consumption? While all may not agree, I believe that, for most people for whom alcohol is not contra-indicated by health, ethical, or religious reasons, there are "intelligent" ways of consuming alcohol that minimize the risks while providing health benefits. If consumed in "moderation" (when that term is defined to exclude binge or irresponsible drinking), alcohol can be considered as a component of a healthy lifestyle (along with not smoking, avoiding obesity, eating a healthy diet, and getting regular exercise).
>
> R. Curtis Ellison, M.D., May 2007[2]

The World Health Organization (WHO) has identified the harmful use of alcohol as "one of the main risk factors for poor health globally."[3] Alcohol in any form—cider, wine, beer, or spirits—can damage one's health and jeopardize public safety if used irresponsibly or excessively. Alcohol-related harm can include, but is not limited to, adverse health effects, intentional and unintentional injuries, crime and public disorder, other anti-social behavior and lost workplace productivity. The specific harm depends on the beverage, its alcoholic strength, the manner of consumption, and the personal attributes of the drinker.

1. Benjamin Rush, An Inquiry into the Effects of Spirituous Liquors 12 (Boston, Thomas & Andrews, 1790).
2. R. Curtis Ellison, Closing Remarks, *in* Health Risks and Benefits of Moderate Alcohol Consumption: Proceedings of an International Symposium, published in 17 Supplement to Annals of Epidemiology S1, S114 (2007).
3. World Health Organization, Strategies to Reduce the Harmful Use of Alcohol, Report of the Secretariat A61/13, 1 (March 20, 2008).

In order to prevent the harmful use of alcohol and control its adverse effects on drinkers and society at large, almost every country, including the United States, regulates the production, sale, and consumption of alcoholic beverages in some manner. The particular approach to alcohol control depends on the country's religious and sociocultural context and on how it balances competing ideological, social, health, and commercial agendas.

In this chapter, I focus first on the public health and safety issues surrounding the sale and consumption of alcoholic beverages generally and wine specifically. I then examine the various legal approaches to reduce the harmful effects of alcoholic beverage consumption and assess their effectiveness. Finally, I propose a model of social responsibility for wine producers to ensure that the product is properly produced and moderately consumed.

A. HEALTH EFFECTS

Excessive alcohol use is the third leading lifestyle-related cause of death in the United States, following tobacco and poor diet/lack of exercise.[4] Approximately 79,000 deaths in the United States are attributable to excessive consumption of alcoholic beverages each year.[5] What is excessive consumption? Generally, it is defined as the opposite of moderate consumption, much like temperance is defined as the opposite of intemperance. There is no universal standard for moderate drinking; the standard varies from country to country.[6] In the United States, the 2010 edition of the *Dietary Guidelines for Americans* (*Dietary Guidelines*) defines moderate drinking as no more than 1 drink per day for women and no more than 2 drinks per day for men.[7] For purposes of defining moderation, a "standard drink" in the United States contains 13.7 grams or 0.6 fluid ounces of pure alcohol, which can be found in 12 fluid ounces of beer (5 percent alcohol by volume), 5 fluid ounces of wine (12 percent alcohol by volume), or 1.5 ounces of 80-proof distilled spirits (40 percent alcohol by volume).[8]

The *Dietary Guidelines* also provide guidance about what constitutes "heavy" or "high-risk" drinking—more than 4 drinks per day or more than 14 drinks per week for men and more than 3 drinks per day or more than 7 drinks per week for women.[9] The *Dietary Guidelines* estimate that 9 percent of

4. A. H. Mokdad et al., Actual Causes of Death in the United States, 2000, 291(10) JAMA 1238 (2004), available at http://jama.ama-assn.org/content/291/10/1238.full.pdf.

5. Fact Sheets: Alcohol Use and Health, Centers for Disease Control and Prevention, http://www.cdc.gov/alcohol/fact-sheets/alcohol-use.htm (last visited October 30, 2010).

6. Some countries recommend no more than 2 drinks per day for men. They include the United States, Poland, Canada, Romania, Slovenia, Sweden, and Switzerland. New Zealand, Portugal, Japan, Italy, and Spain recommend no more than 3 drinks daily as moderate consumption for men. Catalonia, a region in Spain, recommends no more than 4 drinks, and France recommends no more than 5. Judith Brown, Thinking about Drinking: Implementing the Dietary Guideline for Alcoholic Beverages, 43 Nutrition Today 92 (2008).

7. USDA and U.S. Department of Health and Human Services, Dietary Guidelines for Americans 31 (7th ed. 2010), available at www.cnpp.usda.gov/Publications/DietaryGuidelines/2010/Po,icDoc/Chapter3.pdf (last visited February 3, 2011).

8. *Id.* at 21.

9. *Id.* at 31.

men and 4 percent of women in the United States are heavy drinkers who are at risk for adverse health outcomes.[10]

Even moderate consumption is not healthy for everyone. There are some groups of people who should not consume any alcohol according to the *Dietary Guidelines*. At-risk groups include children and adolescents, women who may become pregnant or are pregnant, persons who cannot restrict their alcohol intake, those who plan to drive or engage in other activities that require attention or skill, and persons taking certain medications or with certain medical conditions.[11]

Assessing the health effects of alcoholic beverage consumption—moderate or heavy—is complicated because the threshold effect typically has not been established, and the studies rarely take into account the manner of ingestion (particularly, with or without food). In terms of causation, there often is no straight-line correlation between the volume of alcohol ingested and a particular disease outcome. In some cases, a linear relationship may exist, which means that the body's response is proportional to the dose. Breast cancer and suicide are cited as examples, although no threshold effect has yet been established.[12] In other cases, the so-called dose-response relationship (that is, the mathematical relationship between the dose of a chemical—in this case, ethanol—and the body's reaction to it) accelerates, as with liver cirrhosis. That is, the disease risk rises sharply with increasing numbers of drinks per day. Finally, alcohol may have a beneficial health effect when consumed in moderation. This is the case for coronary heart disease and, in the case of middle-aged and older adults, all-cause mortality (defined as death from any cause) and cognitive function.[13] Yet alcohol is detrimental for those same conditions in heavy doses.[14] This is known as a J-shaped or a U-shaped curve.

Further complicating the analysis of alcohol's health effects is the particular pattern of drinking—for example, moderate daily consumption versus binge drinking. Binge drinking is defined as the consumption of 5 or more drinks by a male, or 4 or more drinks by a female, over a 2-hour time period.[15] Approximately 50 percent of adult Americans are current regular

---

10. *Id.* at 30-31.

11. *Id.* at 31-32. With respect to lactating women, the Dietary Guidelines' recommendation changed from 2005 to 2010. In 2005, lactating women were advised to consume no alcohol. The USDA and the U.S. Department of Health and Human Services, Dietary Gidelines for Americans 44 (6th ed. 2005), available at http://www.health.gov/dietaryguidelines/dga2005/document/html/chapter9.htm (last visited February 4, 2011). In 2010, the Dietary Guidelines advised that, in view of the substantial evidence demonstrating the health benefits of breastfeeding, "occasionally consuming an alcoholic drink does not warrant stopping breastfeeding," but the mother, if she chooses to drink at all, should wait at least 4 hours after consuming a single alcoholic drink before breastfeeding. Dietary Guidelines, *supra* note 7 at 31.

12. Thomas Babor et al., Alcohol: No Ordinary Commodity 57 (2d ed. 2010).

13. Dietary Guidelines, *supra* note 7 at 30-31.

14. Dietary Guidelines Advisory Committee (DGAC), Report of the DGAC on the Dietary Guidelines for Americans, 2010 D7-3–7-4, 7-8–7-10 (2010), available at http://www.cnpp.usda.gov/Publications/DietaryGuidelines/2010/DGAC/Report/D-7-Alcohol.pdf.

15. Dietary Guidelines, *supra* note 7 at 31; see also National Institute on Alcohol Abuse and Alcoholism, NIAAA Newsletter 3, NIAAA Council Approves Definition of Binge Drinking (2004), available at http://pubs.niaaa.nih.gov/publications/newsletter/winter2004/newsletter_number3.pdf (last visited October 30, 2010).

drinkers of alcoholic beverages, and 14 percent are current infrequent drinkers; of those who drink, about 29 percent reported participating in binge drinking within the past month.[16] The incidence of binge drinking is most prevalent among those aged 21 to 25 (46.1 percent), followed by the 18 to 20 age cohort (36.2 percent); the rate decreases beyond young adulthood from 34.2 percent for 26- to 34-year-olds to 18.4 percent for persons 35 or older.[17] Binge drinking rates also vary by gender (e.g., in the 12 to 20 age group, 21.3 percent of males versus 16.5 percent of females binge drink) and race/ethnicity (the highest rate of binge drinking, 31 percent, is among Native Americans and Alaskan natives, and the lowest rate, 11.8 percent, is among Asians).[18]

Youth, according to Professor Philip Cook, are a special case when it comes to alcohol.[19] He reports that "half of high school seniors drink regularly, and the percentage is higher yet for college-aged youths."[20] Binge drinking on college campuses also is widespread. According to a 2005 study, 44 percent of students enrolled at a 4-year college engage in binge drinking.[21]

Compared to abstainers and moderate drinkers, youth who drink heavily are at greater risk of death by unintentional injury, homicide, and suicide, which are the 3 leading causes of death among persons age 15 to 19.[22] A recent study by the Centers for Disease Control and Prevention (CDC) spells out the particular risks in more detail: driving after drinking; riding with a driver who has been drinking; sexual activity and pregnancy of self or partner;

---

16. Dietary Guidelines, *supra* note 7 at 30-1.

17. U.S. Department of Health and Human Services, Substance Abuse and Mental Health Services Administration, Results from the 2006 National Survey on Drug Use and Health: National Findings 32 (2007), available at http://oas.samhsa.gov/nsduh/2k6nsduh/2k6Results.pdf (last visited October 30, 2010).

18. *Id.* at 33 (gender) and 34 (race).

19. Philip Cook, Paying the Tab: The Costs and Benefits of Alcohol Control 179 (2007).

20. *Id.* at 188.

21. Binge Drinking on College Campuses, Center for Science in the Public Interest, www.cspinet.org/booze/collfact1.htm (last visited October 30, 2010). Binge drinking rates differ significantly from one college campus to the next, revealing the importance of one's environment and community. *See, e.g.,* Toben Nelson, Timothy Naimi, Robert Brewer & Henry Wechsler, The State Sets the Rate: The Relationship of College Binge Drinking to State Binge Drinking Rates and Selected State Alcohol Control Policies, 95 American Journal of Public Health 441 (2005). Binge drinking varies by "student subgroups, by the region of the country (higher in northeastern and north-central states, lowest in western states), and by the sets of policies and laws governing alcohol sales and use." Henry Wechsler & Toben F. Nelson, What We Have Learned from the Harvard School of Public Health College Alcohol Study: Focusing Attention on College Student Alcohol Consumption and the Environmental Conditions That Promote It, 69(4) Journal of Studies on Alcohol and Drugs 481, 484 (2008). Other important factors include residential setting, racial composition of the student body, male to female ratio, alcohol price, density of alcohol outlets, and the state in which the college is located. Regarding the last factor, the rate of binge drinking among college students was 32 percent lower in the 10 states with the lowest rates of adult binge drinking compared to the 10 states with the highest rates of adult binge drinking. The State Sets the Rate: The Relationship of College Binge Drinking to State Binge Drinking Rates and Selected State Alcohol Control Policies, *supra*.

22. Data & Statistics (WISQARS), CDC: Injury Prevention and Control, www.cdc.gov/injury/wisqars (last visited October 30, 2010).

tobacco use; interpersonal violence; consideration of or attempt at suicide; and use of marijuana, cocaine, or inhalants.[23]

In general, men are more likely to drink excessively than women[24] and have higher rates of alcohol-related deaths and hospitalizations.[25] In addition, nearly 3 times as many men in the United States (9.8 million) than women (3.9 million) are alcoholics.[26] Nevertheless, according to the National Institute on Alcohol Abuse and Alcoholism (NIAAA), "[a] strong case can be made that heavy drinking is more risky for women than men."[27] Women start to have alcohol-related problems at lower drinking levels than men, even when differences in body weight are taken into account. This is because women have less water in their bodies than men; alcohol disperses in body water, so it is more concentrated in women's bodies than in men's.[28] Alcohol dependence and alcohol-related health problems also tend to progress more rapidly in women than in men.[29]

Women also face the risk of adverse health effects from drinking alcoholic beverages during pregnancy. As stated previously, the *Dietary Guidelines* recommends no use of alcohol by pregnant women or women of childbearing age who may become pregnant. The *Dietary Guidelines* advisory committee reported in 2010: "Heavy drinking during pregnancy can produce a range of behavioral and psychosocial problems, malformations, and cognitive dysfunction in the offspring. [Citations omitted.] Even daily moderate drinking during pregnancy, especially in the first few months or before the pregnancy is recognized, may have behavioral or neurocognitive consequences in the offspring."[30] This is enshrined as the first sentence of the government warning that is carried on the labels of all alcoholic beverages sold in the United States: "According to the Surgeon-General, women should not drink alcoholic beverages during pregnancy because of the risk of birth defects."[31]

Criminologist Mariana Valverde, in *Diseases of the Will: Alcohol and the Dilemmas of Freedom*, questions this absolutist approach to maternal drinking.

> One strange feature of the [Fetal Alcohol Effects] campaign is that information about risks is presented without any attempt at allowing the relevant

---

23. Jacqueline Miller, Timothy Naimi, Robert Brewer & Sherry Everett Jones, Binge Drinking and Associated Health Risk Behaviors among High School Students, 119 Pediatrics 76 (2007), available at http://pediatrics.aappublications.org/cgi/reprint/119/1/76 (last visited October 30, 2010).

24. Fact Sheets: Excessive Alcohol Use and Risks to Men's Health, CDC, www.cdc.gov/alcohol/fact-sheets/mens-health.htm (last visited October 30, 2010).

25. *Id.*

26. Men and Women, Alcoholism-Statistics.com, www.alcoholism-statistics.com/sexes.php (last visited October 30, 2010).

27. U.S. Department of Health and Human Services, NIAAA, Alcohol: A Women's Health Issue 6 (2008), available at http://pubs.niaaa.nih.gov/publications/brochurewomen/women.htm (last visited October 30, 2010).

28. *Id.*; *see also* NIAAA, Rethinking Drinking: Alcohol and Your Health 4 (2010), available at http://pubs.niaaa.nih.gov/publications/RethinkingDrinking/Rethinking_Drinking.pdf (last visited October 30, 2010).

29. NIAAA, Alcohol Alert No. 62, Alcohol: An Important Women's Health Issue 1 (2004), available at http://pubs.niaaa.nih.gov/publications/aa62/aa62.pdf; *see also* FAQs for the General Public, NIAA, www.niaa.nih.gov/FAQs/General-English/default.htm#women (last visited October 30, 2010).

30. Report of the DGAC on the Dietary Guidelines for Americans, 2010, *supra* note 14 at D7-4.

31. *See* 27 U.S.C. §215(a)(1) (2006).

> audience, that is pregnant women, to define the harms and set their own goals in relation to those harms. While, in other fields within child health, parents do have some discretion (e.g. where I live, parents can exempt their children from supposedly universal vaccination programmes), the mother is presented in fetal health discussions not as a responsible parent but as herself the main source of risk. A second peculiar feature of this campaign is that there is very little room for individualized programmes. The advice given is usually universal; particularly in the United States, but increasingly so in other places as well, there is zero tolerance for drinking while pregnant. . . . [W]omen are to forego *all* drinking during pregnancy, even though no epidemiologist has yet produced figures linking occasional moderate drinking during pregnancy with any negative outcomes.[32] [Emphasis in original.]

Although abstaining from drinking during pregnancy is today almost the universal recommendation, some countries have redefined moderate drinking for pregnant women. For example, the United Kingdom's National Institute for Health and Clinical Excellence in its 2008 clinical guideline, *Antenatal Care: Routine Care for the Healthy Pregnant Woman*, advises:

> Pregnant women and women planning a pregnancy should be advised to avoid drinking alcohol in the first three months of pregnancy if possible because it may be associated with an increased risk of miscarriage. If women choose to drink alcohol during pregnancy, they should be advised to drink no more than one to two U.K. units once or twice a week. . . . Although there is uncertainty regarding a safe level of alcohol consumption in pregnancy, at this level there is no evidence of harm to the unborn baby.[33]

One 125 ml glass of wine is equal to 1.5 UK units.

When consumed, alcohol comes into contact with many different parts of the body. About 20 percent of the alcohol is absorbed in the stomach while the rest of it makes its way to the small intestine. After the alcohol is absorbed, it leaves the body either through the lungs, kidney, or liver.

The following is a brief summary of alcohol's health effects.[34]

---

32. Mariana Valverde, Diseases of the Will: Alcohol and the Dilemmas of Freedom 179-181 (1998). Thomas Babor and his co-authors agree with Valverde that "[t]here is still uncertainty as to the intensity and timing of the alcohol exposure needed to produce any type or degree of fetal impairment." Alcohol: No Ordinary Commodity, *supra* note 12 at 15.

33. National Collaborating Centre for Women's and Children's Health, Antenatal Care: Routine Care for the Healthy Pregnant Woman 99 (2008), available at www.nice.org.uk/nicemedia/live/11947/40145/40145.pdf (last visited October 30, 2010).

34. This list is from Alcohol: No Ordinary Commodity, *supra* note 12 at 49. As the authors note,

> [c]onditions are listed only where a causal impact of alcohol on incidence has been established [citations omitted]. Effects are adverse except as noted. Alcohol also plays a causal role in many less common causes of illness and death. Many more conditions have associations with alcohol, such as most neuropsychiatric diseases, but causality has not been established according to standard criteria.

The footnotes in the table are not in the original; they present additional information and explanations.

1. Cancers: head and neck cancers, liver cancer, colorectal cancers, female breast cancer;[35]
2. Neuropsychiatric conditions: alcohol dependence syndrome, alcohol abuse, depression;
3. Diabetes (protective and adverse effects);[36]
4. Cardiovascular conditions: ischaemic heart disease, hypertensive disease, cerebrovascular disease (protective and adverse effects for all cardiovascular conditions);
5. Gastrointestinal conditions: liver cirrhosis, pancreatitis;
6. Infectious diseases: tuberculosis, pneumonia;[37]
7. Maternal and perinatal conditions: low birth weight, fetal alcohol syndrome;
8. Acute toxic effects: alcohol poisoning;
9. Accidents: road and other transport injuries, falls, drowning and burning injuries, occupational and machine injuries;
10. Self-inflicted injuries: suicide;
11. Violent deaths: assault injuries.

There are other deleterious health conditions not listed above for which alcohol is the cause or a contributor. For example, heavy consumption of alcoholic beverages can interfere with the way the body digests and absorbs nutrients from food. Alcohol also can influence the effectiveness of various medications. Alcohol can affect the extent to which the drug reaches its site of action. Sometimes alcohol will compete with the drug for the same set of metabolizing enzymes, which can prolong the amount of time that the drug is activated in the body and thus increase the person's risk of experiencing the harmful side effects of the drug. Alcohol also can do the opposite: activate drug-metabolizing enzymes, which decreases the effectiveness of the drug.

Although alcoholic beverage consumption over time can lead to the development of a variety of health problems, it also can have protective effects for certain health conditions. Perhaps the most celebrated beneficial health effect

---

35. There may be a protective effect of alcohol consumption and, in particular, wine consumption, on cancer. Serge Renaud reports that resveratrol "presents antioxidant and anti-inflammatory activities, inhibits platelet aggregation and cellular events associated with cancer i.e. initiation, promotion and progression [citation omitted]." Serge Renaud, Dominique Lanzmann-Petithory, René Gueguen & Pascale Conard, Alcohol and Mortality from All Causes, 37 Biological Research 183, 185 (2004).

36. The DGAC reports that

> results from comprehensive reviews and meta-analyses suggest that risk of diabetes is significantly lower among moderate drinkers than abstainers. . . . Importantly, compared with moderate consumption, heavy consumption (more than 3 drinks/day) was associated with up to 43 percent increased incidence of T2D (Type 2 Diabetes). Despite the benefit of alcohol when consumed in moderation, when consumed in excess, alcohol can cause serious metabolic disturbances and increase diabetes risk.

Report of the DGAC on the Dietary Guidelines for Americans, 2010, *supra* note 14 at D7-2 and D7-3.

37. Alcohol consumption, particularly heavy drinking, can result in infectious diseases by compromising the immune system. Charles Parry, Jürgen Rehm, Vladimir Poznyak & Robin Room, Alcohol and Infectious Diseases: An Overlooked Causal Linkage? 104 Addiction 331 (2009).

of alcohol is the correlation between moderate alcohol consumption and lower risk of coronary heart disease (CHD), which accounts for 25 percent of total mortality in the United States.[38] This positive health effect was popularized in 1991, when CBS aired its 60 Minutes segment on the "French Paradox." The program revealed that the French have a lower rate of heart disease than Americans, even when controlling for factors such as diet, exercise, and lifestyle choices, and suggested that this is the result of moderate consumption of red wine.[39]

Since that time, studies have revealed that moderate drinkers have rates of CHD-related mortality that are 20 to 40 percent lower than those of abstainers.[40] There are different theories about how alcohol works to lower the risk of CHD. Alcohol may protect the heart by preventing the constriction of the coronary arteries.[41] Moderate alcohol consumption can reduce plaque deposits in the arteries by raising high-density cholesterol (HDL) and lowering low-density cholesterol (LDL), both of which effects can promote heart health.[42] Alcohol also prevents blood clots by thinning the blood.[43]

These beneficial effects do not continue with heavy drinking. Excessive consumption actually increases the risk of other heart-related conditions such as cardiomyopathy, arrhythmias, hemorrhagic stroke, and hypertension.[44]

Moderate consumption of alcoholic beverages also improves all-cause mortality among those aged 45 or more, as Figure 9-1 reveals. This fact is largely, but not exclusively, due to the beneficial effects of alcohol on CHD. Emerging population-based data also suggest that wine, in particular, protects against dementia and some types of cancer.[45] Even risk factors such as high cholesterol and smoking do not impede the protective effect of moderate drinking on all-cause mortality among this age cohort.[46]

---

38. NIAAA, Alcohol Alert No. 45, Alcohol and Coronary Heart Disease (1999), available at http://pubs.niaaa.nih.gov/publications/aa45.htm (last visited October 30, 2010).

39. Richard Mendelson, From Demon to Darling: A Legal History of Wine in America 169 (2009).

40. A. L. Klatsky, Epidemiology of Coronary Heart Disease—Influence of Alcohol, 18 Alcoholism: Clinical and Experimental Research 88, 90-91 (1994); *see also* M. Bobak & M. Marmot, Wine and Heart Disease: A Statistical Approach in Wine: A Scientific Exploration 103 (Merton Sandler & Roger Pinder eds., 2003) ("There is clear evidence that mortality from coronary heart disease is some 20–30% lower among moderate regular drinkers compared with non-drinkers"); Serge Renaud, M. H. Criqui, G. Farchi et al., Alcohol Drinking and Coronary Heart Disease in Health Issues Related to Alcohol Consumption 81-123 (Verschuren, P.M. ed. 1993).

41. E. E. Emeson, V. Manaves, T. Singer et al., Chronic Alcohol Feeding Inhibits Atherogenesis in C57BL/6 Hyperlipidemic Mice, 147 American Journal of Pathology 1749 (1995).

42. Paying the Tab, *supra* note 19 at 110.

43. *Id.* at 110-111.

44. Maureen Storey & Richard Forshee, The Alcohol Dietary Guideline: The Way Forward, 43 Nutrition Today 92 (2008).

45. Wine: A Scientific Exploration, at xv (Merton Sandler & Roger Pinder eds., 2003).

46. Alcohol and Mortality from All Causes, *supra* note 35 at 187.

Figure 9-1
Average daily alcohol consumption and risk of all-cause mortality (females and males aged ≥ 45 years).[47]

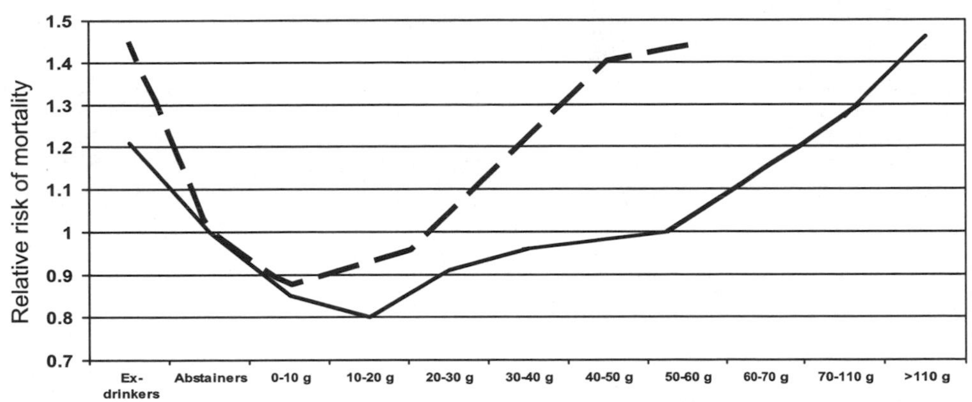

Average daily alcohol consumption
(1 standard drink = 13.7 grams of pure alcohol)

Male
Female

Under the age of 45, the relationship between average daily alcohol consumption and all-cause mortality is linear, as shown in Figure 9-2.

Research by French epidemiologist and nutritionist Serge Renaud, who first espoused the French Paradox, suggests that the health benefits derived from moderate alcohol consumption vary with the type of alcoholic beverage consumed. Typically, alcohol researchers do not address the differences among wine, beer, and spirits; they only measure absolute alcohol (ethanol). This overlooks important differences in composition and manner of ingestion among the different alcoholic beverages. Wine contains compounds such as polyphenols that have been shown to have antioxidant properties and may protect the lining of blood vessels in the heart. One polyphenolic compound in red wine, resveratrol, may help to prevent damage to blood vessels, reduce LDL cholesterol and inflammation, and prevent blood clots. As Dr. Ellison has stated, "Demonstrated have been the effects of wine polyphenolic compounds on coagulation, fibrinolysis, endothelial function, lipid oxidation, glucose metabolism, inflammation, and ventricular function."[48]

---

47. Jürgen Rehm, Elisabeth Gutjahr & Gerhard Gmel, Alcohol and All-Cause Mortality: A Pooled Analysis, 28 Contemporary Drug Problems 337, 350-351 (2001); *see also* Alcohol: No Ordinary Commodity, *supra* note 12 at 56; Charles Holahan, Kathleen Schutte, Penny Brennan, Carole Holahan, Bernice Moos & Rudolf Moos, Late-Life Alcohol Consumption and 20-Year Mortality, 34 Alcoholism: Clinical and Experimental Research 1961 (2010).

48. R. Curtis Ellison, Introduction to Symposium, in Health Risks and Benefits of Moderate Alcohol Consumption: Proceedings of an International Symposium, published in 17 Supplement to Annals of Epidemiology, S1, S1 (2007).

Figure 9-2
Average daily alcohol consumption and risk of all-cause mortality (males aged 45 years).[49]

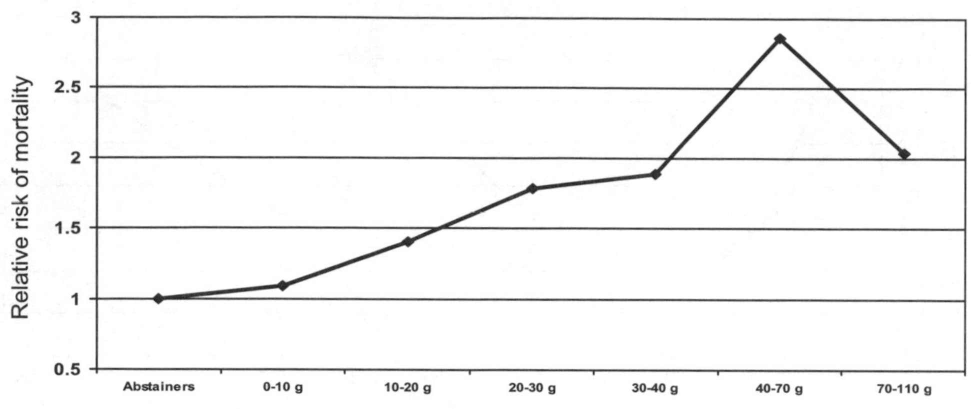

Average daily alcohol consumption
(1 standard drink = 13.7 grams of pure alcohol)

Wine also tends to be consumed with food, which may enhance its beneficial health effects.[50] Creina Stockley, a clinical pharmacologist in Australia, says the following about wine consumed with food:

> This pattern of wine consumption attenuates the blood alcohol concentration achieved, prolongs any short-term plasma anti-oxidative and anti-thrombotic effects, promotes any long-term effects, and prevents any rebound effects of the ethanol and phenolic components of the beverage. Populations that regularly consume a moderate amount of alcohol with a meal, such as those of the Mediterranean countries, and of central and southern France, have a significantly lower risk of cardiovascular disease.[51] [Citations omitted.]

---

49. Jürgen Rehm, Elisabeth Gutjahr & Gerhard Gmel, Alcohol and All-Cause Mortality: A Pooled Analysis, 28 Contemporary Drug Problems 337, 350-351 (2001); *see also* Alcohol: No Ordinary Commodity, *supra* note 12 at 56.

50. Jürgen Rehm et al. report that the consumption of any alcoholic beverage—beer, wine, or spirits—with meals results in a lower risk of coronary heart disease than the consumption of the same alcoholic beverage without meals. Jürgen Rehm et al., Alcohol Use in Comparative Quantification of Health Risks: Global and Regional Burden of Disease Attributable to Selected Major Risk Factors, vol.1, 1020-1021 (Majid Ezzati et al. eds., 2004).

51. Creina Stockley, Evidence of the Specific Benefits of Wine Consumption on Human Health—An Update on the Cardiovascular and Other Physiological Mechanisms, 446 The Australian and New Zealand Grapegrower and Winemaker 72, 77 (2001), available at www.aim-digest.com/gateway/pages/moderate/articles/evidence.htm (last visited October 30, 2010). *See also* Serge Renauc & Michel de Loregeril, Wine, Alcohol, Platelets, and the French Paradox for Coronary Heart Disease, 339 The Lancet 1523, 1525 (1992) (suggesting that "because wine is mostly consumed during meals it is absorbed slowly, and thus has a prolonged protective effect on, for example, blood platelets at a time when they are under the influence of alimentary lipids known to increase their reactivity").

Some researchers contend that the increased health benefits derived from wine are not because of any substance found in wine but because wine drinkers in general tend to live healthier lifestyles than beer or spirits drinkers.[52] Other researchers believe that there is absolutely no difference between wine, beer, and spirits in terms of health effects; they point to studies that show that the consumption of any alcoholic beverage, not just wine, provides some protection against heart disease.[53]

B. PUBLIC SAFETY

While moderate use of alcoholic beverages can have social benefits, harmful use has adverse social consequences, including disorderly conduct, threats to public safety through crime, workplace problems, accidental injuries, other high-risk activities associated with drinking, and intentional self-harm. With respect to all these adverse consequences, heavy drinkers and chronic abusers are at significantly higher risk than moderate drinkers.[54] Yet epidemiological evidence reveals that acute intoxication among all drinkers, both moderate and heavy, is the main cause of alcohol-related injury. That is, the number of heavy-drinking occasions is a stronger predictor of injury than the average level of consumption.[55] As Ingeborg Rossow, et al., write in *Mapping the Social Consequences of Alcohol Consumption*,

> most of the accidents and injuries in established market economies are caused by unusually light to moderate drinkers who were exposed to heavy drinking occasions. Thus, it has been argued that the prevention paradox applies here, namely that preventive measures to reduce the occurrence of accidents and suicidal behavior due to alcohol should take the form of population-based strategies aimed at more moderate drinkers, who contribute the most to alcohol-related accidents and intentional injury.[56]

The fact that alcohol-related harm is "distributed on a continuum throughout the drinking population and is certainly not limited to the small number of consistently heavy drinkers,"[57] however, does not necessitate a population-based strategy to reduce harm. As discussed in more detail in the

---

52. Wine: A Scientific Explanation, supra note 45 at 103: Paying the Tab, *supra* note 19 at 114.

53. Epidemiology of Coronary Heart Disease—Influence of Alcohol, *supra* note 40 at 92; *see also* Wine: A Scientific Explanation, *supra* note 45 at 103; Paying the Tab, *supra* note 19 at 114.

54. Ingeborg Rossow, Kai Pernanen & Jürgen Rehm, Accidents, Suicide and Violence, in Mapping the Social Consequences of Alcohol Consumption 105 (Harald Klingermann & Gerhard Gmel eds., 2001).

55. Jürgen Rehm, Mary Jane Ashley, Robin Room, Eric Single, Susan Bondy, Roberta Ference & Norman Giesbrecht, On the Emerging Paradigm of Drinking Patterns and Their Social and Health Consequences, 91 Addiction 1615, 1619 (1996).

56. Accidents, Suicide and Violence, *supra* note 54 at 105. The prevention paradox exists when a large number of people at small risk contribute more cases of a particular disease outcome than a small number of people at large risk. The paradox has been used to justify population-based approaches to prevention in the case of alcohol, tobacco, obesity, and injury.

57. Tim Stockwell, Eric Single, David Hawks & Jürgen Rehm, Sharpening the Focus of Alcohol Policy from Aggregate Consumption to Harm and Risk Reduction, 5 Addiction Research 1, 4 (1997).

following section, reducing the frequency of heavy drinking rather than reducing overall alcohol consumption may be more prudent and more acceptable to the general public.

C. REGULATIONS AND INTERVENTIONS

Given the array of problems caused by heavy drinking, various policies have been adopted over time to keep the health and social harms to a minimum. This is generally known as "harm reduction," "harm minimization," or the "public health perspective." These alcohol policy measures generally fall into the following 6 categories: access and availability; taxation and pricing; altering the drinking context; drinking and driving; advertising and marketing; and prevention, specifically including education and treatment. Each of these approaches is discussed in turn below.

1. ACCESS AND AVAILABILITY

Perhaps the most heavily relied-upon alcohol control policy is to limit the availability of and access to alcoholic beverages. Supply-side controls can take many forms, from outright prohibition, as occurred (with certain exceptions) during National Prohibition, to government alcohol monopolies such as those that exist today in the 18 control states. As we learned during National Prohibition, a total ban may not be sustainable because of its numerous adverse side effects, including illegal production (moonshining), illegal trade (bootlegging), and a widespread disrespect for the law. By the end of that 13-year period, even John D. Rockefeller, oil magnate, philanthropist, and ardent prohibitionist, had become disillusioned with the "noble experiment."

After studying all the alcohol control systems around the world, Rockefeller proposed that the states establish alcohol monopolies after Repeal. He wrote, "[O]nly as the profit motive is eliminated is there any hope of controlling the liquor traffic in the interest of a decent society. To approach the problem from any other angle is only to tinker with it and to insure failure."[58] Rockefeller believed, as did his researchers Raymond Fosdick and Albert Scott, that the profit motive makes inevitable the stimulation of sales and overconsumption. The "authority plan," which they recommended and which Rockefeller endorsed, would establish a public monopoly in each state over the wholesale and/or retail sale of alcoholic beverages, particularly those with higher alcoholic strength sold for off-premise consumption.[59] The state authority plan, they said, would achieve a social, rather than a profit, objective by curtailing the consumption of alcoholic beverages through price controls,

58. Raymond Fosdick & Albert Scott, Toward Liquor Control, at x (1933).

59. *Id.* at 64. Off-premise consumption refers to alcoholic beverages that are sold in closed containers at a package store (also known as an off-sale premise) and are consumed away from the licensed premise. On-premise or on-sale establishments such as restaurants and bars sell and serve alcoholic beverages for consumption at the licensed premise.

advertising restrictions, educational campaigns, elimination of the saloon, and establishment of carefully located and designed package stores, known today as state stores, run by salaried government employees.

Whether the individual states after Repeal adopted a government monopoly or a licensing system for the private sector, they were able to, and did, restrict the supply of alcoholic beverages through controls on the location and density of on-sale and off-sale premises, the days and hours of sale, and the minimum legal drinking age. Typically, states limit the density of retail outlets by population or geographic area. Certain locations may be prohibited—for example, if they are too close to churches or schools. In the college setting, for example, the numbers of package stores and other sales outlets may be restricted directly by placing a limit on their density within a certain radius of campus.[60] Sometimes these controls are part of the state's alcoholic beverage control laws, or they may be included in state or local land use laws.

All states limit the days and hours during which alcoholic beverages may be sold. The so-called blue laws,[61] originally designed to enforce religious standards, generally prohibit the off-premise sale of alcohol on Sundays. These same states strictly control store hours. For example, in Connecticut, the first state to adopt a blue law, package stores must close by 9:00 p.m. Monday through Saturday. Bars and restaurants can remain open until 1:00 a.m. Sunday through Thursday, and until 2:00 a.m. Friday and Saturday nights.

States, in the exercise of their Twenty-first Amendment rights, also decide which types of retail outlets can sell alcoholic beverages. Some states allow alcoholic beverage sales at drugstores, convenience stores, gas stations, grocery stores, fast food and other restaurants, and sports stadiums. Other states prohibit alcoholic beverage sales at one or more of these locations, or they may specify other products such as food or non-alcoholic beverages that may, may not, or must be sold there.

States may decide to apply specific control measures to specific alcoholic beverages, depending on their alcoholic strength and susceptibility to abuse. For example, state stores in some control states sell only distilled spirits, leaving lower-strength wines and beers to be sold at licensed establishments, including convenience stores and grocery stores. Many state and local jurisdictions through land use laws restrict, in some or all areas, the sale of single bottles of beer, spirits in bottles of one-half pint or less, and more recently, caffeinated alcoholic beverages (alcohol energy drinks).[62]

Another means of restricting access to alcoholic beverages is through the minimum legal drinking age. This is undeniably an effective control mechanism. Today, all 50 states have established 21 as the minimum drinking age,

---

60. Task Force of the NIAAAA, A Call to Action Changing the Culture of Drinking at U.S. Colleges 19 (2002), available at http://www.collegedrinkingprevention.gov/media/TaskForce Report.pdf (last visited October 30, 2010).

61. "Blue laws" are defined by the Oxford English Dictionary as "severe Puritanic laws said to have been enacted last century at New Haven, Connecticut." 2 Oxford English Dictionary 325 (2d ed. 1989), available at http://dictionary.oed.com (s.v. blue) (last visited October 30, 2010).

62. For a review of land use laws related to alcoholic beverages, *see* Chapter 7.

although they vary in terms of the exceptions granted for home consumption or for religious, medical, or educational purposes. In the 1970s and early 1980s, following the adoption of the Twenty-sixth Amendment to the U.S. Constitution,[63] most states adopted 18 or 19 as the minimum drinking age. They accepted the logic that if 18-year-olds can vote and serve in the military, they are old enough to drink alcoholic beverages. In 1982, President Ronald Reagan appointed the Commission on Drunk Driving that recommended, among other things, the establishment of 21 as the national minimum drinking age.[64] This was achieved by withholding federal highway funds from any state that failed to adopt the recommended minimum drinking age. By 1988, all states had done so.

According to Thomas Babor and his co-authors, "[a] comprehensive review [citation omitted] based on all published studies on legal drinking published between 1960 and 2000 (a total of 135 documents) concluded that increasing the legal age for purchase and consumption of alcohol to 21 years is the most effective strategy for reducing drinking and drinking problems among high-school students, college students, and other youth, compared to a wide range of other programmes and efforts."[65]

Yet this has not stopped 135 university presidents and chancellors from joining the Amethyst Initiative—Rethink the Drinking Age, which was launched in July 2008. Their official statement proclaims, "Twenty-one is not working," particularly on college campuses where underage drinkers mingle with students of legal age.[66] They point to an epidemic of binge drinking on college campuses and heavy-drinking norms that are deeply ingrained in the college culture (involving, for instance, fraternities and sororities, athletes, and alumni events). They call for a national debate on the minimum drinking age and its effects.

The specific proposals for lowering the minimum legal drinking age vary widely, including allowing 18- to 20-year-olds to obtain a drinking license after they have completed a mandatory course on alcohol education; allowing them to drink only beer that is 3.2 percent alcohol by volume or less; establishing different purchase ages for beer, wine, and spirits; or even adopting different rules for on-premise and off-premise alcohol purchase and consumption.[67] In response to the Amethyst Initiative, Dr. David Jernigan of the John Hopkins Bloomberg School of Public Health, a long-time alcohol policy advocate, strikes a note of caution. While acknowledging that college administrators have a major problem enforcing the alcohol laws on their campuses, he states, "If this debate they're calling for can lead to more widespread use of solutions that are based in science, then I'm all for the debate. But if it leads us down the

63. Section 1 of the Twenty-sixth Amendment, adopted in 1971, reads, "The right of citizens of the United States, who are eighteen years of age or older, to vote shall not be denied or abridged by the United States or by any State on account of age."

64. Presidential Commission on Drunk Driving: Final Report 10 (1983).

65. Alcohol: No Ordinary Commodity, *supra* note 12 at 140.

66. Statement, Amethyst Initiative: Rethink the Drinking Age, www.amethystinitiative.org (last visited October 30, 2010).

67. Why Sign?, Amethyst Initiative: Rethink the Drinking Age, www.amethystinitiative.org (last visited October 30, 2010).

road to increasing access to alcohol for a group that is hugely at risk of adverse consequences from drinking, then I think it's all a big mistake."[68]

The other supply-side measures discussed in this section have not been as effective as the minimum drinking age in preventing harm, nor are they as widely supported. Certainly, these laws reduce total alcohol consumption. For example, there is strong evidence that state retail monopolies decrease alcohol consumption levels.[69] Between 1997 and 2007, the average annual alcohol consumption in the 18 control states was around 0.65 gallons per capita for people over the age of 14.[70] License states had a higher consumption rate of 0.76 gallons during the same period.[71]

There also is evidence that the elimination of state monopolies leads to increased total annual alcohol consumption. The Alcohol Research Group, in a publication prepared for the National Association of Beverage Control Authorities (NABCA) entitled *Alcohol Control Systems and the Potential Effects of Privatization*, concludes that "privatization results in higher outlet density, greater physical availability, longer and later hours of sale and new elements in the marketing and sales process, such as a greater commercial orientation towards alcohol sales and additional economic vested interests."[72]

There also are data confirming that total alcohol consumption is directly related to adverse health and social consequences. According to Alexander Wagenaar, epidemiologist at the University of Florida's Department of Epidemiology and Health Policy Research, "[i]f you make it easier to drink, people drink more. And if people drink more, we have more alcohol-related problems. It's as simple as that."[73]

This platitude notwithstanding, a population-based strategy designed to reduce total alcohol consumption may be ill advised if it unnecessarily and unfairly burdens moderate drinkers, who far outnumber heavy drinkers. One commentator refers to this approach as "draining the ocean to prevent shark

---

68. Mat Edelson, Proof?, The Magazine of the Johns Hopkins Bloomberg School of Public Health, Summer 2009, at 33, available at http://magazine.jhsph.edu/bin/q/l/Features.pdf (last visited October 31, 2010). Many policy analysts contend that lowering the minimum drinking age will only make matters worse from a public health and safety perspective. Instead, they argue, inter alia, for stricter social host and dram shop liability laws, stricter laws against driving under the influence, banning liquor stores and bars within a given distance of college campuses, mandatory alcohol education, and a crackdown on false identification cards.

69. Thomas Babor, Alcohol Policy and the Public Good: As Simple as One, Two, Three?, in From Science to Action? 100 Years Later—Alcohol Policies Revisited 36 (Richard Miller & Harald Klingermann eds., 2004), citing Alexander Wagenaar, & Harold Holder, Changes in Alcohol Consumption Resulting from the Elimination of Retail Wine Monopolies: Results from Five US states, 56 Journal of Studies on Alcohol 566 (1995).

70. Brian Sonntag, Washington State Auditor, Report No. 1002726, State Government Performance Review: Opportunities for Washington 32 (2010), available at http://www.sao.wa.gov/AuditReports/AuditReportFiles/ar1002726.pdf (last visited October 26, 2010).

71. *Id.*

72. Alcohol Research Group, Alcohol Control Systems and the Potential Effects of Privatization 7 (2009). *See, e.g.,* Changes in Alcohol Consumption Resulting from the Elimination of Retail Wine Monoploies: Results from Five U.S. States, *supra* note 69 at 569-572.

73. Studies Find State Control of Alcohol Protects Public Health, Marin Institute, www.marininstitute.org/site/index.php?option=com_content&view=article&id=538:studies-find-state-control-of-alcohol-good-for-the-publics-health&catid=38&itemid=9 (last visited October 30, 2010).

attacks."[74] Instead, harm reduction might focus on modifying heavy-drinking patterns (chronic or episodic),[75] altering the environments that promote heavy drinking,[76] and promoting beneficial drinking patterns in society. This may be more effective and more politically feasible than the across-the-board alcohol reduction approach.

2. TAXATION AND PRICING

The WHO has asserted that "[p]rice is an important determinant of alcohol consumption and, in many contexts, of the extent of alcohol-related problems."[77] Professor Philip Cook, in *Paying the Tab: The Costs and Benefits of Alcohol Control*, is more direct.

> Quite simply, alcohol taxation and other measures that increase the price of ethanol are effective in promoting public health and safety. Higher prices are conducive to lower rates of underage drinking, traffic fatalities, and sexually transmitted disease. There is less direct evidence on the effects of higher prices on the prevalence of chronic excess drinking and related medical conditions, but the indirect evidence is compelling on that score as well.[78]

Whether price intervention is good public policy depends on how sensitive consumers are to price changes and whether the reduced consumption has a corresponding effect on adverse health and social consequences. Price sensitivity is known as the price elasticity of demand. It is measured as the percentage change in consumption resulting from a 1 percent change in price. For example, a price elasticity of –0.49 for wine, which is a reasonable estimate, means that a 10 percent price increase will cause just under a 5 percent decline in the volume consumed.[79] Wine demand, we would say, is relatively inelastic. This makes intuitive sense because of the number of ways, other than buying

74. Martin Plant, Harm Minimization, in Mapping the Social Consequences of Alcohol, *supra* note 54 at 146.

75. On the Emerging Paradigm of Drinking Patterns and Their Social and Health Consequences, *supra* note 55 at 1619.

76. The Alcohol Research Group's analyses of the NIAAA's National Epidemiologic Survey on Alcohol and Related Conditions indicate that while drinking in bars, taverns, and cocktail lounges accounted for 24 percent of the overall volume reported in 6 drinking contexts, these "on premise" bar settings accounted for 37 percent of the hazardous drinking (5 or more drinks per day). Conversely, restaurants accounted for 14 percent of the total volume but only 3 percent of the volume attributable to hazardous amounts. Thomas Greenfield, Alcohol Policy, presented at the Alcohol and Alcohol Actions (Psychosocial) Lecture Series, Annual Meeting of the Research Society on Alcoholism (June 23-24, 2006), available at http://www.rsalectures.com/pdf/greenfield.doc. Excessive drinking also tends to occur at private parties and in public places such as parking lots and street corners. Patricia McDaniel & Thomas Greenfield, Somewhere between the Bars and Home: Drinking Locations and Drinking Norms among Women and Men in the United States, presented at the 129th Annual Meeting of the American Public Health Association (Oct. 21-25, 2001), abstract available at http://apha.confex.com/apha/129am/techprogram/paper_24218.htm.

77. World Health Organization, Strategies to Reduce the Harmful Use of Alcohol, Document A61/13 4 (March 2008).

78. Paying the Tab, *supra* note 19 at 167.

79. *See* Table 5.2 in Paying the Tab, *supra* note 19 at 72; cf. Table 8.1 in Alcohol: No Ordinary Commodity, *supra* note 12 at 113 (wine elasticities calculated by 3 separate researchers at -0.77, -0.70 and -0.69).

less, in which consumers can compensate for price increases such as drinking more at home, drinking cheaper brands, or substituting other alcoholic beverages. If the price rise is too steep, consumers may turn to illegal alcoholic beverages (adulterated, counterfeit, etc.), as they did during Prohibition.

There have not been many studies of price elasticities for particular groups of drinkers, but it is important in adopting alcohol policies to know which drinkers are affected by a price increase and by how much. One research group found that moderate drinkers are more price sensitive than heavy drinkers, which means that they are affected the most by price increases.[80] If that is correct, the pricing approach may not be equitable or efficient.

In the case of youth, the evidence is more conflicting: they are sensitive to alcoholic beverage prices, more so than adults,[81] but they also engage in substitute behavior such as drinking at home and buying less expensive alcoholic beverages.[82] The Committee on Developing a Strategy to Reduce and Prevent Underage Drinking, created by the National Research Council and the Institute of Medicine (NRC/IOM), concluded in 2004 that higher alcoholic beverage prices achieved by higher excise taxes "are potentially important instruments for preventing underage drinking and its harmful consequences and for generating revenue to fund a broad prevention strategy."[83]

Because of the diversity of research results, the policy prescriptions about alcohol taxation and pricing vary. For example, Godfrey Robson, senior consultant at the International Center for Alcohol Policies, argues that "taxes and price controls are regressive upon responsible consumers while failing to achieve their goal of reducing harm."[84] That is, these measures only distinguish between consumers and abstainers, not between moderate and heavy drinkers. There are other possible disadvantages of taxes as an alcohol control measure. Typically, taxes are imposed for revenue generation, not for prevention. Taxes also may not translate directly into higher prices because of the intervening complex market decisions of producers, wholesalers, and retailers. Finally, high taxes can have unintended negative consequences such as illicit production, adulteration, counterfeiting, and smuggling.

By contrast, Dr. Babor and his co-authors in *Alcohol: No Ordinary Commodity* conclude that "[a]lcohol taxes are thus an attractive instrument of alcohol policy, as they can be used both to generate direct revenue for the state and to reduce alcohol-related harms. Even setting aside their contribution to government revenue, they are among the most cost-effective ways for a government to reduce alcohol-related harm. . . ."[85] The CDC Task Force on Community Preventive Services agrees, finding "strong evidence that raising alcohol

80. Willard Manning & L. Blumberg, The Demand for Alcohol: The Differential Response to Price, 14 J of Health Economics 123 (1995).

81. Reducing Underage Drinking: A Collective Responsibility 243 (Richard Bonnie & Mary Ellen O'Connell eds., 2004).

82. Godfrey Robinson, Pricing Beverage Alcohol, in Working Together to Reduce Harmful Drinking 100-101 (Marcus Grant & Mark Leverton eds., 2010).

83. Reducing Underage Drinking: A Collective Responsibility, *supra* note 81 at 244.

84. *Id.*

85. Alcohol: No Ordinary Commodity, *supra* note 12 at 125.

taxes is an effective strategy for reducing excessive alcohol consumption and related harms."[86]

In terms of the specific measures used to raise prices, the most common is the state, federal, or local excise tax on alcoholic beverages.[87] Because the tax is applied to products that some consider as vices, such as tobacco and gambling, it often is referred to as a "sin tax." Excise taxes are paid by the manufacturer or wholesaler rather than the retailer and are based on the volume of the product, not its value. The amount of excise tax varies depending on the type of alcoholic beverage, with the highest rates imposed on the highest-strength beverages—distilled spirits.[88]

Many policy analysts note that the United States has failed to increase alcoholic beverage excise tax levels to keep pace with inflation. Indeed, the last federal excise tax increase on beer, wine, or spirits was in 1991. This has led to many proposals to index the federal alcoholic beverage excise taxes to inflation, but no such proposal has been adopted.

The excise tax rates on beer, wine, and spirits also are not proportional to their respective levels of absolute alcohol. Specifically, the tax on spirits is far higher than on other alcoholic beverages. This was done purposefully after Repeal to dissuade the consumption of "ardent spirits" in favor of lower-alcohol fermented beverages. In fact, there was a recommended ratio: the excise tax on table wines was one-twentieth of the spirits tax, and the tax on fortified wines was one-tenth of the spirits rate.[89] Not surprisingly, distillers, in particular, want to eliminate this tax discrimination against spirits, but that proposal has had no traction in Congress.

In addition to imposing excise taxes, many states directly or indirectly regulate wine prices. State monopolies can set prices by administrative fiat. License states influence alcoholic beverage prices through a variety of mechanisms, including mandatory markups, impact fees to pay for alcohol-related externalities (health and social services, criminal justice, etc.), minimum prices, resale price maintenance, and price postings.[90] From a policy perspective, not all of these measures have similar effects. Minimum prices, for example, are thought to dampen heavy drinking, while imposing only minimally on moderate wine drinkers. Dr. Chris Record and Professor Chris Day describe the advantages of minimum alcohol pricing in the United Kingdom as follows:

> The current policy of low alcohol prices means that responsible drinkers are subsidi[z]ing the behavior of the 25% of the population who are drinking at

86. Randy lder et al., The Effectiveness of Tax Policy Interventions for Reducing Excessive Alcohol Consumption and Related Harms, 38 American Journal of Preventative Medicine 217, 226 (2010).

87. Environmental Influences on Young Adult Drinking, NIAAA, http://pubs.niaaa.nih.gov/publications/arh284/230-235.htm (last visited April 21, 2010).

88. The excise tax on distilled spirits is disproportionally high compared to beer and wine in relationship to their respective alcoholic strength. Also, Champagne, as a luxury product, is subject to a disproportionately high excise tax.

89. From Demon to Darling, *supra* note 39 at 229 n.10.

90. Price postings on retail prices are equivalent to resale price maintenance because they prevent retailers from lowering their prices below posted levels, although the prices typically can be changed monthly or quarterly.

> hazardous or harmful levels. The introduction of a 50p/unit minimum price would mean that this sector would be selectively targeted and would pay more for the alcohol they consume thus removing the subsidy they are currently enjoying. Alcohol consumption in this group is therefore likely to fall with substantial advantages to public health, law and order.[91]

The states do not have free reign in selecting alcoholic beverage price controls because some of the measures are unlawful. Generally speaking, states increase alcoholic beverage prices in order to decrease demand and promote temperance. Although these are valid goals under the Twenty-first Amendment, state laws may violate federal or state antitrust laws. For example, state fair-trade laws require manufacturers to file fair-trade contracts with the state, including the prices of all their brands; no wholesaler can sell these products to a retailer at prices other than those stated in the contracts. In the 1980 case of *California Retail Liquor Dealers Ass'n v. Midcal Aluminum*, the U.S. Supreme Court invalidated this form of resale price maintenance as a per se violation of the federal Sherman Antitrust Act (Sherman Act).[92] The Supreme Court specifically rejected California's argument that its price-setting program was saved by the Twenty-first Amendment. "The national policy in favor of competition," Justice Lewis Powell wrote, "cannot be thwarted by casting such a gauzy cloak of state involvement over what is essentially a private price-fixing arrangement.[93] *Midcal Aluminum* stood as the law of the land until 2007, when the court, in the case of *Leegin Creative Leather Products v. PSKS, Inc.*, reversed course, holding that resale price maintenance is no longer per se illegal and is to be judged under the so-called rule of reason.[94]

Similarly, "post and hold" pricing provisions have been invalidated by the courts, most recently in the state of Washington. In *Costco Wholesale Corp. v. Maleng*, the Ninth Circuit Court of Appeals invalidated the requirement that wholesalers in that state file with the Washington State Liquor Control Board a listing of all their wholesale prices.[95] Once the prices are posted, they are made public, and the posted prices must be held constant for at least 30 days. The court found the post and hold scheme to be a per se violation of the Sherman Act. While "each wholesaler is only required to adhere to its own posted price and is not compelled to follow others' pricing decisions, the logical result of the restraints is a less uncertain market, a market more conducive to collusive and stabilized pricing, and hence a less competitive market."[96] The restraint, the court concluded, is "highly likely to facilitate horizontal collusion among market participants."[97]

---

91. Chris Record & Chris Day, Britain's Alcohol Market: How Minimum Alcohol Prices Could Stop Moderate Drinkers Subsidizing Those Drinking at Hazardous and Harmful Levels, 9 Clinical Medicine 421, 425 (2009).
92. 445 U.S. 97 (1980); Sherman Antitrust Act, 15 U.S.C. §§1-7 (2006) (original version at ch. 647, 26 Stat. 209 (1890)).
93. *Cal. Retail Liquor Dealers Ass'n.*, 445 U.S. at 106.
94. 551 U.S. 877 (2007).
95. *Costco Wholesale Corp. v. Maleng*, 522 F.3d 874 (9th Cir. 2008).
96. *Id.* at 894.
97. *Id.* at 896.

The court examined whether the Twenty-first Amendment would bar the application of the Sherman Antitrust Act in that case. While acknowledging that the Twenty-first Amendment confers wide latitude upon the states to regulate the intrastate distribution of alcoholic beverages, especially when the goal is to promote temperance, the court found that there was "little empirical evidence" that post and hold had any effect on the rate of alcohol consumption and therefore the state's interest was entitled to less deference than the federal interest in promoting competition.[98]

Price controls are used by some states for purposes other than the promotion of temperance. For example, some state "price affirmation" laws require manufacturers to affirm that they will sell their products to wholesalers at prices that are no higher than the lowest prices that they charge to wholesalers anywhere else in the United States during a prescribed future period, typically one month. These so-called prospective price affirmation laws ensure that consumers in the state will receive the lowest available alcoholic beverage prices, but these laws also interfere with the manufacturers' ability to change their prices in other states during the time that the price affirmation is in effect. The U.S. Supreme Court in 1986 invalidated New York's prospective price affirmation law in *Brown-Forman Distillers v. N.Y. Liquor Authority*, stating: "While New York may regulate the sale of liquor within its borders, and may seek low prices for its residents, it may not 'project its legislation into [other States] by regulating the price to be paid' for liquor in those States."[99] Because of this extra-territorial effect, the Supreme Court found New York's price affirmation law to be unconstitutional under the Commerce Clause.[100]

3. THE DRINKING CONTEXT

Controlling the context in which drinking occurs is an important way to reduce the negative consequences of intoxication. Responsible beverage service (RBS) is a common approach.[101] RBS requires that servers check the identification of anyone appearing to be under the age of 30. Servers learn how to recognize fake identification cards and driver's licenses. They themselves must be over 21. They also learn how to recognize intoxication, to refuse sales to obviously intoxicated patrons, and to deal with problem patrons to prevent violence.[102]

Although RBS programs are important, their effectiveness is modest. As reported in *Alcohol: No Ordinary Commodity*, "[o]verall, the findings suggest that RBS training and house policies [for staff and customers] are likely to have at best a modest effect on alcohol consumption, and this effect will depend on the nature of the programme and the consistency of its

98. *Id.* at 903.

99. *Brown-Forman Distillers Corp. v. N.Y. Liquor Auth.*, 476 U.S. 573, 582-583 (1986) (citing *Baldwin v. G.A.F. Seelig, Inc.*, 294 U.S. 511, 521 (1935)).

100. *See, e.g.*, *Brown-Forman Distillers v. N.Y. Liquor Auth.*, 476 U.S. 573 (1986); *Healy v. U.S. Brewers Assn*, 464 U.S. 909 (1983).

101. *See, e.g.*, National Research Council & Institute of Medicine of the National Academies, Reducing Underage Drinking: A Collective Responsibility 7 (Richard J. Bonnie & Mary Ellen O'Connell eds., 2004).

102. *Id.*; Environmental Influences on Young Adult Drinking, *supra* note 87.

implementation."[103] RBS is greatly enhanced by the active enforcement of alcoholic beverage control laws by alcoholic beverage regulatory authorities and local law enforcement officials.[104]

Community groups also play an important role in controlling the drinking context and enhancing public safety. Community approaches to alcohol control are wide ranging. They include educational programs that seek to modify consumer behavior through changes in knowledge and attitudes, and information and environmental approaches that seek to modify behavior through changes in the social and economic systems within a community.[105] Some communities also have lobbied to change the legal environment, for example, by proposing local ordinances that mandate RBS training for all alcoholic beverage licensees, including their managers, servers, and security staff.[106]

Another way in which states can alter the drinking context is to adopt a dram shop law. Dram shop laws authorize legal actions to be brought against establishments that serve alcohol in a willful, wanton, or reckless manner (e.g., to a minor, an obviously intoxicated person, or after hours) if the intoxicated customer inflicts injury or causes property damage to himself or others. More than 40 states have adopted such laws. The laws vary widely. Some states have imposed damage caps, and others allow a "responsible business practices" or contributory negligence defense. The purpose of these laws is twofold: to compensate persons who suffer harm due to the intoxication of another and to incentivize licensed establishments to be responsible when serving alcoholic beverages to patrons.

Some states also recognize dram shop liability as a common law cause of action for negligence.[107] Early common law principles precluded the imposition of liability on liquor servers because of the requirement of proximate cause. Specifically, the owner of the alcoholic beverage premise was not held liable for damages inflicted by the drinker on himself or a third party because the intoxicated person, not the owner or the server, was the proximate cause of the damage. While this remains the rule in several states, most states now impose liability under a dram shop statute or by following more recent judicial precedent that establishes proximate cause on the basis of public policy rather than foreseeability. As one judge noted, "[t]he law endures no injury, from which damage has ensued, without some remedy."[108]

In some states, dram shop liability principles have been expanded to apply to non-commercial servers of alcohol such as social hosts, employers, fraternities, and other non-licensed entities.[109] Social-host liability is important

103. Alcohol: No Ordinary Commodity, *supra* note 12 at 152.

104. Murray Sim, Elizabeth Morgan & Julie Batchelor, The Impact of Enforcement on Intoxication and Alcohol Related Harm 16 (2005), available at www.police.govt.nz/resources/2005/wgtn-city-alcohol-enforcement-report/wgtn-city-alcohol-enforcement-report.pdf.

105. A compendium of case histories of community action to reform local and state alcoholic beverage laws and policies is Case Histories in Alcohol Policy (Joel Streicker ed., 2002).

106. *See, e.g.*, Ventura County Behavioral Health Department, Best Practices in Responsible Alcoholic Beverage Sales and Service Training with Model Ordinance, Commentary and Resources (Apr. 2008).

107. Ronald Beitman, Practitioner's Guide to Liquor Liability Litigation 2-3 (1987).

108. *Id.* at 5 (citing *Harrison v. Berkley*, 32 S.C.L. (1 Strob.) 525, 47 Am. Dec. 578 (1847)).

109. Alcohol: No Ordinary Commodity, *supra* note 12 at 177.

because, in the post-Repeal era, much drinking has moved from the saloon into the home. Today, for example, underage drinking at a home, hotel, or outdoor area is commonplace. For this reason alone, the social availability of alcoholic beverages needs to be addressed along with commercial availability.[110]

Social-host liability laws typically impose liability on non-commercial individuals who serve alcoholic beverages on property they own, lease, or otherwise control, or who provide the location at which alcohol is served to minors or intoxicated adults who, in turn, inflict some harm to person or property.[111] Generally, social-host liability is of 2 types: criminal, which may include fines or imprisonment, and civil, which may include reimbursement to local government for the cost of law enforcement and emergency services. Social-host laws vary significantly from state to state and locality to locality.[112]

There are other important laws that affect the drinking environment, particularly for youth drinking. Examples include the following: keg registration laws that require the purchaser of a specific numbered keg to be identified at the point of purchase; "shoulder tap"[113] and similar prevention programs that target adults who buy alcoholic beverages for minors; restrictions on drinking in public places such as parks, beaches, parking lots, and sports arenas; and laws that criminalize public drunkenness.[114] Additionally, some states control the activities that can accompany drinking in licensed establishments, such as gambling and nude dancing.[115]

The drinking context also includes the social and physical environment of drinking establishments. The environment includes the physical layout of the premises and the availability of various types of entertainment (gambling, topless or nude dancing, recreational activities such as billiards or darts, etc.), security, transportation options, and food and non-alcoholic beverages. Interestingly, the drinking environment may play a greater role in encouraging aggression and violence than either the pharmacological effects of alcohol or the personality traits of the patrons.[116] Murray Sin, Elizabeth Morgan, and Julie Batchelor, authors of *The Impact of Enforcement on Intoxication and Alcohol Related Harm*, write:

> Aspects of the physical environment that are associated with increased aggression within the licensed premises environment include unclean or poorly maintained venues, poor ventilation, inconvenient access to the bar,

110. *Id.* at 143.

111. *Id.*

112. Underage Drinking: Prohibitions against Hosting Underage Drinking Parties, Alcohol Policy Information System, http://www.alcoholpolicy.niaaa.nih.gov/Prohibitions_Against_Hosting_Underage_Drinking_Parties.html (last visited April 27, 2010).

113. Shoulder tap programs involve a minor decoy who solicits adults outside a liquor store to buy alcoholic beverages for the minor decoy. Any person who furnishes alcohol to the minor decoy is arrested. *See, e.g.,* Cal. Bus. & Prof. Code §25658(a).

114. For a discussion on the laws against public drunkenness, *see* Alcohol and Public Policy: Beyond the Shadow of Prohibition 87-89 (Mark Moore & Dean Gerstein eds., 1981).

115. Challenges to the nude dancing laws at licensed alcoholic beverage establishments have been brought under the First Amendment but generally have failed. *See, e.g., California v. LaRue*, 409 U.S. 109 (1972); *N.Y. State Liquor Auth. v. Bellanca*, 452 U.S. 714 (1981).

116. The Impact of Enforcement on Intoxication and Alcohol Related Harm, *supra* note 104 at 11.

inadequate seating, high noise level, crowding, dancing, and pool playing. The availability of food has been associated with reduced risk of aggression.[117]

History provides some excellent examples of how the drinking environment sets the tenor for the activities that occur there. Norman Clark vividly describes a pre-Prohibition saloon in *Deliver Us from Evil: An Interpretation of American Prohibition:*

> What is difficult . . . to remember is that the saloon was more than an altar of fellowship. It was also a place where dirty old men spat on the floor and conspired toward the subversion of public and private moralities, where the fathers of young children floated away a week's wages that could have gone to food, clothing and education. It was a place where addiction enslaved many a man, insulating him from the lifestyle of decency and responsibility by sinking him into a blurred phantasmagoria of whores, drug fiends, pimps, thieves, and gamblers. Such phrases are in part an exercise in literary license, but they evoke images essential to understanding a reality as it was understood by Prohibitionists. To approach that reality is to fix the mind's eye . . . upon a sort of metaphorical slave ship in middle passage, upon the images of sodden drunks, of hideously fat men sucking stale cigars, of toilets fouled with vomit and urine in the haze of alcoholic narcosis, of the blind idiocy of drunken violence. But the license is not mere local color. To dismiss these images as high camp would be to dismiss the absolute seriousness of millions of men . . . and it would be to ignore a crucial issue in two hundred years of American life.[118]

After Repeal, the universal goal was to prevent the return of the saloon. Some states prohibited saloons outright and only allowed restaurants, hotels, and private clubs.[119] Other states required all on-sale establishments to serve food. Still other states did not allow women to be served at a bar or excluded them altogether from the licensed establishment.[120] States also strictly controlled the activities that could accompany drinking.

For several decades after Repeal, the state stores in the monopoly jurisdictions looked more like pharmacies than modern-day liquor stores. The consumer could not even view the bottles to be purchased, having rather to submit an order form for products that would be taken out of the storage room. There were no floor displays, no point-of-sale materials, and no advertising. All of this affected buying and drinking patterns.

Today, many, if not most, of these post-Repeal restrictions have been relaxed. Yet there still are particular settings that pose a high risk for harmful drinking. In *Alcohol: No Ordinary Commodity*, Dr. Babor and his co-authors suggest that by focusing on particular places such as problem bars, problem drinking can be limited without targeting the drinkers themselves.

> [T]he focus on high-risk environments such as commercial drinking establishments has several advantages. First, it can have a broader impact than individual approaches would have on persons who are at high risk, especially

117. *Id.*
118. Norman Clark, Deliver Us from Evil: An Interpretation of American Prohibition 2 (1976).
119. Randolph Childs, Making Repeal Work 146 (1947).
120. *Id.* at 157.

young people and subcultures with risky drinking practices. Second, a variety of approaches can be applied at one time (e.g., training, enforcement, reduction of environmental risk factors). Finally, most approaches targeting high-risk environments are generally perceived as acceptable in most cultures and may be easier to implement than less-accepted prevention strategies such as general alcohol control and tax measures.[121]

4. DRUNK DRIVING

Considerable attention in the United States has been devoted to reducing the occurrence of drinking and driving. These laws are perhaps the most visible and widely discussed of the various alcohol control policies because of the sobering facts about drinking and driving. In 2008, an estimated 12.4 percent, or roughly 30.9 million, of Americans age 12 and older, drove under the influence of alcohol at least once within the previous year.[122] Drinking alcohol is a factor in approximately 2 out of every 5 injury deaths in the United States,[123] and motor vehicle accidents are the number one cause of death in the United States among persons aged 34 and younger.[124] Based on a 2002 study, in 35 percent of those accidents the driver or pedestrian had a blood alcohol content (BAC) greater than the legal limit of 0.08 percent.[125] On average, the BAC among fatally injured drunk drivers was 0.16.[126] The facts are clear and uncontroverted: drunk drivers are more likely to get into serious crashes than sober drivers, and the relative risk increases with the driver's BAC.[127]

Over the past 30 years, state governments, under strong pressure from Mothers against Drunk Driving and Congress, have made considerable strides in reducing the level of drinking and driving. Many of these state laws revolve around BAC standards. In 1968, many states allowed BAC limits of 0.15 percent. In 1983, President Reagan's Commission on Drunk Driving recommended, among other things, lowering the so-called legal limit for drivers to 0.10 percent BAC, establishing 21 as the minimum legal drinking age, and imposing tough sanctions for all drinking and driving violations. Since that time, there has been a deluge of anti-drunk driving laws.

---

121. Alcohol: No Ordinary Commodity, *supra* note 12 at 162-163.

122. Substance Abuse and Mental Health Services Administration: NSDUH Series H-36, HHS Publication No. SMA 09-4434, Results from the 2008 National Survey on Drug Use and Health: National Findings 36 (2009). Among the different age groups, 21- to 25-year-olds are the most likely to drive while intoxicated, with 26.1 percent of people in that age group having driven while intoxicated within the past year; 18- to 20-year-olds have the next highest rate, at 16.7 percent, followed by 7.2 percent of 16- and 17-year-olds. Gender differences also exist as males are more likely to drive under the influence than females.

123. Paying the Tab, *supra* note 19 at 85.

124. Injury Prevention and Control: Motor Safety, Centers for Disease Control and Prevention, www.cdc.gov/motorvehiclesafety (last visited November 28, 2010).

125. *Id.* (citing Ralph Hingson & Michael Winter, Epidemiology and Consequences of Drinking and Driving, 27 Alcohol Research & Health 63 (2003)). The BAC is usually expressed as a percentage representing the volume of alcohol per volume of blood in the body.

126. National Highway Traffic Safety Administration (NHTSA), NHTSA Budget Overview FY 2007, at 25 (2007).

127. Paying the Tab, *supra* note 19 at 89.

Achieving a national standard on the minimum drinking age and BAC limits is no simple feat. Congress succeeded in establishing 21 as the minimum legal drinking age by offering monetary incentives to the states,[128] a practice that was upheld by the U.S. Supreme Court in 1987.[129] Congress subsequently promised supplemental highway grants to those states that lowered the BAC limit to 0.02 percent for persons under the age of 21.[130] By 1998, all the states had adopted that standard. These so-called zero tolerance laws, according to Dr. Christopher Carpenter, resulted in a 13 to 20 percent decrease in heavy drinking (defined as 5 drinks or more at 1 sitting) and in the overall number of drinks consumed in the previous month by males under the age of 21.[131]

In 2000 Congress imposed reductions in highway funding as a penalty on those states that failed to adopt 0.08 percent as the legal limit for adults by 2004.[132] All the states have now adopted that standard.

According to long-time alcohol policy advocate and attorney Jim Mosher, the deterrent effect on drinking and driving requires 3 components: certainty, swiftness, and severity. More specifically, effective deterrence depends on the drunk driver's *perception* that he or she will be caught and then promptly and harshly punished. For this reason, most state laws focus on open and active enforcement, which has made drunk driving one of the most commonly prosecuted offenses in the lower criminal courts.[133]

The success achieved by these strict laws and enforcement has been enhanced by advances in education and treatment. Currently, 32 states have laws requiring individuals convicted of driving under the influence to be assessed for alcohol abuse or dependence and to attend some kind of alcohol treatment program. Treatment programs reduce the probability that the offender will commit a repeat violation.[134]

There is a wide range of drinking and driving laws and policies in the 50 states. The principal legal interventions include the following: (1) administrative per se laws that authorize the state licensing agency to suspend a driver's license administratively if the driver's BAC exceeds a certain level, separate and apart from a court action for "driving under the influence"

---

128. The National Minimum Drinking Age Act of 1984, 23 U.S.C. §158, also called the Federal Uniform Drinking Age Act, required all states to establish 21 as the minimum age for the purchase and public possession of alcoholic beverages. States that did not comply faced a reduction in highway funds under the Federal Highway Aid Act. Pursuant to the provisions of the Drinking Age Act, many states have adopted specific exceptions for underage consumption when a family member consents or is present and for educational, religious, and medical purposes.

129. *South Dakota v. Dole*, 483 U.S. 203 (1987).

130. 23 U.S.C.A. §410 (1991); 23 U.S.C.A. §161 (1994).

131. Christopher Carpenter, How Do Zero Tolerance Drunk Driving Laws Work?, 23 Journal of Health Economics 61, 81 (2004).

132. 23 U.S.C. §163. The law allows the federal government to withhold 2 percent from federal highway funds, starting in 2004, if the state did not comply with the federal mandate. Each subsequent year, until 2007, an additional 2 percent would be withheld from states that had not complied. Therefore, any state that did not adopt legislation to lower the BAC to 0.08 would have 8 percent of the state's federal funding withheld in 2007. See Christopher O'Neill, Legislating under the Influence: Are Federal Highway Incentives Enough to Induce State Legislatures to Pass a 0.08 Blood Alcohol Concentration Standard?, 28 Seton Hall Legislative Journal 415, 416 (2004).

133. James B. Jacobs, Drunk Driving: An American Dilemma, at xviii (1989).

134. Injury Prevention & Control: Motor Vehicle Safety, *supra* note 124.

(DUI); (2) criminal per se laws that make it a crime to operate a motor vehicle at or above a specified BAC; (3) laws prohibiting plea bargaining between a prosecutor and defense counsel that might otherwise reduce a DUI charge to a lesser offense; (4) laws establishing a mandatory sentence of imprisonment or community service for a first or second DUI conviction; (5) open container laws that prohibit open containers of alcohol inside the passenger portion of a motor vehicle; (6) sobriety checkpoints at which drivers are stopped at random and checked for signs of driving under the influence, which may involve breathalyzer tests to measure the driver's BAC; (7) vehicle impoundment laws that authorize seizure and holding of the driver's vehicle; (8) ignition interlock systems, which are essentially breathalyzers installed on the dashboard of the vehicle, sometimes following a DUI conviction; and (9) zero tolerance laws that impose 0.02 percent BAC on drivers under the age of 21.[135]

All of these interventions, along with the national minimum drinking age of 21, have significantly reduced alcohol-related motor vehicle accidents in the United States and changed the social norms surrounding drinking and driving. Professor Cook reports: "The National Roadside Survey in 1973 found the proportion of drivers with positive BACs was 36 percent on Friday and Saturday night; that percentage dropped to just 17 percent in the National Roadside Survey of 1996. Alcohol-involved traffic fatalities dropped from 60 percent of the total in 1982 to 41 percent in 2002."[136] The reduction has been so dramatic that currently, according to Professor Cook, "the bulk of the damage to public safety from underage drinking is the result of violent crime rather than impaired driving."[137] Any further reductions in drunk driving, according to Jim Mosher, are likely to come from controls on access to alcoholic beverages through increased taxes and a focus on problem bars.

The attitudes surrounding drinking and driving, especially among young adults, are dramatically different than they were 20 years ago. I have witnessed firsthand how my children, now aged 26 and 29, will not drive after drinking and how naturally they and their friends appoint a designated driver or take public or private transportation when they plan to drink.

5. ADVERTISING AND MARKETING

Advertising and marketing of alcoholic beverages occur in both traditional (also known as measured) media — radio, television, magazines, newspapers, outdoor billboards, and signs — and non-traditional (or unmeasured) venues such as the Internet, sponsorship of music concerts and sporting events, consumer contests and giveaways, product placement in movies and television programs, and in-store point-of-sale material and promotional items. Since Repeal, the propriety of alcoholic beverage advertising has been debated in

---

135. William Evans, Doreen Neville & John Graham, General Deterrence of Drunk Driving: Evaluation of Recent American Policies, 11 Risk Analysis 279, 281 (1991).

136. Paying the Tab, *supra* note 19 at 89.

137. *Id.* at 188.

Congress and state legislatures on numerous occasions. In the 1940s and 1950s, there were serious efforts, all unsuccessful, to ban all alcoholic beverage advertising in interstate commerce. Robert Laforge, in his dissertation, *Misplaced Priorities: A History of Federal Alcohol Regulation and Public Health Policy*, writes that

> the proponents of an alcohol ad ban were opposed to the increased volume of alcoholic beverage advertising, to its irrelevant appeals and to the use of puffery and "glamorous" or lifestyle advertising. [They] repeatedly contrasted this type of alcohol promotion with the social damage caused by alcohol, including alcoholism, driving deaths, accidents and family problems.[138]

The same concerns resurfaced in the 1970s and 1980s. Led by the Center for Science in the Public Interest (CSPI),[139] the critics claimed that the beer and spirits industries, in particular, engaged in unfair and deceptive advertising and marketing practices that had significant adverse health and social consequences, especially among underage and heavy drinkers. These lifestyle advertisements, they said, portray alcoholic beverages in conjunction with appealing images of social camaraderie, social success, wealth, elegance, sex, sports, and various risk-taking activities.[140] Regulation was "necessary to protect consumers from the presumed negative effects of advertising of alcoholic beverages—especially those consumers thought to be particularly vulnerable to such effects, such as children and adolescents."[141]

The Treasury Department's alcoholic beverage advertising regulations, which have changed little since 1940, are reviewed in Chapter 3. As a reminder, the TTB does not pre-approve alcoholic beverage advertisements as it does with alcoholic beverage labels. The Bureau prohibits false or misleading statements, statements that are disparaging of a competitor's products, obscene or indecent statements, therapeutic claims, health statements, and statements or designs that create the impression that a wine has intoxicating qualities.[142] But the TTB does not address what are socially acceptable or unacceptable standards for alcoholic beverage advertisements.

In 1983 the CSPI proposed that the federal government expand its regulations of alcoholic beverage advertising. Specifically, the CSPI proposed that (1) the Federal Trade Commission (FTC) or Bureau of Alcohol, Tobacco and Firearms (the TTB's predecessor) should ban all advertising and marketing efforts aimed at heavy drinkers and young people, including activities on college campuses, advertisements on rock music stations and in youth magazines, and commercials on sports broadcasts; (2) advertisements in print or on radio or

138. Robert G. Laforge, Misplaced Priorities: A History of Federal Alcohol Regulation and Public Health Policy 292-293 (1987) (unpublished Ph.D. dissertation, Johns Hopkins University).

139. *See, e.g.*, Michael Jacobson, Robert Atkins & George Hacker, The Booze Merchants: The Inebriating of America (1983).

140. Misplaced Priorities: A History of Federal Alcohol Regulation and Public Health Policy, *supra* note 138 at 415.

141. Sober Reflections: Commerce, Public Health and the Evolution of Alcohol Policy in Canada, 1980-2000, at 209 (Norman Giesbrecht et al. eds., 2006).

142. 27 C.F.R. §4.64. Unlike in the case of wine labels, the TTB does not pre-approve wine industry advertisements.

television should contain, or be balanced by, equally well-disseminated public health information; (3) the Federal Communications Commission should encourage all broadcasters to run health-oriented and other alcohol-related public service announcements in prime-time, sports, and family-viewing time slots; and (4) the content of alcoholic beverage advertisements should be limited to consumer information about the taste, price, and composition of products (known as "tombstone advertising"), with no puffery and no association with social, sexual, or financial success.[143] None of the CSPI's suggestions has ever been adopted.

Nevertheless, the concerns expressed by the CSPI, the Center for Alcohol Marketing and Youth, and other advocacy groups prompted Congress to investigate the impact of alcoholic beverage advertising on underage drinking. In 1998, 2003, and 2008, at Congress' request, the FTC conducted these investigations.[144] Additionally, in 2002 Congress requested the NRC/IOM to develop a national strategy for reducing and preventing youth alcohol problems.[145]

All these reports recommended voluntary self-regulation as the primary strategy for protecting young people from the adverse effects of alcoholic beverage advertising.[146] As the FTC wrote in 1999,

> [s]elf-regulation often can be more prompt, flexible, and effective than government regulation. It can permit application of the accumulated judgment and experience of an industry to issues that are sometimes difficult for the government to define with bright line rules. With respect to advertising practices, self-regulation is an appropriate mechanism because many forms of government intervention raise First Amendment concerns.[147]

In the same report, the FTC pointed out certain weaknesses of industry self-regulation and recommended that industry implement the following best practices: (1) *for advertisement placements*,[148] reduce the percentage of the

---

143. *Id.*

144. FTC, Self-Regulation in the Alcohol Industry: A Review of Industry Efforts to Avoid Promoting Alcohol to Underage Consumers (1999), available at http://www.ftc.gov/reports/alcohol/alcoholreport.shtm (last visited November 27, 2010); FTC, Alcohol Marketing and Advertising: A Report to Congress (2003), available at http://www.ftc.gov/os/2003/09/alcohol08report.pdf (last visited November 27, 2010); FTC, Self-Regulation in the Alcohol Industry: Report of the Federal Trade Commission (2008), available at http://www.ftc.gov/os/2008/06/080626alcoholreport.pdf (last visited November 27, 2010).

145. Reducing Underage Drinking: A Collective Responsibility, *supra* note 81 at 2.

146. Self-regulation takes the form of industry advertising codes. Separate codes have been adopted by the Beer Institute (Brewing Industry Advertising Guidelines), Wine Institute (Code of Advertising Standards), and the Distilled Spirits Council of the United States (Code of Good Practice).

147. Self-Regulation in the Alcohol Industry: A Review of Industry Efforts to Avoid Promoting Alcohol to Underage Consumers, *supra* note 144 at 3

148. Placement restrictions include bans on outdoor alcoholic beverage advertising in locations where children are present such as schools and playgrounds, near colleges and churches, and inside the retail store where point-of-sale advertising and other promotions might stimulate sales, particularly among at-risk groups like such as young adults and problem drinkers. Center for Alcohol Marketing and Youth (CAMY), State Alcohol Advertising Laws: Current Status and Model Policies (2003). For a discussion of point-of-sale advertising, *see* Graeme Willersdorf, Selling and Serving Beverage Alcohol, in Working Together to Reduce Harmful Drinking, *supra* note 82 at 123-125.

underage audience to 30 percent,[149] ban alcoholic beverage advertisements on television series and in other media with the largest underage audiences, and conduct regular audits of previous product placements; (2) *for advertising content*, prohibit advertisements with substantial underage appeal, even if they also appeal to adults or, in the alternative, target advertisements to persons 25 and older; (3) *for product placement in movies and television*, restrict the promotional placement of alcoholic beverages to films rated R and NC-17 and apply to product placement on television the same standards for traditional advertising; (4) *for online advertising*, use available mechanisms to reduce underage access and avoid content that would attract underage consumers; and (5) *for college marketing*, prohibit marketing activities on college campuses (except at licensed establishments) and industry sponsorship of spring break activities such as beach promotions and outdoor concerts. With respect to the youth audience standard, the NRC/IOM recommended that the industry immediately decrease the youth composition in traditional media to 25 percent (cited as a "best practice" in the 1999 FTC report), phasing in a 15 percent standard over time.[150]

In its subsequent reexaminations of alcoholic beverage advertising practices, the FTC again endorsed voluntary advertising codes. But the FTC required industry members to "check reliable audience composition data before placing an ad and . . . make a placement only if that data showed that, historically, at least 70 percent of the audience consisted of adults 21 and older."[151] The FTC also recommended that code compliance be supplemented by an external entity that would review any disputed advertisement to ensure a "consistent, impartial, objective and public resolution of disputes."[152] Finally, the FTC suggested that all supplier websites and online alcohol sales sites use age screening and verification technologies to ensure that alcoholic beverages are not marketed or sold to underage purchasers.[153]

In addition to the federal government, state governments regulate advertising content and placement, typically with the stated goal of achieving temperance. Several of these laws have been carefully scrutinized under the First Amendment to the U.S. Constitution.[154] Generally speaking, restrictions on

149. The wine industry was the first to embrace a 30 percent threshold, that is, not more than 30 percent of the expected viewers shall be under the age of 21. This standard is consistent with the 2000 census data showing that 30 percent of the American public is under the age of 21.

150. Reducing Underage Drinking: A Collective Responsibility, *supra* note 81 at 138.

151. Self-Regulation in the Alcohol Industry: Report of the General Trade Commission, *supra* note 144 at i.

152. *Id.* at ii. Wine Institute did so in 2005. Wine Institute, Code of Advertising Standards Third Party Review Process, approved September 13, 2005.

153. *Id.* at iii.

154. The First Amendment reads in pertinent part: "Congress shall make no law . . . abridging the freedom of speech, or of the press. . . ." The states also must consider federal preemption under Article VI, Section 1, Clause 2 of the U.S. Constitution, also known as the Supremacy Clause ("This Constitution, and the Laws of the United States which shall be made in Pursuance thereof . . . shall be the supreme Law of the Land; and the Judges in every State shall be bound thereby, any Thing in the Constitution or Laws of any State to the Contrary notwithstanding.") *See, e.g., Capital Cities Cable, Inc. v. Crisp*, 467 U.S. 691 (1984) (state cannot

the "time, place, and manner" of alcoholic beverage advertising are more permissible than restrictions on content.[155]

In the seminal 1996 case of *44 Liquormart, Inc. v. Rhode Island,*[156] the Supreme Court invalidated Rhode Island's ban on price advertising of alcoholic beverages. Rhode Island had enacted a law that prohibited licensed vendors inside or outside of the state from advertising the price of any alcoholic beverage offered for sale in the state. The law also prohibited Rhode Island media from publishing or broadcasting any advertisements making reference to alcoholic beverage prices. Not even a placard or sign visible from the exterior of a package store could make reference to alcoholic beverage prices. In fact, Liquormart did not advertise any alcoholic beverage prices; instead, its advertisement included low prices for non-alcoholic items and the word "WOW" in large letters next to pictures of vodka and rum bottles. When the State Liquor Administration imposed a fine, litigation commenced.

To judge the constitutionality of Rhode Island's advertising ban, the Supreme Court applied the 4-part commercial free speech test that it had enunciated in *Central Hudson Gas & Electric Corp v. Public Service Commission of New York*:

1. The speech must concern lawful activity and not be misleading;
2. The government's interest asserted to justify the regulation must be substantial;
3. The regulation must directly advance the government interest asserted; and
4. The regulation must not be more extensive than necessary to serve that interest.[157]

The justices unanimously found that the Rhode Island law did not directly advance the state's substantial interest in promoting temperance and that the ban was more extensive than necessary to serve that interest. Regarding the third prong of the *Central Hudson* test, Justice John Paul Stevens, who authored the unanimous decision, found that "the State has presented no evidence to suggest that its speech prohibition will *significantly* reduce marketwide consumption."[158] With respect to the fourth prong of the test, Justice Stevens added that "it is perfectly obvious that alternative forms of regulation that would not involve any restriction on speech would be likely to achieve the State's goal of promoting temperance. As the State's own expert conceded, higher prices can be maintained by direct regulation or by increased taxation."[159]

---

interfere with the transmission of electronic media signals from outside the state because of the authority granted to the Federal Communications Commission to regulate cable television systems in the United States).

155. "Time, place, and manner" regulations are more acceptable to courts so long as they target a legitimate state interest (e.g., reducing youth exposure) and permit the advertising in at least some venues for the intended (adult) audience. *See, e.g., Metromedia, Inc. v. City of San Diego,* 453 U.S. 490 (1981).

156. 517 U.S. 484 (1996).

157. *Central Hudson Gas & Electric Corp. v. Public Service Comm'n of N.Y.*, 447 U.S. 557, 566 (1980).

158. *Liquormart,* 517 U.S. at 506 (emphasis in the original).

159. *Id.* at 507.

Under *Central Hudson*, a state must have an evidentiary basis for any content-based advertising ban. Where only "anecdotal evidence and educated guesses" support a ban, the Supreme Court will invalidate the law. That occurred in the case of *Rubin v. Coors Brewing Co.*[160] Coors challenged a federal law that prohibited beer labels from displaying alcohol content in order to prevent "strength wars" (battles over whose beer is stronger in alcoholic content).[161] Justice Clarence Thomas, who wrote the unanimous decision, found that the government's interest could be advanced in a less intrusive manner, for example, by directly limiting the alcoholic content of beers, prohibiting marketing that emphasizes high alcoholic strength, and limiting the ban to malt liquors, the segment of the beer market that allegedly is threatened with a "strength war."[162]

Does alcoholic beverage advertising encourage excess consumption, create an environment in which alcoholic beverage consumption is normalized, or simply capture market share?[163] Terrell Rhodes, in *Social and Economic Control of Alcohol: The 21st Amendment in the 21st Century*, argues: "There is little concrete evidence of a positive effect of controls on the advertising or presentation of alcoholic beverages . . . on levels of consumption."[164] Economist Jon Nelson, in "Alcoholic Beverage Advertising and Advertising Bans: A Survey of Research Methods, Results, and Policy Implications," agrees.

> Studies of state-level bans of billboards and publicly visible displays fail to demonstrate that selective bans reduce consumption. Studies of international bans that cover more media and beverages reach the same conclusion for more comprehensive bans. Studies of advertising expenditures fail to find statistically significant effects of advertising on alcohol consumption, despite numerous advances in econometric methods. Studies of brand advertising fail to establish a spillover effect of successful brand advertising on the marketwide demand for alcoholic beverages.[165]

The NRC/IOM reaches the same conclusion about the relationship between alcoholic beverage advertising and youth alcohol consumption.

> [A] causal link between alcoholic beverage advertising and underage alcohol use has not been clearly established. [Citations omitted.] A substantial body of research on the effects of advertising and promotion on alcohol consumption and its consequences, and specifically on underage alcohol consumption, has produced findings that are mixed and inconclusive.[166]

---

160. 514 U.S. 476 (1995).

161. *Id.* at 484.

162. *Id.* at 490-491.

163. Mike MacAvoy & Meg Mackenzie, Government Regulation, Corporate Responsibility, and Personal Pleasure: A Public Health Perspective from New Zealand, in Corporate Social Responsibility and Alcohol: The Need and Potential for Partnership 88 (Marcus Grant & Joyce O'Connor eds., 2005).

164. Terrell Rhodes, Policy, Regulation and Legislation, in Social and Economic Control of Alcohol: The 21st Amendment in the 21st Century 87 (Carole Jurkiewicz & Murphy Painter eds., 2008).

165. Jon Nelson, Alcohol Advertising and Advertising Bans: A Survey of Research Methods, Results, and Policy Implications, in Advertising and Differentiated Products 284-285 (M. R. Baye & Jon Nelson eds., 2001).

166. Reducing Underage Drinking: A Collective Responsibility, *supra* note 81 at 134.

Clearly, more research and monitoring need to be done on overall youth exposure to alcoholic beverage advertising, particularly including unmeasured media such as sponsorships, Internet promotions, and viral marketing. Even in the absence of evidence of advertising's direct effects on young persons' beliefs and behavior, it might be advisable to further limit youth exposure to alcoholic beverage advertising on the basis of the "precautionary principle." That principle prescribes preventive action in the face of uncertainty. How the Supreme Court would react to this policy prescription is another matter altogether.

It is not only advertisements that may lead youth to drink, but products as well. There is no better example than energy drinks that combine beer or spirits with caffeine, inducing what one FDA Commissioner called a state of "wide awake drunk."[167] Products such as Four Loko and Joose have been widely criticized because of their appeal to youth drinkers. As David Jernigan and James O'Hara write in "Alcoholic Beverage Advertising and Promotion,"

> [s]uccessful youth brands not only attach themselves to the subculture, but . . . position themselves to be among its defining features. Some of the newest alcohol products attach themselves to the all-night clubbing scene. Energy drinks, loaded with caffeine, help young people to stay awake through all-night activities like clubbing. Premixed energy drinks were a natural successor to the common practice of mixing nonalcoholic energy drinks such as Red Bull with vodka or other distilled spirits.[168]

In December 2010, following a spate of hospitalizations, including some deaths, of young drinkers and bans of these products in several states, the FDA issued warning letters to 4 manufacturers in which it stated that caffeinated energy drinks are not "Generally Recognized as Safe" (GRAS)[169] and are adulterated under the Federal Food, Drug, and Cosmetic Act.[170]

---

167. Transcript of FDA Media Call on Caffeinated Alcoholic Beverages with Dr. Margaret Hamburg, at 2 (Nov. 17, 2010) available at http://www.fda.gov/downloads/NewsEvents/Newsroom/MediaTranscripts/UCM234483.pdf (last visited November 25, 2010).

168. Reducing Underage Drinking: A Collective Responsibility, *supra* note 81 at 632.

169. The FDA sent warning letters on November 17, 2010, to Phusion Projects, LLC (Four Loko), Charge Beverages Corp. (Core High Gravity HG Green, HG Orange, and Lemon Lime Core Spiked), New Century Brewing Co. (Moonshot), and United Brands Company Inc. (Joose and Max). Each letter states:

> To establish that the use of a substance in food is GRAS under its specific conditions of use (for example, the GRAS status of caffeine when directly added to an alcoholic beverage), there must be consensus among qualified experts that the substance is safe under its conditions of use, based on publicly available data and information. FDA is aware that, based on the publicly available literature, a number of qualified experts have concerns about the safety of caffeinated alcoholic beverages. Moreover, the agency is not aware of data or other information to establish the safety of the relevant conditions of use for your product. Therefore, the criteria for GRAS status have not been met for the caffeine in your beverages.

See, e.g., Letter from Joann M. Given, Acting Director, Office of Compliance, Center for Food Safety and Applied Nutrition, to Tim Baggs, President and CEO, Charge Beverages Corp. (Nov. 17, 2010) (available at www.fda.gov/Food/FoodIngredientsPackaging/ucm190366.htm (last visited November 25, 2010)).

170. 21 U.S.C. §342(a)(2)(C). The FDA's regulations on food additives are located at 21 C.F.R. §170.

6. PREVENTION

Prevention includes both treatment and education. The former involves individualized services and programs for problem drinkers (heavy drinkers, binge drinkers, and alcoholics) as well as screenings for early detection and intervention. Therapeutic interventions include inpatient and outpatient treatment, medications,[171] behavioral counseling, and mutual help groups. In terms of their effectiveness, Dr. Babor writes, "In general, when patients enter treatment, exposure to any treatment is associated with significant reductions in alcohol use and related problems, regardless of the type of intervention used."[172]

Education also can directly influence drinking patterns, although it is generally less effective than treatment. Education may occur in schools, universities, and the home as well as through mass media campaigns and community-based health programs. From a policy perspective, the educational approach is attractive because it does not infringe on consumer sovereignty. Indeed, this was the policy preferred by Ernest Cherrington of the Anti-Saloon League (ASL) before and during Prohibition. But Cherrington was overruled by ASL boss Wayne Wheeler, who believed that Prohibition could not succeed without tough laws and severe sanctions. Wheeler may have been right because there is little direct evidence that education succeeds in any appreciable way.[173] Dr. Babor provides the following details:

> School-based alcohol education programs have been found to increase knowledge and change attitudes toward alcohol and other substances, but actual substance use remains unaffected. [Citations omitted.] Approaches that address values clarification, self-esteem, general social skills, and "alternatives" approaches that provide activities inconsistent with alcohol use (e.g., sports) are equally ineffective. [Citation omitted.] Many contemporary school-based programs include both resistance skills training and normative education, which attempts to correct adolescents' tendency to overestimate the number of their peers who drink. [Citations omitted.] Scientific evaluations of these programs have produced mixed results with generally modest effects that are short-lived unless accompanied by ongoing booster sessions. Some programs include both individual-level education and family- or community-level interventions. Evaluations suggest that even these comprehensive programs may not be sufficient to delay the initiation of drinking, or to sustain a small reduction in drinking beyond the operation of the program.[174]

Health warnings on alcoholic beverage labels are another form of consumer education that supplement public service announcements (PSAs) and counter-advertising. The Government Warning, adopted in 1988, refers to the following alcohol-related risks: birth defects caused by drinking when pregnant, impairment when driving or operating machinery, and health

---

171. Medications for alcohol dependence include benzodiazepines, glutamate inhibitors, and opiate antagonists.

172. Alcohol Policy and the Public Good, in From Science to Action?, *supra* note 69 at 40.

173. Alcohol and Public Policy: Beyond the Shadow of Prohibition, *supra* note 114 at 98.

174. Alcohol Policy and the Public Good, in From Science to Action?, *supra* note 69 at 39.

problems.[175] The evidence, however, suggests that even this explicit warning is generally ineffective in changing drinking behavior,[176] despite the fact that consumer awareness of the warning, in the sense of recalling the wording, is significant and the law is widely accepted.[177]

The message is clear: any single strategy is likely inadequate to address drinking problems and change consumer behavior. But synergies can be achieved in prevention by implementing multi-faceted strategies. The TTB has adopted this approach in the area of wine labeling and advertising. In addition to the health warning on labels, the federal government prohibits any health or therapeutic claim about wine or other alcoholic beverages on labels or in advertising. Even if the claim can be proven, such as "moderate wine consumption reduces the risk of coronary heart disease in persons age 45 or older," the TTB will not allow such a statement because it might mislead particular persons older than 45 for whom any alcohol consumption may be ill advised because of their particular health conditions or genetic propensities. Because we are a polymorphic species, it is inconceivable that information on a wine label could spell out all the possible risks of wine consumption for each and every consumer. For this reason, the only health claims that the TTB has approved in the last decade are so-called health-related directional statements, and even those must be qualified. The pertinent TTB regulations, 27 CFR §§4.39(h) for labels and 4.64(i) for advertising, are identical, and they state:

> A statement that directs consumers to a third party or other source for information regarding the effects on health of wine or alcohol consumption is presumed misleading unless it—
>
> (A) Directs consumers in a neutral or other non-misleading manner to a third party or other source for balanced information regarding the effects on health of wine or alcohol consumption; and
>
> (B)(1) Includes as part of the health-related directional statement the following disclaimer: "This statement should not encourage you to drink or to increase your alcohol consumption for health reasons"; or

---

175. 27 U.S.C. §§213 et seq. The government warning is not required in alcoholic beverage advertising.

176. *Id.*

177. M. Plant, Harm Minimization, in Harald Klingermann & Gerhard Gmel, Mapping Social Consequences of Alcohol Consumption 152 (2001). The health warning serves purposes other than consumer education. It also has legal consequences. Wine Institute chairman John DeLuca recalls the form of the warning label legislation when it was first introduced by Senator Strom Thurmond:

> The Thurmond bill would *not* preempt the other states. In other words, even though the federal government was asking for a warning label, it wasn't going to be preemptive legislation. . . . [Y]ou could have a tank trap system of fifty different states, all desirous of putting on their own warning. We already had experience with Prop 65 that California was in the forefront of the states that wanted to put on warnings.
>
> The most critical aspect of the provisions was a section in the Thurmond bill that indicated that the warning label, if passed, could not be used by any of the companies as a defense in product liability lawsuits. [Emphasis in original.]

Each of these provisions was stricken in the final legislation. John DeLuca, Ph.D., President and CEO of the Wine Institute, 1975-2003, an Oral History Conducted in 1986-2007, by Victor Geraci, Ruth Teiser & Carole Hicke, 90, Regional History Office, The Bancroft Library, University of California, Berkeley, 2007.

> (2) Includes as part of the health-related directional statement some other qualifying statement that the appropriate TTB officer finds is sufficient to dispel any misleading impression conveyed by the health-related directional statement.[178]

In conclusion, policymakers have used many measures to combat the harmful effects of alcoholic beverage consumption. In the 1970s, Selden Bacon, former director of the Center of Alcohol Studies at Rutgers University, summarized the various approaches used in the United States.

> This complex set of problems over the past 150 years has been defined as a moral weakness problem and turned over to the churches, defined as an economic problem and turned over to market and price control authorities, defined as a youth learning problem and turned over to educators, defined as a crime problem and turned over to law enforcement and correction agencies.[179]

The policy debate is ongoing, as is the research. Not surprisingly, on certain subjects there are wide disagreements. To illustrate the range of viewpoints and advance the public discussion of the available policy options, Appendix 9-1 presents a table from "Effectiveness and Cost-Effectiveness of Policies and Programmes to Reduce the Harm Caused by Alcohol" by Peter Anderson, Dan Chisholm, and Daniela Fuhr. The policy measures in that table are not identical to the ones discussed here, but the ratings of the level of evidentiary support and the degree of effectiveness of each measure are useful in the ongoing discussion.

D. A MODEL OF SOCIAL RESPONSIBILITY

Even a cursory review of the positive and negative effects of alcohol consumption and of the effectiveness of the various regulations and interventions discussed in this chapter reveals that there still is considerable debate about the proper selection and mix of policy approaches to prevent and manage alcohol-related problems. No specific course of action is recommended in this section. Rather, a series of principles are presented, which the wine industry might consider as it charts its own course on issues of public health and as it interacts with public health advocates and local, state, national, and international government officials in setting the policy agenda.

A cardinal principle is that drinking does not necessarily lead to problems. Even the precepts that more drinking leads to more serious problems and less drinking reduces the incidence and severity of problems, while empirically correct, are misleading.[180] As Mark Moore and Dean Gerstein wrote in 1981 in *Alcohol and Public Policy: Beyond the Shadow of Prohibition*,

---

178. 27 C.F.R. §§4.39, 4.64 (prohibited labeling and advertising practices, respectively).

179. Quoted in NIAAA, www.utakeitback.org/community/niaaa.html (last visited November 1, 2010).

180. Alcohol and Public Policy: Beyond the Shadow of Prohibition, *supra* note 114 at 19.

> [m]uch seems to depend on how and where alcohol is absorbed in a drinker's life: how much drunkenness is generated and how that drunkenness is fitted into more or less demanding physical and social environments. To be sure, one would expect heavy drinkers to cause and suffer many of the bad consequences of drinking. But moderate and light drinkers could also cause and suffer problems if they consumed their smaller quantities of alcohol in unusually dangerous patterns. . . .
>
> These considerations have two crucial implications for policy. One is that alcohol problems may be distributed over a large segment of the drinking population. They may not be only, or even mainly, problems of alcoholics. To the extent that this is true, focusing exclusively or even primarily on the treatment of alcoholics is not sufficient. A second implication is that there may be other avenues open to controlling alcohol problems besides reducing alcohol consumption. For example, one can think of influencing the drinking practices of individuals so that a given quantity of alcohol could be distributed more safely and appropriately within a given individual's activities, or one can think of altering the structural characteristics of the environment to make it safer for drunken people.[181]

Clearly, the wine industry cannot hide from the problems of alcoholism and chronic drinking in an effort to ward off concerns about alcohol consumption in the broader population. But this does not mean that alcohol control policies should address only—or even primarily—the population at large. Where appropriate, policies should be designed to focus on specific at-risk drinkers, including those who consume alcoholic beverages to excess, those who engage in risky drinking patterns such as binge drinking, and those who drink when they should not, including drunk drivers and underage drinkers.

The question of how to affect drinking patterns so that they do not lead to harmful results is complicated because of the numerous factors that are involved, including individual predispositions, social pressures, commercial practices, and government intervention. Not surprisingly, no single policy is effective in all circumstances. Various measures need to be considered and carefully assessed in terms of their risks and benefits in reducing the harmful effects of alcohol consumption. The wine industry should insist and rely on empirical evidence of policy effectiveness and promote policies that balance benefits and risks in a way that does not "banish" legitimate, moderate drinkers.

The wine industry should promote continued research by independent experts on the harms *and benefits* of moderate wine consumption. The funding sources should be acknowledged by the researchers to ensure transparency and full disclosure of potential conflicts of interest. Additionally, the results should be widely disseminated, and the full effects of drinking wine and the variables that determine those effects should be presented in a clear, accurate, and balanced way, including the amount of alcohol consumed, the pattern of drinking, the characteristics of the consumer, and the circumstances in which the drinking occurs. Because wineries are not allowed to make health claims, the

181. *Id.*

dissemination of research results will need to be done by third parties who are not industry members. Education may not change people's drinking habits overnight, but informed decision making is critical to fostering responsible drinking and empowering responsible choices.

On the subject of education, I am reminded of Margrit Mondavi's foreword in my book *From Demon to Darling: A Legal History of Wine in America*, in which she laments that, although our country has made great strides in transforming wine from an illicit substance to an integral part of our culture, we have not yet taken up the practice in her native Switzerland of introducing wine to children. She writes, "We introduced tiny amounts of wine to the children, diluted for the younger ones, and to me that is the safest and most effective insurance against later alcohol misuse."[182] Perhaps this is because wine still is not a daily beverage in the United States. Roughly one-third of the adult population in the United States abstains, and another third drinks very little over the course of a year.

How, when, and what should young people learn about alcohol? They should know sooner rather than later that wine can be consumed sensibly, provide pleasure, and be healthful; but, if consumed in excess, it can cause harm to the drinker and others. Although this may not alter their risk-taking activities, which often are part of youthful development, adolescents must be made aware of the difference between responsible and irresponsible drinking, the importance of moderation, and the dangers of binge drinking. Clearly, they are not being taught this. In "Drinking Education: Minimizing Negatives or Optimizing Potential," Stanton Peele writes:

> Education in sensible drinking is not being conducted. The Monitoring the Future survey measures students' attitudes toward drinking, as well as their actual drinking. In 2001, although 69% of high school seniors disapproved of taking one or two drinks nearly every day, fewer (63%) disapproved of taking five or six drinks once or twice each weekend. That is, they disapproved as much or more of the kind of drinking likely to prolong life and encourage emotional well-being as they did of the weekend binge drinking so prevalent among the young.[183]

Advertising that associates alcohol with risk-taking activities, sex, and power does not encourage responsible drinking. Self-regulation through an industry advertising code has been an important means to ensure responsible marketing and promotion. But Wine Institute's Code of Advertising Standards must be continuously reviewed and updated to ensure that it is appropriate and effective and to keep up with the ever-expanding ways of communicating over the Internet.

The wine industry must understand that, if its voluntary advertising code is shown to be ineffective, governments can and will intervene with laws on advertising content and placement. Any such laws should include effective

---

182. From Demon to Darling, *supra* note 39 at xiii.

183. Stanton Peele, Drinking Education: Minimizing Negatives or Optimizing Potential?, in Corporate Social Responsibility and Alcohol: The Need and Potential for Partnership, *supra* note 163 at 71.

administrative and deterrence systems for infringements. The laws, however, must not prohibit truthful communication about wine. The First Amendment protects commercial speech, and the wine industry must rely on that protection to invalidate misguided and overreaching advertising restrictions.

Consumers should have access to full and accurate information about the characteristics of the wines offered for sale. Tombstone advertising that would restrict wine labeling and advertising to the product name and type, its price, and where it is available, with no other statements or images that might appeal to youth or heavy drinkers, is unnecessary and should be resisted on the grounds of free speech.

The wine industry should include in its advertising proactive communications about responsible alcohol consumption and the risks associated with misuse. And the industry should be careful not to use marketing and advertising to recruit underage drinkers, lest wine consumption be perceived, as it already is by some, to be part of a wider alcohol or even drug problem. The fact that there are no wine-based energy drinks is a good sign. The industry should remain on this high ground.

To address the drinking environment, the wine industry should work with retailers and community groups to ensure the responsible service of all alcoholic beverages. This includes not serving alcoholic beverages to intoxicated or underage persons and training servers about how to identify and deal with those situations. The consumer should be offered choice and value in the selection of wines but should not be induced in any way to drink to excess. Wherever alcoholic beverages are served, non-alcoholic beverages should be made available as an alternative.

The wine industry also should support reasonable licensing restrictions to limit the availability of and access to alcohol. Restrictions on what, when, where, and how alcohol can be sold are an important way to deter inappropriate drinking (e.g., drinking and driving and sales to minors and those who are intoxicated). But these laws and regulations should not interfere with the right of consumers to buy wine at reasonable prices and drink responsibly. In this respect, governmental tax and pricing policies should take into account the consumers' demand for reasonably priced wines, the government's need for tax revenue, and the demonstrated effects of any particular measure on discouraging inappropriate drinking patterns. Of course, the devil is in the details of any particular licensing, pricing, or taxation scheme, but the guiding principle should be to assess the full set of effects before adopting the measure, lest it have unintended consequences such as substitution or displacement.[184]

On the subject of commerce and trade, the wine industry must support steadfastly the principle, enshrined in the Commerce Clause, that the states cannot discriminate against producers or products from another state unless there is no reasonable, non-discriminatory means to accomplish the state's

---

184. For example, as Graeme Willersdorf, long-time consultant to the International Center for Alcohol Policies, writes, "where a neighboring jurisdiction has cheaper or more widely available alcohol, a state-owned monopoly that restricts availability may shift demand across the border." Graeme Willersdorf, Selling and Serving Beverage Alcohol, in Working Together to Reduce Harmful Drinking, *supra* note 82 at 126.

legitimate objectives. Denying out-of-state wineries the right to ship their wines directly to in-state consumers while granting that same privilege to in-state wineries cannot be condoned, as the Supreme Court held in *Granholm v. Heald*. This is true whether the discrimination is obvious on its face, as was the case in *Granholm*, or in its effects. The states should not be allowed to stand behind platitudes such as "the three-tier system of wine distribution is inviolable," "direct shipping from out of state must be banned to protect youth," and "state tax revenue will be jeopardized if wine is shipped from out of state directly to in-state consumers." Justice Stephen Breyer was brilliant in his questioning of the attorneys general of New York and Michigan at oral argument in *Granholm*. Each time the state tried to rationalize discrimination against out-of-state wineries, whether it was on the basis of preventing underage purchases, collecting taxes, or ensuring an orderly market, Justice Breyer pointed out that the states could adopt reasonable, non-discriminatory measure to achieve their legitimate objectives without discriminating against interstate commerce. Justice Breyer suggested that the states require the shipper to obtain the signature of the adult purchaser at the time the wines are delivered and require the out-of-state producer to obtain a license in the destination state that can be suspended or revoked in the event of a violation; as part of that licensing process, the state could require the producers, in state and out of state, to post a surety bond to ensure excise tax payments to the destination state.

The wine industry must not forget wine's agricultural roots. This tie to the land distinguishes wine from beer and spirits. After Repeal, many states issued licenses to so-called farm wineries (there are no such things as "farm breweries" or "farm distilleries") and afforded them the privilege of direct sales to consumers. The states hoped that wineries would stimulate the local economy and promote agritourism, which they, in fact, did. This agricultural heritage explains in large measure why the direct sales litigation (*Granholm* and its progeny) is about wine, not beer or spirits.

Given wine's special role as an agricultural commodity and a significant one at that (wine is the number one finished agricultural product in California), the wine industry must embrace grapegrowing and winemaking practices that are environmentally, socially, and economically sustainable. This is an essential ingredient of the industry's social responsibility. The California Sustainable Winegrowing Alliance, established by the Wine Institute and the California Association of Winegrape Growers, is taking important steps in that direction. For example, in the field of viticulture, the Alliance addresses such diverse issues as climate change, carbon footprint, pesticide use, and farmworker housing. There are also a variety of certification programs, such as Fish Friendly Farming, that promote environmentally beneficial management practices and carry out important ecological restoration projects.

The enological side of the business is just as important. The wine industry must ensure product quality and integrity and protect consumers from adulterated and contaminated wines. The "green" movement in the United States is here to stay, and wineries should be at the forefront of efforts to conserve water and energy, prevent pollution, and reduce solid waste. Programs such as Napa Green certify both vineyards and wineries that embrace practices advancing the environmental, economic, and social equity goals of sustainability.

In conclusion, wine is now an integral part of American culture. The wine industry must accept its responsibility to address the harms associated with excessive drinking and find ways to promote a responsible role for wine in our society. Of course, there is no single prescription that can be offered. But as a core principle, wineries must accept their role as stewards of responsible corporate behavior and continue to monitor the activities of those in their world, such as tasting room and hospitality staff, brokers, distributors, advertisers, and the like. Of course, the wine industry cannot act alone. It must partner with governments, health care providers, educators, special interest groups, and community groups to achieve and maintain the rightful place of wine in American society as "the temperate, civilized, sacred, romantic mealtime beverage."[185]

185. Larry Walker, The Back Page, Wines & Vines 30 (Jan. 1991). The quote is from the Mondavi Mission Statement that is quoted in Walker's article.

APPENDIX 9-1

SUMMARY OF EFFECT OF POLICY MEASURES, WITH LEVEL OF EVIDENCE RANKED ACCORDING TO AVAILABILITY OF EVIDENCE[186]

Policy Measure	Evidence of Effect	Level of Evidence
Education and information		
School-based education	Some positive effects on increased knowledge and improved attitudes but no sustained effect on behavior. A systematic review of 14 systematic reviews identified 59 high-quality programs, of which only 6 were able to show any evidence of effectiveness.	1
Parenting programs	A systematic review of 14 parenting programs noted reduction in alcohol use in 6 parenting programs.	2

186. Peter Anderson, Dan Chisholm & Daniela Fuhr, Effectiveness and Cost-Effectiveness of Policies and Programmes to Reduce the Harm Caused by Alcohol, 373 The Lancet 2234, 2235-2236 (2009) (citations in the table omitted). Levels of evidence: 1 = more than one systematic review; 2 = one systematic review; 3 = two or more randomized controlled trials; 4 = one randomized controlled trial; 5 = observational evidence; and 6 = not assessed.

Policy Measure	Evidence of Effect	Level of Evidence
Social marketing programs	A systematic review of 15 programs noted 8 of 13 studies with some significant effects on alcohol use in the short term (up to 12 months), 4 of 7 studies with some effect at 1-2 years, and 2 of 4 studies with some effect over 2 years. (Some of the described programs are not strictly social marketing programs, and other reviews have concluded the same programs as ineffective.)	2
Public information campaigns	Little scientific research; individual studies generally ineffective.	5
Counter-advertising	Little scientific research; inconclusive results.	5
Drinking guidelines	No scientifically published assessment.	6
Health warnings	Systematic review of the experience in the USA noted some effect on intentions to change drinking behavior, but no effect on actual behavior change itself.	2
Health-sector response		
Brief advice	A meta-analysis of the effectiveness of brief interventions for hazardous and harmful alcohol consumption noted a positive effect of brief intervention on alcohol consumption, mortality, morbidity, alcohol-related injuries, alcohol-related social consequences, health-care resource use, and laboratory indicators of harmful alcohol use. A systematic review of 12 studies noted that a combination of education and office support programs increased rates of screening and advice giving of primary health-care providers from 32% to 45%.	1 2
Cognitive-behavioral therapies for alcohol dependence	Effective—a systematic review of 17 studies of behavioral self-control training found a combined effect size of 0.33 (SE 0.08) for reduced alcohol consumption and alcohol-related difficulties.	1

Policy Measure	Evidence of Effect	Level of Evidence
Benzodiazepines for alcohol withdrawal	Effective—a systematic review of 57 trial recorded a risk ratio of 0.16 (95% CI 0.04-0.69) for seizures compared with placebo.	1
Glutamate inhibitors for alcohol dependence	Effective—a systematic review of 17 randomized controlled trials reported a risk ratio of point prevalence abstinence of 1.40 (95% CI 1.24-1.59) at 6 months and 1.62 (1.37-1.92) at 12 months.	1
Opiate antagonists for alcohol dependence	Effective—a systematic review of 29 randomized controlled trials reported a significant reduction in relapse, at least in the short term (3 months) (risk ratio 0.64 (95% CI 0.51-0.82)).	1
Community programs		
Media advocacy	Little scientific research; but advocacy in media aimed at uptake of specific policies can lead to increased attention to alcohol on political and public agendas.	5
Community interventions	Evidence of effectiveness of systematic approaches to coordinate community resources to implement effective policies, when backed up by enforcement measures.	5
Workplace policies	A systematic review noted little evidence of effect in changing drinking norms and reducing harmful drinking.	2
Drunk-driving policies and countermeasures		
Introduction and/or reduction of alcohol concentration in the blood	Effective in reducing drunk-driving casualties—a meta-analysis of nine studies in the USA reported implementation of a legal concentration of 0.8 g/l alcohol in the blood resulted in 7% decrease in alcohol-related motor vehicle fatalities.	1
Sobriety checkpoints and unrestrictive (random) breath testing	Effective in reducing alcohol-related injuries and fatalities—a meta-analysis of 23 studies noted that alcohol-related fatal crashes reduced	1

Policy Measure	Evidence of Effect	Level of Evidence
	by 23% after introduction of sobriety checkpoints and by 22% after introduction of random breath testing.	
Restrictions on young or inexperienced drivers (e.g., lower concentrations of alcohol in blood for novice drivers)	Some evidence—a systematic review of three studies of lower alcohol concentrations in the blood detected reductions in fatal crashes of 9%, 17%, and 24%.	2
Mandatory treatment	Evidence of effectiveness—a meta-analysis of 215 assessments of remedial programs noted that they reduced recurrence of alcohol-impaired driving offences and alcohol-related accidents by 8-9%.	2
Alcohol locks	Some evidence—a systematic review of one randomized controlled trial and 13 controlled trials noted that the interlock participants had lower recurrence of offences than did controls, an effect that did not extend once the interlock was removed.	2
Designated driver and safe-ride programs	No evidence for effectiveness. A systematic review of nine studies was unable to draw any conclusions about effectiveness.	2
Addressing the availability of alcohol		
Government monopolies	Effective—privatization followed by higher density outlets, longer hours or more days of sale, changes in price, and an increase in consumption.	2
Minimum purchase age	Effective—a review of 132 studies published between 1960 and 1999 noted that changes in minimum drinking age laws can reduce youth drinking and alcohol-related harm, including road traffic accidents.	2
Outlet density	Effective—a systematic review reported consistent evidence for the effect of outlet density on violence,	2

Policy Measure	Evidence of Effect	Level of Evidence
	harm to others, and drunk-driving fatalities.	
Days and hours of sale	Effective — reviews noted consistent evidence that increases in days and hours of sale increase consumption and harm, and that reductions in days and hours of sale reduce consumption and harm.	3
Addressing the marketing of alcoholic beverages		
Volume of advertising	Effective — a systematic review of 13 studies noted an effect of advertising on youth initiation and heavier drinking among current users. A meta-analysis of 322 estimated advertising expenditure elasticities detected a positive effect of advertising on consumption (coefficient 0.029).	1
Self-regulation of alcohol marketing	No evidence of effectiveness. Studies show that self-regulation does not prevent types of marketing that can affect young people.	5
Pricing policies		
Alcohol taxes	Effective — a meta-analysis of 132 studies noted a median price elasticity for all beverage types of –0.52 in the short term and –0.82 in the long term, elasticities being lower for beer than for wine or spirits. A meta-analysis of 112 studies noted mean price elasticities of –0.46 for beer, –0.69 for wine, and –0.80 for spirits. Increasing taxes reduce acute and chronic alcohol-related harms. Setting minimum prices can reduce acute and chronic harms.	1
Harm reduction		
Training of bar staff, responsible serving practices, security staff in bars, and safety-oriented design of the premise	Little effectiveness. A systematic review detected little effect unless backed up by police enforcement and license inspectors.	2

Policy Measure	Evidence of Effect	Level of Evidence
Reducing the public health effect of illegally and informally produced alcohol		
Informal and surrogate alcohols	Some experience from reducing alcohol-related harm, by, for example, not allowing methanol to be used as denaturing agent.	5
Strict tax labeling	Some evidence of effectiveness drawn from other psychoactive substances (tobacco).	5

CHAPTER 10

INTERNATIONAL INSTITUTIONS AND ACCORDS

Jacques Audier[1]

Numerous international institutions and agreements deal in part with wine, but only one international organization and a few agreements specialize in wine. This specialized organization and the other international organizations with which it interacts (Section A) and these agreements (Section B) are the subject of this chapter.

A. INSTITUTIONS

1. THE OIV

OIV, the acronym for the International Organization of Vine and Wine, is the "old chap" of the vine and wine "family." Before discussing the modern-day institution, it is helpful to understand its long history.

a. Historical Overview

The OIV history can be traced back to an incubation period and two separate births. It begins with the first international event in the wine sector, in 1874, after the phylloxera disaster almost completely destroyed European and later North American viticulture. In that year, the winegrowers of France, Italy, Switzerland, Austria, and Germany held a conference in Montpellier, France, to investigate collaborative measures to eradicate the insidious pest. Thirty-five years later, the phylloxera crisis had been overcome, but the

1. This chapter was written in English by the author, with assistance from Richard Mendelson.

anarchic state of wine production and trade during this period of severe shortages resulted in pervasive fraud that swamped the worldwide market with all sorts of beverages misleadingly labeled "wine."

Two international conferences were held in 1908 and 1909 to examine this worrisome problem. Serious progress was made in developing a first definition of wine, echoing the principles of the Madrid Agreement of April 14, 1891, concerning the repression of false or deceptive "indications of source" on goods.[2]

This evolution continued after the World War I at an international conference of wine-producing countries. The program included the revision of customs tariffs, the regulation of international trade, and the establishment of an international body composed of delegates from wine-exporting and wine-importing countries to arbitrate conflicts that might arise among them.

In 1922 the Society for the Encouragement of Agriculture in France suggested the creation of an international wine organization. This idea was considered at the Genoa Conference in 1923, in which Italy, France, Spain, Greece, and Portugal participated. Later that same year, these five countries met at the First International Conference of Wine. They adopted several important recommendations and a draft resolution on the need for an International Office of Wine:

> Recommendations: Considering the vital interest the International Conference of Wine has for the nations represented to defend viticultural interests and to respond to prohibitionist campaigns,
>
> Considering that when consumed in moderation, wine is a healthy beverage, . . . [the signatories] recommend that the represented states:
>
> (1) collect documentation as quickly as possible to demonstrate the health effects of wine,
>
> (2) organize scientific experiments and complete those experiments presently underway,
>
> (3) make a serious effort to promote the taste of wine (*le goût du vin*),
>
> (4) reserve the denomination "WINE" exclusively for beverages made by the fermentation of fresh grapes or fresh grape juice prepared following local and customary practices that are accepted as being fair and in accordance with health requirements by each of the producer countries. The producer countries should quickly agree on a list of these practices.
>
> (5) adopt legislative initiatives based on a code of standard practices:
>
> a. Guaranteeing the purity and authenticity of products with certificates of origin,
>
> b. Monitoring the wine trade from importation through and including retail sale,
>
> c. Preventing fraud and unfair competition.

2. *See* Madrid Agreement for the Repression of False or Deceptive Indications of Source on Goods, art. 1, §§1-2, April 14, 1989, 15 U.S.C. §1141, 828 U.N.T.S. 389, available at www.wipo.int/treaties/en/ip/madrid/trtdocs_wo032.html#P24_540 (accessed December 14, 2010).

(6) proceed with the creation of an international chemistry bureau with the objective of standardizing the methods of analysis and coordinating the appraisal of product purity.

Draft resolution: The delegates agreed and acknowledged the need for wine producing states to share expenses for maintaining a permanent international office. . . . This Office should function under the authority and the control of a Committee of Delegates appointed by the governments, on which it would be useful to have producer and wine trade representatives.[3]

These recommendations provided an important foundation for an international wine organization. However, no concrete decision was made to create such an organization.

One year later, from June 30 to July 5, 1924, the second session of the International Conference of Wine was held. Austria, Chile, Hungary, Luxembourg, and Mexico joined the initial five member countries. A draft agreement establishing the International Office of Wine was considered and then revised. The lengthy debates attest to the difficulty of overcoming the members' reticence. Finally, on November 29, 1924, Spain, Tunisia, France, Portugal, Hungary, Luxembourg, Greece, and Italy signed the agreement establishing an International Wine Office, also known as the Office International du Vin (OIV). The 1924 agreement was ratified on December 3, 1927, and delegates of the eight member countries assembled for the first International Office of Wine work session.

Thirty years later, on September 4, 1958, the member states decided to change the name of the organization from International Office of Wine to International Office of Vine and Wine, or Office International de la Vigne et du Vin, still known by the acronym OIV.

The name changed again over four decades later to International Organization of Vine and Wine (still OIV), following the replacement of the 1924 agreement with the 2001 Agreement Establishing the International Organisation of Vine and Wine (hereinafter 2001 Agreement). The OIV General Assembly initiated the name change beginning on December 5, 1997, in Buenos Aires, Argentina. As stated in the preamble to the 2001 Agreement,

> [t]he General Assembly 1997 decided to proceed, as necessary, with the adaptation of the International Office of Vine and Wine to the new international environment. This involved adapting its missions, its human, material, and budgetary resources and, as appropriate, its procedures and operating rules, in order to meet the challenges and secure the future of the world vine and wine sector.[4]

3. Procès-verbaux de la conférence internationale des pays exportateurs de vin [Minutes of the International Conference of Wine Exporting Countries], 76 Bulletin de l'OIV 869-870: 541-547 (2003).

4. The 2001 agreement was signed initially by the duly authorized representatives of 35 countries. It was then subjected to different national procedures for approval, acceptance, or ratification. The agreement went into force on January 1, 2004, following the 31st instrument of ratification.

The current OIV members number 44 and include:

Algeria
Argentina
Australia
Austria
Belgium
Bosnia-Herzegovina
Brazil
Bulgaria
Chile
Croatia
Cyprus
Czech Republic
Finland
France
Georgia
Germany
Greece
Hungary
Ireland
Israel
Italy
Lebanon
Luxemburg
Macedonia (the former Yugoslav Republic of)
Malta
Moldavia
Montenegro
Morocco
Netherlands
New Zealand
Norway
Peru
Portugal
Romania
Russia
Serbia
Slovakia
Slovenia
South Africa
Spain
Sweden
Switzerland
Turkey
Uruguay

Together, in 2007 the members accounted for 85 percent of the world's wine production, 75 percent of all vineyards, 92 percent of all exports, and 70 percent of the world's wine consumption.[5] Since the focus and the interests of the member states vary, it is crucial that the OIV adopt a balanced approach to decision making.

Article 1.2 of the 2001 Agreement defines the OIV as an intergovernmental organization of a scientific and technical nature and a recognized authority on vines, wines, wine-based beverages, grapes, raisins, and other vine products. After 86 years of existence, the OIV's mission is well recognized and clearly defined.[6] The organization's objectives are (1) to inform members of proposed measures so that the concerns of producers, consumers, and other actors in the vine and wine products sector may be taken into consideration; (2) to assist other international organizations, both intergovernmental and non-governmental, especially those that carry out standardization activities; and (3) to contribute to international harmonization of existing practices and standards and, as necessary, to prepare new international standards to improve the

5. Author's correspondence with the OIV, dated December 2, 2010. *See* http://news.reseau-concept.net/pls/news/p_entree?i_sid=&i_type_edition_id=20508&i_section_id=&i_lang=33 (accessed December 14, 2010), Report of the Director General of the OIV on the World Vitiviniculture Situation in 2009, and Situation and Statistics of the World Vitiviniculture Sector.

6. Agreement Establishing the International Organisation of Vine and Wine, art. 2, April 3, 2001.

conditions for producing and marketing vine and wine products and to help ensure that the interests of consumers are taken into account.

To attain these objectives, the OIV engages in several important activities. First, the OIV promotes and guides scientific and technical research and experimentation. Second, the OIV makes recommendations and monitors implementation of those recommendations in conjunction with its members, especially in the following areas: conditions for grape production, oenological practices, definition and/or description of products, labeling and marketing conditions, and methods for analyzing and assessing vine products. Third, the OIV submits to its members proposals that (1) guarantee for consumers the authenticity of vine and wine products, especially in connection with the information provided on labels; (2) protect geographical indications, especially vine and wine-growing areas and related appellations of origin, whether designated by geographical names or not, insofar as they do not call into question international agreements relating to trade and intellectual property; and (3) improve scientific and technical criteria for recognizing and protecting new plant varieties. Fourth, the OIV contributes to the harmonization and adaptation of regulations by members or facilitates the mutual recognition of practices, viticultural and oenological, that are integral to the wine industry. Finally, the OIV protects the health of consumers and contributes to food safety by monitoring and scientifically evaluating vine products, promoting and guiding research into appropriate nutritional and health aspects, and disseminating information resulting from such research to the medical and health care professions.

The OIV is headquartered in Paris, France.[7] The organization's official languages are French, Spanish, English, Italian, and German,[8] which facilitates communications among members.[9] Simultaneous translation and interpretation are provided at meetings and for official documents.[10]

The OIV today is governed by a series of laws and regulations, including the 2001 Agreement, consisting of 19 articles and two annexes. The organization also adopted internal rules of procedure in 2004 and 2005, comprising 137 articles and five annexes.

b. Participation

The OIV includes several categories of participants: members, observers, and guests. Each category is discussed below.

i. MEMBERS

The OIV members include sovereign states and international, intergovernmental organizations. Sovereign states that have signed the 2001 Agreement and executed an instrument of acceptance, approval, or ratification are deemed

7. *Id.* at art. 3.6.
8. *Id.* at art. 5.6.
9. *Id.*
10. Internal Rules of Procedure Title I, art. 25., July 3, 2009 (hereinafter Internal Rules).

to be members of the OIV.[11] Other sovereign states may become members of the OIV. India, for example, is in the preliminary stages of accession.

The United States, presently not a member state, first joined the OIV on January 24, 1984, with a "reservation" on the issue of appellations of origin. Although reservations were not mentioned in the 1924 agreement, the OIV granted them with the understanding that the member could participate in OIV discussions on the reserved matter(s) but not vote on them. The United States withdrew as a member of the OIV on July 1, 2001, just before the deadline for the signature of the new agreement establishing the International Organization of Vine and Wine. That withdrawal was unfortunate. The withdrawal letter, signed by then U.S. secretary of state Madeleine Albright, cites no reasons for the withdrawal. It is the author's personal view that the withdrawal was based in part on the actions of certain heads of members' delegations, and it is the author's hope that the United States will rejoin the OIV, as the world's wine sector greatly benefits from the United States' input and opinions, both governmental and professional. The topic of geographical indications, which was heavily discussed at the OIV when the United States was a member, is now under the primary control of the World Trade Organization and the World Intellectual Property Office. As a scientific and technical international organization, the OIV continues to welcome U.S. technicians.

According to Article 8 of the 2001 Agreement, "[a]n international, intergovernmental organization may participate in or be a Member of the OIV and may help to fund the OIV under conditions determined on a case-by-case basis by the General Assembly based on a proposal from the Executive Committee (COMEX)." The European Community (EC) is such an international, intergovernmental organization; it is not presently an OIV member, but it is negotiating for accession.[12] On September 26, 2008, the European Commission published a lengthy and detailed document entitled "Recommendation from the Commission to the Council to Authorize the Commission to Open and Conduct Negotiations with the International Organization of Vine and Wine (OIV) on the Terms and Conditions for the European Community's Accession."[13]

---

11. The member states of the International Office of Vine and Wine that acceded to, but did not sign, the 2001 Agreement can also be members of the OIV, following a simple request to the director general within a prescribed time limit.

12. Article 2.2(b) of the OIV's Rules of Procedure specified in 2004 that an international, intergovernmental organization that fulfills the following conditions may become a member of OIV: (1) its membership is comprised of sovereign states; (2) authority has been transferred to the international, intergovernmental organization by its member states for a range of issues within the jurisdiction of the OIV, including the right to make decisions that are binding on its member states; and (3) the authority of member states of international, intergovernmental organizations is to remain in force for all other issues unless a transfer of national authority has been specifically communicated to the OIV director general more than one month before the meetings of the OIV's decision-making bodies. Following a proposal of the COMEX and the agreement of the General Assembly, a protocol shall be signed between the OIV and each international, intergovernmental organization defining, in each particular case, the specific membership conditions, including, inter alia, voting rights and financial contribution.

13. Recommendation from the Commission to the Council to Authorize the Commission to Open and Conduct Negotiations with the International Organization of Vine and Wine (OIV) on the Terms and Conditions for the European Community's Accession, at 1, COM (2008) 577 final, Official Journal of European Communities (hereinafter OJ), L 148, June 6, 2008, p. 1.

This document contains an Explanatory Memorandum setting forth the OIV's objectives and activities. The Memorandum notes that six of the 27 member states of the European Union are not members of the OIV, including the United Kingdom, Poland, Denmark, Lithuania, Latvia, and Estonia. This fact notwithstanding, the European Commission concludes: "To ensure consistency in the Community's position in its external relations and permit more appropriate coordination of internal measures adopted within the framework of its competencies, accession of the EC to the OIV can be considered legitimate and necessary." The Commission also points out that existing European regulations refer to OIV's oenological practices and methods of analysis. The proposed negotiating directives for OIV membership are as follows: the EC must obtain the status of full member, putting it on an equal footing with other OIV members, and must be able to participate in negotiations and meetings on an equal footing with other OIV members; the EC will not make a financial contribution to the OIV but may agree to cover expenses incurred in its accession, so long as this contribution is not fixed unilaterally by the OIV and is agreed to by the Community. The negotiations for membership are presently underway but have been hindered by complex rules of procedure and extensive discussions on both sides.

The 2001 Agreement endows all OIV members with certain rights, including the right to vote and participate in the work of the General Assembly, the COMEX, commissions, sub-commissions, and groups of experts in accordance with the OIV's procedures.

In terms of voting, consensus is the norm for the adoption of resolutions by the General Assembly and the COMEX. If, following consultations, consensus is not attained, the members vote on the basis of a *qualified majority* of two-thirds plus one of the members present or represented, on a one member, one vote basis.[14] Since 2004, consensus has always been achieved. That being said, voting by consensus can be a shield for dissenting opinions. In any event, OIV resolutions are not, in principle, binding on members.

The election of the OIV president and director general, as well as votes concerning the OIV budget and the members' financial contributions, are done by a *weighted qualified majority*; that is, two-thirds plus one of the weighted votes of the members.[15] Article 4 of the 2001 Agreement describes a weighted vote:

> Each member shall determine the number of its delegates but shall have only two basic votes plus, where relevant, an additional number of votes calculated from objective criteria that determine the relative position of each Member State in the vine and wine sector under the conditions set forth in Annexes 1 and 2 to this Agreement, which form an integral part thereof. The sum of these two figures shall constitute the number of weighted votes.

Annex 1 of the 2001 Agreement specifies the method for determining "the relative position of each Member State in the vine and wine sector." The determination takes into account the member's wine production volume, vineyard

14. 2001 Agreement, *supra* note 6, art. 5.3(a).
15. *Id.* at art. 5.3(b).

plantings, and wine consumption over the last three years. The total number of additional votes is equal to one half the total number of basic votes (44 member states with two basic votes make 88, half of which is 44). These additional votes are allocated, up to that maximum, according to the formula set forth in Annex 1. The sum of each member state's basic votes and additional votes, if any, is the number of its weighted votes. This ensures a balance of power between producing and non-producing members with respect to voting.

All OIV members pay a compulsory financial contribution established each year by the General Assembly.[16] The total amount of compulsory contributions to be paid by the members is calculated based on the budget adopted by the General Assembly. One-third of the total amount is divided equally between the basic votes, and two-thirds are divided in proportion to the additional votes, achieving a balance between "rich" and "poor" members.

The failure to pay dues may result in expulsion from the OIV.[17] Members may withdraw from the organization at any time following a period of six months after a written notice is sent to the OIV's Director General and the Ministry of Foreign Affairs of the French Republic.[18]

ii. OBSERVERS

Observers are of several types. First, a state, a member state of a federation of states, a province, a region, or an international non-governmental organization (NGO) that was granted observer status by the International Office of Vine and Wine remains an OIV observer unless the COMEX decides otherwise or the party elects to withdraw. That is the unique situation of the Chinese province of Yantai.

A non-member state or a territory (or group of territories) belonging to a non-member state that does not conduct its own international relations also may be an OIV observer. Such observers are invited to submit an application to join the organization after no more than five uninterrupted years as an observer.

Each sovereign state observer must pay an annual financial contribution equal to that paid by the member states for their basic votes. Observers may attend the General Assembly and participate in the working sessions of the commissions, sub-commissions, and groups of experts.

An international NGO with an interest in vines, wine, table grapes, raisins, or similar products or issues also may be an OIV observer.[19] All requests for NGO observer status are presented by the Director General to the COMEX for approval. NGO observers may attend the General Assembly and participate in the working sessions of the commissions, sub-commissions, and groups of experts. Presently, there are nine NGO observers: International Federation of Wines and Spirits (FIVS), Assembly of European Wine Growing Regions

---

16. 2001 Agreement, *supra* note 6, art. 6.
17. Internal Rules, *supra* note 10, art. 2.5 et seq.
18. The member is liable for its prorated financial contribution through the effective date of its withdrawal.
19. *Id.* Annex 4 (Guidelines concerning Observer Status of International Non-governmental Organizations in the OIV).

(AREVE), International Union of Oenologists (UIOE), World Federation of Wine Competitions (VINOFED), Amorim Academy, Center for Research on Mountain Viticulture (CERVIM), Wine International University Association (AUIV), Oenological Products and Practices International Association (OEnoppia), and International Wine Law Association (IWLA).

Finally, an international intergovernmental organization (IIGO) may be a special-status observer. Such an observer may not vote[20] but may attend and participate in all OIV meetings,[21] contribute to the making of decisions and help to fund the OIV under conditions determined, on a case-by-case basis, by the General Assembly on a proposal from the COMEX.[22] In 2007, the General Assembly added Annex 3 to the OIV's Internal Rules. Entitled "Protocol of Engagement with International Intergovernmental Organizations," the annex outlines the engagement procedures between the OIV and IIGOs that have expertise and a direct interest in the OIV's objectives or that exercise functions that correspond to those of the OIV, notably the development of standards.[23] Engagement may take the form of special observer status, scientific and technical cooperation and collaboration, and/or occasional or regular invitations to participate in OIV meetings. Examples of IIGOs that are involved to some extent in OIV activities today are the World Trade Organization (WTO), through its Agreement on Agriculture, Agreement on the Application of Sanitary and Phytosanitary Measures, Agreement on Technical Barriers to Trade, and Agreement on Trade-Related Aspects of Intellectual Property Rights; the World Intellectual Property Organization (WIPO), through the Lisbon Agreement for International Registration and Protection of Appellations of Origin; and the Food and Agricultural Organization (FAO) of the United Nations and World Health Organization (WHO), through their food standards and guidelines, known as the Codex Alimentarius.

iii. GUESTS

In the normal course of its scientific and technical activities, the OIV follows all vine and wine scientific news. Sometimes the OIV goes to the source by

20. *Id.* Annex 2.

21. 2001 Agreement, *supra* note 6, art. 8.

22. *Id.* Requests for observer status are addressed in writing to the director general of the OIV and must indicate the nature of organization's activity and the reasons for wishing to obtain observer status. Each request is examined by the COMEX. *Id.* at art. 2.1(b). The COMEX takes into consideration factors such as the activities of the organization, its composition, the number of OIV members belonging to the organization, reciprocity in terms of attending meetings at and receiving documents from the observer, and whether the organization has been associated with the work of the OIV in the past. Following the CODEX's recommendation, the General Assembly, not the COMEX, decides whether to grant special observer status. If granted, a special agreement adopted by the General Assembly identifies the specific conditions for collaboration, including the duration and the amount of any annual financial contribution. Special observer status entitles the party to participate (present documents and opinions, but not vote) in the working sessions of commissions, sub-commissions, and groups of experts, and to attend General Assembly and COMEX meetings addressing issues of direct interest to that party without involvement in decision making. Observer status granted to an international intergovernmental organization may be reviewed if the conditions or the bases on which the OIV granted that status have changed. Decisions to withdraw observer status are made by the General Assembly.

23. Internal Rules, *supra* note 10, Annex 3.

inviting scientific authorities as guests.[24] A non-member state that is not an observer also may be invited by the director general, with the agreement of the OIV president, to attend the General Assembly and commission meetings.

Without prejudice to existing agreements, an IIGO (e.g., the EC, the WTO, and the WIPO) or any other natural or legal entity may be invited by the director general, with the consent of the OIV president, to participate in the working sessions of the General Assembly or the COMEX and/or the meetings of the commissions, sub-commissions, and groups of experts with the agreement of the relevant president. A professor of viticulture, an oenologist, a wine economist, or a lawyer who is neither representing a member state nor part of an observer delegation also may be invited to address a particular topic.[25]

c. Constituent Bodies

The constituent bodies of the OIV are numerous but not excessive in the context of the organization's mission and its scope of work. They include the General Assembly; the president; the vice presidents; the director general; the COMEX; the Scientific and Technical Committee; the Steering Committee; the Secretariat; and various commissions, sub-commissions, and groups of experts.[26] In terms of procedures, these bodies function in an open and transparent manner.[27]

i. THE GENERAL ASSEMBLY

The General Assembly is the OIV's plenary body.[28] As the "supreme body" of the OIV, it is fully empowered.[29] The General Assembly is composed of all the delegates nominated by the members,[30] with each member freely determining the number of its delegates and their qualifications and activities (e.g., public or private, academic or business related).[31] Each member is required to inform the director general of the composition and the head of its delegation at least one month before any meeting of the General Assembly. At the opening

---

24. Internal Rules, *supra* note 10, art. 5.

25. Annex 3 of the Internal Rules related to intergovernmental organizations states specifically that the OIV may invite any cooperating organization with specific expertise of importance to the work of the OIV to attend certain sessions, either occasionally or regularly, in order for that organization to present its own contextually relevant work. However,

> [n]either guest status nor special observer status permits actual participation in OIV proceedings, but merely allows those with such status to intervene in or attend certain OIV bodies without the possibility of presenting proposals or amendments. Neither status entitles the Community to speak on matters falling within its exclusive competence, or to advocate decisions taken at Community level.

Recommendation from the Commission to the Council to Authorise the Commission to Open and Conduct Negotiations with the International Organisation of Vine and Wine (OIV) on the Terms and Conditions for the European Community's Accession, at 3.2, COM (2008) 577 final (Sept. 26, 2008).

26. 2001 Agreement, *supra* note 6, art. 3.1.

27. *Id.* at art. 5.7.

28. *Id.* at art. 3.2.

29. *Id.* at art. 5.2.

30. *Id.* at art. 3.2.

31. Internal Rules, *supra* note 10, at art. 6.2(a).

of each General Assembly, the director general circulates a list of the member states entitled to vote and participate in the sessions as well as the number of their respective votes.[32]

Additionally, each observer informs the director general of its representatives at least one month before any General Assembly. The director general then circulates to the heads of the member state delegations a list of the observer representatives and guests who are attending that General Assembly.[33]

The General Assembly meets once a year[34] at dates and locations determined by the COMEX.[35] The tradition is to hold meetings one year in Paris and the following two years in two different member states. Extraordinary sessions may be convened at the request of one-third of the members.[36]

Only the heads of each delegation — or, in their absence, their substitutes — may speak at a General Assembly. However, a member of a delegation may speak at the request of the head of that delegation, generally to provide a technical explanation.[37]

In the framework of the OIV's objectives and activities, the General Assembly discusses and adopts regulations relating to the organization and working of the OIV; drafts resolutions of a general, scientific, technical, economic, or legal nature; and creates or disbands commissions and sub-commissions.[38] It establishes the budget and audits and approves the organization's accounting. The General Assembly also adopts cooperation and collaboration protocols with various international organizations on matters relating to vine and wine products.[39]

Resolutions are the ultimate work product of the General Assembly. The scientific, technical, economic, and legal work of the OIV and the development of standards are embodied in these resolutions.

Decisions of the General Assembly are based on consensus with three exceptions: (1) the election of the presidents of the OIV, its commissions, and sub-commissions; (2) the election of the director general; and (3) budgetary and financial matters.[40] But it must be underscored that all resolutions of a general, scientific, technical, economic, or legal nature are typically adopted only by the consensus of all 44 member states.

When the General Assembly does not reach consensus on a draft resolution, the president is authorized to consult with members in the intervening period before the next General Assembly in an effort to achieve consensus. If that effort fails, the president calls for a vote on the basis of a qualified majority — a vote of two-thirds plus one of the members on a one member,

32. *Id.* at art. 6.2(b).
33. *Id.* at art. 6.3, 6.4.
34. Heads of delegation from one-third of the members representing at least half the weighted votes constitute a quorum. A head of delegation may represent another member upon written proxy. 2001 Agreement, *supra* note 6, art. 5.2; Internal Rules, *supra* note 10, art. 6.6 *et seq.*
35. Internal Rules, *supra* note 10, art. 7.1(j).
36. 2001 Agreement, *supra* note 6, art. 5.1.
37. Internal Rules, *supra* note 10, art. 6.8.
38. 2001 Agreement, *supra* note 6, art. 2.
39. *Id.* at art. 5.1.
40. *Id.* at art. 5.3.

one vote basis. Nevertheless, the vote will be postponed for a period of one year if a member considers that its essential national interests are at risk.

ii. EXECUTIVE COMMITTEE

The General Assembly may delegate some of its powers to the COMEX, which consists of one delegate per member state.[41] As the executive body of the General Assembly, the COMEX acts on its behalf during the interim period between General Assembly sessions.[42] In this sense, the COMEX is the OIV's governing body.

The COMEX usually meets twice a year, typically at the initiative of the director general and the president, or at the request of one-quarter of its members. The Internal Rules set forth the requirements for a quorum (Article 7.7), the preparation and circulation of an agenda and supporting documents (Article 7.8), and the voting procedures (Article 7.16). The responsibilities of the COMEX are scientific, essentially steering the scientific activities of the OIV; fiscal, serving as OIV's financial advisor; and organizational, deciding on observer status, IIGO protocol, and other administrative matters. Some administrative matters may be entrusted to a steering committee, known as the Bureau, which is essentially the daily cabinet of the COMEX.

The decision-making procedures of the COMEX are set out in Article 5 of the 2001 Agreement.[43] Again, decision by consensus is the norm.

iii. SCIENTIFIC AND TECHNICAL COMMITTEE

The OIV conducts its scientific activities through commissions, sub-commissions, and expert groups, coordinated by a Scientific and Technical Committee (STC) within the framework of a strategic plan approved by the General Assembly.[44] Considering the OIV's role as an "intergovernmental organization of a scientific and technical nature, and a recognized authority on vines, wines, wine-based beverages, grapes, raisins and other vine products,"[45] the STC is at the heart of the organization's activities.

The OIV's Internal Rules provide that the STC be made up of the OIV president serving as president of the STC; the first vice president of the OIV; a vice president appointed among the members of the STC, the presidents of the commissions, sub-commissions, and groups of experts; the vice presidents of the commissions and sub-commissions; the scientific secretaries of the commissions and sub-commissions; the second vice president of the OIV and the former presidents of the OIV; and two qualified persons without voting rights who need not be nationals of OIV member states and who are appointed by the president for his term of office.

---

41. *Id.* at art. 3.2. The COMEX also includes the OIV president, who serves as president of the COMEX, the first vice president of the OIV, who is the first vice president of the COMEX, and the vice president of the Scientific and Technical Committee, who is the second vice president of the COMEX. *Id.* at art. 7.2, 7.4. Only delegates or their substitutes are entitled to vote. *Id.* at art.7.3. At the request of one of the members of the COMEX, a vote may be taken by secret ballot. *Id.* at art. 7.13.

42. Internal Rules, *supra* note 10, art. 7.1.

43. *See id.* at art. 7.9.

44. 2001 Agreement, *supra* note 6, art. 3.3.

45. *Id.* at art. 1.2.

The STC in principle meets twice a year. The STC sessions are private and are reserved exclusively for its members, although the Director General, with the agreement of the president, may invite one or more participants on an exceptional basis.

As the conductor of the OIV's scientific work, defining the scientific policy of the organization, the STC is responsible for the following: (1) developing the draft of a three-year strategic plan that sets forth the general framework of work to be done by the commissions, sub-commissions, and groups of experts according to the main strategic orientations defined by the General Assembly; (2) defining and submitting variations to or updates of the strategic plan to the COMEX within the framework of an annual detailed work program; (3) examining after each work session of the commissions, sub-commissions, and groups of experts the proceedings, reports, and draft agendas presented by their respective presidents; (4) putting forth the names of candidates to chair the commissions and sub-commissions and the names of scientific secretaries to the COMEX; (5) proposing to the COMEX the creation or discontinuance of groups of experts, defining their duties and terms of office; (6) developing and presenting to the COMEX the themes of the OIV world congresses and proposing meetings and symposia that it considers appropriate.

The STC acts by consensus. If the STC is unable to reach a consensus, the STC president is authorized to consult with the members in order to attain agreement prior to the next STC meeting. When all measures designed to reach a consensus have failed, the president refers the matter to the COMEX.[46] If the drafted strategic plan cannot be adopted by consensus, the STC votes by simple majority, that is, one half of the members present or represented plus one, and upon a member's request, by secret ballot.

d. Governance

The president, vice presidents, and the director general are the "[m]ain principals mandated by the Organization."[47] A candidacy for the presidency must be presented by the government or other authority of a member state of which the candidate is a national within a time limit set by the Bureau. Each member of the organization may nominate only one candidate. Candidates, in principle, must have participated in at least two general assemblies. The list of candidates, together with the candidates' curricula vitae, is provided to the members at least six months before the election.

The OIV president is elected by secret ballot for a non-renewable three-year term based on a weighted qualified majority vote, that is, two-thirds plus one of the weighted votes of members, provided that half plus one of the members present or represented have voted for that candidate.[48]

46. Internal Rules, *supra* note 10, art. 8.8.

47. *Id.* at ch. 3.

48. The president assumes his or her duties the day after the election. At the end of the three-year term, the outgoing president has the right to occupy the position of first vice president for a new term of three years.

The current president is Yves Bénard of France. Some years ago a California economist, Kirby Moulton, was president of the OIV. The president serves as the chairperson at meetings of the General Assembly, the COMEX, the STC, and the Bureau. The president also attends the meetings of the other constituent bodies of the organization. The president has no precise responsibility or duties other than to preside. However, as an experienced OIV participant, he or she is generally a wise advisor to those who carry out the organization's work, including, naturally, the director general.

The director general and his or her staff compose the general secretariat of OIV.[49] The current director general is Federico Castellucci of Italy. For the election of the director general, each member within a time limit set by the Bureau can propose one candidate who is a national of that member state. The list of candidates together with the candidates' curricula vitae is sent to the members at least six months before the election.[50]

The General Assembly elects the director general for a five-year term by secret ballot and by a weighted qualified majority. He or she may be re-elected for a second five-year term by the same procedure. The General Assembly also has the right to remove the director general.[51]

The director general is responsible for the internal administration of the OIV and for the recruitment and management of the staff.[52] As the most senior official of the organization, the director general carries out the decisions of the General Assembly and the work program approved by the COMEX. The director general also has important financial responsibilities; the Internal Rules dealing with financial regulations mention the director general 35 times. Overall, the director general is in charge of the management of the OIV's scientific and administrative activities, including all the material and human resources required to run this membership-based organization. The director general must be fit for duty.

e. Scientific Work and Heritage

The OIV conducts its scientific activities through expert groups, commissions, and sub-commissions, coordinated by the STC, within the framework of the strategic plan approved by the General Assembly.[53] The OIV maintains close links with competent international organizations; observes, analyzes, and interprets international vine and wine sector issues and trends, initiatives, and regulations; and coordinates all standardization work undertaken by various international governmental and non-governmental organizations.

The present strategic plan for the OIV covers the period between 2009 and 2012. It is 16 pages long and includes the following 15 strategic research axes: (1) statistical analysis of the vine and wine sectors; (2) economic analysis of

49. Internal Rules, *supra* note 10, tit. III, art. 40 ("Staff Status Regulations").
50. *Id.* at art. 141.
51. 2001 Agreement, *supra* note 6, art. 5.4(b); Internal Rules, *supra* note 10, art. 142.
52. 2001 Agreement, *supra* note 6, art. 3.5; Internal Rules, *supra* note 10, art. 147. Currently, there are 16 General Secretariat members of the OIV, comprising nine different nationalities.
53. 2001 Agreement, *supra* note 6, art. 2.3.

these sectors; (3) viticultural (grape growing), vinicultural (winemaking), biophysical, economic, and social environments; (4) sustainable viticulture and viniculture, "integrated production,"[54] and organic production; (5) climate change and its relationship to viticulture and viniculture; (6) greenhouse effects, including carbon dioxide balance; (7) biodiversity and genetic resources; (8) regulation and impact of biotechnologies; (9) oenological practices and techniques; (10) identification and analytical methods; (11) safety and quality; (12) nutrition and health, both individual and societal; (13) designation and labeling; (14) collection, processing, and dissemination of information; and (15) international cooperation.[55]

The commissions and sub-commissions review all subjects within their respective fields of competency[56] and meet at least once a year.[57] Presently, there are four commissions, enumerated below with the nationality of the current commission president (as of 2009), shown in parentheses:

Commission 1: "Viticulture" (Italy);
Commission 2: "Oenology" (Germany);

54. "Integrated production" is a term of art in France (*agriculture raisonnée*) and Italy (*agricoltura integrata*); it is essentially sustainable, but not organic, agriculture.

55. Each axis of the Strategic Plan is developed with detailed information and result indicators as illustrated by the following examples:

- *Regulation and impact of biotechnologies* is divided into ten subtopics, including analyzing the implications for human health of using genetically modified organisms (GMOs) in viticulture; evaluating the environmental impacts of GMOs; analyzing the socioeconomic impacts of using biotechnologies and the consumer attitudes about the use of biotechnologies; establishing evaluation protocols for vine cultivars and GMOs; and studying and defining taxonomy for genetically modified vines and microorganisms.
- *Sustainable vitiviniculture, integrated production* and organic production contains eight subtopics, including establishing definitions and guidelines for the integrated production of grapes and wine; preparing a guide for implementing sustainable development of all vine products; developing definitions and guidelines for organic production with regard to viticultural and oenological practices; and evaluating the possibility of reducing dependency on phytosanitary inputs and the review of transitional strategies.
- *Viticultural and vinicultural biophysical, economic, and social environments* is dedicated to evaluating geopedological zoning and climate methodologies; analyzing problems related to drought, salinization, and soil density, especially where competition for natural resources is anticipated; defining terroir; and developing official OIV translations of wine and vine vocabulary.
- *Economic analysis of sector* includes collecting existing data and devising methodologies to calculate grape production costs; developing methodologies to calculate the direct costs of grape production and the processing and marketing of viticultural and vinicultural products; and reviewing world consumer behavior and habits.
- *Oenological practices and techniques* evaluates new oenological practices with precise indicators.
- *Denomination and labeling* establishes the criteria for designating wines as organic and updates OIV standards on wine labeling as concerns vintage, grape variety, and food safety and quality.

56. Internal Rules, *supra* note 10, art. 10.1 *et seq.*

57. The commissions and sub-commissions have quorums when one-third plus one of the members who have nominated a delegate and/or an expert are represented. Consensus is the normal method by which the commissions and sub-commissions make decisions. If consensus is not reached, the president of the relevant commission or sub-commission refers the matter to the STC. Each commission is also responsible for preparing the definitive draft resolutions within its field of competence.

Commission 3: "Economy and Law" (New Zealand); and
Commission 4: "Safety and Health" (Croatia).

There are also two sub-commissions: "Methods of Analysis and Appraisal of Wines" (Spain), attached to Commission 2; and "Table grapes, Raisins and Unfermented Vine Products" (Portugal), attached to Commission 1.

According to the strategic plan, Commission 1 conducts important scientific work in the areas of biodiversity and genetic resources, climate change effects on viticulture, sustainable viticulture and viniculture, and the regulation and impact of biotechnologies. The future of viticulture is quite literally within the responsibility of Commission 1.

Commission 2 addresses all matters relating to the composition and production of wines, their storage conditions, packaging, transportation, and consumption.[58] The strategic plan assigns to this commission work on climate change, the evolution and activity of micro-organisms, and the definition of new oenological practices and techniques, including identification and analytical methods with a view to completing and updating the *Compendium of International Methods of Wine and Must Analysis*. Commission 2 and its subcommission on "Methods of Analysis and Appraisal of Wines" play a critical role in the OIV's ongoing scientific work.

Commission 3 deals with all legal, regulatory, economic, and socioeconomic matters related to vine and wine products. The strategic plan charges this commission with monitoring and developing statistics on price and value, the economic situation of the vine and wine sectors, and world consumer behavior and habits, as well as with calculating carbon balances, regulating genetically modified organisms (GMOs), and updating labeling standards.

Commission 4 focuses on the relationships between wine, vine products, and the health of consumers and operators. It is specifically responsible for promoting and focusing research on appropriate nutritional and health issues.[59] Topics include analyzing the implications on human health of using GMOs in viticulture; developing assessment procedures for the toxicological risk of viticultural and vinicultural procedures and treatments, and identifying for evaluation the primary contaminants and toxins; researching, in collaboration with the WHO and other relevant organizations, the effects on human health of consuming wine and other vine products; and setting the direction for research, in collaboration with the FAO and the WHO, on the nutritional potential of all non-alcoholic vine products (grapes, raisins, juice, etc.).

The groups of experts are responsible for studying specific scientific and technical issues at the request of the General Assembly, the COMEX, the STC, commissions, and sub-commissions within the scope of the strategic plan. Appointed by each member, the experts are scientific delegates who are interested in the work of the relevant group and who have a worldwide reputation for expertise in the given field. They propose the components of the strategic

58. Internal Rules, *supra* note 10, art. 10.4.
59. *Id.* at art. 10.5 *bis*.

plan relevant to their work and then report on their research to the STC as well as to the commission or the sub-commission to which they are attached.[60]

The chart of expert groups (as of 2010) within each commission follows:

- Commission 1: "Viticulture," four expert groups:
  - Genetic resources and vine selection,
  - Vine protection,
  - Management and innovation of viticultural techniques, and
  - Viticultural environment and climate change, plus an ad hoc group on raisins.
- Commission 2: "Oenology," three expert groups:
  - Technology,
  - Microbiology, and
  - Specification of oenological products.
- Commission 3: "Economy and Law," four expert groups:
  - Markets and consumption,
  - Economic and situational analysis,
  - Law and consumer information, and
  - Vine- or wine-based spirituous beverages.
- Commission 4: "Safety and Health," two expert groups:
  - Food safety, and
  - Consumption, nutrition and health, plus three ad hoc groups on cartography, innovative biotechnologies, and carbon dioxide balance.

The expert groups meet at least once a year.[61] Consensus is the usual method of decision making. If the group of experts is unable to achieve consensus, the president of the relevant group refers the matter to the president of the commission or the sub-commission to which that group reports.

Draft resolutions, standards, or recommendations prepared by a group of experts are considered in accordance with an elaborate procedure set forth in the Internal Rules.[62] These procedures ensure that all resolutions are the result of intense scrutiny and lengthy debate, spanning three years or more, which establishes their credibility and worth.

All resolutions of a general, scientific, technical, economic, or legal nature are examined in a step-by-step procedure[63] that begins with the preparation of a preliminary draft resolution at the request of one or more of the following: the scientific delegates from the relevant group of experts or sub-commission, the director general, the STC, the COMEX, or the General Assembly. This resolution is then reviewed by the relevant group of experts or sub-commission, following the circulation of any scientific papers relating to the subject and taking into account the opinions of the other interested groups of experts and sub-commissions. If consensus is achieved at this stage, the draft resolution is forwarded by the director general to the members and to the presidents and

60. *Id.* at art. 11.1.
61. *Id.* at art. 11.8.
62. *Id.* at art. 11.13.
63. *Id.* at art. 20.

scientific secretaries of the other commissions and sub-commissions. The text is then modified, edited, or amended, as required, and takes the form of a provisional draft resolution. After further consultations and discussions, a draft resolution is re-examined by the relevant commissions and modified if necessary. Next, a definitive draft resolution is submitted to the General Assembly, where it is examined by the Drafting Committee of the organization, which is responsible for harmonizing all resolutions and ensuring their linguistic coherence. Finally, the General Assembly examines the final draft resolution, discusses it, revises it if necessary, and makes its own decision.[64]

Through this elaborate procedure, the OIV's scientific and technical resolutions are subject to intense scrutiny by all the viticultural and vinicultural institutions, organizations, and professionals of the world wine sector. The consensus of 44 countries, achieved through a democratic procedure, carries great weight in the international arena.

The OIV not only manages its internal scientific work through commissions and expert groups, but it also works with other organizations in a variety of activities. One example is the World Vine and Wine Congress, which is the annual global event of the wine and vine sector. The congress typically is held before the OIV General Assembly. The director general of the OIV delivers an annual report on the world wine and vine situation, including details on vine plantings worldwide, wine production, imports, and exports.

Organizing a World Vine and Wine Congress is the joint responsibility of the inviting member(s) and the OIV.[65] The scientific program and work sessions are under the OIV's control, and the congress is open to any expert or specialist wishing to contribute presentations, papers, posters, or the like that are related to the scientific program.[66]

Other meetings, symposia, and international seminars designed to study in greater depth important issues of general or specific interest to the vine and wine sectors may be organized at the initiative of the OIV, its members, or observers. In some cases, the OIV sponsors the event; in other cases, there is a third-party sponsor.

Each year since 1930, the OIV presents awards to the best original, pertinent works of international scope in the vine and wine sectors that have been published over the previous two years. These works are evaluated by a panel of specialists. The Award Jury is composed of academics, journalists, and scientists designated by the STC, COMEX, and the director general. One award is given in each of the following fields: viticulture; oenology; viticultural or vinicultural economics and law; history, literature, and fine arts; medicine and hygiene related to wine; monographs and specialized studies; and symposium proceedings.[67]

f. OIV Standardization

The OIV 2001 Agreement explicitly recognizes and authorizes the organization's standardization work. Article 2 states that one of the OIV's objectives is

---

64. 2001 Agreement, *supra* note 6, art. 5.
65. Internal Rules, *supra* note 10, art. 22.2.
66. *Id.* at art. 22.4(d), 22.6.
67. *Id.* at art. 12.

to "contribute to international harmonization of existing practices and standards and, as necessary, to the preparation of new international standards in order to improve the conditions for producing and marketing vine and wine products, and to help ensure that the interests of consumers are taken into account." This article further states that the OIV shall "draw up and frame recommendations and monitor implementation of such recommendations in liaison with its Members, especially in the following areas: (1) conditions for grape production; (2) oenological practices; (3) definition and/or description of products, labeling and marketing conditions; and (4) methods for analyzing and assessing vine products."[68]

To accomplish these objectives, the OIV submits to its members proposals in the following areas: "(i) guaranteeing the authenticity of vine products, (ii) protecting geographical indications, . . . insofar as they do not call into question international agreements relating to trade and intellectual property, (iii) improving scientific and technical criteria for recognizing and protecting new viticultural plant varieties."[69] The organization also "[c]ontribute[s] to the harmonization and adaptation of regulations by its Members or, where relevant, facilitate[s] mutual recognition of practices within its field of activities."[70]

As part of its standardized efforts, the OIV publishes so-called Prescriptive Publications classified by subject matter. Sample subjects and publications follow.

i. VITICULTURAL STANDARDS

(1) OIV List of Grape Varieties and Vitis Species (2nd edition, 2009) describes Vitis varieties and species using morphological characteristics (ampelography);

(2) Description of World Vine Varieties describes 128 characteristics of Vitis; and

(3) International List of Vine Varieties and Their Synonyms promotes harmonization of vine varietal designations and identifies procedures for the development of international trade in wines and vines.

ii. OENOLOGICAL STANDARDS

(1) International Oenological Codex is a compilation of the principal chemical products used to make and store wine and the conditions of their use;

(2) *International Code of Oenological Practice* includes instructions and limits on the usage of various chemical products used in winemaking; and

(3) *Compendium of International Methods of Analysis of Wines and Musts* is a two-volume compendium, published in 1962 and re-edited and updated in 2010. It lists all the various international methods of analysis, certificates of analysis models, and maximum acceptable limits of specific substances.

68. 2001 Agreement, *supra* note 6, art. 2.2(b).

69. *Id.* at art. 2.2(c).

70. *Id.* at art. 2.2(d). Mutual recognition also has been included in the 2006 U.S.-European Community (EC) Wine Accord.

iii. ECONOMIC STANDARDS

(1) *International Standard for Labeling of Wine and Spirits of Viticultural or Vinicultural Origin* is the OIV's list of labeling standards recommended for adoption by the member states, designed to facilitate international trade and to ensure straightforward information to the consumer;

(2) *OIV Standard for International Wine and Spirituous Beverages of Viticultural or Vinicultural Origin Competitions*; and

(3) *Guidelines for Sustainable Viticulture and Viniculture: Production, Processing and Packaging of Products*[71] is one of several guidelines published by the OIV.

The OIV's standards are adopted through the passage of resolutions by the General Assembly. These resolutions are simple propositions to members states that have no legally binding effect. Nevertheless, as described above, the resolutions are subject to considerable scrutiny during the step-by-step procedure and are generally voted on by the General Assembly after three years of work involving all 44 member states.

The content of the resolutions varies considerably. A resolution can be a general wish or a specific, technical rule. Typically, a resolution proposes a rule or behavior (action or abstention). However, wishes of the General Assembly have no compulsory effect. Even resolutions of a scientific and technical nature, with specific mandates and prescriptions, are not binding on the member states without their acceptance.

For sovereign states, whether or not they are OIV members,[72] a resolution becomes compulsory when it has been accepted, expressly or tacitly, typically by introducing the OIV recommendation into national or intergovernmental law. As an example, the EC has introduced the OIV's standards directly into its regulations, especially analytical methods, specification of oenological substances, and the names and synonyms of wine grape varieties originating in non-EC countries, except for any conflicting provisions that might be included in a bilateral agreement.[73] The same recognition of, and reference to, OIV

---

71. OIV, Guidelines for Sustainable Viticulture and Viniculture: Production, Processing and Packaging of Products, Resolution CST 1/2008 (June 20, 2008); *see also* R. Tinlot, The OIV Contribution in the International Qualitative Standardization, 69 Bulletin de l'OIV 783-784: 518-524 (1996).

72. The addressees of the OIV resolutions are numerous and varied. They are not restricted to OIV member states but can also include non-members and wine producers or traders. No addressee is obliged to comply with an OIV resolution.

73. Specific examples follow. First, Council Regulation (EC) No. 479/2008 of April 29, 2008, on the common organization of the market in wine, explains in recital 25: "In order to meet the international standards in this field, the Commission should as a general rule base itself on the oenological practices recommended by the International Organization of Vine and Wine (OIV)." Article 30 provides: "When authorizing oenological practices . . . the Commission shall: (a) base its decisions on the oenological practices recommended and published by the International organization of vine and wine (OIV) as well as on the results of any experimental use of as yet unauthorized oenological practices." Second, Article 3 also refers directly to OIV: "The methods of analysis for determining the composition of the products covered by this regulation and the rules whereby it may be established whether these products have undergone processes contrary to the authorized oenological practices shall be those recommended and published by the OIV." Third, for imported wines, Article 82 of this regulation states: "Save as otherwise provided in agreements concluded . . . products referred to in [the regulation] shall be produced in accordance with oenological practices recommended and published by the OIV or authorized by the Community

standards is found in China[74] and in MERCOSUR, a regional trade agreement among Argentina, Brazil, Paraguay, Uruguay, and Venezuela.[75]

---

pursuant to this regulation and its implementing measures." Fourth, EC Regulation No. 606/2009 concerning the categories of grapevine products, oenological practices, and applicable restrictions refers to the OIV's International Oenological Codex or to the Compendium of International Methods of Analysis of Wines and Musts. The regulation provides:

> Whereas (4) Annex V (A) to Regulation (EC) No. 1493/1999 lays down maximum levels of sulphites in wines produced in the Community that are higher than the limits laid down by the International Organization of Vine and Wine (OIV). The limits should be aligned with those of the OIV, which are recognized internationally, and the derogations [exceptions] required for certain sweet wines produced in small quantities because of their higher sugar content and to ensure their good conservation should be retained. In the light of current scientific studies into the reduction and replacement of sulphites in wine and the sulphite intake from wine in the human diet, provision must be made for re-examining the maximum limits at a later date with a view to reducing them. . . . (9) Purity and identification specifications of a large number of substances used in oenological practices are already laid down in the Community rules on foodstuffs and in the *International Oenological Codex* of the OIV. For the purposes of harmonization and clarity, those specifications should be used in the first instance, while providing for additional rules specific to the situation in the Community."

Fifth, this same regulation provides in Appendix 12 ("Requirements for treatment with cation exchangers to ensure the tartaric stabilization of the wine") that the use of cationic resins "must not excessively modify the physico-chemical composition or the organoleptic characteristics of the wine and must comply with the limits set out in point 3 of the *International Oenological Codex* monograph, 'Cation-exchange resins,' published by the OIV." Finally, Commission Regulation No. 607/2009 sets forth detailed rules regarding protected designations of origin and geographical indications, traditional terms, labeling, and presentation of certain wine sector products. This regulation states in article 62 ("Name of wine grape variety"):

> 1. The names of the wine grape varieties or their synonyms . . . may appear on the labels of the products concerned under the conditions laid down in points (a) and (b) of this Article. (a) *For wines produced in the EC*, the names of the wine grape varieties or their synonyms shall be those mentioned in the wine grape varieties classification by Member States. (b) For Member States exempted from the classification obligation . . . the names of the wine grape varieties or synonyms shall be mentioned in the "International list of vine varieties and their synonyms" managed by the International Organization of Vine and Wine (OIV). (c) *For wines originating in third countries*, the conditions of use of the names of the wine grape varieties or their synonyms shall conform with the rules applicable to wine producers in the third country concerned, including those emanating from representative professional organizations, and the names of the wine grape varieties or their synonyms are mentioned in at least one of the following lists: (i) the International Organization of Vine and Wine (OIV); (ii) the Union for the Protection of Plant Varieties (UPOV); (iii) the International Board for Plant Genetic Resources (IBPGR).

74. On May 2, 2006, China notified the WTO of its national standards for wines, issued by the General Administration of Quality Supervision, Inspection and Quarantine of the People's Republic of China and the Standardization Administration of China. *See* WTO Committee on Technical Barriers to Trade (TBT), Notification to the Committee on Technical Barriers to Trade, G/TBT/N/CHM/197 (May 26, 2006); National Standard of the People's Republic of China: Wines, GB15037-200 (May 24, 2006). The standards follow the basic form and substance of, but are not identical to, the OIV rules. The major differences include new wine categories based on sugar content and the limits on citric acid, copper, methanol, and preservatives. The updated standard also bans the use of synthetic colorings, sweeteners, flavorings, and thickeners in wine.

75. Reglamento Vitivinícola del Mercosur [Wine Rules of Mercosur] provides: "1.4. Los Estados Partes armonizarán sus legislaciones básicamente en función de los convenios, principios normativos y recomendaciones de la OIV." ["The Member States shall harmonize their legislation according to agreements, norms and recommendations of the OIV."] MERCOSUR/GMC/RES No. 45/96 (June 26, 1996).

Even those OIV standards that are not adopted by a member have an effect because that member is forced into a defensive posture and must explain its position in OIV meetings or elsewhere on the international stage (e.g., WTO). The member does not become an outlaw but an outsider. Therefore, at the very least, each member state must examine carefully and in a bona fide manner the relevant OIV resolution that represents the consensus of the international organization of which it is a member and whose objectives it has accepted.[76]

OIV resolutions on methods of analysis and the appreciation of wines have an altogether different character. The OIV is charged with enforcing the International Convention on the Standardization of Methods of Wine Analysis and Evaluation (the Convention), signed in Paris, France, on October 13, 1954, by Spain, France, Portugal, Turkey, Greece, Austria, Italy, Chile, Morocco, Yugoslavia, Germany, Argentina, South Africa, Hungary, the United Kingdom, and Brazil. To implement this Convention, the OIV created the sub-commission of methods of analysis and appreciation of wines. This Convention is still in force, and its mandate is integrated into the OIV mission. As such, the United Kingdom, which is not an OIV member but is a signatory to the Convention, is an invited guest at the OIV's sub-commission meetings. Article 1 of the Convention states that the parties "committed themselves to adopting in their national regulations concerning the control of wines destined for international trade the definitions and the methods which are specified in . . . the Convention." These 17 states are therefore bound by the OIV's methods of analysis.

g. Relations with Other International Organizations

The OIV's objectives include "assist[ing] other international organizations, both intergovernmental and non-governmental, especially those that carry out standardization activities"[77] and "contribut[ing] to international harmonization of existing practices and standards."[78] These objectives explicitly envision the OIV's scientific and technical cooperation and collaboration with other intergovernmental organizations. Interestingly, no international intergovernmental organization has been granted observer status by the OIV; yet there are other forms of engagement for the OIV with these organizations.[79]

76. A technical resolution may be enforceable through other means. For example, the OIV's approval of the given competition or meeting can only be obtained if the requesting organization enforces the OIV's rules on the relevant competition and any sponsorship resolutions. OIV, Guidelines for Granting OIV Patronage of International Wine and Spirituous Beverages of Vitivinicultural Origin Competitions, Resolution OIV/Concours 332B/2009 (July 3, 2009); OIV, Guidelines for Granting OIV Sponsorship for Symposia, Meetings and International Seminars, Resolution EGA 5/2007 (Oct. 16, 2007).

77. 2001 Agreement, *supra* note 6, art. 2.1(b).

78. *Id.* at art. 2.1(c).

79. Internal Rules, *supra* note 10, Annex 3. The COMEX, following notification by the STC, may identify an IIGO that has specific expertise of particular importance to the work of the OIV. This organization may be encouraged to take an active part in works of the OIV or projects of mutual interest. *Id.* at art. B1.1. The COMEX authorizes the director general to enter into any negotiations necessary to establish a formal relationship with such organizations. The General Assembly then adopts the relevant memoranda for cooperation and collaboration as proposed by the COMEX. *Id.* at art. B.1.2-3.

The OIV also is authorized to "draw up and frame recommendations . . . protecting geographical indications, especially vine- and wine-growing areas and the related appellations of origin, whether designated by geographical names or not, insofar as they do not call into question international agreements relating to trade and intellectual property."[80] The reference to trade and intellectual property agreements is to the WTO Agreement on Trade-Related Aspects of Intellectual Property Rights (TRIPs Agreement). As such, we must discuss not only the relationship between the OIV and international *organizations* but also the relationship between OIV and international *agreements*, including Codex Alimentarius and the agreements administered by the World Intellectual Property Organization (WIPO) and the WTO.

i. CODEX ALIMENTARIUS COMMISSION

The Codex Alimentarius Commission (CAC) is an intergovernmental body with over 170 members operating within the framework of the Joint Food Standards Program established by the FAO and the WHO. Its purpose is to protect the health of consumers and ensure fair practices in the food trade. The CAC also coordinates all food standards work undertaken by international intergovernmental and non-governmental organizations. The Codex Alimentarius is the work product of the CAC, comprising a collection of internationally adopted food standards, guidelines, codes of practices, and other recommendations.

The CAC's Strategic Plan for 2008-2013 reveals the cooperative and collaborative nature of the organization's activities. Goal 4, Point 15 of the Strategic Plan ("Promoting cooperation between Codex and relevant international organizations") states,

> The CAC must work closely on matters of common interest with other relevant international organizations, including those whose work has indirect but significant implications for food-standard issues. Monitoring by the CAC of activities of other organizations that are relevant to food standards, and coordination with them, where appropriate and consistent with Codex procedures, is necessary to achieve complementarity, avoid duplication, and prevent development of contradictory standards or guidelines. Such collaboration is also critical to the development of health protection and food-trade measures that address the food chain from farm to table in a coherent and seamless manner.[81]

Goal 4, Point 16, underscores the point:

> The WTO recognizes the CAC as the pre-eminent international body for establishing food safety standards. The Commission must, therefore, play a leadership role in establishing international food standards for protecting the health of consumers and ensuring fair practices in food trade, while taking due

80. *Id.* at art. 2.2(c)(ii).

81. *See* Y. Juban, Codex Alimentarius and the World Vitivinicultural Sector, 77 Bulletin de l'OIV 875-876: 84-169 (2004).

account of international regulatory initiatives of international governmental and non-governmental organizations.

The CAC and OIV collaborate through the application of an agreement in the form of an exchange of letters between the FAO and the OIV in 1948, under which the FAO recognized the OIV's specific competence on all questions relating to wine. The CAC made it a rule to not concern itself with wine, but that has now changed. The CAC's new global approach led it to draw up so-called horizontal standards, which include wine. The OIV is working to ensure that the specific place of grape wine is recognized by the CAC's *General Standards on Food Additives*.[82] In this way, the OIV is serving as the spokesperson of the wine sector through the CAC.

ii. WORLD INTELLECTUAL PROPERTY ORGANIZATION

A number of international treaties deal partially or entirely with the protection of trademarks, patents, and geographical indications in wine production and trade. The WIPO manages many of these international treaties that provide general standards of protection, such as the Paris Convention for the Protection of Industrial Property and the Madrid Agreement for the Repression of False or Deceptive Indications of Source on Goods. The WIPO also manages treaties governing registration systems for the international protection of appellations of origin, such as the Lisbon Agreement and the Madrid Agreement. Further, there is the 1995 Agreement between WIPO and the WTO establishing "a mutually supportive relationship."[83] The WIPO has accredited numerous observers, including 11 intergovernmental organizations (e.g., the OIV and the WTO) and 219 international non-governmental organizations (e.g., the International Wine Law Association.)

iii. WORLD TRADE ORGANIZATION

According to its director general, Pascal Lamy, the

> WTO provides a forum for negotiating agreements aimed at reducing obstacles to international trade and ensuring a level playing field for all, thus contributing to economic growth and development. The WTO also provides a legal and institutional framework for the implementation and monitoring of these agreements, as well as for settling disputes arising from their interpretation and application.[84]

Over the past 60 years, the WTO and its predecessor organization, the General Agreement on Tariffs and Trade (GATT), have contributed to global economic growth by helping to create a global trading system. The WTO currently has 153 members, and its activities are supported by a secretariat, led by

---

82. *See* Y. Juban, Oenological Practices: The New Global Situation, 73 Bulletin de l'OIV 827-828: 20-56 (2000).

83. Agreement between the World Intellectual Property Organization and the World Trade Organization, Preamble, Dec. 22, 1995, Preamble, 2d indent.

84. *See* www.wto.org/english/thewto_e/whatis_e/wto_dg_stat_e.htm (accessed November 30, 2010).

the WTO director general, located in Geneva. The WTO has an annual budget of approximately US$180 million. The three official languages of the WTO are English, French, and Spanish.

Decisions of the WTO are made by consensus of the entire membership, which explains the length of its various rounds of negotiations. The supreme institutional body is the Ministerial Conference, which meets roughly every two years. A General Council conducts the organization's work in the intervals between ministerial conferences. Both of these bodies comprise all members. Specialized bodies (councils, committees and sub-committees) administer and monitor the implementation of the various WTO agreements.

More specifically, the WTO's main activities include (1) negotiating the reduction or elimination of obstacles to trade (e.g., import tariffs and other barriers) and agreeing on rules governing the conduct of international trade (e.g., antidumping, subsidies, product standards, etc.); (2) administering and monitoring the application of the WTO's rules for trade in goods, trade in services, and trade-related intellectual property rights; (3) monitoring and reviewing the trade policies of its members, as well as ensuring transparency of regional and bilateral trade agreements; (4) settling disputes among its members regarding the interpretation and application of the agreements; and (5) conducting economic research and collecting and disseminating trade data in support of the WTO's main activities.

The WTO's founding and guiding principles are the pursuit of open borders, the guarantee of most favored nation and non-discriminatory treatment by and among members, and a commitment to transparency in the conduct of its activities.

The WTO deals with goods and services in general, but two agreements, the Technical Barriers to Trade and the Sanitary and Phytosanitary Standards, address the international validity of oenological practices and of labeling and import requirements for wines. Additionally, the TRIPs Agreement contains specific rules for geographical indications concerning wines and spirits, and the WTO's Council of Trade-Related Aspects of Intellectual Property Rights is the forum within the Doha Round for negotiating a multilateral system of notification and registration of geographical indications for wines eligible for protection in those members participating in the system.[85]

B. MULTILATERAL AND BILATERAL AGREEMENTS

The distinction between multilateral and bilateral agreements is formal: the latter involves only two states and the former more than two. When the agreement involves the mutual acceptance of national rules in interstate trade, it is known as a free-trade agreement; when common rules are applied, it is a harmonization agreement. The Free Trade Agreement (FTA) between Canada and

85. Agreement on Trade Related Aspects of Intellectual Property (hereinafter TRIPs Agreement) art. 23.4, Apr. 15, 1994.

the United States is a bilateral free-trade agreement; the North American Free-Trade Agreement (NAFTA) is a multilateral one. MERCOSUR is a multilateral harmonization agreement for some matters, including wine. The best-known multilateral agreements for international trade are the WTO's Plurilateral Trade Agreements. There are numerous other bilateral agreements that address wine to a greater or lesser extent.

1. MULTILATERAL AGREEMENTS

a. The WTO

The GATT came into force in 1948, establishing rules on international trade in all goods. But the GATT rules contained an exception that permitted countries to apply measures "necessary to protect human, animal or plant life or health" as long as these did not unjustifiably discriminate between countries or constitute a disguised restriction to trade. During the GATT's Tokyo Round (1974-1979), the Agreement on Technical Barriers to Trade (TBT Agreement, often referred to as the Standards Code) was negotiated, which inter alia covered technical requirements arising out of food safety and animal and plant health measures.

The TBT Agreement was rewritten during the GATT's Uruguay Round (1986-1994), and a separate agreement covering sanitary and phytosanitary measures was negotiated. Both the current TBT Agreement and the Agreement on the Application of Sanitary and Phytosanitary Measures (SPS Agreement) entered into force with the establishment of the WTO on January 1, 1995.

The respective duties of the WTO and the OIV partially overlap. The agreement establishing the WTO provides in Article II, §1 that "[t]he WTO is the common institutional framework for the conduct of trade relations among its Members in matters related to the Annexes of the Agreement," such as the SPS and TBT agreements (discussed immediately below). By comparison, the OIV 2001 Agreement lists the organization's responsibilities in Article 2.1:

> (b) to assist other international organizations, both intergovernmental and non-governmental, especially those which carry out standardization activities;
> (c) to contribute to international harmonization of existing practices and standards and, as necessary, to the preparation of new international standards in order to improve the conditions for producing and marketing vine and wine products, and to help ensure that the interests of consumers are taken into account.

Article 2.2(b) charges the OIV with an additional task: "to draw up and frame recommendations and monitor implementation of such recommendations in liaison with its members, especially in the following areas: (i) conditions for grape production, (ii) oenological practices, (iii) definition and/or description of products, labeling and marketing conditions, (iv) methods for analyzing and assessing vine products."

i. THE SPS AGREEMENT

The SPS Agreement affirms the right of the WTO members to restrict international trade when necessary to protect human, animal, or plant life or health. At the same time, this agreement aims to ensure that unnecessary health and safety regulations are not used as an excuse for protecting domestic producers from trade competition. To ensure that sanitary and phytosanitary measures are not trade restrictions in disguise, the SPS Agreement requires such measures to be based on science and only to be applied to the minimum extent necessary to protect human, animal, or plant life or health. Also, the measures may not arbitrarily or unjustifiably discriminate between countries where identical or similar conditions prevail.

Members are encouraged to base their measures on internationally developed standards to ensure their scientific justification and advance the harmonization of sanitary and phytosanitary requirements. The SPS Agreement explicitly recognizes the international standards, guidelines, and recommendations established by three intergovernmental organizations: the FAO/WHO's CAC, the International Office of Epizootics, and the FAO's International Plant Protection Convention. Measures based on international standards developed by these organizations are deemed to be consistent with the SPS Agreement. The OIV collaborates with the CAC to avoid "unnecessary duplication."[86] Specifically, OIV standards, guidelines, and recommendations can be used in the harmonization process coordinated by the Committee on Sanitary and Phytosanitary Measures for matters not covered by the aforementioned organizations. This means that the Committee on Sanitary and Phytosanitary Measures can refer to appropriate standards published by other relevant organizations that are open for membership to all WTO members.[87]

In the interest of transparency, members have to publish their sanitary and phytosanitary regulations. In addition, each WTO member must identify a national notification authority and a contact person for inquiries. The members are responsible for submitting notifications to the WTO, providing the full text of sanitary and phytosanitary regulations to interested members and responding to requests for more information about new or existing measures.

WTO members may elect to impose measures that result in a level of protection higher than that of an existing international standard. However, in this case, or when no relevant international standard exists, the measures have to be based on a risk assessment. If asked, members have to explain why the level of protection achieved by an international standard is insufficient and make their risk assessment available to other members.[88]

When preparing their risk assessment, members must take into account available scientific evidence, including the OIV's work. Where relevant scientific evidence is inadequate, members may adopt temporary measures based on the available pertinent information while seeking to obtain the necessary scientific evidence.[89] Although governments have a right to determine the level of health protection that they consider appropriate, they should aim to be consistent in the level of protection sought. Arbitrary or unjustifiable

86. The WTO Agreement on the Application of Sanitary and Phytosanitary Measures (hereinafter SPS Agreement), art. 12, §5.

87. *Id.* at Annex A, §3(d).

88. *Id.* at art. 3, 5.

89. *Id.* at art. 5.7.

differences in levels of protection that result in discrimination or a disguised restriction on trade are to be avoided.[90]

ii. THE TBT AGREEMENT

The TBT Agreement states in its preamble that WTO members "desir[e] therefore to encourage the development of . . . international standards and conformity assessment systems . . . to ensure that technical regulations and standards, including packaging, marking and labeling requirements, and procedures for assessment of conformity with technical regulations and standards do not create unnecessary obstacles to international trade." Vine and wine products are among the agricultural goods subject to the TBT Agreement.[91]

WTO members must use "international standards . . . or the relevant part of them as a basis for their technical regulations except when such international standards or relevant parts would be an ineffective or inappropriate means for the fulfillment of the legitimate objectives pursued, for instance because of fundamental climatic or geographical factors or fundamental technological problems."[92] Any international standard that does not respect a national technical regulation that may have an effect on trade with other WTO members must, upon request, be justified. Conversely, a technical regulation which accords with relevant international standards "shall be rebuttably presumed not to create an unnecessary obstacle to international trade."[93] Thus, the OIV technical standards and resolutions are not refuted by the TBT Agreement; to the contrary, they are a relevant reference.[94]

The TBT Agreement, like the SPS Agreement, encourages the participation of WTO Members in appropriate bodies that develop international standards for products for which they have either adopted, or expect to adopt, technical regulations.[95] On this subject, there can be no better example than the following OIV standards: the *International Oenological Codex*, the *International Code of Oenological Practices*, the *Compendium of International Methods of Analysis of Wines and Musts*, the *Compendium of International Methods of Analysis of Spirituous Beverages*, the *OIV Descriptor List for Grape Varieties and Vitis Species,* and the *International List of Vine Varieties and Their Synonyms*. All these OIV documents are standards under the TBT Agreement. A standard is defined in that agreement as a document approved by a recognized body that provides for common and repeated use, rules, guidelines, or characteristics for products or related processes and production methods, with which compliance is not mandatory. It may also include or deal exclusively with terminology, symbols,

90. *See* J. Audier, Prospective of the Precautionary Principle, 76 Bulletin de l'OIV 869-870: 650-673 (2003).

91. Agreement on Technical Barriers to Trade (hereinafter TBT Agreement), art. 1.3, Jan. 1, 1995.

92. *Id.* at art. 2.4.

93. *Id.* at art. 2.5.

94. *See* Oenological Barriers to Trade, in Y. Juban, Oenological Practice, the New Global Situation, *supra* note 82, at 26.

95. TBT Agreement, *supra* note 89, art. 2.6; SPS Agreement, *supra* note 86, art. 3, §4.

packaging, marking, or labeling requirements that apply to a product, process, or production method.[96]

Finally, it is important to understand the relationship between the SPS and TBT agreements. Because both agreements apply to food in international trade, it is sometimes difficult to decide which one applies to a certain regulation. Although both agreements encourage the use of international standards and share common elements, many of their substantial rules are different. Under the TBT Agreement, governments may decide not to use international standards when they are "ineffective or inappropriate" for achieving a given objective, for example, for technological reasons. Under the SPS Agreement, by contrast, a government can only avoid implementing an international standard by asserting a valid scientific appraisal of potential health risks resulting from its use. Further, the TBT Agreement allows governments to impose technical regulations for many objectives, including the prevention of deceptive practices. The SPS Agreement stipulates that sanitary and phytosanitary measures may only be imposed to the extent necessary to protect human, animal, or plant health on the basis of scientific information.

The scope of the two agreements is different. The TBT Agreement is broader, covering all technical regulations, voluntary standards, and the procedures to ensure that these are met (conformity assessment procedures), except when these are sanitary or phytosanitary measures as defined by the SPS Agreement. The SPS Agreement covers all measures whose purpose is to protect human or animal health from food-borne risks. Thus, the type of measure determines whether it is covered by the TBT Agreement, and the purpose of the measure decides whether it is subject to the SPS Agreement. For instance, measures governing the quality, grading, and labeling of imported grapes or raisins are covered by the TBT Agreement, while regulations on treatment of imported fruit to prevent the spread of pests or on chemical residue levels in the fruit or wine are SPS measures.

iii. THE TRIPS AGREEMENT

The 1994 WTO Act comprises 18 separate agreements, one of which concerns the trade-related aspects of intellectual property rights. The TRIPs Agreement represents a considerable advance from earlier accords and was welcomed by businesses already using a geographical name on their product or hoping to do so.

Part II of the TRIPs Agreement defines "the availability, scope and use of intellectual property rights," and Section 3 contains three fairly substantial articles dealing with geographical indications: Article 22 (protection of geographical indications), Article 23 (additional protection for geographical indications for wines and spirits), and Article 24 (international negotiations and exceptions). The national implementation of the TRIPs Agreement results in domestic protection for geographical indications that is heavily based on national registration. Negotiations for a multilateral system of notification

96. TBT Agreement, *supra* note 91, Annex I.

and registration, called for by Article 23.4 of the TRIPs Agreement, continue to drag on in Geneva.[97]

The former International Office of Vine and Wine adopted several resolutions in the field of geographical indications, covering definitions, relations with trademarks, generic and semi-generic terms, and homonymous names. But the 2001 Agreement includes the following actions among the organization's activities: "(c) to submit to its members all proposals relating to: . . . (ii) protecting geographical indications, especially vine- and wine-growing areas and the related appellations of origin, whether designated by geographical names or not, insofar as they do not call into question international agreements relating to trade and intellectual property."[98] Although the OIV today does not address geographical indications, the organization assists and collaborates with the bodies that implement the TRIPs Agreement and offers input on the geographical names of vine- and wine-growing areas through a world list prepared by its members. This list is useful information for the national authorities in charge of implementing the TRIPs Agreement, who must prevent the use of a geographical indication identifying wines if the wine does not originate in the place indicated by the geographical indication (Article 23.1), refuse the registration of a trademark for wines if that mark contains or consists of a geographical indication for wines or spirits not having that origin (Article 23.2), and detect homonymous geographical indications for wines (Article 23.3).

iv. DISPUTE SETTLEMENT BODY

Inevitably, trade conflicts that invoke the various WTO agreements (SPS, TBT, and TRIPs) will arise. In a few cases, bilateral consultations have helped to clarify misunderstandings and resolve the conflict. But every member has the right to take recourse, at any time, to the formal WTO dispute settlement procedures. The first step of the procedure requires formal consultations among the parties, about which the WTO must be advised. Other interested governments may request to join in the consultations.

If the dispute is not resolved through consultations, a member may request the establishment of an independent panel (known as a "special group" in the Dispute Settlement Body Agreement) to consider the case. Any other member may reserve the right to be a third party to the dispute. A panel is normally composed of three individuals who are not nationals of any party to the dispute and are considered to be unbiased on the issue in dispute. The panel

---

97. *See* R. Mendelson, J.S. Gerien & N. Resnikoff, A Multilateral Register of Geographical Indications for Wines and Spirits: A Summary and Assessment of the Competing Proposals, Oral Presentation before the World Vine and Wine Congress (June 12, 2007); B. O'Connor, Geographical Indications and TRIPs: 10 Years Later . . . A Roadmap for EU GI Holders to Get Protection in other WTO Members, European Commission: Trade (June 22, 2007), available at http://trade.ec.europa.eu/doclib/html/135088.htm (accessed November 29, 2010); J. Audier, TRIPs Agreement: Geographical Indications (Office for Official Publications of the European Communities, 2000); J. Audier, Implementation of the TRIPs Agreement by the WTO Members, 72 Bulletin de l'OIV 821-822: 532-548 (1999).

98. 2001 Agreement, *supra* note 6, art. 2.2.

receives both written and oral arguments from the parties, considers the measure in light of the legal obligations of a member of the WTO, and then issues its findings in a report on the matter. In cases in which the panel finds a violation of a WTO obligation, the usual recommendation is that the member bring its measure(s) into conformity with its obligations.

The recommendations of a dispute settlement panel are considered by the Dispute Settlement Body (DSB), which comprises all WTO members. The panel's recommendations are automatically adopted unless there is a consensus in the DSB not to adopt them. Alternatively, parties to the dispute may appeal the legal interpretations of a panel. In such circumstances, three of the WTO's standing Appellate Body judges will re-examine the case and issue a final decision. As of August 2010, there have been 204 disputes involving the United States (94 as complainants and 110 as respondents) and 152 involving the EU (82 as complainants and 70 as respondents).

In cases in which a member government cannot comply with its WTO obligations within a reasonable time period, it may offer to compensate its trading partners for opportunities subsequently lost. If such compensation is not acceptable, the prevailing party or parties to a dispute may request authorization from the DSB to retaliate against the non-complying government. Both compensation and retaliation normally take the form of increased (or decreased) import access or taxes for products from the other country.[99]

There is one wine-related issue that was referred to a WTO dispute settlement body at the request of Argentina. It concerned former EC Regulation 1493/1999 establishing the common organization of the European market for wines and the provisions applicable to wine trade between the EC and third countries, including approved oenological practices.[100] Argentina's complaint was based on the exclusion of malic acid from the list of permissible acidification products and processes,[101] and it included four claims relating to the permitted and prohibited practices contained in the regulation and their application to wines produced in third-party countries.

The first claim alleges that the requirements of the regulation on approved oenological practices were inconsistent with the requirements of Article 2.2 of the TBT Agreement, which requires member states to ensure that technical regulations are not more trade-restrictive than necessary to fulfill a legitimate objective. It also alleged that the application and enforcement of the regulation's requirements regarding oenological practices (specifically, the use of malic acid) constitutes a violation of Article 12.3 of the TBT Agreement, which requires special consideration of the needs of developing countries to ensure that they do not face unnecessary obstacles in accessing member states' markets.

Argentina's second claim alleged that the EC failed to meet its obligation under Article 2.4 of the TBT Agreement to use relevant international standards

---

99. *See, e.g.*, U.S. v. EC dispute over hormone-treated meat. Appellate Body Report, European Communities—Measures concerning Meat and Meat Products, WT/DS26/AB/R, WT/DS48/AB/R (Jan. 16, 1998).

100. Request for Consultations by Argentina, European Communities—Measures Affecting Imports of Wine, WT/DS263/1 (Sept. 12, 2002).

101. *Id.*

as a basis for its technical regulations and that the EC, when establishing oenological practices authorized for the process of acidification of wines, did not take into account applicable OIV resolutions Oeno 3 and 4/1999, which permit the use of malic acid.[102]

The third and fourth claims alleged that the EC entered bilateral treaties with several member states permitting the use of malic acid and granting other derogations from EC Regulation 1493/1999's acidification regulations and also entered into a bilateral agreement with Chile, the United States, Canada, and Australia[103] that allowed, inter alia, the export of wines made with malic acid from both parties into the other. Thus, refusing to permit importation of Argentinean wines containing malic acid was inconsistent with Article 2.1 of the TBT Agreement, which requires that all member states receive treatment no less favorable than that accorded to domestic producers and to other importing member states' producers.

In March 2003, roughly six months after Argentina filed its complaint, the EC implemented a regulation authorizing the offer and delivery for direct human consumption of wines imported from Argentina that may have undergone oenological processes not provided for in EC Regulation 1493/1999. This regulation expressly permits "[w]ines produced on the territory of Argentina [to] be subject to acidification with malic acid, an oenological practice not authorized by community rules . . . pending the conclusion of [an] agreement [between the EC and Argentina] involving certain oenological practices and the protection of geographical indications."[104]

No panel was ever convened, and the EC allowed wines from Argentina treated with malic acid to be imported into Europe, just as it allowed similarly treated wines from other countries to be imported into the EC.

As a further example, a panel was established at the request of the United States and Australia concerning EC Regulation 2081/92 on the protection of geographical indications and designations of origin for agricultural products and foodstuffs, not including wine.[105] The United States and Australia claimed

102. The International Code of Oenological Practice authorizes the use of malic acid to acidify must and wine. *See* OIV, Acidification Chimique du Mout [Chemical Acidification of Must], Resolution Oeno 3/99 (1999); Acidification Chimique du Vin, Resolution Oeno 4/1999 (1999). MERCOSUR adopted these same resolutions, but the EU did not (R.1493/99). Today, the EU allows the use of malic acid (R.606/2009, Annex I A, Point 12) under the conditions and limits provided by R.479/2008, Annex V, C, and D.

103. Council Decision of January 24, 1994, concerning the conclusion of an Agreement between the EC and Australia on trade in wine, 1994 O.J. (L 086) 1, Annex I (3)(14); Proposal for a Council Decision on the Conclusion of an Agreement between the EC and South Africa on Trade in Wines, EC document 2001/0998 (ACC), 10.12.2001; EU-Chile Association Agreement, OJ 2002 (L352) 3. *See, e.g.*, Agreement between the EC and South Africa on Trade in Wine, 2002 O.J. (L28) 4.

104. Council Regulation 527/2003, authorizing the offer and delivery for direct human consumption of certain wines imported from Argentina that may have undergone oenological processes not provided for in EC Regulation 1493/1999, 2003 O.J. (L 78) 1 (EC).

105. Appellate Body Report, European Communities—Protection of Trademarks and Geographical Indications for Agricultural Products and Foodstuffs, Complaint by United States, WT/DS174 (March 25, 2005) and Appellate Body Report, European Communities—Protection of Trademarks and Geographical Indications for Agricultural Products and Foodstuffs, Complaint by Australia, WT/DS290 (March 25, 2005).

that the European system of geographical indications (GIs) was inconsistent with GATT and TRIPs rules for several reasons, including the lack of equivalent protection for foreign countries (specifically, the EC required that other countries adopt a system of GI protection equivalent to that of the EC and provide reciprocal protection to products from the EC[106]), the application and objection procedures, inspection structures, labeling requirements, and the relationship between GIs and prior trademarks. Subsequently, a new regulation, No. 510/2006 of March 20, 2006, was adopted revising the GI system in the two areas criticized by the panel: first, by formally deleting the requirement for "reciprocity and equivalence" from the EC regulations; and second, by allowing third-country operators to submit applications and objections directly to the EC rather than through their governments. But the panel at the same time upheld the integrity of the EC's GI system and rejected the majority of the claims made by the United States and Australia. In this sense, all parties were able to claim some measure of victory.

In 2008, the EC's GI system for agricultural products and foodstuffs was extended to wine.[107] The EC policy is explained below:

> Whereas (27): The concept of quality wines in the Community is based, *inter alia*, on the specific characteristics attributable to the wine's geographical origin. Such wines are identified for consumers via protected designations of origin and geographical indications, although the current system is not fully developed in this respect. In order to allow for a transparent and more elaborate framework underpinning the claim to quality by the products concerned, a regime should be established under which applications for a designation of origin or a geographical indication are examined in line with the approach followed under the Community's horizontal quality policy applicable to foodstuffs other than wine and spirits in Council Regulation (EC) No. 510/2006 of 20 March 2006 on the protection of geographical indications and designations of origin for agricultural products and foodstuffs.

b. The WIPO

The WIPO is the international organization managing international agreements in the field of intellectual property, including the Paris Convention of March 20, 1883, for the protection of industrial property; the Madrid Agreement of April 14, 1891, for the Repression of False or Deceptive Indications of Source on Goods; and the Lisbon Agreement of October 31, 1958, for the protection of appellations of origin and their international registration. The agreement most directly related to wine is the Lisbon Agreement.

i. THE LISBON AGREEMENT

The Lisbon Agreement, with 26 subscribing parties, defines "appellation of origin" as "the geographical denomination of a country, region or locality

106. United States' first written submission, §22, WTO Doc. WT/DS174, *supra* note 103.

107. Council Regulation 479/2008, on the common organization of the market in wine, art. 33 et seq., 2008 O.J. (L 148) 1 (EC).

which serves to designate a product originating therein, the quality and characteristics of which are due exclusively or essentially to the geographical environment, including natural and human factors."[108] The Lisbon Agreement goes on to state that the country of origin is "the country whose name, or the country in which is situated the region or locality whose name, constitutes the appellation of origin which has given the product its reputation."[109] The registered appellation of origin under this agreement is protected against "any usurpation or imitation, even if the true origin of the product is indicated or if the appellation is used in translated form or accompanied by terms such as 'kind,' 'type,' 'make,' 'imitation' or 'the like.' "[110]

Today, the Lisbon Agreement is not considered to be obsolete. To the contrary, about 70 WTO members (or regional systems implementing the TRIPs Agreement) have copied the Lisbon Agreement's definition of appellation of origin. As a result, the WIPO is currently working to develop a "Lisbon system" that would be extended to all products, perhaps as a substitute for the WTO system of multilateral notification and registration of GIs for wines that would be extended to all products.

Since 1988 the WIPO has organized biannual international symposia dedicated to the subject of geographical indications entitled "Symposium on the International Protection of Geographical Indications." These have been held in Bordeaux, Santenay (France), Wiesbaden, Funchal (Madeira), Melbourne, Eger (Hungary), Cape Town, Montevideo, San Francisco, Parma, Beijing, and Lisbon. The symposia bring together representatives of member states' administrations, producers who use geographical indications to promote their products, and leading experts in the field for an exchange of experiences and views. In addition to offering practical insights into technicalities concerning the use and protection of geographical indications, the symposia contribute constructively to the ongoing debate about geographical indications at the national and international levels.

ii. STANDING COMMITTEE ON THE LAW OF TRADEMARKS, INDUSTRIAL DESIGNS AND GEOGRAPHICAL INDICATIONS

The Standing Committee on the Law of Trademarks, Industrial Designs and Geographical Indications (SCT) was established by a decision of the Assemblies of the Member States of WIPO and the unions administered by the WIPO in March 1998.[111] The SCT is a forum to discuss issues, facilitate

---

108. Lisbon Agreement for the Protection of Appellations of Origin and their International Registration (hereinafter Lisbon Agreement) art. 2(1), Oct. 31, 1958.

109. *Id.* at art. 2(2).

110. *See* M. Geuze, Senior Counselor, Office of the Dir. Gen., WIPO, Let's Have Another Look at the Lisbon Agreement: Its Terms in Their Context and in the Light of Its Object and Purpose, presentation at the International Symposium on Geographical Indications (June 26-28, 2007), in WIPO/GEO/BEI/07/10; WIPO, Working Group on the Development of the Lisbon System: Study on the Relationship between Regional Systems for the Protection of Geographical Indications and the Lisbon System; and on the Conditions for Accession to the Lisbon Agreement by Intergovernmental Organizations, WIPO Doc. LI/WG/DEV/2/3 (Aug. 6, 2010).

111. WIPO, General Report of the Assemblies of the Member States of WIPO, Thirty-Second Series of Meetings, at sec. 93, WIPO Doc. A/32/7 (March 1998).

coordination, and provide guidance concerning the progressive international development of the law of trademarks, industrial designs, and geographical indications, including the harmonization of national laws and procedures. The SCT submits its recommendations and policies to the WIPO General Assembly for approval.

SCT membership is open to all members of the WIPO and of the Paris Union for the Protection of Industrial Property. In addition, participation in an observer capacity is open to all other United Nations member states, intergovernmental organizations, and non-governmental organizations accredited with observer status at the WIPO. SCT documents typically concern the definition and legal nature of rights related to geographical indications.[112]

c. World Wine Trade Group

The World Wine Trade Group Industry Section (WWTG) presents itself as an "informal grouping of industry representatives from wine-producing countries." It was created in 1998 in Zurich. The participants are professional unions of Argentina, Australia, Canada, Chile, Mexico, New Zealand, South Africa, and the United States. The U.S. participants include the Wine Institute, Wine America, and the California Association of Winegrape Growers.

The WWTG shares information and collaborates on various international issues to create an environment for the free trade in wine, often as a counterweight to more trade-restrictive views espoused by some other countries. At the same time, five of the eight originating countries of the WWTG are also member states of the OIV.

The WWTG has functioned successfully as a forum, "Improved Understanding of Global Wine Issues," and also has adopted a Mutual Acceptance Agreement on Oenological Practices. This agreement was discussed from 1999 until it was signed in 2001 by Australia, Canada, Chile, New Zealand, and the United States. Argentina became a signatory of the WWTG's Mutual Acceptance Agreement in December 2002. A WWTG Labeling Agreement also was adopted in 2007 concerning the placement of four mandatory pieces of information—country of origin, product name, net contents, and alcohol content—anywhere on a wine bottle label provided they are presented in a single field of vision. The legal nature of these agreements is somewhat complicated by virtue of the fact that this is more an agreement among professionals than an intergovernmental accord.

2. BILATERAL AGREEMENTS

The gradual implementation of the WTO's multilateral agreements also prompted bilateral trade negotiations. Sometimes these negotiations

112. WIPO Standing Committee on the Law of Trademarks, Industrial Designs and Geographical Indications (SCT), Addendum to Geographical Indications: Historical Background, Nature of Rights, Existing Systems for Protection and Obtaining Protection in Other Countries, SCT 8/5 (April 2, 2002); SCT, Geographical Indications and the Territoriality Principle, SCT 9/5 (Oct. 1, 2001); SCT, Geographical Indications, SCT 10/4 (March 25, 2003).

concerned items not covered by the WTO agreements; in other instances they supplemented those agreements. One such long-standing bilateral negotiation over wine has been between the United States and the EC.

a. The U.S.-EC Wine Accords

The U.S.-EC Wine Accords negotiations included two negotiating rounds, specifically, the letter round and the agreement round. The letter round commenced in 1983 when the U.S. assistant secretary of the Treasury Department addressed a letter to the EC director general for external relations. During this phase of the accord, the EC authorized the importation of U.S. wines made with oenological practices not allowed within the EC and harmonized its import certification requirements. The parties also agreed to enter into wine labeling negotiations. Finally, the EC recognized the names of the American viticultural areas, and the United States agreed to undertake efforts "to prevent erosion of non-generic designations of geographic significance indicating a wine growing area in the European Community." For a non-diplomat, that undertaking was interpreted as a promise by the United States that semi-generics would be phased out. Even this brief history reveals that two issues poisoned the wine negotiations: oenological practices and semi-generics.

Phase One of the Wine Accords ended in 1988 but was extended until 2005, essentially on a year-by-year basis. Following U.S. promises to negotiate on the phaseout of semi-generics and the EC's acceptance of certain U.S. wine-making practices, the negotiations began again in 1999, only to fail in December 2003. The United States applied pressure on the negotiations after Congress passed the Miscellaneous Trade Bill of 2004, which included a "[m]odification to cellar treatment of natural wine," providing that as of November 1, 2005, imported wine with an alcohol content of 0.5 percent to 24 percent, produced after December 31, 2004, in a country that has not ratified a bilateral accord with the United States on oenological practices, must be certified through an official analysis consistent with the U.S. practices.

Phase One was again extended by the EC until December 31, 2005. Finally, the United States and the EC signed the Agreement in the Form of an Exchange of Letters between the European Community and the United States of America on Matters Related to Trade in Wine on November 18, 2005, to serve as a transitional agreement until December 31, 2005.[113] On March 10, 2006, the parties then signed the final Agreement between the European Community and the United States of America on Trade in Wine.[114] This Agreement on Trade in Wine consists of 17 articles, six annexes and a protocol on wine labeling. Not surprisingly, the agreement still bears the traces of the initial poisons, namely, oenological practices and semi-generics.

113. Agreement in the Form of an Exchange of Letters between the European Community and the United States of America on Matters Related to Trade in Wine. 2005 O.J. (L 301) 16 (EC). The agreement is called the Bridge Agreement in the United States.

114. Agreement between the European Community and the United States of America on trade in wine (hereinafter Agreement on Trade in Wine), 2006 O.J. (L 87) 2 (EC).

In terms of objectives, the Agreement on Trade in Wine seeks "to facilitate trade in wine between the Parties, and to improve cooperation in the development and enhance the transparency of regulations affecting such trade."[115] The agreement also "lay[s] the foundation, as the first phase, for broad agreement on trade in wine between the Parties; and . . . provide[s] a framework for continued negotiations in the wine sector."

The Agreement on Trade in Wine is not a complete success. The agreement round remains open to "future negotiations."[116] However, in this regard, the agreement does not appear to implement Article 24.1 of the TRIPs Agreement, which provides: "Members agree to enter into negotiations aimed at increasing the protection of individual geographical indications under Article 23 [Additional Protection for Geographical Indications for Wines and Spirits]."

The Agreement on Trade in Wine defines wine to include

> beverages obtained exclusively from the total or partial alcoholic fermentation of fresh grapes, whether or not crushed, or of grape must, with the possible addition of any constituent parts of fresh grapes authorized in the producing Party, in accordance with wine-making practices authorized under the regulatory mechanisms of the Party in whose territory the wine is produced . . . with an alcohol content of not less than 7% and not more than 22% by volume.

Wine also must contain "no artificial coloring, flavoring or added water beyond technical necessity." Accordingly, the United States gained permission to export to the EC wines with over 15 percent alcohol content.

Title II ("Wine-making practices and specifications") establishes mutual recognition of U.S. and EC winemaking laws and regulations, with a distinction between "present" and "new wine-making practices and specifications."[117] With respect to the "present wine-making practices and specifications" that are authorized, the Agreement affirms that they

> do not change the character of wine arising from its origin in the grapes in a manner inconsistent with good wine-making practices [that] . . . address the reasonable technological or practical need to enhance the keeping or other qualities or stability of the wine and that achieve the winemaker's desired effect, including with respect to not creating an erroneous impression about the product's character and composition.[118]

The Agreement on Trade in Wine echoes the EC rule: "Authorized oenological practices shall only be used for the purposes of ensuring proper vinification, proper preservation or proper refinement of the product."[119]

Article 4.2 of the agreement underscores that

> neither Party shall restrict, on the basis of either wine-making practices or product specifications, the importation, marketing or sale of wine originating

115. *Id.* at art.1, a.
116. *Id.* at art. 10.
117. *Id.* at art. 4-5.
118. *Id.* at art. 4.1 *in fine.*
119. Council Regulation 479/2008, on the common organization of the market in wine, art. 27.2, 2008 O.J. (L 148) 1 (EC).

> in the territory of the other Party that is produced using wine-making practices that are authorized under laws, regulations and requirements of the other Party listed in Annex I and published or communicated to it by that other Party.[120]

According to Article 17, "The provisions of Article 4 . . . shall only apply from the first day of the second month following receipt by the Community of the written notice referred to in Article 6.3," which is "the change in legal status" of the semi-generics and Retsina. By a letter dated February 7, 2007, the United States notified the EC that the change of legal status concerning semi-generics had come into effect. The relevant U.S. legislation is Section 422 of the Tax Relief and Health Care Act of 2006, signed by the U.S. president and enacted into law on December 20, 2006.[121] In accordance with Article 17(2) of the agreement, the provisions concerning winemaking practices and specifications are therefore applicable in the EC as of April 1, 2007.[122]

If the United States or EC

> proposes to authorize for commercial use in its territory a new wine-making practice or modify an existing wine-making practice . . . and it intends to propose the inclusion of the practice among those authorized in the [Agreement on Trade in Wine, specifically, Annex I], it shall provide public notice and specific notice to the other Party and provide a reasonable opportunity for comment and to have those comments considered.

This provision essentially establishes a rulemaking procedure between the United States and the EC. Presumably, the oenological standards of the OIV will be taken into consideration. Further, the "Joint Declarations" to the agreement specify that "[o]n international cooperation, the Parties intend to conduct an exchange of views on issues related to and raised in plurilateral and multilateral organizations involved with wine matters affecting international trade and on how international cooperation on wine matters might best be structured." This could directly implicate the OIV, and the parties very well could exchange points of view about the OIV.

In terms of this rulemaking process, notice of the new or modified winemaking practice must be sent to the other party within 60 days, and the other party can object within 90 days on the ground that the practice is inconsistent with the Agreement's objectives or criteria and, on that basis, request consultations.[123] If no objections are raised (or when they are ultimately resolved), Annex I is then amended "to cover any new winemaking practice

---

120. *See* "Table II: Oenological practices admitted by EU and USA but not in the OIV Code" and "Table III: Oenological practices admitted by OIV and either by the U.S. or by EU" *in* Y. Juban, Oenological Practices: The New Global Situation, *supra* note 82, at 42.

121. Tax Relief and Health Care Act of 2006 §422, 26 U.S.C. §5388 (2006).

122. Commission Communication concerning the Agreement between the European Community and the United States of America on Trade in Wine, 2007 O.J. (C 176/09) 14 (EC). The agreement on winemaking practices and product specifications was a conditional promise. If EU acceptance of U.S. winemaking practices was contingent upon a U.S. legislative change in the status of semi-generic names, what happens in the interim? *See* Impact of the U.S./EU Wine Agreement on Certificates of Label Approval for Wine Labels with a Semi-Generic Name or Retsina, Industry Circular (TTB, Washington, DC), March 6, 2006. The interim period (December 31, 2005, the end of EC derogations, through April 1, 2006) is covered by the Bridge Agreement, *supra* note 111.

123. Agreement on Trade in Wine, *supra* note 112, art. 5.2-5.3.

or modification that has not been subject to objections."[124] This constitutes mutual recognition, not mutual acceptance.

There is a great difference between *mutual recognition* of oenological practices, which applies to specific practices as of a given date, and *mutual acceptance*. Mutual acceptance means that "the Parties shall accept each other's laws, regulations and requirements relating to oenological practices and the mechanisms to regulate them and . . . shall permit the importation of wine produced in the territory of another Party in conformity with that other Party's laws, regulations and requirements relating to oenological practices and the mechanisms to regulate them," except where a wine would compromise human health or safety in accordance with the provisions of the SPS Agreement.[125] Experiments or sanitary and phytosanitary measures are outside the scope of the Agreement on Trade in Wine.

The agreement also addresses semi-generics and other wine-labeling terms. With respect to semi-generics, Article 6.1 states:

> With respect to wine that is sold in the territory of the United States, the United States shall seek to change the legal status of the terms in Annex II [*Burgundy, Chablis, Champagne, Chianti, Claret, Haut Sauterne, Hock, Madeira, Malaga, Marsala, Moselle, Port, Retsina, Rhine, Sauterne, Sherry, and Tokay*] to restrict the use of the terms on wine labels **solely to wine originating in the Community**. Labels for such wines may use the terms in Annex II [*semi-generics*] in a manner consistent with the U.S. wine labeling regulations in force as of September 14, 2005. [Emphasis added.]

What happens when the wine is not sold in the territory of the United States but in third countries? In these situations, the provisions of the TRIPs Agreement apply.[126]

The semi-generics list in Annex II is updated compared to 26 USC §5688. Specifically, *Angelica* is deleted, and *Retsina* is added. The Alcohol and Tobacco Tax and Trade Bureau's (TTB) Industry Circular 2006-1, dated March 10, 2006, explains: "Angelica is a semi-generic name for wine of U.S. origin; however, the Agreement does not affect its use, and it is not subject to any of the information in this circular." Further, "Retsina is a class of wine and is not a semi-generic name; however, under the terms of the Agreement, it is treated the same as the semi-generic names. Its origin is Greece."

Article 6.2 of the Agreement on Trade in Wine provides:

> Paragraph 1 shall not apply with respect to any person or its successor in interest using a term listed in Annex II [semi-generics and Retsina] on a label of a wine not originating in the Community, where such use has occurred in the United States before 13 December 2005, or the date of signature of this Agreement, whichever is later [March 10, 2006]; provided that the term may only be used on labels for wine bearing the brand name, or the brand name and the fanciful name, if any, for which the applicable Certificate of Label Approval [COLA] was issued prior to the later date referred to in this paragraph

124. *Id.* at art. 5.4.
125. Agreement on Mutual Acceptance of Oenological Practices art. 5, Dec. 18, 2001.
126. *See* J. Audier, Generics and Semi-generics, 71 Bulletin de l'OIV 809-810: 608-651 (1998).

> [March 10, 2006] and the term is presented on the label in accordance with the regulations in effect on September 14, 2005.[127]

This constitutes a significant "grandfather clause" for semi-generics used in COLAs issued by the TTB before March 10, 2006. In some sense, it mimics the TRIPs Agreement's grandfather clause at Article 24.5, which provides that a trademark identical or similar to a geographical indication that has been established in good faith and has the necessary priority (usage prior to the implementation of the TRIPs Agreement on January 1, 1995) will remain valid and continue to exist alongside the geographical indication.[128]

Under this exception, U.S. wine and wine from other non-EC countries sold in the United States that use the semi-generic name on a label appearing in a COLA approved prior to March 10, 2006, may continue to use that name. Specifically, "any person or his or her successor in interest may continue to use a semi-generic name or Retsina on a label of a wine not originating in the EC, provided the semi-generic name or Retsina is only used on labels for wine bearing the same brand name, or the brand name and the fanciful name, if any, that appear on a COLA that was issued prior to March 10, 2006."[129] Hence, the COLA holder cannot change the brand name or the fanciful name as they appear on a COLA that was issued before March 10, 2006. "For example, if Company B purchased rights to Company A's grandfathered brand name, Company B may submit a copy of Company A's COLA to support its application."[130] Additionally, COLAs for grandfathered brands that contain a semi-generic name or Retsina are qualified as follows: "Approved under the 'grandfather' provision of the Agreement between the U.S. and the EU on Trade in Wine."

The TTB's Industry Circular 2006-1 also discusses the period between March 10, 2006, and the enactment date of December 20, 2006: "Pending any change to the law, TTB will continue to approve 'new' uses of the semi-generic names and Retsina. Please keep in mind that in order for the U.S. to meet its obligations in the Agreement, the Government must seek to change the law to limit the use of these names on non-EC wine to those brands that were in existence before March 10, 2006."

Article 7.1 of the Agreement on Trade in Wine states that the United States

> shall provide that certain names may be used as names of origin for wine only to designate wines of the origin indicated by such a name, and shall include, among such names, those listed in Annex IV, Part A, names of quality wines produced in specified regions (known by the acronym q.w.p.s.r.) and names of table wines with geographical indications, and Part B, names of Member States.[131]

This ensures that other European terms of origin shall not become generic.

---

127. Provisions enacted by Congress as part of the Tax Relief and Health Care Act of 2006, which was signed into law by President Bush on December 20, 2006.

128. One subject for discussion and ultimate resolution is whether the Agreement can have a different deadline than the one found in TRIPs.

129. TTB Industry Circular, *supra* note 120.

130. *Id.*

131. As of August 1, 2009, q.w.p.s.r. are classified as designations of origin and geographical indications under Regulation No. 479/2008.

In addition, the United States "shall maintain the status of the names listed in Title 27 U.S. Code of Federal Regulations, Section 12.31, set forth in Annex IV, Part C [of the Agreement], as non-generic names of geographic significance that are recognized as distinctive designations of a specific wine of a particular place or region in the Community, distinguishable from all other wines."[132] Examples include Liebfraumilch or Mosel from Germany; Charmes-Chambertin, Châteauneuf-du-Pape, Côte Rotie, and Romanée-Conti from France; Asti Spumante, Barolo, Brunello di Montalcino, Frascati, and Vino Nobile di Montepulciano from Italy; Dao, Oporto, and Porto from Portugal; and Rioja from Spain. The list, with many omissions, includes some winery trademarks and Retsina Attica, Retsina Megaron, etc. The U.S. classification of "non-generic names of geographic significance that are recognized as distinctive designations" is a foreign concept to the WTO members.

Conversely, "[t]he Community shall provide that the names of viticultural significance listed in Annex V may be used as names of origin for wine only to designate wines of the origin indicated by such name."[133] Thus, American viticultural areas, states, and counties are names of viticultural significance and, as such, are geographical indications protected in the EC. Each party's competent authorities are responsible for implementing these provisions and removing from the market any wine not labeled in conformity therewith.[134]

The Agreement on Trade in Wine includes additional labeling standards. First, "[e]ach Party shall provide that labels of wine sold in its territory shall not contain false or misleading information in particular as to character, composition or origin."[135] This standard is akin to the TRIPs Agreement, Article 23:

> Each Member shall provide the legal means for interested parties to prevent use of a geographical indication identifying wines for wines not originating in the place indicated by the geographical indication in question . . . , even where the true origin of the goods is indicated or the geographical indication is used in translation or accompanied by expressions such as "kind," "type," "style," "imitation," or the like.

The Agreement on Trade in Wine thus aims higher than mere origin, taking into account information as to *character, composition* or origin. Nevertheless, the agreement does not prohibit misleading expressions of origin when the true origin or the imitation process is indicated. What does "false or misleading information in particular as to character, composition or origin" mean? What is the "character" of a wine? What is the "composition" of a wine that is naturally composed of more than 700 elements? We shall interpret the agreement simply to mean: "Any false or misleading information is prohibited on wine labels."

The second standard in the Agreement on Trade in Wine deals with optional labeling information. Article 8.2 states that "each Party shall provide that . . . wine may be labeled with optional particulars or additional

132. Agreement on trade in wine, *supra* note 112, art.7.4.
133. *Id.* at art.7.2.
134. *Id.* at art. 7.3.
135. *Id.* at art. 8.1.

information in accordance with the Protocol on Wine Labeling" attached to the agreement. This lengthy protocol with four appendices is an excellent guideline on wine labeling.

For wines originating in the United States, optional particulars on labels include vintage date, varietal name, bottling location, awards, vineyard name, and the so-called traditional expressions, including the words "chateau," "classic," "cream," "crusted/crusting," "late bottled vintage," "ruby," "tawny," "vintage," "vintage character," "fine," "noble," "superior," and "sur lie." Traditional expressions, whose use is restricted under EC regulations, may be used by a U.S. winery on wine sold in the EC provided that the term has been approved for use in a COLA and subject to EC trademark law. The use of these traditional expressions ended on March 10, 2009. However, 13 applications from professional associations in the United States to recognize "traditional terms" were submitted in June, 2010 and published in the Official Journal of the EC, series C, No. 275–278, in October 2010. Optional particulars also include the term "Estate Bottled," the type of product (e.g., for still wines: Dry, Medium dry, Medium sweet, Sweet; and for sparkling wines: Brut nature, Extra brut, Brut, Extra dry, Dry, Medium dry, Sweet), and the production methods such as barrel, oak, or wood aged; fermented; or matured.

Under the third labeling standard in Article 8.3, "[n]either Party shall require that processes, treatments or techniques used in wine making be identified on the label." Thus neither party need frighten the consumer with indications such as "malic acid added," "processed by reverse osmosis," or "processed with potassium ferrocyanide."

The fourth standard in Article 8.4 makes EC producers uneasy. "The United States shall permit the names listed in Annex II [semi-generics and Retsina] to be used as a class or type designation on wines originating in the Community." Presumably, this usage must comply with other portions of the agreement, meaning that no "new" use of semi-generics is allowed.

With respect to wine certifications, the Agreement on Trade in Wine simplifies the process. Wines originating in the parties' countries must be imported, marketed, and sold accompanied by a certification document specified in Annex III (a) for the Community and Annex III (b), COLA, for the United States. Information may be pre-printed and transmitted electronically to the importing country, with the sole exception of the producer's or applicant's signature.[136] The form may be modified by each party after due notice to the other. The agreement does not require any certification that the practices and procedures used to produce wine in EC constitute proper cellar treatment under U.S. law.[137] This is appropriate because wine originating in a country with which the United States has an agreement establishing mutual acceptance of winemaking practices is exempt from this requirement. That is, the mutual recognition of winemaking practices in the Agreement on Trade in Wine exempts the EC from having to certify its wines in the United States.

TTB Industry Circular Number 2007-2, dated June 21, 2007, informs U.S. exporters of wine to the EC of the new simplified certification and analysis

136. *Id.* at art. 9.1-4.
137. *Id.* at art. 9.6.

documentation that the EC requires to accompany each shipment of U.S. grape wine and sparkling grape wine. The new certification and analysis document, instead of the VI-1 form, can be used for wine exports to the EC after April 1, 2007.

The "Final Provisions" of the agreement call for new negotiations "within 90 days of the date of entry into force of the Agreement with a view toward concluding one or more agreements that further facilitate trade in wine between the Parties . . . no later than two years from entry into force of this Agreement." Hence, the agreement round continues and shall be accompanied, insofar as possible, by measurable indicators.

In terms of execution, the EC published Commission Regulation (EC) No. 1416/2006 of September 26, 2006, which sets forth specific rules on the implementation of Article 7(2) of the Agreement on Trade in Wine.[138] The EC allows the names of viticultural significance listed in Annex V of the Agreement on Trade in Wine (AVA, states, and counties) to be used as names of origin only on wines of the origin indicated by such name.

Commission Regulation (EC) No. 113/2009 of February 6, 2009, concerning the use of certain traditional terms on labels for wine imported from the United States implements yet another portion of the Agreement on Trade in Wine.[139] Article 1 provides:

> Wine originating in the United States of America and imported into the Community before 10 March 2009 under the Agreement between the European Community and the United States of America on trade in wine, using terms permitted in accordance with Appendix I to the Protocol on wine labeling as referred to in Article 8(2) of that Agreement [the aforementioned traditional expressions], may be held for sale and put into circulation until stocks are exhausted.

This allowance remained in effect until March 10, 2009, and is automatically extended for additional successive two-year periods unless a party to the agreement provides written notification to the other party that the period should not be extended. However as mentioned previously, 13 applications for the recognition of "traditional terms" were filed by professional organizations in the United States in June 2010.

The United States has implemented the agreement administratively, with the exception of the change in legal status of the EC semi-generic names and Retsina.

Finally, it is important to recite Article 12 of the agreement dealing with the "Relationship to other instruments and laws." This article establishes a "legal shield" or wall between the Agreement on Trade in Wine and the WTO agreements. Specifically, nothing in the Agreement on Trade in Wine affects the rights and obligations of the United States and the EC under the

---

138. Commission Regulation No. 1416/2006, laying down specific rules on the implementation of Article 7(2) of the Agreement between the European Community and the United States of America on trade in wine concerning the protection of U.S. names of origin in the Community, 2006 O.J. (L 267) 22 (EC).

139. Commission Regulation No. 113/2009, concerning the use of certain traditional terms on labels for wine imported from the United States of America, 2009 O.J. (L 38) 25 (EC).

WTO Agreement, and nothing prevents measures allowing "the use of homonymous names of origin where consumers will not be misled" or the "use, in the course of trade, [of] that person's name or the name of that person's predecessor in business in a manner that does not mislead the *consumer*." This is a partial allusion to the TRIPs Agreement, Article 23.3 ("taking into account the need to ensure equitable treatment of the producers concerned") and Article 24.8 ("[t]he provisions of this Section [geographical indications] shall in no way prejudice the *right* of any person to use, in the course of trade, that person's name or the name of that person's predecessor in business, except where such name is used in such a manner as to mislead the *public*"), and preserves the rights of free speech in the United States and in the EC.

The aforementioned legal shield is used again in Article 6 (use of certain terms, semi-generics) and Article 7 (names of origin), which states that the use of these terms lies outside intellectual property rights and "shall not be construed in and of themselves as defining intellectual property or as obligating the Parties to confer or recognize any intellectual property rights." The consequence is that

> the names listed in Annex IV are not necessarily considered, nor excluded from being considered, geographical indications under U.S. law, and the names listed in Annex V are not necessarily considered, nor excluded from being considered, geographical indications under Community law. Furthermore, the terms listed in Annex II are neither considered, nor excluded from being considered in the future, geographical indications of the Community under U.S. law.[140]

Apparently, both Parties forgot the TRIPs Agreement.

3. OTHERS BILATERAL WINE ACCORDS

The EC has a long history of signing bilateral agreements, including accords with Canada in 1989 and 2003, Australia in 1994 and 2008, South Africa in 1999, and Chile in 2002. The same holds true with the United States, which signed free-trade agreements with Australia in 2004, with Chile in 2004, and of course, the trilateral NAFTA with Canada and Mexico in 1994. These agreements are beyond the scope of this chapter.

C. CONCLUSION

We can cast a glance into the future by considering the evolution of wine law to date. Wine law is no longer in an ivory tower; isolationism is over. All vine and wine matters are now subject to the mandates of international trade law, intellectual property law, sanitary and health law, and so on. Additionally, the wine-producing countries of the world are perennially increasing in

---

140. There is a considerable difference between the Agreement on Trade in Wine and the EC-Canada Wine and Spirits Agreement on this point. The latter agreement dedicates an entire title (Title III) to the TRIPs rules.

number. For the foreseeable future, particularly in the face of climate change, the question is whether there will be any countries that are *not* wine producers.

Nor are matters concerning the vine and wine any longer the internal affairs of a private club. Additionally, wines are no longer alone in hoisting the flag of geographical indications, with accompanying notions of origin and quality. The TRIPs Agreement applies to "[g]eographical indications . . . which identify a good as originating in the territory of a Member." Many WTO members understand "product" to include "agricultural, natural, handicraft or industrial" goods. At the same time, questions about "indications of source," which typically are fundamentally different than GIs, are seriously emerging. The wine sector must survey the legal trends of a wider market. Darjeeling (India), Champagne, Napa Valley, Talavera (Mexico), Fuding (China), and TeeJong Mae Chaem (Thailand) are a new family, the GI one, and will constitute an important new lobbying group . . . or war zone.

As we look forward, it is useful to remember the recommendation of the 1923 International Conference of Wine that the represented countries adopt legislative initiatives "guaranteeing the purity and authenticity of products with certificates of origin." The future demands no more and no less. Yet we also must be aware of the role of standards. Nobel Prize–winning economist Joseph E. Stiglitz has said that the place of standards and standardization (or, with a different vocabulary, homogenization) is currently one of Europe's biggest challenges and is crucial for relations between developing and developed countries.[141] Stiglitz sees no reason to compel all consumers to eat the same foodstuffs and spend their money in the same way. With this comment, he goes to the heart of a critical matter for the future of wine in the world: how to balance local standards accompanying products of origin such as wine with globalization and the need for global or regional standards.

141. Joseph Stiglitz, The Roaring Nineties, Le Monde, October 1, 2003; *see also* Joseph Stiglitz, The Roaring Nineties: A New History of the World's Most Prosperous Decade (W. W. Norton 2003).

FOR FURTHER EXPLORATION

Richard Mendelson

Because wine law covers so many fields of law, it is impossible to provide a comprehensive list of books for the wine lawyer's library. In fact, many wine lawyers may never be involved in a case involving land use, intellectual property, or international trade. Some may be litigators and others transactional lawyers. Some may devote their entire careers to federal practice involving TTB, FDA, and the FTC, while others may handle only local or state alcoholic beverage licensing and compliance matters. The nature of a wine lawyer's practice will depend on his or her clients (wineries, wholesalers, retailers, marketing companies, glass manufacturers, barrel makers, etc.), the clients' activities (wine production, wine distribution, wine marketing, direct shipping, auctioneering, import/export), geographic location (urban versus rural and, of course, the particular state in which the lawyer practices), and the lawyer's specific interests and experience.

Notwithstanding the diversity of the field, there are several essentials for any wine lawyer's library. First and foremost, a winery lawyer must keep close at hand copies of the U.S. Constitution, the Federal Alcohol Administration Act (U.S. Code, Title 27), the Internal Revenue Code (U.S. Code, Title 26), and the various regulations, rulings, procedures, industry circulars, and rulemaking activities of the Treasury Department's Alcohol and Tobacco Tax and Trade Bureau (TTB), along with a bookmark to the TTB's excellent website, www.ttb.gov. Each state has its own alcoholic beverage regulatory authority, laws, regulations, policies, and procedures, and these also should be part of the wine lawyer's library, along with any related health and safety, revenue, or penal provisions concerning alcoholic beverages. Commerce Clearing House publishes a worthwhile compendium of state and federal alcoholic beverage laws known as the *CCH Liquor Control Law Reporter*, available on a subscription basis, which includes regular updates. A similar resource is *The Digest of Wine and Spirits Law*, which is also subscription based. While these two resources are excellent, nothing substitutes for personal contacts with the regulators.

Knowledge of the organization and the personnel of each of the various alcoholic beverage regulatory authorities is essential.

A wine lawyer's library should include texts on wine law history generally and Prohibition specifically. There are many excellent books on these subjects by competent academicians, sociologists, historians, economists, and lawyers. I recommend the following: a copy of the National Prohibition Act, known as the Volstead Act (1919); *Report on the Enforcement of the Prohibition Laws of the United States* (1931), by the National Commission on Law Observance and Enforcement; *Legislative History of the FAA Act*, published by the Federal Alcohol Control Administration's Office of General Counsel (September 15, 1935); Raymond Fosdick and Albert Scott's *Toward Liquor Control* (1933); Randolph Childs's *Making Repeal Work* (1947); Thomas Pinney's two-volume set, *A History of Wine in America* (1989 and 2005); my own *From Demon to Darling: A Legal History of Wine in America* (2009); W.J. Rorabaugh's *The Alcohol Republic* (1979); Jack Blocker's *American Temperance Movements: Cycles of Reform* (1989); Richard Hamm's *Shaping the Eighteenth Amendment: Temperance Reform, Legal Culture, and the Polity, 1880-1920* (1995); Norman Clark's *Deliver Us from Evil: An Interpretation of American Prohibition* (1976); and Anne-Marie Szymanski's *Pathways to Prohibition: Radicals, Moderates, and Social Movement Outcomes* (2003).

There are several invaluable websites in addition to that of the TTB. On the domestic front, the National Institute on Alcohol Abuse and Alcoholism (NIAAA) maintains the Alcohol Policy Information System (APIS), at http://alcoholpolicy.niaaa.nih.gov. APIS addresses a variety of alcohol policy issues, including underage drinking, drinking and driving, drinking and pregnancy, alcohol taxation, and retail sales laws. I also recommend the websites maintained by the following associations: Wine Institute, the trade association of California wineries, at www.wineinstitute.org; Wine and Spirits Wholesalers of America (WSWA), the national trade organization representing the wholesale tier of the wine and spirits industry, at www.wswa.org; the National Conference of State Liquor Administrators, at www.ncsla.org; and the National Alcohol Beverage Control Association, representing the control states, at www.nabca.org. These organizations publish useful statistics and also track wine law topics of current interest.

In the area of pubic health, *Alcohol: No Ordinary Commodity*, by Thomas Babor et al. (2d ed. 2010), is the single most important work on the subject. I also recommend *Alcohol and Public Policy: Beyond the Shadow of Prohibition*, edited by Marc Moore and Dean Gerstein (1981), and Philip Cook's *Paying the Tab: The Costs and Benefits of Alcohol Control* (2007). For the perspective of two health prevention advocacy groups, visit the website of the self-styled alcohol industry watchdog the Marin Institute, at www/marininstitute.org, and read *The Booze Merchants: The Inebriating of America*, by the Center for Science in the Public Interest (1983).

In the area of marketing, I recommend Jim Lapsley and Kirby Moulton's *Successful Wine Marketing* (2001), and Liz Thach and Tim Matz's *Wine: A Global Business* (2004), the latter of which also covers a variety of other wine industry topics.

On international wine law topics, there are two excellent websites in English. The first is a public site maintained by the Organisation Internationale de la Vigne et du Vin (International Organization of Vine and Wine, or OIV), an intergovernmental body headquartered in France, at www.oiv.int. The *Bulletin de l'OIV*, its quarterly journal, is available online and includes English translations. OIV also publishes many texts on a wide range of topics involving wine law, history, economics, viticulture, enology, and public health. Second, the Fédération Internationale des Vins and Spiritueux (International Federation of Wines and Spirits, or FIVS), a worldwide organization open to all sectors of the alcoholic beverage industry, maintains an international regulatory database known as FIVS-Abridge that is available on a subscription basis.

I highly recommend the conferences hosted each year by the CLE (Continuing Legal Education) on Wine, Beer and Spirits Law; by the CEB (Continuing Education of the Bar) on California wine law; and by the International Wine Law Association (known by the abbreviation of its French title, AIDV, for Association Internationale des Juristes du Droit de la Vigne et du Vin). The papers presented at these conferences are generally excellent, and the conferences provide a wonderful opportunity to meet other wine law professionals from private law practice, the government, and academia. The American Bar Association also has a Beverage Alcohol Practice Committee within its Section on Administrative Law and Regulatory Practice.

There are several excellent educational programs that include a wine law component. The program that I direct on Wine Law and Policy at the University of California, Berkeley Law, is the only program in the United States, to my knowledge, that focuses specifically on wine law. The University of California at Davis (UC Davis) hosts two annual programs that cursorily address wine law topics: the Wine Marketing Program, jointly sponsored by OIV, UC Davis Extension, and the UC Davis Department of Viticulture and Enology; and the UC Davis Wine Executive Program, sponsored by the Graduate School of Management and the Department of Viticulture and Enology. Finally, several other universities offer courses that address alcoholic beverage law issues, including Sonoma State University, which runs the Wine Business Institute within its School of Business and Economics; the University of Miami School of Law; and the University of Seattle School of Law.

Abroad, the University of Montesquieu–Bordeaux IV and the University Paul Cézanne (Aix-Marseille) each offer a master's degree in Vineyard and Wine Law, and the University of Reims Law School has a Wine and Law program that offers a master's degree in Wine and Spirits Law and a summer program in English on Wine Law. OIV also offers a 16-month post-graduate degree through the University of Paris West in Management of the Wine and Vine Sector, portions of which are taught in various countries.

Of course, knowledge about wine itself, separate and apart from the law, is invaluable. If you cannot work in the industry or make your own wines, I recommend that you keep Jancis Robinson's *The Oxford Companion to Wine* (2006) close at hand and that you get to know the product and the wine market by becoming an avid wine consumer and a serious wine taster.

INDEX

An *f* indicates a figure; *n*, a note; *t*, a table

Access and availability control policies, 360-364, 392-393
  blue laws, 361
  density of retail outlets, 361, 392
  government alcohol monopolies, 360-361, 366, 392. *See also* Control states
  licenses. *See also* Alcoholic beverage license(s)
  minimum legal drinking age, 361-362, 392
  National Prohibition, 3, 4-5, 6, 360, 369-370
  sale days and hours, 361, 393
  specific alcoholic beverages, 361
  state stores, 18, 361, 363
  supply-side controls, 360
  types of retail outlets that can sell alcohol, 361
Adams, Leon, 12
Adelsheim, David, 304
Advertising and marketing of alcoholic beverages, 138-147, 374-380
  associating alcohol with risk-taking activities, 385
  automatic e-mail generation, 146
  caloric or carbohydrate statements, 126-127
  children's protection registry, 145-146
  on college campuses, 377
  and consumption, influence on, 379-380, 393
  content, limits on, 376, 377-379
    44 Liquormart, Inc. v. Rhode Island, 186*n*8, 378
    *Rubin v. Coors Brewing Co.,*379
  counter-advertising, 390
  disparaging statements, 121
  "do not e-mail" laws, 145-146
  efforts to ban, 375-376
  energy drinks combining alcohol and caffeine, 99, 380
  federal monitoring of, advocacy for, 139
  federal regulations concerning, 375
  and First Amendment free speech guarantees, 377-379, 386
    Capital Cities Cable, Inc. v. Crisp, 377*n*154-155
    Central Hudson Gas & Electric Corp. v. Public Service Commission of New York, 378-379

Advertising and marketing of alcoholic beverages (*continued*)
FTC investigation of, 376-377
green claims, 124, 146-147
"Hello Kitty" wine, 140, 141*f*
industry codes, 139-140
Internet promotions, 207, 374, 380
lifestyle ads, 375
non-traditional (unmeasured) venues, 374, 380
obscenity, 121
online, 377
placements, restrictions on, 376*n*148, 377
point-of-sale promotions, 374
pre-approval, 375
price-based, ban on, 378
product categories, differences in, 138
prohibited practices, 121-127
public information campaigns, 390
public service announcements, 376, 381
responsible consumption, proactive communications about, 386
self-regulation
defined, 376*n*146
need for,139, 376, 377, 385-386
weaknesses of, 376-377, 393
Wine Institute's Code of Advertising Standards, 138, 139, 140, 385
social media, 143-145
sponsorships, 374, 380
therapeutic claims, 122-127
time, place, and manner regulations, 378-379
Metromedia, Inc. v. City of San Diego, 378*n*155
"tombstone advertising," 376, 386
traditional (measured) media, 374
and underage drinking, impact on, 376
viral marketing, 380
voluntary advertising codes, 377
"Wide Eye" schnapps and caffeine products, 140, 142
by wine industry, guidelines for, 138, 385-386
youth exposure to, 139, 145-146, 376-377, 379-380, 393
"Agency stores," 18
Agreement on Technical Barriers to Trade (TBT Agreement), 420, 422-423
Agreement on the Application of Sanitary and Phytosanitary Measures (SPS Agreement), 420-422, 423
Agreement on Trade in Wine. *See* U.S.-EC Wine Accords
Agreement on Trade-Related Aspects of Intellectual Property Rights (TRIPS), 217, 218, 419, 423-424, 439
geographical indications
defined, 217*n*2
protection, lack of, 280
non-generic geographical indications, restrictions on, 230-231, 235, 268
intellectual property rights, defined, 217
Uruguay Round Agreements Act (URAA), 230*n*58
Alcohol and Public Policy: Beyond the Shadow of Prohibition, 383-384
Alcohol and Tobacco Tax and Trade Bureau (TTB), 20, 75, 159-161. *See also* American Viticultural Area (AVA); Brand name(s); Certificate of label approval (COLA); Wine labels.
advertising, monitoring of, 21
alternating proprietorships, scrutiny of, 166
basic permit, application process, 160-161
enforcement responsibilities, 21*n*66
federal tied-house laws, enforcement of, 47-49
Notice and Comment Rulemaking, 21
operations and internal structure, 21-22, 160
recordkeeping requirements for wineries, 26
Alcohol consumption
advertising, influence on, 376, 379-380, 393
average daily and risk of all-cause mortality, 357*f*, 358*f*

drinking context, influence of, 368-372, 393
excessive, defined, 350
"Government Warning," effects of, 382
habitual drinking, 4
health effects of, 350-359
heavy (high-risk), defined, 350-351
infectious diseases related to, 355*n*37
license states and, 363
lower average, control states, 19
for medicinal or sacramental use, 5*n*19, 192*n*39
men vs. women, 353
moderate, defined, 350
during National Prohibition, 9
off-premise, defined, 360*n*59
on-premise, defined, 360*n*59
per capita, 4, 12
population-based strategy for reducing, 363-364
during pregnancy, 353, 381
public safety and, 359-360
regulations and interventions related to, 360-383
responsible, lack of consensus on what constitutes, 3
social consequences of, 359
standard drink, defined, 350
taxation and pricing, effects on, 365-366, 368
total domestic, 2*n*4
wines, U.S., 12-13, 123-124, 384-385
zero tolerance laws and, 373

Alcohol content, wine, 108-110

Alcohol control policies, 360-383
access and availability, 360-364, 392-393
advertising and marketing, 374-380, 393
community approaches to, 369, 391
the drinking context, 368-372, 393
drunk driving, 372-374, 391-392
education and information, 389-390
effect, summary of (Appendix 9-1), 389-394
health-sector response, 390-391
illegally and informally produced alcohol, 394
model of social responsibility for the wine industry, 383-388
prevention, 381-383, 389-390
taxation and pricing, 364-368, 393
varying responses to, 350
for wine, 384-385

Alcohol Control Systems and the Potential Effects of Privatization, 363

Alcoholic Beverage Labeling Act (ABLA) of 1988, 81*n*35, 115, 159

Alcoholic beverage license(s) and permit(s)
acquiring for new locations, retail, 305-322
California, 306, 312-322
New York, 306, 310-312
Texas, 306, 308-310
Washington, 306-308
acquiring for winery, 23-27, 156-166
classifications of, retail, defined, 304
off-sale consumption, 18, 304-305, 311-312
on-sale consumption, 16, 18, 304-305, 310-311
controls on existing businesses, retail, California, 16, 322-327
alcohol impact fees, 325-327
"deemed approved" ordinances, 324-325
disorderly house action, 323-324
non-conforming uses, 322-323
control states, 17-19
English system, as a model for, 3-4
license states, 15-17
person-to-person transfer of, 155
restrictions on, 16, 386
retail licensees, defined, 304
suspension/revocation of, 16
tied-house regulation exceptions to, 304-305
undue concentration of licenses, 16
U.S., early history of, 4-5

Alcohol: No Ordinary Commodity, 365, 368, 371-372

Alcohol Research Group, 363

Allergens
Federal Allergen Labeling and Consumer Protection Act (FALCPA) of 2004, 115, 135
labeling, 115, 135-138
major food, categories of, 135
Alternating proprietorship arrangement, 165-168
advantages of, 166
agreement, 167-168
bonded premises, scope of, 167
employees and, 167
federal and state regulation of, 166-167
TTB scrutiny, 166
American Temperance Movement, 8
American Viticultural Area (AVA), 84-86, 251-259
amending names or boundaries, 258-259
boundaries, 257
and brand names, conflicts between, 261-267, 269-271
In re Nantucket, 261*n*186
Sociedad Anomina Vina Santa Rita v. U.S. Treasury Dep't, 262*n*190
brand names featuring, 235-236
defining, 249-259
establishing, procedure for, 251-256
foreign, 251
naming, 256-257
"nested" (sub-appellations), 252, 271-272
overlap, 254
petition, requirements for, 272-274
viticultural distinctiveness, 257-258
Amethyst Initiative-Rethink the Drinking Age, 362
Anti-Saloon League (ASL), 3, 8, 194, 381
Antitrust laws, 32-33
Clayton Antitrust Act of 1914, 32
judicial decisions
Leegin Creative Leather Products, Inc. v. PSKS, Inc., 32
Parker v. Brown, 33
Robinson-Patman Act of 1936, 32-33
Sherman Antitrust Act of 1890, 11, 32, 205, 367-368
Appellations of origin, 83-87, 248-280. *See also* American Viticultural Area (AVA).
defining, 248*n*151, 249-259
foreign, 87, 251
formal system, adoption of in U.S., 248
French *appellations simples*, 256
future of in the U.S., 268-280
history and evolution of, 248
other geographical designations on wine labels
brand names of geographical significance, 260-267
generic, semi-generic, and non-generic names of geographical significance, 267-268
varietal names with geographical significance, 268
vineyard designations, 251*n*157
privatization, 274-280
protecting, 248*n*149, 259-260
regulations, changes to, 269-274
state appellation controls, 95-98
U.S. and European systems compared, 254, 255-256
"Ardent spirits," 2-3, 366
At-rest laws, 29
AVA. *See* American viticultural area (AVA)
AWOL ("alcohol without liquid"), 98

Babor, Dr. Thomas, 362, 365, 371-372, 381
Bacon, Selden, 383
Batchelor, Julie, 370
Beer Institute, 139
Belser, Karl, 286
Berryhill Act. *See* Clare Berryhill Grape Crush Report Act of 1976
Bilateral agreements, 429-438
European Community history of, 438
Free Trade Agreement (FTA), between Canada and the U.S., 419-420
and multilateral agreements compared, 419-420

mutual recognition and mutual acceptance compared, 433
U.S.-EC Wine Accords, 430-438
Binge drinking, 351-352
alcohol control policies to address, 384
on college campuses, 352*n*21
defined, 351
Blocker, Jack, 8
Blood alcohol content (BAC), 372-373
Blue laws, defined, 361*n*61
Bonded Wine Cellar (BWC), 25, 160
Bootlegging, 9-10, 17, 19, 360
Brand name(s), 88-98
and AVA names, conflicts between, 261-267, 269-271
In re Nantucket, 261*n*186
Sociedad Anomina Vina Santa Rita v. U.S. Treasury Dep't, 262*n*190
defined, 219
fictitious, place-sounding names, 94
geographic, or with geographical or viticultural significance, 89-94, 235-236, 260-267, 271
overtaken by viticultural area, 95
state appellation controls, 95-98
sub-brands, 219
as trademarks, 88-89, 219
Brands. *See* Trademark(s); Brand name(s)
Breathalyzer tests, 374
Bricks-and-mortar wineries, 150-161
acquiring an existing facility, 153-156
acquisition process, 154-156
asset purchase, 153-154, 155
equity purchase, 154, 155
merger, 154, 155
structuring the acquisition, 153-154
developing a new facility, 150-152
acquisition process, 150-152
development process, 152
due diligence, 151-152, 155
investigating the property, 151-152
negotiating the sale, 150-151
title review, 152
leasing an existing facility, 156
licenses and permits, 156-161
federal regulation, 159-161
state regulation, 156-159
Broadbent, Michael, 331, 333
Bulk wine, sale of, 165*n*61
Bureau of Alcohol, Tobacco and Firearms (ATF). *See also* Alcohol and Tobacco Tax and Trade Bureau (TTB)
wine appellation system, adoption of, 248
wine labeling and advertising, 75
Business models, 149-182
grape sourcing, 149, 169-182
acquisition process, 170
leasing raw land or existing vineyard, 172-175
legal due diligence concerns, 170-172
non-legal due diligence concerns, 172-175
purchasing grapes, 175-182
purchasing raw land or existing vineyard, 169-170
non-traditional wineries, 161-169
alternating proprietorship, 165-168
custom crush, 161-165
grower custom crush, 168-169
traditional bricks-and-mortar wineries, 150-161
acquiring an existing winery facility, 153-156
developing a new winery facility, 150-152
leasing an existing winery facility, 156
licenses and permits for, 156-161

California
bricks-and-mortar wineries, state licenses and permits required, 157-159
Type 02 Winegrower license, 157-158
Type 29 Winegrower's Storage license, 168, 169

California (*continued*)
free goods law, 57-59
advertising specialties and premiums, 58
case law, 58-59
distribution, defined, 58
statute and regulations, 57
custom crush arrangement, state licenses and permits required, 163
Clare Berryhill Grape Crush Report Act of 1976, 168-169, 178
Type 17 Beer and Wine Wholesaler's license, 163
Type 20 Off-Sale Beer & Wine license, 163
grape sourcing rules, 289*n*30
home rule in, 284, 285
land use, overview, 285-286
Napa County, 170, 286-292
Agricultural Preserve (AP) zoning, 170, 287
Agricultural Watershed (AW) zoning, 170, 288
Bronco Wine Co. v. Jolly, 230*n*57, 264-265
Napa Valley United Farmers v. County Bd. of Supervisors, 287*n*20
restrictions on wineries, and other counties compared, 291-292
retail wine sales, limitations on, 290
Right to Farm Act, adoption of, 288
urban growth boundaries, City of Napa, 288
urban sprawl, efforts to avoid, 268-287, 291
Winery Definition Ordinance (WDO), 151, 289-290
Subdivision Map Act, 152, 174
tied-house regulation, 50-59
case law, 54-56
exceptions to, 51-52
microbreweries, on-sale licenses, 52
restricted benefits laws and exceptions, 53-54
restricted ownership laws and exceptions, 50-52
winegrowers, on-sale licenses, 52
title issues, 171-172
conservation easements, 171-172
Williamson Act contracts, 171
tours and tastings, rules for, 289-290
"winegrower," adoption of term, 51*n*47
wine labeling, controls on, 22-23, 95, 96-97
conjunctive labeling statutes, 96-97
California Alcoholic Beverage Control Act (ABC), 157, 290
California Association of Winegrape Growers, 387
California Department of Alcoholic Beverage Control (ABC), 157-158, 312
alcoholic beverage licenses, power to suspend or revoke, 50
Winegrower's license, application packet for, 157*n*19
California Department of Food and Agriculture (CDFA), 23, 158-159
Wine Grape Inspection Advisory Committee, 23
California Environmental Quality Act (CEQA), 286
California Grape Crush Report, 175*n*91, 178
California Land Conservation (Williamson) Act of 1965, 171*n*82
tax incentives offered by, 287*n*18
California State Board of Equalization (BOE), 159, 312
California Sustainable Winegrowing Alliance, 387
California Water Resources Board, 171*n*79
Carpenter, Christopher, 373
Center for Alcohol Marketing and Youth, 139
Center for Science in the Public Interest (CSPI), opposition to alcohol advertising, 375-376
Certificate of label approval (COLA), 21, 28-29, 77-79, 162, 218
database, 234
defined, 78*n*18
exemption from, 78-79

Public COLA Registry, 78, 89
purpose of, 259-260
trademark protection and, 89, 241
Certification marks, 225-226, 235*n*80, 260-261
Champagne, 98, 232, 267, 433
Cherrington, Ernest, 381
Clare Berryhill Grape Crush Report Act of 1976, 168-169, 178
Clark, Norman, 371
Clayton Antitrust Act of 1914, 32
Codex Alimentarius Commission (CAC), 417-418
COLA. *See* Certificate of label approval (COLA)
Commerce Clause, U.S. Constitution
application of to alcoholic beverages, 6-7, 189-195
discrimination against out-of-state producers and products, 190-191, 386-387
overview, 183-184
capacity cap laws, 211
dormant, 184, 185-186
history and doctrine before the Eighteenth Amendment, 186-189
jurisprudence, 198-202
earliest interpretations of, 186-187
history and evolution of, 186-189
interstate liquor sales, prohibition of, 194
judicial interpretations of, 189-195
Alcohol Div. of Dep't of Fin. & Taxation of Tenn. v. State ex rel. Strawbridge, 7*n*30
Arnold's Wines, Inc. v. Boyle, 215*n*163
Bachus Imports, Ltd. v. Dias, 202-203, 204, 208*n*127, 209*n*134
Bainbridge v. Turner, 208*n*127
Bartmeyer v. Ohio, 190*n*27
Battipaglia v. New York State Liquor Auth., 196*n*56
Baude v. Heath, 214*n*159
Beskind v. Easley, 208*n*124
Black Star Farms LLC v. Oliver, 212-213, 214*n*159
Boston Beer Co. v. Massachusetts, 190*n*27
Bowman v. Chicago and Northwestern Railroad, 7*n*26, 191, 192-193
Bridenbaugh v. Freeman-Wilson, 208
Brooks v. Vassar, 202
Brown v. Maryland, 6, 187, 192
Brown-Forman distillers Corp. v. New York State Liquor Auth., 196*n*56, 204
Carter v. Virginia, 210*n*134
Cherry Hill Vineyard, LLC v. Baldacci, 213*n*154, 214*n*159
Cherry Hill Vineyards, LLC v. Lilly, 214*n*158
City of Philadelphia v. New Jersey, 200, 201*n*85, 202-203
Cooley v. Board of Wardens, 189, 198
Costco Wholesale Corp. v. Hoen (Hoen I), 214*n*160
Costco Wholesale Corp. v. Maleng (Maleng I), 214*n*160
Dickerson v. Bailey, 208*n*127
Family Winemakers of California v. Jenkins, 211-212, 213
Gibbons v. Ogden, 187, 188
Granholm v. Heald, 13, 44*n*4, 183-184, 185-186, 193, 206-214, 387
Heald v. Engler, 208*n*127
Healy v. Beer Institute, 204
Hughes v. Oklahoma, 184, 201*n*85
Indianapolis Brewing Company v. Liquor Control Commission, 196-197
Kassel v. Consolidated Freightways, 199-200
Kleinsmith v. Shurtleff, 214*n*159
Leisy v. Hardin, 7*n*26, 192-193
The License Cases, 6-7, 188-189, 192
Liquor Corp. v. Duffy, 204*n*101
Minnesota v. Clover Leaf Creamery Co., 200
Mugler v. Kansas, 190*n*27
New Energy Co. of Ind. v. Limbach, 200*n*80
North Dakota v. United States, 203, 204
Pike v. Bruce Church, Inc., 199, 202
Rhodes v. Iowa, 7*n*28, 193-194
Scott v. Donald, 193*n*46

Commerce Clause, U.S. Constitution (*continued*)
- *Siesta Vill. Mkt., LLC v. Granholm*, 215*n*165
- *Smith v. Alabama*, 189, 198
- *State Board of Equalization v. Young's Market Company*, 44*n*4, 196, 197
- *Swedenburg v. Kelly*, 208*n*125
- *Walling v. Michigan*, 190
- *Welton v. Missouri*, 184*n*6, 190*n*30
- *Wilkerson v. Rahrer*, 193*n*47
- *Willson v. Black Bird Creek Marsh Co.*, 187*n*12, 188-189
- *Wine Country Gift Baskets.com v. Steen*, 215
- *Wyoming v. Oklahoma*, 200

market participant exception, 202
open borders, Court's defense of, 192-193
"original packages doctrine," 7, 190
price affirmation laws and, 204, 368
scope of, judiciary rulings on, 187-188
and states' authority to regulate trade in alcoholic beverages, 188-189, 196
and the Twenty-first Amendment, 195-206
- competing concerns, 183, 185-186, 197-198
- jurisprudence related to, 202-206, 210*n*134

wholesaler exclusion laws, 211-212

Common law liability, 4-5
- *Rappaport v. Nichols*, 5*n*17

Conservation easements, 171-172
Control state(s), 17-19
- "agency stores," 18
- defined, 17, 306
- interstate commerce with, 19
- list of, 15
- on-premises vs. off-premises sales, 18
- pricing measures, 19*n*58
- privatization of wine sales in, 18
- state stores, 18, 361, 363
- wholesale and retail product distribution (Appendix 1-2), 40-42

Cook, Philip, 352, 364
Copyright, 246-248
- assignment of, 247
- defined, 246
- implied license, 247
  - *Effects Assocs., Inc. v. Cohen*, 247*n*147
- infringement claim, defending, 247
- public domain and, 248*n*148
- and related rights recognized under TRIPS, 217
- registration, 247
- stock images, use of, 248
- third-party use, 248
- work for hire, 247
  - *Cmty. for Creative Non-Violence v. Reid*, 247*n*145

Counterfeit wine, 329-347
- case law impacting the claim, 343-344
  - *La Trace v. Webster*, 344
  - *Weisz v. Parke-Bernet Galleries, Inc.*, 343-344
- classification of 1885, 338
- damages, 344-346
  - breach of contract, 345
  - fraud, 345
  - interest, 346
  - negligence and negligent misrepresentation, 344-345
  - punitive or exemplary damages, 345
- forms of production, 330-331
- industry techniques to respond and protect against, 338-339
- "Jefferson" bottles, 332-334
- lawsuits, 334-338
  - *Frye v. The Wine Library Inc.*, 337*n*47, 338*n*48
  - *Koch v. Acker Merrall & Condit Company*, 336
  - *Koch v. Chicago Wine Company*, 335-336
  - *Koch v. Christie's International PLC*, 334*n*11, 337-338
  - *Koch v. Greenberg*, 334-335
  - *Koch v. Rodenstock*, 334
  - *Koch v. Rud Kurniawan*, 336-337
  - *Zeller v. E & J Gallo Winery, Inc.*, 337*n*45
- legal claims associated with, 341-342
  - breach of contract, 341
  - breach of warranty, 341

fraud, 342
negligence, 341
negligent misrepresentation, 342
unfair business practices, 342
legal issues and litigation of a case, 339-347
case law impacting the claim, 343-344
damages, 344-346
discovery, 342-343
expert testimony, 340-341
legal claims associated with counterfeit wine, 341-342
trial, 346-347
proving or establishing lack of authenticity, 330
recent history, overview of, 332-334
trial, jury selection, 346-347
Custom crush arrangement, 161-165
advantages of, 162
agreements, 163-164
defined, 161
federal and state regulation of, 163
host winery, responsibilities of, 161, 162, 164
licensing required, 163*n*56
négociant model, 164-165

"Damp/moist" establishments, 15, 308
"Deemed approved" ordinances, 324-325
Deliver Us from Evil: An Interpretation of American Prohibition, 371
Dessert wine, 98, 101
Dietary Guidelines for Americans
heavy (high-risk) drinking, defined, 350-351
moderate drinking, defined, 123, 350
Dillon's rule, 283, 284, 293
Diseases of the Will: Alcohol and the Dilemmas of Freedom, 353-354
Disorderly house, 282, 323-324
Dispute Settlement Body (DSB), 424-427
Distilled Spirits Council of the United States (DISCUS), 139
Distribution and marketing, 29-33
antitrust laws, 33-33
at-rest laws, 29
"bright-line" standards, 29
broker and wholesaler, distinction between 29*n*109
dualing, 31
interstate commerce, restrictions on, 6-7, 30, 387
Parker immunity doctrine, 33
"primary source" laws, 17, 31-32
rule of reason, 32
state alcoholic beverage franchise laws, 17, 31
state trade practice provisions, 30
three-tiered system of, 13, 29, 59, 207, 209, 214-215, 304, 387
Dow, Neal, 5
Dram shop laws, 4-5, 369-370
contributory negligence defense, 369
damage caps, 369
social-host liability, 369-370
Drinking context, control of, 368-372, 393
activities that accompany drinking, attempts to control, 370-371
California v. LaRue, 370
common law liability, 4-5
community groups, role of, 369
dram shop laws, 4-5, 369-370
problem bars, 371-372
public drunkenness, criminalization of, 3, 370
responsible beverage service (RBS), 368-369, 386, 393
restrictions on drinking in public places, 370
social and physical environment of drinking establishments, 370-371
social-host liability, 369-370
underage drinking, 370
Drunk driving, 372-374
alcohol control policies to address, 384
blood alcohol content (BAC), 372-373, 391
federal highway funds, link to, 373*n*132
legal limit, recommendations for lowering, 372

Drunk driving (*continued*)
national standards for, 373
underage drinkers, 372, 392
breathalyzer tests, 374
designated driver, 374, 392
deterrent effect, necessary components of, 373
driver's license, suspension of, 373
DUI, mandatory imprisonment, 374
ignition interlock systems, use of, 374, 392
legal interventions, 372, 373-374, 392
minimum legal drinking age, 372-373, 392
open container laws, 374
plea bargaining, prohibition on, 374
Reagan Commission on, 362, 372
safe-ride programs, 392
sobriety checkpoints, 374, 391-392
social norms and attitudes toward, changes in, 374
statistics related to, 372
treatment programs, 373
vehicle impoundment, 374
zero tolerance laws, 373, 374
Dry states, 5, 184
Due Process Clause, U.S. Constitution
state land use authority, limitations on, 285
Wisconsin v. Constantineau, 186*n*8

Eighteenth Amendment, U.S. Constitution, 8-9
adoption and ratification of, 194
dormant Commerce Clause, history and doctrine prior to, 186-189
Ellison, R. Curtis, 349
Energy drinks combining alcohol and caffeine, 99, 380
Equal Protection Clause, U.S. Constitution
California v. LaRue, 186
Craig v. Boren, 186n8
N.Y. State Liquor Auth. v. Bellanca, 186
state land use authority, limitations on, 285
Establishment Clause, U.S. Constitution
Larkin v. Grendel's Den, Inc., 186*n*8
"Estate Bottled" designation, use of, 86-87, 173
Excise tax(es), 4, 23-25, 160-161, 364-366. *See also* "Sin taxes"
bond requirement, 25-26
defined, 4*n*13
federal rates for alcoholic beverages, 24*t*
history, 20*n*61. *See also* 1*n*1
Small Producer's Tax Credit, 161, 166
tax rate, calculation of, 161*n*48
variations in rate by state, 159*n*35
Existing vineyard or raw land, leasing, 172-175
"crop share" lease, 175
landowner's motivation to lease, 173
lease term issues, 174-175
process, 174
rent issues, 175
sale-leaseback transactions, 173-174
subdivision map concerns (California), 174
unique vineyard development lease elements, 174
vineyard improvements, 175
vintner's motivation to lease, 173
Existing winery facility, acquiring, 153-156
acquisition process, 154-156
structuring the acquisition
asset purchase, 153-154, 155
equity purchase, 154, 155
merger, 154, 155
Existing winery facility, leasing, 156
use permits
Cohn v. County Bd. of Supervisors of L.A., 156*n*15
County of Imperial v. McDougal, 156*n*15

FAA. *See* Federal Alcohol Administration (FAA) Act of 1935
Fair-trade laws, 367. *See also* Antitrust laws

Fair use, doctrine of, 180, 246, 261
Farm winery(ies)
  direct sales to consumers by, 387
  history and evolution of, 11, 207, 282-283
  New York, Farm Winery Law 1976), 282-283
  Virginia, 292-293, 294, 295
FDA. *See* Food and Drug Administration (FDA)
Federal Alcohol Administration (FAA) Act of 1935, 45, 159
  geographical indications under, 218
  labeling regulations, 76
  purpose of, 20-21, 249
  tied-house provision of, 46-47
  and wine, regulation of, 27-28
Federal Alcohol Control Administration (FACA), 27*n*94
Federal Allergen Labeling and Consumer Protection Act (FALCPA) of 2004, 115, 135
Federal Highway Aid Act, 373*n*128
Federal Trade Commission (FTC), 75
  alcoholic beverage advertising, conclusions re:, 376-377
  Green Claims Guide, 146-147
  wine, definition of, 75*n*2
Fifth Amendment, takings provision, 285
First Amendment
  free speech guarantees, 285, 377-379, 386
  44 Liquormart, Inc. v. Rhode Island, 186*n*8, 378
Flavored wine products, 98, 99
Food Allergen Labeling and Consumer Protection Act (FALCPA), 115, 135
Food and Drug Administration (FDA), 21, 161
  GRAS standards, 22, 380
  warnings re: energy drinks combining alcohol and caffeine, 380
  wine labeling and advertising, 74-75
Forbes, Christopher, 333
Fourteenth Amendment, 6, 190
  Due Process clause, 186*n*8, 285
  Equal Protection clause, 186*n*8, 285
  Prohibitory laws under, 190
Franchise law, alcoholic beverage, state, 17, 31
Fraud, 396. *See also* Counterfeit wine
  Zeller v. E&J Gallo Winery, Inc., 337*n*45
Free goods laws, 11, 43
  California, 57-59
    advertising specialties and premiums, 58
    distribution, defined, 58
    statute and regulations, 57
  case law, 58-59
    Coors Brewing v. Stroh, 59
    Department of Alcoholic Beverage Control v. Alcoholic Beverage Control Appeals Bd. (Anheuser-Busch, Inc.), 58-59
    Gonzales & Co., Inc., v. Department of Alcoholic Beverage Control, 58
    Miller Brewing Co. v. Department of Alcoholic Beverage Control, 58
    People ex rel. Department of Alcoholic Beverage Control v. Miller Brewing Co., 58
Free lunch, 11
Free Trade Agreement (FTA), between Canada and the U.S., 419-420
"French Paradox," 122, 356, 357
From Demon to Darling: A Legal History of Wine in America, 385
Fruit wine, 98
FTC. *See* Federal Trade Commission (FTC)

General Agreement on Tariffs and Trade (GATT), 418, 420
Generally Recognized as Safe (GRAS) standards, Food and Drug Administration (FDA), 22, 380
Generic names, 231-232, 267
Geographical indications, 217-218. *See also* Appellations of origin
  defined, 217*n*2
  under U.S. law, 218
Geographic brand names. *See* Brand name(s).
Gerstein, Dean, 383
Goût de terroir, 11, 282

"Government Warning" requirement, 21*n*66, 82*f*, 115-117, 353, 381-382
Grape purchase agreement (GPA), 176-182
  farming practice and viticultural control, 180-181
  grower's liens, 181-182
    Frazier Nuts, Inc. v. American Ag Credit, 182*n*105
  harvest, delivery, and risk of loss, 181
  preamble and recitals, 176
  pricing and payment, 178-179
    bottle pricing, 179
    per-acre pricing, 178
    price adjustments, 179
    price per ton, 178
    timing of payment, 179
  quality, 177
    grape defects, 177
    material other than grapes (MOG), percentage of, 177, 179
  quantity, 177
  term and termination, 176-177
  vineyard designation, 180
Grape sourcing, 169-182
  leasing raw land or an existing vineyard, 172-175
    landowner's motivation to lease, 173
    lease term issues, 174-175
    rent issues, 175
    sale-leaseback transactions, 173-174
    Subdivision Map Act concerns (California), 174
    unique vineyard development lease elements, 174
    vineyard improvements, 175-182
    vintner's motivation to lease, 173
  purchasing raw land or an existing vineyard, 169-172
    acquisition process, 170
    legal due diligence concerns, 170-172
    non-legal due diligence concerns, 172
  title issues, 171-172
  water rights, 170-171
  zoning laws, 170
Grape varietals. *See* Varietal designation
GRAS standards. *See* Generally Recognized as Safe (GRAS) standards
Green claims, 124, 146-147
"Green light" acts, 48
"Green" practices, 277-278, 387
Grower custom crush arrangement, 168-169
  sale of grapes, 168-169
  sale of wine, 168
Growing degree days (GDDs), 258*n*174

Health effects of alcohol consumption, 123-124, 350-359. *See also* Public Health.
  assessing, difficulty of, 351
  Bacardi Rum advertisement, 126-127
  binge drinking, 351-352
  death, risk of, 350, 352-353
  dose-response relationship, 351
  excessive consumption, 350, 356
  "French Paradox," 122, 356, 357
  health-related directional statements, 123-124, 382-383
  J- or U-shaped curve, 351
  medications and, 355
  men vs. women, 353
  moderate consumption, 123, 351, 356
  mortality, 356
  pattern of drinking and, 351
  pregnancy and, 353, 381
  protective effects, 351, 355-356
  summary of, 354-355
  threshold effect, 351
  total alcohol consumption, data re:, 363, 364*n*76
  wine, special properties of, 357-358
Heavy (high-risk) drinking, defined, 350-351
The History of Liquor Licensing in England Principally from 1700 to 1830, 3-4
Holder, Harold, 18
Homeland Security Act of 2002, 20*n*62, 248*n*152
Home rule, 283, 284
Hybrid grapes, 2

Imitation wine, 98, 101
The Impact of Enforcement on Intoxication and Alcohol Related Harm, 370-371
Import-Export Clause, U.S. Constitution
  Dep't of Revenue v. James B. Beam Distilling Co., 186*n*8
Industrial property rights, 217. *See also* Geographical indications; Trademarks
Intellectual property rights, 217, 280
Internal Revenue Code (IRC), 20, 25-26, 159
International institutions and accords, 395-439
  bilateral agreements, 429-438
  future of, 438-439
  International Organization of Vine and Wine (OIV), 395-419
  multilateral agreements, 420-429
  multilateral and bilateral agreements compared, 419-420
International Organization of Vine and Wine (OIV), 395-419
  constituent bodies, 404-407
    Executive Committee (COMEX), 406
    General Assembly, 404-406
    Scientific and Technical Committee (STC), 406-407
  governance, 407-408
  history and evolution of, 395-399
  member countries, list of, 398
  mission and purpose, 398-399, 412-413
  standardization work, 412-416
    economic standards, 414-416
    oenological standards, 413
    viticultural standards, 413
  participants, categories of, 399-404
    guests, 403-404
    members, 399-402
    observers, 402-403
    requests for observer status, 403*n*22
  relations with other international organizations, 416-419
    Codex Alimentarius Commission (CAC), 417-418
    World Intellectual Property Organization (WIPO), 418
    World Trade Organization (WTO), 418-419
  scientific work and heritage, 408-412
  voting protocols, 401-402
International Wine Law Association, 418
Interstate commerce, 6-7. *See also* Commerce Clause, U.S. Constitution
  direct and indirect burdens on, distinguishing between, 189
  discrimination against, 201, 387
    C & A Carbone, Inc. v. Town of Clarkstown, 201
    Dean Milk Co. v. Madison, Wisconsin, 201
    Granholm v. Heald, 13, 183-184, 185-186, 206-214, 387
    Hunt v. Washington State Apple Advertising Comm'n, 201, 202
    Maine v. Taylor, 201, 202
  laws that are protectionist in purpose, 201
    West Lynn Creamery v. Healy, 201
  Pike balancing test, 199-200, 202, 210, 212
  reciprocity laws, 207-208
    Indianapolis Brewing Company v. Liquor Control Commission, 207*n*121
  restrictions on, 30

Janes, Kathleen, 18
Jefferson, Thomas, 3, 331, 332

Keg registration laws, 370
Kentucky, local option law, 14
Koch, William ("Bill") I., 331-332, 334-338, 339

Labeling. *See* Wine labels
Laforge, Robert, 375
Land use, 281-327
  conditional use permit (CUP), 284
  constitutional limits to state/municipal authority, 285

Land use (*continued*)
controls, 281-282
Dillon's rule, 283, 284, 293
home rule, 283, 284
laws, 152
mixed uses, 283
regulation, as police power, 283
Associated Home Builders Inc. v. City of Livermore, 283*n*7
Berman v. Parker, 283*n*7
Candid Enterprises, Inc. v. Grossmont Union High School District, 284*n*10
Clark v. City of DesMoines, 283*n*9
Miller v. Bd. of Pub. Works, 283*n*7
Village of Belle Terre v. Boraas, 283*n*7
rural wineries, 282-304
in California, 295-292
history and evolution of, 282-283
land use basics, 283-285
in Oregon, 300-304
in Virginia, 292-300
urban retailers, 304-327
existing businesses, controls on, 322-327
impact fee, 325-327
new locations, 305-322
variance, 284
zoning, 284
Village of Euclid v. Amber Realty Co., 284*n*11
Lanham Act
commerce, defined, 233
geographical certification marks, 218, 226, 235, 260-261, 267
trademark, defined, 218-219, 225
trademark registration, use in commerce requirement, 233-234
and TRIPS Article 23, potential conflicts with, 235
Licenses/licensing. *See* Alcoholic beverage license(s)
License states, 15-17, 363
Liquor Control Board of Ontario (LCBO), 137
Lisbon Agreement, 418, 427-428
Local option, 10, 14-15
"damp/moist" establishments, 15, 308
elections, 5
Kentucky, 14
popularity of, 10
Texas, 308-309
U.S. jurisdictions (Appendix 1-1), 34-39

Madrid Agreement for the Repression of False or Deceptive Indications of Source on Goods/Madrid Protocol, 238-239, 396, 418
Maine Law of 1851, 5-6, 190
Mapping the Social Consequences of Alcohol Consumption, 359
Mark(s). *See* Trademark(s)
Mill, John Stuart, 5*n*20
Minimum legal drinking age, 361-362, 392
exceptions to, 362
and federal highway funds, link to, 362, 373*n*, 128
National Minimum Drinking Age Act of 1984, 373*n*128
proposals for lowering, 362-363, 363*n*68
Misplaced Priorities: A History of Federal Alcohol Regulation and Public Health Policy, 375
Moderate drinking, defined, 123, 350
Mondavi, Margrit, 385
Moonshining, 360
Moore, Mark, 383
Morgan, Elizabeth, 370
Mosher, Jim, 373, 374
Mothers against Drunk Driving (MADD), 372
Multilateral agreements, 420-429
and bilateral agreements compared, 419-420
MERCOSUR, 420
North American Free Trade Agreement (NAFTA), 420, 438
Pluralateral Trade Agreements, WTO, 420
World Intellectual Property Organization (WIPO), 427-429
World Trade Organization (WTO), 420-427
World Wine Trade Group (WWTG), 429

Nation, Carrie, 8
National Association of Beverage Control Authorities (NABCA), 363
National Conference on Weights and Measures (NCWM), 112
National Grape Registry, 107
National Grapevine Importation Program, 106
National Industrial Recovery Act (NIRA), 27*n*94, 45
  A.L.A. Schechter Poultry Corp. v. United States, 27*n*45
National Institute of Standards and Technology, 113
National Minimum Drinking Age Act of 1984, 373*n*128
National Prohibition, 3, 360. *See also* Eighteenth Amendment, U.S. Constitution
  alcohol consumption during, 9
  bootlegging, 9-10, 19
  commercial winemaking and, 9
  cost of, 10
  early attempts at
    Maine Law of 1851, 4-5, 369-370
    Mugler v. Kansas, 6
  efforts to enforce, failure of, 195
  groups advocating repeal of, 195
  illegal liquor production and sale during, 195
  negative consequences of, 10
  repeal of. *See* Twenty-first Amendment, U.S. Constitution
National Prohibition Act, 9
Négociant model, 164-165
Net contents
  authorized bottle sizes for wine, 110*f*, 111-113
New winery facility, acquiring
  due diligence and title review, 151-152, 155
  negotiating the sale, 150-151
    "as is" property condition, 151
    purchase and sale agreement, 150-151
  term sheet or letter of intent, 150
New York
  alcoholic beverage licensing, new retail locations, 310-312
    off-premises license, 311-312
    on-premises license, 310-311
    self-certification, 311
    source-of-funds documentation, 310
  case law
    People (New York) v. Bacardi U.S.A., et al., 67*n*181
  Farm Winery Law 1976), 282-283
  State Liquor Authority (SLA), 65
  trade practice law, 65-70
Non-generic wines, 230-231, 268, 435
Non-traditional wineries, 161-169
  alternating proprietorship, 165-168
  custom crush arrangement, 161-165
  grower custom crush, 168-169
Nutrition Labeling and Education Act (NLEA), 133-134

Office International de la Vigne et du Vin. *See* International Organization of Vine and Wine (OIV)
Office of the United States Trade Representative, 21
Off-premises, 18, 304, 311-312, 360*n*59
On-premises, 16, 18, 304, 310-311, 360*n*59
Open container laws, 374
Oregon
  accessory uses, regulation of, 303
  conditional option, 303-304
  custom crush arrangement, licenses required, 163*n*56
  exclusive farm use (EFU) zoning, 300-301
  express option, 303*n*83
  farm crops, defined, 302
  farm processing facilities, 301
  farm stands, 302
  land use planning in, 300-301
  limited-service restaurants on winery premises, 301
  Measures 37 and 49, 303-304
  regulations re: production and sale of wine, 158*n*29
  sale of incidental items and services at wineries, restrictions on, 301-302
  special events on winery property, 302

Oregon (*continued*)
urban growth boundaries, 300
wine labeling, controls on, 22, 95
Oregon Land Conservation and Development Commission (OLCDC), 300
Oregon Liquor Control Commission (OLCC), 158*n*29
"Organic" wine, 115, 124
Original Packages Act. *See* Wilson Act of 1890
"Original packages doctrine," 7, 190

Paris Convention for the Protection of Industrial Property, 238, 248*n*149, 418, 427
Parker, Robert, 101, 333
Parker immunity doctrine, 33
Patents, 217
Patient Protection and Affordable Care Act of 2010, 134
Paying the Tab: The Costs and Benefits of Alcohol Control, 364
Peatman, Joseph, 287
Phylloxera crisis, 395
Polyphenols, health effects of, 357
Prevention efforts, 381-383
drunk driving, strict laws and enforcement, 373
education, 381
school-based programs, 381, 389
health-related directional statements, 123-124, 382-383
health warnings on alcoholic beverage labels, 381-382
therapeutic interventions, 381
treatment, 373, 381
Pricing, 364-368
mandatory markups, 366
minimum prices, 366
"post and hold" pricing provisions, 367
Costco Wholesale Corp. v. Maleng, 367
price affirmation laws, 368
Brown-Forman Distillers v. N.Y. Liquor Authority, 204, 368
California Retail Liquor Dealers Association v. Midcal Aluminum, Inc., 205
Costco Wholesale Corp. v. Maleng (Maleng II), 205, 206n114
price-based advertising, ban on, 378
44 Liquormart, Inc. v. Rhode Island, 186*n*8, 378
price controls, 4
price elasticity of demand, 364-365, 393
price postings, 366
resale price maintenance, 366, 367
California Retail Liquor Dealers Ass'n v. Midcal Aluminum, 367
Leegin Creative Leather Products v. PSKS, Inc., 367
"Primary source" laws, 17, 31-32
Prohibition, U.S.
Anti-Saloon League (ASL), 3, 8, 194, 381
cycles of, 8
history of, as a process of local gradualism, 8
legally mandated. *See* Eighteenth Amendment, U.S. Constitution; National Prohibition
state-level laws, enactment of, 184
Proof gallon, defined, 24*n*78
Public drunkenness, criminalization of, 3, 370
Public health, 349-394. *See also* Health effects of alcohol consumption.
at-risk drinkers, policies to address, 384
effect of policy measures, summary of (Appendix 9-1), 389-394
model of social responsibility for the wine industry, 383-388
regulations and interventions, 360-383
access and availability, 360-364, 392-393
advertising and marketing, 374-380, 393
the drinking context, 368-372, 393
drunk driving, 372-374, 391-392
prevention, 381-383, 389-390
taxation and pricing, 364-368, 393

Public Health Security and Bioterrorism Preparedness and Response Act of 2002, 161
Public safety, 359-360
  alcohol-related harm, 349-350, 359-360
  social consequences of alcohol consumption, 359

Racketeering, 19
Reciprocity laws, interstate commerce, 207
"Red light" acts, 48
Renaud, Serge, 357
Responsible beverage service (RBS), 368-369, 386, 393
Resveratrol, 357
Revenue Reconciliation Act of 1990, 20*n*60
Rhodes, Terrell, 379
Robinson-Patman Act of 1936, 32-33
Robson, Godfrey, 364
Rodenstock, Hardy, 331, 332-333
Rossow, Ingeborg, 359
Rural wineries, 282-304. *See also* Farm winery(ies)
  in California, 285-292
  concepts of *terroir* and *goût de terroir,* 11, 282
  history and evolution of, 282-283
  land use basics, 283-285
  in Oregon, 300-304
  in Virginia, 292-300
Rush, Dr. Benjamin, 2-3, 349

School-based alcohol education programs, 389
Semi-generic wines, 267-268, 433-434
Service marks, 225
Serving facts, 127-135
Sherman Antitrust Act of 1890, 11, 32, 205, 367-368
Sin, Murray, 370
"Sin taxes," 4, 325, 366
Small Producer's Wine Tax Credit, 161, 166
Sobriety checkpoints, 374
Social and Economic Control of Alcohol: The 21st Amendment in the 21st Century, 379
Social-host liability, 369-370
Sparkling wine, 98, 232
SPS Agreement. *See* Agreement on the Application of Sanitary and Phytosanitary Measures (SPS Agreement)
"Standard drink," defined, 350
Standards Code. *See* Agreement on Technical Barriers to Trade (TBT Agreement)
Standing Committee on the Law of Trademarks, Industrial Designs, and Geographical Indications (SCT), 428-429
State monopolies, 15, 363, 366. *See also* Control states
State stores, 18, 361, 363
Sulfites, declaration of, 81*n*34, 114-115
Sumptuary laws, defined, 4
Supremacy Clause, U.S. Constitution
  Capital Cities Cable, Inc. v. Crisp, 186*n*8, 377*n*154-155
  Gibbons v. Ogden, 187, 188
Szymanski, Anne-Marie, 8

Table wine, 101, 109
Tasting rooms, 156, 289, 305
Taxation. *See* Excise tax(es).
TBT Agreement. *See* Agreement on Technical Barriers to Trade (TBT Agreement)
Teetotalism, 3
Temperance
  ardent spirits, 2-3, 366
  defined, 11, 206*n*113, 350
    Costco Wholesale Corp. v. Hoen (Hoen II), 206*n*113
  price controls as means to promote, 367-368
  restrictions on advertising content and, 378
Temperance movement, U.S.
  Maine Law of 1851, 190
  "original packages doctrine," effects of, 7, 190
  origins of, 2-3
Tenth Amendment, U.S. Constitution, 6, 283*n*6
Terroir, 11, 282
Texas
  alcoholic beverage licensing, new retail locations, 308-310

Texas (*continued*)
central business district, defined, 309*n*105
grounds for denial, 310
late hours, 309*n*104
license application, notice of filing, 309-310
local option, 308-309
number of permits issued, 309
public hearings, 310
wineries, tied-house exception, 305*n*85
Food and Beverage Certificates, 310*n*108
Texas Alcoholic Beverage Commission (TABC), 308
Three-tiered system of distribution, 13, 29, 59, 207, 209, 214-215, 304, 387
Tied-house law(s)
amendments, 71-72
in California, 15-16, 50-59
restricted benefits laws and exceptions, 53-54
restricted ownership laws and exceptions, 50-52
case law
Cal. Beer & Wine Wholesalers Ass'n. v. Dep't of Alcoholic Beverage Control, 56*n*100
California Beer Wholesalers Assn., Inc. v. Alcoholic Bev. Control Appeals Bd., 44*n*6, 54-56
Department of Alcoholic Beverage Control v. Alcoholic Beverage Control Appeals Board (Deleuze), 55
Department of Alcoholic Beverage Control v. Alcoholic Beverage Control Appeals Board (Schieffelin & Somerset Co.), 55-56
Fedway Associates, Inc. v. United States Treasury Department Bureau of Alcohol, Tobacco and Firearms, 46-47
In the matter of Allied Domecq Spirits and Wine, 56*n*99
In the matter of Anheuser-Busch, Inc., 56*n*98
National Distrib. Co., Inc. v. U.S. Treasury Dep't, Bureau of Alcohol, Tobacco and Firearms, 44*n*11
People ex rel. Dep't of Alcoholic Beverage Control v. Miller Brewing Co., 56*n*99
Stein Distributing Company, Inc. v. Department of the Treasury Bureau of Alcohol, Tobacco & Firearms, 49-50
and control of retailers, 45, 72
defined, 304-305
evolution of, 70
exceptions to, 304-305
California, 45, 50-52
New Jersey wineries, 305*n*86
Texas wineries, 305*n*85
federal regulation, 45-50
Federal Alcohol Administration (FAA) Act of 1935, 45, 46-47
"green light" acts, 48
preemption, 49-50
"red light" acts, 48
"yellow light" acts, 48-49
purpose of, 44
supplier-sponsored exceptions, 71
temperance movement and, 44-45
variations in by state, 15-16
wholesalers and, 70-71
Tippling, restrictions on, 4
Tombstone advertising, 376, 386
Trade practices, 30, 43-72
"alcoholic beverages," use of term, 43*n*2
California free goods laws, 43
California tied-house regulation, 50-59
federal tied-house regulation, 45-50
historical background, 43-45
New York law trade practice, 65-70
tied-house laws, 43
Washington (state) trade practice law, 59-64
Trademark(s), 217
adoption and registration of, 232-241
Grupo Gigane SA DeCV v. Dallo & Co., Inc., 232*n*65
Hanover Star Milling Co. v. Metcalf, 232*n*65
application, federal trademark registration, 236-240
filing, bases for, 237

intent-to-use (ITU), 237
Madrid Agreement/Madrid Protocol and, 238-239, 396, 418
Paris Convention and, 238, 418
use-based, 237, 238
USPTO Trademark Electronic Search System, 89, 234-235, 236, 239
arbitrary, 227
brand name as, 88-89, 219
business value of, 241
catalog covers, 220, 223, 224*f*
certification marks, defined, 225-226, 235*n*80, 260-261
classification of, 225-227
clearance search, 234
collective marks, defined, 226
color as, 224
Freixenet v. Admiral Wine, 225*n*16
Qualitex Co. v. Jacobson Prods. Co., 225*n*14
Sazerac Co. v. Skyy Spirits, 225*n*16
Wal-Mart Stores v. Samara Bros., 225*n*15
defined, 218-219, 225, 246
descriptive, 229, 231
E. & J. Gallo Winery v. Gallo Cattle Co., 229*n*51
Friend v. H.A. Friend & Co., 229*n*47
In re Uncle Sam Chemical Co., 231*n*61
Yankee Candle Co. v. Bridgewater Candle Co., 231*n*62
dilution, 244
distinctive, 227
enforcement of, 241-244
fair use, concept of, 180, 246, 261
fanciful, 227
federal registration, use in commerce requirement, 233-234
Dawn Donut co. v. Hart's Food Stores, Inc., 234*n*76
foreign wineries, relief from, 238
Geovision, Inc. v. Geovision Corp., 233*n*75
Giant Foods, Inc. v. Nation's Foodservice, Inc., 233*n*66
In re Stellar Int'l Inc., 233*n*72
Richardson-Vicks, Inc. v. Franklin Mint Corp., 233*n*74
generic, 231-232
Door Systems, Inc. v. Pro-Line Door Systems, Inc., 232*n*64
Kendall-Jackson v. E. & J. Gallo, 232
geographical certification marks, defined, 218, 226, 235, 260-261
with geographical significance, restrictions on, 235-236, 260
graphic presentations, 220
highly-suggestive, 228
Minnesota Mining & Mfg. Co. v. Johnson & Johnson, 228*n*44
infringement
Acad. Of Motion Picture Arts & Scis. v. Creative House Promotions, Inc., 219*n*7
Am. Ass'n for Advancement of Sci. v. Hearts Corp., 242*n*117
AMF, Inc. v. Sleekcraft Boats, 242*n*117
Banfi Products Corp. v. Kendall-Jackson Winery, Ltd., 243*n*123, 126, 128
Bd. of Regents, Univ. of Texas Sys. ex rel. Univ. of Texas at Austin v. KST Elec., Ltd., 244*n*133
Chanel Inc. v. Savannah-Chanel, 244*n*136
and dilution, compared, 244
E. & J. Gallo Winery v. Ben R. Goltsman & Co., 243*n*123
E. & J. Gallo Winery v. Consorzio del Gallo Nero, 242*n*119, 243*n*125
E. & J. Gallo Winery v. Gallo Cattle Co., 242*n*119
Frehling Enterprises, Inc. v. Int'l Select Group, Inc., 242*n*117
Frisch's Rests v. Elby's Big Boy, 242*n*117
Helen Curtis Indus., Inc. v. Church & Dwight Co., 242*n*117
In re E.I. DuPont Nemours & Co., 242*n*117
In re Saviah Rose Winery, LLC, 243*n*122
In re Vina La Miranda Limitada, 242*n*119
Interpace Crop. V. Lapp, Inc., 242*n*117
legal systems providing no protection against, 241
Maker's Mark Distillery, Inc. v. Diageo N. Am., Inc., 244*n*135

Trademark(s) (*continued*)
Nike, Inc. v. Nikepal Int'l, Inc., 244*n*133
Nova Wines, Inc. v. Adler Fels Winery LLC, 242*n*119, 243*n*124
One Industries v. Jim O'Neal Distrib., Inc., 219*n*7
Palm Bay Imps. Inc. v. Veuve Clicquot Ponsardin Maison Fondee en 1772, 243*n*120
Park N' Fly, Inc. v. Dollar Park and Fly, Inc., 240*n*109
Pepsico, Inc. v. #1 Wholesale, LLC, 244*n*133
Pignons S.A. de Mecanique de Precision v. Polaroid Corp., 242*n*117
Pizzeria Uno Corp. v. Temple, 242*n*117
Polaroid Corp. v. Polaroid Electronics Corp., 242*n*117
Roto-Rooter Corp. v. O'Neal, 242*n*117
Russell v. Caesar, 211-242
SquirtCo v. Seven-Up Co., 242*n*117
Sutter Home Winery, Inc. v. Madrona Vineyards, L.P., 243*n*126, 244*n*129
Taylor Wine Co. v. Bully Hill Vineyards, Inc., 242*n*119
Team Tires Plus, Ltd. v. Tires Plus, Inc., 242*n*117
tests of, 242-44
Vigeron Partners, LLC v. Woop Woop Wines Pty. Ltd., 243*n* 121, 128
Internet domain, registration of, 241
Lanham Act, 218-219, 225, 226, 233-234, 235, 260-261, 267
licensing of, 244-246
Barcamerica Int'l USA Trust v. Tyfield Imps., Inc., 245*n*137
Embedded Moments, Inc. v. Int'l Silver Co., 245*n*140
logos, 220
misdescriptive, 229-230, 260
"naked license," 245
non-distinctive, 227-228, 231
packaging elements, 220, 223, 224*f*
protectability and spectrum of, 227-232
primarily geographically descriptive, 229-230
Bronco Wine Co. v. Jolly, 230*n*57, 264-265
In re Brouwerij Nacional Balashi NV, 230*n*53
registration
cancellation of, 239
declaration of current use, 240
declaration of renewal, 240
federal, application process for, 226-240
In re Fisons, Ltd., 238*n*98
maintenance of, 239-240
Oromeccanica, Inc. v. Ottmar Botzenhardt GmbH & Co. KG, 238*n*101
state, 240
screening, 234-236
service marks, defined, 225
sound and smell, 225
statistics re:, 218
statutory protection for, 241
sub-brands, 219
tag line, 219-220
trade dress, 221
Kendall-Jackson v. E. & J. Gallo, 222-223
trademark law, overview, 218-225
viticultural significance and, 90-94, 235-236, 262-263, 271, 435
Trademark Trial and Appeal Board, USPTO, 239
Trezise, Jim, 282-283
TRIPS Agreement. *See* Agreement on Trade-Related Aspects of Intellectual Property Rights (TRIPS)
TTB. *See* Alcohol and Tobacco Tax and Trade Bureau (TTB)
Twenty-first Amendment, U.S. Constitution, 8*n*30, 10
and the Commerce Clause, competing concerns, 183, 185-186, 197-198, 367, 368
Hostetter v. Idlewilde Bon Voyage Liquor Corporation, 197-198, 204*n*101
North Dakota v. United States, 198*n*63

judicial challenges to, 202-206, 210*n*134
ratification of, special provisions for, 195*n*53
and states' role in regulating wine sales and distribution, 43-44, 49-50
and various other provisions of the Constitution, 186*n*8
Twenty-sixth Amendment, U.S. Constitution, 362

Underage drinking
alcohol control policies to address, 384
alcoholic beverage advertising and, 376-377, 379-380
Committee on Developing a Strategy to Reduce and Prevent Underage Drinking, 365
and laws affecting the drinking environment, 370
price increases, influence on, 365
"shoulder tap" programs, 384
social-host liability and, 370
United States Patent and Trademark Office (USPTO)
federal trademark registration, process, 239
non-generic geographical indications, treatment of, 230-231, 268, 435
Trademark Electronic Search System, 89, 234-235, 236, 239
trademark maintenance, 239-240
Trademark Trial and Appeal Board (TTAB), 239
U.S. Constitution
Commerce Clause, 6-7, 183-215
Eighteenth Amendment, 8-9, 186-189, 194
Establishment Clause, 186*n*8
Fifth Amendment, takings provision, 285
First Amendment, free speech guarantees, 285, 377-379, 386
Fourteenth Amendment, 6, 190
Due Process clause, 186*n*8, 285
Equal Protection clause, 186*n*8, 285
Import-Export Clause, 186*n*8
Supremacy Clause, 186*n*8, 187, 377*n*154-155
Tenth Amendment, 6, 283*n*6
Twenty-first Amendment, 8*n*30, 10, 43-44, 49-50, 183, 185-186, 195-206, 210*n*134, 367, 368
Twenty-sixth Amendment, 362
U.S.-EC Wine Accords, 21, 430-438
U.S. Metric Association, Inc., 113
USPTO. *See* United States Patent and Trademark Office (USPTO)

Valverde, Mariana, 353
Varietal designation, 22, 77, 88, 101-120
approval of, 105*n*125
foreign varietal and geographic label claims, validating, 107-108
Foundation Plant Service, UC-David, 106-107
fraud convictions re:, 107
Grenache Noir, recognition of, 106
National Grapevine Importation Program, 106
National Grape Registry, 107
new varietals, recognition of, 106-107
Petite Sirah vs. Durif situation, 104-105
prime vs. alternative names, 102
records to substantiate, 104
rulemaking activities, chronology of, 103*f*
Zinfandel vs. Primitivo situation, 105-106
Vineyard designation, 180, 219, 250-251
Vintage date, 88, 117-120
percentages, major winemaking countries, 119*f*
Virginia
Agritourism Liability Act, 294, 299
building code exemption and ancillary uses, 297-299
farm winery, defined, 292-293, 294
Class A designation, 295
Class B designation, 295
land use basics, 292-293
Paradise Springs Winery in Fairfax County, case study of, 299-300
Right to Farm Act, 294, 295-296

Virginia (*continued*)
rural wineries in, 292-300
source of authority for localities, 293-294
Board of Supervisors v. Pumphrey, 293
City of Norfolk v. Tiny House, Inc., 294
County of Chesterfield v. Windy Hill Ltd., 294
Dillon's rule, 283, 284, 293
King v. County of Arlington, 293*n*49
statutory benefits of licensed farm wineries, 294-295
statutory protection for on-site marketing and sales, 296-297
Virginia Department of Alcoholic Beverage Control (ABVC), 293
Viticultural practices, 22-23
Viticultural significance, 90-94, 235-236, 262-263, 271, 435
Volstead, Andrew, 9
Volstead Act. *See* National Prohibition Act

Wagenaar, Alexander, 363
Washington (state)
alcoholic beverage licensing, new retail locations, 306-308
license application packet, 307
potential hurdles, 306
public notice, requirements for, 307
special conditions applied to, 307-308
alcohol impact area (AIA), 307
bar licenses, treatment of as personal property, 306
custom crush arrangement, licenses required, 163*n*56
new nightclub license, 308
regulations re: production and sale of wine, 158*n*30
trade practice law, 59-64
analysis of, 62-63
Costco Wholesale Corp. v. Maleng, 60-61
privatization movement, 63-64
tied-house statute, 59-60
Washington State Liquor Control Board (WSLCB), 158*n*30, 306
Webb, Sidney and Beatrice, 3
Webb-Kenyon Act of 1913, 7-8, 21*n*66, 159, 194, 209, 215
judicial challenges to (*James Clark Distilling Co. v. Western Maryland Railway Co.*), 194*n*51
Wheeler, Wayne, 3, 381
Whiskey Rebellion 1794), 20*n*61, 325*n*169
Whiskey Trust, 11
Willard, Frances, 8
Williamson Act. *See* California Land Conservation (Williamson) Act of 1965
Wilson Act of 1890, 7, 193-194, 209, 215
judicial challenges to (*Wilkerson v. Rahrer*), 194*n*51
Wine certifications, U.S.-EC Wine Accords, 436-437
Wine coolers, 98
Wine gallon, defined, 24*n*80
Wine Institute, 88-89, 112, 117-118, 387
Code of Advertising Standards, 138, 139, 140, 385
logo, 88-89
Wine labels. *See also* Appellations of origin; American Viticultural Area (AVA); Brand name(s); Certificate of label approval (COLA).
alcohol content, 108-110
and Alcoholic Beverage Labeling Act of 1988, 81*n*35
allergens, notice of, 115, 135-138
approval
"Black Death" Vodka example, 76, 78
exemption from, 78-79
statistics re:, 80
"use-up" permission, 79
bare-bones, construction of, 79-120
brand label, requirements for, 81
caloric or carbohydrate statements, 125
classes of wine, 98
conjunctive labeling statutes, 96-97
consumer deception, efforts to prevent, 75-77
"Contains Sulfites" disclosure statement, 81*n*34, 114-115

"Estate Bottled" designation, use of, 86-87, 173
"flag" labels, 121-122
flavored wine products, 98, 99, 101
geographical designations, 260-268
brand names of geographical significance, 260-267
generic, semi-generic, and non-generic names of geographical significance, 267-268, 433-434
varietal names with geographical significance, 268
"Government Warning" requirement, 21, 82*f*, 115-117, 353, 381-382
green claims, 124, 146-147
health-related directional statements, 124, 382-383
health warnings, 381-382, 390
imitation wine, 98, 101
judicial decisions
Bronco Wine Co. v. Jolly, 96*n*79
Cabo Distrib. Co. v. Brady, 76*n*8
Wawszkiewicz v. Dep't of the Treasury, 76-77, 94*n*74
jurisdiction, 74-75
mandatory information, 22, 88-120
name and address, 117
net contents, 110-113
non-generic names of geographical significance, 230-231, 268, 435
optional statements, standards for, 117, 435-436
"Blended," 117
"Cellared," "Vinted," or "Prepared," 117
"Produced" or "Made," 117
pending issues, 127-138
allergen labeling, 135-138
serving facts, 127-135
prohibited practices, 121-127
disparaging statements, 121
"flag" labels, 121-122
obscenity, 121, 122*f*
therapeutic claims, 122-127, 382
varietal designation, 22, 77, 88, 101-120
approval of, 105*n*125
foreign varietal and geographic label claims, validating, 107-108
Foundation Plant Service, UC-Davis, 106-107
fraud convictions re:, 107
Grenache Noir, recognition of, 106
National Grape Registry, 107
National Grapevine Importation Program, 106
new varietals, recognition of, 106-107
Petite Sirah vs. Durif situation, 104-105
prime vs. alternative names, 102
records to substantiate, 104
rulemaking activities, chronology of, 103*f*
Zinfandel vs. Primitivo situation, 105-106
vineyard designation, 180, 219, 250-251
vintage date, 88, 117-120
"Vintner/Proprietor Grown" designation, 87
vitamin claims, 125
Wine Renaissance, 249
Wine Revolution, 12, 282
"Winery within a winery." *See* Alternating proprietorship arrangement
The Wines of America, 12
Winkler, Albert, 258
WIPO. *See* World Intellectual Property Organization (WIPO)
Woman's Christian Temperance Union (WCTU), 8, 194
World Health Organization (WHO)
harmful use of alcohol and poor health, correlation between, 349-350
World Intellectual Property Organization (WIPO), 418, 427-429
Lisbon Agreement, 418, 427-428
Madrid Agreement for the Repression of False or Deceptive Indications of Source on Goods, 238-239, 396, 418, 427
Paris Convention for the Protection of Industrial Property, 238, 248*n*149, 418, 427
Standing Committee on the Law of Trademarks, Industrial Designs, and Geographical Indications (SCT), 428-429

World Trade Organization (WTO). *See also* General Agreement on Tariffs and Trade (GATT)
  Agreement on Technical Barriers to Trade (TBT Agreement), 420, 422-423
  Agreement on the Application of Sanitary and Phytosanitary Measures (SPS Agreement), 420-422, 423
  Agreement on Trade-Related Aspects of Intellectual Property Rights (TRIPS), 217, 280, 419, 423-424, 439
  Dispute Settlement Body (DSB), 424-427
  and International Organization of Vine and Wine (OIV), relations with, 418-419
  multilateral agreements, overview, 420
  Standards Code. *See* Agreement on Technical Barriers to Trade (TBT Agreement)
World Wine Trade Group (WWTG), 429
WTO. *See* World Trade Organization (WTO)

"Yellow light" acts, 48-49

Zero tolerance laws, 373, 374
Zoning, 152, 284
  entertainment zones, 321
  exceptions to, 284
  local ordinances, Virginia, 294
  mixed-use, 283, 284
  new bars and liquor stores, California, 314-315
  non-conforming (grandfathered) uses, California, 322-323
  variance, 284
  Village of Euclid v. Amber Realty Co., 284*n*11